KB035572

우루과이라운드

협상 동향 및
무역협상위원회
회의 3

우루과이라운드

협상 동향 및 무역협상위원회 회의 3

한국학중앙연구원

| 머리말

우루과이라운드는 국제적 교역 질서를 수립하려는 다각적 무역 교섭으로서, 각국의 보호무역 추세를 보다 완화하고 다자무역체제를 강화하기 위해 출범되었다. 1986년 9월 개시가 선언되었으며, 15개 분야의 교섭을 1990년 말까지 진행하기로 했다. 그러나 각 분야의 중간 교섭이 이루어진 1989년 이후에도 농산물, 지적소유권, 서비스무역, 섬유, 긴급수입제한 등 많은 분야에서 대립하며 1992년이 돼서야 타결에 이를 수 있었다. 한국은 특히 농산물 분야에서 기존 수입 제한 품목 대부분을 개방해야 했기에 큰 경쟁력 하락을 겪었고, 관세와 기술 장벽 완화, 보조금 및 수입 규제 정책의 변화로 제조업 수출입에도 많은 변화가 있었다.

본 총서는 우루과이라운드 협상이 막바지에 다다랐던 1991~1992년 사이 외교부에서 작성한 관련 자료를 담고 있다. 관련 협상의 치열했던 후반기 동향과 관계부처회의, 무역협상위원회 회의, 실무대책회의, 규범 및 제도, 투자회의, 특히나 가장 많은 논란이 있었던 농산물과 서비스 분야 협상 등의 자료를 포함해 총 28권으로 구성되었다. 전체 분량은 약 1만 3천여 쪽에 이른다.

2024년 3월
한국학술정보(주)

| 일러두기

· 본 총서에 실린 자료는 2022년 4월과 2023년 4월에 각각 공개한 외교문서 4,827권, 76만여 쪽 가운데 일부를 발췌한 것이다.

· 각 권의 제목과 순서는 공개된 원본을 최대한 반영하였으나, 주제에 따라 일부는 적절히 변경하였다.

· 원본 자료는 A4 판형에 맞게 축소하거나 원본 비율을 유지한 채 A4 페이지 안에 삽입하였다. 또한 현재 시점에선 공개되지 않아 '공란'이란 표기만 있는 페이지 역시 그대로 실었다.

· 외교부가 공개한 문서 각 권의 첫 페이지에는 '정리 보존 문서 목록'이란 이름으로 기록물 종류, 일자, 명칭, 간단한 내용 등의 정보가 수록되어 있으며, 이를 기준으로 0001번부터 번호가 매겨져 있다. 이는 삭제하지 않고 총서에 그대로 수록하였다.

· 보고서 내용에 관한 더 자세한 정보가 필요하다면, 외교부가 온라인상에 제공하는 『대한민국 외교사료요약집』 1991년과 1992년 자료를 참조할 수 있다.

| 차례

\multicolumn{7}{c}{**정 리 보 존 문 서 목 록**}						
기록물종류	일반공문서철	등록번호	2020030177	등록일자	2020-03-16	
분류번호	764.51	국가코드		보존기간	영구	
명 칭	\multicolumn{6}{l}{UR(우루과이라운드) 협상 동향 및 TNC(무역협상위원회) 회의, 1992. 전5권}					
생 산 과	통상기구과	생산년도	1992~1992	담당그룹		
권 차 명	\multicolumn{6}{l}{V.1 1월}					
내용목차	\multicolumn{6}{l}{...}					

정 리 보 존 문 서 목 록

기록물종류	일반공문서철	등록번호	2020030177	등록일자	2020-03-16
분류번호	764.51	국가코드		보존기간	영구
명 칭	UR(우루과이라운드) 협상 동향 및 TNC(무역협상위원회) 회의, 1992. 전5권				
생 산 과	통상기구과	생산년도	1992~1992	담당그룹	
권 차 명	V.1 1월				

내용목차	* 1.13. TNC 회의
	    - 수석대표: 조일호 농림수산부 농업협력통상관
	    - Dunkel 협정문 초안(91.12.20.)을 기초로 협상(양자.다자) 추진 결정
	    - 4 track(상품 양허, 서비스 양허, 협정조문 법적 정비, 협정초안 수정 작업) 협상 전략 제시
	11.10. TNC 회의
	    - 미국.EC 간 양자협상 타결 촉구
	11.20. 미국.EC 농산물 협상 타결
	    - 공산품, 서비스 등 여타 분야 협상 결렬
	11.26. TNC 회의
	    - 협정문안 연내 확정 일정 승인
	12.18. TNC 회의
	    - 1992년 초 협상재개 결정				

0001

UR(우루과이라운드) 협상 동향 및 TNC(무역협상위원회) 회의, 1992. 전5권(V.1 1월)　　7

외 무 부

종 별 :

번 호 : USW-0025   일 시 : 92 0103 1818

수 신 : 장 관(봉기,봉이,경기원,농수산부,상공부,경제수석)

발 신 : 주 미 대사대리   사본: 주미대사,주제네바대사,주EC대사-본부중계요

제 목 : UR 협상 관련 동향

DUNKEL 사무총장의 협정안에 대한 주재국내각계의 최근 동향을 하기 추보함.

1. 미 정부 동향

0 미 농무부에서는 DUNKEL TEXT 내용대로 농업개혁이 진행될 경우 미국 농업에 미칠 영향에 관한 연구 보고서를 작성중인 것으로 알려지고 있음.

0 동 연구 내용의 일부는 1.7 개최될 대통령 농업정책 자문위에 보고되어 DUNKEL TEXT 에 대한 행정부 내부 협의를 가진후, 1.9 개최 예정인 하원 농업위 청문회에서 행정부 내부 협의를 가진후 1.9 개최 예정인 하원 농업위 청문회에서 행정부 (USTR 및 농무부), 업계 및 의회보좌관들 참석하에 보다 섧게 의견을 수렴할 예정이라함.

2. 미 농업계 동향

0 U.S. FARM BUREAU 측은 지난 12.22 자로 발표한 -예비적 분석- (별전 INSIDE U.S. TRADE 게재전문 참조)을 통하여 DUNKEL 사무총장의 노력을 치하하면서도, 동 TEXT 는 아직 개선의 여지가 있다는 반응을 보였음.

0 그러나, 미 농업계 인사들도 현재의 TEXT 가 EC, 일본, 한국등의 반대 때문에 향후 교섭과정에서 약화되는것이 불가피하다는것을 인정하고 있는 형편이며, 따라서 미 농업계의 애매한태도 표명은 향후 EC 등의 반대에 대한 견제로서의 성격도 있는 것으로 관측되고 있음.

3. 미국내 DUNKEL TEXT 반대 세력

0 영화업계는 지적 소유권 (저작권) 부분에 대한 반대를 분명히 하고 있으며, 이미 DUNKEL TEXT 의저작권 부분에 대한 나름대로의 대체안을 작성, USTR 에 제시 하였다함.

0 의약업계도 지적 소유권 부분에 대해 반대를 표하고 개도국에 대한 과다한 특혜 (장기적인 이행기간 부여등)에 대해 불만을 표하면서, 특히 선진국과 동등 수준에서

통상국   2차보   통상국   청와대   경기원   농수부   상공부   증거필   미주국

경쟁하고 있는 선발 개도국들에게 특혜를 부여할 필요성에 대해 의문을 제기하고 있음.

0 반덤핑과 관련, 철강등 국내 업계는 DUNKELTEXT 상의 반덤핑 관련 조항이 너무 엄격하여 미국의 반덤핑 관련 국내 규정의 발동을 사실상 어렵게 한다는 측면에서 반대를 표하고 있으며, 한편 미국의 수출 업계 및 해외 진출 다국적기업들은 유럽에서의 반덤핑 규제 남용을 방지할 제도적 안전 장치를 마련치 못하고 있다는 철강업계와는 상반댄 이유로 반덤핑 관련부분을 반대하고 있어 상호 댈조를 이루고 있음. (철강 업계는 동 TEXT 상 우회 덤핑 방지도 미흡하다고 주장하나, 수출 업계는 동 TEXT 상 우회덤핑 방지가 충분히 포함되어 있다고 평가)

0 상계 관세 부분도 대체로 반덤핑 과 유사한 반대에 직면하고 있는바, 특히 미국내 업계는 개도국에 대한 특혜 조항에 대해 불만을 표하고있는 것으로 알려짐.

첨부: USW(F)-0050

(대사대리 김봉규 - 실장)

주 미 대 사 관

USW(F) : **0050**   년월일 :   시간 :

수 신 : 장 관 (통재.통가.경기원 농수산식.상상부. 경재사)
        사본: 죽미대사, 죽계네바 대사, 죽한 대사

발 신 : 주 미 대 사

제 목 : USW - **0025** 의 청부.

(출처 :   )

보 안
통 제

(0050 - 29 - 1)

외신 1과
통 제

0004

Inside U.S. Trade

An exclusive weekly report on major government and industry tra.

Vol. 10 No. 1 - January 3, 1992

U.S. DOMESTIC INDUSTRY CHALLENGES EXEMPTIONS IN DRAFT SUBSIDIES CODE

Draft Uruguay Round rules aimed at curbing trade-distorting subsidies have come under heavy criticism by U.S. domestic industry for exempting regional assistance as well as research & development from countervailing duty cases in addition to creating special rules for developing countries. At the same time, representatives of U.S. multinationals insist the draft code tabled on Dec. 20 is a dramatic improvement because it caps most subsidies at 5 percent.

This means that subsidies beyond that threshold are presumed to cause "serious prejudice" to trading partners whatever their justification. These disciplines on subsidies represent a "revolutionary" shift in political thinking despite the exceptions the draft agreement would allow, according to one private-sector source. They would make it impossible for governments to undertake corporate bailouts such as those

continued on page 10

U.S. INDUSTRY FIGHTS PROPOSED RETALIATION AGAINST PRC, BACKED BY HONG KONG

The majority of U.S. industry representatives commenting on a proposed retaliation list of exports from the People's Republic of China are urging the Office of the U.S. Trade Representative not to penalize the country for its failure to protect U.S. intellectual property rights, according to comments filed with USTR. Supporting retaliation are General Motors Corporation because Chinese companies infringed on a patent of a magnet it developed as well as members of the U.S. luggage and leather industry who cited the country's poor trademark protection.

GM pointed out that it is losing sales in the U.S. and royalty income as a result of Chinese infringement of its patent for electromagnets, according to its comments. Chinese company sales of these magnets to the U.S. range from $10 to $20-billion, and worldwide sales are expected to top $400-million

continued on page 16

FARM GROUPS SEE DRAFT GATT PACT AS MINIMAL IMPROVEMENT OVER STATUS QUO

After a preliminary assessment, selected U.S. agriculture groups see the draft Uruguay Round farm pact at best as offering minimal improvements in agricultural trade. The draft text as presented by the top official of the General Agreement on Tariffs & Trade on Dec. 20 would minimally increase market access and would cut the volume and expenses for export subsidies in a way that would allow most of them to stay in place until 1999, these groups say.

The Agricultural Policy Advisory Committee, along with other formal industry advisory groups, expect to be briefed on Jan. 7 by Administration officials on the details of the draft agreement relevant to the respective sectors. Many agriculture industry advisors point out that their final assessment will largely be influenced by the analysis to be performed by the U.S. Dept. of Agriculture, but a preliminary assessment

continued on page 11

SIA IMPLORES BUSH TO PRESS FOR MORE OPEN JAPANESE CHIP MARKET DURING TALKS

The Semiconductor Industry Assn. (SIA) urged President Bush in a Dec. 30 letter to tell Japanese Prime Minister Miyazawa during his upcoming trip to East Asia that Japan will have to do much more to comply with a bilateral semiconductor agreement calling for a 20% foreign share in its market by 1992.

"Mr. President, we implore you to tell Prime Minister Miyazawa in no uncertain terms that this agreement must be strictly abided by and U.S. firms must be given a full and free opportunity to compete in Japan," the letter said.

Written by SIA president Andrew Procassini, the letter stresses that gaining access to Japan's $20-billion market is "particularly vital" for U.S. manufacturers. It says that while the Reagan Administration negotiated an agreement with Japan in 1986 that reversed a decline in the U.S. share of Japan's

0050 - 29 - 2

Special Report: Analysis of Draft GATT Antidumping Agreement

0005

semiconductor market, the pact fell short of solving the problems of U.S. firms.

The Bush Administration then negotiated a second agreement calling for a full opening of Japan's market and a 20% foreign share by the end of 1992. But the foreign share of Japan's market is reported at only 14.3% for the third quarter of 1991, and sales have been stagnant or falling for over a year, according to the letter. "With a full open market, the U.S. industry would have much more than 20% of the Japanese market," the letter to Bush said. "A totally open market is our goal, but we will need your help to achieve that goal."

The Office of the U.S. Trade Representative and the Commerce Dept. announced the 14.3% figure on Dec. 24, saying it indicates that foreign share of the Japanese semiconductor market "has increased significantly over the past few years." But USTR and Commerce stressed that Japan needs to take much more aggressive action. USTR Carla Hills said in a statement that the U.S. will "need to see a marked improvement in access to the Japanese market over the coming months if we are to successfully implement the Semiconductor Arrangement." Michael Farren, the under secretary for international trade at Commerce, said in a statement that while the 14.3% figure finally shows some meaningful movement on the part of the Japanese, the December 1992 deadline for meeting the 20% goal "poses a real challenge."

The 14.3% figure is the first official foreign market share number calculated by U.S. and Japanese government experts under the new U.S.-Japan Semiconductor Arrangement, which took effect Aug. 1, 1991. The next market share figures are scheduled to be released by the Administration in early March.

The letter, reprinted below, says that the U.S. industry is far more competitive than the 20% market share goal indicates. Procassini told Bush that the U.S. industry's share of the world market excluding Japan in 1990 was over 57% and over was 72% in the U.S. Procassini said that the 20% figure was chosen as a "very low estimate" of the share that foreign semiconductors would have of Japan's market if it were more open. SIA maintains that if the Japanese market were more fully open to U.S. semiconductors, U.S. sales would increase by more than $1-billion a year.

While the letter does not ask Bush to take specific actions to increase the foreign market share, industry sources point out that elevating the issue to the Presidential level would put additional pressure on the Japanese. For example, the U.S. and Japan hold regular consultations under the semiconductor agreement, and direct involvement by Bush could make the Japanese more willing to act on U.S. requests at these meetings to increase foreign market share. One industry source said it is highly likely that Bush will raise the issue with Miyazawa.

SIA Letter to Bush

December 30, 1991

The Honorable George H.W. Bush
President
1600 Pennsylvania Ave., N.W.
Washington, D.C. 20500

Dear Mr. President:

The U.S. Semiconductor Industry Association applauds your trip to East Asia. Obtaining greater market access for U.S. products must be a cornerstone of U.S. economic policy.

For the semiconductor industry, free market access to the $20 billion Japanese market -- the world's largest -- is particularly vital. Without the opportunity to compete freely and fairly in Japan, we will be seriously handicapped in our efforts to meet the competitive challenge facing our industry in an ever more complex global market.

Nor do we need to remind you of the critical role that a competitive semiconductor industry plays in both national security and economic security. If we are given a fair opportunity, Mr. President, I assure you that we will maintain the vital and competitive industry that our nation needs.

Unfortunately, fully opening Japan's market has proved no simple task. In 1986, the Reagan-Bush Administration negotiated a market-opening agreement that reversed a decline in the already small U.S. share of Japan's market (then 8.5%) and contributed to the ability of the U.S. industry to reverse the decline in its share of the world semiconductor market in 1990.

That agreement, however, did not solve the problem. Thus, your Administration negotiated a second agreement calling for a full opening of Japan's market and a 20% foreign share of that market by the end of 1992. In actuality, the U.S. industry is far more competitive than the 20% figure would indicate. By comparison, the U.S. industry's share of the world market excluding Japan in 1990 was over 57% and over 72% in the United States, the world's most open market. The 20% figure was chosen as a very low estimate of the share that foreign semiconductors would have of Japan's market if the market were more fully open. What the agreement sought was merely a fair chance to compete for greater share.

Unfortunately, foreign share of Japan's market has again stagnated. It is now reported (using a new calculation system) at 14.3% for the third quarter of 1991, but sales have been stagnant or falling for over a year.

Mr. President, we implore you to tell Prime Minister Miyazawa in no uncertain terms that this agreement must be strictly abided by and U.S. firms must be given a full and free opportunity to compete in Japan. With a fully open market, the U.S. industry would have much more than 20% of the Japanese market. A totally open market is our goal, but we will need your help to achieve that goal.

Good luck in the new year! The nation needs your success.

Sincerely,

Andrew A. Procassini
President, Semiconductor Industry Association

2   0050 -29-3

이영화문제, 내△상품의 TRIPS 관계문서┘ #2수권④상정 (동기.동.1) 상,13

MOTION PICTURE INDUSTRY PRESSING FOR MAJOR CHANGES IN DUNKEL TEXT ON TRIPs

The motion picture industry is strongly pressing the Office of the U.S. Trade Representative to reject key provisions on trade-related intellectual property (TRIPs) contained in a draft Uruguay Round text prepared by Arthur Dunkel, the director general of the General Agreement on Tariffs & Trade. The industry is particularly vociferous about the need to better protect copyrights of U.S. motion pictures in Western Europe and guarantee that U.S. firms are compensated by a royalty system that industry says is substantially tilted against them in the draft Dunkel text.

Meanwhile, the U.S. pharmaceutical industry is gearing up to make a case to USTR that a clause in the Dunkel TRIPS text that was requested by India would allow countries to produce a pharmaceutical product without a license if the countries fail to negotiate a license at a reasonable price.

The Motion Picture Association of America (MPAA) contends that the TRIPs provisions in the Dunkel draft fall far short of protecting copyrights for motion pictures in Western Europe. At the heart of the dispute is a basic difference between the copyright systems in the U.S. and most Western European countries. While Western Europe looks to protect individual authors of a work, the U.S. generally protects legal entities that acquire copyright ownership through contractual agreements, according to an MPAA official.

This distinction is particularly acute for the U.S. motion picture industry because movies do not have one author. Unlike the author of a book, there are scores of people who contribute artistically to motion pictures. "The U.S. copyright owner is a corporate entity, and the TRIPs agreement does not recognize our system of corporate ownership," he said.

The MPAA wants to be assured that the U.S. copyright system and the legitimacy of contractual relationships in the U.S. will be recognized in Uruguay Round negotiations. If not, the GATT will invite discrimination for U.S. motion pictures, according to the MPAA.

The MPAA official said his group already has communicated its concerns about the Dunkel draft to USTR, which he said appears to be very receptive. The group provided U.S. negotiators with specific language that it hopes will be adopted in place of the Dunkel provisions on TRIPs. The source added that there will have to be substantial modifications in the TRIPs provisions in the Dunkel text before Congress supports it. He emphasized that even a good agreement will be difficult to get through Congress because a "groundswell of protectionism" appears to be developing in light of the recession. The source acknowledged that the European Community will fight to keep much of the TRIPs language in tact but added that "everything is negotiable."

The Dunkel draft also does little to prevent the passage of European laws that cut U.S. copyright owners out of all or a substantial portion of special levies designed to compensate authors of a copyrighted work, according to the MPAA official. Such a royalty system of compensation is either in existence in Western Europe or is being considered by virtually every Western European country, he said. For example, France has a home taping levy that raises a pool of money that is then divided among copyright owners of the taped material, the source pointed out.

France divides the proceeds of the levy into four portions, the first being to help the arts in France. U.S. copyright owners are automatically shut out of this portion. The remaining three portions are divided among the author, performers and video grand producers, which are the French distributors of material.

While U.S. companies can qualify to receive some of the author's portion, they are prevented from receiving any of the money raised to compensate the performer since it can only go to individual artists, the source said. The U.S. firms also do not qualify for the compensation of grand producers, meaning U.S. motion picture companies can qualify for compensation for one only of the four categories. The MPAA official said U.S. companies should at least be eligible to receive royalties for three categories since U.S. firms are automatically excluded from the fund contributing to the arts in France.

The Pharmaceutical Manufacturers Association (PMA) is highly concerned that patent protection will be seriously jeopardized if the Dunkel text is not substantially altered. Allowing companies to make a pharmaceutical product without a license if a reasonable price for a license cannot be negotiated is "an attack on patent protection," according to an industry source. "We have a very serious problem with that," he said. The PMA is also very concerned about language in the Dunkel draft saying that developing countries such as India would be given 20 years before being forced to give patent protection to U.S. drugs. Such language would turn the GATT into a "protectionist organ for developing countries at the expense of Western nations," the source said. The PMA has not yet submitted its criticisms to the USTR but will do so soon, he added.

0056-29-4

이·가 표는 (동이)

U.S. EXPANDS SCOPE OF CANADIAN LUMBER INVESTIGATION TO CONSIDER EXPORT BAN

The Commerce Dept. is expanding the scope of its countervailing duty investigation on Canadian softwood lumber to determine whether a Canadian export "ban" on logs constitutes a subsidy.

The U.S. lumber industry maintains that federal and provincial restrictions in Canada on log exports have the effect of driving the price of logs down by artificially increasing the domestic supply. Canada does this in order to "subsidize" the domestic wood processing industry, U.S. sources claim.

A counsel to the Canadian government has submitted comments challenging a petition filed on behalf of the U.S. lumber industry by the Coalition for Fair Lumber Imports. The Coalition has not proven in its petition that the export ban actually leads to price reductions, according to a Canadian source. Canada has also taken issue with the methodology used by the Coalition for calculating price distortions.

The Commerce Dept. sent a questionnaire with a list of 25 question to Canadian authorities on Dec. 24 to determine if the export ban warranted action. A response to the questionnaire is due Jan. 14. The Commerce Dept. is expected to make a preliminary decision Feb. 24 on whether countervailing duties should be imposed and may include an assessment at that time whether a ban on lumber exports is a subsidy. The Canadian's have requested an extension in the case. If the extension is granted a preliminary decision will be due March 30.

The export ban goes hand in hand with federal and provincial practices of allocating timber at below-market value, U.S. lumber representatives claim. The Commerce Dept. investigation originally just focused on the system of timber allocation practiced in the provinces, especially British Colombia, where the U.S. lumber industry maintains that timber on provincial land is sold to Canadian loggers by as much as 35% below market value. This, they claim, is a direct subsidy by the provincial governments. The International Trade Commission voted Dec. 12 that there was reason to believe that U.S. industry was either injured or was threatened with injury by this practice.

In order to export logs out of Canada, a license must be obtained from both the federal and the provincial authorities, and these licenses are granted only under certain conditions. In addition, in British Colombia, the province with the largest timber industry, a 100% tax is levied on the profits made from selling logs into the export market for use in a foreign lumber industry. For logs slated for the foreign paper and pulp industry, British Colombia collects a 40% tax on profits. The U.S. lumber industry maintains that the license restrictions constitutes an export ban, and the British Colombian tax shows that the ban is directed at the foreign lumber industry in particular.

The Commerce Dept. self-initiated the investigation on Oct. 31, 1991 after Canada withdrew from a 1986 memorandum of understanding governing lumber trade between the two countries. Under the terms of the MOU, the Canadian government was required to levy an export tax of up to 15% to offset the subsidized prices Canadian industry enjoyed from provincial authorities. The provinces were also allowed to adopt other measures in lieu of the federal government's export tariff.

The MOU did not deal with the issue of the export ban, in part because there was no precedent for setting countervailing duties on an export ban. However, in 1990 the Commerce Dept. imposed countervailing duties on Argentine leather hides, which are subject to an export ban in Argentina. This case provided the precedent that the U.S. lumber industry cites in pressing for the investigation into the Canadian log export restrictions.

공능 수출 자유화제 연방간치 (동이) 상징

ADMINISTRATION GRANTS TWO-YEAR, PHASED-OUT EXTENSION ON MACHINE TOOL VRAs

President Bush last week directed the Office of the U.S. Trade Representative to negotiate a two-year, phased-out extension of the voluntary restraint agreements (VRAs) on machine tools with Japan and Taiwan. As part of the new VRAs, the restrictions would be removed progressively beginning in January 1992.

The domestic industry has been lobbying USTR to begin the phase out in the second year of the extension rather than having it begin immediately. According to sources, the schedule for phasing out the VRAs has yet to be decided and will be the subject of talks next week when U.S. negotiators travel to Taiwan and Japan.

However, in conjunction with the phase-out, the President directed on Dec. 27 that export control regulations should be reviewed to "ensure that restrictions on machine tools are kept to the minimum consistent with national security," according to a statement by the White House Press Secretary. The Administration will also actively pursue a number of initiatives to promote and protect the domestic machine tool industry.

To allow sufficient time for negotiations with concerned countries over the phase-out schedule, the Administration has requested that Japan and Taiwan extend the current VRAs that expired Dec. 31 for an

0050-29-5

additional 30 days. The VRAs cover —computer controlled lathes, punching ▪ ◼ ═ ing machine tools and milling machine tools.

As part of the Administration's efforts, the Commerce Dept., along with the departments of Defense and Labor, will designate officials at the assistant secretary level to monitor the industry's performance and consult with industry representatives. In addition, the departments of Commerce and Defense will continue an ongoing Domestic Action Plan to help the industry, which includes support for the National Center for Manufacturing Sciences and the Defense Dept.'s Manufacturing Technology (MANTECH) R&D program. Government support for the Center amounted to $50-million during fiscal years 1988 to 1991, and more than $33-million has been spent for research on machine tools and related technologies under the MANTECH program over the past three years, according to the Administration. Funding for related technologies is estimated at $82-million over FY-91 to FY-95.

In addition, the departments of Commerce and Energy will examine R&D efforts in the national laboratories and recommend investment and technology transfers to the industry. At the same time, the President has directed the Labor Dept. to help the machine tool industry improve technical training, human resource management and the utilization of new and emerging technologies.

The Commerce Dept., as chair of the Trade Promotion Coordinating Committee, is directed by the President to focus on ways to promote machine tool exports. Commerce also is directed to continue efforts under the May 1990 U.S.-Japan Cooperation Plan to promote U.S. products to Japanese machine tool users and their subsidiaries in the U.S.

The domestic machine tool industry had been urging a five-year extension of the VRAs, and in a Dec. 27 statement by the Association for Manufacturing Technology, which represents the domestic machine tool industry, the association indicated its support for the two-year extension. The VRAs that were originally negotiated in 1987 provided "breathing space" to the industry, and the two year extension will give more time to the industry to continue its investment strategies, according to the statement.

In the years between 1987 and 1989, the U.S. machine tool industry averaged productivity gains of 11.3% — among the highest productivity growth of any industrial sector, according to the association. Over the five-year period from 1987, annual investment in U.S.-based, VRA-affected companies grew by 78%, and R&D spending grew by 23% between 1987 and 1990.

Over 196 members of Congress contacted President Bush in support of the VRA extension. The association emphasized that its push for a VRA extension was strongly backed by a bipartisan group of senators and representatives, including Sens. Alfonse D'Amato (R-NY), Bob Kasten (R-WI), John Glenn (D-OH), Charles Grassley (R-IA), Don Riegle (D-MI), John Danforth (R-MO), Alan Dixon (D-IL), Jesse Helms (R-NC), James Jeffords (R-VT) and Jay Rockefeller (D-WV). The House members include Reps. Nancy Johnson (R-CT), Barbara Kennelly (D-CT), Les Aspin (D-WI), Helen Bentley (R-MD), William Broomfield (R-MI), Rod Chandler (R-WA), John Dingell (D-MI), Duncan Hunter (R-CA), Henry Hyde (R-IL), Marcy Kaptur (D-OH), Joe Moakley (D-MA), John Murtha (D-PA), Dan Rostenkowski (D-IL), Marty Russo (D-IL), Guy Vander Jagt (R-MI). At the state level, the association pointed to the efforts of Govs. Tommy Thompson (R-WI) and George Voinovich (R-OH) and Secretary of State George Ryan (R-IL).

USTR ANNOUNCES PLANS TO RETALIATE AGAINST CANADIAN BEER, ALCOHOL BY APRIL 10

The Office of the U.S. Trade Representative last week announced that it will raise duties on Canadian beer and alcohol by April 10 because trade barriers maintained by provincial authorities violated the rules of the General Agreement on Tariffs & Trade. USTR based its determination on a September 1991 report by a GATT dispute settlement panel that was established at the request of the U.S.

The Dec. 27 USTR decision not to take action until April 10 will allow Canada to concur in the adoption of a panel report at the next GATT Council meeting in February. The U.S. will continue to consult with the Canadian government to avoid taking retaliatory action under the authority of a section 301 investigation, according to a statement by USTR.

The decision by the U.S. to delay unilateral trade action was hailed by the Brewers Association of Canada. "We are pleased the United States has decided to work within the GATT process which they launched and not to move unilaterally," said Sandy Morrison, president of the association, in a Dec. 27 statement.

The panel has outlined a plan for Canada to do away with its inconsistent trade practices in two steps in March and July. Because the trade barriers are the result of rules enacted by the provinces, the Canadian government has been consulting with provincial authorities over how to phase out these practices, Canadian sources say.

The panel found that certain listing, pricing and distribution practices maintained by Canadian provincial liquor boards discriminate against imported beer and violate the GATT. The panel also found that Canada failed to take "serious, persistent and convincing efforts" to ensure compliance by provincial authorities of a 1988 GATT panel that found discriminatory practices by the provinces. The U.S. argues that since that time, provincial authorities have instituted new, more restrictive practices.

The investigation was initiated by USTR on June 29, 1990 in response to a 302 petition filed by the G. Heileman Brewing Company. The petition was later joined by a petition for a 301 investigation on Sept. 14, 1990 by the Stroh Brewery Company against discriminatory practices of Ontario authorities.

Canada is expecting by the end of January the report of another GATT panel currently investigating complaints about discriminatory U.S. federal and state beer taxation, marketing and distribution practices. The Canadian complaint was launched earlier this year challenging a change in U.S. excise taxes that allegedly favor all but seven of the largest U.S. brewers. More than 200 U.S. brewers are eligible for the favorable treatment, but no foreign brewers are eligible, according to the Canadian presentation to the GATT council. A GATT panel was appointed to decide the complaint on May 29.

The excise tax rate in the U.S. is $18 per barrel and this rate applies to imports as well. But for U.S. brewers producing less than 2-million barrels per year, the excise tax rate is only $7 for the first 60,000 barrels of production.

Canada is also complaining against discriminatory practices at the state level, charging that in eight states there are special tax exemptions for in-state brewers. These eight states include Ohio, Oregon, Kentucky, Illinois, Minnesota, Rhode Island, Texas and Wisconsin. In five states, preferential tax treatment is extended to beer containing less than 4% alcohol. Canadian producers say this discriminates against regular Canadian beer that contains 5% alcohol.

Further, in most states, local brewers can sell directly to retailers, licensees and distributors. This gives in-state brewers a competitive advantage over foreign brewers who are required to sell first to an importer or distributor in that state. In addition, a number of states require special labels that are different from state to state. This, Canada claims, impairs the efficiency of distribution of foreign brewers. In contrast, Canada has one national labeling requirement.

Stroh, G. Heileman and Pabst are in the process of appealing a dumping and injury determination made by Canadian authorities against them. The U.S. brewers have applied for a binational panel to review the decision. Briefs on the margin determination are due Jan. 28 and on the injury determination by Feb. 17. Pabst is only listed as an "interested party" in the margin counter appeal, but all three brewers are plaintiffs in appealing the injury determination.

Final oral arguments on the margin determination are due to be heard no later than May 14, and for the injury decision no later than June 5.

Canadian and U.S. distillers have complained to USTR about its decision to include Canadian exports of distilled spirits in the retaliation. International Distillers & Vintners North America (IDA), in a Dec. 29 letter to USTR, claims that U.S. retaliation "will not contribute in any meaningful way to the correction of trading inequities which may presently exist." Moreover, U.S. sanctions will impact U.S. importers of Canadian beverages and lead to economic hardship, according to IDV. This concern is echoed in a Dec. 23 letter by the National Association of Beverage Importers and the Distilled Spirits Council of the United States.

The Association of Canadian Distillers add in a Dec. 16 letter to USTR that the GATT panel report involved only discriminatory practices against beer and not against distilled spirits. Moreover, U.S. trade sanctions against Canadian distilled spirits would "undermine the regime for distilled spirits established in Chapter 8 of the Free Trade Agreement," it said. The letter goes on to add that "this regime is working well and we know of no complaints concerning Canada-U.S. trade in distilled spirits raised by either the Canadian or U.S. industries." By Alkman Granitsas

BENTSEN SEES MEXICAN IMPORT BANS VIOLATING THE SPIRIT AND GOALS OF NAFTA

Sen. Lloyd Bentsen (D-TX) this week told the Mexican trade minister in a letter that his country's imposition of import bans for live swine and tree fruit from the U.S. "raises serious concerns" about its commitment to freer trade between the two countries. The import bans imposed in December are only the latest instances where Mexico has imposed or threatened to impose measures that are clearly at odds with the "spirit and the goals" of the North American free-trade agreement, Bentsen said in a Dec. 30 letter.

"Whether these measures affect a land transport firm such as Mexico Express seeking to expand its services between our two countries, U.S. petrochemical producers or U.S. swine producers or fruit growers, they are bound to call into question ... Mexico's genuine desire for expanded, more open two-way trade," Bentsen said in his letter to Mexican trade minister Jaime Serra Puche. Copies of the letter were also sent to U.S. Trade Representative Carla Hills and U.S. Agriculture Secretary Ed Madigan, sources said.

After Mexico imposed import bans on U.S. tree fruit effective Dec. 2 and on live swine effective Dec. 15, governments for the two sides have been trying to negotiate an agreement that would create transparent procedures for imposing steps limiting cross border farm trade for animal and plant health reasons (*Inside U.S. Trade*, Special Report, Dec. 20, 1991). Bentsen acknowledged in his letter that the U.S. and Mexico have reached tentative agreements to allow some exports of tree fruit to Mexico and have made progress on establishing procedures for certifying entry of live swine from the U.S. to Mexico. But the import ban imposed by Mexico effective Dec. 15 to prevent swine infertility & respiratory syndrome will stay in place until an agreement is final, according to the letter.

Given the importance of agricultural trade between Mexico and the U.S., it is "essential" for NAFTA to include adequate rules dealing with the imposition of sanitary and phytosanitary measures, the letter said. In the meantime, it is "absolutely critical" that no animal and plant health measures be imposed without adequate justification and without sufficient prior notice to the other party, Bentsen said in the letter.

Bentsen Letter to Mexican Trade Minister

December 30, 1991

The Honorable
Jaime Serra Puche
Secretario
Secretaria de Comercio y Fomento Industrial
Alfonso Reyes 30, Piso 10
Col. Condesa
06140 Mexico, D.F.

Dear Mr. Secretary:

I am writing to bring to your attention my concern about the Government of Mexico's recently-imposed bans on imports of live swine and certain tree fruits from the United States

I understand that, after the import bans took effect, Mexican and U.S. agricultural officials met and reached tentative agreements intended to allow U.S. exports of some of the tree fruit products to Mexico to resume. I understand further that Mexico now has proposed certain procedures for certifying entries of live swine from the United States, but that the swine import ban will remain in place until an agreement can be reached. Still, notwithstanding whatever progress has been made, the imposition of these import bans itself raises serious concerns about Mexico's commitment to freer trade with the United States.

Mexican and U.S. agricultural officials apparently differ on whether these import bans can be justified on sanitary and phytosanitary grounds. That kind of dispute is bound to occur from time to time in light of the substantial two-way agricultural trade between our two countries. Given the importance of this trade for both the United States and Mexico, it will be essential that any North American free trade agreement include adequate

measures to deal with the imposition of sanitary and phytosanitary measures.

In the meantime, it is absolutely critical that any such measures not be imposed without adequate justification and without sufficient prior notice to the other party. Here, one of the import bans took effect before any notice was provided to the U.S. Government, and the other was implemented less than a week after notice was given. Clearly, this procedure was wholly inadequate to allow U.S. Government and industry experts to respond to Mexico's health and sanitary claims and to enable bilateral consultations to then take place before U.S. producers were adversely affected.

These import bans also raise broader concerns. They are only the latest instances in which Mexico has imposed or threatened to impose measures that, in my view, are clearly at odds with both the spirit and the goals of a North American free trade agreement. Whether these measures affect a land transport firm such as Mexico Express seeking to expand its services between our two countries, U.S. petrochemical producers, or U.S. swine producers and fruit growers, they are bound to call into question — including among firms and industries that support closer bilateral trade relations — Mexico's genuine desire for expanded, more open two-way trade.

I know that you remain committed to the goal of a North American free trade agreement that can benefit the economies of both of our countries. With that objective in mind, I hope that you will actively oppose measures, including those noted above, that restrict rather than expedite freer trade between the United States and Mexico.

Sincerely,

Lloyd Bentsen

SUBSCRIPTIONS:
703-892-8500 or
Toll-free 800-424-9068

NEWS OFFICE
703-892-1014

FAX: 703-685-2606

Publisher: Joe Burey
Chief Editor: Jutta Hennig
Associate Editor: Alkman Granitsas

Inside U.S. Trade is published every Friday by Inside Washington Publishers, P.O. Box 7167, Ben Franklin Station, Washington, D.C. 20044. Subscription rates: $685/yr in U.S. and Canada; $735/yr elsewhere (air mail). Copyright 1992 by Inside Washington Publishers. All rights reserved. Reproduction in any form whatsoever forbidden without express permission of the copyright owners.

0050 - 29

EC, 대한건비 후로 2동2동구 항상을 부분 기부 [택]. 중1. 동산P.행인생, 상기

EC REJECTS DRAFT URUGUAY ROUND FARM AGREEMENT FOR THREE MAJOR REASONS

European Community rejection of a draft agriculture agreement emerging from the Uruguay Round is based on the fact that it would ask trading partners to cut internal support payments, including those that are meant to compensate farmers for price reductions. In addition, the EC opposes the proposed cuts in export subsidies and the fact that market access for grain substitutes could not be curbed, according to EC sources.

Cutting internal support payments by the proposed 20% reductions starting in 1993 based on an average of the 1986-1988 levels would undermine the planned changes in the Common Agricultural Policy, EC sources argue. Most member states would oppose the price cuts foreseen in the Commission's CAP reform proposals without having farm income supported by direct payments. As a result, the EC has insisted in international negotiations that all these payments should be placed in a "green category" exempt from cuts because farmers have to participate in a set aside program in order to be eligible. At one point, U.S. and EC negotiators considered a separate category of domestic supports that would only be subject to ceiling limits, not actual cuts (*Inside U.S. Trade*, Dec. 13 p 1). However, that idea is not reflected in the draft Uruguay Round agreement.

Regarding the internal supports, the EC strongly rejects the draft agreement's demands that cuts in internal supports must take place based on individual commodities, and cannot be based on sector-wide commodity groups. Such an arrangement would give trading partners more flexibility to shift cuts to less sensitive commodities within a group, according to one agriculture source. In addition, EC member states have raised objections to a draft agreement on plant and animal health rules, sources said.

EC trade and economics ministers formally opposed the draft agriculture agreement in a Dec. 23 council meeting attended by several agriculture ministers. They demanded that the Commission negotiate "further necessary improvements" to it in the General Agreement on Tariffs & Trade because the draft calls into question the EC's agricultural policy, according to a communique from the Council meeting reprinted below. At the same time, the communique emphasized the importance of a successful conclusion of the Uruguay Round to remedy the threat of a world economic recession and to help countries moving toward a more market-oriented economy.

The EC formal assessment on the overall Uruguay Round package was more cautious, emphasizing the need to study the "extensive and complicated text," the communique said. A final assessment is only possible after the outcome of the specific market access negotiations that are planned, according to the communique. However, EC Commission officials at the Dec. 23 council meeting were said to raise objections because the agreement would not guarantee that the U.S. could not act unilaterally under section 301 and criticized the proposed antidumping and subsidies agreement, sources said. Member states are expected to meet again at the 113-committee level on Jan. 10, three days before the Trade Negotiations Committee of the Uruguay Round is scheduled to meet, sources said.

Text of EC Statement on Uruguay Round

**Communiqué
General Council
23 December 1991**

• Recalling the conclusions of the European Council meeting in Maastricht, the Council stressed the importance of a successful conclusion of the Uruguay Round. A further opening up of markets and improvement of the rules and disciplines governing world trade are an indispensable element in the strategy to remedy the threat of world economic recession. More specifically the need for success is addressed by the beneficial effects an opening up of world trade will have on those countries that are in the process of transforming their economies into a more market oriented direction.

• The Council discussed the "Dunkel paper" on the basis of a first evaluation by the Commission. The Council shared the view of the Commission that at this stage a final assessment is premature. More time is needed to study the extensive and complicated text.

• Moreover the Council noted that a final assessment of the "Dunkel paper" is only possible after, and will be influenced by, the pending outcome of the outstanding specific negotiations planned for and resulting from the "Dunkel paper."

• The Council's concerns focused on the proposed result on agriculture. Insofar as the "Dunkel paper" calls into question the foundation of the Community's agricultural policy, the paper is not acceptable and therefore has to be modified. Since the Community has embarked upon a far-reaching reform process of its agriculture policy, the proposed text was in particular evaluated in this light.

• Although the Council recognized that the paper contains some positive elements as it stands now, the Council is of the opinion that the paper is not balanced in total and therefore invites the Commission to negotiate further necessary improvements to it.

• Also genuine efforts from some major trading partners, especially US and Japan, should be obtained to ensure mutual advantages and to increase benefits to all participants.

0050 - 29 - 9

8

0012

559 P01   WDI

'92-01-04 09:23

18   우루과이라운드 협상 동향 및 무역협상위원회 회의 3

STUDY FINDS JAPAN LEADS FOREIGN INVESTMENT IN U.S. HIGH-TECHNOLOGY INDUSTRIES

Japanese investment in the U.S. high-technology sector is seven times greater than the investments by the UK, the next largest foreign investor, according to a report by the Economic Strategy Institute (ESI). The Washington, DC-based think tank announced last month that Japanese investment in U.S. high-technology companies continues to greatly outstrip all other countries. Japanese companies account for 363 investments in high-technology industries compared with 51 by the United Kingdom. In a related development, another study by the Whalen Company found that foreign direct investment is plunging.

The ESI study, conducted by ESI over the period May to October 1991, shows that the biggest increase in foreign investment during that time was in the chemicals sector, followed by new investments in electronics, telecommunications and computers. Over the period of October 1988 to October 1991, high-technology acquisitions by foreign investors totaled 536, with Japan accounting for 363 of them, according to ESI. Next was the United Kingdom with 51, France with 31, Canada with 14, Taiwan with 12 and Germany with 11.

According to the study, foreign investment in chemicals increased by 68%, with 21 new investments over the period from May to October 1991. Over that same period, foreign investment in electronics increased 41%, with 14 new investments, and in telecommunications it increased by 34%, with 15 new investments. In computers, foreign investment over the same period increased 27% with 28 new investments, according to the report.

Overall by industry, since 1988 foreign investment is directed primarily at the computer sector, which accounted for 133 of the high-technology acquisitions, followed by telecommunications (59), semiconductors (53), chemicals (52), electronics and advanced materials (48 each), and semiconductor equipment (37).

Of the Japanese firms investing in high-technology companies, 171 made investments that resulted in majority ownership and 140 resulted in minority ownership, according to the ESI survey.

Foreign direct investment took a nosedive according to the report by the Whalen Company. The report finds that foreign direct investment in U.S. enterprises plummeted from $71-billion in 1989 to $37-billion in 1990 -- a decline of 48%. And based on the first half of 1991, in which foreigners invested only $7.6 billion -- one-third the level of the first half of 1990 -- the total for 1991 is expected to amount to only about $15-billion, a decline of 59%.

In 1990, foreign direct investment from European countries amounted to only $13-billion, down dramatically from the $40-billion average between 1987 and 1989. Only the Japanese held even at about $16-billion, according to the report. In the first half of 1991, however, investment from Japan, which is beset by problems in its financial markets, has also plummeted to $850-million from $12-billion in the first half of 1990, a decline of 93%. The Japanese invested in only 55 companies in the first half of 1991, half the number of the same period last year. And investment from Europe declined 36%, from $8.5-billion to $5.4-billion, according to the report.

Foreign direct investment refers to ownership of 10% or more of a U.S. enterprise and does not include investment in Treasury bonds and notes. The reasons for the slowdown, according to the report, are because of a weak U.S. economy and problems with Japan's banks, stock market and real estate, which has reduced funds available in that country for overseas investments. By far the largest share of foreign investment, 40%, has gone into manufacturing, with the wholesale and retail trades second at 17.8%.

The report notes "the slowdown in foreign investment comes at a time when the U.S., which is short of domestic savings and investment of its own, badly needs foreign investment to help sustain the economic recovery."

The Whalen Company is a political consulting and communications firm founded in 1970 under the name of WIRES.

미래산자전러, 수출부분및 청측적능정동증정는 ㄴ동비 상.B

NAM STRESSES NEED FOR EXPORT DRIVE, ADOPTION OF EXCHANGE RATE POLICY

The U.S. must commit itself to an aggressive national export campaign if it hopes to continue winnowing down the trade deficit because the U.S. economy has many "serious structural problems" and economic growth abroad is much stronger, according to a new report by the National Association of Manufacturers. The analysis, entitled *Can the U.S. Export Drive Continue?*, also says the Administration and Congress must adopt an exchange rate policy, in cooperation with major industrial countries, that does not allow an overvaluation of the dollar to "short-circuit" a further reduction of the U.S. trade deficit.

Elements of a national export campaign being advocated by NAM include increasing funding for the Export-Import Bank by $4-billion; aggressively using Ex-Im funds to enforce a recent international agreement on "tied aid;" increasing funding for export promotion at the Commerce Dept. by $10-15-million for the next fiscal year; appointing a Presidential task force to develop recommendations for a

005b - 29 - 10

INSIDE U.S. TRADE - January 3, 1992   9 complete overhaul of the export control system in the next two years; and increasing funding for the State Dept.'s Trade & Development Program to $55-million, which would be an additional $20-million in budget outlays.

NAM president Jerry Jasinowski said at a Dec. 17 press conference that there is "no question" that the exchange rate reduction is the big reason for improved U.S. exports during the past few years. He said that by 1989 the U.S. gained back over half the export share it had lost because of the high dollar. But the benefits of the shifting exchange rate will be significantly less in the future, he said. This is why it is critical to adopt a monetary policy that does not permit an overvaluation of the dollar, he said. The report also calls for additional measures to stimulate export growth, including efforts to reduce corporate costs and improve service and quality; intensify bilateral and multilateral negotiations to open foreign markets; reduce outdated commercial export controls; strengthen export financing and promotion; and increase national savings and investment, with a special emphasis on enacting a research & development tax credit.

Jasinowski said it is critical for the U.S. to take forceful action to ensure that the export-led growth in recent years "keeps rolling along at a fast pace." He said that if the recommendations in the analysis are adopted by Congress and the Administration, he is optimistic that the U.S. will be able to maintain a high rate of export growth.

The author of the report, Stephen Cooney, pointed out at the press briefing that U.S. exports to France have increased over $4-billion over the last two years, a 33% jump, despite a slowing of growth in France. One of the reasons for that is the restructuring of the French economy, he said. Job layoffs in Europe resulting from the slowdown in growth and to some degree the forming of a unified market in 1992 are occurring at the same time as increased U.S. capital goods exports to Europe. He said this is "probably part of the same phenomenon, a restructuring phenomenon in European industry." And even if the growth rates in Europe over the next few years slow somewhat, exporting to Europe will still be a "better bet" for U.S. industry than selling in the U.S. and elsewhere, he said.

The report concludes that the U.S. is becoming an export-led economy, and the strong export growth in manufactured goods has accounted for most of the $100-billion reduction in the U.S. trade deficit since 1987, according to Jasinowski. The report also says that the most competitive U.S.-based exporters have been in high-technology products, which Jasinowski said "belies the widespread myth that we are losing out in all the industries of the future."

The analysis also pointed to "hot markets" for U.S. exports. It said that over the past five years, Europe, Japan and other East Asian countries have accounted for over $100-billion in increased U.S. exports. It said this pattern should continue in the future. In addition, there are strong signs that a successful effort to create a U.S.-Canada-Mexico free trade area will strengthen a recent recovery in U.S. exports to Mexico, the analysis said. Within the context of that three-country agreement, Canada also may resume its growth as a U.S. export market after the end of the North American economic recession, according to the report. New markets, especially China, Eastern Europe, the Soviet Union and India, may also be developed, but that process is a longer way off, according to the analysis.

DRAFT SUBSIDIES CODE INVITES CONFLICTING COMMENTS...begins on page 1

aimed at saving Chrysler or Lockheed, he added. The draft agreement was released Dec. 20 by Arthur Dunkel, the Director General of the General Agreement on Tariffs & Trade (GATT).

A representative for some U.S. multinationals downplayed the significance of permitting R&D subsidies because of relatively tight constraints the draft agreement places on subsidies to the developmental side of technology research. The draft agreement caps R&D subsidies at 50 percent of the costs of basic industrial research and at 25 percent of applied research. He did concede that permitting regional development subsidies is an important step because they are seen as trade distorting, but emphasized that their inclusion in the agreement was a deal breaker for the European Community. These subsidies will be limited to poor regions, which in the EC includes Scotland, Ireland, Greece, Portugal and Spain, sources said.

He also pointed out that the draft's exemption for developing countries is not as significant as some critics charge because most of them do not have the resources necessary for significant trade-distorting subsidization. This is particularly true for import substitution, which the source said has gone "out of fashion" in the developing world.

Domestic industry sources oppose the special treatment of developing countries, which they said is tantamount to virtually exempting them from the rules altogether. They implied that they would not object

0050 – 29 – 11

10   INSIDE U.S. TRADE - January 3, 1992

.as much to exemptions for least developed countries, but that special rules are inappropriate for middle-income countries, particularly the newly industrialized ones, which are already world class producers of some products.

The subsidies draft gives developing world countries eight years to phase out their export promotion and import substitution subsidies, compared with three years for the developed world. Non-market economies are also permitted a longer time frame to phase out their subsidies.

U.S. domestic producers also attacked the so-called "sunset" clause in the subsidies agreement that would terminate countervailing duties after a five year period. Like in the anti-dumping section of the draft agreement, petitioners would bear the burden of proof to demonstrate they would be injured if the duties were lifted (see related story in the *Special Report*).

The draft agreement does not explicitly recognize the right of unions to bring cases against subsidies, something which critics say could be narrowly interpreted by a GATT panel to exclude them as potential petitioners. Critics also charge that restrictive requirements on standing and prerequisites for pressing a case are similar to those in the anti-dumping section of the draft. In the section on anti-dumping, U.S. domestic producers object to rules that potential petitioners must first canvass the industry, a time-consuming task, and prove majority support for the petition before pressing the case. At the same time there is no language on what constitutes the majority of an industry, which like the case with labor unions, gives a GATT panel too much discretion in determining standing, critics pointed out.

The draft creates de minimis provisions on subsidized exports below which countervailing duties cannot be imposed. Under the terms of the draft agreement countervailing duties could not be erected on subsidies of less than 1% from developed world exporters, and 2% for the developing world. Also if the volume of subsidized imports constituted less than 4% of the market share in the home country, a countervailing duty could not be levied. This is similar to a provision in the anti-dumping section of the agreement. But critics charge that in some markets, such as commodities markets, a 2% dumping margin can be enough to drive U.S. producers out of business.

Calculations used to determine a subsidy are vague and incomplete, according to domestic industry sources. The definition does not cover a situation where a government may pressure private banks to lend to industries at preferential rates, they pointed out. Moreover, the issue of how to handle parastatal companies is left open, they said. Other observers challenge this assessment, however, and argue that the definition does in fact cover preferential treatment by banks.

DUNKEL FARM DRAFT OFFERS FEW REFORMS...begins on page 1

by the American Farm Bureau Federation calls for a good faith negotiating effort by all countries to have the agreement achieve a more substantial cutback in export subsidies and market access barriers.

The group acknowledges that may be hard to do in light of opposition from the European Community, Canada, Japan, Korea and the Nordic countries, according to the preliminary analysis reprinted below. The group points out that the Dec. 20 text is an improvement over a Dec. 12 draft agriculture text, which led it to call for a rejection of the farm deal (*Inside U.S. Trade*, Dec. 20, p 1). The new text offers a stronger commitment to continue farm reforms after six years than the Dec. 12 draft (*Inside U.S. Trade*, Special Report, Dec. 20, pS-1).

It also does not appear to limit countries' rights to protect their trade under the General Agreement on Tariffs & Trade, the Farm Bureau said in an analysis reprinted below. The text also stipulates that domestic supports listed in Annex 2 of the agreement cannot be offset with countervailing duties, but are not exempt from other trade measures, according to Article 7 of the draft agreement.

Several farm group representatives this week pointed out that in light of the EC opposition, it will be difficult to prevent further weakening of the text from its current version which some major commodity groups now assess as minimally acceptable.

USDA is assessing the impact of the proposed cuts and changes for each commodity, Secretary Ed Madigan told reporters this week. The analysis will then be discussed with Congress, private-sector advisors and farm leaders, Madigan said. He said he hoped USDA will complete its analysis by Jan. 13, when all nations meet again in the General Agreement on Tariffs & Trade "to begin deliberations" on this text. He refused to assess the draft, but when specifically pressed about its impact on commodities protected under section 22, Madigan offered a brief analysis for crops grown in Louisiana. He said he did not see sugar and tobacco producers getting hurt under the agreement and identified rice as a beneficiary from the agreement. Madigan did concede that peanut producers may have some complaints, but emphasized that peanuts entering the U.S. under a quota would still sell in excess of $400 a ton, maybe as high as

0015

The Jan. 7 briefings are also expected to provide groups with a better deadline for having to submit their assessment of the draft Uruguay Round agreement to the Administration, sources said. The Administration_is likely to provide briefings to congressional staff before Jan. 13, but direct meetings between high-level Administration officials and members of Congress are not likely to take place before Jan. 20, when Congress returns from recess, congressional sources said. The House Agriculture Committee is scheduled to hold hearings on the draft agreement on Jan. 9, where the Administration will be represented by USDA Under Secretary Richard Crowder, according to a tentative witness list issued by the panel. It is expected that Deputy U.S. Trade Representative Julius Katz will represent the Administration, although it is still possible that U.S. Trade Representative Carla Hills may testify, according to a committee source. Other witnesses on the tentative list include representatives of the American Farm Bureau, the National Council of Farmer Cooperatives, the American Soybean Assn., the National Farmers Union, the American Sugarbeet Growers Assn., the Associated Milk Producers, the National Cotton Council and the National Peanuts Growers Group.

The incremental cuts of export subsidies would leave most of the subsidies in place until 1999, farm groups pointed out. Under the GATT text, export subsidies would have to be cut 24 percent by volume and 36 percent by budgetary expenses from a 1986-1990 base period over the six years of the farm agreement. But the cuts would take place at different rates as specified in the text of Annex 8, paragraph five, farm groups pointed out. Assuming that the draft proposes a six-year transition arrangement, the budgetary cuts would have to be made at the level of six percent in the first year, they pointed out. In the following four years, the cuts would have to be made at least at the level of 3 percent and in the final year, the cuts would have to be made at a level that the 36 percent threshold would be met. The same stages would apply to the 24 percent volume reduction.

The farm groups' assessments will further be influenced by the outcome of the market access negotiations, including the details of how quotas and other barriers will be converted to tariffs. On tariffication, the EC may build in such a level of preference that the required tariff cuts of 36 percent by 1999 will lead to little increases in imports because they would start from a maximum levels, some farm representatives said.

Such padding is possible because most of the EC's current import barriers are variable levies which are not as transparent as quotas and are not internationally negotiated as are the tariffs of other countries, the sources said. One source pointed out that 80 percent of agricultural product categories in the U.S. are covered by internationally negotiated tariffs, while the EC has 80 percent of its product categories covered by a variable levy. All lists of concessions for individual commodities and supporting calculations must be submitted no later than March 1, 1992, according to the draft text. They will be classified as secret documents unless otherwise stipulated and will be made available only to trading partners that have submitted lists, the text said. The lists shall form the basis for the establishment of final country schedules no later than March 31, 1992, the text said.

The National Association of Wheat Growers is likely to raise the issue of freight and transport charges that are defined as export subsidies subject to reduction, according to the sources. In its comments to the Administration, NAWG is likely to insist that the definition of freight subsidies contained in Article 9 of the draft text be changed to read "internal transport and freight charges on export shipments provided or mandated by governments," one source said. The current definition would only count these charges if they are extended on "terms more favorable than for domestic shipments," according the text. If that definition is allowed to stand, it may allow Canada to backslide on the commitments it made in the free-trade agreement and would allow the so-called Crow's Nest rail subsidies to continue, NAWG has charged.

By Jutta Hennig

>> *Text of Farm Bureau Analysis starts on page 13* <<

0050 -29-13

0016

559 P05   WOI   '92-01-04 09:27

Farm Bureau Preliminary Analysis of GATT Farm Pact

Preliminary Farm Bureau Reaction
To GATT Director General Dunkel's Paper
On Agriculture

December 22, 1991

Farm Bureau has had only a brief opportunity to review the long and complicated proposed agricultural agreement offered by GATT Director General Arthur Dunkel on December 20.

Farm Bureau's principal goals in the trade talks have always been to achieve a substantial cutback in the use of export subsidies and to obtain a significant opening of foreign markets. Our preliminary assessment of the proposal from the GATT is that it would only partially achieve these objectives.

At the same time, we recognize that this document represents the net result of over five years of frustrating and often fruitless talks between countries with widely different and strongly held positions on agricultural trade. Mr. Dunkel is to be commended for his efforts to find a compromise solution in this sector that achieves the agreed objective of "a fair and market-oriented agricultural trading system."

We believe it is still possible to strengthen the agreement with good faith negotiating efforts by all countries and yet come out with a final text that better addresses all of our objectives. Unfortunately, we also have to recognize that some nations will find the proposal too far-reaching and may, instead, seek to weaken certain provisions.

Regardless of the eventual outcome of any further bilateral and multilateral negotiations on this text, a complete and careful examination of the full 74-page agreement will have to be completed before Farm Bureau's leaders can judge its overall merits.

In this connection, we will also be looking for analysis from the Department of Agriculture regarding the economic impact of the proposed agreement on U.S. agriculture and the benefits to our trade.

Summary of Key Elements

Below is a brief summary of some of the key elements of the proposed agreement. This summary was prepared in a short amount of time and may contain some inaccuracies, misinterpretations or omissions for which we apologize.

1. Proposed reforms are to begin in 1993. The proposed transition or implementation period covers the period beginning in 1993 and ending in the year 1999 (some reforms run from marketing year to marketing year and that must be the reason for the reference to "ending in 1999"). It is, therefore, a six-year transition arrangement.

A "continuation clause" is included in the proposed agreement, which reads in part as follows: "... the participants agree that the negotiations for continuing the [reform] process will be initiated one year before the end of the implementation period..." This language is somewhat stronger that the language in the draft text, which simply called for a "review" of the draft text, which simply called for a "review" of the reform process by a certain date and for the establishment of a program for continuing the reforms.

2. A very limited "peace treaty" is included in a form that would not appear to impair the rights of countries to pursue their

GATT rights in trade disputes. The proposed agreement states explicitly that existing GATT dispute settlement articles "shall apply to consultations and the settlement of disputes under this Agreement." It goes on to say that countries should "exercise due restraint" in the application of their GATT rights in relation to products included in this reform program.

3. Export subsidy expenditures are to be reduced by 36 percent over 6 years. The tonnage of commodities exported with subsidies will be reduced by 24 percent over the same period. Reductions will be made from a 1986-1990 base period (average).

Export subsidies to be covered include direct government payments to any firm or organization contingent on export performance, the disposal of publicly owned stocks at a price below the price on the domestic market, export subsidies financed by levies on producers imposed as a result of government action, subsidies to reduce the cost of marketing (other than generally available export promotion advisory services), internal transport charges on terms more favorable than for domestic shipments, and subsidies on primary products contingent on their incorporation in exported processed products.

Export credit and guarantees will continue to be subject to existing disciplines in the GATT. Food aid will continue to be subject to existing disciplines under the Food and Agriculture Organization (FAO).

Commitments on export subsidies will include undertakings not to introduce or re-introduce subsidies on commodities that did not receive subsidies during the base period. Also, commitments may be negotiated among the participants to limit or avoid subsidies on exports to specific markets or regions of the world.

4. As an overall objective, import barriers are to be lowered by 36 percent over 6 years.

For tariffs, reductions will be made from bound levels or, if unbound, from the level applied on September 1, 1986. On average, tariff reductions will be of 6 percent each year from 1993 through 1998. However, although tariffs on individual products may be reduced more than 36 percent, no tariffs may be reduced less than 15 percent.

Non-tariff barriers, such as variable levies and quotas, will be converted to "tariff quotas" under the so-called tariffication plan. There are no exceptions which means all non-tariff barriers will be covered, including Japan's rice barrier.

Tariff quotas will operate as follows: For a given commodity, the same level of imports will be allowed to enter as entered during the base period 1986-88 (average). A non-restrictive tariff may be applied to these imports (this will probably be the current tariff for products now subject to quotas). After that level of imports is reached in a given year, a higher tariff will be imposed to restrict additional imports.

This higher tariff will be essentially the difference between the internal and world prices during the base period so as to provide, at least initially, the same level of price protection from imports as exists under the current restrictions. However, both this tariff and the lower tariff on imports under the quota level will be gradually lowered according to the reduction plan for regular tariffs, 36 percent reductions by 1999.

In addition, in cases where imports during the 1986-1988 base period exceeded 3 percent of domestic consumption, the

0050 - 29 - IK

0017

559 P06   WOI   '92-01-04 09:28

tariff quota level is to be "maintained and increased" over the implementation period. How and to what extent they will be increased is not specified. Presumably, increases are to be negotiated through direct requests and offers among the participating countries. This provision is meant to address concerns in the U.S. and elsewhere that the agreement provide for increases in "current access opportunities."

In cases where imports of a given commodity during the 1986-88 base period were below 3 percent of domestic consumption, countries would have to establish an initial "minimum access" tariff quota at 3 percent of domestic consumption, and this would have to increase to 5 percent by 1999.

There is no "rebalancing" provision. The only provision that would allow consideration of positive export undertakings in the establishment of new import commitments reads: "...in relation to the expansion of current access, due account shall be taken of reduction commitments in the export area." This would not apply to soybeans and corn gluten feed, however, since both are subject only to tariffs, and, therefore, not to these "current access" expansion provisions.

A safeguard mechanism may also be used to temporarily limit imports under tariffication, if (1) the volume of imports during the marketing year exceeds 125 percent of the average of the three preceding years, or 125 percent of the agreed access minimums, whichever is higher; or (2) the import price of the commodity in question falls below the average price during the 1986-1988 base period. There are limits on both the time such a safeguard may be imposed and the level of the tariff safeguard employed.

5. Domestic supports fall into two categories: those that are minimally or non-trade distorting and, therefore, not subject to GATT disciplines; and those that are trade distorting and, therefore, subject to gradual reductions.

Domestic supports not subject to reductions must meet the fundamental requirement that they have no, or at most minimal, trade distorting or production effects. Examples of such non-trade distorting domestic subsidies include: disaster relief, domestic food aid programs, food security stockholding, income insurance, structural adjustment and long term land retirement programs, environmental payments, regional assistance, research, pest and disease control, training services, extension services, inspection services, promotion services, infrastructural works and services, and direct or de-coupled payments to producers.

Under the GATT proposal, trade distorting internal subsidies will be subject to 20 percent reductions in their respective "aggregate measurements of support" (AMS) over 6 years. The AMS, to greatly oversimplify, is the difference between the supported internal price of the commodity and the fixed external reference price for the same commodity during the base period 1986-1988 (average) multiplied by the quantity of production eligible for the support. Domestic supports that do not exceed 5 percent of the total value of production of a product or product sector will not be subject to reduction requirements.

6. An agreement on sanitary and phytosanitary measures in agricultural trade is included in the GATT paper. This will be reviewed in a separate report.

7. Special and differential treatment will be afforded developing countries in the length of transition period, the level of reductions and the treatment of their exports by developed countries. Details will be spelled out in a future report.

8. A Committee on Agriculture will be established to monitor progress in the reform process.

9. All lists of concessions and supporting calculations (AMS, subsidy levels, etc.) for individual commodities must be submitted no later than March 1, 1992, and final schedules of all concessions must be submitted by March 31, 1991.

Preliminary Evaluation

A preliminary evaluation of the paper suggests the following impacts on world agricultural trade (this is not in any way intended to be an all-encompassing analysis).

Continuation Clause:

* The so-called "continuation clause" that would extend export subsidy and other subsidy cuts beyond 1999 is stronger than what was suggested in the original draft text. While it is still marginal in our view, it may now be too strong for the EC. The EC had sought a simple review after 5 years, whereas the U.S. would prefer that the reforms be continued almost automatically for a total of 10 years.

Peace Treaty:

* The "peace treaty" language should not be objectionable, since it does not weaken any country's right to traditional dispute settlement procedures. The current U.S. complaint against EC oilseed subsidies should, therefore, not be affected.

Export Subsidies:

* Subsidized EC exports could be reduced substantially from current levels by 1999. The effect of a 36 percent reduction in subsidy expenditures and a 24 percent reduction in actual tonnages will have to be studied, however, for each of the many commodities sold with subsidies on the world market by the EC. The EC currently uses export subsidies for wheat, flour, most other grains, dairy products, beef, pork, sugar, poultry, and a wide range of other products.

* The 1986-1990 base period for export subsidy calculations is clearly a compromise. Applying the proposed percentage reductions to an earlier period, say 1986, when EC exports were generally lower, would have meant a more substantial real cut in subsidies from current (higher) levels. By the same token, applying the cuts to a more recent period, say 1990, would have resulted in smaller subsidy cuts. Basically, if subsidized EC exports were lower during the base period than they are today, the tonnage cut required will actually be greater, in some cases substantially, than the nominal 24 percent proposed.

* Providing for both tonnage and budgetary limits on export subsidies is an improvement over the first draft circulated last week. In that text, the emphasis was heavily on budgetary cuts. We have insisted on cuts in tonnage as well as in expenditures. Budgetary restraints become limiting when world prices are low and the EC cannot make up the difference between its prices and external prices. In such situations, the EC will become more of a residual supplier on the world market.

* Most U.S. export programs will be exempt from disciplines. The exception, of course, is the Export Enhancement Program (EEP). The budgetary reductions will likely be more limiting than the quantity limits for the U.S., since exports under the EEP since 1985 have been relatively stable. A guesstimate of average U.S. expenditures on EEP from 1986 to 1990 would be about $800 million annually. If this is in the ball park, the

0050 -29-'5

559 P07   WOI

'92-01-04 09:29

0018

program would have to be reduced to $752 million in 1993, and to $512 million by 1998.

* EC sugar exports will be covered even though the subsidy payments are financed by the producers. Canada's transportation subsidies will also be included--if they do not find another way to make the same kind of shipping payments. Differential export taxes used by Argentina on oilseed products are not included. In any case, Canada's transportation subsidies and Argentina's differential export taxes need to be eliminated, not simply reduced by 36 percent over 6 years.

* The commitments not to introduce new subsidies on commodities is more constraining for the U.S. than for the EC, since many more, if not most, EC exports are already subsidized. This provision will mean that the U.S. will not be able to subsidize exports of some products during the implementation period, even though the EC can. It would be more valuable to the U.S. to have commitments not to use subsidies into new markets or regions of the world. The GATT paper provides for this, but such commitments must be negotiated bilaterally and then included in the final list of concessions.

Market Access:

* Most U.S. agricultural imports are subject to tariffs, and these are generally low or already zero. The 36 percent tariff cuts by 1999 will not have a major impact on most producers. Where U.S. tariffs are high (mainly in the fruit and vegetable sector), 36 percent cuts could be significant, but these will be phased in over 6 years at 6 percentage points each year.

* For sensitive products, it will be possible to limit the cuts to a total of 15 percent by 1999. However, deeper cuts will have to be made in tariffs on other products to reach the aggregate 36 percent cut mandated.

* Tariffication will mean that U.S. Section 22 quotas will be converted to tariff rate quotas. Minimum access will have to [be] given to imports equaling 3 percent of domestic consumption in 1993, rising to 5 percent by 1999. This does not mean the U.S. must import this amount; it means that the U.S. must allow this amount if the foreign products can compete.

* This provision will affect peanuts, and individual dairy and sugar products where imports are less than 3 percent of consumption. The calculations and commitments will be done on a 4-digit tariff line bases (this means, for example, on butter, cheddar cheese, brie cheese, etc., rather than on a sector-wide basis). In many cases, these individual products may already be above the minimum access levels.

* One advantage of tariff quotas over quotas is that they are legal in the GATT and do not require a waiver to be maintained.

* Where imports already exceed the minimum access levels, the existing quotas will be converted to tariff quotas at current access levels. The tariff applied to imports allowed under the tariff quota, and the high tariff above the quota, will be reduced by 36 percent by 1999. In most cases, this degree of tariff cut will not result in substantial increases in imports. Any increase in the quota level itself would have to be negotiated in response to requests from other countries; it will not be automatic.

* This provision for non-automatic expansion in current access may be a relief to Section 22 producers, but it will be view negatively by U.S. producers of commodities seeking more access in foreign markets. The EC will not be likely to negotiate increases in current access unless such increases are required under an automatic GATT formula.

* The methodology of calculating tariff levels under tariffication could give the EC an advantage over other countries. The EC has calculated tariff equivalents of its variable levies in a manner that maximizes the level of the new above-quota tariff. The EC can "pad" its calculations because most of its current import barriers are variable levies which are not nearly as transparent as quotas and which are not bound in GATT. Most other countries utilize tariffs which are bound.

* The fact that a rebalancing clause was not included in the GATT paper is significant. The U.S. could not have accepted any paper that included rebalancing. Rebalancing would have permitted the EC to erect new import restrictions on corn gluten feed and other products, and would have set an extremely bad precedent for future trade negotiations.

* The concept of tariffication was rejected at the last minute last week by a number of countries that rely on quotas or outright import prohibitions — Canada (dairy and poultry), Japan (rice), Korea (rice and beef), and the Nordic countries (a number of commodities). Inclusion of the concept in this paper will raise questions about whether they will accept the text.

* The safeguard mechanism needs careful study in terms of its impact on specific products. The notion of a price-based safeguard originated with the EC, which wanted to retain a mechanism that would operate much like the variable levy that the tariff quotas were meant to replace. If the safeguards are allowed to operate too quickly, they will be too trade inhibiting. The establishment of the price base of 1986-1988 will prevent the use of safeguard tariffs unless import prices are below the average price during that period. The impact will vary from commodity to commodity depending on the relationship between those prices and prices today, and in the future.

Domestic Supports:

* Trade distorting domestic supports are to be reduced by 20 percent over 6 years, beginning in 1993 and using the average level of support in 1986-1988 as the starting point. Therefore, where supports were higher during the base period than today, no reductions will be required, at least not immediately. In addition, credit will be given for reductions made since 1986. The text does not explain how this would be done in addition to the "credit" automatically received by setting the base period at 1986-1988.

* Most U.S. commodities would receive sufficient credit to avoid cuts for a number of years, given the cuts that were made in the 1985 and 1990 farm bills. Interestingly, the U.S. 1995 farm bill will be written long before most commodities would face any cuts resulting from the GATT agreement. Exceptions, obviously, would be commodities that did not absorb support cuts in either recent farm bill.

* Domestic support cuts are not actually made in the support price, itself, but rather in the gap (the AMS) between the supported internal price and the external reference price. The gap depends not only on the level of government support, but also on the reference price level during the 1986-1988 base period. In any case, the 20 percent cut in the gap by 1999 would result in annual reductions in the gap of 3.3 percent beginning in 1993.

* To determine the actual effect on support prices, the external reference prices would have to be known. However, assuming that the domestic price is no more than a third higher

0050 - 29 - 16

than the external price, the effect is likely to be no more than a one percent reduction in the support price each year.

*The GATT paper would allow any lost income to producers from these cuts to be offset by direct income payments that may be tied to environmental or other similar activities, but may not be tied to production.

* The 20 percent reduction figure is probably a reflection of the sensitivity of reducing internal farm supports. Earlier discussions in Geneva pointed to a reduction of 30 to 35 percent.

* The idea (discussed between the U.S. and the EC) of a separate category of domestic supports that would be subject only to ceiling limits -- as opposed to actual cuts -- did not find its way into the GATT paper. This idea would have allowed virtually all new EC support programs (under the EC's Common Agricultural Policy reforms) to be exempt. It would have also allowed most U.S. programs to be exempt.

U.S., HONG KONG INDUSTRIES OPPOSE RETALIATION AGAINST PRC...begins on page 1

in 1991, according to the company.

Opponents of retaliation were backed by industry representatives from Hong Kong, who also argued that the retaliation will hurt U.S. consumers and industries by driving up prices. They also insisted that retaliation would largely be ineffective in forcing the hand of the Chinese government, according to the comments filed.

A hearing on the proposed $1.5-billion retaliation list is scheduled for Jan. 6 & 7, with rebuttals to be filed on Jan. 13, according to a USTR announcement. U.S. Trade Representative Carla Hills announced last month that Jan. 16 is the firm deadline for retaliation (*Inside U.S. Trade*, Dec. 20, p 14). More than 60 witnesses are expected to testify at the hearings, according to a tentative witness list reprinted below.

U.S. and Chinese authorities continue to negotiate on intellectual property protection, Administration sources said this week. However, Dec. 21 & 22 talks between USTR and the Chinese government appear to have resulted in a widening of differences between the two sides, with the U.S. charging that the PRC has been backing off from prior commitments to improve intellectual property protection.

In a Dec. 16 briefing, Hills said the U.S. wants meaningful protection of patents including for pharmaceuticals as well as meaningful protection for copyrights. She emphasized the need for "some specificity" of when and how promised protection would be extended. Hills added that the Chinese had indicated they were prepared to join the Berne Convention, but were not prepared to say when they would put in place its obligations. She also said that the PRC had indicated that "it was prepared in general" to join the Geneva Phonograph Convention, but would not specify when it would put in place the protections demanded of this agreement. She said there was "no real change," in the Chinese position. Under the Special 301 case in question, the U.S. has charged China with inadequate copyright protection, deficient patent laws, inadequate protection of trade secrets and trademarks.

Raising tariffs on Chinese made goods would be especially harmful to U.S. commercial and consumer interests given the current recession, according to a comment filed by the National Retail Federation and the Retail Industry Trade Action Coalition. The higher cost to U.S. consumers would have the effect of reducing consumer spending just as both Congress and the Administration are trying to devise ways to stimulate it to help the economy. The higher prices would hit low-income consumers especially hard, the groups argue.

The retaliation would also deal a financial blow to the U.S. retail industry that could lead to job losses, especially since it would follow crippling losses over the past two year. Moreover, retaliation against consumer products would not have the desired effect of forcing the government of the PRC to improve its intellectual property laws, according to the comments. The groups also ask that retailers get at least 270 days to prepare for the higher prices, if USTR goes forward with the retaliation.

Comments made by the retailers groups are echoed by the Footwear Distributors and Retailers of America, which insist that retaliation will not influence Chinese government policy. They argue that in the footwear industry the value added in China is extremely small and consists almost exclusively of labor payment. All of the profit and most of the material costs of the industry do not remain in China.

On the other hand, the retaliation would harm U.S. commercial interests as well as the commercial interests of Hong Kong, Taiwan and the southern Chinese provinces and thereby contribute to instability in the region, according to the group.

Also filing comments opposing the retaliation, particularly because of its impact on Hong Kong, were the Hong Kong Electronics Association, the Hong Kong Leather Goods Manufacturers Trade Association, the Ad Hoc Committee of Manufacturers of Electrical Appliances of Hong Kong, and the Hong Kong Electronics Industry Council. A number of Hong Kong footwear associations and the Hong Kong Watch Manufacturers Association are also expected to give testimony at the hearing against the retaliation.

0050-29-19

continued on next page

INSIDE U.S. TRADE - January 3, 1992

January 7, 1992
2:00 p.m.

Kansky Associates Inc.	Motor fuels	National Dauch, Ltd.	
		Hollies Enterprises, Ltd.	
Westport Corporation	4202.31.60	Winning Star Enterprises, Ltd.	
Fashion Accessories Shippers Association, Inc.	4201.31.60	Wolverine World Wide, Inc.	Footwear
	4201.11.00	Isaco	Silk apparel
Timex Corporation	9102.12.80	Penn, Wright and Manson	Silk apparel
Hong Kong Watch Manufacturers Association Ltd.	9102.12.80	Mast Industries and The Limited, Inc.	Silk apparel
National Electronics Holdings Ltd.	9102.11.80	Magnadyne Corporation (USA)	Electronic products
National Electronics & Watch Co., Ltd.			

단가판단의 복지해가격 결정 (동기, 동이) 상당히 끼치는

DRAFT GATT TEXT HAS STRONG DISPUTE SETTLEMENT MECHANISM, WEAK RULES

A preliminary assessment of a draft Uruguay Round agreement on dispute settlement procedures reveals that negotiators agreed on a strong mechanism for resolving disputes, but struck weak rules on the scope of review for dispute panels of the General Agreement on Tariffs & Trade (GATT). The U.S. failure to achieve such standards means that the draft dispute settlement agreement will be a "mixed bag" for U.S. industry seeking to protect its rights, sources say.

The principal strengthening in the dispute settlement mechanism is that it would provide for automatic adoption of a dispute panel report after 60 days. A consensus would have to be built to block a panel report rather than the current system where a consensus must exist to adopt one. An appeal must be filed within 60 days, and the decision is automatically adopted after 30 days unless it is unanimously rejected. With these tight timetables, it would be unlikely that U.S. section 301 provisions triggering unilateral retaliation would kick in, sources said. Current U.S. law allows unilateral action even if a case has been taken to the GATT, if that process does not produce a timely result. At the same time, it does not appear that the draft agreement would require changes in the section 301 law, some sources said.

According to a Dec. 23 letter sent to members of Congress by the American Iron and Steel Institute, this absence of standards for review will have the effect of displacing U.S. government authority in dispute settlement (see related story in *Special Report*). "By failing to set forth an acceptable standard or scope of review, the new texts allow GATT panels when reviewing trade cases to substitute their judgement for that of the U.S. government," the letter states.

The draft text proscribes the use of unilateral trade remedies in areas covered by the GATT, but this is not tantamount to an outright ban on U.S. use of section 301 provisions, according to a private-sector source. Section 21 of the draft text states that contracting parties shall not make determinations that violations have occurred or that their trade rights have been nullified except through the multilateral process. According to the AISI letter, however, the draft text would outright prohibit use of section 301 law and prevent the U.S. from using it as a lever to open up overseas markets. The AISI letter concludes that "exclusive GATT jurisdiction over trade disputes and weak substantive GATT rules will deprive the United States of a proven means for defending its rights."

0050-29-19

Inside U.S. Trade

An exclusive weekly report on major government and industry trade action

January 3, 1992

Special Report

대체(초·5)의 반면정 추청기 간초 비 교개 반흥 (동가.동나) 상,땅

ANTIDUMPING DRAFT INVITES CONFLICTING COMMENTS FROM EXPORTERS, PRODUCERS

Representatives of domestic industries this week claimed that changes in international antidumping rules proposed in the Uruguay Round would seriously weaken U.S. law, particularly by allowing foreign producers regional sales at unfairly low prices and by placing new burdens on domestic firms seeking to keep antidumping duties in place for longer than five years. They also insist that the draft antidumping agreement tabled by the top official of the General Agreement on Tariffs & Trade on Dec. 20 would make it harder to bring and win antidumping cases.

But representatives of U.S. multinational corporations contradict that assessment, saying that the proposed draft could bring small improvements for U.S. producers seeking to use antidumping law. They also highlight that they consider the draft agreement to be a victory for the European Community because it would legitimize two of its controversial antidumping practices. One of them gives governments "excessive" leeway in calculating the profit margins of U.S. exporters in antidumping calculations, one private-sector source said. The other makes foreign exporters responsible for the dumping practices of their unrelated retailers, he said. Representatives of multinationals argue that the Dunkel text fails to protect them from abuses of antidumping law by foreign governments.

The complaints of domestic producers were also highlighted in a Dec. 23 letter sent by the American Iron and Steel Institute to all members of Congress (see related story). The letter points to five areas in the antidumping section of the Dunkel text that jeopardizes U.S. trade law including changes in the methodology for calculating dumping margins, the absence of "cumulative injury" provisions, restrictive definitions of standing, high de minimis levels on foreign dumping, and the automatic termination of antidumping duties after five years.

The letter also argues that in the Dunkel text the U.S. has not achieved its key goals of strengthening rules against circumvention of duty orders, and against repeat offenders. This assessment is challenged, however, by U.S. exporters who claim that the text contains three new provisions to fight circumvention.

Domestic industry representatives argue that the draft would allow region-specific dumping or predatory dumping against domestic firms. According to these sources dumping margins would be calculated in the importing country by averaging the nationwide sales prices for a product of an exporting company under investigation, instead of taking prices on a region by region basis as is now the case under U.S. law. This means that an exporting company could sell product at less than fair value in one region and offset those sales by selling at a higher price in another region, they claim. Domestic critics of the Dunkel anti-dumping section also charge that a whole series of methodologies used for calculating margins are being changed, which when added together, will reduce or eliminate dumping margins in many cases. These sources particularly attacked changes made in the cost of production calculations.

The draft agreement does adopt a current U.S. practice that allows exporters at least 60 days to adjust prices in response to sustained changes in the exchange rate. Originally U.S. multinationals had been pressing for a 90 period to adjust prices.

The Dunkel text could sharply curtail efforts by a domestic industry to bring antidumping cases by narrowing the definition of standing, and requiring a petitioner to show industry-wide support for a petition before an investigation is launched. According to sources, the narrow definition of standing could potentially exclude labor unions as legitimate plaintiffs. The text also lacks a definition of what constitutes the "majority" of an industry, which critics say gives a GATT panel too much discretion.

Under current U.S. law, a petitioner may prompt an antidumping investigation which, once underway, can be halted with a successful challenge to the petitioner's standing. But in the Dunkel text, a petitioner would have to show industry support for the petition before the investigation could be launched. If an industry with thousands of producers had to be canvassed before an antidumping investigation could be

005b —29 —2 o

continued on page 8

>> AISI Letter on Uruguay Round begins page S-10 <<

0022

Exporters' Analysis of GATT Antidumping Draft

Memorandum

Date: December 27, 1991

To:

From:

Subject: Analysis of December 20, 1991 GATT Antidumping Draft

Introduction

The December 20, 1991 GATT Antidumping Code is, in a word, disappointing. On every major issue, it fails to include the safeguards against abuse which would protect U.S. industry from unfair foreign antidumping duties in our major export markets (except, perhaps, Canada, which is the only country other than the U.S. which has an organization similar to our International Trade Commission to exercise some minimal restraint on unbridled executive discretion to impose duties whenever and in whatever amount is desired). The clear winner in the negotiation is the European Communities (EC), which was able to use U.S. pressure to enshrine in the code certain of the more bizarre and protectionist current EC antidumping practices (such as requiring foreign exporters, but not domestic producers, to fix prices of unrelated customers down to the [retail] level; and preserving the EC ability to impute whatever level of profit is necessary to find dumping margins). The main losers will be U.S. exporters, who will be the most exposed to abuse of antidumping laws in their export markets. Minor winners include protection-seeking U.S. companies -- many of which, oddly enough, are foreign-owned (e.g., steel (Japan) and typewriters (United Kingdom)).

Key Points

• The cost of production provisions have serious flaws. The failure to include in this draft some of the detail included in earlier texts (such as the prohibition of customs authorities claiming that start-up periods are less than six months) exposes both high-tech and heavy machinery U.S. exporters to substantial vulnerability to foreign antidumping duties, simply because of declines in demand. In addition, the method of measuring the profit margin to be imputed to U.S. exporters leaves foreign governments with virtually unfettered discretion (such as is already applied by the EC).

• The "averaging" provisions appear to continue to allow foreign governments, if they wish, to find dumping where prices in both markets are identical.

• The injury standard contains nothing to protect U.S. exporters from being found to cause injury, even when the U.S. company is selling at a price much higher than the local company. This has been the experience of U.S. exporters of processed agricultural products in Israel, Korea, Taiwan and Japan, and now Thailand and Nigeria.

• Nothing in the transparency provisions will improve transparency in such major U.S. export markets as the EC or Canada.

• The procedural provisions do not prevent use of antidumping laws to harass U.S. exporters, in particular in smaller markets where the cost of defending the case may exceed the value of the market.

• The only major positive aspect appears to be in the dispute resolution area, where adoption of the U.S. proposal for general GATT dispute resolution would ensure that U.S. exporters have the same access to review as foreign exporters (at present, foreign exporters to the U.S. get fairly good judicial review in the U.S. Court of International Trade, while U.S. exporters to the EC, Canada, and other countries confront a virtually unbeatable standard of high judicial deference to the administrators). Some attempts were made to reduce the degree of GATT review of antidumping determinations; this threatened to spread to other negotiating groups, where it would have seriously undermined U.S. gains in the "new areas" of GATT, such as TRIP's.

In addition, there were minor gains in the de minimis margin level, which was set at 2%. This is not a major gain for U.S. exporters, because the EC and Canada already applied a 1.5-2.5% level, but it may help some of the new antidumping user countries (e.g., Korea, Colombia, Venezuela, Israel, Taiwan, Mexico, Nigeria) which do not have fixed de minimis levels.

I attach a more detailed memorandum reviewing the major items.

Cost of Production

A new section (Art. 2.2.1) was added expressly permitting antidumping authorities to attack sales below full (variable plus fixed) cost. The section is drawn directly from the U.S. statute.

Prices may be considered below cost if the average price is lower than the average cost, or if 20 percent of prices are below average cost.

To avoid dumping charges, sales must be made above full cost plus profit. "Profit" will not usually be calculated from the profit only on profitable sales, rather than the profit on all sales of the product (Art. 2.2.2). This replaces the U.S. statute with the EC rule.

Costs will now be adjusted to reflect start-up periods (Art. 2.2.1.1), but there is no definition of start-up period and no minimum length of such period.

Anticircumvention Measures

The most significant change from the existing Antidumping Code is the addition of all three anticircumvention measures advocated by the U.S. Authorities may apply duties to parts and components exported from the country subject to the antidumping duty for assembly in the U.S. without conducting an investigation to determine whether such parts and components are dumped or causing injury (Art. 12). The reverses a 1989 GATT panel decision in favor of Japan against the EC.

Parts and components exported for assembly in third countries may be subject to retroactive antidumping duties after an investigation of dumping and injury. (Art. 10.5)

"Country-hopping" (the shifting of sources by a multinational company from one country to another after an antidumping case is initiated will be subject to similar controls (Art. 10.4).

Calculation of Dumping Margins

The text (Art. 2.4.2) continues the 1979 Code's requirement of a fair comparison between the export price and the normal value to calculate a dumping margin.

Current U.S. practice on currency conversions has been

0050 - 29 -21

0023

559 P13   WOI   '92-01-04 09:35

adopted (Art. 2.4.1), which allows exporters at least 60 days to adjust prices in response to sustained changes in exchange rates.

With respect to averaging, the Secretariat's text is a compromise between Mexico's consistent practice of comparing weighted-average prices in the importing country and the EC's practice of comparing a single transaction in the importing country to a weighted-average in the exporting country. (Since 1984, U.S. law has permitted both options.)

The text requires authorities to compare averages-to-averages, or transaction-to-transaction (Art. 2.4.2), except when there are low prices in the export market, in which case individual export prices may be compared to a weighted-average home market price without regard to whether there are comparable prices in the home market.

De Minimis Margins/Negligible Imports

Article 5.8 for the first time sets an explicit standard for de minimis dumping margins of 2 percent. De minimis margins are currently 1.5 to 2.5 percent in practice in the EC and Canada and 0.5 percent by regulation in the U.S.

For purposes of injury analysis, Article 5.8 also provides a negligibility guideline -- i.e. if the volume of dumped imports from a particular country account for less than one percent of domestic market share, they shall be considered negligible and the case shall be terminated, unless the total market share of negligible suppliers exceeds 2.5 percent, in which case those suppliers remain in the case.

Sunset

An EC and Canadian procedure for reviewing antidumping orders after 5 years was adopted (in place of some proposals for automatic termination).

Injury

The injury provisions generally unchanged, except for inclusion of a Canadian proposal that the size of the margin of dumping be a factor to be evaluated in deciding whether the dumping caused material injury.

Standing

Antidumping authorities will now be required to check standing before initiation (5.7) (as already done by the EC and Canada, and as required by a 1990 GATT panel ruling in a case brought by Sweden), but no specific percentage of support is required.

Duty Collection

The EC will be allowed to continue to double-count certain costs in calculating duties (thus increasing them) (Art. 9.3.3). The EC practice is allegedly aimed at Japanese multinationals, although it also applies to U.S. exporters to Europe. USTR Formally objected to this practice in 1985.

Industrial Users and Consumer Interests

A provision was added requiring authorities to allow industrial users and, in a limited number of cases, consumer groups to express views on certain issues (Art. 6.12).

Dispute Resolution

Disputes under the Antidumping Code will be handled under the new Dispute Resolution Code, which is based on U.S. and EC proposals (Art. 18).

Excerpt From GATT Dumping Text
Analysis done by Steptoe & Johnson

DUNKEL DRAFT

[ARTICLE 11
DURATION AND REVIEW
OF ANTI-DUMPING DUTIES
AND PRICE UNDERTAKINGS]

11.1 An anti-dumping duty shall remain in force only as long as and to the extent necessary to counteract dumping which is causing injury.

11.2 The authorities shall review the need for the continued imposition of the duty, where warranted, on their own initiative or,

provided that a reasonable period of time has elapsed since the imposition of the definitive anti-dumping duty, upon request by any interested party which submits positive information substantiating the need for a review.[1]

Interested parties shall have the right to request the authorities to examine whether the continued imposition of the duty is necessary to offset dumping, whether recurrence of the injury would occur if the duty were removed or varied, or both. If, as a result of the review under this paragraph, the authorities determine that the anti-dumping duty is no longer

0050 - 29 - 22

0024

SS9 P14   WOI   '92-01-04   09:36

warranted, it shall be terminated immediately.

11.3 Notwithstanding the provisions of paragraphs 1 and 2, any definitive anti-dumping duty shall be terminated on a date not later than five years from its imposition (or from the date of the most recent review under paragraph 2 if that review has covered both dumping and injury, or under this paragraph), unless the authorities determine, in a review initiated before that date on their own initiative or upon a duly substantiated request made by or on behalf of the domestic industry within a reasonable period of time prior to that date, that the continued imposition of

the duty is necessary to prevent the continuation or recurrence of injury by dumped imports.[2/] The duty may remain in force pending the outcome of such a review.

11.4 The provisions of Article 6 regarding evidence and procedure shall apply to any review carried out under this Article. Any such review shall be carried out expeditiously and shall normally be concluded within twelve months of the date of initiation of the review.

11.5 The provisions of this Article shall *mutatis mutandis* apply to price undertakings accepted under Article 8.]

[1/] A determination of final liability for payment of anti-dumping duties as provided for in Article 9.3 does not by itself constitute a review within the meaning of this Article.

[2/] When the amount of the anti-dumping duty is assessed on a retrospective basis, a finding in the most recent assessment proceeding under Article 9.3.1 that no duty is to be levied shall not by itself require the authorities to determine under this paragraph that the continued imposition of the anti-dumping duty is not necessary.

ARTICLE 2
DETERMINATION OF DUMPING

2.1 For the purpose of this Code a product is to be considered as being dumped, i.e., introduced into the commerce of another country at less than its normal value, if the export price of the product exported from one country to another is less than the comparable price, in the ordinary course of trade, for the like product when destined for consumption in the exporting country.

[2.6 Throughout this Code the term "like product" ("produit similaire") shall be interpreted to mean a product

which is identical, i.e., alike in all respects to the product under consideration, or in the absence of such a product, another product which although not alike in all respects, has characteristics closely resembling those of the product under consideration.]

[2.5 In the case where products are not imported directly from the country of origin but are exported to the country of importation from an intermediate country, the price at which the products are sold from the country of export to the country of importation shall normally be compared with the comparable

price in the country of
export. However, comparison
may be made with the price in
the country of origin, if, for
example, the products are
merely trans-shipped through
the country of export, or such
products are not produced in
the country of export, or
there is no comparable price
for them in the country of
export.]

2.2   When there are no
sales of the like product in
the ordinary course of trade
in the domestic market of the
exporting country or when,
because of the particular
market situation
or the low volume of the sales
in the domestic market of the
exporting country,[2]
such sales do not permit a
proper comparison; the margin
of dumping shall be determined
by comparison with a
comparable price of the like
product when exported to an
appropriate third country
provided that this price is
representative,
or with the cost of production
in the country of origin plus
a reasonable amount for
administrative, selling and
any other costs and for
profits.

2.2.1 Sales of the like
product in the domestic market
of the exporting country or
sales to a third country at
prices below per unit (fixed
and variable) costs of
production plus selling,
general and administrative
costs may be treated as not
being in the ordinary course
of trade by reason of price
and may be disregarded in
determining normal value only
if the authorities[3] determine
that such sales are made
within an extended period of
time[4] in substantial
quantities[3] and are at prices
which do not provide for the

recovery of all costs within a
reasonable period of time. If
prices which are below costs
at the time of sale are above
weighted average costs for the
period of investigation, such
prices shall be considered to
provide for recovery of costs
within a reasonable period of
time.

2.2.1.1 For the purpose
of paragraph 2.2, costs shall
normally be calculated on the
basis of records kept by the
exporter or producer under
investigation, provided that
such records are in accordance
with the generally accepted
accounting principles of the
exporting country and
reasonably reflect the costs
associated with the production
and sale of the product under
consideration. Authorities
shall consider all available
evidence on the proper
allocation of costs, including
that which is made available
by the exporter or producer in
the course of the
investigation provided that
such allocations have been
historically utilized by the
exporter or producer, in
particular in relation to
establishing appropriate
amortization and depreciation
periods and allowances for
capital expenditures and other
development costs. Unless
already reflected in the cost
allocations under this sub-
paragraph, costs shall be
adjusted appropriately for
those non-recurring items of
cost which benefit future
and/or current production, or
for circumstances in which
costs during the period of
investigation are affected by
start-up operations.[5]

2.2.2 For the purpose of
paragraph 2 of this Article,
the amounts for administrative
selling and any other costs
and for profits shall be based

0050 -29-26

0026

SSS P16   WOI   '92-01-04 09:37

on actual data pertaining to production and sales in the ordinary course of trade of the like product by the exporter or producer under investigation. When such amounts cannot be determined on this basis, the amounts may be determined on the basis of:

(i) the actual amounts incurred and realized by the exporter or producer in question in respect of production and sales in the domestic market of the country of origin of the same general category of products;

(ii) the weighted average of the actual amounts incurred and realized by other exporters or producers subject to investigation in respect of production and sales of the like product in the domestic market of the country of origin;

(iii) any other reasonable method, provided that the amount for profit so established shall not exceed the profit normally realized by other exporters or producers on sales of products of the same general category in the domestic market of the country of origin.

2.3 In cases where there is no export price or where it appears to the authorities concerned that the export price is unreliable because of association or a compensatory arrangement between the exporter and the importer or a third party, the export price may be constructed on the basis of the price at which the imported products are first resold to an independent

buyer, or if the products are not resold to an independent buyer, or not resold in the condition as imported, on such reasonable basis as the authorities may determine.

2.4 A fair comparison shall be made between the export price and the normal value.

The two prices shall be compared at the same level of trade, normally at the ex-factory level, and in respect of sales made at as nearly as possible the same time. Due allowance shall be made in each case, on its merits, for differences which affect price comparability, including differences in conditions and terms of sale, taxation, levels of trade, quantities, physical characteristics, and any other differences which are also demonstrated to affect price comparability. In the cases referred to in paragraph 3 of Article 2, allowances for costs, including duties and taxes, incurred between importation and resale, and for profits accruing, should also be made. If in these cases, price comparability has been affected, the authorities shall establish the normal value at a level of trade equivalent to the level of trade of the constructed export price, or make due allowance as warranted under this paragraph. The authorities shall indicate to the parties in question what information is necessary to ensure a fair comparison and shall not impose an unreasonable burden of proof on those parties.

2.4.1 When the price comparison under this paragraph requires a

0050 -29 -25

conversion of currencies, such
conversion should be made
using the rate of exchange on
the date of sale,[3/] provided
that when a sale of foreign
currency on forward markets is
directly linked to the export
sale involved, the rate of
exchange in the forward sale
shall be used: Fluctuations in
exchange rates shall be
ignored and, in an
investigation the authorities
shall allow exporters at least
60 days to have adjusted their
export prices to reflect
sustained movements during the
period of investigation.

2.4.2 Subject to the
provisions governing fair
comparison in paragraph 2.4,
the existence of margins of
dumping during the
investigation phase shall
normally be established on the
basis of a comparison of a
weighted average normal value
with a weighted average of
prices of all export
transactions or by a
comparison of normal value and
export prices on a transaction
to transaction basis. A
normal value established on a
weighted average basis may be
compared to prices of
individual export transactions
if the authorities find a
pattern of export prices which
differ significantly among
different purchasers, regions
or time periods and if an
explanation is provided why
such differences cannot be
taken into account
appropriately by the use of a
weighted average-to-weighted

average or transaction-to-
transaction comparison.

2.5 In the case where
products are not imported
directly from the country of
origin but are exported to the
country of importation from an
intermediate country, the
price at which the products
are sold from the country of
export to the country of
importation shall normally be
compared with the comparable
price in the country of
export. However, comparison
may be made with the price in
the country of origin, if, for
example, the products are
merely trans-shipped through
the country of export, or such
products are not produced in
the country of export, or
there is no comparable price
for them in the country of
export.

2.6 Throughout this Code
the term "like product"
("produit similaire") shall be
interpreted to mean a product
which is identical, i.e.,
alike in all respects to the
product under consideration,
or in the absence of such a
product, another product which
although not alike in all
respects, has characteristics
closely resembling those of
the product under
consideration.

2.7 This Article is
without prejudice to the
second Supplementary Provision
to paragraph I of Article VI
in Annex L to the General
Agreement.

[1/] When in this Code the term 'authorities' is used, it shall
be interpreted as meaning authorities at an appropriate, senior
level.

[2/] Sales of the like product destined for consumption in the
domestic market of the exporting country shall normally be
considered a sufficient quantity for the determination of the

.normal value if such sales constitute 5 per cent or more of the sales of the product under consideration to the importing country, provided that a lower ratio should be acceptable where the evidence demonstrates that domestic sales at such lower ratio are nonetheless of sufficient magnitude to provide for a proper comparison.

3/   When in this Code the term "authorities" is used, it shall be interpreted as meaning authorities at an appropriate senior level.

4/   The extended period of time should normally be one year but shall in no case be less than six months.

5/   Sales below per unit cost are made in substantial quantities when the authorities establish that the weighted average selling price of the transactions under consideration for the determination of the normal value is below the weighted average unit cost or that the volume of sales below per unit costs represents not less than 20 per cent of the transactions under consideration for the determination of the normal value.

6/   The adjustment made for start-up operations shall reflect the costs at the end of the start-up period or, if that period extends beyond the period of investigation, the most recent costs which can reasonably be taken into account by the authorities during the investigation.

7/   It is understood that some of the above factors may overlap, and authorities shall ensure that they do not duplicate adjustments that have been already made under this provision.

8/   Normally, the date of sale would be the date of contract, purchase order, order confirmation, or invoice, whichever establishes the material terms of sale.

DUNKEL DRAFT WOULD CHANGE U.S. ANTIDUMPING LAWS . . . begins page S1

launched, this would give an offender time to cease dumping or build domestic inventory before the investigation began, critics say. The text does allow the use of sampling procedures to survey the industry, but this would still be a burden, one source added.

Related to this is how "neutral" companies would be tallied in gauging industry support. Under U.S. law, companies that have expressed neither support or opposition to the investigation are counted as being in favor of it. This is because many companies may choose to remain neutral -- even though they are in favor of an investigation -- in order not to "rock the boat," one source explained. In the Dunkel text, however, the neutral companies would not be counted, making it potentially harder to demonstrate support.

The draft also fails to make any provision for a "cumulative" assessment of injury in antidumping cases, as allowed under U.S. law. Under U.S. law, injury can be determined by adding together the impact of dumped imports from several countries. In the Dunkel text, a separate determination of injury would have to be made for each country.

The draft allows for de minimis dumping where the margin is less than two percent, but critics charge that can be injurious particularly in commodities markets where a 2% difference in price can be significant. The U.S. allows 0.5% de minimis dumping, compared to the European Community and Canada, where de minimis dumping margins between 1.5% and 2.5% are allowed. Given these differences, the Dunkel draft represents a minor gain for U.S. exporters, one private-sector supporter of the change said. This is especially true for cases that would be brought by countries, such as Korea and Mexico, which are just beginning to use antidumping laws against foreign exporters and do not have any fixed de minimis levels,

0029

559 P19   WOI   '92-01-04 09:40

The draft also includes in a new concept for allowing de minimis dumping calculated by volume rather than price. Specifically, if the volume of dumped imports accounts for less than 1% of an exporter's home market, an antidumping case will be dropped, unless the total market share of negligible suppliers exceeds 2.5%.--

The draft would end anti-dumping duty orders automatically after five years -- a "sunset" clause, according to the Dunkel text. In order for the duty to be kept in place, the domestic industries would have to prove that it would be injured by the lifting of the antidumping orders. Under U.S. law, there is no time limit on duty orders, and an order may only be lifted if it can be demonstrated that there has been no sales by an exporter at less than fair value for at least the two most recent years.

The draft agreement would shift the burden of proof for extending a dumping order to the petitioner. But the case is made harder for the petitioner because in trying to show probable injury resulting from lifting the duty, there would be no "track record" for the preceding five years, opponents of the change argue. Thus proof of injury would become very speculative and difficult to produce, they said.

The U.S. failed to get any strong rules in the Dunkel text to help curb circumvention and violations by repeat offenders, domestic industry critics charge. In order to combat circumvention, U.S. law sets forth a series of criteria to expand the scope of a duty order against an exporting company to its U.S. assembly plants. These criteria include determining the business relationship between the transplant and the exporting company in the home country, and the percentage of parts made in the home country and shipped for assembly in the transplant.

But the Dunkel text sets forth specific numbers, requiring that the parts content from the exporting company to the transplant be 70% or more before a country can expand a duty order to products from an assembly plant. In effect, the provisions in the draft tend to treat an investigation of products from a transplant as a wholly new case, whereas current U.S. law considers such an investigation as part of the same case. The Dunkel draft does allow for duties to be collected retroactively for 150 days if an investigation shows proof of circumvention.

In contrast, representatives of U.S. multinational corporations insist that the U.S. succeeded in adding to the text all three anticircumvention measures it had been advocating. In addition to gaining retroactivity on duty orders against transplants, authorities may expand duties to parts and components exported to the U.S. for assembly without conducting an investigation on whether those parts and components cause injury or are being dumped. The text also proscribes attempts by multinational companies to "country hop," -- shifting sources of supply from one country to another after an antidumping case has been initiated.

There are no provisions in the text for handling the case of repeat offenders, domestic industry sources say. The U.S. had been pressing for rules on repeat offenders, as well as for expedited procedures to combat dumping in products with a relatively short life-cycle such as semiconductors. But these demands were defeated in the face of fierce resistance from other trading partners, according to sources.

A major gain for U.S. exporters was the inclusion of a U.S. proposal to strengthen GATT review of antidumping disputes. Historically, foreign exporters have enjoyed better judicial review of their cases in the U.S. than U.S. exporters to the EC, Canada and other countries, a private-sector representative for U.S. multinationals said. But the draft does not make any procedural changes that would limit harassment of U.S. exporters with antidumping cases, nor does that draft push the EC or Canada towards greater transparency, he said.

U.S. exporters failed to achieve a provision in the draft that would have guaranteed them protection from antidumping investigations when they sold exports above the prices of local producers. Also, major capital equipment producers, such as in aircraft or construction equipment, failed in another effort to secure a guarantee that they would not be considered to dump a product if they failed to recover its cost of production in the first year. Finally, U.S. exporters were seeking a "short supply" provision where if a domestic producer could not meet demand, imports above the capacity of the producer should not be subject to antidumping duties. *By Alkman Granitsas*

0050 - 29 - 28

I CHARGES GATT DRAFT AGREEMENT UNDERMINES U.S. TRADE LA

The American Iron and Steel Institute (AISI) last week charged in a letter to all members of Congress that U.S. manufacturing would suffer "serious damage" if a draft Uruguay Round agreement were accepted in its current form. The AISI president urged members of Congress to forestall the proposed changes in the areas of antidumping, subsidies and dispute settlement, according to a copy of the Dec. 23 letter reprinted below.

Separately, Sen. Lloyd Bentsen (D-TX), chairman of the Senate Finance Committee, said in a Dec. 20 statement that he would pay "particular attention" in his assessment of the draft agreement to whether it permits the U.S. to preserve "tough trade laws." Those laws are essential to the U.S. trading future and must be preserved by any agreement, Bentsen said in a three-paragraph statement that emphasized he has not fully reviewed the text.

AISI Letter on Uruguay Round Draft

American Iron and Steel Institute

December 23, 1991

he Honorable Daniel Rostenkowski
ouse of Representatives
ayburn House Office Bldg., Rm. 2111
/ashington, D.C. 20515-1308

ear Congressman Rostenkowski:

I am writing to alert you to a very ominous situation that is eveloping in the Uruguay Round negotiations in Geneva. The ;ATT bureaucrats have drafted a paper which we are told can nly be modified in very minor respects. This paper devastates asic U.S. laws against unfair trade -- antidumping laws, ountervailing duty laws and Section 301. If this text is allowed become final and is implemented into U.S. law, serious amage will be done to U.S. manufacturing.

Enclosed is a brief paper describing some of the technical roblems with the text. We will be in further contact with you ater when our analysis is more complete, but we wanted you to now as soon as possible of our concerns on this matter. In the ieantime, anything you can do to forestall the Administration's ccepting this text would be appreciated by us and would be in ie interest of millions of workers in the U.S. manufacturing ector.

incerely yours,

Ailton Deaner
President

The Uruguay Round and the Trade Laws

GATT Director General Dunkel has prepared a "final" draft Uruguay Round agreement. With respect to trade law ssues, the United States failed to achieve its key objectives. At he same time, the texts would, if implemented, undermine U.S. rade law remedies.

The United States Failed to Achieve Its Key Objectives

• In the dumping area, the key U.S. goals -- special rules against repeat dumpers, recognition of U.S. rules to prevent circumvention of dumping duty orders -- have not been achieved.

• In the subsidies area, new disciplines are extremely limited at best, and developing countries are virtually exempted from the rules altogether.

The Texts Contain Major Substantive Limits on Trade Remedies

• In the subsidies area, the draft text contains new rules "green-lighting" (making non-countervailable) regional and research subsidies. Instead of an agreement that bans subsidies, the draft text explicitly authorizes many subsidies, even when they injure U.S. industry.

• In the dumping area, the draft text contains changes in the method of calculating dumping (especially regarding sales below cost) that will reduce or eliminate dumping margins in many cases.

• The draft dumping text fails to recognize the right to add together ("cumulate") injury caused by dumped imports from multiple countries.

The Texts Contain Damaging Procedural Limitations on Trade Remedies

• The texts would likely be interpreted to prevent labor unions from bringing trade cases.

• Both the subsidies and dumping texts set higher de minimis levels (both for dumping/subsidization and import volumes) below which duties cannot be imposed. In the subsidies area, special de minimis rules apply to developing countries.

• The texts provide for automatic termination of AD/CVD orders after five years, requiring a U.S. industry to re-litigate a case and prove that "but for" the AD/CVD order it would still be injured by the unfairly trade goods.

Dispute Resolution Provisions Are Flawed

• GATT panels recently have held that U.S. trade remedies must be strictly construed. By failing to set forth an acceptable standard or scope of review, the new texts allow GATT panels when reviewing trade cases to substitute their judgement for that of the U.S. Government.

• The dispute resolution text would prohibit the use of Section 301 to remedy GATT violations. This would prevent the United States from using access to its market as a lever to open foreign markets. A combination of exclusive GATT jurisdiction over trade disputes and weak substantive GATT rules will deprive the United States of a proven means for defending its rights.

The Dunkel drafts would require major detrimental changes in every U.S. law relating to unfair trade practices. It would shift control over U.S. trade laws from Congress to GATT dispute resolution panels. Congress should make clear that it will not approve an Uruguay Round agreement that undermines the effectiveness of U.S. trade laws.

면 담 요 록

1. 면 담 자

   ○ 주한 호주 대사관 Rod Smith 1등서기관

   ○ 주한 뉴질랜드 대사관 Guy Lewis 2등서기관

   ○ 홍종기 통상기구과장

   ○ 조 현 통상기구과 서기관

2. 면담일시 및 장소 : 1991.1.3(금) 11:00-11:30, 통상기구과

3. 면담내용 :

Smith 서기관

○ 호주는 던켈 총장이 90.12.20 제시한 UR 협상/최종 협정 초안이 균형잡힌
  것으로 평가하고 있음.

  - 약간 실망스러운 분야도 있으나 농업부문등 대체로 만족스럽게 생각함.

○ 지난주 경제기획원 UR 업무 담당자와 접촉, 최종 협정 초안에 대한 한국의
  평가를 문의한 바, 농업부문, 특히 예외없는 관세화를 문제점으로 지적하였음.
  협정 초안에 대한 한국측의 전체적인 평가는 ?

통상기구과장

○ 협정 초안에 대한 각 분야별 평가는 현재 관련부처별로 검토중이며, 1.13
  TNC 전에 입장을 정할 계획으로 있는바, 협상 결과의 국내적 수용상의 문제와
  UR 협상 타결을 위한 한국의 역할이라는 두가지 요소가 한국의 최종 입장
  정립에 고려될 것임.

○ 우선 1차적인 검토 결과, 긍정적인 요소도 많이 있으나 농산물 분야에 있어서
  예외없는 관세화, 최소 시장접근, 기준년도 등에 문제점이 있는 것으로
  판단됨.

0032

Lewis 서기관

o 최종 협정 초안에 대한 뉴질랜드 입장에 관해 아직 통보 받은바 없으나
  대체로 호주와 비슷한 입장을 취할 것으로 생각됨.

o 협정 초안에 대한 미국, EC, 일본의 입장과 최종 협정 초안에 대한 추가
  협상 여부는 ?

통상기구과장

o EC, 일본은 최종 협정 초안에 대해 뚜렷한 입장 표명을 유보하고 있는
  것으로 파악됨.

o 추가 협상 여부에 대한 전망도 1.13 TNC 이후 가시화 될 것임.   끝.

0033

	분류번호	보존기간

발 신 전 보

WBR-0004   920104 1544 DW

번   호 :   종별 :

수   신 : 주 수신처 참조   대사. 총영사/   WSG -0003   WTH -0008
                                                  WHG -0005   WND-0009

발   신 : 장 관 (통 기)

제   목 : UR 협상 동향

1. UR 협상은 91.12.20 TNC 회의에서 던켈 총장이 최종 협정 초안을 제시하고
   협상초안 수석에게를 밝히고
   92.1.13. TNC 회의시까지 각국 정부가 동 협정 초안을 검토, 이후 수주일이 내에
   UR 협상을 종결한다는 계획을 발표함에 따라, 막바지에 접어들고 있으며 오는
   1.13 TNC 회의에서 향후 협상 전망이 구체화 될 것으로 예견되고 있음.

2. 상기 던켈 총장의 최종 협정 초안에 대한 아국 입장 정립에 참고코자 하니
   동 협정 초안에 대한 귀주재국의 종합 평가 및 전체 협정 초안(package) 수용
   여부에 대한 최근 동향을 파악 가능한대로 수시 보고바람.

3. 아울러 1.13 개최되는 TNC에 파견할 귀주재국 대표단의 수준 및 규모(수석대표
   직위 포함)도 가능하면 파악 보고바람.   끝.   (통상국장 김 용 규)

수신처 : 주 브라질, 인도, 싱가폴, 태국, 헝가리 대사

| 예고문에 의거 분류 1992.6.30. 직위   성명 이시홍경 | |

	보안통제	

앙고재	92년 1월 6일	통기과	기안자 성명 조천		과장	심의관	국장 전결	차관	장관		외신과통제

0034

	분류번호	보존기간

발 신 전 보

WCN-0004   920104 0857 BE

번   호 :   종별 :

	WGE -0004	WFR -0008
	WAU -0005	WUS -0015
	WJA -0013	WEC -0004
	WGV -0004	

수   신 : 주   수신처 참조   대사. /총영사/

발   신 : 장 관 (통 기)

제   목 : UR 협상 동향

연 : WUS-5781, WJA-5714, WEC-0837, WCN-1478, WGE-1983, WFR-2660,

WAU-0967, WGV-1867

1. 연호, 91.12.20 UR/TNC 회의에서 제시된 던켈 총장의 최종 협정 초안에 대한 아국

입장 정립에 참고코자 하니 동 협정 초안에 대한 귀주재국의 종합 평가 및 전체 협정 초안

(Package) 수용 여부를 에대한 검토동향을 파악 가능한대로 수시 보고바라며, 가능하면 각 협상 분야별

세부쟁점에 대한 주재국 입장에 특히 기존 입장에 관해서도 파악, 보고바람.

2. 아울러 1.13 개최되는 TNC에 파견한 귀 주재국 대표단의 규모 (수석대표 직위 포함)도 가능하면

파악 보고바람. 끝.   수로 밀) (통상국장 김 용 규)

수신처 : 주 카나다, 독일, 불란서, 호주 대사

주 미국, 일본, EC 대사 (A불 : 주제네바 대사)

~~주 브라질, 인도, 싱가폴, 태국 대사~~

예고문에 의거 재.분류 1992.6.30.
직위   성명 이시영

	보 안 통 제		

앙고재	92년1월3일	통기과	기안자 성명 조현	과장	심의관	국장 전결	차관	장관	외신과통제

최근 UR 협상 동향

1992. 1. 6.
통상기구과

1. 협상 현황

    ㅇ 던켈 갓트 사무총장은 91.12.20 무역협상위원회(TNC)에서 UR 최종 협정 초안
      및 향후 협상 계획 제시

      - 각국 정부에 대해 동 최종 협정 초안을 검토, 92.1.13 무역협상위원회에서
        이에 대한 평가 및 입장을 밝히도록 요청

      - 시장접근, 서비스 분야 양자협상등 기술적 협의는 92.1.13 이후 수주일
        동안 계속 실시, 전체 UR 협상을 종결한다는 계획 제시

2. 최종 협정 초안의 성격

    ㅇ 90.12. 브랏셀 각료회의 이후 각 협상 분야별 쟁점 타결을 위한 집중적 협상
      결과를 종합한 문서로서, 외형상으로는 합의된 형태를 취함.

    ㅇ 실제로 일부 분야에서 협상 참가국간 합의를 이루지 못하여 협상그룹 의장이
      독자적 책임하에 타협안을 제시

      - 농산물 분야에서는 우리나라등 수개국가의 반대에도 불구, 모든 품목의
        관세화와 최소 시장접근(3%) 의무를 수용

3. 최종협정 초안에 대한 각국 반응. (상세 각국 반응 : 별첨)

    가. 미 국

      ㅇ 부시 대통령, 아시아 순방시 각국에 UR 협상의 성공적 타결을 위해서는
        던켈 협정 초안이 기초가 되어야 할 것임을 강조

      ㅇ 반덤핑, 상계관세등 일부 불만을 표시한 부문이 있으나, 농산물을 포함,
        전체적으로 만족 표시

0036

나. E C *협정초안에 대한 최종 입장표명은 유보하면서* (handwritten)

　　ㅇ 농산물 부문에 대해 강한 불만 표시

　　ㅇ 1.10경 EC 각료이사회 개최, 최종 입장 정립 예정
　　　　-11경 (handwritten)

다. 일　본

　　ㅇ 1.13 TNC에서 협정 초안에 대한 입장 표명 유보 예상

　　ㅇ *어느 선에서든지 타협점을 찾아야 하므로 ~~협정~~ 협정초안 은 존중되어야* (handwritten)

라. 카나다　　　　　　　　　　　　*한다는 입장이지만, 농산물분야에 대해서도* (handwritten)
　　　　　　　　　　　　　　　　　　　　강한 불만 표시 (handwritten)

　　ㅇ 농산물 부문에 불만 표시 (낙농, 가금, 계란에 대한 보호규정 미흡)

　　ㅇ 협정 초안에 대한 입장과 관련 주정부와 협의중

마. 호주, 뉴질랜드

　　ㅇ 협정 초안에 대체로 만족 표시

바. *핀란드, 노르웨이* (handwritten)
　　　　ㅇ *협정 초안에 대체로 만족 하나, 농산물분야에 대해 불만 표시* (handwritten)
4. 협상 전망

ㅇ EC가 협정 초안을 그대로 수락하기 어렵다는 1차적 반응을 보였으며,
　　미결쟁점이 적지 않음에 비추어 1.13 무역협상위원회에서 협상 문서 수락
　　여부에 대한 결정이 유보된채 협상 문서의 전체적 균형을 깨뜨리지 않는
　　제한된 범위내에서 일부 내용 수정을 위한 협상이 이루어질 가능성이 있음.

ㅇ 다만, 미결 쟁점에도 불구, 각국 정부가 국제무역 체제의 장래에 대한 고려
　　및 협상 대세에 따라 최종 협정 초안 수락을 일괄 거부하지는 않을 것이라는
　　것이 일반적인 관측임.　　　　　　　　　　　　　끝.

ㅇ 1.7 Andriessen EC 집행위 부위원장, 워싱톤 방문, (handwritten)
*　　Baker 국무, Hills USTR과 면담; UR 협상 타개의 방안 협의 예정* (handwritten)
*　　- McSharry EC 농업담당 집행위원도 Madigan 미 농무장관과* (handwritten)
*　　　전화접촉, 계속 협의* (handwritten)

0037

최종협정 초안에 대한 각국 반응

1992. 1. 6.
통상기구과

1. 미 국

   o 부시 대통령, 아시아 순방시 던켈 협정 초안을 기초로 UR 협상을 성공적으로 타결하는 노력에 동참할 것을 촉구

   o 농산물 초안에 대해서는 농무성이 1차적으로 만족 표명

   o 농산물을 포함한 각 협상 분야별 입장은 의회 청문회(1.6-8) 및 업계와의 협의후 구체화 될 것으로 전망

2. E C

   o 91.12.23. 무역상, 농상 합동 각료이사회에서 최종 입장 표명은 유보한채, 농산물 초안은 수락할 수 없으므로 수정되어야 하며, 전체적으로도 균형되어 있지 않다는 1차적인 평가 제시

   o 1.2 폴투갈(92년 상반기 EC 의장국) 외무장관, 1.13 무역협상위원회에서 UR 협상의 확정적 결과가 도출될 가능성은 희박하다고 하고, 6개월이내 UR 협상이 합의될 전망은 밝지 않다는 견해 표명

   o 1.10-11간 EC 각료이사회에서 최종 입장 정립 예정

3. 일 본

   o 어느선에서든지 타협점을 찾아야 하므로 협정 초안은 존중되어야 한다는 입장이지만, 농산물 부문에 대해서는 강한 불만 표시

   o 그러나 1.13 TNC에서는 협정 초안에 대한 입장 표명을 유보할 가능성이 있는 것으로 예상

4. 카 나 다

   o 농산물 부문에 불만 표시 (낙농, 가금, 계란에 대한 보호규정 미흡)

   o 협정 초안에 대한 입장과 관련 주정부와 협의중

5. 호주, 뉴질랜드등 케언즈그룹

   o 협정 초안에 대체로 만족 표시

6. 핀란드, 노르웨이

   o 협정 초안에 대체로 만족하나, 농산물 분야에 대해 불만 표시

7. 개 도 국

   o 미 상.   끝.   0038

종 별 :

번 호 : ECW-0015   일   시 : 92 0106 1800

수 신 : 장관(봉기, 경기원, 재무부, 농림수산부, 상공부)

발 신 : 주 EC 대사   사본: 주 미, 제네바-중계필

제 목 : GATT/UR 협상

최근 표제협상 동향을 하기 보고함

1. 1.6. EC 집행위 대변인에 의하면 1.7(화) ANDRIESSEN 부위원장이 워싱턴을 방문, BAKER 국무및 HILLS 대표를 만나 소련의 원조문제 이외에 표제협상의 마무리 방안에대해 협의할 것이라고 말함. 동인은 구체적으로 협의될 내용에 대하여는 언급을 회피하면서 동 회담과는 별도로 MACSHARRY 위원도 MADIGAN 농무장관과 전화접촉을 봉하여 동건 협의를 가질것임을 확인함

2. 한편, 1.5. MERMAZ 불란서 농무장관은 EC 회원국들은 GATT 협상에서 타협하기를 계속 거부할 것으로 확신한다고 말하고, EC 로서 필요한것은 DUNKEL PAPER 에 대해 가중다수결로 거부하는 것이며, 지난해 12.23. 이사회 결정이 1.10-11 개최되는 이사회에서도 재확인되길 희망한다고 말함. 또한 ANDRIESSEN 부위원장은 표제협상의 해결전망에 대해 현재로서는 무엇이라 말하기 어려우며, 미-EC 간 타협이 이루어지지 않을 경우, 양측 모두에게 책임이 있는 것이라고 말함

3. 한편, PINHEIRO 폴투갈 외무장관은 1.2. 가진 기자회견에서 1.13 GATT 이사회에서 확정적인 결과가 도출될 가능성은 희박하다는 견해를 피력하면서 자국의 EC 의장국으로 재임하는 6 개월 이내에 표제협상이 합의될 전망은 낙관적으로 볼수 없다고 말함. 끝

(대사 권동만-국장)

예고: 92.6.30 까지

예고문에 의거 분류 1992.6.30.   이시행

통상국	장관	차관	2차보	구주국	외정실	분석관	청와대	안기부
경기원	재무부	농수부	상공부	중계				

PAGE 1   92.01.07   05:00

외신 2과 통제관 FM

0039

외 무 부

종 별 :

번 호 : ECW-0016   일 시 : 92 0106 1800

수 신 : 장 관(동구일,동구이,통기,통삼,구일)사본:주제네바대사-직송필

발 신 : 주 EC 대사

제 목 : EC 일반 각료이사회

   1. EC 일반 각료이사회가 92.1.10(금)-11(토) 간브랏셀에서 개최될 예정임

   2. 1.10. 회의에서는 회원국 외무장관간 유고내공화국의 독립 승인문제와 워싱턴개최 대소지원 국제회의에 대한 EC 입장이논의될 예정이며, 1.11. 회의에서는 통상장 관및 농무장관간 UR 관련 DUNKEL 문서에 대한EC 의 최종입장이 논의될 예정인바, 회의 결과 파악되는 대로 보고위계임. 끝

   (대사 권동만-국장)

구주국   구주국   구주국   통상국   통상국

PAGE 1   92.01.07   07:51 FO

외신 1과 통제관

0040

면 담 요 록

1. 면 담 자

   ○ 주한 핀란드 대사관 Hanna Bjorkman 2등서기관

   ○ 통상기구과장

2. 면담일시 및 장소 : 1992.1.7(화) 11:00-11:30, 통상기구과

3. 면담내용 :

Bjorkman 서기관

○ 던켈 최종 협정 초안에 대한 한국 입장 문의

   - 한국이 동 협정 초안에 대해 반대한다는 언론보도에 대한 확인 요청

통상기구과장

○ 던켈 협정 초안에 대한 한국 정부의 입장은 현재 관계부처간 협의를 통해 정립 단계에 있음.

○ 통상기구과에서 1차적으로 검토한 바로는 던켈 초안에 긍정적 요소가 많이 있으나 농산물 분야에서 한국 입장에 반하는 기초식량의 전면 시장개방 및 최소 시장접근이 포함되어 있어서 문제가 있다고 생각함.

Bjorkman 서기관

○ take-it-or-leave-it이 되는 경우 한국은 던켈 협정 초안을 받아들일 것인지?

○ 최근 일본이 관세화를 수용할 것이라는 보도가 있었는바, 일본이 협정 초안을 받아들이는 경우 한국은 어떤 입장을 취할 것인지 ?

○ 금번 부시 대통령의 방한기간중 UR 협상 및 쌀시장 개방에 관한 논의는 있었는지 ?

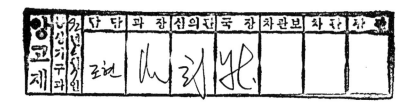

0041

<u>통상기구과장</u>

o 한국이 협정 초안을 받아들일 것인지는 아직 말할 수 없으며, 한국의 기본
   입장이 협정에 반영되도록 계속 노력할 것임.

o 일본이 보다 유연한 입장을 취할 것이라는 보도가 있었으나 아직 확인된바
   없음. 한국은 경제력이나 농산물 개방이 사회에 미치는 민감한 정도에
   있어서도 일본과는 큰 차이가 있으므로 일본이 양보한다고 하더라도 한국도
   동일한 입장을 취할수는 없음.

o 한.미 정상회담에서 미국은 성공적인 UR 협상 타결을 위한 한국의 협조를
   요청 하였으며 한국은 UR 협상 타결을 위해 가능한 최선의 노력을 다하되
   농산물의 전면 개방은 어려우며 이러한 한국 입장이 협정에 반영되도록
   미국이 협조해 줄 것을 요청한 것으로 보도되었음.

o (부시 대통령이 협정 초안을 받아들이도록 요청했는지 질문에 대하여)
   부시 대통령이 직접 이러한 요청을 한바 없는 것으로 알고 있으며, 다만
   국회 연설에서 모든 순방국들에게 던켈 협정 초안이 기초가 되어야 할 것임을
   강조 함으로써 이를 간접적으로 시사 하였다고 생각함.

<u>Bjorkman 서기관</u>

o 한국은 갓트 차원의 다자주의를 택하는 것이 미.EC등과의 쌍무적 협상보다
   유리하다는 KIET의 연구보고서를 보았는바, 이에 대한 견해는 ?

o 협정 초안의 다른 분야에서의 문제점은 ?

<u>통상기구과장</u>

o 한국은 과거 미국과의 301조 협상 경험도 있으므로 다자주의를 선호함.

o 협정 초안의 다른 분야, 즉 rule-making, safeguard, 보조금등에 문제가
   있다고 보나 이는 농산물에 비하면 큰 문제는 아니라고 생각함.

<u>Bjorkman 서기관</u>

o 핀란드는 협정 초안을 대체로 긍정적으로 평가하고 있으나 농산물 분야에
   문제가 있다고 보고 있으며, 반덤핑, 시장접근 분야에도 약간의 문제점이
   있는 것으로 평가하고 있음. 다만, 협정 초안에 대한 명확한 입장은 아직
   결정되지 않았으며 여타국과 마찬가지로 다른나라의 입장 표명 결과를 예의
   주시하고 있는 것으로 보임.

2

※ 1.7(화) 10:00 주한 노르웨이 대사관 Oedegaard 서기관, 통상기구과
조현 서기관과 통화, 던켈 협정 초안에 대한 한국 입장 문의

- 상기 면담내용과 같은 선에서 답변
- 노르웨이는 던켈 협정 초안을 긍정적으로 평가하나 농산물 분야에
  문제가 있는 것으로 보고 있다고 설명.   끝.

3

외 무 부

종 별 : 지 급

번 호 : GVW-0017   일   시 : 92 0107 1600

수 신 : 장 관(통기,경기원,재무부,농림수산부,상공부,특허청)

발 신 : 주 제네바 차석대사   사본:박수길대사

제 목 : 그린룸 회의

    금 1.7(화) 던켈깟트 사무총장은 1.13(월)개최예정인 TNC 회의 준비를 위해 1.9(목) 16:30 수석대표급 비공식 그린룸회의를 소집하였음을 당관에 통보하여 왔음.끝

    (차석대사 김삼훈-국장)

통상국   2차보   구주국   청와대   안기부   경기원   재무부   농수부   상공부
특허청

PAGE 1   92.01.08   02:03 FN

                                               외신 1과 통제관

                                                     0044

외　무　부

종　별 : 지급

번　호 : GVW-0018　　　　　　　　　　일　시 : 92 0107 1600

수　신 : 장 관(박수길 주제네바대사)

발　신 : 주 제네바 차석대사(김삼훈) 사본: 홍종기 통상기구과장

제　목 : 엽연

1. 서울에서 여러가지로 바쁘실줄 압니다.

2. 1.6 부터 업무가 재개되었으나 갓트사무국이나 주요공관의 담당자들이 부재중인 경우가 많은 실정 입니다만 전 직원이 가능한한 동향 파악코저 노력중이며 현재로서는 특히할 만한 진전이 없습니다.

3. 금(1.7)일 GATT 로 부터 1.9(목) 16:30 수석대표급 그린룸 비공식 협의 개최(1명 참석) 통보가 왔으며 한편 개도국 회의는 1.10(금) 오후 4:00 로 확정 통보가 왔읍니다.

4. 1.9(목) 그린룸 회의와 관련 대사님 일정에 참고 하시기 바라며, 지시사항 있으면 하시해 주시기 바랍니다. 갓트사무국에 확인한바, 동 그린룸 협의는 40여개국에 참 석토록 통보되었다 하며 주요국의 입장 사전 파악등 1.13. TNC 회의운영에 대비한 사전 협의 목적인 것으로 파악되고있습니다.

5. 김용식 전장관님이 1.8(수) 당지 10:00 도착, 1.9(목) 11:00 오슬로로 향발 예정입니다. 끝

구주국　　통상국

PAGE 1

외 무 부

종 별 :

번 호 : GVW-0016　　　　　　　　　　　　　일 시 : 92 0107 1600

수 신 : 장 관(봉기)

발 신 : 주 제네바대사대리

제 목 : UR/개도국 비공식 그룹회의

　　연: GVW-2752

　　연호, 표제회의가 1.10(금) 오후 4:00 개최되어 UR 진전 현황을 검토할 예정임.끝
　　(차석대사 김삼훈-국장)

통상국

PAGE 1　　　　　　　　　　　　　　　　　　　　　　　92.01.08　　07:53 WH

　　　　　　　　　　　　　　　　　　　　　　　　　　　외신 1과 통제관

　　　　　　　　　　　　　　　　　　　　　　　　　　　　　0046

원 본

외 무 부

종 별 :

번 호 : NDW-0039   일 시 : 92 0107 1900

수 신 : 장 관(봉기)

발 신 : 주 인도 대사

제 목 : UR 협상 동향

대:WND-0009

1. 대호관련, 당관 임재홍서기관은 금 1.7(화) 주재국 상무부 GATT 및 UR 담당 MR. P.S. RANDHAWA 부국장(동인은 외무부 소속직원으로서 제네바에서 UR 협상 담당자로서 근무한 후 본부에 귀임, 상무부에 파견중임)을 방문, 던켈총장의 최종협정 초안에 대한 인도측 입장을 타진하였는바, 동요지 아래와 같이 보고함.

가. 던켈총장 협정안에 대한 인도정부 기본입장

0 인도정부는 그간 수년에 걸쳐 진행되어온 UR 협상 타결에 인도가 장애물로서 작용하지 않는 다는 것이 기본원칙임. 다만 지난 수년간에 걸쳐 15 개 분야의 UR 협상을 통해 우리가 현재 어디에 와 있는지를 잘 알고 있으므로 그 바탕위에서 좀더 나은 것을 얻기 위해서 노력할 생각임.

0 상기 던켈총장 협정안에 인도정부가 각 관련부처에서 현재 검토중에 있으며 금주 말경에야 동협정안에 대한 인도정부 입장이 최종 마무리 될수 있을 것으로 전망됨.

나. 던켈총장 협정안에 대한 작년 12 월말 현재 잠정 검토결과는 전체적으로 불만족 스럽다(UNHAPPY AND UNSATISFACTORY)고 말할수 있을 것 같으며 특히 섬유와 지적소유권 분야에서 인도측에 불리한 내용을 발견할수 있었음.

1) 인도측에 유리한 점

0 2003 년 1 월 1 까지 식품, 화학제품(CHEMICALS), 의약품에 대한 생산특허(PRODUCT PATENT)를 제공하지 않아도 되는 점

0 의무허가(COMPULSORY LICENSING)규정이 충분히 광범위하고 유연하기 때문에 인도가 국내법을 통해서 수용할수 있다는 점

0 현존 특허권에 의한 생산물에 대하여 EXCLUSIVE MARKETING RIGHTS(소위 PIPELINE PROTECTION)를 주지 않아도 된다는 점

통상국   장관   차관   1차보   분석관   청와대   안기부

PAGE 1   92.01.08   05:10

2) 인도측에 불리한 점

가) 섬유분야

0 MFA 를 10 년내에 서서히 종결시킨다고 하였으나 그것이 10 년의 전반부 부분에서 많이 종결시키는 것이 아니라 인도측 입장에서 볼때는 <u>7 년째가 되어야겨우 종결되기 시작한다</u>는 점

나) 지적소유권 분야

0 생산특허를 식물(PLANTS)및 동물등 예외를 제외하고는 모든 발명품(INVENTIONS)에 주어야 한다는 점

0 특허기간이 모든분야에서 동일하게 20 년 이라는 점

0 식품과 약품분야에서 의무허가(COMPULSORY LICENSING)에 대한 어떠한 예외규정일지라도 초안에 규정된 한계(PARAMENTERS)내에서 이루어져야 한다는 점

0 중간과정 특허(PROCESS PATENTS)의 경우, 입증책임이 소위 위반자에게로 전환된다는 점

다. 1.13. 개최 TNC 회의 대표단 파견문제

0 표제회의는 끝갑회의가 아니라 던켈총장 협정안에 대한 각국의 입장을 밝히는 회의인 관계로 반드시 대표단을 델리에서 파견해야 할 필요성이 있다고 보지 않기 때문에 현재로서는 대표단 파견계획이 없으며 <u>주제네바 대사가 대표로 참석할수 있을것임.</u>

또한 상무부로서는 현재 인도정부가 당면한 외환부족으로 인한 공무원 해외출장규제조치도 고려해야 할 것임.

2. 한편 인도 상공회의소연합(아국의 상공회의소와 비슷한 성격의 경제단체)은 1.4. 인도정부가 던켈총장 협정안에 대해 긍정적인 입장(POSITIVE VIEW)를 취하여 줄것을 요구하였는바, 동 주요내용은 아래와 같음.

0 인도정부는 인도의 수출증진에 결정적으로 중요한 장기적 무역평화를 위해서 던켈협정안에 긍정적 입장을 취하여야 함.

0 UR 협상의 실패는 다자주의보다는 양자주의에 더욱 의존케 함으로서 인도와 같은 개도국이 세계시장에서 발판을 얻을 수 있는 기회를 위협할 것임.

0 던켈협정안은 장기적 관점에서 인도에 유리한 내용을 많이 포함하고 있음.

- 농산물 보조금의 점진적 철폐

- ANTI-DUMPING DUTY 부과조건의 완화

PAGE 2

- 국민소득 1000 불이하이고 세계시장의 2.5%이하점유 개도국의 경우 수출보조금 계속지원 가능
- GATT 의 분쟁 해결기능과 무역 감시활동의 강화
- 던켈협정안에 생산 특허규정이 포함되어는 있지만 2003 년 이후에야 시행된다는 점
- 식품과 화학산업에 대해서는 의무허가 규정이 없으며, 또한 이분야에 대한 협정안이 광범위하고 유연하기 때문에 국가이익을 최대한 도모할 수 있음.

(대사 -국장)

예고:92.6.30 까지

관리 번호	92-8

외 무 부

종 별 : 지급

번 호 : GVW-0020

일 시 : 92 0107 2100

수 신 : 장관(통기, 경기원, 재무부, 농림수산부, 상공부, 특허청)사본: 주미, 주이씨

발 신 : 주 제네바차석 대사   대사(본부중계필)

제 목 : UR 협상 동향

연: GVW-0016, 0017

1. 금 1.7(화) 싱가폴대표부에서 홍콩, 싱가폴, 노리딕 3 국, 브라질, 헝가리 및 아국등 협상실무자들이 모여 UR/ 반덤핑 협정안에 대한 비공식 협의를 하였는바, 대부분의 참석자들은 현 TEXT 가 수출국 입장에서 수용가능하다는 입장이었으나 싱가폴만은 재협상이 필요하다는 강한 입장을 피력하였음(강상무관 참석)

2. 금일 회의에 참석한 대표부 실무자들은 아직 UR 최종협상안에 대한 각국정부의 입장이 확정되지 못한 상태에 있어 1.9(목) 그린룸협의 및 1.13(월) TNC 회의에 어떤 반응들이 나오게 될지 예측하기 어렵다는 견해이었음.

3. 인도 대표는 던켈총장이 갑자기 1.9(목) 그린룸 협의를 소집한 이유는 특히 농산물 협상과 관련 불란서측의 강경한 반대입장을 고려 동 회의를 통해 EC측에 DUNKEL 초안을 수용토록 압력을 가하려는 것일수도 있다고 하고, DUNKEL 총장이 동 회의에서 1.13. TNC 회의시 각국이 각협상 분야에 대해 구체적인 COMMENT 를 자제하고 정치적인 결단을 해줄것을 요청할 가능성이 있다는 의견을 피력함.

4. NORDIC 대표는 TNC 회의에서 시장접근 분야 협상이 남아있는 상태인 만큼 그결과를 본후에야 수용여부 판단이 가능하다는 입장을 밝히게 될것으로 본다고 하였음.

5. 참석자들에 의하면 각국은 미국.이씨가 어떠한 반응을 보일것인가를 우선 예의 주시하려는 듯한 입장이었으며, 자국의 입장은 유보하는 태도였음.

6. 년말연시 휴가이후 갓트 사무국 및 각국대표가 1.6(월) 업무를 재개하였으나 사무국의 주요국장들이 아직 휴가중인 경우가 많고 각국 대표부도 본국정부의 최종입장이 결정되지 않은 상황하에서 1.13. TNC 회의에 대비한 뚜렷한 움직임이 없는 실정임.

통상국 특허청	장관 중계	차관	1차보	2차보	경기원	재무부	농수부	상공부

PAGE 1

7. 한편 김대사는 1.8(수) 갓트사무국의 HUSSEIN 차장과 오찬 예정인바, 동인 접촉후 특기사항 있으면 보고하겠음. 끝

(차석대사 김삼훈-국장)

예고:92.6.30 까지

네고문 내개
제본족   92.6.30 해제

手書き: 3, 홍 (경과부, 재씨씨)

관리 번호	92-18

외 무 부

원 본

종   별 :

번   호 : FRW-0032   일   시 : 92 0107 1830

수   신 : 장관(봉기)

발   신 : 주 불 대사

제   목 : UR 협상 동향

대:WFR-0008

연:FRW-2732,2772

1. 1.13(월) TNC 회의관련, EC 입장 정립을 위한 EC 농업 및 봉상장관 회의가 1.11(토) 브랏셀에서 개최될 예정이며, 주재국의 TNC 수석대표는 동 회의 결과를 보아 결정될 것이나 대외봉상 교섭권한이 EC 로 위임되었음에 비추어 수석대표를 각료급으로 할 가능성은 적음.(이경우 주제네바대사 예상)

2. DUNKEL 안에 대한 종합평가: 연호 참조

3. 주요 분야별 평가

가. 농산물

0 수출 보조금 감축

- 던켈안이 6 년간 수출물량의 24 프로, 보조금액의 36 프로 감축을 명시하고 있으나, 불란서는 물량감축 비율 명시에는 반대함.

- 이와관련, 기존 EC 소맥 수출물량 20 백만톤을 CAP 개혁과 연계하여 15 백만톤선까지 축소하는 것은 최대 양보선 임. 물량감축은 대부분 불란서 희생하에 이루어질 것이므로 MACSHARRY EC 농무집행위원의 13 백만톤 수준 타협입장을 수락할수 없음.

- 특히 DUNKEL 안에서 REBALANCING 이 인정되지 않고 GREEN-BOX LIST 에 대농민 직접소득 보상 조치가 명확히 반영되지 않은것은 EC 의 CAP 개혁관련 도저히 수용할수 없음.

0 시장접근

- 국경조치(BORDER MECHANISM) 만으로는 EC 농산물 선호수준(역내가격과 개입가격의 10 프로 차이 부여)을 유지할수 없으며

통상국	장관	차관	1차보	2차보	구주국	경제국	외정실	분석관
청와대	안기부							

PAGE 1

92.01.08   18:01

외신 2과 통제관 BW

0052

- 각농산물에 대해 (5 년에) 걸쳐 3-5 프로 수준의 시장개방 허용은 과잉생산분야(돼지고기, 가금등)에 심각한 결과 초래가 우려됨.

나. 분쟁해결

0 불란서(EC)는 미국 봉상법 301 조에 의한 일방적 보복조치 철폐를 요구하고 있으나, DUNKEL 안은 이러한 독단적 조치를 간접적으로 자제해 줄것을 요청하는 정도로 되어있음.

다. 저작권

0 EC, 특히 불란서는 문화적 특수성을 고려, AUDIOVISUAL 분야를 특별히 취급하여 최혜국대우(MFN)에서 제외시키도록 협정부속서에 이를 명시함으로써 현재운영되고 있는 EC 산 프로그램 쿼타 제도를 계속 유지코자 함.

0 또한 저작권에 있어 저작자의 권한을 강조하는 EC 와 계약만을 인정하는 미국입장이 상충되고 있음.

라. 보조금

0 비록 DUNKEL 안의 GREEN-BOX LIST 에 연구 및 지역개발 항목이 포함되어 있으나 환경 및 구조조정분야 뿐아니라 특정산업분야 보조금(예:OECD 선박)도 명시되어야 함.

마. 시장접근

0 EC 의 관세 30 프로 GLOBAL REDUCTION 입장과 미국의 REQUEST/OFFER 방식이 대립되고 있으나, 동건은 추후 협상과정을 거쳐 DUNKEL 안에 부록으로 추가될내용이므로 시간을 두고 절충될수 있을 것임.

4. 전망

0 DUNKEL 안은 (전반적)으로 미국입장을 옹호하고 EC 를 사실상 세계무역자유화의 "문제아" 취급하고 있으므로 이를 수용할수 없다는 것이 불란서의 기본입장이며, EC 여타 회원국도 동 내용이 "이해의 균형"(BALANCE)이 이루어지지 않았다는 데는 전반적으로 공감하고 있음.

0 불란서는 여사한 입장을 1.11 EC 봉상 농업장관 회담에서도 계속 강력히 견지할 것인바, 미국의 양보가 없는한 1.13 TNC 회의를 계기로 전반적 타결수준에 접근키는 어려울 것으로 전망됨.

0 불란서는 미국이 농산물 문제에 있어 EC 의 현실적 양보한계와 여타 국제문제(예:동구 및 구소련 지원)등에 있어 EC 의 협조가 긴요하다는 점을 충분히 인식하고 있으므로 EC 를 필요이상으로 자극하지는 않을 것으로도 계산함. 끝.

PAGE 2

0053

(대사 노영찬-국장)
예고:92.12.31. 까지

PAGE 3

0054

長官報告事項

1992. 1. 8.
通 商 局
通商機構課(2)

題 目 : UR 協商 關聯 駐 제네바 大使의 出入記者團 懇談會 要旨 (1.8. 10:10)

1. 懇談會 槪要

　○ 1. 8.(水) 10:10~10:40 (記者 約 15名 參席 기자

　○ 通商局長, 公報官, 通商機構課長 陪席

2. 駐 제네바 大使 言及 要旨

가. UR 協商 現況 및 展望

　○ 1.13. TNC 會議에서 Dunkel 協定 草案에 대한 各國의 評價 聽取한후 이후 협상일정 논의

　　3月까지 市場接近, 서비스 分野의 讓許協商 進行

　○ 協商이 순조로울 境遇, 4.15경 閣僚級 TNC 會議 開催, 協定案 一括 採擇

　○ 미국.EC間의 農産物 分野에서의 合意가 協商 妥結의 關鍵

　○ 協定 草案은 綜合 妥結案으로서, 各國의 利害關係를 폭넓게 反映 하였으며,

　　各國이 肯定的인 反應을 보일 可能性이 큼 (妥結 可能性은 50:50)

　○ 協商 參加國의 主流는 農産物의 包括的 關稅化를 支持

　○ 協定 草案에 대해 EC.日本은 일단 유보적인 反應을 보이고 있으나, 1.13

　　以後 本質的인 協商이 再開될지는 不確實

나. 우리의 對策

　○ 韓國의 立場에서 볼때 協商이 완전히 終結 되었다고 볼 수 없으며, 남은

　　協商을 통해 利害 一致國과의 協調등을 통해 農産物을 包含한 우리 立場

　　反映을 위해 최선의 努力을 경주

3. 기자 질의 반응 :

4. 國會 및 言論對策 : 該當事項 없음.　　　　　　　　끝.

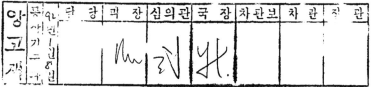

0055

면담 요록

1992. 1. 8.
통상기구과

1. 면담일시 및 장소 : 92.1.8(수) 14:30-15:20, 통상국 심의관실

2. 면담자 :

   ○ 최혁 통상국 심의관

   ○ MACINTOSH 주한 카나다 대사관 참사관

3. 면담요지

   가. 카측 언급요지

      ○ 1.13 TNC 회의와 관련하여 Dunkel Paper에 대한 카측 입장 정립을 위해
        고위급의 정치적 결정을 기다리고 있는 상황이나 지역 무역 Bloc의 대두,
        미국내 UR협상에 대한 관심 저하에 대한 심각한 우려 때문에 UR협상이
        조기에 성공적으로 타결되어야 한다는 데에는 확고한 인식을 갖고 있음.

      ○ 다만, 농산물 분야의 예외없는 관세화, 국내보조 감축 기준년도('86-'88)에
        문제가 있어 동문제로 인해 상당히 어려운 결정을 내려야 할 입장임.

      ○ 1.13 TNC 회의에서는 참가국들이 Dunkel paper 수락 여부에 대한 가부
        입장을 밝히는 것이 아니고 구체적인 문제점을 제시하는 것이 불가피할
        것으로 봄.

      ○ 카측이 보기에는 91.12.23. EC 합동 각료이사회 성명이 반드시 전체
        Package를 못 받겠다는 입장이 아니며, 일본도 농산물 분야를 결국 받을
        가능성이 있음.

공람	통상기구과	92년 1월 8일	담당	과장	심의관	국장	차관보	차관	장관
			송봉헌						

0056

o '부쉬' 대통령의 금번 아시아, 태평양 지역 4개국 순방에서 미측이
  Dunkel Paper에 대해 긍정적인 입장을 표명하고 있기 때문에 전체
  Package 수락을 아무도 거부하지 못하지만 각국이 갖고 있는 수락하기
  어려운 문제점을 어떻게 1.13 TNC 회의에서 표명하고 1.13이후 이를
  어떻게 처리해 나가느냐가 주요 관심사임.

o 딴 나라도 마찬가지이겠지만 시장접근에 대한 전체 협상결과가 도출되어야
  참가국의 최종수락 여부에 대한 Package를 의회등 국내에 제시 가능하므로
  남은 시장접근 협상이 매우 중요함. 이와 관련, 상품, 서비스, 농산물 분야
  협상 guideline에 대한 완전한 합의가 이루어지지 않은 상태에서 협상을
  추진해야 하는 문제점이 있기 때문에 동문제점도 해결해야 될 과제임.

나. 아측 언급요지

o 1.13 TNC 회의 관련 아국 최종입장은 상부의 결정 과정이 남아 있고
  여타국의 동향도 고려해야 하기 때문에 아직 결정되지 않음.

o 그러나, 아국은 UR협상 타결을 위해 남은 협상에 계속 적극적인 자세로
  임할 예정임. 다만, 국내적으로 Package가 수락 가능한 것이 되기 위해서는
  농산물 분야의 예외없는 관세화등을 포함하여 협상결과가 보다 균형된
  것이 되어야 할 필요가 있다고 봄.

o 금번 한.미 정상회담에서는 쌀문제, NAFTA 문제가 거론된 바 없음.
  (카측 질의에 대한 답변) 끝.

분류번호	보존기간

발 신 전 보

WGV-0023   920108 1813 ED

번   호 :   종별 :

수   신 : 주   제네바   대사. 총영사/

발   신 : 장 관 (통 기)

제   목 : UR/그린룸 협의 및 개도국 비공식 그룹회의

대 : GVW-2752, 0017

1. 표제회의 대책 관련 12.20자 최종 협정 초안에 대한 평가는 명 1.9 타전 예정이니
   참고바람.

2. 협정 초안상의 분야별 개도국 우대조항중 아국 관심사항에 관한 본부의 평가
   내용을 아래 통보하니, 1.10 개도국 비공식 회의 대비에 참고바람.

   가. 시장접근 및 서비스

     ㅇ 시장접근 및 서비스 분야에서는 개도국 우대가 원칙적인 선에서 언급
        되었을뿐, 구체적 이행장치는 미비한바, 실질적인 개도국 우대를 보장하기
        위해서는 향후 시장접근 및 서비스 분야의 양자협상 과정에서 개도국에 대한
        실질적 우대가 공여될 수 있도록 협상 상대국 선진에 대해 들의 특별한 배려를 요함.
        추구하여야 할 것임.

   나. 농 산 물

     ㅇ 농산물 일부 분야에서 수출국과 수입국, 선진국과 개발도상국의 이해가
        균형을 이루지 못한 것은 유감임.

		보 안 통 제	

앙고재	92년 1월 8일	통기과	기안자성명	과 장	심의관	국 장	차 관	장 관
			조천			전결		

외신과통제

0058

o 개별국가의 특수성, 특히 농산물 순수입국의 취약한 농업 기반을 보호할
  수 있는 장치가 전혀 고려되지 않은 「예외없는 관세화」에 대해 반대하며,
  식량안보 관련 기초식량에 대한 관세화의 예외가 인정되어야 할것임.

o 개도국의 사회 여건상 받아들이기 곤란한 사항에 대해서는 예외가
  인정되어야 할 것인바, ~~한국의 경우 쌀에 대한 최소 시장접근은 불가능하며~~
  ~~기타 품목의~~ 최소 시장접근 보장에 있어서도 개도국 우대원칙이 적용되어야
  함.

o 개도국에 대해서는 국내보조 동결조치가 적용되지 않았음에도 불구하고
  수출보조 분야와는 달리 시장접근 및 국내보조 감축상의 기준년도를
  1986-88년간으로 설정한 것은 실질적으로 선진국보다 더 큰 부담을
  지우는 것으로서 불합리한바, 개도국에 대해서는 통계적으로 자료산정이
  가능한 최근년도(1991년)을 적용토록 함이 타당함.

다. 규 법

o 보조금 분야의 수출보조금 철폐 의무와 관련, 개도국을 1인당 국민소득을
  기준에 따라 세분하지 않고 최빈개도국을 제외한 여타 모든 개도국에게
  일률 적용, 8년동안 수출보조금을 점진적으로 축소, 철폐하도록 한것은
  개도국을 자의적으로 구분, 차별 대우를 ~~함으로써 개도국간의 단합과~~ 하려는
  ~~여건 도출을 방해하고저~~ 하는 일부 선진국의 기도~~가 좌절된~~ 결과로서
  환영하는 바임.

o 보조금 및 상계관세 분야에 있어 구조 조정의 촉진을 위한 정부보조금을
  허용보조금으로 인정하지 않는 것은 급속한 산업구조 조정 단계에 있는
  대부분의 개도국들의 효율적인 고용.산업정책을 저해하므로 구조 조정에
  필요한 보조금 지급은 허용되어야 함.

o 긴급 수입제한 조치에 있어 국별 선택 적용이 가능한 쿼타 ~~감축~~ 조정 (Quota
  Modulation) 제도는 다자간 협상의 무차별 원칙에 어긋나며 ~~선택 적용~~ 쿼타조정
  대상이 대부분 개도국이 될 것임을 감안할때 금지되어야 함.

3. EC의 아국, 홍콩, 싱가폴에 대한 개도국 우대 적용 배제 의사 표명과 관련,
   홍콩이나 싱가폴측이 동건을 거론하는 경우, 아국도 동조 발언할 수 있도록 하는등
   ~~준비, 필요시~~ 적절히 대처바람.   끝.   (통상국장 김 용 규)

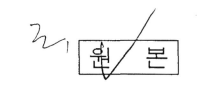

```
┌──────┐
│ 관리 │
│ 번호 │ 92-11
└──────┘
```

외   무   부

종   별 : 지급

번   호 : NDW-0040   일   시 : 92 0108 1200

수   신 : 장 관(봉기)

발   신 : 주 인도 대사대리

제   목 : UR 협상 동향

    대:WND-0009

    연:NDW-0039

    1. 연호관련, 인도 연합상공회의소는 1.7(화) 던켈협정안이 인도의 장기적 무역에 이익이 되므로 이를 전반적으로 수락할 것을 요구하는 성명을 발표하였는바, 동 요지는 아래와 같음.

    0 던켈협정안은 개괄적이고(BROAD) 유연할 뿐 아니라, 동 협정안에 대한 지지는 무역분야에서의 다자간 협조체제를 강화하는 것이 될 것이며, 이는 인도와 같은 개도국의 세계시장 접근에 필요한 것임.

    0 던켈 협정안은 TRIPS, 섬유무역및 시장접근(MARKET ACESS)에 있어 과거 선진국이 취해온 강경한 입장에서 탈피, 개도국을 위해 일보 전진한 면이있음.

    - 식품, 의약품, 화학제품및 동 관련 제품에 대한 PRODUCT PATENTS 시행의 10 년간 잠정유예기간 설정

    - 식물(PLANTS)및 동물등에 대한 특허권제도에서의 제외

    - 인도가 철폐를 주장해온 MFA 체제의 10 년내 철폐

    - 무역관련 법규제정, 시장접근및 수출보조금 삭감분야에서의 개선

    - 천연자원 중간재및 자본재에 대한 30% 관세인하

    2. 상기와 관련, 1.8. 자 당지 HINDUSTAN TIMES 는 인도 상공업자 협회에서던켈협정안 지지입장을 공개적으로 표명, 정부의 던켈협정안에 대한 미온적 태도(HARD STANCE)에 반대함으로써 인도정부는 동 협정안에 대한 정부입장 정립과 관련 난처한 처지에 빠지게 되었다고 보도함.

    3. 한편 당지 최대일간지인 TIMES OF INDIA(1.6. 자 기사)와 최대 경제지인ECONOMIC TIMES(1.1. 자)는 제네바 주재 특파원 및 해설기사에서

통상국 농수부	장관 상공부	차관	1차보	분석관	청와대	안기부	경기원	재무부

PAGE 1   92.01.08   16:13

던켈협정안은인도 상품및 서어비스와 세계시장 접근잠재력이라는 관점에서 검토되어야
할 것이며, UR 협상이 실패할 경우, 인도를 비롯한 개도국에 대해서는 성공시의
이점을 훨씬 상회하는 타격을 초래하게 될 것이고, 또한 상호 적대적 지역경제주의가
팽배해 질 것인바 그경우 어떠한 지역 경제블럭에도 가담되어 있지 않은 인도로서는 큰
곤경에 처하게 될 것이기 때문에 동 협정안을 가급적 받아들여야 할 것이라고 설명하고
있음. 특히 현 인도정부가 대외지향적 경제정책을 추진하고 있는 시점에서는
자유무역의 다자경제체제 유지가 동 정책의 성공여부에 중요한 관건이라고 논평하고
있음.

(대사대리-국장)

예고:92.6.30 일반

메고문에새
재분류 92.6.30 夏

판리 번호	92-10

외 무 부

종 별 : 지 급

번 호 : AUW-0020

일 시 : 92 0108 1040

수 신 : 장관(통기)

발 신 : 주 호주 대사

제 목 : UR 협상동향

대:WAU-0005

1. KERIN 외무장관 대리는 1.7 호주정부는 대호 던켈 총장의 최종협정초안을수락키로 결정했다고 발표함.

2 KERIN 무역및 해외개발장관은 동 초안이 농산물및 서비스분야를 포함하여호주에 긍정적인 영향을 미칠것으로 판단하며, 비록 최상의 목표에는 못미치지만 모든 참가국에게 실제적 혜택을 가져다줄것으로 보기때문에 UR 협상 종료를 위한 수락가능한 기초로 받아들인다고 밝힘.

3. 동장관의 언론 발표문 및 관련 신문기사 별첨" FAX(AUWF-0001)" 송부함.끝.(대사 이창범-국장)

예고:92.6.30. 까지.

예고문에게
개방류 92.6.30 종

통상국	장관	차관	1차보	2차보	아주국	분석관	청와대	안기부

경기원, 재무, 농수산, 상공.

92.01.08   09:39

외신 2과 통제관 CA

0062

주 호 주 대 사 관

AUW(F) : 0003   년월일 : 20108   시간 : 1100
~~0004~~

수 신 : 장   관 (통기   )

발 신 : 주 호주 대사

제 목 : UR

보 안	8/3
복 제	

(출처 :   )

Page

(1 - 5 - 1)

외신 1과	
복 제	

0063

MINISTER FOR FOREIGN AFFAIRS AND TRADE

NEWS RELEASE

No.	Date
M3	7/1/92

GOVERNMENT ENDORSES DUNKEL PACKAGE

Acting Minister for Foreign Affairs & Trade, John Kerin, announced today that the Australian Government had endorsed the draft package presented by Director-General Dunkel of the GATT as a means of finalising negotiations in the Uruguay Round of multilateral trade negotiations.

"Cabinet today agreed that the document provides an acceptable basis for concluding the Uruguay Round," Mr Kerin said.

"It contains the elements of a positive outcome for Australia, including on agriculture and services.   A final assessment of the impact of the package on Australia will depend on the outcome of detailed tariff and market access negotiations over coming weeks."

Mr Kerin said the positive aspects of the package include:

* international commitments for the reduction of agricultural export subsidies and domestic supports and the adoption of bound tariff protection with no exceptions for the first time in a GATT negotiation,

* a services agreement which will contain clear rules governing access and non-discriminatory treatment in foreign markets,

* improvement to the existing system for the protection of intellectual property rights,

* an overall agreed target of a one third bound reduction in tariffs, to cover all sectors,

* commitments on reductions in import barriers and subsidies on coal in the EC and Japan,

* an improved GATT dispute settlement procedure which discourages unilateral action,

* significant strengthening of the trading system by the establishment of a Multilateral Trade Organisation.

"While not realising the maximum objectives of all concerned, the proposed outcome delivers real benefits for all participating countries across the whole spectrum of negotiations," Mr Kerin said.

"On balance, this package would open the way for a realistic outcome for the Uruguay Round and deliver positive benefits for Australia."

0064

1 - 5 - 2

Mr Kerin said he would inform all his Cairns Group Ministerial
colleagues of the Government's decision today.

"I will be encouraging them to take a similar stand to enable the
Cairns Group to take a coordinated approach in support of the Dunkel
package at the Trade Negotiations Committee meeting in Geneva next
week and secure the earliest possible completion of the Uruguay
Round negotiations."

For more information contact:

Simon Grose
Media Adviser
06 2777 420

1-5-3

0065

4

NATIONAL

Financial Review, Wednes

Cabinet backs last ditch deal on GATT

By BINA BROWN

Keen to end the Uruguay Round of multi-lateral trade negotiations, Australia yesterday agreed formally to a "take it or leave it" proposal aimed at freeing up world trade and reducing agricultural export subsidies.

Federal Cabinet endorsed the draft package presented by the Director-General of the General Agreement on Tariffs and Trade, Mr Arthur Dunkel, as a means of finalising five years of negotiations.

While not entirely happy with the package, Cabinet agreed it opened the way for positive benefits for Australia.

"Cabinet agreed that the document provides an acceptable basis for concluding the Uruguay Round," the Acting Minister for Foreign Affairs and Trade, Mr Kerin said.

Australia's farm sector, the industry group most directly affected by domestic price support systems and export subsidies, said it was the "bare minimum".

The executive director of the National Farmers Federation, Mr Rick Farley, said he would make sure Australia was involved in negotiations of schedules surrounding the principles of the package.

Mr Kerin agreed that the final assessment of the impact of the package on Australia would depend on the outcome of detailed tariff and market access negotiations over coming weeks.

Mr Dunkel asked all 108 member countries of the GATT to state their position on the package by January 13 when the Trade Negotiations Committee is scheduled to meet in Geneva.

Mr Kerin, who admitted that the proposal fell short of Australia's aims, said every country involved would benefit to some degree.

"While not realising the maximum objectives of all concerned, the proposed outcome delivers real benefits for all participating countries across the whole spectrum of negotiations," he said.

He said the positive aspects of the package included:
□ International commitments for the reduction of agricultural export subsidies and domestic supports and the adoption of bound tariff protection with no exceptions for the first time in a GATT negotiation.

□ A services agreement which would contain clear rules governing access and non-discriminatory treatment of foreign markets.
□ Improvement to the existing system for the protection of intellectual property rights.
□ A reduction of bound tariffs by one third across all sectors.
□ Commitments on reductions in import barriers and subsidies on coal in the EC and Japan.
□ The establishment of a multilateral trade organisation.

As head of the seven members of the fair-trade grouping of countries – the Cairns Group – Australia would be looking for support on its decision from the rest of the group.

Mr DUNKEL

"I will be encouraging them to take a similar stand to enable the Cairns group to take a co-ordinated approach and secure the earliest possible completion of the Uruguay Round Negotiations," Mr Kerin said.

But hostility to the package among members of the European Community, particularly France, threatens to see the collapse of the negotiations.

There is wide concern that the EC would not accept the package and seek to negotiate the package further.

It is directly affected by a move to a 20 per cent cut in domestic support payments over six years.

Mr Farley said the details surrounding the schedule of the package remained "tremendously important".

"It's not all over on January 13 even if everyone agrees," he said.

In particular the NFF would like to see higher levels of cuts to domestic support arrangements, new markets excluded from exports subsidies and a guarantee for greater than 5 per cent access by the year 2000 to new markets.

Financial Review 1.8.

1-5-4.

0066

Draft GATT package endorsed

By KATRINA IFFLAND,
Environment and
Rural Reporter

The Australian Government endorsed yesterday a draft GATT package — the Dunkel report — in an attempt to help finalise negotiations in the Uruguay Round of multilateral trade negotiations.

The 448-page Dunkel report, named after the director-general of the GATT talks, Arthur Dunkel, proposed that agricultural subsidies be cut by 36 per cent over six years, plus a 20 per cent cut in domestic support systems and a 36 per cent cut in export subsidies.

If realised, the successful finalisation of GATT would result in forcing open markets for Australian produce such as farm products, coal, steel and manufactured goods. It could result in the eventual death of the controversial Export Enhancement Program.

"Cabinet agreed that the document provided an acceptable basis for concluding the Uruguay Round," the Minister for Trade and Overseas Development, John Kerin, said yesterday. "It contains the elements of a positive outcome for Australia including agriculture and services.

"A final assessment of the package on Australia will depend on the outcome of detailed tariff and market-access negotiations over the coming weeks."

Mr Kerin noted that among the most positive points of the package, which will be debated on January 13 in Geneva, were international commitments for the reduction of agricultural export subsidies and domestic support systems and the adoption of bound tariff protection with no exceptions — a first, since the GATT talks began five years ago.

He also noted the services agreement that will clear rules governing access and non-discriminatory treatment in foreign markets; and improvements were to be made to the existing system for the protection of intellectual property rights.

Commitments on reductions in import barriers and subsidies on coal in the EC and Japan had also been included, as well as dispute settlement procedures.

Mr Kerin added that while the draft proposal had not realised the maximum objectives of all Australia's concerns, the proposed outcome delivered real benefits for all 105 participating countries.

John Kerin: contains the elements of a positive outcome.

A spokesman for Mr Kerin said yesterday that he would not comment on speculation that GATT might fail. He would not comment on whether the Government had a contingency plan in place if this was the case.

While the Federal Opposition also accepted the Dunkel package, it believed the Government should go further about entering "a range of reservations it has about the deal".

The Opposition spokesman on trade, Alexander Downer, said that although the Dunkel package would provide some relief for Australian farmers, the proposal would not have a major impact on world farm prices and access to Third World markets for several years.

Mr Downer said that Australia should make its reservations clear about the fact that the EC and the US will not be prevented from extending their export subsidies to new markets, even though they will be prevented from extending the subsidies to new commodities.

"Secondly, while the 36 per cent reduction in tariffs on farm imports sounds good, in reality the 36 per cent is an average, leaving some tariffs to be reduced by only 15 per cent," he said. "Thirdly, agricultural protectionists will be able to resort to a safeguards clause . . . they may still be able to keep Australian products out of their markets."

Canberra Times 1.8.

0067

외 무 부

종 별 :

번 호 : AUW-0021

일 시 : 92 0108 1100

수 신 : 장관(봉기)

발 신 : 주 호주 대사

제 목 : UR협상 동향

대:WAU-0005

김의택 서기관이 1.8 외무성 MAY 가트과장에게 확인한바, 호주정부는 1.13 제네바 개최 TNC 에 HAWKES 주제네바대사를 수석대표로 참석시킬예정이라함. 끝. (대사 이창범-국장)

예고:92.6.30. 까지.

예고문에게 재분류
92.6.30 종료

통상국

PAGE 1

92.01.08   13:23

외신 2과   통제관 BD

0068

3.8 (차세문서, ~~~)

관리 번호	92-13

원 본

외 무 부

종 별 : 지급

번 호 : THW-0042   일 시 : 92 0108 0800

수 신 : 장 관(봉기)

발 신 : 주 태 국 대사대리

제 목 : UR협상동향

대 : WTH-0008

1. 박윤준서기관은 1.7 상무부 상업경제국 APIRADI 무역정책과장을 접촉, 대호 문의한바 동과장은 현재까지 태국정부의 최종입장및 대표단 명단이 결정되지 않았으며 확정되는대로 동결과를 알려주겠다고 하였음

2. 한편 동과장은 AMARET 상무장관이 12.26 기자회견에서 밝혔듯이, 태국으로서는 던켈총장의 최종협정초안이 현상황하에서는 가장 좋은 타협안으로 보고있으며 수용하지 못할 이유가 없다고 언급하였음. 상기관련 AMARET 상무장관의 동 회견요지 아래 보고함

가. 던켈총장 초안이 태국이 희망한 농산물교역의 완전자유화 입장을 반영하지는 못하였지만 EC. 일본등 농업보호국과 미국 CAIRNS GROUP 등의 농산물 수출국간의 이견이 지속되는 상황에서 도출해낼수있는 가장 좋은 타협안인것으로 평가되며, 태국으로서는 던켈 초안의 수용이 가능함. 호주도 12.25 동 초안수락가능함을 태국에 통보하여옴

나. 특히 동 초안이 수산물 위생규제에 관한 신규범을 포함하고 있으며, 섬유및 봉제품의 자유화를 제안하고 있는 것을 환영함

다. 일본과 EC 가 동초안에 반대입장을 표명하고있는데 우려를 표명하고 수락을 촉구함

3. 상기관련 태국측요청이 있으니 동 최종협정초안에 대한 아국 기본입장 및 대표단 명단이 확정되는대로 당관에 통보바람

(대사대리 주진엽-국장)

예고 : 92.6.30 까지

예고문에게 재분류
92. 6.30

통상국	장관	차관	1차보	2차보	아주국	경제국	외정실	분석관
청와대	안기부							

PAGE 1   92.01.08   14:20

외신 2과 통제관 BW

0069

관리
번호 *92-15*

외 무 부

종 별 : 지 급

번 호 : GVW-0026   일 시 : 92 0108 2100

수 신 : 장관(통기,경기원,재무부,농림수산부,상공부,특허청,경제수석)

발 신 : 주 제네바 대사대리 사본:박수길대사,주미,이씨,일,카나다,호주대사,

제 목 : UR 협상 동향   (본부중계필)

연: GVW-0020

1. 김대사는 금 1.8(수) HUSSEIN 갓트 사무차장보를 오찬에 초대 1.9 그린룸회의 및 1.13 TNC 회의와 관련 관심사를 논의한바 동 차장보의 언급요지는 아래와 같음.(오찬사관 동석)

가. 1.9 비공식 그린룸협의 개최 변경

1) 던켈 총장으로서는 1.13.TNC 회의에서 각국이 12.20 자 협상안에 대해 구체적인 분야별 COMMENT 를 하게될 경우 UR 협상타결에 결코 도움이되지 못하다는 판단하에 가능한한 짧고 효율적인 회의가 되기를 바라고 있음.

2) 따라서 아래와 같은 던켈 총장자신의 협상추진 전략을 밝히고 각국이 1.13. 까지 본국정부와 협의, 동 총장이 구상하는 빠른시일내의 협상종결을 위한 협조를 구하기 위한 전략의 일환으로 1.9 그린룸협의 개최를 결정한 것임.

(가) 1.13. TNC 회의는 협상을 위한 회의가 아님

(나) 아직 시장접근, 서비스분야에서의 양자 협상이 남아있어 협상이 종결된 것이 아니므로 UR 협상의 최종결과(RESULT)가 나와 있지 않은 현시점에서 UR 협상 결과를 최종 가부평가 할수는 없는 것임.

(다) 따라서 1.13. 회의는 UR 협상결과에 대한 수락 여부를 밝히는 회의가 아니며, 12.20 자 협상안을 기초로 수주내에 아래 협상 작업 계획(FOUR TRACK)으로 UR 협상을 진행코자함

- 상품분야(농산물포함) 시장접근 양허 협상
- 서비스 분야 양허협상
- 12.20 자 협상안의 법률문서화 작업(용어의 일치화등)
- 분야별 협상그룹은 해체되었으므로 던켈총장이 주재하는 TNC 차원의 일부분야별

통상국	장관	차관	1차보	2차보	국기국	분석관	청와대	안기부
경기원	재무부	농수부	상공부	특허청	중계			

외신 2과 통제관 CA

0070

조정작업(FINE TUNING)

(라) 그러나 만약 1.13.TNC 회의를 기점으로 12.20 자 협상안이 UR 협상을 조기에 타결하는데 충분한 기초가 되지 못한다고 이를 거부한다면 던켈총장으로서는 4-5 일후에 TNC 를 개최, UR 의 실패를 선언할수 밖에 없을 것임.

나. 1.13.TNC 회의

- TNC 회의를 짧고 효율적으로 운영하겠다는 던켈총장의 의도에도 불구하고 각국이 관심분야에 대한 COMMENT 등 발언 기회가 부여될것임

- 갓트사무국의 판단으로는(본인이 던켈총장과의 협의결과임을 강조) 미국,카나다, 북구, 인도, 멕시코, 일본등 많은 나라가 일부 분야에서 어려움이 있어 일부 COMMENT 가 예상되나 결국 12.20 자 협상안을 UR 협상 조기타결을 위한 기초로 받아들이는 입장을 보일 것으로 알고 있음.

- 문제는 EC 의 태도이며, 1.13. 오전 EC 이사회에서 어떤 결정을 내리게 될것인지 알수 없으나 EC 도 EC 때문에 협상이 실패했다는 비난을 감수하기는 어려울 것이므로 결국 던켈의 전략에 동의해올 가능성이 있다고 봄.

- EC 가 적극적으로 반대하는 경우 UR 협상은 결렬될 것인바, 한국으로서는 1.13.TNC 회의시 농산물 분야에서의 어려움등 관심분야를 언급은 하되 다자무역체제의 신장지지, UR 협상 조기타결 필요성등 전반적으로 긍정적이고 LOW PROFILE COMMENT 를 하는 것이 좋을 것으로 생각함.

다. 1.13. TNC 회의 이후의 추가협상 전망

- 던켈총장이 TNC 차원에서의 조정작업(FINE TUNING)을 위한 추가협상의 가능성을 남겨두고 있기는 하나 협상 참가국이 동의하고 전체협상안의 균형을 유지하는 차원에서만 가능할 것임.

(실제로 문호는 개방하되 사실상 실질적 수정 가능성은 없음을 시사)

2. 판단 및 건의

가. 1.9 개최되는 그린룸협의는 EC 측이 1.13.TNC 회의에서 12.20 자 협상안을 전적으로 거부하지 못하도록 하려는 의도가 있다고 보여짐.

나. 1.9 그린룸회의에서는 던켈총장의 협상추진 전략을 청취하고, 각국은 자국입장 개진을 자제할 것으로 보이며, 따라서 당관으로서도 발언을 자제코져하며, 부득이 발언이 강요되는 경우에는 본국정부로 부터의 훈령이 없다는 선에서 대응코져함.

다. EC 가 결국 12.20 자 협상안을 협상의 기초로 받아들이기를 거부하여 UR

PAGE 2

협상이 결렬될 가능성도 배제할수 없으므로 아국으로서는 협상결렬의 책임을
공유하게되는 어려운 입장에 처하게되는 상황은 발생하지 않도록 대처하는 것이
중요하다고 판단됨. 끝

    (차석대사 김삼훈-차관)

    예고:92.6.30 까지

예고문에게
재분류 92.6.30

외 무 부

종 별 :

번 호 : HGW-0019   일 시 : 92 0108 1800

수 신 : 장 관(봉기)

발 신 : 주 헝가리 대사

제 목 : UR 협상동향

대:WHG-0005

1. 대호 당관 오영환 1 등서기관은 1.8. 대외경제부 VARKONYI 과장을 접촉,1.13. 로 예정된 TNC 회의 헝측대표단, DUNKEL 안에 대한 헝측 입장등에 관해 청취한바, 동인의 발언요지 아래 보고함.

   가. 대표단

   0 본국에서 별도의 대표단은 파견하지 않고 주제네바 대표부의 상주대표인 SZEPESI 특명전권공사를 수석대표로 동 대표부의 상무관실 직원(전원 대외경제부 소속)으로 대표단 구성예정

   나.DUNKEL 안에 대하 평가 및 입장

   0 헝정부 최종입장은 아직 정하지 않았으며, 1.10. 로 예정된 관계부처 회의에서 입장이 정해질 것으로 봄. DUNKEL 안에 관해 현재까지 검토한바로는 기본적으로 큰 문제점은 없는 것으로 보고 있으나, 농업, 지적소유권, 보조금등 분야에서 다소 기술적인 문제가 있는 것으로 보고 있음.

   0 농업에 있어서는 미국과 헝가리가 속한 CAIRNS 구룹의 입장이 상당 반영된 것으로 보아 기본적으로 수용가능하다고 보고 있으나, 보조금문제를 둘러싼 EC 의 반발, 일본,한국,카나다. 스위스등 농산물 수입국의 예외없는 관세화 문제에 대한 강한 반대등으로 인해 앞으로의 교섭에서 미국이 이런문제에 있어 다소 타협할 가능성이 있을수 있다고 보고, 헝정부로서는 우려를 갖고 주시하고 있음.

   0 지적소유권에 관하여는 주로 시행기간상의 신축성 확보에 관심을갖고 있으며, 보조금문제는 그 인정범위를 확대할 경우 경제규모와 예산규모가 적은 헝가리로서는 불리한 입장에 서게되므로, 가급적 엄격한 감축을 희망하고 있음.

   2. 한편, 동과장은 사견임을 전제로 이번 TNC 회의에서 전 회원국이 DUNKEL안을

통상국	장관	차관	1차보	2차보	외정실	분석관	정와대	안기부

PAGE 1

수용할 가능성은 거의 없다고 보며, 농업등 주요쟁점에 관한 수정교섭이 계속될것으로 전망하고, 특히 농업문제에 있어 보조금 삭감문제에 관한 불란서등일부 EC 회원국의 입장이 강경하고, 예외없는 관세화에 대하여 농산물 수입국이 반대입장을 견지하고 있으며, 또한 대통령선거를 앞둔 미정부로서도 의회, 농민으로부터 더이상의 양보는 곤란하다는 강한 압력을 받고있어 조속한 시일내에 농업교섭 타결전망은 불부명하다는 의견을 피력하였음. 동인으 또한 UR 의 성공적 타결을 위해서는 미대통령 선거전이 본격화되는 3-4 월까지는 교섭이 매듭지어져야 할것이라는 개인적인 관측을 표명하였음.

　3. 당과관찰

　　헝가리는 현재 시장경제로의 이행과 국제경제사회의 완전한 일원으로서의 복귀를 기치로 각종 경제개혁과 수출확대 노력을 경주하고 있는바, 이를 위해서는 UR 을 봉한 다자간 자유무역 환경을 보장하는 분명한 루을의 확립이 중요하다고 보고 있으며, 특히 농산물 수출국으로서 EC, 아프리카등 안정된 수출시장을 확보하기 위한 자유로운 농업교역의 보장에 역점을 두고 교섭에 임하고 있는 것으로 관측됨. 따라서 UR 교섭의 장기화나 결렬로 인해 미, 일, EC 등 상호간 봉상마찰이 격화되거나, 지역, 보호주의 경향이 확산되는것을 크게 경계하고 있으며, 농업문제에 있어 자국과 입장이 비슷한 현재의 DUNKEL 안이 크게 후퇴하지 않는 선에서 타결되기를 기대하고 있는 것으로 보여짐.끝.

　　(대사 박영우-국장)

　　예고:92.6.30. 까지

예고문 의거 재분류
92. 6. 30 홍

외 무 부

종   별 :

번   호 : BRW-0031   일   시 : 92 0108 1900

수   신 : 장 관(봉기,미남)

발   신 : 주 브라질 대사

제   목 : UR 협상 동향

(자료응신 92-2)

1. 당관 임수영참사관은 1.7 오후 주재국 외무부 봉상정책과 THAIS 과장 차석 CARLOS MARCIO 서기관을 방문, 대호 DUNKEL 총장의 최종 협정 초안에 대한 주재국 입장을 문의한바, 동인들은 년말 년시 관계로 금주에 관계부처와 각각 부문별 회의를 소집할 것으로 예정되어 있는바, 동 초안을 검토한바로는 주로 미국과 EC 간에 첨예한 대립이 계속되고 있으나, 브라질은 동 초안에 대해 대체적으로 긍정적 수용을 할것임을 피력함.

2. 한편 당지 O ESTADO DE SAO PAULO 유수 일간지와 GAZETA MERCANTIL 경제 일간지에도 각각 브라질 정부는 DUNKEL 협정 초안이 이상과 거리는 있다 할지라도 전반적으로 이를 수용할것으로 보도하였음. 끝

(대사 한철수-국장)

봉상국   차관   2차보   미주국   경제국   외정실   분석관   청와대   안기부

외 무 부

종 별 :

번 호 : GVW-0023 일 시 : 92 0108 1700

수 신 : 장관(통기)

발 신 : 주제네바차석대사

제 목 : 모로코대표부 공한

　　1. 당지 모로코대표부는 별첨공한을 통해 무역을담당하고 있는 부처장관명 및 주소를 알려줄것을 요청하여 왔음.

　　2. 동 대표부 담당관에 확인한바 상기 요청은 모로코가 UR 협상을 마무리짓는 TNC 각료회의 개최준비와 무관하지 않다고 하니 참고 바람.

　　첨부: 모로코대표부 공한사본(NO.1683).끝.(GVW-0006)

　　(차석대사 김삼훈-국장)

통상국　　2차보

PAGE 1 92.01.09 08:02 BX

외신 1과 통제관

0076

PERMANENT MISSION OF

KINGDOM OF MOROCCO

No /ㅇ??

The Permanent Mission of Kingdom of Morocco to the United Nations Office at Geneva and other International Organizations in Switzerland presents its compliments to all the Permanent Missions at Geneva and has the honour to request transmitting to it the name and address of their Ministers in charge of Foreign Trade.

The Permanent Mission of the Kingdom of Morocco avails itself of this opportunity to renew to all the Permanent Missions at Geneva the assurances of its highest consideration.

Geneva, 24 December 1991.

To all the
PERMANENT MISSIONS
- G E N E V A -

0077ᐧ

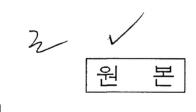

외　무　부

종　별 :

번　호 : USW-0098　　　　　　　　　일　시 : 92 0108 1817

수　신 : 장 관 (봉기,봉이,미일,경기원,상공부)

발　신 : 주 미국 대사대리

제　목 : UR 협상동향 (DUNKEL TEXT 에 대한 반응)

대: WUS-0015

1. 금 1.8. 미 제조업자 협회(NAM: NATIONAL ASSOCIATION OF MANUFACTURERS)는 금번 DUNKEL 의 UR 협상안이 농업분야의 교착상태를 벗어나게 하고 모든 분야에서 진지한 토론이 가능토록 하였다고 지적하면서, 미 협상팀이 동 안을 UR 협상의 기초로 수용하여야 할 것이라고 주장하였음.

2. 그러나 동 협회는 동 안이 상품미 서비스 시장접근 분야에서 미흡함을 지적하고 특히 지적소유권, 반덤핑및 상계관세, 시장접근, 정부조달등의 분야에서 추가적인 발전이 있어야 한다고 언급하였음.

3. 상기관련, 동 협회의 JERRY JASINOWSKI 회장의 CARLA HILLS USTR 대표앞 서한을 별첨 송부하여 상기 보완이 요구되는 분야에 대한 동 협회 입장 파악되는대로 추보코자함.

첨부: USW(F)-0127. 끝.

(대사대리 김봉규-국장)

예고: 92.6.30. 까지

예고문 의거 재분류
92. 6. 30

통상국	장관	차관	1차보	2차보	미주국	통상국	외정실	분석관
청와대	안기부	경기원	상공부					

PAGE 1　　　　　　　　　　　　　　　　　92.01.09　　09:11

외신 2과 통제관 BS

0078

주 미 대 사 관

USW(E) : 0/27   년월일 : 1.8   시간 : 18:00

수 신 : 장 관 (통기. 통이. 비닙, 경기원, 상공부)

발 신 : 주미대사

제 목 : UR 협상 동향

보동 안처 ✓

(출처 :   )

NAM

National Association
of Manufacturers

JERRY J. JASINOWSKI
President

January 8, 1992

The Honorable Carla A. Hills
U.S. Trade Representative
Executive Office of the President
600 17th Street, NW
Washington, DC 20506

Dear Carla:

NAM RESPONSE TO THE DUNKEL DRAFT

I know that you and your staff have been working very hard to assess the Draft Final Act Embodying the results of the Uruguay Round of Multilateral Trade Negotiations, which was released by GATT Director General Arthur Dunkel on December 20. I want to thank you for that and to commend you for the genuine effort that you and your staff have made to share USTR's knowledge and insights with the private sector and to encourage individual firms and associations to share their assessments of the Dunkel draft with you.

The Dunkel draft reflects clear progress in some areas and unwelcome concessions in others. It is going to take some time for NAM to have a solid understanding of all of its key elements and their likely effects on U.S. manufacturers. There are, however, some important responses to the draft that can and should be expressed now.

NAM has consistently held to the view that the maintenance of a multilateral trading system based on the General Agreement on Tariffs and Trade is critical to American manufacturers and to the advancement of the trading interests of the United States. For more than five years, we have urged all concerned to move toward a successful conclusion of the Uruguay Round. This position was based on the belief that, if the GATT were not strengthened and modernized, its importance as the mainstay of discipline in the world trading system would inevitably erode.

From Punta del Este on, we have supported the objectives associated with all of the major elements of the Uruguay Round negotiations — including those relating to market access, rules, and the new areas of intellectual property rights protection, services, and agricultural trade. We have repeatedly stated, however, that the GATT itself is more important than any individual improvement that might result from these negotiations.

The Dunkel draft, complete with proposed language for almost all areas of the negotiations, has created a new and unprecedented situation. Never before has such a full and substantive document been made publicly available prior to the conclusion of major negotiations. Tactically, this text has moved the negotiations beyond the agricultural deadlock and made it possible for serious talks to occur in all areas. We congratulate those of you who worked with Director

1331 Pennsylvania Avenue, NW
Suite 1500—North Lobby
Washington, DC 20004-1703
(202) 637-3100
Fax: (202) 637-3182

027-3-2

0080

The Honorable Carla A. Hills
January 8, 1992
Page 2

General Dunkel on this achievement. The draft as such has major problems. Nevertheless, because of it, a final, constructive Uruguay Round agreement is now foreseeable in a way that it has not been before.

With this goal in mind, we urge the U.S. negotiators to accept the Dunkel text as the basis for further negotiation when the negotiations reconvene in Geneva on January 13.

In making this recommendation, NAM is expressing its hope that a successful conclusion can be reached. Obviously, however, the Association cannot pledge its support for an agreement that does not yet exist. This is especially true in view of the fact that the Dunkel draft is without language in the critical areas of market access for goods and market access for services. In addition, there are a number of areas where we believe there is a clear need for improvement.

It is, therefore, our hope that the final agreement will reflect further progress in the following areas, among others:

- protection for intellectual property rights;

- antidumping rules;

- market access, including significant progress in the zero-for-zero negotiations;

- subsidies and countervailing measures; and

- government procurement.

Like Congress and other interested parties, NAM will have to judge the final Uruguay Round document on its merits and as a single package. We hope to be able to support it. If in our judgment, however, the final agreement does not advance the interests of American manufacturers, we will oppose it.

It is perhaps fair to say that the Uruguay Round negotiations have proven more difficult than most of us expected them to be in September of 1986. Yet significant progress has been made. On behalf of NAM, I want to thank you for the leadership that has made that progress possible and to wish you the very best of luck in the difficult negotiations that lie ahead.

Sincerely,

Jerry Jasinowski
President
National Association of Manufacturers

0(27-3-3

관리 번호	92~24

외 무 부

종 별 :

번 호 : USW-0095   일 시 : 92 0108 1751

수 신 : 장 관(통기,통이,미일,경기원,농수산부,상공부,경제수석)

발 신 : 주 미국 대사대리   사본: 주제네바,EC 대사(중계필)

제 목 : UR 협상관련 미 의회 동향

연: USW-0025

1. 당관 조태열 서기관은 금 1.18. JOHN ZIOLKOWSKI 상원 농업위 전문위원을 면담, DUNKEL 텍스트에 대한 의회의 반응및 각계의 동향을 탐문한바, 동 요지아래 보고함.

가. 미 의회 동향

- BENTSEN 상원 금융위원장, ROSTENKOWSKI 하원 세입위원장등 대외 경제문제에 있어 미 의회에서 가장 큰 영향력을 행사하고 있는 민주당 의원들은 동 텍스크가 제출되기 전날인 12.19 직접 DUNKEL 사무총장에게 전화를 걸어 동 텍스트에 포함된 반덤핑, 상계관세 관련 조항이 미 국내법을 약화시킨다는 이유를 들어삭제를 요구하는등 벌써부터 민감한 반응을 보인바 있음.

- GEPHARDT 하원의원, RIEGLE, BAUCUS 상원의원등 민주당의 여타 인사들도 불만족스러운 협상결과를 수용할 수 없다는 강경입장을 분명히 하고 있는바, 이는 비단 민주당 의원들에게만 국한된 것이 아님. 국내 경기악화 및 금년도 선거정국과 맞물려 공화당 의원들 조차도 현 협상안을 그대로 수락하기 어려운 입장에 있음. 자신이 보좌하고 있는 LUGAR 상원위원(상원 농업위 공화당 간사)도 지역구 이해가 걸려있는 철강, 섬유분야에서의 입장때문에 현 협상안을 그대로 지지하기는 어려운 입장임.

- 하원 세입위 주요 전문위원들도 1.7. 행정부측에 대해 반덤핑, 보조금 관련 조항등 현 텍스트의 상당부분에 대해 반대입장을 표명한 것으로 알고 있음.

- 따라서, 향후 협상결과 다소 개선된 선에서 협상이 타결된다 하더라도 동 협상안이 의회를 통과할 수 있을지는 매우 회의적임. 자신의 견해로는 현재 43명의 공화당 상원의원중 적어도 15 명은 정치적 이유등으로 지지입장에서 이탈할 것으로

통상국 분석관	장관 청와대	차관 청와대	1차보 안기부	2차보 경기원	미주국 농수부	경제국 상공부	통상국 중계	외정실

PAGE 1

봄. 민주당의 BENTSEN 상원의원과 ROSTENKOWSKI 하원의원의 태도가 향후 협상안의 의회 통과 여부에 관건이 될 것인바, 동 의원들이 지난해 FAST TRACK 권한 연장문제에서는 행정부 입장을 지지하였으나, UR 협상결과는 동 의원들의 정치적 이해와 직결되어 있고, 더구나 시기적으로도 금년이 선거의 해임을 감안할때, 이번에도 행정부 입장을 지지하기는 어려울 것으로 봄.

나. 미 농업계 동향

- 1.7. 개최된 연호 대통령 농업정책 자문위원회에서는 땅콩, 설탕, 낙농업계 등 주로 갓트 22 조 작물업계에서 현 협상안에 대해 강한 반대입장을 보였으나, 설탕업계의 반대입장은 예상했던 것만큼 강하지는 않았음.

- 옥수수, 밀, 육류, 유지업계등은 대체로 긍정적인 반응이었으며, 특히 식물 검역 부분에 있어서는 전혀 이의가 제기되지 않았음.

- 농산물 관세화의 수준이 어느선에서 타결될지 아직 분명치 않고, EC 의 보조금 감축도 만족스런 수준이 아니어서 어느업계도 현 텍스트에 대해 ENTHUSIASTIC 한 것으로 보이지는 않았으나, 협상타결의 기초로 수용할수 있다는게 일반적인 반응이었음.

다. 미 행정부 동향

- 농무부는 기본적으로 합의가 없는 것보다는 다소 불만스럽더라도 합의가 있는 것이 낫다는 입장이므로 DUNKEL 텍스트에 대해 대체로 긍정적인 반응을 보이고 있는 것으로 알고 있으나, 최종 협상결과 농업보조금 감축수준이나 REBALANCING 문제에서 현 협상안보다 후퇴한다면 이를 받아들일수 없을 것임.

- 여타분야에서는 의약품, 섬유, 철강, 영화업계 등에서 현 텍스트에 대해 강한 반발을 보이고 있어 행정부로서는 1.13. 이후 재개될 협상에서 이들을 납득시킬만한 결과를 얻어내야할 입장에 있음. 따라서, 금주는 그간의 협상경과를 설명하고, 업계를 설득하기 위한 EDUCATION WEEK 가 될 것임. (행정부는 금주부터 의회, 업계등을 상대로 계속 브리핑 실시중)

- 향후 협상과정에서 행정부가 여하한 범위에서 현 텍스트의 수정을 시도할것인지는 현단계에서는 판단하기 어려움. 업계와 의회의 반대를 무마하기 위해서는 상당한 수정이 이루어져야 할 것으로 보나, 이경우 EC 와 일본등의 연쇄적 수정요구를 초래, 협상이 원점으로 되돌아갈 것이라는데 문제가 있음. 자신의 견해로는 농업분야에서는 현 텍스트가 미측으로서는 수용 가능한 최저수준이라고 봄.

PAGE 2

0083

라. EC 및 일본의 반응

- 1.10-11 일 양일간 본격적인 EC 내부협의가 이루어질 것으로 아는바, 현재로서는 불란서가 계속 강한 반대입장을 보일 것이라는 사실외에는 EC 측 반응을 예측키 어려움.

- 일본은 결국 쌀시장 개방문제에서 관세화를 수용할 것이라는게 행정부측의 일반적인 관측임.

마. 개도국 우대 적용문제

- 개도국 우대문제에 있어서는 특히 보조금 감축및 지적재산권 보호기간과 관련, 미관련 업계에서 불만이 있으나, 개도국을 여하히 정의할 것인가에 대해서는 행정부측도 명확한 입장을 갖고 있지 못한 것으로 보임. 지적재산권 관련 업계에서는 UN 의 개도국 정의를 원용할 것을 주장하고 있는 것으로 암.

- 한국이 특히 농업분야에서 개도국 우대를 받을 필요가 있다는 점은 충분히 이해하나, 이를 분야별로 분리 적용할 수 없다는데 문제가 있다고봄.

바. 협상타결 전망

- 당초 기대했던 2-3 월경 타결은 현실적으로 어려울 것으로 봄. 자신이 1.7. 상기 농업정책 자문위에서 접촉한 KATZ USTR 부대표에 의하면, DUNKEL 사무총장이 최종협상안 가서명(INITIAL) 시기를 4.15 경으로 잡고 있다함.

- 그러나, 협상이 타결된다 하더라도 상기한 바와 같이 의회통과등 동 협상안의 국내수용 가능여부가 또다른 문제로 대두될 것인바, 시기적으로 국내선거가 본격화될 시점이어서 의회내 격론이 예상되며, 시간이 갈수록 SIDE-ISSUE 화 할 것으로 봄.

2. 당관 평가및 전망

- 국내 경제문제가 금년도 선거의 최대 이슈로 등장하고 있고, 이에따라, 대외통상문제(특히, 대일관계)도 민주당측의 대 행정부 정치공세의 표적이 되고 있는 상황에서 UR 협상이 불만족스런 수준에서 타결될 경우 동 협상안이 민주당 지배 의회를 통과하기는 매우 어려운 상황임.

- 부시 행정부로서는 협상의 성공적 타결을 통해 선거정국을 유리한 국면으로 몰아가기 위해 총력을 기울이고 있으나, 협상결과가 만족스럽지 못할 경우 오히려 선거에 치명적인 타격(POLITICAL DISASTER)이 될 것이라는 견해가 공화당 내부에서 조차 대두되고 있음.

- 따라서, 부시 행정부는 협상타결을 위하여 주요 교역국을 설득하여야 하는

PAGE 3

0084

부담과 동시에 이의 국내적 수용을 위한 대의회및 업계설득이라는 이중부담을안고 있으므로, 최종협상 타결과정에서 기대이상의 신축성을 보이기는 어려울 것으로 판단됨. 끝.

　　(대사대리 김봉규-과장)

　　예고: 92.6.30. 까지

메고를 내 재분류
92. 6. 30 중

외 무 부

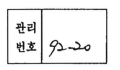

종 별 :

번 호 : ECW-0023   일 시 : 92 0108 1800

수 신 : 장 관(봉기,경기원,재무부,농림수산부,상공부,기정동문)

발 신 : 주 EC 대사   사본: 주 미,제네바-본부중계필

제 목 : GATT/UR 협상

연: ECW-1175

표제협상 관련, 당관이 파악한 EC 의 최근동향 아래 보고함

1. DUNKEL 협상안 제출이후 UR 협상에대한 EC 의 기본입장

가. 소연방의 해체를 비롯한 동구의 변혁등 현 국제사회가 직면하고 있는 정치.경제적 현황및 미국의 대통령 선거일정등을 감안할때, UR 협상은 늦어도 92.3 월말 이전에 완전 타결되야 한다는것이 EC 의 기본입장이며, 이러한 대전제하에서 UR 협상의 성공적 타결을위해 최선의 노력을 경주하고 있음

나. UR 협상이 3 월이전 타결되지 않을 경우, 현 상태에서 잠정동결, 92 년말 또는 93 년초에 재개하는 방안이 제기되고 있으나 격변하는 세계정세및 각 회원국의 상이한 정치및 경제적 우선순위 등에 비추어 협상의 연기는 사실상 협상의 실패를 초래하게 될것으로 봄

다. DUNKEL 협상안을 TAKE IT OR LEAVE IT 성격의 최종안으로 보지 않으나,동 내용에 대한 실질적인 (SUBSTANTIAL) 수정을 가할경우 협상이 원점으로 환원되어 PANDORA BOX 를 다시 여는것과 마찬가지이므로 수정의 폭을 어느정도까지허용하느냐가 최대의 관건임

라. 한편, EC 이사회 의장인 폴부갈 외무장관은 1.7. 리스본에서 영국 외무장관과 회담후 가진 기자회견에서 2 월말까지 UR 협상이 종결될수 있도록 농산물문제가 해결되기를 희망한다고 말하고, 동 협상이 실패할 경우 세계정세는 어려운 국면에 처하게 될것이라고 경고함

2. 향후 EC 내부의 협의전망

가. EC 회원국들의 1.9(목) 대사급 COREPER 회의, 1.10(금) 113 위원회, 1.11(토) 무역및 농업장관회의등 일련의 고위실무급및 각료회의를 거쳐 각국의 이해관계를

통상국 안기부	장관 경기원	차관 재무부	1차보 농수부	2차보 상공부	경제국 중계	외정실	분석관	청와대

PAGE 1   92.01.09   03:50

외신 2과 통제관 FI

0086

조정, DUNKEL 안에대한 EC 의 최종입장을 도출하기 위해 노력할 것임

　나. 그러나 농산물 분야에서의 불란서의 강력한 반대입장으로 1.13. TNC 회의에 맞추어 EC 의 최종입장이 마련되기는 현실적으로 어려울 것이며, 농산물 분야에서의 상당한 수정을 위하여 미국및 GATT 사무총장과 막바지 협의를 계속할 것으로 보임. 끝

　　(대사 권동만-국장)

　　예고: 92.6.30 까지

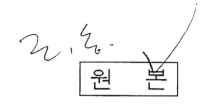

관리 번호	92~22

외 무 부

종 별 :

번 호 : USW-0100   일 시 : 92 0108 1843

수 신 : 장 관(봉기),봉이,농수산부,경제수석)   사본:주미대사

발 신 : 주 미국 대사 대리   사본:주제네바,EC대사-중계필

제 목 : UR 협상

사본; 주미대사, 주제네바대사, 주 EC 대사-본부 중계요

연;USW-6457,0025

당관 장기호 참사관은 1.8. S.EARLY USTR 농업 담당 대표보를 면담, UR 농산물 협상 관련 동향에 관하여 협의한바, 동 결과 요지 하기 보고함(서용현 서기관 동석)

1.UR 관련 미국내 동향

0 EARLY 대표보는 DUNKEL TEXT 중 농산물 분야에 대한 미측의 구체적 입장은 아직도 검토단계에 있고 마지막 단계에서나 정리가 될것으로 본다고 하고, DUNKEL TEXT 는 당초 미국이 기대한것 보다는 미흡하지만 대체적으로 향후협상의 좋은 기초로 본다고 언급하였음.

0 동 대표보는 이어서 미국이 동 협정안에 대해 여러가지 실질적 변경(SUBSTANTIAL CHANGE)을 추진하게 되면 여타 국가의 연쇄적인 개정 요구를 초래하게되어 결국 UR 협상을 실패로 이끌게 될 우려가 있다고 하였음. 그러나 이러한 고려에 입각하여 미측이 일단 DUNKEL TEXT 를 당분간 현 상태에서 큰 수정없이 수락하고 시장 접근 협상을 진전시킨 다음에 DUNKEL TEXT 와 시장 접근 협상 결과를 묶어서 최종 타결을 짓는다는 시나리오를 염두에 둘수 있지 않겠느냐고 지적한데 대하여는 동 대표보는 확정적인 답변을 회피함.

0 동 대표보는 이러한 상황에서 명 1.9 개최 예정인 하원 농업위 청문회는 DUNKEL TEXT 에 대한 미국내 여론의 향배를 저울질 할수 있는 계기가 될것이라고 하였음.

0 한편, 당지 언론 보도에 의하면 미국내에서 DUNKEL TEXT 에 대한 찬반이 엇갈리는 가운데 UR 협상을 지지하는 다국적 기업들의 연합체인 MTN COALITION 은 시장 접근 협상의 결과를 알수 있을때까지는 DUNKEL TEXT 의 수락 또는 불수락을 논할 계제가 아니라고 지적하면서 반대 세력들이 의회에 영향력을 행사 하기 전에 하루빨리

통상국 외정실	장관 분석관	차관 청와대	1차보 청와대	2차보 안기부	미주국 농수부	미주국 중계	경제국	통상국

PAGE 1   92.01.09   09:45

협사을 진행시켜 나가는것이 UR 협상을 성공리에 마무리지을 수 있는 길이라고 주장하였는바, 이러한 친 UR 세력의 언급은 향후 미측의 UR 협상 전략의 방향과도 무관치 않을것으로 보임.

2. 여타 국가의 관계

O EARLY 대표보는 작 1.7 당지를 방문중인 ANDRIESSEN EC 대외 무역상과 HILLS 대표간 회담 결과에 대하여는 아직 파악치 못하고 있으나 동 회담이 EC 외무, 통상관계 각료 회의와 거의 동시에 진행되어 ANDRIESSEN 대외 무역상이 새로운 MANDATE 를 지침할수 없었을것이므로 동 회담에서 구체적인 진전이 있었을 것으로는 기대되지 않는다고 말함.

O EARLY 대표보는 DUNKEL TEXT 의 농산물 부문은 사실후 미국으로서도 수용할수 있는 최저선이기 때문에, EC 가 요구하고 있는것과 같은 실질적인 변경은 수락될수 없는것으로 본다고 강조하고 앞으로 EC 측의 반응이 동 협상의 성과를 가름할 것이라고 하여 미측으로서는 더이상의 양보를 하기 어렵다는 반응을 보였음.

O 또한 동 대표보는 1.13 TNC 회의에서 EC 측은 대외적으로 강경한 입장을 표할것이나, 일본, 한국은 일단 EC 와는 달리 보다 유보적인 태도를 보일것으로 예상한다고 언급함.

3. 농산물 분야 세부 사항에 관한 협상 전망

O EARLY 대표보는 현재의 DUNKEL TEXT 내용중에는 관세화의 구체적 시행 방법, SAFEGUARD 가 최소 시장 접근외에 관세화에도 적용되는것인지 여부등 아직도세부 사항에 관하여 불확실한 부분이 있다고 하면서 1.13 이후의 회의에서는 우선 이러한것들을 명확히 해야할것이라고 언급함.

O 또한 시장접근 협상에 관하여도, 각국의 양허 스케줄 제시 시한이 너무 늦게 잡혀 있어 1.20 부터 개시될 시장 접근 협상에서 무엇을 기초로 하여 협상을 진행할수 있을 것인지도 모호하다고 지적함.끝.

(대사 대리 김봉규-국장)

예고: 92.6.30 까지

PAGE 2

0089

통화 요록

1992. 1. 9.
통상기구과

1. 통화일시 : 92.1.9(목) 10:00

2. 통 화 자 :

    ㅇ 최혁 통상국 심의관

    ㅇ '시모구치' 주한 일본 대사관 참사관

3. 통화요록

    가. 일측 언급요지

    ㅇ 1.13 TNC 대책과 관련, 일정부에서는 최종 입장을 검토중에 있는바,
       쌀문제는 계속 검토중이며 여타 협상요소에 대한 일정부의 1차 검토
       결과, 문제점이 있는 사항은 아래와 같음.

       - 농산물 : 예외없는 관세화, 국내 허용 보조범위 제한, 수출보조의
                  감축 의무 미흡

       - 반덤핑 : averaging, sales below costs 산정, comparison of fair
                  price의 허점으로 인한 남용 가능성, anti-circumvention
                  규율 미흡

       - 세이프가드 : quota modulation이 선별적 세이프가드를 허용할 가능성

       - 보조금 : 개발지원이 허용보조로 분류되어야 할 필요

       - TRIPs : 대체로 만족

    ㅇ 쌀에 대한 일정부 입장은 결정대로 알려주겠음.

    나. 아측 언급요지

    ㅇ 1차적 평가는 완료되어 상부 보고중에 있음.

공람	통상기구과 92년1월9일	담당	과 장	심의관	국 장	차관보	차 관	장 관
		농봉헌						

0030

ㅇ 1.13 TNC 회의는 최종 협정안 수락 여부에 대한 입장을 표명하는
   회의가 안될 것이므로 ~~구체적~~ 입장은 밝히지 않을 것이나, 국내적으로
   수용 가능한 package가 되기 위해서는 예외없는 관세화등을 포함하여
   농산물 협상 결과가 보다 균형된 것이 되어야 한다는 입장을 밝혀야
   될 것으로 봄.

ㅇ 농산물 분야 이외에도 보조금 분야에서 허용보조 범위 제한, 세이프가드
   분야에서 quota modulation에 따른 문제점이 있음.   끝.

외 무 부

관리
번호 92-31

종 별 :

번 호 : JAW-0107

일 시 : 92 0109 1441

수 신 : 장관(봉기)

발 신 : 주 일 대사(일경)

제 목 : UR 협상

대:WJA-0013

대:JAW-7169

대호, 당관 조태영 서기관은 1.8(수) "이시카와"외무성 국제기관 1 과 차석을 면담, 던켈 최종 협정 초안에 대한 일측의 입장을 문의한바, 동인의 발언요지를 다음 보고함.

1. 일측의 종합 평가

0 일본으로서 던켈 초안에 만족하지 못하는 부분이 상당히 있음.

0 가장 큰 문제는 역시 농업분야 초안으로서 현재의 초안대로는 동의하기가 어려운 상황임.

- 그러나 던켈 초안상의 관세화안은 원래 미국측이 주장하던 관세화안 보다훨씬 완화된 것으로서 이를 평가하고, 어느정도 긍정적인 대응이 필요하다는 견해가 일부 있는 것은 사실임.

- 이와관련, 최근 언론에 와따나베 외상이 일본이 완전 관세화안의 수용을 포함하여 대응방안을 검토 예정이라고 보도된 것은 와전으로서, 와따나베 외상은완전 관세화안을 포함하여 각종안이 일본에 있어 어떤 영향을 미치는 지를 철저히 검토할 필요가 있다고 언급함으로써 문제 제기를 한데 불과함.

0 반덤핑 분야에서 일본이 주장해온 반덤핑 조치 남용방지를 위한 규율강화가 충분히 받아 들여지지 않은 점등에 일측은 불만임.

0 한편, 미국의 통상법 301 조등 일방적 제재조치에 대해 좀더 강한 규제를 기대했던 것은 사실이나, 금번 협정초안 정도로 된 것은 GATT 의 성격상 최대한이라고 보고 있음.

0 금번 합의초안에 대해 완전히 만족하고 있는 국가는 별로 없지만, 또한 완전히

통상국 안기부	장관	차관	1차보	2차보	경제국	외정실	분석관	청와대

92.01.09 16:28

외신 2과 통제관 CD

0092

불만인 나라도 많지 않은 점에서 1.13. 의 무역협상 위원회에서는 일단 모든 나라들이 긍정적인 반응을 보이되 조건을 붙이는 반응을 보이지 않을까 생각함.

2. 향후 협상 전망

0 현재 원산지 규정 관련 부분은 이미 합의가 거의 완료된 상태이고, 기준, 인증부분은 거의 합의에 가까운 상태이나, 농업, 시장접근 분야등은 아직도 쟁점이 많이 남아 있는 등 협상 분야별로 진전도에 상당한 차가 있다는 점에서 92.3월까지 협상이 완료될까는 예측 불가능한 상황이라고 봄.

3.1.13 TNC 에 대한 일본의 대표단 규모

0 일본으로서는 엔도오 외무성 국제무역, 경제담당대사를 단장으로 본부에서 12-3 명의 대표단을 파견 예정이며, 제네바 주재 대표부의 관계관이 이에 참여할 예정임.끝.

(대사 오재희-국장)

예고:92.6.30. 일반

예고들 의거 재분류
92.6.30 강

관리
번호 92-32

외 무 부

종 별 :

번 호 : NZW-0007

일 시 : 92 0109 1815

수 신 : 장관(봉기,아동,사본:주제네바대사-중계필)

발 신 : 주 뉴질랜드대사

제 목 : GATT 던켈안에 대한 주재국반응

1. 주재국 MCKINNON 부수상겸 외상은 1.9 BURDON 상무장관및 FALLOON 농업장관과 GATT 무역자유화 협상관련 협의를 가진후 뉴정부는 DUNKEL PAPER 를 공식적으로 지지한다는 주재국정부 입장을 발표하였음.

2. MCKINNON 외상은 또한 동 PAPER 의 채택을위해 CAIRNS 그룹 국가들과 긴밀히 협조할 것이라고 말하고, 동 PAPER 가 채택되더라도 U/R 이 종결되기 까지에는 동 PAPER 를 구체화 시키는 협상이 계속 필요하다고 언급하였음.

3. 세계 주요 축산국가의 하나인 주재국 정부는 CAIRNS GROUP 일원으로 GATT 농산물 교역자유화의 조기타결을 적극 지지해오고 있음을 참고바람.

4. 상기관련 언론발표문 파편송부 예정임.끝.

(대사 운영엽-국장)

예고:92.6.30 까지

예고문에 재분류
92.6.30. 종

통상국	장관	차관	1차보	2차보	아주국	경제국	외정실	분석관
정와대	안기부	중계						

92.01.09   15:22

외신 2과 통제관 BW
0094

관리 번호	92-30

외 무 부

종 별 :

번 호 : SGW-0025
　　　　　　　　　　　　　　　　　　　일 시 : 92 0109 1730

수 신 : 장관(봉기, 아동)

발 신 : 주 싱가포르 대사

제 목 : UR 협상 동향

대: WSG-3

　　1. 대호건 당관 황정일 1 등서기관이 MS TAN 외무부 국제기구국 UR 담당관 및 무역개발청 UR 담당관들과 접촉 파악한바, 주재국측은 DUNKEL PACKAGE 중 일부 분야에 대하여 유보적이기는 하나 전반적으로 동 PACKAGE 를 실행 가능한 (WORKABLE) 것으로 받아 들이고 있으며, UR 협상이 더이상 지연되지 않고 성공적으로 타결되기를 원하고 있는 실정임.

　　2. DUNKEL PACKAGE 중 주재국측이 관심을 갖고 있는분야는 보조금, 상계관세, 반덤핑, SAFAGUARDS, 시장및 서비스 개방등 5 개 분야로 특히 상계관세, 반덤핑, SAFEGUARDS 등 분야와 관련해서는 미, EC 등이 과거 이를 빈번히 발동하는등 남용해온 사례가 있음에 비추어 이들의 발동요건 및 절차등을 제한하는 방향으로 대처하고 하고 있음.

　　3. 1.13. 의 TNC 회의 참가 주재국 대표단은 주제네바대사를 수석대표로 하고, 외무부및 무역개발청 관리들로 구성될 것이라 함.

　　4. 주재국은, 아국과같이 제조업이나 농업이 산업의 기초가 아니며, 해운, 금융등 서비스가 주된 경제분야로서, 국제교역이 자유롭고 물자 이동이 많을수록 국익이 된다는 입장에서 UR 에대하여는 처음부터 적극 지지하는 입장임을 첨언함. 끝.

　　(대사-국장)

　　예고: 92.12.31. 까지

통상국	장관	차관	2차보	아주국	분석관	청와대	안기부

　　　　　　　　　　　　　　　　　　　　92.01.09　　20:53
　　　　　　　　　　　　　　　　　　　　외신 2과 통제관 CD
　　　　　　　　　　　　　　　　　　　　　　　　0095

관리
번호 92-34

외 무 부

종 별 :

번 호 : CNW-0039

일 시 : 92 0109 1000

수 신 : 장 관(봉기,상공부)

발 신 : 주 캐나다 대사

제 목 : UR 협상 동향

대 : WCN-0004

GATT 던켈 총장의 협상안 관련 주재국 평가 및 반응(주재국 정부 관계관, 봉상전문가등 의견을 기초로 한 당관 평가)등을 아래와 같이 보고함.

1. 주재국은 던켈 총장의 협상안에 대하여 양자 택일적으로 전면 수용 또는 전면 거부 입장을 가지고 있지는 않는 것으로 평가됨. 주재국의 관점에서 볼때동 협상안은 협상분야에 따라 긍정적인 측면과 함께 부정적인 측면도 함께 지니고 있는 것으로 분석되고 있는 것으로 알려지고 있음. 그러나 주재국 정부는 동 협상안에 대해 일부 분야를 제외하고는 원칙적으로 수용 가능한 것(협상 타결을 위한 기초)으로 받아 들이고 있는 것으로 보임.

2. 동 협상안에 포함된 무역규범 관련 규정은 카나다 상품 및 서비스의 대외시장 진출기회를 확대할 것으로 기대되고 있으며, 분쟁처리 절차규정 및 보조금 정의의 명료화는 대체적으로 일보 진전된 것으로 관측되고 있음. 시장접근 분야에서는 던켈 초안에 가시적인 내용이 없고 92.3 월말이 되어야 구체적인 내용이 도출될수 있을 것으로 보고있음.

3. 농산물 분야는 세부내용에 따라 엇갈린 평가를 받고 있는데 동 협상안에 포함된 수출 보조금 감축등 관련 내용은 주재국의 입장에서 볼때 흡족한 수준에 이르는 것은 아니지만 대체적으로 보아 괜찮은 시발점으로 환영하고 있으며, 특히 서부지역에 생산 기반을 둔 곡물의 가격 상승에 긍정적인 영향을 미칠 것으로 기대되고 있음. 반면에 동 초안이 예외없는 관세화를 들고 나옴에 따라 GATT 제 11 조의 규정에 근거한 SUPPLY MANAGEMENT SYSTEM 의 존립기반이 위협을 받게 되고 그 결과 퀘벡 및 온타리오에 집중되어 있는 낙농, 가금류 및 양계 농가의 생계에 심각한 영향을 미치는 것으로 보고 있음. 특히 퀘벡의 분리문제가 대두되고 있는 현 시점에서 보수당 정부가 예외없는

| 통상국 | 장관 | 차관 | 1차보 | 2차보 | 미주국 | 경제국 | 외정실 | 분석관 |
| 정와대 | 안기부 | 상공부 | | | | | | |

PAGE 1

관세화를 받아들일경우 정치적으로도 어려움에 봉착할 것으로 예상되기 때문에 1.13. 개최 예정인 TNC 에서 동 협상안중 이부문에 대한 반대 입장을 밝힐것으로 봄.

4. 1.13. 개최예정인 TNC 에는 SHANNON 제네바 (MTN) 대사를 수석대표로 하여 일부 관계관이 참석할 예정임.끝.

(대사-국장)

예고문 : 92.6.30. 까지

예고문 에게 재분류
92.6.30

PAGE 2

0097

외 무 부

종   별 :

번   호 : BRW-0035

일   시 : 92 0109 1910

수   신 : 장관(봉기)

발   신 : 주 브라질 대사

제   목 : UR 협상동향

(자료응신 92-3)

대:WBR-0004

연:BRW-0031

1. 주재국 정부는 1.8 경제부, 외무부, 농무부, 3 개장관간 DUNKEL 총장의 최종 협정 초안에 대하여 협의한후 공식적으로 DUNKEL 초안의 수용을 발표하면서 협상 5 년을 끌어온 현 시점에서 최선의 해결책은 현행 DUNKEL 안을 수용, 협상 종결시키는 것임을 부연함.

2. 당지 발간 1.9 자 일간지에 보도된바에 의하면 REZEK 외무장관은 서구국가들이 1.13 동 차안을 거부할 경우, UR 협상은 종결의 기회를 상실할지도 모든다고 피력하였고, 또한 1.7 GAIRNS 그룹내의 호주동 동 DUNKEL 총장의 안을 수용키로 결정하였다함.

3. 대호 3 항 1.13 개최되는 TNC 에 파견될 주재국 대표단은 CELSO AMORIM 제네바 주재 대사가 수석대표로 되고, 실무직원 3 명 정도가 수행할 것이라함. 끝

(대사 한철수-국장)

예고:92.6.30

예고문 의거 재분류
92. 6. 30

통상국	차관	2차보	외정실	분석관	청와대	안기부

외 무 부

종   별 : 긴 급

번   호 : GVW-0049   일   시 : 92 0109 2110

수   신 : 장관(봉기, 경기원, 재무부, 농림수산부, 상공부, 특허청, 경제수석)

발   신 : 주 제네바 대사대리   사본: 주 미, 주이씨, 주일, 주카나대사(중계필)

제   목 : UR/그린룸회의

1. 금 1.9(목) 16:00-18:00 간 예정대로 수석대표급 비공식 그린룸회의가 개최되었음. 던켈 사무총장은 연호로 보고한바와 같이 1.13. 개최되는 TNC 회의는 UR 협상 결과를 최종 가부평가하는 회의가 아님을 강조하고 참석 각국의 반대가 없는한 12.20 자 (협상안을 기초로) 아래 FOUR TRACK 협상전략에 따라 UR 협상을 진행할것을 제의하고 각국의 입장을 문의한바, 각국의 입장은 1) 12:20 자 협상안을 전적으로 수용하고 던켈총장의 전략을 지지하겠다는 국가 2) 협상안에 대한 본국의 검토가 아직 끝나지 않았으나 수용 가능하며 던켈총장의 전략을 지지한다는 국가 3) 본국정부의 던켈 전략을 보고하겠다는 국가 4) 대사 부재로 입장개진이 어렵다는 국가로 대별되었는바 어느 국가도 던켈총장의 전략에 반대의사를 표명한 국가는 없었음.

- 아래-

- 시장접근(농산물 포함) 양허협상

- 서비스 양허협상

- 12.20 자 협상안 법률문서화 작업

- 협상 참가국이 동의하고 전체 협상안의 균형이 유지되는 차원에서 일부 조정작업(FINE TUNING)

2. 금일 회의에서는 미국, EC 대사 포함 40 여국의 대표가 참석하였으며 아국도 김대사, 오참사관이 참석하였는바, 카나다, 일본, 말련, 항가리를 포함 다수 국가가 차석이 참석함.

3. 던켈총장은 회의 서두에 지난 연말 이후 지금까지 각국 수도의 주요인사와 각국대표단을 접촉한 결과, 대부분의 국가가 12.20 자 협상안을 기초로 앞으로 수주내에 UR 협상을 마루리 지어야 한다는 긍정적인 입장이었다는 점을 밝히고 금일 회의 소집 목적은 13 일회의 이후 12.20 자 협상안을 기초로 FOUR TRACK에 의해

통상국 재무부	장관 농수부	차관 상공부	2차보 특허청	외정실 중계	분석관	청와대	안기부	경기원

협상을 계속할 것인지, 12.20 자 협상안을 기초로 협상을 계속할수 없다는 입장인지 여부를 본국정부와 시간을 가지고 협의, 1.13. TNC 회의에서 밝혀주도록 요청하기 위해 소집한 것이라고 하였음. (1.13. TNC 회의는 15:00 개최예정)

　　4. 각국대표 발언요지

　　0 이집트

　　- 시장접근 결과가 나와있지 않으므로 구체적으로 언급하기 어려우나 협상안이 개도국 입장에서 볼때 만족스럽지 못하므로 좀더 협의가 있어야 됨

　　0 EC

　　- 사무총장의 전략에 협조하도록 본부에 건의하겠음.

　　0 협상 참가국뿐아니라 회원국 국민들에 대해서도 책임있게 행동해야 하는 점이 있음.

　　0 스위스

　　- TNC 회의에서 협상안에 대한 일반적 평가를 하겠음.

　　0 호주

　　- 12.20 협상안을 수용하며, 던켈전략을 지지함.

　　- 일부 조정작업 관련 제기할 문제점은 있을수 있음.

　　0 미국

　　- 12.20 자 협상안을 기초로 수주내에 협상 종결을 희망하여 일부 협상 분야별 조정작업 관련 관심사항을 표명 예정임.

　　0 태국

　　- 던켈 총장 전략을 지지하며, 조정작업 관련 관심분야를 표명 예정임

　　0 캐나다

　　- 던켈 전략을 본국정부에 보고하겠음

　　0 아르헨티나, 브라질, 콜롬비아

　　- 협상안은 수용가능하며 던켈전략을 지지함

　　0 멕시코

　　- 기본적으로 협상안을 수용할 수 있으며, 던켈 전략을 지지하나 조정작업관련 주요 문제가 협의되기를 희망함

　　0 일본

　　- 본국정부의 협상 검토가 끝나지 않았으나 협상안이 UR 협상 성공을 위한 중요한

PAGE 2

0100

단계로 볼수 있으며, 동 협상안을 최종적인 것으로 보지않으며 좀더 현실적으로 일부분야가 조정되어야 함

　　- UR 협상 성공을 위해 협력할 용의가 있음

　0 우루과이

　　- 서비스, TRIPS 등 푼타 선언과 관련 비교할때 균형을 이루지 못함.

　　- 던켈 총장의 전략을 지지함.

　0 한국

　　- 다자 무역체제의 신장과 UR 협상의 조기 타결을 지지해왔음.

　　- 12.20 자 협상안에 대해서는 본국정부에서 신중히 검토중에 있음.

　　- TNC 차원의 협의를 통해 모든 국가가 수용할수 있는 공정하고 균형된 협상결과가 도출되기를 기대함.

　　- 던켈총장의 전략을 본국정부에 보고하겠음. (전반적인 회의 분위기가 특정분야에 대한 언급을 하기 어려운 상황이라고 판단, TNC 를 통한 추가협상 필요성을 언급, 아국관심 사항을 간접적으로 표명하였는바, 회의 종료후 갓트사무국측에 확인한바 미국 및 EC 도 특정문제를 거론하도록 훈령을 받았으나 회의 분위기를 감안 언급을 자제하였다함)

　　0 인도

　　- 협상안에 부정적인 요소가 있다고 보며 TNC 회의에서 일반적인 평가를 하겠음.

　　0 뉴질랜드

　　- 협상안을 수용하며 던켈전략을 지지함.

　　0 페루

　　- 던켈전략을 지지함.

　　0 항가리

　　- 협상안을 본국정부에서 검토중이나 던켈전략을 지지함.

　　0 오지리

　　- 본국정부가 협상안 검토중이며 일부 문제가 있다고 보나 던켈 전략을 지지함

　　0 나이지리아

　　- 던켈 전략을 지지함.

　4. 관찰 및 평가

　1.13.TNC 회의에서는 EC 의 태도가 큰 변수로 작용하게될 것이나 금일회의

분위기를 보아 각국으로 부터 불만족스러운 일부분야에 대한 언급은 있을
것으로보이나 던켈 총장의 전략을 반대하는 분위기는 아닐것으로 예상되는바 아국입장
개진에 참고 바람. 끝

　　　(차석대사 김삼훈-차관)

　　　예고:92.6.30 까지

	분류번호	보존기간

발 신 전 보

WGV—0031   920109 1130 BE   종별: 지급

번   호 :

수   신 : 주   제네바   대사. 총영사/

발   신 : 장   관 (통 기)

제   목 : UR/그린룸 협의

대 : GVW-26

1. 대호 그린룸 협의시 각국이 Dunkel 총장의 협상 추진 전략을 청취하고 자국
    입장 개진을 자제할 경우 귀관 건의대로 아국도 발언을 자제하기 바람.

2. 다만, 여러나라가 자국의 어려운 문제점을 지적할 경우 아국으로서도 농산물
    분야에서 ~~전체~~ 수출, 수입국간의 균형 차원 및 식량안보 측면에서 예외없는
    관세화를 수용하기가 극히 어려우며 따라서 금후 협상에서 ~~₩~~ 이러한 문제점을
    해결하는 노력이 필요함을 간략히 언급하는 선에서 대처바람.   끝.

(통상국장 김 용 규)

								보 안 통 제	

앙 고 재	92 년 1 월 9 일	통 상 국 과	기안자 성 명 송봉헌		과 장	심의관	국 장		차 관	장 관		외신과통제

분류번호	보존기간

발 신 전 보

WGV-0040   920110 1006 FO

번   호 : _____   종별 : _____

수   신 : 주   제네바   대사. ~~총영사~~ ~~표~~(사본: 주 ~~제네바~~, 일본 대사)   WUS -0107 WEC -0028

발   신 : 장 관 (통 기)

제   목 : UR/TNC 회의

대: GVW-0049

1. 1.13 TNC 회의 대책(수석대표 연설요지 포함)을 아래 타전함.

  가. 기본적인 대응방향

    1) 기본적인 대응방향

      - 금번 TNC 회의에서는 전체 최종 협상 문안에 대한 우리의 1차적 평가와
        함께 농산물 분야에서의 기존 입장 재확인

      - 농산물 분야이외의 사항에 대한 우리의 입장 표명은 1.13을 전후한
        주요국의 동향 및 현지 회의 분위기를 검토하여 다음 대안별로 대처

        (대안 I) 대부분의 협상 참가국들이 자국의 관심사항을 구체적으로
                  개진하는 경우

        (대안 II) 발언국이 소수에 불과하고 추가 협상 필요성등 기본적
                  입장만을 간단히 언급하는 경우

      - 이와같은 대안으로도 대응키 곤란한 새로운 상황이 전개되거나
        동 입장의 명시적 표명이 부적절하다고 판단될 경우에는 본부에
        별도의 지침을 청훈하여 대응

    2) 우리 입장의 개진에 앞서 주요국의 입장을 사전에 파악토록 하며 농산물
       분야에서는 유사한 입장을 가진 나라들과 공동 대응 방안을 사전 협의

제2차관보 :

통제	
사전협의	

앙고고재	72년 1월 1일 통기과	기안자성명 조천		과장	심의관	국장 전결	차관	장관		외신과통제

나. 수석대표 발언요지

(대안 I : 대부분의 협상 참가국들이 자국의 관심사항을 구체적으로
　　　　개진하는 경우)

- 이번에 제시된 최종 협정 문안은 지난 5년간의 협상 결과를 잘 집약시킨
  것으로 평가하며 GATT 사무국을 비롯한 각 분야별 협상그룹 의장들의
  노고를 치하함.

- 특히 국제무역규범의 개선, 섬유교역의 GATT 체제로의 복귀, GATT 기능
  강화 및 제도분야에서의 협상 진전은 UR 협상의 타결에 도움이 될 것이라는
  것이 한국 정부의 1차적 평가임.

- 한국 정부는 앞으로의 최종 협상 단계에서 우리가 계속 주장해온 농산물등
  주요쟁점에서 보다 균형있는 합의의 도출이 필요하다고 보며 이를 전제로
  금후 협상에 계속 적극적인 자세로 참여할 것임.

  ① 농산물 일부분야에서 수출국과 수입국, 선진국과 개도국의 이해가
     균형을 이루지 못한 것은 유감임.

     ㅇ 개별국가의 특수성, 특히 농산물 순수입국의 취약한 농업 기반을
        보호할 수 있는 장치가 전혀 고려되지 않은 「예외없는 관세화」에
        반대

        . 식량안보 관련 기초식량에 대해서는 관세화 예외인정 필요

     ㅇ 쌀에 대한 최소 시장접근은 불가하며 기타품목의 최소 시장접근에
        있어서의 개도국 우대원칙이 적용되어서 함.

     ㅇ 개도국에 대하여는 국내보조 동결 조치가 적용되지 않았음에도
        불구하고 수출보조 분야와는 달리 시장접근 및 국내보조 감축상의
        기준년도를 1986-88년간으로 설정한 것은 실질적으로 선진국보다
        더 큰 부담을 지우는 것으로 불합리하기 때문에 개도국에 대해서는
        통계적으로 자료산정이 가능한 최근년도(1991년)을 적용토록 함이
        타당함.

  ② 관세인하에 있어서는 몬트리올 합의 목표가 우선적으로 달성되어야 함.

  ③ 긴급 수입제한 조치에 있어 국별 선택 적용이 가능한 Quota Modulation
     제도는 다자간 협상의 무차별 원칙에 어긋나므로 폐지되어야 함.

ㅗ

0105

④ 보조금 및 상계관세 분야에 있어서 구조 조정의 촉진을 위한 정부 보조금을 허용보조금으로 인정하지 않는 것은 급속한 산업구조 조정 단계에 있는 국가들의 효율적인 고용·산업정책을 저해하므로 구조 조정에 필요한 보조금 지급은 허용되어야 함.

⑤ 서비스 협상분야에서 MFN 원칙은 일반원칙으로서 준수되어야 함.

- 한국 정부는 과거와 마찬가지로 앞으로도 UR 협상의 성공적 마무리를 위한 시장접근 및 서비스 분야 양허협상에 적극 참여할 것이며 동 양허협상이 각국의 기준 개방 수준을 고려하고 경제적 능력의 범위내에서 균형있게 이루어질 것을 기대함.

(대안 Ⅱ : 발언국이 소수에 불과하고 추가 협상 필요성등 기본 입장만을 간단히 언급하는 경우)

- 상기 대안 Ⅰ과 동일하나, 다만 농산물외 분야(②, ③, ④, ⑤)는 통합하여 아래 표현으로 대체

② 이밖에도 한국정부는 상당수준의 관세인하가 이루어져야 하며 긴급 수입제한 조치, 보조금 및 상계관세등 분야에서 추가적인 협상이 필요하다는 입장임.

2. 아울러 12.20 던켈 총장의 최종협정 초안에 대한 본부의 평가를 별첨 송부하니 참고바람.

3. 대호 던켈총장의 four track 협상 전략에 대한 별도 대응이 필요한 경우, 이는 추보하겠음.

첨 부 : 최종 협정 초안에 대한 평가 1부(2매) 끝.   (통상국장 김 용 규)

(fax) GVF-14, USF-17, ECF-7, JAF-5.

예고문에 의거 개봉독
92.6.30 종

발 신 전 보

WGV-0043   920110 1425 FL

번   호 : _____   종별 : _____

수   신 : 주   제네바   대사. 총영사/

발   신 : 장   관 (통 기)

제   목 : UR/최종협정 초안

12.20자 최종 협정 초안과 관련, 주한대사(관으)로부터의 아국 입장 문의 및 자국 입장
표명 현황을 아래 통보하니 참고바람 (괄호안은 접촉일자) (외정)

　　ㅇ 스위스 (12.30)

　　　- 협정 초안은 균형되지 않았으나 이에 대한 최종 입장은 미정 상태임.

　　　- 농산물 협정 이행은 스위스의 희생이 따르게 될 것임.

　　　- 보조금, Safeguards, 지적재산권, 서비스등 여타분야는 수용 가능함.

　　ㅇ 호주, 뉴질랜드 (1.3)

　　　- 약간 실망스러운 분야도 있으나 농업부문등 대체로 만족스럽게 생각함.

　　ㅇ 핀랜드, 노르웨이 (1.7)

　　　- 협정 초안을 대체로 긍정적으로 평가하고 있으나, 농산물 분야에서
　　　　문제가 있으며, 반덤핑, 시장접근 분야에도 약간의 문제점이 있는 것으로
　　　　평가하고 있음.

　　ㅇ 카나다 (1.8)

　　　- 협정 초안에 대한 카나다의 입장 정립을 위해 고위급의 정치적 결정을
　　　　기다리고 있는 상태임.

　　　- 농산물 분야의 예외없는 관세화, 국내보조 감축 기준년도에 문제가
　　　　있어 상당히 어려운 결정을 내려야 할 입장임.

0107

- 시장접근에 대한 전체 협상 결과가 도출되어야 최종 수락 여부에 대한
  Package를 의회등 국내에 제시할 수 있으므로 남은 시장접근 협상이 매우
  중요함. 이와 관련, 상품, 서비스, 농산물 분야 협상 guideline에 대한
  완전한 합의가 이루어지지 않은 상태에서 협상을 추진해야 하는 문제점이
  있기 때문에 동 문제점도 해결해야 될 과제임.

ㅇ 일본 (1.9)

- 1.13 TNC 대책과 관련, 일본 정부에서는 최종 입장을 검토중에 있는바,
  쌀문제는 계속 검토중이며 여타 협상 요소에 대한 1차 검토 결과 ~~문제점이~~
  ~~없는 사항은~~ 아래와 같음.

  . 농산물 : 예외없는 관세화, 국내 허용 보조범위 제한, 수출보조의
            감축 의무 미흡

  . 반덤핑 : averaging, sales below costs 산정, comparison of fair
            price의 허점으로 인한 남용 가능성, anti-circumvention
            규율 미흡

  . 세이프가드 : quota modulation이 선별적 세이프가드를 허용할 가능성

  . 보조금 : 개발지원이 허용보조로 분류되어야 할 필요

  . TRIPs : 대체로 만족

- 쌀에 대한 일정부 입장은 결정되는대로 알려주겠음.

ㅇ 영국 (1.10)

- 협정 초안이 균형된 것으로 평가하며 UR 협상 성공을 위한 기초가
  되어야 할 것임.

- 한국도 가능하면 동 초안을 UR 협상 성공을 위한 기초로 해주기 바람.

                              끝.   (통상국장 김용규)

0108

면 담 요 록

1. 면 담 자

    ㅇ Brian Wilson 주한 뉴질랜드 대사관 참사관

    ㅇ 통상기구과장

2. 면담일시 및 장소 : 1992.1.10(금) 16:00-16:20, 통상기구과

3. 면담내용 :

Wilson 참사관

    ㅇ UR/던켈 협정 초안에 대한 뉴질랜드 정부 입장 전달 (별첨)

    ㅇ 한국측 입장 및 협상 전망 문의

통상기구과장

    ㅇ 최종 협정 초안에 대한 한국 입장은 아직 확정되지 않았음.

       - 일차 검토 결과 농산물 분야에서 어려운 문제가 있다고 보며, 앞으로의
         협상에서 시정되어야 할 것임.

    ㅇ 향후 UR 협상은 미.EC간 협상이 관건이며, 던켈 총장은 일방 상품, 서비스
       분야의 시장접근 협상을 계획대로 진행하며, 미.EC간 협상 결과를 기다릴
       것으로 보임.   끝.

양 고 재	통상기구과	92 년 산 일 일	담 당	과 장	심의관	국 장	차관보	차 관	장 관
			조이						

0109

GATT: URUGUAY ROUND: SECRETARY GENERAL DUNKEL'S PAPER: NEW ZEALAND'S VIEWS

The New Zealand Government would like to convey to the Government of the Republic of Korea the following views concerning GATT Secretary General Dunkel's draft Uruguay Round agreement:

1   All GATT Contracting Parties should endorse the text of Secretary General Dunkel's paper unaltered as the basis for concluding the Uruguay Round. It is not a practical proposition for countries to endorse the text in part only. Any attempt to reopen the text at this stage would risk unravelling the five years of hard work which has gone into bringing the Uruguay Round to the point it has reached now, and would place in jeopardy the future of the GATT system.

2   Director General Dunkel faced an extremely difficult task in trying to reconcile the differing positions of the parties involved in the Uruguay Round negotiations. In the end he had no choice but to prepare a paper himself because of the inability of Contracting Parties to arrive at a compromise among themselves. The Dunkel paper represents the best hope for achieving a satisfactory conclusion to the Uruguay Round negotiations. It would be impractical for any Contracting Party to try to reopen areas of the negotiations where agreement has hitherto been impossible.

3   The "selected adjustments" to the text which some countries have called for would result in a worse result overall because they would lower the level of ambition for the liberalisation of global trade.

4   The Dunkel paper represents a turning point in respect of world trade in agriculture. It is an opportunity which is too good to be missed, both by countries which protect their agricultural sectors and by those which do not. It is time that agriculture was brought within GATT rules and the Dunkel paper may be the last chance for years to do so. New Zealand, like most other countries, has difficulties with some parts of the text (for instance, we consider the disciplines proposed for internal support measures are too loose), but the package represents the best balance of country interests which can be found.

0110

5   The inclusion in the Dunkel paper of a complete GATS framework in respect of services is a considerable achievement. While the text is flawed in that it leaves wide scope for MFN derogations, this need not render the rest of the framework inoperative provided countries do not misuse it and are prepared individually to sign on to worthwhile packages of commitments in the next phase of the negotiations.

6   The Dunkel paper includes also advances in the areas of market access for non-agricultural goods, trade rules and dispute settlement procedures, and the protection of intellectual property. These will strengthen the international trading system to ensure that trade relations between countries proceed on a more certain and stable basis and thereby bring benefits to all countries.

7   New Zealand hopes that the Republic of Korea will support the Dunkel text when the Trade Negotiations Committee reconvenes on 13 January.

New Zealand Embassy
SEOUL

10 January 1992

0111

외 무 부

110-760 서울 종로구 세종로 77번지 / (02)720-2188 / (02)725-1737

문서번호 통기 20644-

시행일자 1992. 1.10.(   )

취급		차 관	장 관
보존			
국 장	버.		
심의관	부재중	제2차관보	
과 장		기획관리실장	
		총무과장	
기안	현철승	기획운영담당관	협조

수신   내부결재

참조

제목   UR/무역협상위원회(TNC) 정부대표 임명

        92.1.13. 스위스 제네바에서 개최되는 UR/TNC에 참가할 정부 본부대표를
"정부대표 및 특별사절의 임명과 권한에 관한 법률"에 의거 아래와 같이 임명할 것을
건의하니 재가하여 주시기 바랍니다.

                        - 아   래 -

1. 회 의 명 : Uruguay Round 무역협상위원회(Trade Negotiations Committee)
              및 UR 관련 비공식 협의

2. 기간 및 장소 : 1992. 1.13-14, 스위스 제네바

3. 본부대표 : 홍종기 통상기구과장

4. 출장기간 : 1992. 1.11(토)-16(목) (5박6일)

5. 소요예산

    - 항공료 (서울 → 제네바 2등왕복) : $2,128

    - 체재비

      . 숙박비 : $66 X 5 = $330

      . 식 비 : ($20+$42) X 6 = $372

    - 총 액 : $2,830

    - 지변항목 : 경제활동 국외여비

                                                        0112

6. 훈   령

　ｏ 기본적 대응방안

　　　- 금번 TNC 회의에서는 전체 최종 협상 문안에 대한 우리의 1차적
　　　　평가와 함께 농산물 분야에서의 기존 입장을 재확인

　　　- 농산물 이외의 사항에 대한 우리의 입장 표명은 1.13을 전후한
　　　　주요국의 동향 및 현지 회의 분위기를 검토하여 다음 대안별로 대처

　　　　. 대안 I : 대부분의 협상 참가국들이 자국의 관심사항을
　　　　　　　　　　　구체적으로 개진하는 경우

　　　　. 대안 II : 발언국이 소수에 불과하고 추가 협상 필요성등
　　　　　　　　　　　기본적 입장만을 간단히 언급하는 경우

　　　- 이와같은 대안으로도 대응키 곤란한 새로운 상황이 전개되거나
　　　　동 입장의 명시적 표명이 부적절하다고 판단될 경우에는 본부에
　　　　별도의 지침을 청훈하여 대응

　ｏ 우리 입장의 개진에 앞서 주요국의 입장을 사전에 파악토록 하며
　　　농산물 분야에서는 유사한 입장을 가진 나라들과 공동 대응 방안을
　　　사전 협의.　　　　　　　　　　　끝.

외　무　부　장　관

0113

외 무 부

110-760 서울 종로구 세종로 77번지   / (02)720-2188   / (02)725-1737

문서번호 통기 20644- 10

시행일자 1992. 1. 11. (   )

취급		장 관	
보존			
국장	전결	代 (서명)	/
심의관			
과장			
기안	송봉헌		협조

수신 농림수산부장관

참조

제목 UR/무역협상위원회 정부대표 임명 통보

─────────────────────────────────────

    92.1.13. 스위스 제네바에서 개최되는 UR/TNC 회의에 참가할 정부대표가

"정부대표 및 특별사절의 임명과 권한에 관한 법률"에 의거 아래와 같이 임명 되었음을

알려 드립니다.

- 아   래 -

1. 회 의 명 : UR/TNC 회의 및 UR 관련 비공식 협의

2. 회의기간 및 장소 : 92.1.13-14, 스위스 제네바

3. 정부대표(본부) : 조일호 농림수산부 농업협력통상관

4. 출장기간 : 92.1.12(일)-16(목)

5. 소요예산 : 소속부처 소관예산

6. 출장 결과 보고 : 귀국후 20일 이내.   끝.

외 무 부 장 관

농 림 수 산 부

우 427-760 / 주소 경기 과천시 중앙동 1번지 / 전화 (02) 503-7227 / 전송 503-7249

문서번호 국협20644-28

시행일자 1992.1 .11 (년)

(경유)

수신 외무부장관

참조 통상국장

선결			지시	
접수	일자 시간	19 . .	결재 공람	
	번호			
	처리과			
	담당자			

제목 UR/TNC회의 참석

---

1. '92.1.13 개최예정인 UR/TNC회의에 다음과 같이 당부대표를 파견코자 하오니 협조하여 주시기 바랍니다(참가대책은 대외협력위원회의 결정사항에 따름).

- 다   음 -

가. 당부대표

구 분	소 속	직 위	성 명	비 고
대 표	농업협력통상관실	농업협력통상관	조 일 호	

나. 출장기간 및 출장지 : '92.1.12(일)-1.16(목), 스위스 제네바

다. 출장목적 : UR TNC회의 참석 및 각국의 협상동향 파악

라. 소요경비 : 농림수산부 부담

마. 기   타
　　O TNC회의 참석대책은 대외협력위원의 결정사항에 따라 대처함

첨부 : 출장일정 및 소요경비 내역 1부. 끝.

농 림 수 산 부 장

0115

출장일정 및 소요경비내역

가. 출장일정

'92.1. 12(일) 12:40 서 울 발(KE 901)
                18:10 파 리 착
                20:45 파 리 발(SR 729)
                21:45 제네바 착

'92.1. 13(월)   THC회의 참석

'92.1. 14(화)   각국동향 파악 및 향후 대책협의

'91.1. 15(수) 10:55 제네바 발(LH 1855)
                12:15 프랑크푸르트 착
                13:50 프랑크루트 발(KE 904)

'91.1. 16(목) 10:20 서 울 착

나. 소요경비

(1) 국외여비

0 항공료 : $2,109

0 체재비 : $546
  - 일 비 : $25 X 5일 = $125
  - 숙박비 : $79 X 3일 = $237
  - 식 비 : $46 X 4일 = $184

0 합 계 : $2,655(1113-213)

0116

관리 번호	92-41

외 무 부

종 별 :

번 호 : THW-0074

일 시 : 92 0110 1600

수 신 : 장 관(통기)

발 신 : 주 태 국 대사대리

제 목 : UR 협상동향

대 : WTH-0088

연 : THW-0042

연호, TNC 회의참가 태국 수석대표는 주제네바 태국대사라고 함

(대사대리 주진엽-국장)

예고 : 92.6.30 까지

대외공개 재분류
92.6.30 〃

통상국   차관   2차보

92.01.10   19:40

외신 2과 통제관 CD

0117

관리 번호	92-43

외 무 부

종 별 :

번 호 : GVW-0066   일 시 : 92 0110 2330

수 신 : 장 관(봉기,경기원,재무부,농수산부,상공부,특허청)

발 신 : 주 제네바 대사   사본:주미,주EC대사(중계필)

제 목 : UR/개도국 비공식 그룹 회의

연: GVW-0049

1. 표제회의가 1.10(금) 16:00-18:00 간 BENHIMA 의장주재로 개최되어 1.13 TNC 회의 대책을 협의하였는바, 금일 회의에서는 12.20 자 최종 의정서 초안에 대한 평가와 1.9 그린룸회의시 던켈 사무총장이 제시한 FOUR TRACK 협상전략에 관하여 로 협의하였음. (본직, 김봉주 서기관 참석)

2. 12.20 자 최종의정서 초안에 대하여 아세안(인니 대변)은 일부 분야에서 미진한 부분이 있기는 하나 향후 계속적인 작업의 기초(AS A REASONABLE BASIS TO CONTINUE FURTHER WORK)로 본다는 입장을 개진한 반면, 인도, 이집트, 콜롬비아등 다수 참가국들은 시장접근 및 서비스 분야의 양허 협상이 끝난 다음에 구체적인 평가가 가능할 것이라는 태도를 보였으며, 동 초안을 협상의 기초로 할수 없다는 반대의사를 표명한 국가는 없었음.

3. 던켈 총장의 향후 협상 전략과 관련, 라틴 아메리카 및 카리브해 연안 국가를 대표한 멕시코가 던켈 총장 전략중 네번째 전략에 강한 이의를 제기하고 만일 일부 분야에 조정작업(FINE TUNING)을 하기 시작하면 걷잡을수 없는 혼란이 초래된다는 의견을 개진하였으며, 이에 인도 및 우루과이, 브라질등 라틴아메리카 국가 대표들이 동조함.(라틴 그룹 제안문을 별첨 하며, 동 제안문은 채택된 것은 아님)

4. 본직은 아국으로서는 농산물 분야의 어려움으로 인하여 1.9 그린룸 협의시 던켈 총장의 협상전략 특히 4 번째 TRACK 을 지지한다고 전제하고 현 최종의정서 초안을 수정할수 있는 협상 참가국들의 권리를 제한하는 어떠한 제안도 수락할수 없음을 밝히고 BENHIMA 의장이 1.13 TNC 회의에서 개도국 비공식 그룹의 입장을 발표할때 현 최종의정서 초안을 수정할수 있는 협상 참가국들의 권리를 제한하는 어떠한 내용도 포함시켜서는 안된다는 입장을 개진하였는바, 이집트, 튜니지아등이 이에 동조함.

통상국 안기부	장관 경기원	차관 재무부	1차보 농수부	2차보 상공부	경제국 특허청	외정실 중계	분석관	정와대

PAGE 1

92.01.11   08:11

외신 2과 통제관 BS

0118

5. 의장은 금일 회의결과를 종합하여 1.13 TNC 회의시 개도국들의 입장을 밝히기로 하였으며, 이러한 의장의 개도국 비공식 그룹의 입장 개진에도 불구하고 각 협상 참가국들은 각자 입장을 별도 개진할수 있도록 하고 회의를 종료함.

6. 회의 종료후 멕시코 대표와 접촉한 결과 상기 멕시코 입장은 1.13 TNC 회의에서 EC 를 고립시키는 것이 그 목적이라고 하였음을 참고로 첨언함. 끝.

첨부: 라틴 그룹 제안문 1 부(GVW(F)-15)

(대사 박수길-국장)

예고 92.6.30 까지

예고문에 의거 분류 1992.6.30.)
기위 성명 이시형

The Latin American and Caribbean countries wish to propose that the Informal Group of Developing Countries deliver a statement at the TNC Meeting scheduled for January 13, 1992, along the following lines:

The developing countries participants in the Uruguay Round have listened with great attention to the proposal presented by the Chairman of the TNC. In this regard and on behalf of the Informal Group of Developing Countries I would like to state the following:

1. The first three tracks of the proposal reflect the work program that was implicit in the Draft Final Act circulated on 20 december, 1991, namely, (i) the need to finalize, or indeed conduct, the market access negotiations on goods; (ii) to similarly conduct the negotiations concerning the initial commitments on services; and (iii) to tidy up the texts in order to ensure their legal consistency.

2. It is the fourth track now proposed which requires our careful consideration at this stage. With respect to this issue, I would like to make three points:

First, the Draft Final Act contains serious deficiencies from the point of view of our expectations and interests.

Nevertheless, it represents a carefully crafted package, reflecting the balance in the negotiating positions, as read by the Chairman of the TNC after over five years of delicate, fragile negotiations.

Second, to now reopen the texts could unleash a process of changes and revisions with unforeseen consequences which could jeopardize the entire negotiating effort. Participants wishing to do so would have to bear the full political responsibility of such a step.

Third, should the texts be reopened, this could not be done in a partial and restricted manner, as it would necessarily have to involve modifications in all areas in order to reflect the serious difficulties that the preliminary results pose for our countries.

(∫ − 2 − 2

0120

관리 번호	92-44

외 무 부

종 별 :

번 호 : ECW-0043   일 시 : 92 0111 1900

수 신 : 장 관(통기, 경기원, 재무부, 농림수산부, 상공부)

발 신 : 주 EC 대사   사본: 주 미, 제네바대사-중계요필

제 목 : 갓트/UR 협상

연: ECW-0023

1. EC 무역이사회 (농업각료들도 참석) 는 1.10. 만찬부터 1.11. 새벽까지 DUNKEL 협상안에 대해 토의를 가진후 (당초 예정이었던 1.11. 이사회는 취소) 아래요지의 성명을 발표함 (별전 FAX 송부)

가. 이사회는 동협상안에 대한 EC 의 기본입장이 작년 12.23. 무역이사회에서 합의된바와 같음을 재확인하며, 동 협상안의 분야별 문제점들에 관한 입장을 정리한바, 1.13. TNC 이후 개최될 표제협상에서 EC 집행위가 이러한 입장이 균형되고 실질적으로 반영될수 있도록 노력할 것을 요청함

나. UR 협상의 조속한 종결은 세계경제발전에 긴요하며 모든 협상 참여국들은 UR 협상의 성공을위해 현실적인 입장을 취해줄것을 촉구하며, 특히 시장접근, 서비스분야에서 시장개방 협상결과는 MONTREAL 중간평가회의 합의를 달성할수 있는지 여부를 결정하는 관건임

2. 상기회의 결과와 관련, 향후 EC 의 대 UR 협상전략에 관한 당관의 관찰내용은 아래와 같음

가. 동 이사회가 당초 계획된 회의일정을 축소하고, DUNKEL 협상안에 대한 구체적인 입장을 공표하지 않은 이유는 DUNKEL 총장이 표제협상 종료시점을 부활절 (4.19) 까지로 재조정하고 동기한까지 이해당사국들간의 협상을 추진할것을 촉구하고 있음에 비추어 협상참여 주요국들의 입장이 표출될때까지 EC 의 구체적인 협상입장 노출을 방지하기 위한것으로 보임

나. 따라서 1.13. TNC 회의에서도 분야별 문제점에 대한 EC 의 구체적 입장보다는 DUNKEL 협상안 전반에대한 개괄적인 평가및 검토의견을 개진하게 될것으로 보임

다. 농산물 분야에 있어서는 GREEN BOX, 보조금감축 기준, REBALANCING, PEACE

통상국 안기부	장관 경기원	차관 재무부	1차보 농수부	2차보 상공부	경제국	외정실	분석관	정와대

PAGE 1

CLAUSE 등 4 개 항목에대한 EC 의 입장이 최대한 반영되도록 재협상을 시도할 것으로 보임. 그러나, UR 협상 조기타결의 중요성을 감안하여 앞으로의 협상과정에서 미국, 호주등의 협상자세에 따라 상당한 융통성을 갖고 대처할 것으로 전망됨. 끝

　　(대사 권동만-국장)
　　예고: 92.6.30. 까지

92.6.30 예고들에게 재분류
종

주 뉴 질 랜 드 대 사 관

예고문 에 의거 재분류(92. 6. 30.)
직위 5급 성명 김태진

주뉴 20650- 002   1992 . 1 . 9

수신 : 장 관

참조 : 통상국장

제목 : GATT 던켈안에 대한 주재국 반응

     연 : NZW - 0007

     연호 주재국 Don McKinnon 부수상겸 외상의 던켈안 지지입장
표명 관련 언론발표문을 별첨과 같이 송부합니다.

     첨부 : 상기 언론 발표문 1부. 끝.

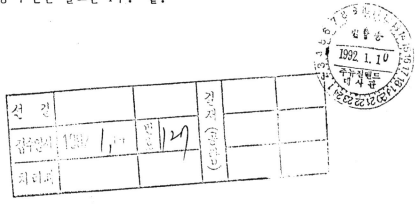

     주 뉴 질 랜 드 대 사

THE MINISTER *of* EXTERNAL RELATIONS *and* TRADE

PARLIAMENT BUILDINGS, WELLINGTON, NEW ZEALAND

9 January 1992

MEDIA RELEASE

GATT : NEW ZEALAND ACCEPTS DUNKEL PACKAGE

The Minister of External Relations and Trade, Hon Don McKinnon, announced today that New Zealand would accept the draft Uruguay Round package contained in the paper tabled by GATT Director-General Arthur Dunkel in Geneva on 20 December 1991.

Mr McKinnon was speaking on behalf of the three Ministers - the Minister for Trade Negotiations, Hon Philip Burdon, the Minister of Agriculture, Hon John Falloon, and himself - who had considered the Dunkel paper this morning.

"It is our assessment that the Dunkel paper will provide net benefits to New Zealand," Mr McKinnon said. "The text on agriculture provides for the first time a framework under the GATT for the reduction of agricultural protection."

Mr McKinnon said that the paper also contained advances in the areas of market access for non-agricultural goods, trade rules and dispute settlement procedures, the protection of intellectual property and trade in services. These would strengthen the international trading system and bring benefits to New Zealand.

"Like all countries, New Zealand has difficulties with some parts of the text," Mr McKinnon said, "but the package needs to be considered as a whole, taking into account the future of the international trading system."

0124

TELEPHONE: 0064 4 471-9997   FAX: 0064 4 471-1444

Mr McKinnon noted that acceptance of the paper by Uruguay Round participants would not mark the conclusion of negotiations. Further detailed negotiations will be required to translate the Dunkel paper into commitments, tariff line by tariff line, product by product. A final binding decision on the Uruguay Round results will not be taken by Ministers until these negotiations are successfully concluded.

Mr McKinnon said New Zealand would be working closely with other Cairns Group countries to achieve the adoption of the Dunkel paper when negotiations recommence in Geneva on 13 January 1992. "Any attempts to reopen the text at this stage would risk the unravelling of five years of hard work," he said.

Simon Gimson   Press Secretary   4719848

0125

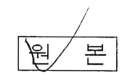

외 무 부

종 별 : 긴 급

번 호 : GVW-0073   일 시 : 92 0114 0210

수 신 : 장관(봉기,경기원,재무부,농림수산부,상공부,특허청)

발 신 : 사본: 주 미,EC,일,호주,불,영,카나다,독대사중계요필

제 목 : 주제네바대사

TNC 회의개최

　연:GVW-0049

1. 1.13(월) 15:00-19:00 간 표제회의가 DUNKEL TNC 의장 주재로 개최되었는바, 의장은 금일 회의는 협상결과의 수락여부를 결정하려는 것이 목적이 아니라 12.20 협상안이 UR 협상을 조기에 종료시킬수 있는 기초가 될 수 있는지 여부를 결정하기 위한 것이라고 전제하고, 그동안 각국의 반응은 긍정적이었다고 하고 모든 참가국들이 상기 초안을 협상의 기초로 수락할 경우 FOUR TRACK 협상전략(연호 보고)에 따라 향후 협상을 추진할 예정임을 밝히고 이에 대한 참가국의 의견을 문의함.

2. 금일 회의에는 39 개국이 발언한바, 대부분의 발언국들이 12.20 자 협상안을 UR 협상 조기 타결을 위한 기초로 수락한다는 입장을 표명하였으며, 동초안을 협상의 기초로 수락할 수 없다는 반대입장을 표명한 참가국은 없었음.

3. 던켈의장이 제시한 FOUR TRACK 협상 전략에 대해서는 대부분의 발언국들이 첫째, 둘째, 세째 TRACK 에 대해서는 아무런 이의를 제기치 않았으며 네째(FOURTH) TRACK 과 관련하여 미국 및 호주, 알젠틴등 케언즈 그룹을 포함한 대다수국가들이 일부 조정작업(FINE TUNING)은 매우 제한된 분야에 국한되어야 하며 현 협상 결과를 해체시키지 않는(AVOID UNRAVELING) 범위내에서 이루어져야 한다는 입장을 표명한 반면, EC 는 던켈의 협상전략을 지지한다는 점을 명백히 하면서도 협상안의 대폭적인 개선(SERIOUSLY IMPROVE)이 불가피하다는 입장을 개진함

4. 본직은 12.20 자 협상안이 특히 농산물분야에서 수입국, 수출국 및 선진국, 개도국들간의 이익이 균형있게 반영되지 않은 점이 유감이며, 예외없는 관세화는 식량수입국의 농업특성을 간과하고 있어 아국으로서는 심각한 어려움이 있다는 점을 지적하고 기초식량을 위한 예외가 설정되도록 협상안의 개선되어야 한다고 하였으며,

통상국 안기부	장관 경기원	차관 재무부	1차보 농수부	2차보 상공부	경제국 특허청	외정실 중계	분석관	청와대

PAGE 1   92.01.14   11:38

이러한 전제하에 향후 협상에 적극 참여할 것이라고 하였음.

또한 본직은 던켈 총장의 4 TRACK 협상 전략에 대한 지지를 표명, 4 번째 TRACK 은 제한적으로 운영하되 각국의 핵심 관심사항을 반영할 유용한기회로 활용할수 있는 유일한 방법이므로 동 TRACK 의 유용성은 평가되어야 함을지적함.(발언문 별첨)

5. 던켈총장은 금일 회의를 마무리 하면서 금일 회의에서 참가국들은 대체로 12.20 자 협상안을 UR 협상 조기타결을 위한 기초로 수용하겠다는 입장을 표명하였으며, 4 가지 TRACK 에 의한 협상전략에 대해서도 지지의사를 밝힌 것으로평가한다고 하고 이에따라 앞으로 시장접근분야, 서비스분야, 양자, 다자간 협상을 조속히 추진하겠다고 밝히고 TRACK 4 에 따른 조정작업과 관련 아래와 같이부연설명함.

- TRACK 4 는 GLOBAL TRACK 으로선 전체 협상의 BALANCE 를 유지하는 선에서 이루어지는 것이며 협상이 이루어지더라도 전문가들에 의한 분야별 협상은 있을 수 없고, 협상 전체를 관장하는 대표차원에서 이루어질 수 있는 극히 제한적인 성격의 것임.

- 각국은 TRACK 4 와 관련 협상을 RE-OPEN 하지 않도록 자제해야 함.

- 협상 과정의 명료성을 확보하겠으며, 자신은 성실한 중재자의 역할을 수행하겠음.

- 특히 협상의 부재로 인하여 부득이 의장안이반영된 초안을 REOPEN 하고져할 경우에는 모든 관계국의 동의가 전제되어야 할것임.

6. 관찰 및 평가

가. 금일 회의의 전반적인 분위기는 던켈총장의 회의결과를 평가한바와 같이 대부분의 국가가 12.20 자 협상안을 UR 협상 타결의 기초로 수용할 수 있으며, 던켈총장의 FOUR TRACK 작업계획에 의거 UR 협상을 조기에 타결해야 한다는 것이었음.

나. 미국은 당초 예상대로 12.20 자 협상안 및 던켈 협상전략에 아주 긍정적인 반응을 보였으며, EC 는 1.10 EC 무역및 농업장관 회의결과에 따라 12.20 자 협상안, 특히 농산물 분야에 심각한 어려움이 있다는 점을 지적하고 대폭 수정(SERIOUSLY IMPROVED)되어야 한다고 주장하면서도 던켈총장의 협상전략을 지지하였는바, 이는 동총장의 협상전략 TRACK 4 가 추가협상의 여지를 남겨두고 있다는 점, 시장접근 및 써비스 쌍무 UR 협상결과등이 나와있지는 않은 현시점에서 협상결렬의 책임을 지지 않겠다는 고려하에서 취해진 입장으로 보여짐.

다. 일본도 UR 협상의 조기타결 필요성을 강조하면서 예외없는 관세화등에 심각한 문제점(EXTREMELY DIFFCULT)은 있으나 12.20 자 협상안을 UR 협상 타결을위한 중요한 계기로 평가하고, 던켈총장의 전략을 지지한 것은 부쉬 미대통령의 일본 방문 결과와 무관하지 않으며, 브라셀 회의시의 경험을 감안한 입장인 것으로 관측됨(일부 회의 참석자들은 일본의 입장이 완화된 것으로 평가)

　　라. 많은 개도국들도 시장접근 분야에서의 쌍무 또는 다자협상결과의 중요성을 강조하고 동 협상안을 UR 협상 타결을 위한 기초로 받아들일수 있다는 입장을 밝혔으며, 네번째 TRACK 운영에 관해서는 명료성의 보장 및 제한성을 강조함.

　　마.1.9 그린룸협의 및 금일 TNC 회의에서의 던켈총장의 언동에 비추어볼때 협상결과수용여부를 결정할 시기는 시장접근 및 서비스 쌍무협상결과가 마무리될3 월말-4 월 중순경이 될 가능성이 있음.

　　바. 그러나 상기에도 불구하고 UR 협상의 타결 은 협상을 지금까지 주도해온 미국, EC 의 특히 농산물 분야에서의 타협이 전제가되고 있으므로 현싯점에서는 그전망을 정확히 예단키는 극히 어려운 형편임.

　　사. 다른한편 금일 회의에서 예외없는 관세화에 반대내지 유보를 표명한 국가는 아국을 비롯, 멕시코, 일본, 스위스, 카나다, 이스라엘등 수개국에 국한되었으며 또한 반대의 강도도 현저히 저하된듯한 인상이었음.

　　아. 당관으로서는 내주부터 본격화될 시장접근, 서비스분야에서의 양자협상에 철저히 대비함과 아울러 예외없는 관세화에 반대하는 국가들과 계속 긴밀협력, 사태발전에 대처코져함.

　　(GVW-00074 로 계속됨)

외 무 부

종 별 : 긴 급

번 호 : GVW-0074 일 시 : 92 0114 02100

수 신 : 장관(봉기,경기원,재무부,농림수산부,상공부,특허청,경제수석)

발 신 : 주 제네바 대사 사본:주미,EC,일,호주,불,영,카나다,독대사본부중계필

제 목 : GVW-0073 의 계속

7. 주요 협상국들의 발언요지는 하기와 같음.

0 미국: 현 초안은 UR 협상의 성공적인 타결을 위한 협상의 기초가 되며, 서비스분야 및 시장접근 분야 협상이 조속히 완결되어야 함.

0 EC : 의장의 협상 일정에 따라 협상을 계속할 용의가 있으며(READY TO CONTINUE AND COMPLETE NEGOTIATION), 현 초안에 대한 전반적인 검토는 아직 끝나지 않았으나 12.20 자 협상안이 대폭적으로 개선되어야 함.

0 일본: 모든 협상이 완결된 후에 구체적인 평가가 가능할 것이나 농산물 분야에서는 균형이 결여되어 있고 예외없는 관세화는 수용하기 어려우며 던켈 총장의 4 TRACK 전략에 따라 관심사가 반영되길 희망함.

0 카나다: 12.20 자 협상안을 협상의 기초로 수락키로 하였음. 그러나 11 조 2 항과 관련 예외없는 관세화에 대한 우려가 반영되지 않았음을 지적코자함.

0 호주: 협상의 기초로 수락하며, 협상은 조속히 종결되어야 함. 4 번째 TRACK 은 협상결과 전제를 UNRAVEL 할 위험이 있음.

0 알젠틴: 초안의 수정은 최소한에 그쳐야 함.

0 북구(핀랜드): 12.20 자 협상안을 기초로 4 TRACK 에 의한 협상 용의가 있음. 농산물, 서비스 분야 관련 입장을 유보함.

0 인도: 개도국 우대문제, TRIPS, 섬유분야등에서 어려움이 있기는 하나(4 번째 TRACK 에 의한 협의 용의 표시)

UR 협상의 성공적 종결을 위해 최선을 다할것임.

0 아세안(인니) : TRIPS, 규범, 농산물등 불만족한 분야가 있지만 12.20 자협상안을 기초로 수락하며, 4 번째 TRACK 과 관련 협상결과를 해체시켜서는 안됨.

네번째 TRACK 과 관련 협상추진 방법이 극히 모호함.

통상국 청와대	장관 안기부	차관 경기원	1차보 재무부	2차보 농수부	경제국 상공부	외정실 특허청	분석관	청와대

PAGE 1

O 스위스: 예외없는 관세화 수용이 어려우며, 정치적으로 수용가능한 결과를 위해 FOUR TRACK 협상전략을 지지함.

(대사 박수길-차관)

첨부: 1. 아국발언문 1 부

2. 던켈총장 회의서두 언급내용 1 부.

(GVW(F)-0018). 끝.

예고: 92.6.30 까지

주 제 네 바 대 표 부

번 호 : GVW(F) - *0018*   년월일 : *920114*   시간 : *02/0*

수 신 : 장   관 *(통기, 경기원, 재무부, 농림수산부, 상광부, 특허청, 경제유)*

발 신 : 주 제네바대사   *사본 : 주미, EC, 일, 호주, 분, 영, 카나다, 독인*
                                              대사
제 목 : *첨 부*

총 *12* 매(표지포함)

보 안 통 제	

외신관 통 제	

18-12-1

1. My delegation would like to express its sincere gratitude
    for the efforts made by you, Mr. Chairman together with the
    Chairman of each negotiating group and the GATT Secretariat
    to prepare the draft Final Act presented at the TNC meeting
    of 20th of last December. Let me also take this occasion
    to express my support to the statement made by the Ambassador
    of Morocco who spoke on behalf of the group of developing
    countries.

2. Like previous speakers I also would like to emphasize the critical
    importance of bringing the Uruguay Round negotiations to a successful
    conclusion as early as possible. To this end my delegation wishes
    to reaffirm its firm commitment and continued efforts.

3. My Government appreciates the draft Final Act as the consolidation
    of the results of five years of the Uruguay Round negotiations.
    The Korean Government views that many elements contained in the
    draft agreement, such as improvements on various trade rules and
    disciplines, integration of textiles and clothing sector into the
    GATT system, and strengthening of the function and institution of
    GATT would contribute positively to the successful conclusion of
    the Uruguay Round.

- 1 -

18-12-2

0132

4. With regard to some of the core issues in the draft agreements, including those in the agriculture sector, however, the Korean Government believes that further improvements should be made to achieve a more balanced package of agreements. With this understanding, Korea will continue to participate actively in the future process of negotiations.

a. In agriculture, it is regretable that the interests of not agricultural importing and exporting countries as well as less developed and developed countries are not reflected in a balanced manner.

My Government continues to have serious difficulties with regard to the idea of comprehensive tariffication because it tends to ignore the specific characteristics of agriculture in the individual food importing countries and further fails to safeguard the fragile agricultural production base against collapse. For this reason, it is our considered view that a carefully defined exception from tariffication should be established for the basic food stuffs vital for food security.

- As importantly, we also have serious difficulties in permitting the minimum access to all products across the board.

- 2 -

/8 - /2 -3

0133

- Despite the fact that under the Mid-term Agreement the commitment on standstill of domestic support and market access did not apply to the less developed countries, using 1986 - 1988 as the base period for the calculation of commitments in the market access and domestic support would in fact impose greater burden on the less developed countries than the developed. Therefore, in the case of less developed countries, it would be more reasonable to take as the base period the most recent year for which statistical data are available.

b. As regards other issues, Korea would like to emphasize that the tariff reduction target agreed upon at the Montreal Mid- term Review must be achieved on a priority basis before negotiating additional reductions, and that further adjustments are needed in the areas of safeguards, subsidies and countervailing duties.

5. Turning to the four track approach you put forward to this meeting, I express my support to it. In its continuing support to contribute toward a successful conclusion of the UR, my Government will actively participate in the negotiations in the field of market access and services.

I hope that future negotiations will be conducted with due consideration given to participants' existing level of market opening and their economic capabilities. The negotiations in these field will certainly figure importantly in our overall assessment of the package.

- 3 -

18-12-4

0134

As regards the fourth track of your work program, I agree with your
view that an exercise under this track should be precise, limited and
expedious. In this regard I would like to echo the concern of
those who stressed the need for transparency. We believe this
track will eventually prove to be extremely useful in achieving
our common objectives, because it is this track that will present
the last opportunity to address the preoccupation of those countries
which still have serious difficulties with some hard-core issues.

In concluding, Mr. Chairman I would like to pledge the fullest
cooperation of this delegation toward the successful conclusion
of the UR negotiations.

- 4 -

18-12-5

43

13.1.1992

TRADE NEGOTIATIONS COMMITTEE
Meeting at Official Level
13 January 1992

NOTE FOR CHAIRMAN

1.   When preparing for this meeting, I could not but think
back to the days of the Punta del Este Ministerial Meeting
when the Uruguay Round was launched. In doing so, what I find
most impressive is the fact that, during these five years, all
participants in these negotiations have made major and,
sometimes, totally unexpected - adjustments in their positions
to bring us to the very high level of consensus which supports
the Draft Final Act, MTN.TNC/W/FA, now before us.

2.   We are now, very clearly, in the concluding phase of the
Round. Therefore, our efforts today and in the weeks
following have to be well coordinated and directed towards the
sole objective of bringing the Uruguay Round to a successful
and quick conclusion. I assume we are all in agreement here.
More so because my contacts with representatives in Geneva and
in capitals during the Christmas and New Year break have left
me with the clear impression that all participants are ready
to carry the negotiating process forward constructively and
expeditiously, and work intensively in the coming weeks in a
result-oriented manner.

3.   In this context - and before I give you the floor - allow
me to share with you my own thoughts on the purpose of today's
meeting.

18-12-6

0136

- 2 -

4.   To begin with, let me say what this meeting is <u>not</u> intended to be:

   (a)   It is <u>not</u> the occasion for governments participating in the Uruguay Round to accept or reject the <u>results</u> of the Round. Before this stage is reached, a number of essential steps must be taken. I described the work which still remains to be done quite clearly in my statement to this Committee on 20 December. This work is also outlined in the cover-note to the Draft Final Act. I will come back to this in a minute.

   (b)   This meeting is also <u>not</u> a negotiating meeting. You should not, therefore, spend your time enumerating detailed lists of all kinds of specific concerns related to this or that paragraph of this or that agreement in the Draft Final Act.

      As Chairman, I would consider this counter-productive. For one, if this were to happen, we would be sitting here for days with each of the 108 participants bringing his own shopping list!!! But, even more importantly, this would inevitably result in an uncontrollable unravelling of the "package" I presented in December in keeping with the working procedure agreed by you - and, consequently, the conclusion that an expeditious end to the Uruguay Round is ruled out.

0137

- 3 -

5.   These remarks bring me to the real question - what then,
is our intention today. You will recall that I had indicated
this at our last meeting on 20 December when I said that our
aim, today, is to conclude the intensive consultations which
Dr. Gros Espiell, Chairman of the Committee at Ministerial
level, had asked me to carry forward at the end of the
Brussels Ministerial meeting on 7 December 1990.

6.   The implication is, therefore, clear: today is when,
individually and collectively, governments must **either** agree
to push the negotiating process forward so as to conclude the
Uruguay Round in the weeks ahead **or** admit that the stage we
had reached last December does not offer the basis for an
early conclusion.

7.   As I said earlier, all the signals I have so far received
lead me to believe that governments prefer the first option.
If so, this TNC Session will be expected to approve a work
plan for the period that lies ahead. I have some concrete
proposals to make in this regard. But before I come to these,
I would, once again, ask you to go over my TNC statement of
last December. In particular, I would stress three points:

> **One**, the presentation of a complete and consolidated
> document bringing together the results of five years of
> effort was announced. This text has been with your
> governments since 20 December. It is numbered
> MTN.TNC/W/FA.

18-12-8

0138

- 4 -

Let me remind you that in presenting it I had said
that it sought to strike the best possible balance
across-the-board of the long negotiating agenda of this
Round. This is still true.

Let me also remind you that this document is,
foremost, the result of intensive negotiations. In fact
the major part of the texts are the result of protracted
negotiation in the well-established tradition of "give
and take". On some outstanding points, where arbitration
and conciliation have appeared unavoidable, the text is
based on informed and conscientious decisions that I and
my colleagues, the Chairmen of the former negotiating
groups, had no alternative but to take.

Here again, to the best of my knowledge, the
situation has not changed today. I have no new - or
better - solutions to offer on my own.

Two: I had stated that our work from January onwards
will be based on a global approach; and

Three: I had reminded you that being a single
undertaking in accordance with the Punta del Este
Declaration, our negotiations are governed by the
principle that nothing is final until everything is
agreed.

8. It is in this context that I now come to my proposals on
how to organize the work that still needs to be done. And, as

0139

18 - 12 - P

- 5 -

each of you are surely aware, there is still a lot to
accomplish. I would propose, therefore, that we all get down
to serious work simultaneously and immediately on a four-track
approach:

Track one: Intensive, non-stop bilateral, plurilateral
and multilateral negotiations on market access. An enormous
effort is required here by all participants to ensure
substantial and overall meaningful results. On this will
depend final agreement to the Final Act. As you are aware the
Market Access Group is the only group still in existence under
the GNG. It is charged with the specific task of concluding
the Market Access negotiations expeditiously. As I informed
the TNC in December, I include in the area of market access,
the negotiations on specific commitments on internal support
and export competition in agriculture. The Chairman,
Mr. Germain Denis is in Geneva to overview these negotiations.
His intention will be to put maximum pressure on delegations
and not leave the process to only bilateral efforts. What we
envisage is a series of rounds with continuous multilateral
monitoring to ensure that the process is going in the right
direction. Needless to say all the facilities of the GATT
Secretariat will be available for this purpose.

Track two: Intensive non-stop negotiations, again, with
continuous multilateral monitoring, on initial commitments in
services under the GNS which, as you know, also remains in
place. Substantial and meaningful results for all parties in
this area are also necessary for final agreement by parties to
the total package.

18-12-10

0140

- 6 -

Track three: Work to ensure the legal conformity and
internal consistency of the agreements constituting the Final
Act. As I said in December this process is important and
unavoidable though it should not lead to changes in the
balance of rights and obligations established in the
agreements and, finally,

Track four: Work at the level of the Trade Negotiations
Committee with a view to examining whether and if it is
possible to adjust the package in certain specific places.

I hesitate to even mention this fourth track to you for
fear of creating misunderstandings. So let me make myself as
clear as I can at this stage. This exercise must be very
precise and concentrated entirely on what we all can
collectively agree to without unravelling the package. This
exercise must also be conducted rapidly in a low-key and
professional manner in full consciousness of the very limited
time available to us. I have said earlier, and I would wish
to repeat this now, the Draft Final Act presented to you in
December is the expression of the most informed and
conscientious evaluation of the level of consensus achievable
after a one-year extension of the dead-line for finalizing
this Round. I consider it my duty, however, to be ready to
serve as "honest broker" in the resolution of outstanding
differences should this be considered necessary.

9.   If you agree with this work plan I would expect this
meeting to be brief, and your interventions to be of a general

- 7 -

and political nature rather than devoted to all kinds of specific points.

10.   Finally, the Trade Negotiations Committee should approve the negotiating strategy I have just outlined and thus enable us to resume work immediately in a business-like manner.

11.   I need hardly say that this Committee remains on call to meet periodically to review progress in our work and to take such decisions as may be necessary for the future of this Round.

0142.

18-12-12

PREPARED STATEMENT
FOR AMBASSADOR RUFUS YERXA
JANUARY 13, 1992

AFTER FIVE LONG YEARS OF WORK ON THE MOST COMPLEX TRADE
ACCORD EVER ATTEMPTED, WE FINALLY HAVE BEFORE US A
COMPREHENSIVE DRAFT OF THE FINAL AGREEMENT. CHAIRMAN DUNKEL
AND HIS ENTIRE TEAM -- THE OTHER CHAIRMEN AND THE SECRETARIAT
STAFF -- DESERVE OUR ADMIRATION AND RESPECT. WHERE THE
PARTICIPANTS COULD NOT NEGOTIATE THE DEAL IN THE TIME
ALLOTTED, THE CHAIRMAN AND HIS TEAM FACED A DIFFICULT TASK --
TO PRODUCE A TEXT COVERING ALL AREAS OF THE NEGOTIATIONS AND
TO MAKE IT ACCEPTABLE TO ALL PARTICIPANTS. IT IS OBVIOUS
FROM THEIR EFFORTS THAT THIS DEDICATED GROUP OF INDIVIDUALS
WANTED TO SUGGEST WORKABLE COMPROMISES TO THE DIFFERENCES
THAT REMAINED BETWEEN US WHEN NEGOTIATIONS ENDED ON THE 19TH
OF DECEMBER.

THE QUESTION NOW BEFORE US IS SIMPLE: DOES THE DRAFT FINAL
AGREEMENT PROVIDE US WITH THE BASIC INGREDIENTS FOR
FINALIZING THE URUGUAY ROUND? FOR THE UNITED STATES, THE
ANSWER IS "YES."

PRESIDENT BUSH SAID IN SINGAPORE LAST WEEK THAT, "I AM URGING
THE WORLD'S TRADING NATIONS TO JOIN WITH US IN MAKING GATT
DIRECTOR GENERAL DUNKEL'S PROPOSED DRAFT AGREEMENT THE BASIS
FOR THE SUCCESSFUL CONCLUSION OF THE URUGUAY ROUND. WHILE
ALL OF US HAVE PROBLEMS WITH PORTIONS OF THAT DRAFT, NONE OF
US CAN AFFORD TO LET THE PROGRESS IT REPRESENTS SLIP AWAY
INTO THE PAST. NOW IS THE MOMENT FOR A STRONG COLLECTIVE
RESPONSE."

WE SEE MUCH TO BE GAINED FROM THE AGREEMENT NOW EMERGING: A
REDUCTION OF TRADE-DISTORTING SUBSIDIES AND TIGHTER
DISCIPLINES IN THIS AREA; A NEW REGIME FOR AGRICULTURE;
PROHIBITION OF CERTAIN TRADE-DISTORTING INVESTMENT POLICIES;
A MORE CREDIBLE INSTITUTIONAL FRAMEWORK FOR RESOLVING TRADE
DISPUTES BASED ON INTERNATIONAL RULES; AND MANY OTHER
POSITIVE ELEMENTS.

ON THE OTHER HAND, WE FIND CERTAIN SECTIONS OF THE PAPER
DEFICIENT. IN SOME CASES, WE BELIEVE THAT THE TEXT DOES NOT
GO FAR ENOUGH IN REDUCING BARRIERS, SETTING RIGOROUS
STANDARDS, OR PROVIDING STRONG DISCIPLINES AND REMEDIES
AGAINST UNFAIR BEHAVIOR. THE UNITED STATES STRONGLY BELIEVES
THAT, IF THERE ARE CHANGES TO BE MADE, THEY SHOULD SERVE ONLY
TO STRENGTHEN THE DISCIPLINES AND/OR LEAD TO GREATER MARKET
LIBERALIZATION.

0143

MORE IMPORTANTLY, THERE IS THE QUESTION OF THE UPCOMING
MARKET ACCESS NEGOTIATIONS ON GOODS, ESPECIALLY OUR
ZERO-FOR-ZERO PROPOSALS AND, AS THE CHAIRMAN NOTED, IMPROVED
ACCESS FOR AGRICULTURE AND TEXTILES AND CLOTHING.
FURTHERMORE, WE MUST ACHIEVE A SERVICES AGREEMENT THAT
SECURES SUBSTANTIAL LIBERALIZATION AND MARKET ACCESS,
PARTICULARLY FOR FINANCIAL SERVICES. WITHOUT GOOD RESULTS IN
THESE AREAS, THE UNITED STATES WILL NOT FIND THE OVERALL
PACKAGE ACCEPTABLE.

WEIGHING ALL OF THESE FACTORS, WE BELIEVE THAT MUCH PROGRESS
HAS BEEN MADE TOWARD A SIGNIFICANT REFORM OF THE GATT
SYSTEM. WE BELIEVE THAT THE DRAFT FINAL AGREEMENT DOES
PROVIDE US -- AS PRESIDENT BUSH SAID -- WITH AN OPPORTUNITY
TO SUCCESSFULLY CONCLUDE THE URUGUAY ROUND. WE ARE PREPARED
TO WORK WITH OTHERS TOWARD THAT OBJECTIVE, BUT TIME IS OF THE
ESSENCE.

IF THE ROUND IS TO BE COMPLETED AND ENTER INTO FORCE BY EARLY
1993, WE MUST MOVE FORWARD VIGOROUSLY. THE NEXT FEW WEEKS
WILL BE CRITICAL. IF DIFFERENCES PERSIST BEYOND THAT
TIME-FRAME, WE WILL NOT BE ABLE TO MEET THE TARGET FOR
IMPLEMENTATION.

AND, WE MUST BEGIN IMMEDIATELY TO ACCELERATE THE PACE OF THE
TARIFF NEGOTIATIONS AND THE COMPLETION OF SERVICES
COMMITMENTS. MUCH WORK REMAINS AND THERE CAN BE NO MORE
EXCUSES FOR ANY PARTY FAILING TO NEGOTIATE IN ALL MARKET
ACCESS SECTORS.

WE STAND READY TO ENGAGE IN INTENSIVE EFFORTS TO TURN THIS
DRAFT AGREEMENT INTO A REALITY. WE MUST AVOID UNRAVELING IT,
AND WE MUST BE READY TO WORK OUT OUR REMAINING DIFFERENCES.
TO DO OTHERWISE WOULD PLACE THE ENTIRE MULTILATERAL TRADING
SYSTEM INTO A STATE OF CONSIDERABLE UNCERTAINTY.

COMMON SENSE DICTATES THAT WE MAKE EVERY EFFORT TO CREATE A
STRENGTHENED, EFFECTIVE, AND MULTILATERAL SYSTEM FOR
PROMOTING WORLD TRADE. I URGE ALL PARTIES TO WORK WITH US
TOWARDS THIS OBJECTIVE.

0144

長官報告事項

報 告 畢

1992. 1. 14.
通 商 局
通商機構課(4)

題 目 : UR/TNC 會議 結果

제네바에서 1.13(月) 15:15-19:05間 開催된 UR 貿易協商委員會(TNC) 會議 結果를 아래 報告 드립니다.

---

1. 會議 進行 要旨

    ○ 던켈 總長은 各國이 最終 協定 草案에 대한 受諾 與否보다 이를 기초로 four track approach 協商을 進行하는데 同意하는지 與否를 言及할 것을 要請

    ※ four track approach

    - 商品分野의 讓許協商(農産物의 補助金 減縮 計劃 包含)

    - 서비스 分野의 讓許協商

    - 協定 草案의 法的인 整備作業

    - 特定事項의 調整 必要性 檢討

    ○ 모든 발언국(39個國)이 上記 던켈 總長의 協商 戰略에 同意 表示

    - 케언즈 國家等 多數國은 最終 協定 草案의 受諾을 명시적으로 言及

    ○ 主要國 反應

    - 美國 : 協定 草案을 다시 全面 재협상하지는 않아야 하며 일부 修正 하더라도 貿易自由化를 擴大하는 方向으로만 修正하여야 함.

    - E C : 던켈 總長의 協商 戰略에 의거, 協商을 繼續할 用意가 있으며, 協定 草案中 農産物 分野에 問題가 있으므로 修正이 必要함.

    - 日本 : 農産物 分野에서 市場開放과 補助金 減縮 義務間의 不均衡이 있으며, 특히 包括的 關稅化에 큰 問題가 있음.

    - 北歐 : 서비스, 農産物, 規範分野에 問題가 있음.

0145

- 케언즈그룹 : 最終 協定 草案을 受諾하며 동 草案의 修正에 反對함.
- 餘他 開途國 : 向後 市場接近 分野 協商에 關心이 있으며, 協定 草案의
  修正에 反對함.

o 例外없는 關稅化 問題 : 멕시코, 카나다, 이스라엘, 오지리, 스위스, 韓國이
  反對 (멕시코, 韓國이 가장 강하게 反對)

o 我國 首席代表 發言 要旨
- 協定 草案에 여러가지 肯定的 要所가 있으나 農産物 分野에서 問題가
  있으며 修正이 必要함.
- 특히 例外없는 關稅化 및 最小 市場接近에 심각한 問題가 있으며 市場接近,
  國內 補助의 基準年度에도 問題가 있음.
- 던켈 總長의 協商 戰略을 支持하며 向後 市場接近, 서비스 協商에
  적극 參加할 計劃임.
- 그러나 4번째 track(特定事項의 調整)은 核心爭點에 어려움이 있는 國家의
  問題點을 解決하기 위한 마지막 機會가 되어야 할 것임.

o 던켈 總長의 會議 結論
- 모든 國家가 自身이 提示한 協商 戰略을 支持 하였으며, 向後 수주간
  協商을 促進(push forward)하기로 合意하였음.
- 네번째 track에 대해 不明確한 점이 있으나, 아래 原則이 지켜질 것임.
  1) 明瞭性 : 막후 協商이 아닌 公開 協商
  2) 극히 制限된 範圍내에서 모든 나라가 合意하는 이슈에 대해서만 協商
  3) 全體 協商 次元(global track)에서 協商 進行

2. 評 價

o 모든 國家가 던켈 總長의 協商 戰略을 支持 하였으며, 全般的으로 協商의
  妥結 必要性에 共感하는 雰圍氣였음.
o 또한 제4 track(特定事項의 調整, 協商)의 水準과 폭이 어떻게 進行될
  것인지가 協商 妥結 與否 및 協商 結果의 關鍵이 될 것임.
o 我國 關心事項과 關聯, 앞으로 제4 track下의 協商이 극히 制限된 範圍內에서의
  協商이 될 可能性이 있음에 비추어 면밀한 對備가 必要함.   끝.

0146

長官報告事項

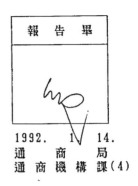

報告畢

1992. 1. 14.
通商局
通商機構課(4)

題目 : UR/TNC 會議 結果

제네바에서 1.13(月) 15:15-19:05間 開催된 UR 貿易協商委員會(TNC)
會議 結果를 아래 報告 드립니다.

---

1. 會議 進行 要旨

 ㅇ 던켈 總長은 各國이 最終 協定 草案에 대한 受諾 與否보다 이를 기초로
   four track approach 協商을 進行하는데 同意하는지 與否를 言及할 것을 要請
   ※ four track approach
   - 商品分野의 讓許協商(農産物의 補助金 減縮 計劃 包含)
   - 서비스 分野의 讓許協商
   - 協定 草案의 法的인 整備作業
   - 特定事項의 調整 必要性 檢討

 ㅇ 모든 발언국(39個國)이 上記 던켈 總長의 協商 戰略에 同意 表示
   - 케언즈 國家等 多數國은 最終 協定 草案의 受諾을 명시적으로 言及

 ㅇ 主要國 反應
   - 美國 : 協定 草案을 다시 全面 재협상하지는 않아야 하며 일부 修正
          하더라도 貿易自由化를 擴大하는 方向으로만 修正하여야 함.
   - E C : 던켈 總長의 協商 戰略에 의거, 協商을 繼續할 用意가 있으며,
          協定 草案中 農産物 分野에 問題가 있으므로 修正이 必要함.
   - 日本 : 農産物 分野에서 市場開放과 補助金 減縮 義務間의 不均衡이
          있으며, 특히 包括的 關稅化에 큰 問題가 있음.
   - 北歐 : 서비스, 農産物, 規範分野에 問題가 있음.

0147

- 케언즈그룹 : 最終 協定 草案을 受諾하며 동 草案의 修正에 反對함.
- 餘他 開途國 : 向後 市場接近 分野 協商에 關心이 있으며, 協定 草案의
修正에 反對함.

○ 例外없는 關稅化 問題 : 멕시코, 카나다, 이스라엘, 오지리, 스위스, 韓國이
反對 (멕시코, 韓國이 가장 강하게 反對)

○ 我國 首席代表 發言 要旨
- 協定 草案에 여러가지 肯定的 要所가 있으나 農産物 分野에서 問題가
있으며 修正이 必要함.
- 특히 例外없는 關稅化 및 最小 市場接近에 심각한 問題가 있으며 市場接近,
國內 補助의 基準年度에도 問題가 있음.
- 던켈 總長의 協商 戰略을 支持하며 向後 市場接近, 서비스 協商에
적극 參加할 計劃임.
- 그러나 4번째 track(特定事項의 調整)은 核心爭點에 어려움이 있는 國家의
問題點을 解決하기 위한 마지막 機會가 되어야 할 것임.

○ 던켈 總長의 會議 結論
- 모든 國家가 自身이 提示한 協商 戰略을 支持 하였으며, 向後 수주간
協商을 促進(push forward)하기로 合意하였음.
- 네번째 track에 대해 不明確한 점이 있으나, 아래 原則이 지켜질 것임.
1) 明瞭性 : 막후 協商이 아닌 公開 協商
2) 극히 制限된 範圍내에서 모든 나라가 合意하는 이슈에 대해서만 協商
3) 全體 協商 次元(global track)에서 協商 進行

2. 評 價

○ 모든 國家가 던켈 總長의 協商 戰略을 支持 하였으며, 全般的으로 協商의
妥結 必要性에 共感하는 雰圍氣였음.
○ 또한 제4 track(特定事項의 調整, 協商)의 水準과 폭이 어떻게 進行될
것인지가 協商 妥結 與否 및 協商 結果의 關鍵이 될 것임.
○ 我國 關心事項과 關聯, 앞으로 제4 track下의 協商이 극히 制限된 範圍內에서의
協商이 될 可能性이 있음에 비추어 면밀한 對備가 必要함.   끝.

UR 貿易委員會(1.13) 會議動向

- '92. 1. 14 -

1. '92.1.13(월) 오후 15:00(제네바 시간)부터 약 4시간동안 개최된 우루과이라운드 貿易協商委員會는 작년 12.20 Dunkel 갓트 사무총장이 제시한 우루과이라운드 최종협정문안을 기초로 협상을 조기에 종료하기 위해 앞으로 수주간에 걸쳐 4원(4 track)협상을 진행한다는 Dunkel 總長의 協商計劃을 채택하였음.

   ※ Dunkel 總長의 4원 協商計劃(4 track approach)

   (1) 商品分野의 讓許協商(농산물의 보조금 감축계획 포함)

   (2) 서비스분야의 양허협상

   (3) 협정조문의 법적인 정비작업

   (4) 특정사항의 조정필요성 검토(Fine Tuning)

2. 이날 회의에서 모든 참가국은 비록 12.20자 협정초안을 최종적으로 수락한 것은 아니나, 우루과이라운드 협상의 성공적 타결 필요성에 공감하고, Dunkel 총장의 4원 協商計劃을 지지하였음. 이러한 Dunkel 총장의 협상계획은 협상이 순조롭게 진행될 경우 4월 중순경 모든 분야에 걸친 협상안 채택을 예정하고 있으나 협상참가국들이 앞으로의 협상에서 각국의 관심사항반영을 위해 실질문제의 재협상을 어느정도 폭넓게 추진할 것인지 특히 미국과 EC간의 농산물분야 이견조정 가능여부가 중요한 관건이 될 것으로 전망됨.

   ※ 이날 회의에서, 일부국가들은 협정초안에 반영되지 않은 자국의 관심사항을 거론하고 이중 앞으로의 협상을 통해 반영할 것을 희망하였으나, 많은 국가들이 실질문제에 대해 협상이 재개될 경우 協定草案全體가 붕괴될 수도 있다는 우려를 제기하였음.

0149

3. 우리 대표단은 우루과이라운드 협상의 성공적 타결 필요성을
   강조하고 最終協定草案이 그간의 협상결과를 잘 집약한 것으로
   평가하였으나 농산물의 예외없는 관세화와 모든 품목의 최소
   시장접근등 분야에서 심각한 문제점이 있음을 지적하고 이를
   앞으로의 협상에서 시정할 것을 주장하였음.
   (별도 발언요지 참조)

4. 農産物分野의 예외없는 관세화에 대하여는 우리나라를 비롯,
   멕시코, 카나다, 스위스, 오지리, 이스라엘등이 반대의사를
   표시하였음.

0150

〈 參考 〉 금번 TNC회의에서 우리의 發言內容要約

- 한국대표단은 UR협상의 성공적 타결이 중요하다는 점을 강조함.

- 지난 5년간의 협상결과로 집약된 最終協定文案에 있어 國際 交易規範의 改善, 纖維交易의 GATT體制로의 復歸, GATT機能 强化 및 制度分野에서의 協商進展은 UR협상의 타결에 도움이 될 것이라는 것이 韓國政府의 평가임.

- 韓國政府는 앞으로의 最終協商段階에서 우리가 계속 주장해온 農産物등 主要爭點에서 보다 균형있는 合意導出을 위한 개선이 있어야 함을 전제로 금후협상에 계속 적극적인 자세로 참여할 것임.

  i) 農産物 一部分野에서 輸出國과 輸入國, 先進國과 開發 途上國의 이해가 균형을 이루지 못한 것은 유감임.

    ○ 個別國家의 特殊性, 특히 農産物 純輸入國의 취약한 농업 기반을 보호할 수 있는 장치가 전혀 고려되지 않은 「例外 없는 關稅化」의 수용에 심각한 어려움이 있으며 식량안보 관련 基礎食糧에 대해서는 關稅化 例外認定이 필요함.

    ○ 또한 우리는 모든 農産物品目에 대한 최소시장접근 허용에 심각한 어려움이 있음.

    ○ 開發途上國에 대하여는 國內補助 凍結措置가 적용되지 않았음에도 불구하고 輸出補助分野와는 달리 市場接近 및 國內補助減縮上의 基準年度를 1986~88년간으로 설정한 것은 실질적으로 선진국보다 더 큰 부담을 지우는 것으로 불합리하기 때문에 開發途上國에 대해서는 統計的으로 資料算定이 가능한 最近年度를 적용토록 함이 타당함.

0151

ii) 이밖에도 韓國政府는 關稅分野에 있어 協商參加國들이
    1차적으로 몬트리올 合意目標를 우선적으로 달성하여야
    하며 緊急輸入制限措置, 補助金 및 相計關稅등 분야에서
    追加的인 협상이 필요하다는 입장임.

- 韓國政府는 과거와 마찬가지로 앞으로도 UR협상의 성공적
  마무리를 위한 市場接近 및 서비스分野 讓許協商에 적극
  참여할 것이며 同 讓許協商이 각국의 기존 개방수준을 고려
  하고 경제적 능력의 범위내에서 균형있게 이루어 질 것을
  기대함.

0152

관리 번호	92-내

원 본

외 무 부

종 별 :

번 호 : CNW-0057   일 시 : 92 0114 1715

수 신 : 장 관(통기,상공부)

발 신 : 주 캐나다 대사

제 목 : UR 협상 동향 및 전망

연 : CNW-0039,0048

대 : WCN-0004,0029

하명근 상무관은 1.14. 주재국 외무무역부 MTN BRANCH MARIO STE-MARIE 부조정관과 최근 TNC 회의 결과등 UR 협상 동향 및 전망관련 협의한바, 동인의 발언 요지를 아래와 같이 보고함.

1. 1.13. 개최 TNC 회의는 카나다정부가 당초 예상한대로 거의 모든 참가국이 DUNKEL 협상안을 UR 협상의 조기타결을 위한 기초로 받아들인 결과로 되었음. 부분적으로 일부분야(특히 농산물)에 대한 이의를 제기한 국가도 있었으나 동 초안을 전면적으로 거부한 국가가 없었다는 점에서 이를 긍정적으로 평가함.

2. 카나다의 경우 예외없는 관세화 및 금융서비스 시장 개방 미흡등에 대한 우려를 표명하였으며, 동 입장은 앞으로도 계속 견지해 나갈 방침임. 다만 최근들어 예외없는 관세화에 대한 참가국간 반대 분위기가 차츰 감소되는 추세에 있는 것으로 느껴지며, 카나다내 주정부 및 농업 단체내에서도 이의 불가피성에 대한 인식이 싹트기 시작하는 것으로 관측되고 있음.

3. 만약 예외없는 관세화가 압도적인 대세의 흐름으로 판단되고 협상 타결이라는 대 전제를 위하 카나다가 이를 수락하지 않을수 없는 경우에 처하게되는 가정하에서 카 정부로서는 GATT 제 11 조 2 항 대신 차선책으로 다른 수단에 의해서라도 SUPPLY MANAGEMENT PROGRAM 을 유지해 나가는 방안을 모색 할것임. 이경우 차선책으로 생각할수 있는 수단으로는 낙농, 가금 및 계란 품목에 대한 고율 TE(국제, 국내가 차액이상의)의 설정 및 SPECIAL SAFEGUARDS 활용등을 상정할수있고 DUNKEL 총장의 협상안에 포함된 최소시장 접근은 허용하는데에 큰 어려움이 없을 것임. EC 의 경우에도 낙농제품에 대한 SUPPLY MANAGEMENT PROGRAM 유지를 위해 상기 수단을

통상국	장관	차관	1차보	2차보	미주국	경제국	외정실	분석관
정와대	안기부	상공부						

PAGE 1

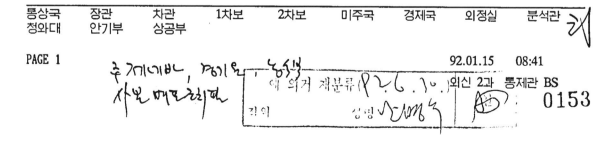

92.01.15   08:41

외신 2과 통제관 BS

0153

채택할 것으로 전망되고 있음.

4. 향후 협상 전망관련, 3 월초 까지의 시장접근(농산물 포함) 및 서비스 양허협상을 거쳐 늦어도 4 월 중순까지는 쟁점분야에 대한 완전 타결이 이루어져야 UR 결렬내지 장기지연을 방지할 가능성이 큰 것으로 평가되고 있음. 이는 미국의 대통령 선거시기(92.11)를 감안할때, 적어도 6 월말까지는 협정안이 의회에제출되어야 한다는 고려에 기초를 둔 것임.

5. 현재로서는 DUNKEL 협상안의 조정작업은 제한된 분야를 제외하고는 용이하지 않는 것으로 참가국간에 받아들여지고 있기때문에 향후 미국, EC 간의 농산물 협상에서 미국이 보다 유리한 입장에 서게 될 것으로 전망되며, 만약 EC 가 동 협상안의 대폭적인 개선을 고수, 타협이 이루어지지 않는경우 그책임이 EC 측에 전가될 공산이 큼. 일본으로서도 쌀에 대한 최소시장 접근은 협상 최종 단계에서 수락이 불가피 할 것으로 관망됨. 끝.

(대사-국장)

예고문 : 92.6.30. 까지

PAGE 2

0154

외 무 부

종 별 :

번 호 : ECW-0052 일 시 : 92 0114 1800

수 신 : 장관 (롱기,경기원,재부부,농림수산부,상공부)

발 신 : 주 EC 대사   사본: 주 미,제네바-중계필

제 목 : GATT/UR 협상

대: WEC-0837

연: ECW-0023

1.13-14 당관이 EC 회원국 대표부를 접촉 파악한 EC 의 표제협상 관련동향과, 1.10 무역이사회에서 개진된 회원국의 던켈협상안에 대한 입장을 아래 보고함

1. EC 의 동향

가. 1.10. 이사회에서 각 회원국들은 DUNKEL 협상안에 대해 폭넓게 의견을 개진한바 있으나 집행위에 부여된 일반적인 MANDATE 에 감축율등 구체적인 내용이 포함되어 있지 않음. 따라서 1.13. TNC 이후 MACSHARRY 등 EC 의 협상주역들은 상당한 결정권한 (LEEWAY) 을 갖고, 융통성있게 협상에 임할것임

나. EC 로서는 표제협상의 타결관건이 농산물분야에 있다고 보며 향후 농산물협상에서 EC 가 가장 큰 관심을 갖고 협상에 임할 분야는 수출보조금과 국내보조금의 감축율을 동등하게 맞추는 문제와 수출보조금을 수출물량 기준하여 감축하는 경우 수출물량이 증가하고 있는 소맥등 품목에대한 어려움을 협상에 반영하는 문제임

다. 이제까지 EC 의 어려운 분야로 제기되어온 GREEN BOX 에 대하여는 독일및 남부국가들이 관심을 갖고있고 REBALANCING 반영문제에 대하여는 불란서가 강경입장을 취하고 있는것은 사실이나 보조금 감축율과 수출보조금 감축 기준문제가 해결될 경우 다소 협상의 여지가 있을것임 (회원국간 여타문제와 관련 TRADE-OFF 가 있을것임을 시사하는 것으로 볼수있음)

라. EC 는 최근 DUNKEL 이 제시한 협상타결 시한 (부활절 이전) 까지 협상종결 여부에대해 낙관적이라 할수는 없으나 긍정적으로 보고 이에 대처해 나갈것임

2. EC 회원국등의 입장

롱상국 정와대	장관 안기부	차관 경기원	1차보 재무부	2차보 농수부	구주국 상공부	경제국 중계	외정실	분석관

92.01.15 18:47

외신 2과 롱제관 BW

0155

가. 회원국별 의견

O DUNKEL 협상안중 12 개 회원국 모두 (특히 덴마크, 영국, 불란서및 화란은강경, 벨지움, 아일랜드및 룩셈부르그는 다소 유연한 입장)가 수출물량의 감축문제에 대해 반대입장을 취함

O 독일은 농산물 보호수준의 감축이 농산물 가격에 미칠영향을 우려하면서 GREEN BOX 와 EC 산 농산물 우선취급원칙 (COMMUNITY PREFERENCES) 이 고려되고있지 않음을 지적함

O 불란서는 아일랜드와 함께 DUNKEL 협상안을 협상기초로 수락하는 것 자체를 반대하면서 물량기준의 수출보조감축 조항은 허용될수 없으며 GREEN BOX 개념을 인정하는 것은 일종의 함정이므로 동 개념에는 생산량을 제한하기 위한 보조만 허용되어야 한다는 입장을 보임. 한편 공산품분야에 대하여는 협상국들에 대한 홍보활동이 필요할 것이라는 입장을 보임

O 영국은 농산물분야에 대해 일부 수정이 필요한 것 이외에는 동 협상안에 대해 대체적으로 호의적임

O 화란은 물량기준의 수출보조금 감축이 낙농제품 수출에 미치는 영향에대해 우려를 표시하고 환경보전 조치를위한 보조금이 GREEN BOX 에 포함되어야 할것을 주장함

O 덴마크와 그리스는 해운산업 관련한 협상안에 반대함

O 아일랜드와 폴투갈은 섬유분야에 대한 협상안에 반대입장을 표명함

O 스페인은 섬유, 보조금및 원산지문제에 대한 내용이 개정되어야 하며 농산물분야및 섬유분야에 있어 EC 산 우선 취급원칙이 빠져있는 것에 대해 반대입장을 표명함

O 이태리는 농산물및 섬유분야 전반에대해 일보 후퇴한 협상안이라고 비난함

나. EC 경제단체의 입장

O EC 경제인연합회 (UNICE) 는 UR 협상 실패 가능성에대해 우려를 표명하고EC 는 DUNKEL 협상안을 협상의 기초로 받아들일것을 촉구하면서 시장접근및 서비스분야에서 수락가능한 결과가 도출될것을 희망하고 농산물분야에서도 균형있는 해결방안이 강구되어야 한다고 주장함

O 유럽 소비자연맹(BEUC) 은 EC 무역이사회 의장(폴투갈 무역장관) 에게 발송한 서한에서 EC 가 농산물 협상에서 타협하는 방안을 강구하는 것이 UR 협상을살리는

PAGE 2

길이며 동 협상의 실패는 보호주의, 무역분재, 실업율증가및 물가인상을 초래할
것이라고 경고함

　　O 한편, EC 의 농업단체인 COPA 와 COGECA 는 EC 이사회가 DUNKEL 협상안
(농산물분야) 을 거부한 것을 환영하면서 주요사항에 대한 재협상을 촉구함. 끝

　　(대사 권동만-국장)

　　예고: 92.6.30 까지

메모은 내게 재보록
92.6.30

원 본

외 무 부

종 별 :

번 호 : HGW-0034

일 시 : 92 0114 1800

수 신 : 장관(봉기)

발 신 : 주 형가리 대사

제 목 : UR 협상 동향

대: WHG-0005

연: HGW-0019

본직은 금 1.14.대외경제부 MAJOR 차관보를 오찬에 초청, UR 협상등에 관해 논의한바,동인 발언요지 아래 보고함.

1. 던켈안중 농산물 분야에 관하여는 수용 가능하다고 보며,TRIPS 및 써비스분야에서도기본적으로 전향적 입장이지만 세부사항에 있어서는 개방대상 및 범위등 양허에 어려움이 많음.

2. UR 협상의 성공을 위해서는 관건인 농업분야에서 미.EC 간 합의가 필요하나,EC 국가중 불란서가 반대하고,영,덴마크등 비교적 온건국가들도 이에 동조하고 있으며,미국도던켈안에 불만을 표하고 있는 실정이므로 타결을 낙관하기 어려움. 미.EC 간 합의가 이루어질 경우 일본은 책임있는 무역대국으로서 협상타결을 가로막는 행동은 하지 않을 것으로봄.

3.과거 도꾜라운드도 10년 가까이 걸린바 있지만,이번 협상이 쉽게 타결을 보지 못하고 있는 것은 TRIPS 및 써비스등 신분야까지 포괄하고 있어 협상분야가 넓을뿐 아니라목표가 높아 모든 협상국들이 사실상 과중한 부담을 느끼고 있기 때문임. 특히 과거 동서간 대결시절에는 다자간 무역체제의 주도국인 미국이 군사,안보상 EC 국가들에 대해 LEVERAGE를 행사할수 있었으나,동서 냉전체제가 붕괴된 지금 미국의 압력수단이 현저히축소되어 있고, EC 는 단일시장과 동구권 국가들을 포괄하는 광역구주시장 출현에 더 관심을 쏟고 있는데다가,미국도 금년이 대통령 선거해가 되어 농업분야에서 양보가 더 어려워진 상황이기 때문에 협상타결 전망은 반반으로 볼수밖에 없음. 4.형가리로서는 사회주의 체제로부터 시장경제로의 전환을 위한 구조개편노력을 경주하고 있는 현시점에서 형+리가 중시하고 있는 농산물등 상품의

통상국	장관	차관	1차보	2차보	외정실	분석관	정와대	안기부

자유무역을 보장하기위한 다자간 국제루울의 확립과 보호주의 경향의 확산방지 조치가 필요하다고 보고 있으며,따라서 UR 로 인해 분야에 따라 시장개방의 부담을 더 지게되는 고통이 있다 하더라도 협상이 성공할수 있도록 최선을 다하고 있음.끝.

(대사 박영우-국장)

예고:92.6.30.까지

예고문 의거 재분류
92.6.30 한

외 무 부

종 별 :

번 호 : GEW-0101

일 시 : 92 0115 1730

수 신 : 장 관(봉기) 사본:주 제네바 대사(직송필)

발 신 : 주 독 대사

제 목 : UR 협상동향

대:WGE-0004

연: 삽-2559

대호관련, 당관 정참사관및 장일형 상무관은 금 1.15. 주재국 경제부 UR 담당 DR.KIESOW 부과장(농산물)및 DR.BARTH 부과장(서비스, 지적재산권)을 오찬 초청, 주재국입장등에 관해 탐문한바, 아래 보고함

1. 지적재산권

- 금번 던켄총장 초안은 선진국과 개도국의 이해가 균형있게(WELL BALANCED)반영된 안으로서 주재국 정부는 이를 적극 수용할수 있음.

- 즉 컴퓨터 프로그램보호, 반도체칩 보호, 국경조치등에 관한 새로운 규정도입은 괄목할만한 발전으로 평가함

- 이와관련 미국 영화업계등 지적재산권 관련 단체들이 개도국에 대한 경과규정등에 대해 강한 반대를 표시하고 있는 것은 지나친 요구라고 봄

2. 서비스 분야

- 주재국은 서비스시장 개방에 많은 중점을 두고 있는바, 특히 해운및 운송분야에 있어서는 조속한 타결을 원하나 금번 초안에 부속서가 작성되지 못하였음은 유감임.

- AUDIO-VISUAL 분야 관련 주재국의 경우 TV, 라디오 방송등은 헌법상 주정부관할 사항으로서 UR 협의결과를 주정부에 강요할수 없는 어려움이 있음

- 금융분야에 있어서는 분쟁해결과 관련 금융서비스 기구가 충분한 결정권한을 가지 못하고 있는등 금융부속서의 내용이 불충분한 것으로 봄

3. 농산물 분야

- 1.13.TNC 회의시 미국대표의 긍정적 반응과는 대조적으로 부시 미 대통령이

1.13. 컨서스시티에서 행한 강한어조의 연설은, 국내 정치적 목적에 주안이 있는

통상국 정와대	장관 안기부	차관	1차보	2차보	구주국	경제국	외정실	분석관

PAGE 1

92.01.16 03:00

외신 2과 통제관 FI

0160

것으로 봄

- 던켈 초안 관련 미국은 수출보조 36 프로 삭감율 상향조정과 기술적, 세부적 사항의 개선이외 기타에 관해서는 상금 적극적인 반대입장 표명은 없음

- 불란서및 아일랜드의 반대로 EC 입장조정에 어려움이 있으나, 끝까지 반대하여 협상결렬의 책임을 안게되는 정치적 부담을 질려고는 하지 않을 것으로 보므로 결국 불란서도 EC 내 다수의견에 추종할 것으로 전망함.

(대사-국장)

예고:92.6.30. 까지

예고문에 개방분류
92.6.30 함

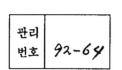

외　무　부

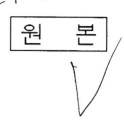

원　본

종　별 :

번　호 : FRW-0118

일　시 : 92 0116 1700

수　신 : 장관(통기)

발　신 : 주불 대사

제　목 : UR협상

대:WFR-0008

연:FRW-0032

(란난문서로 재분류(1992 . 12. 31)

1. 미테랑 대통령은 1.15 각료회의 주재석상에서 DUNKEL 안은 불란서 국익에 반하므로 이를 수락할수 없다는 입장을 분명히 밝히고, 불란서는 미국의 요구나 여타 비유럽국의 이해에 부합키위해 양보하지 않을것임을 천명함.

2. MERMAZ 농업장관도 DUNKEL 안은 여러면에서 문제점이 있으나 농산물 분야는 전적으로 수락할수 없는 내용이며, EC 집행위가 미측의 상응한 양보없이 수출 보조 삭감에 동의코자 할경우 엄청난 결과를 초래 할것이라고 경고함.

3. DUMAS 외상 역시 현상태로서의 DUNKEL 안을 거부할수 밖에 없다고 말하고, EC 집행위가 기부여된 협상 MANDATE 에서 이탈하지 않도록 촉구할 예정이라 밝힘.

4. 불란서가 상기와 같이 DUNKEL 안에 대해 재차 반대 입장을 확고히 표명하는것은

가. 1.13 부시 미 대통령의 EC 농산물 보호 장벽 비난에 대한 반박 입장을 분명히 표시하고

나. 1.13 TNC 회의시 EC 측은 DDUNKEL 안에 대해 예상보다 다소 완화된 입장을 표시한것으로 판다하여, 향후 EC 집행위나 여타 회원국의 유화적 협상 상태도 가능성을 사전에 견제하는 한편

다. 1/4 분기중 자치 단체선거에 직면한 국내 상황에서 당분간 강경 자세를고수하지 않을수 밖에 없는 사정으로 분석됨.

5. 동건 관련 사항 추보함. 끝

(대사 노영찬- 국장)

예고: 92.12.31 까지

92.6.30

통상국 안기부	장관	차관	1차보	2차보	구주국	외정실	분석관	청와대

UR 협상 동향

1. 협상 현황

o 던켈 갓트 사무총장은 91.12.20 무역협상위원회(TNC)에서 UR 최종 협상 문서
  및 협상 계획 제시
  - 각국 정부에 대해 동 최종 협상 문서를 검토, 92.1.13 무역협상위원회에서
    협상을 종결한다는 계획을 제시
  - 시장접근, 서비스 분야 양자협상등 기술적 협의는 92.1.13 이후에도 계속
    실시

o 최종 협상 문서(Dunkel Text)의 성격
  - 90.12. 브랏셀 각료회의 이후 각 협상 분야별 쟁점 타결을 위한 집중적
    협상 결과를 종합한 문서로서, 외형상으로는 합의된 형태를 취함.
  - 실제로 일부 분야에서 협상 참가국간 합의를 이루지 못하여 협상그룹
    의장이 독자적 책임하에 타협안을 제시
    . 농산물 분야에서는 우리나라등 수개국가의 반대에도 불구, 모든 품목의
      관세화와 최소 시장접근(3%) 의무를 수용

o 1.13 무역협상위원회(TNC) 회의 결과
  - 하기 협상 전략에 따라 작년 12.20 제시된 협정 초안을 기초로 수주간
    양자, 다자간 협상을 추진키로 결정
    1) 농산물등 상품분야의 양허협상 (농산물의 보조금 감축 계획 포함)
    2) 서비스 분야의 양허협상
    3) 협정 초안의 법적인 정비작업
    4) 협정 초안 내용중 특정사항의 조정 필요성 검토

o 동 회의에서는 UR 협상 종결 시한을 명시적으로 정하지 않았으나, Dunkel
  갓트 사무총장은 4월중순을 협상 종결 시한으로 정하고 있는 것으로 관측

0163

향후 협상 전망

o 현단계에서는 정확한 예측이 어려우나 3월말까지 농산물등 상품분야 및
  서비스 분야에 대한 집중적 양허협상을 전개, 동 협상 결과에 따라 UR 협상
  타결 여부에 대한 윤곽이 드러날 전망

o 그러나, 농산물 보조금 감축을 위요한 미·EC간 타결 여부 및 예외없는
  관세화등 민감사안에 대한 협정 초안 수정 가능 여부등이 UR 협상 조기
  타결에 변수로 작용할 전망.   끝.

0164

외 무 부

종   별 :

번   호 : NDW-0070   일   시 : 92 0115 1130

수   신 : 장 관(통기)

발   신 : 주 인도 대사

제   목 : UR 협상동향

연:NDW-0040

대:WND-0009

1. 연호, 당관 임재홍서기관은 금 1.15(수) 주재국 상무부 GATT 및 UR 담당 MR. P.S. RANDBAWA 부국장과 접촉, 던켈총장 협정안에 대한 인도측 입장의 확정 여부를 문의한바, 동 부국장은 현재 인도측 입장이 최종 마무리 되지 않았으며 확정되기까지에는 2-3 주 더 걸릴것으로 예상된다고 답한 후 1.13. 개최된 TNC 회의에 본국 대표단은 파견치 않았다고 부언함.

2. 한편 최근 UR 협상관련 주재국의 주요동향은 아래와 같음.

0 1.10. 주재국 특허권법 활동그룹(THE NATIONAL WORKING GROUP ON PATENT LAWS)은 던켈협정안이 개도국의 이익을 팔아 선진국의 세계경제에서의 독점적 지위를 확보하도록 할 뿐 이라고 강력히 비난하고 인도정부가 국민적 합의없이 던켈협정안에 서명치 않토록 권고하였으며, 또한 인도 정계, 경제계, 법조계등 저명인사 40 여명도 인도정부에 대해 GATT 든 IMF 든 인도정부의 경제적 주권을 손상시키는 국제압력에는 절대 굴복하지 말 것으로 촉구하는 성명을 발표함.

0 1.11. 주재국 야당지도자 V.P. SINGH 전수상은 던켈협정안은 외국기업들이 사실상 인도내에서 무제한 활동할수 있도록하고 있다고 주장하면서, 정부가 던켈협정안에 서명할 경우 인도는 경제적 노예상태에 처하게 될 것이라고 경고하고 동 협정안에 서명하지 말도록 권고함.(만약 서명경우 전야당이 연대하여 부쟁할 것임을 공언)

(대사 이정빈-국장)

예고:92.6.30 일반

예고문 의계재 보류
92.6.30 종결

통상국	장관	차관	1차보	2차보	아주국	분석관	정와대	안기부

외 무 부

종 별 :

번 호 : ECW-0059　　　　　　　　　　　일　시 : 92 0115 1700

수 신 : 장관 (통기,통삼,미일)

발 신 : 주EC 대사(사본: 주제네바,주미대사-중계요망)

제 목 : UR 관련 동향

21.15. EC 집행위 FRANS ANDRIESSEN 부위원장은 BUSH 미대통령이 1.13. KANSAS CITY 에서 행한연설중 EC 에 대하여 언급한 부분에 대하여아래 성명을 발표하고, BUSH대통령이 사용한표현중 COLD WAR 또는 IRON CURTAIN 등의표현은 현 EC-미국관계를제대로 반영하지못한 것이라고 불쾌한 놀라움을 표시함

- 아래 -

REACTION DU VICE-PRESIDENT ANDRIESSEN A LA DECLARATION DUPRESIDENT BUSH RELATIVE A LA POLITIQUE COMMERCIALE ETAGRICOLE DE LA COMMUNAUTE

LE VICE-PRESIDENT ANDRIESSEN EST DESAGREABLEMENT SURPRISPAR LA TONALITE DESREMARQUES PRONONCEES PAR LE PRESIDENTBUSH LE 13 JANVIER DERNIER A KANSAS CITY (MISSOURI)

M. ANDRIESSEN TIENT A RAPPELER QUE LA COMMUNAUTE, SURTOUTDANS LES DERNIERS MOIS, A CONTRIBUE D'UNE FACON TRES ACTIVE,NOTAMMENT DANS LE CADRE DE L URUGUAY ROUND, A LA RECHERCHEDES SOLUTIONS APPROPRIEES ET EQUITABLES ASSURANT DEMEILLEURES CONDITIONS AUX ECHANGES INTERNATIONAUX, Y COMPRISEN AGRICULTURE.

LA COMMUNAUTE PARTICIPE A CES DERNIERES NEGOCIATIONS AVECUN ESPRIT DE COOPERATION ET DE CONSULTATION. EN CE QUICONCERNE LA COMMISSION, LES TERMES DE GUERRE FROIDE ET DERIDEAU DE FER NE REFLETENT PAS LES RELATIONS ENTRE LESETATS-UNIS ET LA COMMUNAUTE TELLES QU ELLE LES VOIT.

(대사 권동만-국장)

통상국　　2차보　　미주국　　통상국

PAGE 1　　　　　　　　　　　　　　　　　92.01.16　05:46 FE

외신 1과 통제관

0166

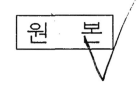

관리 번호	92-58

외 무 부

종 별 : 지급

번 호 : GVW-0100   일 시 : 92 0115 2000

수 신 : 장관(봉기, 경기원, 재무부, 농림수산부, 상공부)   사본: 주미대사 (오참관)

발 신 : 주 제네바 대사   주일대사

제 목 : UR 협상(일본 외무성 UR 담당 대사 오찬 면담)

   1. 본직은 1.15(수) 당지 방문중인 ENDO 일본 외무성 UR 담당대사와 UR 협상 관련 상호 관심사를 논의한바, 동인의 주요 언급 내용은 아래와 같음. (오참사관 동석)

   가. 예외없는 관세화에 대한 일본의 입장

   - 일본 정계 일각등에서 예외없는 관세화를 포함하고 있는 12.20 자 농산물협상안이 당초 우려했던것 보다는 경제적인 시각에서 크게 우려할 것이 못되며, 11 조 2 항 C 에 따른 수입규제 가능성을 허용하면서 대신 10 % 정도의 최소시장 접근 의무를 부과하는 것 보다는 차라리 어려움이 덜 하다는 입장을 보이는경우도 있음.

   - 그러나, 일본 정부로서는 융통성이 없는 현행대로의 예외없는 관세화는 식량관리법을 개정해야만 이행이 가능하다는 점, 금년 7 월 참의원 선거가 예정되어 있는 상황에서 정치적으로 받아들일수 없다는 입장임.

   - 1.13 TNC 회의에서 예외없는 관세화 문제에 심각한 어려움에도 불구하고 UR 협상 타결에 일본이 방해가 된다는 인상을 주지 않기 위해 12.20 자 협상안이 최종적인 것은 아니며, UR 협상 타결을 위한 주요한 계기가 된다고 하고, 던켈의 4 TRACK 협상 전략을 지지한다고 밝힌바 있음.

   나. 일본으로서의 향후 대책

   일반문서로 재분류(1992 12. 31

   - 일본 농무성 관리들은 미국도 WAIVER 포기에 매우 어려움이 있는 만큼, 각국의 제일 민감한 품목(예: 미국의 땅콩, 일본의 쌀등)을 예외로 인정되도록 끝까지 노력해야 한다는 주장을 하고 있으나, 설령 미국 농무부로서는 수용하고저 하더라도 USTR 로서는 받아들이기 어려운 사항인만큼 추진키 어려운 것으로 판단하고 있음.

   - 던켈 총장의 4 번째 TRACK 조정과정에서 관세화 문제에 대한 조정작업이 이루어질 가능성은 극히 희박하다고 보고 있지만, FLEXIBILITY 가 확보되는 방향으로 개선되도록 노력할 예정임.

롱상국 경기원	장관 재무부	차관 농수부	1차보 상공부	2차보	외정실	분석관	청와대	안기부

PAGE 1   92.01.16   07:50

                                          외신 2과 통제관 BD

                                          0167

- 일본 농산성 시와꾸 심의관(차관급)이 TNC 회의 참석후 미국을 방문중이며, ENDO 대사 자신도 내주에 미국을 방문(아주마 농무성 국제 부장은 현재 브랏셀 방문중)한후 다시 GENEVA 에 돌아올 예정임.

　　다. EC 측의 입장

- EC 로서는 각 회원국의 입장을 내부조정하는데 어려움이 있는듯하며, 1.10 무역 및 농업 이사회도 작년 12.23 이사회시의 입장을 재확인 하였을뿐 구체적인 추후 대처방안을 제시하지 않았으므로 EC 로서는 1.13 TNC 회의시 12.20 자 협상안이 대폭 개선(SERIOUS IMPROVEMENT)되어야 한다는 점만 밝히고 던켈의 4 TRACK 전략을 지지한바 있음.(SERIOUS AMENDAMENT 가 아닌 SERIOUS IMPROVEMENT 에는 뉴앙스상 큰 차이가 있음을 지적)

- 만약 EC 이사회가 QUALIFIED VOTE 를 하지 않으면 안되는 상황이 올때 불란서측이 독일을 비롯 각국의 입장을 감안한 구체적인 안을 제시할 경우 불란서만이 고립되는 상황이 되지 않을수도 있다고 봄.

- 불란서로서는 지방선거(92.3 월경)후에는 현재보다 다소 완화된 입장을 제시할수도 있을 것으로 보나, 그 이전에는 강경입장을 고수할 것으로 보여짐.

　　라. 3 월말, 4 월 중순 UR 협상 타결 전망

- EC 측의 강경한 입장을 감안, 던켈 총장으로서는 아마도 1 월 말경 다시한번 CRISIS 를 조성, EC 측에 압력을 가할 가능성이 있는 것으로 보고있음.

- 미국으로서는 시장접근 분야에서의 양자 협상에서 실질적인 성과를 거두어야 하며, 서비스 분야 양허 협상도 매우 복잡한 사안임을 감안할때 3 월말까지협상을 마무리 하는 것도 간단치 않다고 봄.

- 자기로서는 4 월 중순까지 UR 협상을 종결지을 가능성을 예측한다면 그 가능성은 50:50 으로 보고있음.

　　2. 동 대사는 관세화문제와 관련, 한국의 경우에는 농가소득의 50 % 이상을쌀에 의존하고 있으나 일본은 20 %에 그치고 있는 점에 비추어 일본과 한국을 별도로 취급해야 한다는 견해도 있고, 특히 한국과 미국이 비공식 접촉을 통해 예외 인정에 합의했다는 소문을 듣고 있다고 하였음. 본직은 이에 대해 아국이 미측에 아국의 어려운 입장을 설명해오고 있으나 그러한 합의가 이루어진것은 없으며, 와전된 것이라고 답변하였음.

　　3. 본직과 ENDO 대사는 앞으로 던켈 총장의 4 번째 TRACK 협의를 통해 예외없는

PAGE 2

0168

관세화 문제와 관련 개선점이 이루어지도록 양국이 긴밀히 협조하여 대체키로 하였음.
끝

    (대사 박수길-국장) 예고 :92.12 31까지

외 무 부

종   별 :

번   호 : NDW-0096   일   시 : 92 0117 1740

수   신 : 장 관(봉기)

발   신 : 주 인 도 대사

제   목 : UR 협상동향

연:NDW-0070

1. 연호관련, 주재국 정부는 던켈협정안에 대한 국내여론이 긍정적 수용과 부정적 비판으로 대립되고 있는 현실을 고려, 정치권을 비롯 상공무역업자및 지식층을 포함한 여론형성층과의 광범위한 의견수렴을 통해 던켈협정안에 대한 합의된 인도입장 도출을 위하여 최근 ARJUN SINGH 인력개발장관을 의장으로하는 던켈협정안에 대한 관계부처장관 협의회(외무, 재무, 상무, 보건, 농업부및 화학제품과 비료담당부장관으로 구성됨)를 구성하였음.

2. 동 장관협의회는 던켈협정안중 인도가 가장 큰 관심을 갖고 있는 MFA 와TRIPS 에 대해 집중검토할 것으로 보이며, 최종적 인도입장은 내각의 승인을 득한후 확정될 전망이므로 던켈협정안에 대한 인도측 입장정립에는 다소 시간이 걸릴 것으로 예상되고 있음.

(대사 이정빈-국장)

통상국	장관	차관	1차보	2차보	아주국	분석관	청와대	안기부

PAGE 1

발 신 전 보

WUS-0218   920117 1455 DQ

번   호 : _____   종별 : _____

WGV -0086   WJA -0192

수   신 : 주   미   대사. 총영사 (사본 : 주 제네바 대사, 주일 대사)

발   신 : 장 관 (통 기)

제   목 : UR 협상

연 : GVW-0100

1. 연호 주 제네바 대사의 Endo 일본 UR 협상 대표와의 면담 보고에 의하면 일본은
    UR 협상에서 예외없는 관세화 제의에 대한 수정 작업이 이루어질 가능성은 극히
    희박한 것으로 보고, 예외없는 관세화를 수용하는 경우 flexibility를 확보하는
    방향(관세화 실시의 유예기간 확보, 최소 시장접근 비율 하향 조정등을 고려할 수
    있을것임.)으로 막후 협상을 추진할 가능성이 있는 것으로 시사되고 있는바,
    아국으로서는 이와 관련한 일본의 동향을 예의 주시할 필요가 있다고 판단됨.

2. ~~상기~~ ENDO ~~일본 외무성 UR 담당~~ 대사에 의하면 일본 농산성 시와꾸 심의관(차관급)이
    TNC 회의 참석후 방미중이며, ENDO 대사도 1.21 주간에 미국을 방문 예정이라는바,
    이와 관련 미·일간의 접촉 내용(특히 농산물의 관세화 문제와 관련한 막후 협상이
    있는 경우 동 내용)애 관해 가급적 간접적인 방법을 통해 은밀히 파악 보고바람.

끝.   (통상국장 김 용 규)

예고문 의거 재보류 ÷6
92.6.30
제2차-관보:

앙 고 재	91년 1월 8일	통 기 과	기안자 성명		과 장	심의관	국 장		차 관	장 관	
			조철				전결				

0171

원 본

외 무 부

종 별 :

번 호 : ECW-0073

일 시 : 92 0117 1830

수 신 : 장관 (봉기, 경기원, 농수산부, 기정동문)

발 신 : 주 EC 대사 사본: 주 미, 제네바-중계필

제 목 : UR 협상동향

    당관 김광동참사관이 금 1.17. EC 집행위 DE PASCALE UR 담당총괄 과장을 접촉, 표제협상 관련 협의한바, 동 과장의 반응 아래 보고함

    1. 동 과장은 먼저 91.12.23. EC 각료회의 이후 지금까지 EC 의 입장에 한치의 변화도 없으며 오히려 최근의 분위기는 DUNKEL 텍스트가 나오기 이전보다 더욱 경직되고 있는것으로 감지된다고 전제한후 다음주부터 제네바에서 재개되는양자 또는 다자협상 과정에서 과거 EC 의 입장을 고수, DUNKEL 텍스트가 재작성 또는 대폭 수정되도록 현지협상 대표에 지시하였다 함

    2. 동 과장은 1.13. 제네바 TNC 회의시 EC 는 UR 협상 결렬의 책임문제와 관련, 비교적 완곡한 표현으로 DUNKEL TEXT 에 대하여 실질적 변경 또는 상당한 개선을 요구하는 선에서 EC 의 입장을 표명하였으나, 1.10-11 EC 무역및 농업이사회에서 대부분의 참석각료들은 DUNKEL TEXT 가 수출물량 기준감축, GREEN BOX, REBALANCING 등 EC 의 입장을 전혀 반영치 않고 미국의 입장만을 편향하게 반영, 작성되었다는데 강한 불만을 표시하고 보다 강경한 입장을 표명해야 한다는 주장이 팽배하였었다는 점을 지적함

    3. 동 과장은 협상타결 시한이 4.19. 부활절까지로 약 2 개월간 연장되었으나, UR 협상타결의 관건인 농산물에 대한 미.EC 간의 근본적인 입장차이가 2 개월 동안에 조정될 가능성은 희박하다고 보며, 미.EC 양측은 농산물협상에 관한한더 이상 양보할수 없는 입장의 한계를 서로 잘 인식하고 있기 때문에 브랏셀 또는 워싱톤에서 다시 협의할 필요성이 현재로서는 거의 없다고 말함. 동 과장은불란서가 그동안 협상결렬의 책임, EC 회원국내에서의 고립문제등을 고려, 국내 정치용으로 형식적인 반대입장을 보이며 정치동맹 추진및 EC 기구의 유치 (EP의 스트라스부르그 잔류및 구주은행 본부) 등으로 타협적인 자세를 보였으나, 협상타결 시한이 연장되고 다수의

롱상국 정와대	장관 안기부	차관 경기원	1차보 농수부	2차보	구주국	경제국	외정실	분석관

PAGE 1

92.01.18 07:12

외신 2과 통제관 BD

0172

국가들이 DUNKEL TEXT 에 대한 불만을 표시하고 수정의 불가피성을 주장함에 따라 강경입장으로 선회하고 아일랜드, 덴마크등이 동조하게 되어 회원국간의 입장조정이 더욱 어려워져 UR 협상 타결전망이 밝지않다고 언급함

4. 동 과장은 특히 1.13. 미대통령의 KANSAS CITY 연설내용중 EC 관련부분및 미.일 정상회담 결과등과 관련, 냉전시대의 종식에 따라 국제정치, 경제적으로 크게 제고된 EC 의 위상을 간과하고, 모든 문제에서 미국이 자국의 이익에 합치되는 방향으로 EC 를 끌고 가려는 자세에 대하여 회원국들이 불만을 표시하였으며, 특히 불란서는 미국의 태도에 대하여 노골적으로 감정섞인 불만을 표시하고 있는바, 1.16. 미테랑 대통령은 DUNKEL TEXT 를 협상의 기초로 받아들일수 없으며 거부한다고 밝힌데 대하여 일부 회원국이 동조하는 입장을 취하고 또 여타 국가는 이러한 불란서의 강경입장 선회를 비난하는등 EC 회원국간에도 입장이 분열되어 UR 협상이 더욱 어려운 국면에 접어들게 될 것이라고 말함

5. 동 과장은 자신의 이름이 인용되기를 원치 않는다고 전제하고 지금까지 UR 협상 없이도 EC 는 그런대로 안정성장을 지속해온 사실을 주목할 필요가 있다고 하면서, EC 회원국 전체 또는 일부 회원국의 이익을 희생하면서 까지 불만족스러운 협상결과를 수용할수 없는것이 변함없는 EC 의 기본입장이며 이러한 EC의 기본입장을 협상 참가국들이 인정하지 않는한 성공적인 UR 타결은 불가능한바, 세계최대의 무역주체인 EC 의 입장이 무시되는 것은 있을수 없는 일이라고 말함. 이에대하여 김참사관이 EC 가 UR 의 결렬까지도 감수하겠다는 것을 의미 하느냐고 반문한데 대하여는 언급을 회피함. 끝

(대사 권동만-국장)
예고: 92.6.30. 까지

예고문 의거 재분류
92.6.30 종결

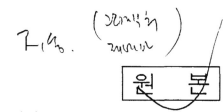

외 무 부

<table>
<tr><td>관리
번호</td><td>92-66</td></tr>
</table>

종 별 :

번 호 : FRW-0136

일 시 : 92 0117 1850

수 신 : 장관(봉기)

발 신 : 주 불 대사

제 목 : UR 협상동향

연 : FRW-0032

대 : WFR-0008

일반문서로 재분류 (1992. 12. 31. 都)

당관 조참사관은 1.17 외무성 경제국 DENIS SIMONEAU UR 담당관과 접촉, 1.13 TNC 회의 관련, 불측이 보는 UR 협상동향에 관해 의견교환한 바, 주요내용 아래 보고함.

1. 1.13 TNC 회의 분위기

0 DUNKEL 안 수락여부를 놓고 아래와 같이 3 개그룹으로 반응이 나뉘어졌으나, 전반적으로 협상의 기초로 수락할수 있다는 분위기 였음.

- 미국, 케언즈 그룹, 일부 중남미국 : DUNKEL 안에 매우 호의적인 반응이었으며 이를 기초로 협상이 종료되어도 사실상 무방하다는 인상임.

- 브라질, 인도등 주요 개도국 : DUNKEL 안에 어려운점이 상당히 있으나 모든협상을 재개할수 없으며 차선책이 없는 현실에서 수락할 가능성이 큼.

- EC, 한국, 일본, 멕시코, EFTA 국 : DUNKEL 안을 수락키 매우 어려우며 FOUR TRACK 에 의해 분야별로 수정되어야 함.

0 1.13 EC 봉상농업장관 회담시, 독.영등은 TNC 회의시 DUNKEL 안을 "협상의 기초"로 할수 있다는 입장 표명을 주장하였으나 불란서가 강경히 반대함에 따라 결국 EC 는 DUNKEL 안을 "협상의 참고"(REFERENCE OF NEGOTIATION)로 한다는 모호한 입장을 표명함.

0 또한 EC 는 DUNKEL 안의 협상전략에 반대하지는 않으나 자국입장이 충분히 반영되지 않을 경우 4 월중순 까지 협상을 종결해야 할 당위성은 없다고 봄.

2. 불란서 입장

0 UR 타결이 지연되는 이유는 미.EC 간 대립뿐아니라 EC 내부에서도 농산물문제에 있어 의견이 상충되기 때문임.

<table>
<tr><td>통상국
청와대</td><td>장관
안기부</td><td>차관</td><td>1차보</td><td>2차보</td><td>구주국</td><td>경제국</td><td>외정실</td><td>분석관</td></tr>
</table>

PAGE 1

92.01.18   08:10

외신 2과 통제관 BD

0174

O 불란서의 경우 수출보조금 삭감, REBALANCING 등은 극히 민감한 사항으로자국입장이 필히 반영되어야 함. 반면 EC 내 가장 경쟁력있는 자국 농업사정에비추어 GREEN BOX LIST 는 가능한한 축소되는 것이 바람직하며 CAP 개혁에 따른 "직접 소득보상'이 GREEN BOX 에 포함되지 않아도 이를 수락할수 있다는 입장임.(영국도 입장 유사)

 - 반면, 독일을 포함한 상당수 EC 국가와 EC 집행위는 "직접 소득보상"을 포함한 GREEN BOX LIST 의 확대를 주장하고 있으며, 독일의 경우 동건이 포함될 경우 DUNKEL 안을 수락할 가능성도 있음.

O 이와관련, 불란서는 미국이 GREEN BOX 내 직접 소득보상을 포함시키는 댓가로 EC 의 양보, 특히 독일의 태도변경을 추구할 가능성을 가장 우려하고 있음.

O 연호(2) 미테랑 대통령을 비롯한 불정부 인사의 강경한 입장 천명은 국내정치적 목적도 있으나, EC 집행위의 양보협상 및 독일의 이탈가능성을 사전에 견제키 위한 것으로 봄.

3. 향후 전망

O 불란서가 기존입장을 고수하는데는 독일의 협조가 절대적으로 긴요하며 독일 이탈시 사실상 불란서와 아일랜드만으로 고립되어 더이상의 강경입장 유지는 불가능할 것으로 예상됨.

O DUNKEL 안 발표이후 전반적 대세가 동안에 호의적이며 또한 독일도 다소 유화적인 UR 협상 가능성을 보임에 다라, 불란서는 무엇보다도 EC 내에서 계속 독일의 지지확보를 위해 주력하는 한편, 이에 실패할 경우 불란서의 양보를 댓가로 CAP 개혁, EC 산업정책등 EC 내 여타 불란서 관심분야에서 이에 상응하는 보상을 추구할 것으로 보임.

O 한편 1.13 TNC 회의 이후 1.24 고위급 113 조 위원회가,1.28 농업이사회가 각각 브랏셀에서 개최될 예정이며, 불란서는 EC 집행위에 대한 새로운 협상 MANDATE 부여 거부등 강경자세를 당분간 고수할 것으로 보임.끝.

 (대사 노영찬-국장)

 예고:92.12.31. 까지

PAGE 2

0175

UR(우루과이라운드) 협상 동향 및 TNC(무역협상위원회) 회의, 1992. 전5권(V.1 1월) 181

외 무 부

관리
번호 92-78

종 별 :

번 호 : ECW-0080   일 시 : 92 0120 1800

수 신 : 장 관(통기,경기원,재무부,농림수산부,상공부,기정동문)

발 신 : 주 EC 대사 사본: 주 미,일,제네바-중계필

제 목 : GATT/UR 협상

최근 표제협상 관련 당지동향을 아래보고함

1. 일본-EC 접촉동향

가. 1.20. 당관 이관용농무관이 당지 일본대표부의 하라구찌 농무관및 EC 집행위 농업총국 OLSEN 담당관과 접촉, 최근 EC-일본 접촉 동향에 대하여 문의한바에 의하면 지난주 일본 농무성의 아즈마심의관이 당지를 방문, MOHLER 농업부총국장에게 농산물협상에 대한 일본의 입장을 설명하고, 미-EC 간의 양자접촉등 향후 협상전망에 대해 의견교환을 가진바 있다고 함. 하라구치농무관은 상기관련, 쌀문제에 대한 일본입장이 바뀐바 없으며, 아즈마 심의관의 당지방문이 쌀문제에 대한 EC 측의 입장 타진이나 지지를 요청하기 위한것이 아니고, 표제협상 추진전망등 일본적인 의견교환에 목적이 있었다고 말함

나. 한편 또다른 일본대표단이 워싱본을 방문, CROWDER 농무차관및 KATZ 부대표를 만났으나, 미측은 UR 협상의 향후전망 등에 관하여 구체적인 의견개진을 자제하는 태도를 보였다 함

2. 불란서 입장

1.17. DUMAS 불란서 외무장관은 리스본에서 PINHEIRO 폴무갈 외무장관과 회담후 가진 기자회견에서 UR 협상의 성공을위해 자국의 농업을 희생시킬수 없다는불란서정부의 강경입장을 재천명함. 동인은 불란서도 UR 협상의 실패를 원하는초강경론자는 아니며, 실질적인 협상을 바라고 있으나 지금까지 제시되고 있는협상국들의 입장은 대화보다는 압력이라고 지적하면서, 그러한 압력 (특히 미국으로 부터의)에 굴복할수 없으며 불란서는 자국및 EC 의 이익을 옹호해 나갈 것이라고 말함

3. 독일입장

통상국	장관 경기원	차관 재무부	1차보 농수부	2차보 상공부	외정실 중계	분석관	청와대	안기부

PAGE 1   92.01.21   05:01

외신 2과 통제관 FK

0176

1.16. MOELLEMANN 독일 경제장관은 EC 와 그 회원국들이 UR 협상의 성공을 봉쇄하고 있다고 비난하면서, G-7 및 EC 는 이제까지 계속 밝힌바와 같이 UR 협상의 성공적인 종결을 위한 제반조치를 취해야 할 것이라고 말함. 끝

(대사 권동만-국장)

예고: 92.6.30 까지

예고문 의거 개비분류
92.6.30 중

관리
번호 *92-73*

외 무 부

종 별 :

번 호 : GVW-0138   일 시 : 92 0120 2000

수 신 : 장관(통기, 경기원, 재무부, 농림수산부, 상공부)

발 신 : 주 제네바 대사 (사본:주미, 주이씨대사(중계필))

제 목 : UR 협상 동향(RAMSAUER 스위스 공사 오찬 면담)

　　김대사는 1.20 UR 규범 제정 분야 협상 그룹의장 보좌관으로서 반덤핑 분야협상 TEXT 를 성안한 RAMSAUER 당지 스위스공사와 UR 협상 전망등에 관해 의견을 교환한바, 동인 언급요지 아래 보고함.

　　1. 던켈 총장의 4 번째 TRACK 과 관련한 견해

　　- 작년 12.20 협상안 제출시 UR 협상 그룹의장단들의 의견은 동 협상안을 거의 TAKE OR LEAVE IT TEXT 로 하고 각 협상 그룹을 해체할 것을 던켈 총장에게건의한바 있으나, 던켈 총장이 1.13 TNC 회의에서 4 TRACK 전략을 제시 모든 나라가 반대하지 않도록 하는 현명한 조치를 취했다고 봄.

　　- 그러나 4 번째 TRACK 이 어면식으로 운영될지에 대해서는 현재로서는 예단키 어려우며, 자신의 판단으로는 각국이 던켈 총장에게 어떤 사안을 제기할 경우 던켈 총장으로서는 관련국과 협의, 동의를 구하라고 대응할 것으로 예상할수 있으며, 따라서 4 번째 TRACK 에 의한 협상안의 실질내용 수정 가능성은 극히 희박하다고 봄.

　　2. 반덤핑등 규범제정 분야

　　- 미국으로서 가장 큰 관심을 갖고 있는 분야인바, 특히 반덤핑 분야에서 CIRCUMVENTION DE MINIMUS 조항등 관련 미국이 가장 강한 반대입장을 보이고 있고, EC 로서도 불만족스러운 분야이나 협상이 재개되어 개정될 가능성은 없다고 보고있음.

　　- AVERAGING 관련 TARGETED DUMPING 요건, 수입국 조립 우회덤핑 요건에 있어서의 부가가치 개념 불규정등 다소 불명확하고 애매한 측면이 있다는 것을 인정하지만 앞으로 어떤 형식으로 수정이 가능할지, 자신이 관여하게될지 여부도 현재로서는 아는바 없음.

　　- 자신의 판단으로는 반덤핑 보다 보조금 상계관세, 세이프가드 분야가 문제점이 많은 분야로 보고있음.

통상국	장관	차관	1차보	2차보	외정실	분석관	청와대	안기부
경기원	재무부	농수부	상공부					

PAGE 1   92.01.21   06:12

3. 농산물 분야

- UR 협상 성공을 위해서는 농산물 협상안의 일부 수정이 불가피하다고 보여지나, 자신의 생각으로는 수출 보조분야는 수정이 어렵다고 보며, 독일과 미국이 다같이 관심을 갖고 있는 국내 보조분야에 대한 일부 조정 가능성은 있을수 있다고 봄.

- 예외없는 관세화 문제는 일본, 카나다, 이스라엘등이 이를 수용하는 방향으로 움직이듯 하며, 서로 관심사항은 다르지만 한국, 스위스, 멕시코등이 계속 반대의사를 보이고 있으나 미국, EC 가 이미 합의하고 있는 사항으로서 앞으로 수정가능성은 별로 없다고 보고있음.

(스위스로서는 예외없는 관세화, 세이프가드 조항, 상대적 단기간의 이행기간등에 문제가 있다고 보고있음.)

- 아직 양자협의의 기초가 마련되지 않은 상태에서 시장접근 분야협상(TRACK 1)을 어떻게 진행할수 있을지에 대해 스위스 정부로서도 확실한 방안을 갖고 있지 못함.

- EC 의 농산물 협상 대표인 MULLER 가 금주중 방미, 미.EC 간 협의가 있는것으로 알고 있음.

4. UR 협상의 조기 타결 가능성 전망

- EC 내에서는 농업분야에서 불란서의 반대입장이 강하며, 독일로서도 국내보조문제와 관련 반대입장을 보이고 있고, 미국으로서도 12.20 자 협상안 제시후 규범제정분야(반덤핑, 보조금, 상계관세) 분쟁해결등 분야에서의 미국내법 상충문제, TRIPS 분야에서의 반대 (영화, 의약품, 오디오 비쥬얼 등)와 아울러 농업, 섬유분야에서의 일부 반대도 있어 의회에서의 지지획득 여부가 다소 불투명한 상태에 있음.

- 4 번째 TRACK 과 관련 4 월중순까지의 협상 완결 여부는 현시점에서 예산키 어려우나, 다른 분야에서의 문제점에 불구 미.EC 간 농어분야에서의 일부 조정등에 합의가 이루어지는 경우 UR 타결 가능성이 있다고 봄.

- 4 월 중순까지 타결되지 않을 경우에는 미의회의 하계휴가 이전 협상안제출이 어렵게 되는바, 미국선거 이후로 미루어지게 될지 아니면 UR 협상 실패로 종결지워질지 알수 없으나 자기로서는 던켈 총장의 임기와는 무관하다고 봄. 끝

(대사 박수길-국장)

예고 92.6.20 까지

외교톤에 재보류

92. 6. 30. ㅎ

관리 번호	92-76

외 무 부

종   별 :

번   호 : GVW-0139   일   시 : 92 0120 2000

수   신 : 장관(통기,경기원,재무부,농림수산부,상공부,경제수석)

발   신 : 주 제네바 대사

제   목 : CALISLE 사무차장의 협상 UR 협상 전망

1. 본직은 1.17(금) 카라일 갓트 사무차장을 오찬에 초대 UR 전망등에 관하여 의견 교환한바 요지 아래 보고함.

가. BUSH 대통령이 아무리 선거운동의 일환이긴 하지만 EC 가 "보호주의 철의 장막"을 쳤다는 언급은 EC 당국을 크게 자극하는 결과를 가져와 미테랑 대통령으로 하여금 DUNKEL 초안을 수락할수 없다는 발언을 하게 하였는바, 이는 UR 타결을 앞두고 EC 미국간에 불필요한 마찰을 이르케 하였음.

나. DUNKEL 초안은 미국입장에서 전체적으로 평가할때 "최소한의 기준"은 충족시키고 있으나 EC 의 입장에선 농산물 분야에 관한한 "최소한"에 미달이므로앞으로 TRACK 4 를 운영함에 있어서 DUNKEL 총장으로서는 이점에 역점을 둘 것이나 문제의 민감성에 비추어 TRACK 4 의 활용은 오직 마지막 단계에서만 활용, 가능할 것임.

다. TRACK 의 존재에도 불구하고 일본, 한국등이 관심을 갖는 예외없는 관세화 문제는 사실상 재론이 극히 어려우며, 또한 미국의 의회가 많은 불만을 제기하고 있는 보조금, 상계관세, 반덤핑, PIPELINE PRODUCTS 보호문제등도 재론은불가능하므로 TRACK 4 는 사실상 EC 가 불만을 갖고 있는 국내 보조문제를 제한적으로 반영하는데만 활용될 가능성이 많음. (자기도 1,2 일 와싱본에서 HILLS대표와 회동한바 HILLS 대표도 SPECIAL INTERESTS 반발때문에 상당한 우려를 표명했다함)

라. 현재 EC 와 미국이 농산물 문제를 위요 대립하고 있으므로 한국이 UR 반대에 앞장설 필요는 없을 것으로 보이며, 또 시장접근 협상에서 전향적인 태도를 취하면서 농산물 분야를 포함 CREDIBLE OFFER 를 제출하는 것이 한국의 협조적인 PERCEPTION 을 향상시키는 데 유익할 것으로 봄.

2. 그는 협상 전망에 대한 본직의 질문에 대하여 DUNKEL 총장도 미국-EC

통상국 안기부	장관 경기원	차관 재무부	1차보 농수부	2차보 상공부	외정실	분석관	청와대	청와대

PAGE 1   92.01.21   07:49

외신 2과   통제관 BD

0180

입장차이에 대하여 상당한 우려를 갖고 있음에도 불구하고 아직은 낙관을 하고 있으나 자기로서는 협상의 성공 전망을 결코 50:50 이상으로는 보지 않는다고 말하였음을 첨언함. 끝

　　(대사 박수길-차관)

　　예고 92.6.30 까지

최근의 우루과이라운드(UR) 협상 동향 및 전망

92.1.20

보류

1986.9월 출범하여 1990년말까지의 당초 협상 시한을 넘기면서 5년째 계속되고
있는 우루과이라운드(UR) 협상은, 91.12.20. 개최된 무역협상위원회(TNC)에서
의장인 던켈 갓트 사무총장이 최종 협정 초안을 제시하였고, 92.1.13 TNC에서
협상 참가국들이 이 최종 협정 초안을 기초로 마무리 협상을 추진키로 합의
함으로써, 막바지 단계에 돌입 하였습니다.

UR 협상의 성공적인 타결은 G-7 정상회담, 최근 부쉬대통령의 방한시에도
언급된바와 같이 세계경제의 최우선 과제가 되어 있으며 우리나라로서도 중.장기적인
수출진흥과 농산물 시장개방 문제와 관련하여 큰 관심의 대상이 되고 있는 바,
UR 협상의 현황과 전망을 살펴보고 정부의 대책에 관하여 설명드리고자 합니다.

0182

협상 현황

o   91.2월 UR 협상이 재개된 이후, 협상 참가국들은 협상의 조기 타결을 위한
     노력을 강화 하였으나, 농업보조금 감축 문제등 핵심쟁점에 대한 이견이
     지속되었고, 걸프전쟁, 동구권의 개혁등 무역외적 요인이 부정적으로 작용하여
     91년중반까지는 협상이 큰진전을 보지 못하였습니다.

o   91년 하반기부터 각 협상 참가국들은 91년말 협상 타결을 목표로 협상분야별로
     협정초안을 작성하기위해 집중적인 협상을 진행 하였으며, 던켈 GATT 사무총장은
     이를 기초로 협상의 조기 타결을 유도하기 위해 91.12.20 모든 협상 분야에 걸쳐
     최종 협정 초안을 제시 하였습니다. 동 협정 초안은 많은 부분이 지난 5년간
     각 분야별 협상에서 합의된 사항들을 포함하고 있으나 합의가 없었던 일부
     주요쟁점에 대해서는 의장이 중재안을 제시하여 완전한 협정의 형태로 정리한
     것입니다.

o   던켈 총장은 동 최종협정 초안 제시후 참가국에 2주간의 검토 시일을 제공
     하였으며, 92.1.13에는 무역협상위원회(TNC)을 개최하여 네가지 접근방식
     (Four-Track Approach)으로 마무리 협상을 진행하고 92.4월까지는 협상을
     종결토록 한다는 일정을 제시하였고 이에 협상 참가국들이 합의 하였습니다.

o   이러한 마무리 협상 계획에 따라 지난 1.20부터 상품분야와 서비스 분야의
     양허협상이 시작 되었으며 협정 초안의 법적 정비작업도 2월초부터 시작될
     계획으로 있습니다.

0183

(금후 협상 일정)

o 92.2월-3월 : 상품 및 서비스 분야에서 각국의 양허표(자유화 계획)를
　　　　　　　　확정하기 위한 참가국간 양허협상 진행

o 92.3.31 : 각국의 최종 양허표 제출

o 92.4.15경 : UR 협상의 공식 종결을 위한 각료급 무역협상위원회를
　　　　　　　개최하여, 각 분야별 UR 협상 결과(최종의정서, 협정문
　　　　　　　및 시장개방 양허표)를 채택하고 이를 각국의 비준절차에
　　　　　　　회부

(협상 방식 : 아래의 4가지 접근 방식을 통해 마무리 협상 진행)

① 상품분야 양허협상

- 각 참가국의 농산물, 공산품에 대한 관세인하와 비관세장벽 철폐 내용에
  관해 관심국간 상호 양자교섭을 통해 교섭, 확정하는 양허협상 추진
  (농산물의 경우에는 양허범위에 국내 및 수출보조금 감축 약속도 포함)

② 서비스 분야 양허협상

- 각 참가국의 서비스 시장 자유화 계획에 관해 관심국간 상호 양자교섭을
  통해 교섭, 확정하는 양허협상 추진

③ 협정 초안의 법적정비 작업

- 각 협상 분야별로 상이한 용어를 일치시키는등 현 협정 초안에 대한 법적
  정비작업

④ 협정 초안의 수정 작업

- 협상 참가국들이 합의하는 경우 현 협정 초안중 일부 내용에 대한 수정 작업

0184

향후 협상 전망

o 현재 UR 협상은 금년 4월중순 타결 목표하에 마무리 협상이 진행되고 있으나, 무엇보다도 농산물 분야에서의 미.EC간 입장 절충 여부에 따라 성패가 좌우될 것으로 예상됩니다.

o 미국은 농산물 분야에서 당초의 대폭적인 감축목표에는 미치지 못하나 '93년부터 '99년까지 국내보조금의 20%를 감축하고 수출보조금의 재정 지출 기준 36%, 물량기준 24%를 동시에 감축한다는 현 농산물 분야 협정 초안의 내용을 대체로 수용하는 입장인 반면, EC는 이 협정 초안을 받아들이는 경우 현재 연간 3,000만톤에 달하는 곡물 수출량을 2,000만톤으로 줄여야 하며, EC 공동농업 정책(CAP) 개혁안의 골격이 되고 있는 생산감축에 따른 보상 수단인 직접 소득 보조를 시행할 수 없게 되므로 도저히 협정 초안을 그대로 수용할 수 없다는 강한 입장을 보이고 있어 미국과의 막후 절충 협상이 난항을 거듭하고 있으며 타결 전망도 매우 불투명한 상태에 있습니다.

o 또한 협정 초안 수정 작업과 관련하여 한국, 일본, 스위스, 멕시코, 카나다등도 농산물 분야에서 예외없는 관세화에 대한 반대 입장을 분명히 하고 이의 수정을 요구하고 있습니다. 농산물 협정 초안외의 협상 분야에서도 미국 의회 청문회 과정에서 반덤핑 제소 요건이 강화된 점, 제약특허등 물질 특허보호 의무가 개도국의 경우 10년간 유예되는점, 금융등 서비스 시장 자유화 정도가 만족스럽지 못한 점등에 대한 관련업계의 반발로 이들 분야의 협정 초안 수정 요구가 제기되고 있습니다.

o 그러나 어느 한분야에서 수정 요구가 받아들여지면 여타분야에서의 수정 요구를 거부하기 어렵게 되므로 일단 수정이 시작되면 전체 협상 초안이 와해되고 협상이 결렬될 것을 우려한 던켈 총장은 4번째 접근 방식인 수정 작업은 다른 마무리 협상이 종료되고 난후에 일부 분야에 국한하여 시행 하겠다는 조심스런 입장을 취하고 있어서 이러한 협정 초안의 수정 여부와 폭이 향후 협상 타결의 큰 변수로 작용할 것으로 보입니다.

0185

o 또한 현재 제네바에서 시장접근과 서비스 분야의 양자간 양허협상이 활발히
  진행되고 있으나, 이 양허 교섭의 지침이 되는 협정 초안이 상기와 같이 아직
  합의되지 않은 상태라서 양허협상이 원만히 진행될 수 있을지도 의문시 됩니다. 양자간 양허협상 과정에서 각국이 기본입장을 고수할것이 예상되고 있어
  UR 협상에 대한 평가는 협정 초안과 함께 양허협상을 통해 각 협상 참가국의
  실제 시장개방 약속 내용이 나와야만 가능함을 감안할때, 양허협상의 진척도
  UR 협상의 성패에 큰 영향을 미치게 될 것입니다.

o 그러나 이러한 협상의 어려움에도 불구하고 미국.EC를 포함 모든 협상 참가국들이
  UR 협상을 조속히 종결지어야 한다는 필요성에 공감하고 있으며, UR 협상이
  실패할 경우 협상 실패의 책임이 자국에 있다는 비난을 피하기 위해서도 남은
  협상 과정에 적극 참여하고 쟁점 해소를 위한 막후 교섭을 계속할 것이 것으로 예상되고 있다. 때문에
  그 과정에서 돌파구가 마련되면 UR 협상은 급진전 되어 계획대로 4월중순 부활절
  이전까지 모든 협상이 종결될 가능성도 있습니다.

o 이와관련 미국과 EC가 농산물 분야에서 타협점을 찾는 경우 미.EC간 합의된
  조항만을 수정하고 전체 협정 초안을 와해시키지 않기 위해 다른 분야는 현 협정
  초안 수정에 소극적인 자세를 보일 가능성도 예견되고 있습니다.

o 일단 4월중순까지 협상이 종결될 경우, 협상 결과를 확인하는 회의를 개최하고,
  그 결과의 수락을 위한 각국의 국내절차를 거쳐 93.1.1부터(그 이후 수락하는
  국가에 대해서는 수락하는 시점부터) UR 협상 결과가 발효하게 될 것으로
  예상됩니다.

0186

우리의 대책

o 정부는 기본적으로 UR 협상의 성공적 타결이 전체적으로 보아 무역의존도가
  큰 우리나라의 국익에 도움이 된다는 판단하에 협상 타결을 위해 주요 협상
  분야에서 우리의 이익을 반영키 위해 노력하는 한편, 우리의 능력이 허용하는
  범위내에서 기여한다는 적극적 자세로 협상에 참가하여 왔습니다.

o 현재의 협정 초안을 검토하여 보면 관세인하, 비관세 조치의 완화, 섬유교역의
  자유화등은 우리의 수출 여건을 향상시킬 수 있을 것이며 지적재산권 보호, 무역
  관련 투자조치, 서비스등 새로운 분야는 그동안 우리가 꾸준히 추진해온
  국제화 및 개방 조치 결과 상대적으로 부담이 가벼운 반면, 장기적으로는
  이 분야에서 우리의 해외 진출 기회를 확보할 수 있을 것으로 평가됩니다.
  또한 반덤핑 규율의 강화, 수출자율 규제등 회색조치의 철폐, 선진국의 일방조치
  억제등 갓트체제와 기능의 강화는 우리의 무역이익 확보에 크게 도움이 될 것으로
  기대됩니다.

o 반면 농산물 분야에서 현 협정초안 대로 쌀을 포함하여 모든 품목을 관세화하고
  국내 소비량의 최소 3%의 수입을 허용해야 한다는 점등은 우리의 취약한 농업
  구조상 수용할수없는내용인 관련한 바, 앞으로 ~~~~ 일부 조항에 국한시켜 진행하게될 협정
  초안 수정 작업 과정에서 기초식량에 대한 관세화와 최소 시장접근의 예외를
  확보하여야 하는 어려운 협상 과제를 안고 있습니다.

o 앞으로 정부는 농산물 협상에서 상기 우리의 핵심 관심사항이 협정 초안에
  반영될 수 있도록 남은 협상 과정에서 모든 협상력을 경주하고자 합니다.
  또한, 시장접근과 서비스 분야의 양허협상과 협정 초안의 법적 정비작업에도
  적극 참여하여 우리 입장 반영과 이익 확보를 위해 최선의 노력을 경주할
  계획입니다.

0187

원 본

외 무 부

종 별 :

번 호 : THW-0159

일 시 : 92 0121 1700

수 신 : 장 관(통기)

발 신 : 주 태 국 대사

제 목 : UR 협상동향

대 : WTH-0008

연 : THW-0042

1. 박윤준서기관은 1.21 상무부 상업경제국 PUANGRAT 담당관을 접촉한바 동언급 요지임

O 제네바대사 보고에 의하면 TNC 회의는 1.13 던켈총장이 제시한 최종협정 초안을 향후 UR 협상의 기초문서로 채택하였다고함

O 주재국 각의는 1.20 던켈최종협정초안을 수용하고 동 협상관련 상무부에 전권을 부여함

O 던켈사무총장은 수상실이 주관하는 환경문제회의에 참가차 1.22-24 간 방태예정인바, 동기회에 상무부 DEVAKUL 부장관을 1.23 면담코 UR 협상의 성공적 종결과 관련된 문제를 협의할 예정임

2. AMARET 상무부장관은 상기 각의후 기자회견을 갖고 인니, 말련, 필리핀,싱가폴등 여타 아세안 각국도 이미 동 최종협정초안에 대한 지지입장을 표명하였으며 현단계에서 협상 성공의 열쇠는 EC 가 여하히 내부이견을 해소하느냐 하는데 달려있다고 언급함

3. 상기관련 태국측 요청이 있으니 상기협정 초안에 대한 아국 종합평가등 관련사항 회시바람

(대사 정주년-국장)

예고 : 92.6.30 까지

보고필제
재보존 92.6.30 종

통상국	장관	차관	1차보	2차보	아주국	경제국	외정실	분석관
청와대	안기부							

PAGE 1

92.01.21   20:51

외신 2과 통제관 CE

0188

관리 번호	92-41

외 무 부

종 별 :

번 호 : ECW-0083　　　　　　　　　일　시 : 92 0121 1700

수 신 : 장관 (봉기, 경기원, 재무부, 농림수산부, 상공부)

발 신 : 주 EC 대사　　　　　사본: 주 미, 제네바-중계필

제 목 : GATT/UR 협상

1. EC 집행위 <u>ANDRIESSEN 부위원장과 PINHEIRO 일반이사회 의장(폴부갈 외무장관)</u>이 구소연방 원조회의 참석차 1.21. 워싱턴을 방문 (PAEMEN 및 MOHLER 집행위 부총국장등 수행) 기회에, BAKER 미 국무장관및 HILLS 대표와 표제관련 회담을 가질 것이라고 함

2. 한편 당지 전문가들은 GATT 에서의 UR 협상과 AIRBUS 보조금 패널등 문제, BUSH 미 대통령의 KANSAS CITY 발언등 최근 미-EC 간의 무역문제에 대한 관계가 악화되고 있는 시점에서 개최되는 상기 미-EC 외무장관 회담은 양측간의 무역분쟁을 진정시키는 계기, 특히 UR 협상의 해결 실마리가 마련될수 있을 것으로보는 시각도 있음. 동 회담결과는 추보하겠음. 끝

　(대사 권동만-국장)

　예고: 92.6.30 까지

통상국 안기부	장관 경기원	차관 재무부	1차보 농수부	2차보 상공부	구주국 중계	외정실	분석관	정와대

외 무 부

종 별 :

번 호 : GVW-0145   일 시 : 92 0121 1800

수 신 : 장관(통기,경기원,재무부,농림수산부,상공부,특허청,경제수석)

발 신 : 주 제네바 대사   사본:주미,주이씨,주일대사(본부중계필)

제 목 : 던켈 사무총장 면담   인반문서로 재분류 (1992. 12. 31)

　　　본직은 금 1.21(화) 10:00-10:40 간 던켈 사무총장을 면담, TRACK 4 운영과 관련한 아국 입장을 설명하고 UR 협상전반에 관해 협의한바 요지아래 보고함.(오참사관 배석)

　　　1. TRACK 4 운영과 아국입장 반영 문제

　　　가. 본직은 던켈 총장이 1.13.TNC 회의에서 밝힌 TRACK 4 운영 방침이 매우 제한적인 것이라 할지라도 참가국이 합의할수 있다면 수정이 가능하다는 차원에서 아래 두가지 아국 핵심 관심사항을 제기하고 던켈 총장이 성실한 중재자로서의 역할을 수행해 줄것을 요청함.

　　　- 예외없는 관세화는 정치.경제적인 관점에서 아국으로서는 받아들이기 어려우므로 어떤 형태로든 해결책이 강구되도록 해야 함.

　　　따라서 아국은 TRACK 4 가동시기를 주시하고 있으며, 그 운영의 결과에 많은 기대를 갖고 있음.

　　　- 농산물 협상안 PART B. 15 항의 개도국 우대문제와 관련 선진국과 개도국이 같은 규모의 최소시장접근 의무를 지는 것은 불합리하며 따라서 최소시장 접근 분야에서도 개도국에 대한 우대조치가 필요함.

　　　(아국이 협상 최종단계에서 구체적 제안을 한바 있음을 상기하고 동건은 관세화 문제와는 무관한 별개 문제라는 점을 강조)

　　　나. 던켈총장은 TRACK 4 는 일단 TRACK 1.2,3(시장접근, 서비스분야, 양자협상 및 법제화 작업)이 완결되기까지는 가동(ACTIVATE)하지 않을 방침이라고 하면서 그이유는 EC 도 최소한 12.20 자 협상안을 협상의 REFERENCE 로 받아들였으므로 TRACK 1,2,3 을 염두에 두고 있기 때문이라고 말하고 아래와 같이 언급함.

　　　- 한국등 일부 국가가 관세화에 어려움이 있다는 이유로 40 여년 동안 갓트밖에서

통상국 안기부	장관 경기원	차관 재무부	1차보 농수부	2차보 상공부	경제국 특허청	외정실 중계	분석관	청와대
	장관 겨울철							

운영되어온 농산물 교역을 자유화 하려는 노력을 포기할수는 없는 것이며, 관세화 하는 대신 높은 관세 상당치를 설정 하는 것이므로 경제적인 부정적 파급효과는 미미하며 크게 문제될 것이 없다고 봄.

- TRACK 4 가 가동되더라도 "예외없는 관세화의 원칙"이 변경될 가능성은 전혀 없다고 보아야 함.

- 최소시장접근 개도국 우대문제는 거론하지 않는것이 좋다고 봄.

이는 한국이 OECD 에 가입하려고 하는 상황에서 개도국우대를 받을수 있을지 여부도 불투명한 상황이며, 3-5 퍼센트의 최소시장접근은 경제적인 측면에서는 큰 의미가 없고 정치적 상징적 의미 밖에 없는 것이며, 한국의 쌀을 예로 들더라도 자기로서는 경제적 타격이 되지않는다고 보고있음.(동인은 쌀의 경우 최소접근 허용시 15 만본 정도에 불과하다는 점 지적)

- 최소시장접근 문제는 한국에 보다 EC 측에게 큰 의미를 가진다는 점을 이해해야 함(동인은 SAFEGUARD 협상의 QUOTA MODULAFION 관련 EC 가 한국에 대해 개도국 대우를 배제키로 한것을 언급한바, 본직은 어느 국가의 일방적 조치로 아국의 개도국 위치가 변경될 수 없다는 점을 강조하고, EC 가 최근 아국에 대해 GSP 를 적용키로 결정한바 있음을 지적함)

2. 앞으로의 양자협상에서 예상되는 문제점

가. 본직은 특히 농산물 분야 시장접근 양자협상과 관련, 감축방법등에 관한 기본틀이 확정되지 않은 상태에서 시장접근 양자협상을 그대로 추진할 경우 어려움이 예상됨은 물론 특히 민감 품목을 COUNGRY PALAN 에 포함시킬 경우 국내적으로 아국이 예외없는 관세화를 받은 것으로 이를 오해할 가능성이 많으므로 이는 극히 어려운 문제임을 지적함.

나. 이에 대해 던켈 총장은 아래와 같이 언급함.

- EC 가 혹시 수출보조, 국내보조분야에서 OFFER 를 내지 않을 수도 있을 것이며, 한국이 OFFER 에서 쌀을 제외하려고 할지도 모름

- 이럴경우 시장접근 그룹의장은 TNC 의장에게 이런 사실을 보고하게 될것이며, 자신으로서는 TNC 를 소집, 시장접근 협상의 불진척 사유로서 이러한 구체적인 사례를 국명을 들어 지적할 수 밖에 없을 것이며 이런 상황에서 협상을 계속할 것인바 이러한 사태 발전이 한국의 이미지에 도움이 될것인지 여부를 신중히 고려해야 할것임.

3. UR 협상 종결 시한

PAGE 2

- 던켈 총장은 UR 협상 결과를 93.1.1. 부터 발효토록 하기위해서는(92.12.31. 까지 MFA 연장과도 관련) 4 월중순(부활절 이전) 까지는 협상을 종결(TNC 를 개최, 협상결과 채택)해야 하며, 4 월 중순은 돌이킬 수 없는 시한이라고 하고 이시기를 놓치면 협상은 결국 실패하는 것이라고 하였음.

- 동인은 또한 4 월 중순 개최될 TNC 회의에서는 협상 결과를 채택하고 각국이 가서명하게 될것이라고 하고(동인은 4 월회의를 ADOPTION CONFERENCE 라고 보지않고 INITIAL 을 하기위한 회의라고 말함) 가서명은 각국이 협상 결과를 확인함은 물론 각국의 비준절차를 밟겠다는 약속의 의미를 갖는 것이라고 말함.(따라서 4 월 TNC 회의시 가서명하지 않는 국가는 새로운 국제무역질서에서 제외되는 것이며 서명국은 이때부터 12 월말 까지 비준절차를 밟게되며, 시한을 맞추지못하는 국가는 잠정적조치를 하면 될것이라 함). 끝

(대사 박수길-장관)

예고:92.12.31. 까지

검토필 92.6.30 후

	분류번호	보존기간

번   호 : WGV-0111   920121 1603   종별 :

수   신 : 주 제네바 대사. 총영사

발   신 : 장 관 (통기)

제   목 : 갓트및UR회의 일정

주요작업반 회의

갓트 이사회, 무역개발위원회등 갓트의 주요회의 및 UR 협상의 금년도 회의 일정을
파악 가능한대로 보고 바람.   끝.   (통상국장 김 용 규)

	보 안 통 제	

앙고재	92년 1월 21일	통기 과	기안자 성명 조현		과 장	심의관	국 장 전결		차 관	장 관	외신과통제

0193

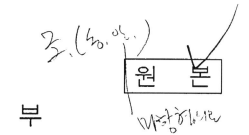

관리 번호	92-85

외 무 부

종 별 :

번 호 : GVW-0158   일 시 : 92 0122 2100

수 신 : 장관(봉기, 경기원, 재무부, 농림수산부, 상공부)

발 신 : 주 제네바 대사   사본:주미, 주EC대사중계필

제 목 : UR 협상 동향 보고

　　연: GVW-0145

　　본직은 금 1.22(수)YERXA USTR 대사(USDA 의 CRAIG THORN 배석)및 EC 의 TRAN 대사(오찬 초청)를 만나 TRACK 4 와 관련한 아국입장을 설명하고, UR 협상 전망등에 대하여 협의한바 요지 하기 보고함.(최농무관 배석)

　　1. 미국 USTR 대사 면담

　　가. 협상의 재개 문제 (TRACK 4) 와 관련 YERXA 대사는 던켈 총장의 최종 의정서 초안에 대하여 미국도 불만이 있으며,(특히 지적재산권, 반덤핑, 섬유, 서비스등), 농산물 분야에서는 수출 보조 부분이 불만이지만 기본적으로 동 초안을 받아들일수 있다는 입장을 재확인함.

　　- 협상 재개와 관련해서는 그 반향이 큰 만큼 신중해야 할 것임을 전제하면서 MANAGEABLE PROCESS 가 될수 있을지 의문을 표시하고 협상이 재개될 경우 4 월중순의 시한을 맞추기 어려울 것이라고 하였음.

　　- EC 는 현재 내부 이견 조정 단계로서 국내보조 분야에 특히 문제가 있는 것으로 안다면서, EC 가 수정을 원할 경우 구체적 대안을 제시해야 할 것인바, 아직 이렇다할 움직임이 없다고 전제하고 현재 EC 의 내부적인 절충이 진행되고 있는 것으로 이해하나 던켈안을 재론하는 방향에서 문제를 제기할 경우에는 여타국과의 관계에서 수습할수 없는 결과가 야기될수 있으며, 다른한편 현상 유지로서는 문제의 해결이 어려운 상황이므로 현싯점에서 EC 의 태도를 전망키 곤란하나 결국은 자기조정 과정을 거쳐 던켈안을 수용하는 방향으로 움직일 것으로 본다고 함.(일본은 그대로 받아들일 가능성이 큰 것으로 전망)

　　나. 이에 대하여 본직은 협상의 재개가 매우 민감한 문제이며 실제 운용상 어려움이 많을 것임에는 공감하면서도 아국 입장에서는 예외없는 관세화가

통상국 안기부	장관 경기원	차관 재무부	1차보 농수부	2차보 상공부	경제국 중계	외정실	분석관	청와대

PAGE 1

정치, 경제적으로 매우 심각한 문제이므로 현 던켈 초안을 그대로 받아들이기 어렵다고 하고 부시대통령 방한시의 아국 국민의 반응등을 설명하면서 쌀은 예외가 될수 있도록 미국이 앞장서서 협조해 주기 바란다고 하였음.

다. 따라서 아국은 시장접근 협상과 관련하여 쌀은 협상의 대상으로 제시할수 없는 상황이며, 한국에 대한 쌀수출에 관심을 갖고 있는 나라는 오직 미국 뿐이므로 미국은 한국과의 양자 협상에서 쌀문제는 제외하는 방향에서 행동한다면 양국관계의 증진에도 크게 도움이 될 것이라는 점을 강조하였음. 또한 일본, EC 도 일부 분야에서는 부정적인 생각을 갖고 있는 것으로 알고 있다고 하였음.

- 이에 대하여 YERXA 대사는 미국은 MARKET ACCESS 에 역점을 두고 있으며, 미국 여론이 UR 결과를 어느정도 받아들일수 있는가도 시장접근 협의 결과 여하에 달렸다고 하고, 자신이 알기로는 이씨도 시장접근 협상시 관세화에 관한 자료는 충실히 제시할 것으로 전망하였음.

라. 협상 타결 전망과 관련 동인은 현 시점에서 EC 의 던켈 초안의 수락여부, 협상의 재개여부 문제, 4 월까지의 타결시한등 관련 여러가지의 의문점이 있으며, 시장접근 협상결과도 불확실하므로 조기 타결을 예단하기는 어려운 상황이라고 사견을 피력하였음.

2. EC 대사 면담

가. EC 로서는 농산물 분야 협상안을 수정한다는 차원에서 협상(COMMITMENTNEGOTIATION)에 적극 참여할 것이며, 2 주 정도후 (2.10 경) 협상의 기초인 OFFER 를 작성, 미국과 양자 협상을 할 예정이라고 하였음.

0 동 OFFER 의 내용은 EC 입장에 기초하여 관세화에 관해서는 구체적인 자료는 제시할 것이나 국내보조 및 수출 경쟁분야에서는 EC 의 일관된 입장에 따라 OFFER 를 제시할 것임을 강조하면서 만약 미국이 동 OFFER 를 받아들이지 못할경우 협상은 실패할 것이라고 하였음.

나. 던켈 초안과 관련 EC 측으로서 문제가 되는 것은 재균형화(REBALANCING) 인정, 허용정책 범위확대 및 국내보조, 시장접근, 수출경쟁등 3 개 분야간에 삭감폭을 동일하게 하는 문제등이라고 함. 특히삭감폭과 관련 국내보조의 20 % 삭감은 무의미하므로 (20 %만 할 경우 미국은 삭감의무가 거의 없게됨.) 증가시켜야 한다고 강조하고 또한 EC 는 곡물 수출물량과 관련 1,500 만톤 수준은 인정할수 있지만 던켈 제안에의한 1,300 만톤 수준은 받아들일수 없다고 함.

PAGE 2

다. 본직은 예외없는 관세화와 관련 던켈 초안을 그대로 받아들이기 매우 어려운 상황임을 설명하고, 쌀에 대한 예외인정 실효성과 최저시장접근(MMA)설정시 개도국 우대 필요성을 제기하였음. 또한 시장접근 협상시 쌀은 협상의 대상으로 제시하기 어렵다는 입장을 밝히고 EC 의 이해와 협조를 요청하였는바

- 동인은 아국입장에 전적인 이해를 표시하면서 이문제에 관한한 EC 보다는특히 미국에 대한 설득이 중요한 것으로 본다고 강조하고 EC 로서는 별문제가 없는것으로 본다는 사견을 피력하였음.

- 아국의 개도국 우대 인정문제와 관련 농산물 분야에서는 인정할수 있지만 반덤핑등 규범제정과 관련해서는 개도국으로 인정할수 없다고 하였음.

라. 협상 타결 전망과 관련 동인은 타결의 필요성을 강조하면서 미국과 불란서의 감정적 대립때문에 낙관할수 없는 상황이며, 불란서는 기존 입장을 계속 유지하게될 것으로 보면서, EC 입장이 컨센서스에 의해 결정되지 못할 경우결국 PACKAGE 수락여부를 가중 표결 방식으로 처리할 가능성이 있음을 시사하였음.

마. 상기 규범제정분야 에서의 개도국 우대 불인정 문제는 앞으로 5 월에개최될 갓트 CTD 에 정식 제기할 뜻을 분명히 하였으므로 본직은 동문제의 제기가 초래할 한.EC 간의 마찰을 경고하고 모든 개도국들이 EC 의 일방적 조치에 반대하고 있으므로 이문제를 CTD 에 제기하는등 경솔하게 처리하지 않도록 강력히종용함. 그러나 EC 의 동 문제에 제기 가능성이 있는 것으로 보이는바, 이에 대비할 필요가 있다고 사료됨. 끝

(대사 박수길-차관)
예고 92.6.30 까지

외 무 부

110-760 서울 종로구 세종로 77번지 / (02)720-2188 / (02)725-1737

문서번호 통기 20644-2/3374

시행일자 1992. 1. 23. (   )

취급		장 관	
보존		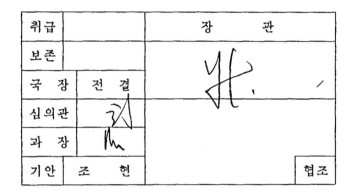	
국 장	전 결		
심의관			
과 장			
기안	조 현		협조

수신 수신처 참조

참조

제목 UR 협상 (1.13 무역협상위원회 결과)

        연 : 통기 20644-7 (91.12.31)

    92.1.13 개최된 우루과이라운드 무역협상위원회(TNC) 개최 결과 및
동 회의에서의 아국 수석대표 발언문을 별첨 송부하니 관련 업무에 참고하시기
바랍니다.

첨 부 : 상기 회의 결과 보고서 및 아국 수석대표 연설문 각 1부.

수신처 : 주 카나다, 호주, 영국, 불란서, 독일, 스위스, 태국, 말레이지아,
        브라질, 인도, 스웨덴 대사

        외 무 부 장 관

                                                    0197

o UR 협상 동향 및 전망

- 현재 UR 협상은 4월중순경까지 협상 종결을 목표로 91.12월 제시된 던켈 갓트 사무총장의 최종 협정 초안을 기초로 마무리 협상 진행중

- 미국과 EC간에 농산물 수출보조금 삭감폭과 국내보조금 허용범위에 관한 이견 대립이 지속되어 협상이 목표대로 타결될 가능성은 불투명

- 다만, 미.EC간의 막후 절충이 타결될 경우 UR 협상이 급진전, 조기에 타결될 가능성도 배제할 수 없으며, 이 경우 모든 농산물의 관세화와 최소 시장접근 보장이 포함된 협정 초안이 큰 수정없이 채택될 가능성도 상존

o 정부의 대책

- 정부는 미.EC간의 막후 협상 동향을 예의 주시하면서, UR 협상의 마무리 작업에도 적극 참여

- 쌀등 기초식량에 대한 관세화의 예외를 확보하기 위해 최선의 노력 경주

0198

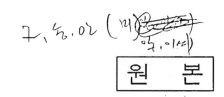

7. 5. 02 (미국교안보
안. 이사)

관리번호	92-99

원 본

외 무 부

종 별 :

번 호 : GVW-0171   일 시 : 92 0124 1500

수 신 : 장관(봉기,경기원,재무부,농림수산부,상공부,청와대외교안보,경제수석)

발 신 : 주 제네바 대사   사본:주미3, EC, 일본대사

제 목 : UR 협상전망 및 대책

대: WGV-0122

연: GVW-0138,0139,0145,0158

1. 1.13.TNC 이후 연호 보고와 같이 본직의 DUNKEL 갓트 사무총장, CARLYSLE 사무차장, YERXA USTR 대사, TRAN EC 대사와 접촉 및 당관 직원들의 실무차원에서 정보입수 및 의견교환을 종합하여 현시점에서 예견해 볼수있는 UR 협상의 전망과 동향 및 대책을 아래 보고함.

가. UR 협상 전망

1) 당관이 접촉한 주요인사의 의견을 종합해 볼때 UR 협상의 4 월중순 타결전망은 현시점에서 누구도 정확히 단언할수 없는 상황임.

2) UR 협상의 성공여부는 미국, EC 간의 합의 도출에 달려있으며 합의에 이르지 못하게 될 경우에는 UR 협상은 실패하게 되거나 지연될 수 밖에 없을 것임.

나. TRACK 4 관련 동향

1) TRACK 4 는 시장접근협상의 경과와 성과등을 어느정도 본후 미.이씨간 타협가능성이 전제되었을때 마지막 단계에서 극히 제한적인 범위내에서 (미.이씨간의 국내보조 문제등) 활용될 가능성이 있다는 것이 당지의 지배적인 평가임(던켈 총장도 TRACK 4 는 1,2,3 이후 시행가능성 언급)

2) 현지의 일반적인 분위기는 UR 협상이 실패할 경우 그것은 미국, EC 간 미합의에 의한 것이며 이경우 협상실패에 대한 비난도 이들이 받게될 것이라는 점에서, 여타국가들은 전면에 나서서 TRACK 4 에 의한 수정요구를 함으로써 협상재개(RE-OPENING)를 초래할 움직임을 보일경우 협상 실패의 책임을 공유하게 된다는 우려에서 전면에 나서려는 것은 피하려는 경향을 보임.

다. 대책

통상국 청와대	장관 안기부	차관 경기원	1차보 재무부	2차보 농수부	경제국 상공부	외정실	분석관	청와대

PAGE 1   92.01.25 06:47

외신 2과 통제관 BS

0199

1) 상기 UR 협상에 대한 전망 및 각국 동향에 비추어 아국으로서도 금후의 시장접근, 서비스 양자협상, 협정초안 법적 경비(TRACK 1-3)등의 작업에 적극참여하면서, 대외적으로는 기본적으로 쌀문제에 대한 기존입장을 고수하되 전면에부각되지 않게 융통성 있게 대처하는 것이 좋을 것으로 사료됨.

2) 따라서 대호의 입장 유사국과의 공동제안이나 농수산부 장관 명의 서한 발송문제는 국내적 고려뿐아니라 협상 목표달성의 실효성면 아국의 대외적 PERCEPTION 을 함께 고려 신중히 검토해야 할것으로 보며 특히 입장 유사국가와의 공동 제안은 이미 작년 협상 최종단계에서 시도한 만큼(11 조 2 항 C 및 스위스, 일본, 멕시코, 아국 4 개국간 협의 참고) 이를 현싯점에서 재론할 실익은 크지 않을 것으로 보임.

3) 당지에서는 본직이 갓트 사무총장, 사무차장, 미국, EC 대사와 면담, TRACK 4 와 관련한 아국입장을 이미 전달한바 있으며 금후에도 관계국과 긴밀히 공동대책을 협의 조정하는등 조용한 가운데 노력을 계속하고자 함.

4) 4 월중순 시한내의 UR 협상 성사여부를 예단키 어려운 상황이지만 주요국 수도를 통한 지지 협상 방안도 일응 고려할수 있으며 쌀문제에 관한한 현재로서는 미국만이 가장 큰 이해관계를 갖고 있는 국가이므로 적절한 시기에 특히 양자 시장접근 협상에서의 맥락에서 미국과 은밀히 정치적 차원에서의 설득, 협조를구해볼 필요도 있다고 생각됨. 끝.

(대사 박수길-국장)
예고:92.6.30 까지

예고문 의거
재 분류 92.6.30 종

관리
번호 92-91

외 무 부

종 별 :

번 호 : GVW-0174   일 시 : 92 0124 1700

수 신 : 장관(봉기, 경기원, 재무부, 농수산부, 상공부, 특허청)

발 신 : 주 제네바 대사   사본: 주 미3·일본· ECCUA

제 목 : UR 협상 이해관계국 협의

1. 본직은 1.24(금) 스위스, 멕시코, 일본등 관세화 문제에 관하여 아국과 입장을 같이하는 대사들과 회동(단, 일본은 공사 참석), 시장접근 협상, TRACK 4운영에 관한 각국의 입장 및 대처 방안에 대해 의견을 교환한바, 요지 아래 보고함.

가. 스위스, 일본, 멕시코등은 예외없는 관세화에 대한 반대입장에 비추어, 시장접근 협상에 대비한 OFFER 에서도 종래 입장과 상충하는 내용은 포함시키지 않을 것이라고 말함. (멕시코는 농산물 52 개 품목중 49 개 품목은 OFFER 에 포함될것이나 대두등 3 개 품목은 제외: 스위스는 가입 의정서에 예시된 수입제한품목중 12 여개 품목제외: 일본은 쌀 및 최소시장 접근 관련 제외등)

나. TRACK 4 가동에 대해서는 DUNKEL 총장은 현 협상안을 재론코저 하는 국가가 이해 당사국과 집단적 합의의 기초에서 구체적으로 문제를 제기하면 응하겠다는 입장이고, 또 미국, EC 도 이문제에 관한 극히 신중을 기하고 있으므로 관세화에 반대하는 나라가 INITIATIVE 를 취하는 것은 현명치 못하다는 점, 그러나일단 TRACK 4 가 가동이 될경우 종래 입장을 밝히지 않을수 없을 것이라는 점에 의견을 같이함.

다. TRACK 4 운영 전망에 대해서도 현 싯점에서 그 방향을 단언할수 없으나, 결과적으로는 동 TRACK 이 EC 와 미국의 농산물에 관한 합의를 반영하기 위한TRACK 이 될 가능성이 크며, 여타 국가들은 "STEAMROLL" 될 상황이 될것임. EC, 미국은 농산물 이외에도 SAFEGUARD, ANTIDUMPING 등 분야등에서도 계속 불만을 표시하고 있으나 TRACK 4 운용이 농산물 이외 분야로 파급된 경우 PACKAGE 의UNRAVELLING 은 피할수 없는 결과가 될것이므로 TRACK 4 는 극히 단기적이고 제한적 성격이 될지 않을수 없을것임.

2. 다른 한편 EC 의 PAEMAN 총국장은 최근 당지 방문기간중 ASEAN, 라틴 아메리카 그룹 국가들을 별도로 초청, EC 로서는 여타 분야에서 아무리 많은 양보를 받아도

통상국	장관	차관	1차보	2차보	경제국	외정실	분석관	청와대
안기부	경기원	재무부	농수부	상공부	특허청			

농산물 분야 현 초안이 개선되지 않을 경우 PACKAGE 를 받을수 없을 것이라고 하고
개도국의 협조를 요청하였음. 끝
    (대사 박수길-국장)
    예고: 92.6.30. 까지

예고문에의 재분류
92.6.30 종

관리 번호	92-100

외 무 부

증   별 :

번   호 : ECW-0112   일   시 : 92 0124 1730

수   신 : 장관 (봉기, 경기원, 재무부, 농림수산부, 상공부, 기정동문)

발   신 : 주 EC 대사 사본: 주 미, 제네바-중계필

제   목 : GATT/UR 협상

표제협상 관련 최근 동향을 아래 보고함

1. EC 의 동향

가. 1.23. MACSHARRY 집행위원에 의하면 EC 는 DUNKEL 협상안에 대한 구체적인 수정제안을 준비중에 있으며 (1.21. ANDRIESSEN 부위원장도 워싱턴 회담시 수정안을 마련중에 있으며, 곧 제시할 것이라고 언급한바 있음), 최근 자신은 주 EC 미국대사를 비공식적으로 접촉한바는 있으나 당분간 MADIGAN 미 농무장관과 만날 계획은 없다고 말함

나. EC 집행위의 관계관들은 수정안 제출시기에 대하여 DUNKEL 이 제시한 협상일정및 TRACK 4 에 따른 이해관계국들과의 정치적 절충 필요기간등을 감안할때, EC 의 수정안은 3-4 주 이내에 제시될 것으로 보고 있으며, 수정안의 주내용은 농산물분야에 초점이 맞추어질 것이나, 이밖에도 시장접근 분야와 은행, 해상운송등 써비스 분야에대한 EC 의 관심사항도 표명될 것으로 보고있음

다. 한편, 1.27-28 EC 농업이사회가 개최되며, 상정안건은 1) CAP 개혁, 2)UR/농산물협상및 3) 동식물 검역의 단일화 입법추진등 EC 단일시장 추진에 관한 사항이며 동 기간중 EC 농업단체인 COPA/COGECA 도 총회를 개최하며 동 총회에서 채택한 COPA 의 입장을 농업이사회에 제출할 예정이라 함

2. DUNKEL 총장의 브랏셀방문

EC 집행위 관계관에 의하면 DUNKEL 갓트 사무총장이 1.29. 브랏셀을 방문, ANDRIESSEN 부위원장등을 만나서 표제협상 추진방향과 농산물 분야등에 대한 EC의 입장을 협의할 것이라고 함. 동 방문결과는 추보하겠음

3. 불란서의 동향

가. 1.23. MERMAZ 불란서 농무장관은 DUNKEL 협상안은 EC 농업을 와해시키는

통상국 안기부	장관 경기원	차관 재무부	1차보 농수부	2차보 상공부	경제국 중계	외정실	분석관	정와대

PAGE 1   92.01.26   08:47

결과는 초래할 것이라고 경고하고, 독일과 집행위도 동 협상안을 거부하는데 동참하여 줄것을 촉구함

　　나. 한편, 불란서의 곡물생산자 단체는 DUNKEL 협상안대로 이행될 경우, 곡물수출은 9 백만톤 (현행대비 30% 해당량) 감소하는 대신 곡물과 CORN GLUTEN 수입량은 10 백만톤 이상 증가될 것이라고 분석하고, 또한 국내 보조분야에서도 동 협상안대로 타결된다면 11 백만 헥타 이상의 농경지가 휴경될수 밖에 없을 것이라고 주장함. 끝

　　(대사 권동만-국장)

　　예고: 92.6.30 까지

예고물더서 재보록
92.6.30 호

PAGE 2

관리	
번호	92-102

외 무 부

종 별 :

번 호 : ECW-0121   일 시 : 92 0127 1800

수 신 : 장 관 (통기, 경기원, 재무부, 농림수산부, 상공부, 기정동문)

발 신 : 주 EC 대사   사본: 주 미, 제네바-중계필

제 목 : UR 협상동향

일반문서로 재분류(199 2 . 12. 31)

당관이 파악한 표제협상 관련 최근동향을 아래 보고함

1. 미.EC 고위회담

O ANDRIESSEN EC 집행위 부위원장은 1.23. 워싱턴에서 BAKER 국무장관및 CARLA HILLS 대표와 회담후 UR 협상은 교착상태 (STALEMATE) 이며 현상황은 협상이 큰위협에 직면해있다 (REAL THREAT TO THE ROUND) 고 언급하고 미-EC 양측간 상이한 입장을 재확인하였으며 결론적으로 DUNKEL 협상안은 EC 측이 수용 가능하도록 운용의 한계(MARGIN OF MANOEUVRE) 를 최대한 확대하는 것이 긴요할 것이라고 강조함

O 동 부위원장은 농업문제의 해결이 협상타결에 유일한 분야가 아니며 EC 측으로서는 시장접근, 보조금, 서비스 (특히 해상운송및 은행)분야에서도 DUNKEL안을 수용하기 어려운바 농업분야에서의 타협이 이루어지지 않을 경우 개도국과의 시장접근및 서비스분야의 협상은 아주 어려울 것이라고 농산물 수출국을 겨냥하여 언급함

O 한편, 집행위 대변인은 1.27 일, 4.15 이전 협상을 완료하는 문제와 관련, 농산물분야에서의 타결이 선행되는 경우에만 가능할 것이며 EC 는 곧 제네바에서 DUNKEL 협상안의 수정에대한 구체적인 입장을 제시할 것이라고 말하고, 이와관련 DUNKEL GATT 사무총장이 1.29. 당지를 방문, ANDRIESSEN 부위원장과 만날 계획이라고 말함

2. 한편 MACSHARRY EC 집행위원은 1.24. 구주의회 농산물 분과위에서 DUNKEL 협상안에 대한 기존의 EC 입장을 재확인하고 CAP 개혁과 UR 협상에 직접적인 관련이 있다면 향후 CAP 개혁을 위태롭게 하는 DUNKEL 협상은은 절대로 받아들일수 없다고 말함. 동 집행위원은 EC 는 4.15. 까지 협상타결을 위해 최선을 다할것 이나 수출물량기준 감축수준, REBALANCING, 시장접근, 수출보조및 국내보조금 감축폭의

통상국 안기부	장관 경기원	차관 재무부	1차보 농수부	2차보 상공부	구주국 중계	외정실	문석관	정와대

PAGE 1   92.01.28   06:17

외신 2과 통제관 BS

0205

일관성유지 (COHERENCE) 와 특히 GREEN BOX 인정등 EC 의 입장이 반영된 DUNKEL 수정안이 나오지 않는한 EC 는 협상실패의 책임을 질수 없다고 말함

　　3. DELORS EC 집행위원장은 1.24. 프랑스의 CHATEAUROUX 에서 개최된 농업관계 세미나에서 연설을 통하여 UR 농산물 협상에서 프랑스측이 타협의 자세를 보이지않고 무조건 반대입장을 보이고 있는데 대하여 비난하고 농산물때문에 UR 협상이 실패한다면 프랑스를 포함한 모든 회원국이 큰 손실을 겪게 될것이며, EC내에서 프랑스가 고립되고 있음을 경고함. 동 위원장은 또한 미국이 EC 측의 현실을 수용하여 양보하지 않는한 UR 협상은 실패할 것이라고 미국을 비난함. 또한 동인은 DUNKEL 협상안이 EC 의 입장을 제대로 반영하지 않고 미국의 입장에 편향되게 작성된데 대하여 강력 비난하고 EC 의 입장이 반영된 수정안이 재작성되지 않는한 계속 거부입장을 견지할 것이라고 말함. 끝.

　　(대사 권동만-국장)

　　예고: 92.12.31. 까지

0206

외 무 부

종 별 :

번 호 : USW-0444 　　　　　　　　일 시 : 92 0128 1721

수 신 : 장관 (통기)

발 신 : 주미 대사

제 목 : UR 협상결과 FAST TRACK 처리

대: WUS-0330

1. 당관 김중근 서기관은 1.28. USTR MARY RYCKMANMTN 과장을 면담, 대호 미측 입장을 타진한바, 동 과장은 금년 하반기 대통령 선거를 감안할때, 의회가 하계 휴회 이전에 UR협정및 동 시행법안을 승인하는 것이 바람직하기는 하나, 현재의 UR 협상 추이를 살펴볼때 이는 거의 난망시된다고 전망함.

2. 즉, 4월 중순 협상이 종결된다 할지라도

가. 이것이 의회를 만족시킬 만한 결과가 되지못할 경우에는 사전에 대의회 설득작업이 필요하므로 의회에 협정 참여의사를 통고하는 시일이 늦추어질 수도 있으며

나. 대의회 통고후 최소 90일 호기일 기간동안에 의회와 비공식 협의를 거쳐, 의회는 행정부가 제출하는 UR 협상 및 관련 시행법안에 대해 60회기일 이내에 승인 여부를 결정하여야 하나, 하계휴회 일정으로 빨라야 가을에 들어서야 승인여부 결정이 가능할 것으로 보인다 하며

다. 현재 행정부로서는 금년중 의회 승인을 목표로 하고 있으나 선거준비를 위한 휴회 (10.2.회기종료 예상) 일정을 감안한다면 내년 새로운 회기에 UR 협정및 관련 시행법안의 승인이 이루어질 가능성도 배제할수 없다함.

3. 상기관련 의회 동향등 관련사항 추보하겠으며, 금년 의회 일정을 별첨 송부하니 참고바람.끝.

첨부: USW(F)-0498(2 매).끝.

(대사 현홍주-국장)

통상국

PAGE 1 　　　　　　　　　　　　　　　　　　　　92.01.29　　08:35 WG

외신 1과 통제관

0207

1992 Congressional Schedule

Congressional recesses are in boldface type
Dates are inclusive

SENATE		HOUSE	
Jan. 21	Senate Reconvenes	Jan. 22	House Reconvenes
Feb. 10-17	Senate not in session	Feb. 10-17	District Work Period
Feb. 10	Lincoln's Birthday	Feb. 12	Lincoln's Birthday
Feb. 17	President's Day	Feb. 17	President's Day
March 9-13	Senate not in session		
April 13-24	Senate not in session	April 13-24	District Work Period
April 17	Good Friday	April 17	Good Friday
April 18	Passover	April 18	Passover
April 19	Easter	April 19	Easter
May 25-29	Senate not in session	May 22-25	District Work Period
May 25	Memorial Day	May 25	Memorial Day
		July 3-6	District Work Period
July 4	Independence Day	July 4	Independence Day
July 8-17	Senate not in session	July 13-17	House not in session
July 13-16	Democratic National Convention	July 13-16	Democratic National Convention
Aug. 13-Sept. 7	Senate not in session	Aug. 13-Sept. 8	District Work Period
Aug. 17-20	Republican National Convention	Aug. 17-20	Republican National Convention
Sept. 7	Labor Day	Sept. 7	Labor Day
Sept. 28	Rosh Hashana	Sept. 28	Rosh Hashana
		Oct. 2	Adjournment Target Date
Oct. 7	Yom Kippur	Oct. 7	Yom Kippur
Oct. 12	Columbus Day	Oct. 12	Columbus Day
Nov. 3	Election Day	Nov. 3	Election Day

SOURCE: Senate Majority Leader, House Majority Whip

Dates to Watch

Jan. 28	President Bush delivers State of the Union message to Congress
Jan. 29	Administration unveils fiscal 1993 budget proposal
Feb. 10	Iowa caucuses
Feb. 18	New Hampshire presidential primary
March 10	"Super Tuesday" presidential primaries
July 13-16	Democratic National Convention in New York
Aug. 17-20	Republican National Convention in Houston
Nov. 3	Election Day

0208

외 무 부

종   별 :

번   호 : USW-0477   일   시 : 92 0129 1632

수   신 : 장 관(통기,통이,통삼)사본:상공부,경기원,농수산부

발   신 : 주 미 대사

제   목 : UR 동향

　　UR 협상 추진 관련 최근 미측 평가 및 분야별입장을 정리한 당지 법률 회사인
SIDLEY ANDAUSTIN 사의 메모를 별첨 FAX 송하니 미측입장 판단에 참고 바람.

　　첨부: USW(F)-0506

　　(대사 현홍주-국장)

주 미 대 사 관

USW(F) : 0506 년월일 :   시간 :

수 신 : 장 관 (통기, 통이, 통상) 사본: 상공우,

발 신 : 주미대사 경기원, 농수산우

제 목 : USW - 0477 천우 (4mm)

보 안
통 제

(출처 :   )

(0506 - 4 - 1)

외신 1과
통 제

0210

MEMORANDUM

FROM: Alan F. Holmer and Judith H. Bello

RE: Uruguay Round Update

DATE: January 28, 1992

This memorandum responds to your fax of January 23, 1992 and provides a report on the perspective of U.S. Government officials in Washington regarding the current state of the Uruguay Round negotiations.

U.S. officials report that the two meetings between Ambassador Hills and Mr. Andriessen in January were "remarkably unproductive." Uruguay Round negotiations in Geneva in January have not moved the process forward. Generally, the sense in Washington is that a general malaise pervades the negotiations. It appears to the U.S. that most countries will not be fielding their negotiating teams until February.

As always, the key to the negotiations is agriculture and the key to agriculture is the EC. While many Administration officials are increasingly skeptical about achieving (and implementing in the Congress) a Uruguay Round agreement in 1992, other officials continue to be optimistic and believe that a good Uruguay Round package can still be a winning issue for President Bush both legislatively and politically in 1992. Such officials remain hopeful that with strong leadership from Washington, a Uruguay Round package can be agreed to in the next few months. Some in the Administration fear that after 1992, there will be new trade officials in the EC, possibly a new U.S. Trade Representative, and that such changes would significantly slow the negotiating process. However, there seems to be a recognition that in order for the negotiations to be completed, it will be necessary for the U.S. to precipitate further negotiations with the EC on agriculture and other issues.

The following is a snapshot of a number of key negotiating areas from the U.S. perspective.

Agriculture

U.S. officials are confused regarding (1) who they must deal with in the EC on agriculture, and (2) what the real substantive issues are.

It is becoming clear to U.S. officials that Mr. Andriessen is not the key to the agriculture negotiations.

0506-4-2

Increasingly, U.S. officials believe that these issues must be pursued with Mr. MacSharry and Mr. Delors.

U.S. officials hear about three different EC priority concerns on agriculture, depending on who they talk to:

1. **Green Box**: Mr. MacSharry has focused on the inadequacy of the "green box" of permissible internal supports (because the green box doesn't encompass all CAP payments). The U.S. concern is that by placing such programs in the green box, they are creating something that does not now exist, i.e., international agreement that such programs are consistent with GATT rules and immune from national CVD actions or GATT challenge.

2. **Rebalancing**, i.e., precluding the EC from effectively reducing imports of some agricultural products by liberalizing access to its market for others.

3. **Export Subsidies**: The Dutch and French indicate that they cannot live with the export subsidy numbers contained in the Dunkel text.

In addition to these issues, the U.S. continues to be dissatisfied with the EC response to the Oilseeds case; this is an issue which U.S. officials believe must be addressed in the context of the GATT negotiations.

In short, U.S. officials are attempting to determine who among the EC negotiators they have to please and how they have to please them. The frustration from the U.S. side is that U.S. negotiators believe that EC officials do not yet know exactly what has to be changed in the Dunkel text and by how much. U.S. officials expect that during the next few weeks, EC officials will be trying to sort out their own positions.

With respect to the U.S. agricultural private sector, U.S. negotiators believe that the U.S. agricultural community in general will be willing to accept the Dunkel text, but they cannot be pushed far; support by those interests will be lost if U.S. negotiators move very far beyond the Dunkel text.

Services

U.S. negotiators are quite concerned that the services market access negotiations are not going very well. USTR has sent tailored cables to various embassies around the world in hopes of moving those negotiations forward. But thus far, the market access negotiations have been a disappointment.

This is particularly true with respect to financial services. The Treasury Department is concerned about "free riders" in the negotiations. U.S. officials recognize that in order to achieve their objectives on financial services, they

-2-

0212

need to obtain additional leverage in the negotiations. One
solution in this area is to use the "carrot" of access to the
U.S. textiles market as a means of inducing key LDCs to sign up
for market access for financial services.

Intellectual Property

The U.S. continues to have major problems with the
draft Dunkel TRIPS text, particularly with respect to the lengthy
transition provisions, and the failure to provide "pipeline
protection" for already patented pharmaceutical products and
products for which application already has been filed.

U.S. officials continue to be optimistic that a
solution can be achieved in this area. The U.S. faces upcoming
deadlines with respect to bilateral intellectual property
negotiations with India and Thailand, as well as announcements
regarding future "special 301" targets by April 30, 1992. It can
be expected that those bilateral initiatives will be used
aggressively by the U.S. in an attempt to place pressure on the
GATT negotiations. U.S. officials also discuss using access to
the U.S. textiles market as a further leverage tool.

Antidumping Reform

There are a number of areas in which U.S. officials
would like to seek changes to improve the Dunkel text from the
perspective of petitioning U.S. industries. Areas of possible
change include: anticircumvention, cumulation, standing, sunset,
and standard of review. We have not yet been able to determine
the precise areas which will be proposed by U.S. negotiators.
(We believe they have not yet reached agreement in this respect.)
Presumably, the U.S. and EC have many similar problems with
respect to the Dunkel text. If they work together, the U.S. and
the EC can be a powerful combination in this area. However, so
long as the EC is considered by the U.S. and many LDCs as being
the "bad guy" in the agriculture negotiations, it is likely that
they will not at the same time press hard against the LDCs as the
"bad guy" (along with the U.S.) in the antidumping negotiations.
If possible, the EC will prefer to let the U.S. carry that banner
on its own.

0506-4-K

AFH92A47.SED (1/28/92 2:36pm)

-3-

0213

정 리 보 존 문 서 목 록					
기록물종류	일반공문서철	등록번호	2020030178	등록일자	2020-03-16
분류번호	764.51	국가코드		보존기간	영구
명 칭	UR(우루과이라운드) 협상 동향 및 TNC(무역협상위원회) 회의, 1992. 전5권				
생 산 과	통상기구과	생산년도	1992~1992	담당그룹	
권 차 명	V.2 2-6월				

내용목차	* 1.13. TNC 회의
	    - 수석대표: 조일호 농림수산부 농업협력통상관
	    - Dunkel 협정문 초안(91.12.20.)을 기초로 협상(양자.다자) 추진 결정
	    - 4 track(상품 양허, 서비스 양허, 협정조문 법적 정비, 협정초안 수정 작업) 협상 전략 제시
	11.10. TNC 회의
	    - 미국.EC 간 양자협상 타결 촉구
	11.20. 미국.EC 농산물 협상 타결
	    - 공산품, 서비스 등 여타 분야 협상 결렬
	11.26. TNC 회의
	    - 협정문안 연내 확정 일정 승인
	12.18. TNC 회의
	    - 1992년 초 협상재개 결정				

0001

외 무 부

원 본

종 별 :

번 호 : NDW-0183   일 시 : 92 0203 1630

수 신 : 장 관(봉기)

발 신 : 주 인도 대사

제 목 : UR 동향

연;NDW-0096

1. 연호 주재국의 던켈협정안에 대한 관계부처 장관협의회 구성관련, 당관 임재홍서기관은 2.3(월) 상무부 GATT 및 UR 담당 MR. P.S. RANDHAWA 부국장과 접촉, 동 협의회에서 진행되고 있는 던켈협정안에 대한 청문회 내용을 파악하였는 바, 동 부국장의 답변요지는 아래와 같음.

가. 전체적 평가

0 청문회에 참석, 진술한 대부분의 정치인, 경제학자, 관련 및 의약품 제조업자협회등 이익단체들은 한결같이 던켈협정안 반대의견을 피력하였으나, 상기 반대 그룹중 어느누구도 인도경제의 VULNERABIBITY 와 현국제정세하에 인도의 국가이익과 현재 추진중에 있는 신경제 개방무역체제속에서 인도 무역에 이익이 될수 있는 신뢰성 있는 대안을 제시하지는 못했음.

0 반대의견은 주로 던켈협정안이 IMF 나 IBRD 의 구조조정책을 세계적으로 제도화하고 특허권분야에서는 선진국에의 완전한 굴복과 다국적기업에 의한 서비스분야의 압도적 지배및 서구선진국으로부터의 추가농산물덤핑에 따른 농업분야의 마비등을 기도하고 있다고 비난하고, 이경우 인도의 경제적 주권은 손상되고 지난 40 년간 인도가 쌓아온 사회서어비스분야는 파괴될 것이라고 주장하고 있음.

0 긍정적 입장을 피력하고 있는 측은 상공회의소연합등 상공무역업자 단체및 인사들인바, 이들은 던켈협정안을 수용은 하되, MFA, COMPULSORY LICENSING, 서어비스및 특허권 보장기간등 인도측에 불리한 내용은 교섭을 통해 개선해야 한다는 입장을 보이고 있음.

나. 상무부 입장

0 상무부로서는 인도가 과거 동경 라운드에 불참함으로써 그 댓가를

통상국	장관	차관	1차보	2차보	아주국	분석관	청와대	안기부

상당히치루었기 때문에 던켈안에 대한 국내반대가 거세더라도 금번 우루과이 라운드에서는 과거의 전철을 밟을 수는 없다는 입장임.

O 현재 상무부에서 큰 관심을 갖고 있는 분야는 TRIPS 와 MFA 분야이며, TRIPS 의 경우에는 크게 3 가지 문제점이 있다고 말할수 있음.

- 인도 특허권법에는 생산과정 특허는 있으나, 물질특허는 없음. 던켈안에서 물질특허 도입시까지 10 년의 잠정기간을 설정하고 있는 바, 이기간이 인도에대해 충분한 기간인지 여부는 계속 검토중임.(개인적으로는 20 년이 적정치 않은가 하는 생각도 있음)

- 인도 특허권법에는 생산과정 특허보장 기간이 대상에 따라 5-14 년으로 짧게 되어 있으나, 던켈안은 모든 대상을 20 년 보장으로 하고 있음.

- 인도 특허권법에는 특허를 갖고 있는 자가 3 년이내에 동 특허제품을 생산치 않을 경우, 정부에서 강제적으로 제 3 자에게 특허권을 부여할수 있는 바(소위 COMPULSORY LICENSING), 던켈안에는 이에 대해 분명치가 않음.

O MFA 분야는 인도의 최관심분야로서 과거부터 MFA 의 폐지를 주장해 왔으나, 금번 던켈안은 MFA 를 2003 년까지 서서히 폐지하는 것으로 되어 있으며, 그것도 2000 년이 되어야 겨우 폐지되기 시작한다고 말할수 있으므로 인도측 입장이 충분히 반영되었다고는 볼수 없음.(개인적으로는 5 년이내 폐지가 좋다고 봄)

다. 인도측 입장 확정시기

O 동 청문회 종료후, 인도측 입장이 정립될 수 있을 것으로 보이나, 야당에서는 국회에서 충분한 토의및 UR 협상에 대한 백서제출을 요구하는 등 국내적으로 반대입장이 심각히 존재하고 있는 현실에 비추어, 입장정립까지는 상당한 시간이 소요될 수도 있을 것임.

2. 상기 청문회등을 통해 부각된 던켈안의 각분야별 인도에 대한 긍정적 측면및 부정적 측면보고서는 파편 송부예정임.

(대사 이정빈-국장)

예고:92.6.30 일반

예규등 의거 재분류
92. 6. 30

관리
번호 92-126

외 무 부

종 별 :

번 호 : GVW-0297   일 시 : 92 0206 1830

수 신 : 장관(통기,경기원,재무부,농림수산부,상공부)

발 신 : 주 제네바 대사대리   사본:박수길대사(주콜롬비아 대사관 경유

제 목 : UR 동향   (본부중계필)

연: GVW-0287, GVW-0288

1. 카나다 대표부 GOSSLIN 공사에 의하면 작 2.5(수) 저녁 미, 이씨, 일, 카나다 4
국의 UR 협상 대표가 당지에서 회동하였으며,(미국 LABORELL USTR 대사, 카나다 DENIS
차관보, 이씨 PAEMAN 부총국장, 일본 ENDO 본부대사 참석) 동 협의과정에서 미국, EC
간 농산물 분야 협상관련 의견 접근이 이루어지고 있는 것으로 나타났다고 함.

2. 상기는 2.6(목) 김대사와 동 공사와의 오찬(카측 초청)시 제반 상호 관심사를
논의하는 과정에서 동 공사가 김대사 문의에 답하면서 언급한 내용인바, 동인에
의하면 EC 의 PAEMAN 부총국장과 일본의 ENDO 대사는 동회동을 위해 본국에서 당지에
출장하였다함.

3. 김대사가 미, EC 접근 동향 관련 미국과 EC (특히 독일)가 국내보조 분야에서
TRACK 4 에 의한 협의를 하게될 것이라는 관측이 있는 것으로 안다고 하였던바,
동공사는 농산물에 관해 전문가가 아니라 기술적인 내용은 잘 모르나, 미. 이씨측은
TRACK 1 (시장접근 양자 협상)과정을 통해 문제를 해결할수 있을 것으로 보고 있다고
동회동 참석자로 부터 들었다고 하고, TRACK 4 는 가동하기 어려울 것이라는 견해를
밝히고, 내주경에는 미.이씨의 동향이 좀더 가시화 될것으로 보고 있다고 하였음. (최
농무관이 추후 당지 일본 대표부 하야시 참사관에확인한바, 동회등은 사실이지만
결과에 대해서는 알지 못하고 있다고 하면서 일본은 동회동시 TRACK 1 과 TRACK 4 가
동시에 가동되어야 한다는 입장을 밝혔다고 하며, 내주에 G-8 기술적 협의가 당지에서
개최될 것으로 알고 있다 있다함)

4. 김대사가 11 조 2 항 C 관련 카나다측이 작일 6 개국 협의시 입장변화가없음을
밝힌데 대해 문의한바, 동공사는 카나다로서는 11 조 2 항 C 가 개선되는 것이
바람직하다는 입장이지만 관세화문제도 동시에 검토하고 있다고 하였음.

통상국	2차보	청와대	안기부	경기원	재무부	농수부	상공부	중계

PAGE 1

92.02.07   06:41

외신 2과 롱제관 CA

0004

5. 상기 미.이씨 의견 접근 동향에 관한 동공사의 언급 내용은 그간 언론보도나 당지에 알려져 있던 내용과는 다소 거리가 있는 것인바, 동향을 예의 주시하겠으며, 내주 EC 측 및 갓트 사무국측과 접촉, 관련 사항을 파악 보고하겠음. 끝

(차석대사 김삼훈-국장)

예고 : 92.6.30 까지

예고문 의거

재분류 92.6.30 종

速報 KOTRA 海外市場   대한무역진흥공사
KOREA TRADE PROMOTION CORPORATION
서울・江南區三成洞159番地
(代表電話 : 551・4181)

第5104 號   1992・2・6・

던켈총장, 美・EC간 농산물 협상 입장조정에 실패

- Katz USTR 부대표, 4월중순이 UR 타결을 위한 절대적인 시한은 아니라고 밝혀 -

[워싱턴 무역관 보고]

I. 情報要約

가. 던켈 GATT 사무총장은 1월 29일 부터 3일간 EC 집행위 관계자들과 연쇄적인
접촉을 갖고, EC측에 대해 미국을 비롯한 농산물 수출국들의 입장을 감안하여
종래의 입장을 수정해 줄 것을 요청하였으나, 아무런 성과가 없었던 것으로
알려지고 있어 UR협상의 타결을 둘러싼 앞으로의 전망이 더욱 불투명해 질
것으로 보임・

나. 이에따라, 던켈총장이 당초 예상했던 UR협상의 4월중순 타결 계획은 현실적
으로 어려울 것이라는 분석도 나오고 있는데, 지난 1월 30일부터 8일간의 일정
으로 스위스 다보스에서 개최되고 있는 '92 WEF (World Economic Forum)연차
총회에 참석 중인 각국의 경제지도자들은 난항을 거듭하고 있는 UR협상을 타개
하기 위해서 금년 봄 G7회담을 개최할 것을 제안하고 있음・

다. 한편, Katz USTR 부대표는 지난 1월 30일 워싱턴 D・C・ 소재 Commodity Club
에서 행한 연설에서 던켈총장이 제시한 4월중순이라는 시한은 바람직한 시한
이지 결코 UR타결의 절대적 시한은 아니라고 밝히고, 하지만 4월을 넘기게
되면 곧바로 닥치게될 선거로 인해 협상의 순조로운 진행이 어려울 것이라는
점을 강조하면서, 점차 고조되고 있는 미 의회의 분위기를 감안, 금년 봄을
넘기지 않는 것이 보다 바람직하다는 미국의 입장을 밝혔음・

0006

라. 미국측 협상 관계자들은, 현재의 상황이 최종협정 초안의 농산물 분야에 대한
실질적인 개정을 주장하는 EC와 약간의 조정 혹은 더이상의 조정이 불필요하다
는 미국을 비롯한 일부 국가의 주장이 대립되고 있는 상태라고 지적하면서,
EC측의 주장이 너무 독선적이라는 견해를 표명하고 있음.

마. '92 WEF 연차총회에 참석하고 있는 많은 인사들도 EC경제의 5%도 채되지 않는
비중을 차지하고 있는 농업부문이 UR협상 전체를 좌지우지하는 것은 아이러니
이며, 이제 EC는 UR 협상이 결렬될 경우 예상되는 파급효과에 대해서 고려해
나가야할 것이라고 강조하였음.

2. 評價

가. 현재 미국은 당초 던켈총장이 제안했던 4월 중순을 UR타결을 위한 적기로 판단
하고 있는 것으로 알려지고 있음.

나. 동 시한까지 협상이 타결되지 못할 경우에도 미국은 협상을 계속해 나갈 것
으로 보이나, 금년 중반기이후로 예정되어 있는 상·하원선거, 대통령 선거 등
일련의 정치적 부담이 따르는 행사들로 인해 협상을 제대로 수행해 나가지는
못할 것이라는 것이 일반적인 예상임.

0007

다. 따라서 이러한 제반상황들을 고려할 때, 농산물 협상과 관련한 금년 ─

외　무　부

원　본

종　별 :

번　호 : FRW-0271　　　　　　　　　　일　시 : 92 0207 0930

수　신 : 장 관 (봉기)

발　신 : 주 불 대사

제　목 : UR 협상

　　UR 협상전망 관련, ANDRIESSEN EC 집행위대외관계 담당 부위원장이 2.4 당지 FIGARO지와 기자회견 내용 아래 보고함.

　　1. G-7 특별 정상회담 소집

　　0 UR 협상은 2월이 가장 중요한 시기로서 현재의 협상 담당자가 이를 계속하도록 하는것이 바람직하다는 의사를 표명함으로써 DAVOS 회의 기간중 MOELLEMANN 독일 경제장관이 주장한 G-7특별정상회담 소집 필요성에 소극적 반응을보임. (현재 대외협상권을 보유하고 있는 EC로서는 EC 협상의 주도권이 EC 회원국으로 돌아가는데 대한 부정적 입장으로 해석됨)

　　2. DUNKEL 제안

　　0 EC 의 입장이 반영되지 않은 균형을 잃은 내용으로 GREENBOX LIST 는 EC/CAP개혁에 오히려 문제점을 제기함.

　　0 최근 DUNKEL 사무총장의 EC 방문시 EC측은 DUNKEL 안에 대한 불만을 토로하였으나 본인은 자신 제안에 대한 수정 가능성은 배제하고 이해관계국간 직접협상으로합의에 이르기를 바란다는 반응을 보임.

　　0 이와관련,EC 집행위는 REBALANCING 을 포함하고 수출물량 삭감내용을 수정한대안을 현재 준비중이며, 조만간 미측과 교섭에 착수할 예정임.

　　3. 농산물 분야 협상

　　0 농산물 분야는 GATT 체제에 점진적, 단계별로 통합되어야 하며 비록 1단계 타결내용이 온건하다 하여도 향후 추가교섭을 위한 정치적 타협의지로 해석해야 함.

　　0 현재 각 협상국은 미국이 PUNTA DEL ESTE 선언내용을 과도하게 해석함에 따라자승자박되었다며, 미국의 지나친 요구가 현실적 가능한 수준의 타결을 어렵게 하였는바, 이러한 견지에서 DUNKEL 의 최종안도 EC 로서는 무리한 요구임.

통상국　　2차보　　국기국　　청와대　　안기부

PAGE 1　　　　　　　　　　　　　　　　92.02.07　21:04 DU

외신 1과 통제관

0008

O UR 협상의 성공이 궁극적으로 보다 많은 고용기회 창출을 위한것이라고
볼때,농산물문제 때문에 여타분야의 협상타결(특히,유럽내 60프로의 고용효과를
갖고있는 서비스 분야)이 지장을 받아서는 안됨.끝.

(대사 노영찬-국장)

외 무 부

원 본

종 별 :

번 호 : USW-0665   일 시 : 92 0207 1851

수 신 : 장 관 (통기,통이,경기원,상공부,농수산부,경제수석)

발 신 : 주 미 대사 사본: 주 제네바, EC대사(본부중계필)

제 목 : UR 협상관련 의회 동향

    BENTSEN 상원 재무위 위원장(D-텍사스)은 2.6. 상원 본회의 연설을 통해 DUNKEL
텍스트에 대한 아래 요지의 견해를 표명하였음. (텍스트 팩시편 별송)

    1. DUNKEL 총장이 제시한 4.15. 협상시한까지 협상이 종료되길 기대하나, 현재
상원내 분위기와 업계의 반응에 비추어 현 DUNKEL 텍스트로는 상원의 승인을 얻기
어려움. 국내 경기 악화로 통상문제는 전례없이 중요한 정치 쟁점이 되어 있으며,
통상정책에 대한 의회의 시각도 매우 회의적임.(SKEPTICAL CONGRESS). 따라서, UR
협상 결과를 포함, 여하한 통상협정도 의회와 미국민의 높은 기대수준을 만족시키기
어려운 상황임.(TOUGH SELL). 본인은 동 텍스트가 제출되기전 DUNKEL 총장에게 현
텍스트로는 미 의회 통과가 어렵다는 점을 경고한바 있음. 일단 협상이 타결되면
의회내 대단한(HOT AND HEAVY) 격론이 예상됨.

    2. 최종 협상안이 의회를 통과하기 위해서는 남은 협상기간중 아래와 같은
문제점이 개선되어야함.

    가. 지적재산권, 서비스, 농산물 교역등 핵심분야에서의 충분하고도
신속한시장개방이 확보되어야함. 현 텍스트는 이점에 있어 많은 결함을 가지고
있으며, 개별국가의 구체적 공약(COUNTRY-BY-COUNTRY COMMITMENTS)도 결여되어 있음.

    나. 반덤핑, 보조금, 301 조등 미 통상법 규정의 유지, 강화를 통해 미국 기업을
불공정 경쟁으로 보호할 능력을 계속 보유할수 있어야함.

    다. 모든 국가가 최종 협상 결과에 참여하여야 하며, FREE RIDER 를 허용해서는
않됨. 과거에는 미, 일, 카나다, 유럽등 주요 교역국들이 관세인하등에 합의하면
여타국가들은 MFN 원칙에 따라 그 혜택을 향유할수 있었음. 그러나 동경라운드 이후
국제무역 환경은 크게 변화하였으며, 한국등 아시아 NICS, 브라질, 알젠틴, 인니,
태국등 교역국들이 중요한 비중을 차지하게 되었음. 이러한 국가들은 BIG LEAGUES 에

통상국   장관   차관   1차보   2차보   통상국   분석관   청와대   안기부
경기원   농수부   상공부

PAGE 1   92.02.08   09:48

외신 2과 통제관 CA

0010

230 우루과이라운드 협상 동향 및 무역협상위원회 회의 3

들어온 만큼 이에 상응하는 책임을 부담하여야함. 이러한 관점에서 DUNKEL 텍스트가 다자무역기구(MTO) 설립을 재사하고 있는 점을 환영함.

라. 효과적이고 신속한 분쟁해결 제도는 그동안 미국의 주요 협상목표의 하나였음. 그러나, 행정부는 이러한 목표를 추구하되, 여타 교역 상대국의 상응하는 제도와 시장개방 의지가 확보될 경우에 한하여 강력한 분쟁해결 제도에 합의할 것이라는 점을 분명히 하여 왔음. 규범 자체가 불완전할 경우 그 효율적 집행도 기대할 수 없다는 것은 당연한 이치임. 그러나, 이러한 측면에서 볼때 현 텍스트의 분쟁해결 제도는 아직 상당한 개선을 요함.

3. 상기 문제점 해결을 위한 협상이 쉬운 것이 아니라는 점은 인정하나 최종 협정안의 의회 통과를 위해 필수적이라는 점을 분명히 하지 않을수 없음.

첨부: USW(F)-0732(4 매). 끝.

(대사 현홍주-국장)

예고: 92.6.30. 까지

PAGE 2

USW(F) : 732   년월일 : 0204   시간 : 1857

수 신 : 장 관 (종기, 통이, 경기진 상화부, 조사2과, 경제수석) 사본 : 주제네바- 즉 든다 대사

발 신 : 주미대사

보안 동제 ᆢ

제 목 : UR 협상관련 Bentsen 상원의원 발언   (출처 :   )

THE URUGUAY ROUND

Mr. BENTSEN. Mr. President, I rise today to discuss an issue that I think is going to affect the well-being of Americans well into the next century. I am talking about the Uruguay round of multilateral trade negotiations. What a name. But it gets down to what is going to happen to the standard of living of our people over this next decade. It gets down to the point, are we going to go more and more in debt to other countries? Or are we going to turn that trade deficit around?

Those negotiations are now at a very important stage. Just before the Christmas holidays, the Director General of the General Agreement on Tariffs and Trade, Arthur Dunkel, released his draft of a comprehensive multilateral trade agreement. His text, some 451 pages, covers most of the topics that our negotiators have been debating since the Uruguay round negotiations began over 5 years ago.

He has set out an ambitious schedule. I understand his concerns. We need deadlines to try to get things moving. What he is calling for is a final phase of the negotiations. He set April 15 as the target date for countries to initial the final agreement.

I hope we can reach agreement by that date. I certainly urge our negotiators to press these negotiations as hard as they can. But we have some awfully tough negotiations remaining because once an agreement is reached, of course, then it has to come back to the Congress for approval, and only the Congress can implement this agreement. So it makes sense to take stock of whether the Dunkel text as it now stands can pass muster in the Congress.

I have taken soundings from many of my Senate colleagues. I have heard from many of the industry groups that have a stake in this process. I must say, Mr. President—and the time to say it is now, not when it is too late—I do not believe the Senate would approve the current text. Let me be clear. Let me state it again. The text simply is not good enough in its present form to pass the Senate, in my opinion.

And that certainly concerns me. As my colleagues know, I fought long and hard last spring to extend the President's so-called fast-track negotiating authority. I did it because I believed strongly that the President must have the ability to negotiate the elimina-

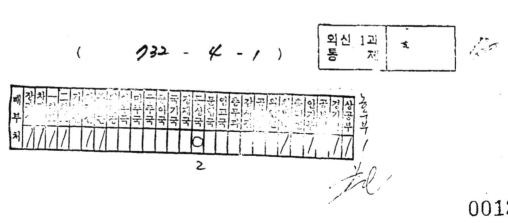

(732 - 4 - 1)

외신 1과 통 제

2

0012

tion of unfair foreign trade barriers. I do not believe a congressional body by itself can do that in negotiating with these other countries. I felt last spring, and I believe now, that the Uruguay round offers us an opportunity to get the biggest bang for our buck, negotiating with over 100 countries in one comprehensive negotiation, instead of trying to eliminate those barriers through a piecemeal, country-by-country approach.

I still believe that these negotiations are important. But we also have to face the facts. Today our economy is in a rut; it is in a ditch. We have a prolonged recession; that means that any agreement that comes back is going to face a very skeptical Congress. There are serious questions. Will we have a net increase in jobs when we sign this agreement, or are we going to have a net decease in jobs?

The fact is that trade policy has assumed an importance in our political debate that we have not seen in the past, and that is good. It is about time it did. Whatever we think about the President's trip to Japan, it certainly made crystal clear the link between international trade and jobs here at home. Trade has become prime time fare. That is good, but that also means that the Uruguay round is going to undergo as close a scrutiny as any trade agreement ever has and that any agreement is going to be held to a very high standard by the Senate and by the citizens of this country.

It all adds up to one central point. This Congress is going to be a tough sell when the Uruguay round agreement is sent up for approval. Under the Constitution that responsibility is ours. As it is currently drafted, I am convinced that the Dunkel text just will not pass muster. I warned the Director General about this before he put that text out. Once an agreement is reached, then we are going to have it here before us and the debate will be hot and heavy.

Today, it is not my objective to list all the deficiencies in the current text, but I do think it is important to make clear that any agreement is likely to be measured against certain guideposts. As it currently stands, I think the Dunkel text falls short in many respects.

Any agreement must open up foreign markets and provide substantial export opportunities for competitive American industries, but we are not there yet. The current text simply is not strong enough in key areas. In critical areas—like intellectual property, services trade, and agriculture—the current text does not assure us that we will open up foreign markets sufficiently or quickly enough. Our negotiators need to redouble their efforts to ensure that the deficiencies in the text are remedied.

Even more important is to talk about what is not in the text. In several key areas, the Dunkel text only provides a framework of rules for eliminating barriers. Specific commitments by the individual countries are yet to come. We must see substantial progress in reducing foreign tariffs and opening up those foreign services markets. In agriculture, we still have some very important negotiations ahead on what the framework of liberalization should be. Do you think Senators from farm States are going to approve it in its present form if it comes back without the concessions that have to be made, when we changed our agriculture program in this country to cut back on subsidies, to try to show good faith to the European Community? Well, there are going to be some tough negotiations that have to take place to get the country-by-country commitments.

In my view, these market access negotiations are the linchpin of the entire Uruguay round. Without substantial progress in these areas, I do not see how a Uruguay round agreement is going to win congressional approval.

172-4-2

Second, it is critical that any agreement preserves and strengthens our remedies against dumping ███ subsidies, and other unfair trade p█████es. That is one of the key negotiating objectives that we put into the 1988 Trade Act. It is still of importance, not just to me, but to the entire body of the Congress. It is essential that we retain the ability to protect any and all industries injured by unfair competition.

Third, the key objective of this round must be to ensure that all countries participate, all, we cut out the free riders. In the past, GATT rounds have largely involved agreements among a limited group of countries. That cannot be the case in this round because in many of the areas in which we want to see progress—services, intellectual property, market access, and investment—barriers are found in the developing countries.

For years, we have given many of these countries a "free ride" in the trading system. In the past GATT rounds, the big players, the United States, Canada, Japan, and the Europeans, would negotiate steep tariff cuts, but there was no incentive for many of the others to play along because the most-favored-nation principle guaranteed that everyone, everyone, would get the benefit of a tariff reduction. The result: At the beginning of the Uruguay round, the United States" average tariff was less than 5 percent; India's was 118 percent.

This round offers us an opportunity to correct that kind of an imbalance. The world has dramatically changed. The players have changed. The magnitude of their involvement in world trade has changed since the Tokyo round. Countries that were not major players in world trade are assuming increased importance today. Since the Tokyo round, our trade with the four newly industrialized countries of Asia—Hong Kong, Korea, Taiwan, Singapore—has tripled. Brazil, Argentina, Indonesia, Thailand are flexing their trade muscles, and that is fine. They are all in the big leagues now. It is important they act like they are in the big leagues and assume some of the responsibilities that go along with it.

This is the time to do it. We probably will not have another big round of multilateral negotiations for another 10 years. Those countries are important today, and they will be even more important when you look at the trend line 10 years from now. That is why we have to lock in the benefits today. That means no more free riders.

In the past, countries did not need to sign on to all parts of the GATT agreements. That left some of the countries free to sign up for the benefits, but not to grant full concessions. The Dunkel text tries a new approach, and I congratulate him for that.

I have been talking about having GATT plus, so countries willing to assume greater obligations would get greater benefits. That would move us more toward free trade, but the free riders should be setaside.

So Dunkel's text works toward that. He establishes a new organization called the Multilateral Trade Organization, MTO, and the price of admission to the new organization is that a country must sign onto the entire agreement. And that part is good.

In other words, if a country wants to get the benefits of our tariff cuts or liberalization of our textile markets, it has to reduce tariffs in its markets, open its services markets and protect the intellectual property rights of U.S. companies. The dues to join this club are pretty stiff, but that is the way it ought to be. If a country does not want to pay the dues, they can make that choice, but it sure should not get the benefits of club membership. That is strong leverage. Any country left out of the club will be at a serious disadvantage in world trade. And that leverage might help remedy our free rider problem. But you know what that is going to depend on. That is going to depend on the political courage, on the fortitude of the administration to use the stick that the MTO will provide and actually deny benefits to the countries that are not willing to meet the new Uruguay round standards.

732-4-3

And finally, I will be taking a close look at how the Uruguay round agreements will be enforced. In the 1988 Trade Act, we told our negotiators that providing for a more effective and expeditious GATT dispute settlement mechanism was one of our very principal negotiating objectives. But the catch is this: If we want tough rules and a fast and effective dispute settlement system when we are plaintiffs in a case, we also have to live with the same rules when we are the defendants.

The administration has assured us all along that they would agree to a tough, binding dispute settlement system, but only if we also secured strong rules and good commitments from our trading partners to open their markets. After all, it does not help to have tough enforcement, if the rules you are enforcing are no good. Frankly, looking at the Dunkel text, I think we still have a good distance to go.

Mr. President, I support the concept of the Uruguay round. I sure hope we can reach a successful conclusion. But any agreement that is reached must gain the support of the U.S. Congress. And right now I simply do not think that support is there.

I am an optimist by nature. I believe the round can succeed. I think it is terribly important that it does. I do not see any cakewalk. I know our negotiators have worked hard. I have confidence in them. But we need to start with tough negotiations in the months ahead—negotiations that address every area that I have mentioned today; negotiations that produce an agreement that can be sold to a skeptical Congress in a time of recession. And that is no easy task. But it is absolutely essential if this Congress is to approve a Uruguay round agreement.

732-4-4

0015

UR(우루과이라운드) 협상 동향 및 TNC(무역협상위원회) 회의, 1992. 전5권(V.2 2-6월) 235

외 무 부

종   별 :

번   호 : ECW-0185   일   시 : 92 0211 1600

수   신 : 장 관 (봉기, 경기원, 재무부, 농림수산부, 상공부)

발   신 : 주 EC 대사   사본: 주 미, 제네바-중계필

제   목 : 갓트/UR 협상

표제협상 관련한 당지의 최근동향을 아래보고함

1. 미.EC 양자협상

가. 폴투갈 외무성은 OLIVEIRA 폴투갈 외무장관 (EC 일반이사회 의장) 이 콜롬비아에서 개최되는 UNCTAD 총회 참석에 즈음, 2.10 DUNKEL 갓트 사무총장과 표제관련 회담을 가질것이며, 2.12. 에는 워싱턴을 방문하여 HILLS 대표와 회담할 것이라고 발표함

나. 2.10 EC 집행위의 관계관은 2.13-14 미국과 EC 는 워싱턴에서 표제관련 양자회담을 가질것이며, EC 측 대표로는 LEGRAS 농업총국장, PAEMEN 대외총국 부총국장과 ANDRIESSEN 위원및 MACSHARRY 위원의 보좌관등이 참석할 것이라고말함

2. EC 의 동향

가. 2.9. 뮨헨에서 개최된 NATO 세미나에서 QUAYLE 미부통령, COHEN, LUGAR미 상원의원등이 경제와 안보의 연계시사등 표제협상과 관련하여 강한 입장을 보인데 대하여 EC 는 다음과같은 반응을 보임

O 2.10 EC 집행위 대변인은 무역협상과 안보는 별개의 것이며, UR 협상이 민감한 상황에 처해 있다는 점을 고려할때, 그러한 발언은 동 협상 성공노력에 도움이 되지 않을 것이라고 논평함

O 2.9. VAN DEN BROEK 화란 외무장관은 모든 갓트협상 참여자들은 타협노력을 기울이는 것이 중요하며, EC 의 보호무역에 대한 비난은 과장되고 있으며, 미국의 결손보조금도 EC 가 볼때에는 보호무역과 같은 것이라고 말함

O 2.10. 농업이사회에 참석중인 EC 농업각료들은 NATO 문제와 갓트협상을 연계시키려는 의도를 받아드릴수 없다는 입장을 분명히하면서 그러한 발언은 EC 측 보다는 미국측에 해로운 결과를 초래할 것이라는 견해를 피력함

통상국 정와대	장관 안기부	차관 경기원	1차보 재무부	2차보 농수부	구주국 상공부	경제국 중계	외정실	분석관

92.02.12   17:58

외신 2과   통제관 BS

0016

O 2.10 독일정부 대변인은 이제까지 EC 는 UR 협상에서 타협을 시도해 왔으며, EC 가 농산물분야에서의 협상준비를 갖추어가고 있으므로 미국측도 탄력적인 입장을 보아야 할것이라고 말함

O 2.9. KIECHLE 독일 농무장관은 미국이 타협할 준비가 되어있다면 UR 협상은 6 월 개최되는 뮨헨 G-7 정상회담을 계기로 종료될수도 있을 것이라고 말하고 미국도 타협가능성을 보여야 할것이라고 주장함

나. 한편, 최근 ANDRIESSEN 집행위원은 MOELLEMAN 독일 경제장관이 DAVOS 세계경제 FORUM 에서 제의한바 있는 UR 협상 종결을위한 특별경제정상회담 개최에 반대한다고 말하고, UR 협상은 현재의 협상자들에게 맡겨야 하며 G-7 에서 다루는 것은 문제해결을 더욱 복잡하게 할 것이라고 말한바 있음. 끝.

(대사 권동만-국장)

예고: 92.6.30 까지

예고문 의거 재분류
92.6.30 함

조,안

관리
번호 92-137

외 무 부

종   별 :

번   호 : GVW-0334   일   시 : 92 0211 1730

수   신 : 장관(통기, 경기원, 재무, 농수산, 상공부)

발   신 : 주 제네바 대사대리

제   목 : EC 협상 담당관 접촉

　　1. 김삼훈 차석대사는 금 2.11. EC 대표부 JOHN BECK 차석대표 및 K.F.FALKENBERG 참사관과 오찬을 갖고 UR 협상 동향 및 전망에 관한 의견을 교환함. (최농무관 이참사관 동석)

　　2. 상기 양인은 전반적으로 극히 신중한 태도를 유지하면서 협상 동향 및 전망에 관해 아래와같은 의견을 조심스럽게 피력함.

　　O 2.5. 개최된 QUAD 회의결과에 관심을 표명한바, 동인은 UR 협상 타결의 관건이 결국은 미.EC 간 이견 조정 및 타협성패 여부에 달려 있다고 보기 때문에QUAD 회의가 큰 역할을 수행할 것으로는 보지 않는다는 견해를 표명하였음.

　　O TRACK 4 협상 가동 전망에 관해서는 4 TRACK 방식이 1.13. 시점에서 GATT 사무국에게 유용한 동시 유일한 방편이긴 하였지만, 과연 액면 대로의 의미가 있는것인지의 여부에 대해서는 다소 회의적으로 본다하였으며, 미.EC 간 농산물 분야에서 TRACK 1 을 활용 사실상 문제를 해결할 수도 있을 것이라는 의견도 있는 것으로 안다는 질문에 대해서는 이를 부인치 않았음.

　　O 부활절 이전 협상 타결 전망에 대해서는 실무선에서 정확한 판단을 내리기는 어려운 상황임을 전제한후 약 50 퍼센트 정도의 확율이 있지 않겠느냐는 의견과 함께 협상 성패와는 관계없이 내주부터 실무진 바빠지게 될것으로 본다고 언급함.

　　3. 한편 EC LEGRAS 농업총국장 및 PAEMAN 부총국장이 2.13-14 워싱본을 방문 미측과 협의를 갖는 것으로 확인됨. 끝

　　(차석대사 김삼훈-국장)

　　예고: 92.6.30 까지

통상국	장관	차관	1차보	2차보	외정실	분석관	청와대	안기부
경기원	재무부	상공부	상공부	농수산				

PAGE 1   92.02.12   05:06

외신 2과 통제관 FM

0018

7,알

관리 번호	92-182

외 무 부

종   별 :

번   호 : GVW-0346   일   시 : 92 0212 1900

수   신 : 장관(통기, 경기원, 재무부, 농림수산부, 상공부)

발   신 : 주 제네바 대사대리   사본:주미,주EC대사-중계필

제   목 : UR 협상동향

    1. 김대사는 92.2.12(수) GATT 사무국 후세인차장보와 오찬을 갖고 UR 협상동향과 향후 전망등에 대하여 의견을 교환한바 동인 언급 요지 아래와 같음.

    가. 대부분의 참여국과 GATT 사무국은 TRACK 4 를 개방(OPEN)해서는 문제를수습할수 없을 것이라는 견해를 갖고 있으며 T 4 의 OPEN 을 강력히 요구하는 나라는 그로 인하여 야기될 모든 문제의 책임을 져야 할 것이라는 것임.

    나. 지난주 4 극 회담에서 일본은 T 4 가동없이는 TRACK 1 협상에 적극 참여할 수 없다는 강경 입장을 개진한 것으로 알고 있으나 비록 일본이 국내정치적고려를 염두에 두고 있다고 해도 UR 성패여부가 미.EC 간의 협의 여하에 달려 있는 점에 비추어 보아 그와같은 국제적 대응은 서투른 것으로 봄.

    다. EC 로서는 현 TEXT 의 수정없이 그대로 받아들이기 매우 어려울 것으로보며, 일단 던켈 총장은 지난번 BRUSSELS 방문시 EC 측에게 미국과 먼저 협상의 합의점을 찾아 보도록 권고한바 있으며 내일부터 와싱톤에서 미.EC 협의가 있을 예정임.

    라. 현시점에서 부활절 이전까지의 일정에 따른 협상 타결 여부는 솔질히 예단키 어려우며 결국 미.EC 간 협의의 성패 여부가 중요한바 조속한 미.EC 간 합의 도출이 없는 경우 UR 협상은 일단 SUSPEND 될수 밖에 없다고봄.

    마. 이러한 상황판단하에서 각국은 현재 진행중인 TRACK 1 에의 적극 참여와 특히 3.1 까지로 예정된 국별계획표(NATIONAL SCHEDULE)를 성의를 다하여 제출하는 것이 중요하다고 봄.

    2. 김대사는 한국은 계획된 기간내에 NATIONAL SCHEDULE 을 제출하기 위하여 신중한 검토를 하고 있으며 성의를 다할 것이나 주지하는 바와같이 특정 품목은 포함시키기 어려울 것이라는 견해를 표명한바 동인은 동문제점은 예외없는 관세화에 반대하는 국가 특히 스위스와 같은 나라가 여하히 기술적으로 대처하는 가를 파악해

통상국	장관	차관	1차보	2차보	외정실	분석관	청와대	안기부
경기원	재무부	농수부	상공부	중계				

PAGE 1   92.02.13   04:49

보는 것도 좋을 것이라는 반응을 보였음.

3. T 4 를 가동치 않고 TRACK 1 을 봉해서 미.EC 간 농산물 문제를 해결할 가능성을 문의한데 대하여 동인은 그가능성에 대하여 어려울 것으로 본다는 부정적 반응을 보였음.

4. TNC 개최 시기와 가능성을 문의한데 대하여 현재로서는 계획된바 없으며NATIONAL SCHEDULE 제출 이후 그결과 여하에 따라 검토될 수 있을 것으로 본다고 하였음.

(차석대사 김삼훈-국장)

예고:92.6.30 까지

예고의거
재분류 92.6.30 종결

PAGE 2

외 무 부

종 별 :

번 호 : USW-0774   일 시 : 92 0214 1850

수 신 : 장 관 (통기,통이,경기원,재무부,농수부)

발 신 : 주 미 대사

제 목 : UR 협상관련 동향

당관 장기호 참사관은 2.14. D. DWOSKIN USTR GATT 담당 부대표와 면담, 표제협상 관련 동향을 타진한바, 동 결과 하기 보고함. (서용현 서기관 동석)

1. 미/EC 간 양자협상

- 2.13-14 간 당지에서 개최되고 있는 미-EC 고위 실무협상의 결과는 아직 나오지 않았다함.

- 동 대표보는 미-EC 간 협상이 난항에 부닥치고 있다는 항간의 소문에 대하여, 사실상 EC 도 UR 의 성공에 미국 못지않게 큰 이해를 가지고 있으며, 금번고위 실무회담 개최를 EC 측이 먼저 제의한 것도 이러한 이유에서 비롯된 것이라고 강조함.

- 동 대표보는 EC 가 DUNKEL 협정안에 직접적으로 반대함으로써 UR 실패의 책임을 지는 것은 피하면서 동시에 DUNKEL 협정안의 일부 수정을 도모하여야 하는 어려움을 안고 있는 것으로 이해한다며, 과거 협상 막바지까지 난국에 봉착하였다가 종국적으로 타협을 모색해낸 미-EC 간 각종 협상의 경험에 비추어 볼때 금번 미-EC 간 협상도 비관적으로만 볼수는 없다고 언급함.

2. DUNKEL 협정안에 대한 미국정부의 대업계 협의 결과

- DUNKEL 협정안에 관한 대업계 협의과정에서 업계가 가장 큰 반발을 보인 것은 금융서비스 분야임. 업계는 홍콩등 일부 국가의 무임승차(FREE RIDE)를 방지하기 위하여 상응한 양허를 제공치 않는 국가에 대해서는 금융서비스 부분 협상 결과를 적용하지 않아 강력하게 요구하고 있으며, 한국의 금융시장 개방수준에 대해서도 미 업계의 불만이 아직 큰 것으로 알고 있다고 언급함.

. 이에대해 장참사관은 우리 금융시장의 점진적인 개방조치를 설명하고 각국의 발전 정도를 도외시하고 각국의 금융시장 개방 수준을 평면적으로 비교하는것은 무의미함을 강조하였으나, DWOSKIN 부대표보는 한국 금융개방에 대한 미업계의 인식이

통상국	장관	차관	1차보	2차보	통상국	분석관	정와대	안기부
경기원	재무부	농수부						

매우 저조하므로 한국측이 금융서비스 부문 OFFER 를 제출함에 있어 가급적 구체저긴 개방 계획을 포함시켜야 할 것이라고 말함.

  - 기타 덤핑및 상계관세 부분과 지적소유권(특히 PIPELINE PRODUCTS 보호) 부분등이 업계및 의회의 UR 패키지 수용에 어려움을 초래하고 있다고 언급함.

  3. 한. 미 경제협의회에서의 UR 문제 토의

  - 동 부대표보는 2.24. 한. 미 경제협의회에 참가할 USTR 측 대표(MOSCOW 부대표 또는 기타 인사)는 UR 과 관련하여 하기 사항을 거론할 것으로 본다고 말함.

  . 상품분야 시장접근: 2.25. 개최 예정인 한. 미간 상품분야 시장접근 양자협의와 관련, 미측은 ZERO-TO-ZERO 무관세화(전자, 건설장비, 목제품등) 제의를 재차 강조할 것이며, 한국측의 분야별 관세인하 OFFER 에 대해 몇가지 질문(예: 한국이 완제품보다 부품 분야에서 관세를 더 많이 인하시켜 역 관세구조를 취하려 하는 이유등)을 할수도 있을 것임.

  . 서비스분야 시장접근: 한국측이 당초 제출기한(2.10)이 경과했는데도 아직 제출치 않고 있는 서비스분야 수정 OFFER 제출을 촉구하고, 특히 금융서비스 분야에서 한국측의 적극저긴 노력을 촉구하게 될것임.

  . 그밖에 오는 3.1. 까지 제출케 되어 있는 농업분야 COUNTRY LIST 와 관련한 한국측의 입장을 타진하게 될 가능성도 있음. 끝.

  (대사 현홍주-국장)

  예고: 92.6.30. 까지

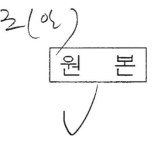

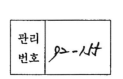

관리
번호

외 무 부

종   별 :

번   호 : FRW-0369

일   시 : 92 0219 1700

수   신 : 장관(통기)

발   신 : 주 불 대사

제   목 : UR 협상 동향

일반문서로 재분류(1992. 12. 31)

연:FRW-0136

　　조참사관이 2.19 DENIS SIMONNEAU 외무성 경제국 UR 담당관으로 부터 파악한 UR 협상 관련 최근동향 아래 보고함.

　　1. 불.독 정상회담시 협의내용(2.13 파리 개최)

　　0 콜 독일총리는 UR 협상이 92.7 월초 G-7 정상회담(독일이 의장국) 이전에타결되기를 희망하고 이를 위한 불란서의 보다 유연한 협상자세를 요망함.

　　0 미테랑 대통령은 UR 협상의 조기타결은 바람직하나 BAD AGREEMENT 는 받아들일수 없으며 미국이 유럽에 있어 농업의 중요성에 대한 올바른 인식을 갖고 EC 에 대한 지나친 요구를 우선적으로 수정해야 한다고 말한바, 콜 총리도 이에동감함.(미테랑 대통령은 1.31 유엔 안보리 정상회의시에도 BUSH 대통령에 UR 타개를 위한 미국의 우선적 태도 변경을 요망하였다 함)

　　0 양국 정상은 2.9 QUALE 미 부통령의 UR 협상과 유럽안보를 연계한 발언에대해 대외적으로 양국 결속을 재과시할 필요가 있다고 보고 정상회담후 양국이UR 협상에 공동으로 대처한다는 기본입장을 표명함.

　　0 동 정상회담후 일부 언론에서 "양국은 농업분야를 제외한 UR 협상의 우선타결을 추진키로 합의했다"는 보도와 관련, 이는 사실이 아니며 불란서와 EC 의 "GLOBAL 협상에 의한 일시, 완전 UR 타결" 입장에 변함이 없음.

　　2. EC, 미국 양자 협상

　　0 EC 집행위 GUY LEGRAS 농업국장과 HUGO PAMEN 대외관계 부총국장이 2.13 미국을 방문 양자협상을 갖은바 미측은 EC 공동농업정책 개혁 관련 직접소득 보조금을 GREEN BOX 에 포함시키고, EC 회원국내 EC 농산물이 선호될수 있도록(국제가격과 10 프로 차이) 관세를 조정하는 문제에 있어 EC 측의 요청을 수락할 의향을 보였다 함.

통상국	장관	차관	1차보	2차보	외정실	분석관	청와대	안기부

PAGE 1

92.02.20　　04:29

외신 2과　통제관 FK

0023

- 미국이 양보의사를 표명한 관세조정 문제와 아국이 요구하는 TARIFFICATION 에서의 예외조치와는 관련이 없다함.

0 EC 집행위측은 상기 미측의 태도변경을 적극적으로 평가하는 입장인 바, 이에대한 EC 의 대처입장을 협의키 위해 2.20-21 간 EC 회원국 113 조 위원회가 브랏셀에서 개최 예정임.

0 불란서로서는 상기 미측의 수정제의 내용은 자국 관심분야가 아니므로(연호 2 항 참조) EC 의 기존입장 고수를 주장할 예정이나 여타 회원국이 어떠한 동향을 보일지가 주목됨.

- 특히 GREEN BOX 건은 독일의 주요 관심사로 동건이 해결된다면 독일의 태도변경 가능성을 배제할수 없음.

0 다만, 현 EC 의장인 CAVACO SILVA 폴투갈 총리가 미테랑 대통령에게 EC 의 UR 협상 입장 수정여부는 회원국간 CONSENSUS 에 의해 결정될 것임을 약속했으므로 불란서의 동의없는 EC 의 독자적인 양보는 있을수 없을 것으로 봄.

4. 불란서의 협상 입장

0 미국이 제의한 양보내용이 불란서로서는 SUBSTANCE 가 없는 내용으로 독일을 겨냥하여 EC 내 불란서를 고립시키기 위한 전략일 가능성으로 보고 EC 집행위 및 일부국가가 유화적 입장을 보일 가능성을 적극 견제토록 노력할 것임.

0 특히 3.22 지방선거를 앞두고 인기가 하락세인 현 정부로서는 농산물과 같이 민감한 분야에서 실익없이 양보할 입장이 아니며, DUNKEL 사무총장의 4 월초 타결시한도 별다른 부담을 갖고 있지 않음.

0 불란서는 현실적으로 동 시한중 타결될 전망이 크지 않을 것으로 보고 지방선거이후 개각등 국내정국 추이, 독일의 태도변경 여부등을 고려, 92.7. G-7 정상회담시까지 다소 시간적 여유를 두고 협상에 임할 것으로 보임.끝.

(대사 노영찬-국장)

예고: 92.12.31. 까지

김도팔 92.6.30 김

PAGE 2

외 무 부

종 별 :

번 호 : FRW-0419   일 시 : 92 0226 1800

수 신 : 장관 (통기)

발 신 : 주 불 대사

제 목 : UR 협상 동향

당지 2.27자 LE MONDE 지에 게재된 최근 UR협상 동향에 관한 기사내용 아래 요약보고함.

1. 4.15 UR 협상 타결시한이 다가오는 가운데 EC 의 통신분야 공공시장에 대한 차별적 개방 움직임에 대해 미국이 2.24 보복조치 가능성을 언급하는등 미.EC 간 긴장이 고조되고 있음.

2. UR 협상 관련 DUNKEL 사무총장 복안대로 EC 집행위는 EC 측 OFFER LIST 안을 작성하였으며 3.2-3간 브랏셀 개최 EC 외무,농업장관 회의시 토의 예정이나,1차로 전문가 수준 협의시 영국과 독일을 제외한 10개국 대표는 동 내용이 DUNKEL 총장의 논리를 지나치게 수용하였으며 EC 각료이사회가 수락하지 않는 내용에 대해서도 양보하였다면서 EC 집행위를 비난함.

3. 영국과 독일은 EC 집행위 오퍼리스트내용을 거의 그대로 수용할수 있는 태도를 보였으며,특히 독일은 불란서와 거의 상반되는 입장을 취했음.

4. 한편 2.25 미국을 방문한 STRAUSS-KAHN 불상공장관은 미국이 농산물 문제에 지나치게 집착하여 서비스,지적소유권등 여타 주요분야 협상까지 교착상태를 만들고 있음을 비난하고,농산물 보조금 삭감은 수용할수 있으나 농산물 수출물량을 규제하는것은 GATT 의 무역자유화 기본정신에 위배되므로 수락할수 없다는 뜻을 미측에 전달함.

5. 동 장관은 방미 목적이 EC 의 입장을 미측에 이해시키는데 있다고 말하고,수주내 상당한 협상진전이 없을 경우 UR 협상은 미대통령 선거일정에 비추어 년말까지 지연될것으로 예상한다고 말함.끝.

(대사 노영찬-국장)

통상국   2차보   외정실   분석관

PAGE 1   92.02.27   07:46 DQ

외신 1과 통제관

0025

관리
번호 92-138

외 무 부

종 별 :

번 호 : GVW-0450   일   시 : 92 0227 1700

수 신 : 장관(봉기, 경기원, 재무부, 농수산부, 상공부)

발 신 : 주 제네바 대사

제 목 : DUNKEL 총장 면담

   본직은 금 2.27(목) 공관장회의등 대비 DUNKEL 사무총장을 면담한바, 동 결과 아래
보고함.

   1. 면담내용

   가. 본직은 우선 업무 협의 일시 귀국에 앞서 UR 협상 진전 동향 및 전망과관련한
DUNKEL 총장의 직접적인 평가를 듣기 위한 것임을 전제하고 아래 2 가지 사항에 대한
동 총장의 견해 또는 계획을 문의함.

   (1) 최근 양허 계획표 제출 시한 연기 움직임등 시장접근 협상이 별다른 진전을
보이지 않고 있는 상황하에서 부활절 시한이 지켜질수 있을 지 여부

   (2) 아국의 농산물 관련 T 4 협상 전망 및 T 4 가동 시기

   나. DUNKEL 총장은 양허 계획표 제출이 3.1 이후로 지연될 가능성에
우려를표명하고, 이경우 3 월중에 TNC 를 소집하는 것도 하나의 OPTION 으로 고려하고
있은 확실한 것은 1-2 주 더 지켜보고 결정할 의향임을 시사함.

   TNC 회의가 소집될 경우에는 T1 , T2 의장으로 하여금 협상 현황을 소상히 보고케
하여 전체적 윤곽 및 국별 책임 소재를 명확히하고 자신도 별도의 기자회견을 갖고
문제의 심각도 및 그 원인을 분명히 밝힐 예정이라고 함.

   다. T 4 가동 여부에 관해서는 한국, 일본, 스위스등이 관심을 갖고 있는 것으로
아나, 자신으로서는 주요 협상 참가국들이 상호 협의, 협상 전분야에 걸쳐 합의를
이루어 동 결과를 가져오지 않는한 가동할 계획이 전혀 없다는 것이 확고한 입장이며,
따라서 T1, T2 협상 완료전 가동은 있을수 없으며, T4 를 가동하더라도 그것은 극히
제한적이고 단기적이어야 함으로 가동시한은 24 시간이면 충분하다고 본다함.

   라. 한국, 일본의 관세화 예외인정 문제에 관해서는 EC 의 바나나를 예로 들면서
인정되는 경우 연쇄효과를 가져올 것이 명약관화 하므로 자신의 입장은 단호하며,

통상국   장관   차관   1차보   2차보   외정실   분석관   정와대   안기부
경기원   재무부   농수부   상공부

PAGE 1   92.02.28   05:46

한국, 일본등 제국도 이점을 확실히 인식해야 할것이라함.

마. 부활적 시한 준수 가능성 여부는 각국의 국내 비준 절차의 상이등으로 기본적으로 협상 참가국에 달려 있기 때문에 단정할수는 없으나, 자신으로서는 93.1.1 발효 목표에 변함이 없다 하면서, 아국의 비준 소요 기간을 문의함.

사. 이에 대해 본직은 쌀 문제가 현실적으로 대단히 심각한 문제이기 때문에 비준 소요기간 문제는 아국으로서는 부차적인 문제라고 전제하고, 쌀 문제에 대한 아국 입장이 반영된다면 순수 법적, 기술적 측면에서는 6-8 개월 이면 가능할 것이라고 답변한후, 아국이 UR 협상의 타결에 장애가 되지 않도록 개인적으로최대한 노력하고 있으나 이에는 쌀문제 해결이 관건이라고 언급, 동 문제의 중요성을 재차 강조함.

아. 본직은 또한 양허 계획표의 시한내 제출을 계속 정부에 건의해 왔고 동결과 공산품 분야에서는 제출 준비가 되어 있다고 하면서 시장접근 협상의 부진은 분야별 무관세, 관세조화등과 관련 미.EC 양측에 주된 협상의 부진은 분야별 무관세, 관세조화등과 관련 미.EC 양측에주된 책임이 있다고 언급하고, 한국을 부정적 시각에서 보는 것은 옳지 못하다고 지적한바, 동 총장은 최근 핀랜드,놀웨이의 태도 완화를 예로 들면서 한국, 일본 양국이 조속 결단을 내려 그들의 전향적 입장을 대외적으로 천명함으로써 협상 진전의 자극제가 되어 주기를 희망함.

자. 한편 HUSSEIN 차장보는 부활절 시한 준수 관련 아직 비관할 단계는 아니며 현재 미.EC 간 협의가 상당한 (SUBSTANTIAL) 진전이 있는 것으로 알고 있기때문에 내주가 중대한 국면이 될것으로 본다는 의견을 표명함.

3. 관찰

가. DUNKEL 의장은 12.20 TEXT 제출 및 1.13 TNC 회의를 계기로 자신의 책임은 일단 완수했고 현재의 시장접근 협상 부진 현상 및 향후 협상 성패 여부는 예외없는 관세화등에 반대하는 나라들의 태도에 달려있다고 강조하면서 전반적으로는 최근의 시장접근 협상 부진 현상등과 관련 1.13 에 비해 상당히 자신감을 상실한 인상을 풍김.

나. 상기 DUNKEL 의장의 태도, 미.EC 타협 부진 상황에 비추어 부활절 시한준수가 어렵겠다는 미국대사의 언급 및 6-7 월 시한설이 당지에 대두되고 있는사실등에 비추어 현 상황하에서는 부활절 시한 준수가 점점 어려워 지는 방향으로 가고 있는 것으로 판단됨.

다. 그러나 시한 연기등과 관련 동 책임소재를 타국 또는 특정국에 전가시킬

PAGE 2

가능성(상기 1 항 "나" DUNKEL 의 총장 언급 내용 포함)에 대비하여 양허 계획표 제출 시기문제등과 관련 주요국 동정을 면밀히 주시하면서 아국도 가능한한최선을 다하여 아국의 NATIONAL SCHEDULE 제출이 제출 약속 시한에서 크게 늦어지지 않도록 세심한 노력이 필요할 것으로 판단됨. 끝

(대사 박수길-국장)

예고 92.6.30 까지

長 官 報 告 事 項

報 告 畢

1992. 2. 27.
通　商　局
通 商 機 構 課(12)

題 目 : UR 協商 時限에 관한 Baucus 美 上院議員 發言內容

　　　　93年 6月까지 UR 協商의 延期가 불가피하다는 Baucus 美 上院議員(民主黨, 上院 財務委 貿易小委員長)의 發言에 관한 2.25자 Journal of Commerce 報道 內容 (2.27 一部 國內言論 전재)에 대해 아래 報告 드립니다.

1.　發言內容

　　○ 現在의 부진한 UR 協商 進行狀況으로 보아 4.15 協商 妥結 日程은 지켜지기 어려울 것임.

　　○ 實質的 協商 時限은 美 行政府의 Fast Track이 完了되는 93.6月이 될것임.

　　○ 부시 大統領은 UR 協定에 대한 議會 討論으로 이 問題가 選擧爭點化 하는 것을 希望하지 않는 것으로 보임.

2.　評　價

　　○ 最近 제네바에서 進行되고 있는 兩者協商의 不振相에 비추어 볼때 各國의 農産物 減縮 移行 計劃을 包含한 市場接近 分野의 讓許 計劃書 提出이 다소 遲延되고, 旣存 提出 時限(3.1)의 延期 可能性이 높은 것으로 展望됨.

　　○ 따라서 4月中旬까지 協商 妥結도 事實上 不可能하다는 見解도 조심스럽게 대두되고 있으나, Baucus 議員의 觀測대로 來年 6月까지 延期될 것인지는 速斷키 어려움.

3.　言論 및 國會 對策 : 關聯없음.

添　附 : Journal of Commerce 記事 寫本 1부.　　　　　　　　끝.

0029

주 미 대 사 관

USW(F) :   년월일 :   시간 :

수 신 : 장   관

발 신 : 주 미 대 사

제 목 : UR동향 (통가 동이)   (출처 : JOC. 2/25)

GATT Talks Will Not Meet April Deadline, Baucus Says

By JOHN MAGGS
Journal of Commerce Staff

WASHINGTON — Negotiators are unlikely to meet an April 15 deadline for completing the Uruguay Round of world trade talks, and the new deadline may be June 1993, Sen. Max Baucus, D-Mont., said Monday.

Sen. Baucus, chairman of the trade subcommittee of the Finance Committee, said that the talks are moving too slowly to be completed by April 15, the deadline imposed by Arthur Dunkel, director general of the General Agreement on Tariffs and Trade, the body that governs most world trade.

He added that President Bush probably does not want a congressional debate on the pact to complicate his relection campaign. "It's an election year, and I think the administration is reluctant to bring back a trade agreement" that would be opposed by some industries, Sen Baucus said. "It's possible the real deadline is when current fast-track authority expires," in June 1993.

President Bush today is scheduled to unveil his plans for protecting the environment from the effects of a North American free trade agreement, and Sen. Baucus said Mexico must make more of a commitment to border-area cleanup in a joint border plan that will be part of that announcement.

Sen. Baucus touted his plan to impose restraints on Japanese car sales in the United States if U.S. car makers steadily improve their international competitiveness. He denied that the plan, if enacted, would violate international trade rules

He commended a proposal by Attorney General William Barr to extend U.S. antitrust law to cover some unfair trade practices by Japanese corporations.

(1062-3-3)

외신 1과
주제

長 官 報 告 事 項

題 目 : UR 協商 動向 (協商 時限 延長 問題)

1. 2.26 UR/市場接近 非公式 協議 結果

   ○ 美國, EC, 濠洲, 스위스, 오지리 等이 3.1까지 修正 讓許 계획표(農産物 分野 履行 計劃書 包含) 提出이 어렵다는 立場 表明

     - 美國, 濠洲는 工産品 : EC, 스위스, 오지리등은 農産物 分野에서 어려움이 있음을 表明

   ○ Denis 議長은 別途 時限은 정하지 않은채 讓許 計劃表 提出 時限 延期가 불가피하다고 結論짓고, 다만 農産物의 境遇에는 3月初旬까지 基礎資料라도 提出할 것을 要請

2. 評 價

   ○ 讓許 計劃表 提出 時限(3.1)은 일단 약 2주간 延期가 確實視되지만 美.EC間의 農産物 및 無税化에 대한 合意 與否가 提出 時限의 決定的 關鍵임.

   ○ UR 協商 妥結 時限(4月中旬)에 대해서는 아직 어느나라도 延期 問題를 公式的으로 擧論하지 않고 있으나, 앞으로 市場接近, 서비스 讓許協商의 複雜性에 비추어 4月中旬의 妥結 時限도 다소 延期될 可能性이 있음.

     - 最近, Baucus 美 上院 貿易小委員長은 實質的인 UR 協商 時限은 美國 Fast Track 終了 時點인 93.6月이 될 可能性이 있다고 言及

3. 措置 計劃 : 我國의 讓許 계획표 提出 時期는 主要國의 動向을 감안, 關係部處와 協議 決定

4. 言論 및 國會 對策 : 別途 措置 不要.   끝.

0031

우루과이라운드 協商 動向

1992. 3. 2.

外 務 部

> 最近 協商 時限 延期説이 擧論되고 있는 우루과이라운드
> 協商 動向을 아래 報告 드립니다.

(現 況)

○ 92. 1. 13. 우루과이라운드 貿易協商委員會에서 92. 4月中旬까지
  協商을 終結하기 위해 92. 3. 1까지 農産物 및 工産品에 대한
  各國의 讓許計劃表(市場開放 및 農産物 補助 減縮 計劃)을
  提出키로 合意

○ 우리의 讓許計劃表 提出과 關聯, 農産物 市場開放의
  敏感性을 감안, 提出 時期와 쌀등 一部 基礎食糧에 대한
  開放 및 關税化 例外 確保 方案에 대하여 關係部處間 對策
  協議中

(最近의 動向)

○ 3. 1 讓許計劃表 提出 時限과 關聯, 最近 美國. EC등 主要協商
  參加國이 時限 遵守가 어렵다는 立場을 表明함으로써,
  同 時限이 약 2週間 延期될 것으로 展望
  - 美國은 工産品 分野 關税引下 協商 부진을 理由로 提示
  - EC等 農産物 輸入國들은 農産物 分野에 合意 不在로 讓許
    計劃 作成에 어려움이 있음을 表明

- 1 -

0032

o 4月中旬 協商 終結 目標와 關聯, 상금 公式 擧論되지는 않고
　있으나, 一角에서 同 時限의 延期가 불가피하다는 意見 擡頭
　- Baucus 美 上院 貿易小委員長은 93.6月 (美國 議會의 迅速
　　處理 權限 終了 時點)을 協商 妥結 時限으로 擧論
　- Kohl 獨逸 首相은 時限 延期 불가피성을 認識, 92.7月 先進
　　7個國 頂上會談에서 協商 妥結 方案을 協議할 것을 非公式
　　提議
　- 제네바 協商 專門家들간에 6-7月 時限說 擡頭

(評價 및 對策)

o 讓許計劃表 提出 時限(3.1)이 延期됨에 따라 우루과이라운드
　協商 終結 時限(4月中旬)도 연기될 것으로 豫想
　- 美國, EC間 農産物 補助金 分野 合意가 協商의 長期化
　　與否의 決定的 關鍵

o 農産物 開放 計劃 提出과 關聯, 國內 政治 日程上 어려움이
　큰 우리나라로서는 提出 時限의 延期로 다소 時間的 餘裕를
　갖고 對處하는데 도움

o 우리나라의 讓許表 提出 內容 및 時期는 主要國의 動向을
　보아 決定할 計劃이나, 全體 協商 妥結에 消極的이라는
　印象을 주지 않도록 신중 對處 豫定.　　　　　　　끝.

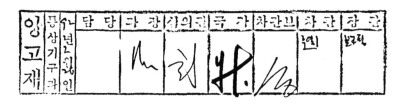

2

```
관리
번호  92-188
```

외   무   부

종   별 :

번   호 : FRW-0467   일   시 : 92 0304 1900

수   신 : 장관(봉기),사본:주불대사

발   신 : 주 불 대사대리

제   목 : UR 협상 동향

연:FRW-0369

3.2-3 간 브랏셀에서 개최된 EC 외무, 무역, 농업장관 회의 결과, EC 집행위는 불란서의 유보적 입장에도 불구하고 농산물 수출물량 감축, 최소 시장접근등이 포함된 오퍼리스트를 GATT 사무국에 제출키로 하였는바, 이에대한 주재국 정부 반응 아래 보고함.(조참사관 3.4 SIMONEAU 외무성 UR 담당관 접촉)

1. 불란서는 금번회의의 중요성에 비추어 EC 의 기존입장 유지를 위해 최대한 노력하였으며 회의 첫날 상당수 회원국의 동조를 기대이상으로 확보한듯 하였으나, EC 집행위의 오퍼리스트 초안 수정을 위한 전문가회의 협의과정에서 기존 리스트가 별다른 수정없이 재작성됨에 따라 상당한 당혹감과 실망을 금치 못함.

2. 상기와 같은 불란서의 고립은 당초 예상되기는 하였으나, 대부분의 회원국과 EC 집행위가 오퍼리스트 마저 EC 가 제출하지 못할 경우 UR 교착의 책임을 면할수 없다는 인식이 강해진 가운데 독일이 기존의 대불 공동입장에서 이탈하는 태도를 분명히 취한점에 기인함.

3. 동 회의후 불란서 MERMAZ 농업장관은 EC 집행위가 동 오퍼리스트를 기초로 하여 협상을 타결했을 경우 거부입장을 강력히 표명하였으나 금번회의를 계기로 EC 내 불란서의 고립양상이 더욱 가속화될 것으로 보임.

4. 또한 EC 집행위는 불란서가 적극 반대한 수출물량 감축 입장을 오퍼리스트에 포함시킴으로써(숫자는 불명시) 향후 EC 집행위의 협상 MANDATE 및 타결내용 수락 여부를 놓고 불란서와 충돌이 예상됨.

5. 한편 불란서로서는 독일의 이탈이 명백해진 이상, 새로운 협상 전략을 수립치 않을수 없는 입장이나 국내정치적으로 3.22 지방 총선을 앞두고 기존입장을 선회하기는 극히 어려운 형편임.

롱상국	장관	차관	1차보	2차보	구주국	외정실	분석관	안기부

PAGE 1   92.03.05   06:08

6. 이와관련 불정부는 내주부터 주요 협상국에 대한 EC 입장 설명을 위해 알젠틴, 브라질, 인도, 파키스탄, 스웨덴, 스위스, 인니, 홍콩, 모로코, 코트디브와르, 호주, 뉴질랜드등에 대해 의회사절단을 파견할 예정이었으나 금번회의 결과 EC 입장이 아닌 불란서 입장을 해명하는 결과가 될듯하여 시기적으로 늦은 감이 있음.

7. 한편 외무성 UR 담당관은 개인적인 의견임을 전제하고, 지방총선후 개각등 국내정세 동향과 3 월중 UR 협상 동향을 보아 미테랑대통령이 BUSH 대통령과 UR 협상을 놓고 직접 정치적 교섭에 임할 가능성을 언급함. 끝.

   (대사대리 김성식-국장)

   예고:92.12.31. 까지

외 무 부

종 별 :

번 호 : ECW-0307   일 시 : 92 0305 1700

수 신 : 장관 (봉기, 경기원, 재무부, 농림수산부, 상공부)

발 신 : 주 EC 대사대리   사본: 주제네바대사-직송필, 주EC 권동만 대사

제 목 : 갓트/UR 협상

　　　표제 관련 최근 당지의 동향을 아래 보고함
　　1. 독일의 동향
　　가. 3.4 KOHL 독일수상의 대변인은 최근 표면화되어 온 UR 협상 관련한 독,불간의 의견 마찰문제에 대한 KOHL 수상의 입장을 설명하면서, 독일은 UR 협상에서 불란서와 의견을 같이 할것이며, 불란서나 독일이 UR 협상 추진을 막고있다는 비난의 대상이될 수 없다고 말함
　　나. 동인은 UR 협상의 성공이 독일 경제발전에 주요계기가 될 것이므로 이달중에 동협상타결 계기가 마련되길 희망한다고 말하고 콜수상은 미국과 불란서와 정기적으로 접촉할의사를 갖고 있으며 특별 경제정상회담 (G-7)개최가 UR 협상 타결에 도움이 될 것으로 보고 있지 않다고 말함
　　다. 한편, 독일연립내각 구성에 참여하고 있는 정당대표인 LAMBSDORF 는 지역선거가 개최되는 3월 이전까지 불란서는 EC 회원국 대다수가 찬성하고 있는 EC 의 농산물협상안을 봉쇄할 것이라고 주장하면서 특별 경제정상회담을 조기에 개최할 것을 요구함
　　2. EC 집행위 관계관에 의하면 차기 미,EC양자협상은 내주말경 개최될 것이며, 양측은 단계적으로 의견을 조정하여 나가고 있다 함
　　3. 한편 불란서 농민연맹은 EC 집행위가 농산물보조금등 감축 LIST 를 제출한데대해 반발하면서 UR 협상을 미대통령 선거가 끝나는 금년 11월 이후로 연기할 것을요구함. 끝
　　(공사 정의용-국장)

통상국　　2차보　　경기원　　재무부　　농수부　　상공부 구조국

PAGE 1   92.03.06   07:29 DQ

외신 1과 몽제관

0036

256 우루과이라운드 협상 동향 및 무역협상위원회 회의 3

외 무 부

종 별 :

번 호 : GVW-0502   일 시 : 92 0305 1100

수 신 : 장 관(봉기, 경기원 재무부, 농수부, 상공부) 사본:박수길대사

발 신 : 주 제네바대사대리

제 목 : UR 관련 노르딕 성명

　　노르딕 대외무역 장관들은 3.4 헬싱키에서 모임을 갖고 UR 의 조속한 타결을 촉구하는 별첨성명을 채택하였음.

　　첨부: 상기 성명 1부

　　(GVW(F)-154)

　　(차석대사 김삼훈-국장)

롱상국　　경기원　　재무부　　농수부　　상공부　　국기록　　2차1관

PAGE 1   92.03.06   08:44 WH

주 제 네 바 대 표 부

번 호 : GVW(F) - 6154   년월일 : 20308   시간 : 1100

수 신 : 장   관(동기、경기원、상공부、재무부、농림수산부) (사본 : 박수길대사)

발 신 : 주 제네바대사

제 목 :

총 2 매(표지포함)

보 안 통 제	

외신과 통 제	

1154-2-1.

NORDIC STATEMENT ON THE GATT NEGOTIATIONS

The Ministers for Foreign Trade of Finland, Iceland, Norway and Sweden met in Helsinki on 4 March 1992 under the chairmanship of Mr. Pertti Salolainen, Minister for Foreign Trade of Finland.

As one of their topics the Ministers discussed the current situation in the ongoing GATT negotiations. They noted that negotiations had advanced very far in a number of important fields. The Ministers stressed that the remaining problems should not prevent a rapid and successful conclusion of the negotiations. This would give an important positive impulse to world trade and hence increase the dynamism of the world economy.

The Nordic countries will on their part contribute to a positive outcome of the Uruguay Round. Furthermore, the Ministers decided to jointly urge the parties holding a key position in the negotiations to do their utmost in view of finding a rapid solution to the remaining focal issues.

In the meeting participated Mr. Pertti Salolainen, Minister for Foreign Trade, Mr. Jón Sigurdsson, Minister of Trade and Industry, Mr. Bjørn Tore Godal, Minister of Trade and Mr. Ulf Dinkelspiel, Minister for Europe and for Foreign Trade.

154 - 2 - 2

외 무 부

종 별 :

번 호 : FRW-0505
일 시 : 92 0310 1700

수 신 : 장 관 (봉기)

발 신 : 주 불 대사대리

제 목 : UR 협상동향

　　최근 EC 내 UR 협상에 있어 독일의 유화적 입장과 관련 3.10자 당지 경제 일간지 LA TRIBUNE에 게재된 기사내용 아래 요약 보고함.

　　1. KOHL 독일총리는 92.7월 뮌헨 개최 G-7정상회담이 UR 문제로 인해 영향받는 것을 원치않는바, 이를 위해 가능한한 4월말 이전이라도 UR 협상의 조기타결을 위해 본인이 직접 전력하고 있으며, 3.20로 예정된 BUSH대통령과의 정상회담시에도 미국의 타협 필요성을 마지막으로 재강조할 예정임.

　　2. GNP 의 30프로, 고용인구의 1/3을 수출에 의존하고 있는 독일의 산업계 입장에서 보면 UR 의 실패는 독일경제에 치명적인 국제무역전쟁의 야기와 함께 세계경제의 침체가속화로 이어질것을 극히 우려하고 있으며, 이러한 문제를 다분히 과소평가하고있는 불란서의 태도에 당혹감을 갖고 있음.

　　3. 독일의 전반적 시각은 UR 협상기한이 불란서, 영국, 미국의 국내정치 일정으로 재차 연기된다 하여도 협상여건이 크게 달라질 것으로 확신할수 없다고 보나, 각료급인사들은 3.22 불 지방선거, 4.5 독일 BADE-WURTEMBERG 및 SCHLESWIG-HOLSTEIN 지역 선거가 끝나면 여하한 형태로든 변화가 있을 것으로 기대하고 있음.

　　4. 독일은 불란서가 반대하는 EC 농산물 수출물량 감축을 수락할 태세가 되어있음. 이와관련, EC 가 공동 농업정책(CAP) 개혁에 있어 기존 농산물 가격체제의 전반적인하에 합의시 불란서 잉여 농산물의 대독일 수출이 증가할수 있으므로 이를 댓가로 UR 협상에서 불란석 양보할 가능성이 있다고 봄.

　　5. 이경우 독 농민(전체인구 3프로)의 상당한 반발이 예상되나 각국의 타협을 통한 UR 협상타결을 위해 불가피하다고 보며 여하한 경우에도 대외적으로 EC 의 분열상을 보이는 것은 피하여야 됨. 끝.

통상국　　2차보　　구주국

PAGE 1
92.03.11　02:30

외신 1과 통제관

0040

외 무 부

종 별 :

번 호 : FRW-0514

일 시 : 92 0311 1550

수 신 : 장관(통삼,경일,통기)

발 신 : 주 불 대사

제 목 : 불 상공장관 방한 평가

일반문서로 재분류 (1982. 12. 31)

대:통삼 20655-341

92.2 STRAUSS-KAHN 불 상공장관의 방한 관련, 불측의 평가 아래 보고함.(3.11 조참사관, BENTEJAC 장관 국제문제담당보좌관 접촉)

1. 방한 소감

0 장관으로서는 최초의 방한이었으나 한국의 경제역량을 재인식하는 좋은 기회였으며, 한국측의 환대와 주요 경제각료와의 면담내용에 크게 만족하고 있음.

0 STRAUSS-KAHN 장관은 지난주 아국 상공장관에 발송한 사의표명 서한에서 한장관의 방불을 초청하였음.

2. 양국간 통상경제 현안

0 불장관 방한시 아측에 요청한 사안중 한국정부가 즉시 머린제린사에 대한 부자인가 조치를 취해준데 대해 사의를 표함.

0 특히 불측은 아국 자동차 수입허가 이후 한국정부가 즉각적으로 화답하여준데 만족하고 있으며 이와같이 상호 호혜적 조치가 계속되기를 기대함.

3. UR 협상

0 금번 방한기간중 UR 협상 현안에 대한 양측간 협의가 상당히 유익했으며 특히 불측으로서는 쌀시장 개방 문제에 있어 한국이 처한 현실적 어려움을 새삼 인식하는 계기가 되었음.

0 현재 EC 의 기본입장인 "예외없는 곤세화 원칙"을 불란서가 변경할수는 없으나 추후 EC 내 관련사항 협의 기회시 한국측 입장이 유념될수 있도록 언급하겠음.

4. 기술이전

0 불측은 금번 방한을 통해 한국의 현 경제발전단계에 있어 가장 긴요한 선진기술 전수를 위해 적극 협력할 용의를 표망한바 있음.

통상국	장관	차관	2차보	경제국	통상국	분석관

O 불란서는 대형 프로젝트에 관련된 기술이전뿐 아니라 현재 APRODI 와 중소기업 중앙회간 추진되고 있는 중소규모 기업간 기술협력 사업도 내용면에서 보다 충실해 지도록 보완내지는 재검토할 의향이 있음.

5. 민간협력

O 향후 양국간 협력은 민간분야가 선도해 나가야 할것인바 이와 관련 불정부는 금년 파리 개최예정인 한. 불 최고경영자 클럽 총회가 민간경협의 새로운 계기가 될것으로 기대함.

O 일본 경단련 회장등 재계 핵심인사로 구성된 대표단(약 50 명 규모)이 3.9-11 간 불란서를 방문하며 미테랑 대통령, 크레송 총리 예방과 주요 경제각료 면담 및 불 전경련측과의 회동을 통해 상호 투자촉진 및 이해증진의 기회로 활용하였으며 불측은 동 성과에 만족하고 있음.

O 한. 불 통상교류 내용은 일본에 비해 보다 호혜균형적인 바, 한국측에서 한. 불 경영자 클럽총회에 다수의 고위 경제인단을 파견시 불정부는 한국 대표단이 방불 성과에 만족할수 있도록 최대한 협조 예정임.끝.

(대사 노영찬-국장)

예고:92.12.31. 까지

PAGE 2

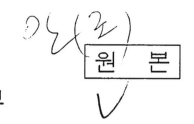

외 무 부

종 별 :

번 호 : ECW-0345   일 시 : 92 0311 1900

수 신 : 장 관(봉기, 경기원, 재무부, 농림수산부, 상공부, 기정동문)

발 신 : 주 EC대사대리(권동만) 사본:주미, 주제네바대사(중계요망)
대사   중계원

제 목 : 갓트/UR 협상

연: ECW-0307

표제 관련한 최근의 미.EC 양자협상 동향등을 아래 보고함

1. NATO/NACC 회의참석차 당지방문중인 BAKER 미 국무장관은 3.10 DELORS EC 집행위원장을 만나 UR 농산물협상과 관련한 미측의 새로운 입장을 전달한 것으로 알려짐. 한편, 상기제안과 관련 금 3.11 당지에서 미.EC 고위급협상이 개최되었는 바, 동협의내용은 상금 파악되지 않고 있음 (미.EC 양측은 동 협의 진전사항에 관해 당분간 보안 유지키로 한 것으로 보도되고 있음)

2. 이와관련, 당지 전문가들은 최근 BUSH대통령이 DELORS 위원장에게 보낸 서한에서 농산물 보조감축 문제에 대해 미국은 탄력성있는 입장을 취한다는 입장을 전달한바 있음을 상기시키면서, 금번 고위협상에서 미측은 EC가 CAP 개혁의 일환으로 시행코자 하는 직접소득보조를 감축대상 보조에서 제외하는 방법을 제시한 것으로 추정하고 있으며 그 구체적 방법으로 EC의 직접 소득보조를 GREEN BOX 에 포함하는 것이 아니라 BLUE BOX를 새로이 설정하고 이의 정확한 개념 및 운영방법을 협의할 것으로 보고 있음. 그러나 REBALANCING 문제에 대해서는 미측의 입장이 변경된바 없는 것으로 보임.

3. ANDRIESSEN 집행위원은 3.11 미측의 새로운 제안내용을 신중히 검토한후 자신의 입장을 밝힐수 있을 것이라는 반응을 보였으며, MACSHARRY 집행위원은 CAP 개혁안에 제시된 소득보조가 감축대상에서 제외될수 있는 제안이라면 이를 환영한다고 말함. 끝

(공사 정의용-국장)

통상국   안기부   경기원   재무부   농수부   상공부   2차보   구주국

PAGE 1   92.03.12   09:21 WH
                                                   외신 1과 통제관

                                                        0043

외 무 부

관리
번호 92-206

종 별 :

번 호 : ECW-0373   일 시 : 92 0316 1830

수 신 : 장관 (봉기, 경기원, 재무부, 농림수산부, 상공부)

발 신 : 주 EC 대사대리   사본: 주 미, 제네바대사(중계요망)

제 목 : 갓트/UR 협상

    당관 정공사는 금 3.16 EC 집행위 대외총국 (DGI) 수석심의관 JACQUES DUGIMONT (UR 협상 실무조정총괄) 을 면담, UR 협상 진전상황에 관해 협의한바 주요내용 아래 보고함 (이관용농무관, WASSOLS 한국담당관 동석)

    1. 미.EC 양자협상및 UR 타결전망

    가. 동 심의관은 미.EC 양측 모두 DUNKEL 총장이 제시한 시한내 협상이 종결되지 않을 경우, 미 대통령선거등 정치일정으로 협상타결이 어려워질 것이라는 사실을 인식하고, 타협안을 도출해 내기위해 최대한 노력하고 있으며, 동시한전 UR 협상 타결가능성이 전혀 없는것은 아니라고 말함

    나. 동인은 이어 현재 협상이 계속 진행 (금주중 워싱턴에게 재개) 되고있어 동내용을 사전에 설명할수 없으나, EC 의 직접소득보조 문제만 타결되면 여타문제는 쉽게 해결할수 있을 것이라고 언급함

    다. 정공사는 UR 협상과정의 원활한 진행을 위해서는 여타 주요협상참여국에 대한 미.EC 양자협상 과정의 TRANSPARENCY 가 필요함을 지적한바, 동 심의관은 한.EC 양측이 제네바대표부를 통해 긴밀히 협력하고 있는데 대해 만족을 표시하고 가급적 조속하고 적절한 시기에 제네바대표부를 통해 미.EC 간 협상내용을 한국측에 설명토록 하겠다고 답변함

    2. 아국 관련문제

    가. 동 심의관은 한국의 쌀문제에 대한 입장은 충분히 이해하며 또한 EC 로서는 직접적인 관련이 없는 문제이긴 하나 일본이 궁극적으로 쌀관세화를 수락하는 경우 한국도 이를 수용할수 밖에 없지 않겠느냐고 반문함

    나. 정공사는 EC 가 한국을 기타 개도국과는 다르게 취급하려고 하는 움직임이 있으며 특히 긴급 수입규제와 관련, SELECTIVITY 의 적용을 주장하고 있는것에 대한

───

통상국   장관   차관   1차보   2차보   분석관   안기부   경기원   재무부
농수부   상공부 중계

PAGE 1   92.03.17   05:48

우려를 표명한바, 동 심의관은 SELECTIVITY 적용에대한 EC 의 입장은 이미 오래전에 결정되어 있는것으로, 이에대한 입장변경은 회원국간 합의를 이루기 힘들것이며 93 년부터 EC 단일시장 출범에 따라 회원국들의 개별 수량규제 조치가 불가능하게 됨을 고려할때 긴급수입규제에 있어 SELECTIVITY 적용은 불가피할 것이라는 견해를 표명함. 끝

(공사 정의용-국장)

예고: 92.12.31 까지

외 무 부

종 별 :

번 호 : ECW-0379 일 시 : 92 0317 1800

수 신 : 장 관 (통삼,통기,경과,아동,정보,농수산부)

발 신 : 주 EC 대사대리 사본: 주제네바,호주대사(중계필)

제 목 : EC-호주 각료회담 개최동정(자료응신 92-12호)

1. 80년 이후 개최되어온 EC-호주 연례 각료회담이 3.16(월) 브랏셀에서 개최되었는바 동 회담에 EC 측에서는 ANDRIESSEN 대외담당 집행위원과 PANDOLFI 과학및 연구개발담당 집행위원이, 호주측에서는 EVANS 외무통상장관과 KERIN 통상및 해외개발담당장관이 참석하였음

2. 회담종료후 발표된 공동성명등에 나타난 주요협의 요지 아래 보고함

가. UR 협상

O EVANS 장관은 DUNKEL 안이 세계무역 자유화와 UR 협상의 기본목표를 달성할수있는 것으로 판단, 호주는 이를 적극 수용하고 있다고 밝히고, UR 협상의 현실적인 타결을 위해 EC 측도 이를 받아드릴 것을 권고한바, ANDRIESSEN 집행위원은 DUNKEL안이 특히, 농산물 분야에 있어 크게 불균형 되어있어 필요한 수정을 추진하고 있다고 설명함

O 그러나 양측은 UR 협상의 성공적 타결이 매우 중요함에 인식을 같이하고 UR 협상 종료시한(부활절전) 의 준수를 위해 최선의 노력을 다할것에 합의함

O EVANS 장관은 호주를 포함한 CAIRNS 그룹은 농산물 보조금중 수출보조및 시장접근 분야는 불가능하나, 국내보조 부문에 대해서는 FLEXIBILITY를 보일수 있다면서 EC 측도 보다 탄력적인 입장을 보일것을 촉구하였음. ANDRIESSEN 집행위원은 EC-미국간 양자협상에 진전이 있을 경우 CAIRNS GROUP 도 타협안 작성에 참여할수 있도록 하겠다고 약속함

O 동 회의후 ANDRIESSEN 집행위원은 부활절전 UR 타결시한이 지켜지지 않을 경우에 대한 기자들의 질문에 대해 그 경우는 전체 UR협상의 실패가능성이 있다고 하면서부활절전에 타결이 되지 않는다면, 연말까지도 타결이 어려울 것이라고 답변함

나. 양자문제

통상국	1차보	2차보	아주국	구주국	경제국	통상국	외정실	농수부

92.03.18 06:45 FN

외신 1과 통제관

0046

1) 과기협력협정 추진

0 양측은 과학기술분야의 협력강화를 위해 86년 서명된 과기협력 약정을 일반협력 협정(FRAMEWORK AGREEMENT FOR COOPERATION IN SCIENCE ANDTECHNOLOGY) 으로 확대할 것에 합의함

2) 산업협력 강화

0 양측은 산업정책에 관한 정보교환강화를 위해 산업협력 공동그룹 (JOINT GROUPONINDUSTRIAL COOPERATION) 을 구성하기로 합의하고 양측간 중소기업분야 협력증대를 위해 EC 의 BC-NET (BUSINESS COOPERATION NETWORK) 에 하주가 가입하는 약정에 서명함으로서 양측기업간 협력및 정보교환을 보다 확대할수 있는 기반을 마련함

3) 기타 협력강화

0 양측은 에너지, 환경, 개발원조 등의분야에서의 협력을 보다 강화키로 하였으며, 표준및 인증의 상호인정을 위해 양자협의를 강화할것에 합의함

3. 동 회담시 협의된 상세사항은 EC집행위와 접촉, 파악한후 추보 예정임. 끝

(공사 정의용-국장)

외 무 부

관리번호 92-221

종 별 :

번 호 : ECW-0384   일 시 : 92 0319 1600

수 신 : 장 관(봉기, 경기원, 농수산부, 상공부) 사본: 주미, 일, 제네바대사 중계필

발 신 : 주 EC 대사대리

제 목 : UR 협상동향

　　1. HELMUT KOHL 독일수상이 금주말 미국을 방문, 3.21(토) CAMP DAVID 에서 BUSH 미국대통령과 만나, 교착상태에 있는 UR 협상의 마지막 정치적 타결을 시도할 것으로 알려짐.

　　2. KOHL 수상은 그간 불란서, 영국을 포함한 EC 주요 회원국과 사전협의를 통하여 UR 농산물 협상타결의 최대난제로 알려진 수출물량 기준 감축과 관련 일정기간동안 미국이 대 EC 대체곡물 수출을 동결한다는 조건으로 EC 측이 수출물량기준 감축을 받아들인다는데 대체적인 합의를 이루고 이를 미측에 타협안으로 제기할 것이라고 함. 한편 EC 관계관은 BAKER 미국무장관이 EC 측에 제의한 직접소득 보조허용과 관련 GREEN BOX 대신 SAFE BOX (BLUE BOX) 제도에 대하여 미국이 상기 KOHL 수상의 타협안을 수락하는 경우 PACKAGE 로 처리될수 있는 것이므로 향후 UR 협상전망을 긍정적으로 평가한다고 언급하면서도 3.17 미 농업국 (US FARM BUREAU) 이 여사한 대 EC 대체곡물 수출동결에 반대한다는 의견을 분명히한점을 들어 금번 KOHL 수상의 방미결과를 낙관할수만은 없다고 덧붙임

　　3. 한편 3.18 당지 일본대표부 SATO 참사관은 김참사관에게 상기 KOHL 수상의 방미가 UR 협상타결의 결정적인 계기가 될 것이며, 미.EC 의 합의에 따라 협상시 한인 부활절이전 타결가능성도 있음으로 농산물협상 관련 미.EC 동향을 예의 주시하고 UR 협상의 마무리 (WRAP-UP) 단계에 돌입하도록 지시를 받았다고 하면서 한국이 쌀문제에 관하여 일본이 마지막까지 기존의 일관된 입장을 유지하리라고 오해하지 않기를 바란다고 언급함. 끝

　　(공사 정의용-국장)

　　예고: 92.12.31 까지

검　통상표현(19 9.2. .6. 30)

통상국	장관	차관	1차보	2차보	외정실	분석관	청와대	안기부
경기원	농수부	상공부	중계					

외 무 부

종 별 :

번 호 : GEW-0531   일 시 : 92 0320 1630

수 신 : 장 관(통기, 구일)

발 신 : 주 독대사

제 목 : 독.미 정상간 UR 관련 협의보도

　　주재국 일간지 금 3.20.자는 주재국 KOHL 수상이 금주말 CAMP DAVID 에서 미국 BUSH 대통령과 회동시 미. EC간 UR농산물 협상관련 타협안 도출을 모색할 것으로 보도하고 있는 바, 관계기사 별첨 FAX 송부하니 참고바람

　　별첨: GEW(F)-050

　　(대사-국장)

통상국　　　구주국

주 독 일 대 사 관

GEW(F) - 050   2032016530

<table>
<tr><td>보안
동계</td><td>∨</td></tr>
</table>

(출처 :   )

수 신 : 장 관 (통기, 구인)

발 신 : 주 독 대 사

제 목 : GEW - 0531 의 별첨

　　　　(표지 포함 총 3 매)

0050

Am Kamin von Camp David will Bush Kohl an GATT erinnern

Das Allgemeine Zoll- und Handelsabkommen ist das große Thema zwischen Deutschland und den Vereinigten Staaten

Von unserem Korrespondenten
Siegfried Maruhn

Washington. Der Rahmen ist inoffiziell, fast familiär. Bundeskanzler Kohl und Frau Hannelore kommen mit kleiner Begleitung. Präsident Bush hat beide zu einem Wochenendbesuch auf seinen Feriensitz nach Camp David eingeladen. Doch am Kamin in den Catoctin-Bergen dürfte es heiß hergehen.

Der Präsident wird den Kanzler an sein Versprechen von Houston erinnern. Damals, beim Weltwirtschaftsgipfel vor zwei Jahren hatte Kohl zugesagt, sich bei Frankreichs Staatspräsident Mitterand für einen erfolgreichen Abschluß der Uruguay-Runde einzusetzen. Nun drängt die Zeit, drängt auch der Präsident.

Seit Monaten gibt es in den deutsch-amerikanischen Beziehungen kaum ein anderes Thema. GATT, das Allgemeine Abkommen über Handel und Tarife, beherrscht die Diskussion. In der Uruguay-Runde (so benannt nach dem Konferenzort, an dem sie begonnen wurde) soll eine Fülle von Verbesserungen beschlossen werden, mit denen der Welthandel vereinfacht und ausgedehnt werden soll. Einer der Kernpunkte ist die Landwirtschaft, zumindest aus der Sicht Amerikas, des Großexporteurs von Agrarprodukten. Europa soll die wettbewerbsverfälschende Überproduktion verringern und seine Exportsubventionen abschaffen oder zumindest senken. Dazu ist es nur unter Schmerzen und auf Raten bereit. Statt der Exporte sollen irgendwann in der Zukunft die Produzenten subventioniert werden. Das wäre wettbewerbsneutral. Doch die Umstellung fordert Zeit, wie auch die Bundesregierung argumentiert. Haupthindernis ist Frankreich, das auf seine Bauern Rücksicht nimmt. Deutschland, so meint Amerika, müßte eigentlich wegen seiner auf den Export angewiesenen Industrie auf der Seite der USA stehen.

In der Diskussion am Kamin wird Bundeskanzler Kohl auch noch anderes Argumente hören. Für Präsident Bush ist die Uruguay-Runde, ist der Außenhandel überhaupt ein wichtiges Wahlkampfthema. Er muß sich gegen Vorwürfe wehren, daß er amerikanische Interessen vernachlässige. Wer George Bush als Präsidenten behalten möchte, so könnte die Botschaft lauten, muß jetzt etwas für ihn tun, auch wenn es bedeutet, einem anderen engen Freund, François Mitterand, auf die Füße zu treten.

Im Wahlkampf kommt Deutschland gemeinsam mit Japan recht häufig vor. Manchmal als gutes, nachahmenswertes Beispiel, wenn es um Krankenversicherung oder Berufsausbildung geht. Meist jedoch als Gefahr von morgen, als Konkurrent. Präsident Bush macht da keine Ausnahme. Im Autostaat Michigan warf er seinem Konkurrenten Buchanan vor, als angeblich guter Amerikaner kein amerikanisches sondern ein Importauto zu fahren. Im Hintergrund zeigte der Fernsehspot dazu einen Mercedes-Stern. Gegenüber der Kritik hat Bush einen schweren Stand, wenn er das Freihandelsabkommen mit Mexiko vertritt oder seinerseits für Zugeständ-nisse an Amerikas Handelspartner in Uruguay-Runde wirbt. Druck auf Japan t Deutschland soll einen Ausgleich schaff „Der Präsident kümmert sich praktisch t lich darum," verteidigt ihn sein Stabsc Skinner. „Das wird das Thema einiger I kussionen an diesem Wochenende in Ca David sein. Wir werden nicht für irgend. GATT-Abkommen kämpfen, sondern für Abkommen, das Sinn macht und die Märl überall öffnet."

Ermahnungen seien fehl am Platze, he es vorbeugend von deutscher Seite. Die U guay-Runde werde wie vorgesehen zu Er geführt. Doch Kompromißformeln, die : Bonn avisiert worden waren, werden von Handelsbeauftragten des Präsidenten, Ca Hills, bereits als unzureichend bezeichn. „Wir glauben nicht, daß es Sinn macht, Tar die in der Vergangenheit herunterverhand worden, wieder zu erhöhen", kritisiert sie d Vorschlag, einen neuen Ausgleich zu sch fen. Allerdings wird Frau Hills, wie sie zug am Wochenende in Camp David nicht dal sein.

General Anzeiger 3.20.zr.

Seite 8 — HANDELSBLATT   3.20. 카

USA / Kanzler Kohl beim Präsidenten in Camp David

Im Handelsstreit kann sich George Bush kaum bewegen

Von VIOLA HERMS DRATH

HANDELSBLATT, Donnerstag, 19.3.1992

WASHINGTON. Ungeachtet der heftigen Kontroversen über das Gatt, den westlichen Beitrag für die GUS-Republiken sowie die wachsenden internationalen Verantwortung Deutschlands in der Welt und in dem kollektiven europäischen Sicherheitsnetz sind die deutsch-amerikanischen Beziehungen intakt. Wenn Kanzler Kohl mit Präsident George Bush am Wochenende nach Camp David zu Gesprächen fliegt, dann liegen diesem Privatbesuch keinerlei aktuelle Krisen und bilateralen Probleme zu Grunde.

Allerdings mangelt es an europäisch-amerikanischen Verstimmungen nicht. An erster Stelle der Traktandenliste steht fraglos Washingtons zunehmende Unzufriedenheit mit der stagnierenden Welthandelsrunde des Gatt und den Klagen, daß die Reformen zur Liberalisierung des Welthandels, insbesondere des stark subventionierten Welt-Agarmarktes, zu wünschen übrig lassen.

Kürzlich von Vizepräsident Dan Quayle und einigen Senatoren darauf aufmerksam gemacht, daß zwischen Gatt und Sicherheitspolitik gewisse Verbindungen bestehen, dürfte von beiden Gesprächspartnern ein Kompromiß angesteuert werden, der die von Kohl versprochenen Restriktionen des subventionierten Exportes überschüssiger europäischer Agrarprodukte zum Ziel hat. Doch ob der angeblich von der Europäischen Kommission gebilligte Vorschlag, den europäischen Markt im Gegenzug durch das Einfrieren amerikanischer Getreide-Ersatz-Exporte zu schützen, für Bush akzeptabel ist, erscheint in diesem Wahljahr ebenso fraglich wie ein

Verzicht von Frankreichs Präsident Mitterand auf Subventionen bei seiner Agrarpolitik.

Die langfristige Stabilisierung der GUS-Republiken, die einen Zugang zur Weltbank und dem Währungsfonds voraussetzt und damit eine finanzielle Aufstockung und Neuverteilung der Quoten erfordert, ist angesichts der gigantischen innenpolitischen Probleme Amerikas ein Thema, dem vor der Präsidentenwahl im November gleichermaßen geringe Erfolgschancen beigemessen werden.

Weniger frustrierend sieht es für den deutschen Gast im sicherheitspolitischen Bereich aus. Während die Bush-Administration ihr starkes Engagement in Europa erneut zum Ausdruck gebracht hat und mit dem Verbleiben von 150000 US-Soldaten unterstreicht, dürfte es Kohl vermutlich daran gelegen sein, seinem Gesprächspartner klarzumachen, daß es in der deutschen Sicherheitspolitik kein „entweder oder" zwischen Nato und der von Frankreich bevorzugten WEU geben kann, sondern nur ein „sowohl als auch".

Kohls wirtschaftspolitischer Einsatz in Osteuropa wird ihn jedoch einer schlüssigen Antwort auf die Frage nach vermehrter Verantwortung beim globalen „burden sharing" kaum entheben. Zu diesem Schwerpunkt gehört zugleich die deutsche Beteiligung an den Uno-Friedensmissionen.

So bedauerlich die gezielt veröffentlichte Pentagon-Studie sein mag, in der dem deutschen Bündnispartner vertragsbrechende nukleare Ambitionen unterstellt werden, so beleuchtet dieser inzwischen schnell zu den Akten gelegte Vorfall doch, wie wichtig die Vermeidung falscher Signale ist, wie sie bisweilen aus Bonn mit der Verfolgung von Alleingängen — siehe Golfkrieg, Türkei, Jugolawien — gesetzt wurden.

0052

외　무　부

종　별 :

번　호 : GEW-0545　　　　　　　　　　일　시 : 92 0323 1700

수　신 : 장관(구일,동구일,미일,통기)

발　신 : 주 독 대사

제　목 : 콜 수상방미(자료응신 26호)

　　1. 연호 콜 수상은 3.21-22. 에 걸쳐 부쉬 대통령과 CAMP DAQVID 에서 회담한 바,
동 결과에 관한 당지 언론보도내용을 아래 보고함

　　2. 양국 정상은 UR 협상이 조속히 타결되어야 한다는데 의견을 같이하였다하며,
특히 독일측은 금년 7 월 뮌헨에서 개최예정인 G-7 정상회의가 UR 문제에 치중되는
일이 없도록 할것이라 함. 백악관 대변인은 이와 관련 DUNDEL GATT 사무총장이 정한
UR 타결시한인 4.15. 까지 타결될 것이라는 낙관론을 제기하였음

　　3. 양국 정상은 CIS 정세및 대 CIS. 유고지원 문제도 협의한바, 부쉬 대통령은 구
쏘연방의 핵잠재력 통제문제에 있어 콜 수상의 중요한 역할을 강조하였음. 콜 수상은
미국이 CIS 국가들에 대한 지원을 늘릴 것을 촉구하였음. 부쉬 대통령은 콜수상의
도착에 앞서 우크라이나및 아르메니아 대통령과 통화를 가졌으며, 이들 CIS 국
대통령들은 3.20. 키에프에서 개최된 CIS 정상회의 결과를 부시대통령에게 설명하고,
이를 콜 수상에게 전달해 줄것을 요청하였다 함

　　4. 기타 양국 정상들은 중근동, 이락및 유고정세에 관해서도 의견을 교환하였음.
특히 독.미관계에 있어, 최근 유고사태들에 있어 양국간의 이견이 있어 왔다는
언론보도와 관련, 미 고위관리는 미국이 독일의 적극적인 외교정책(ASSERTIVENESS)
시현에 대해 우려하고 있지 않으며, 오히려 구주에서의 독일의 역할및 독. 미
동반자관계에 만족하고 있다고 밝힌 것으로 보도되고 있음.

　　5. 콜 수상의 금번 방미는 이미 작년 크리스마스 이전 부쉬 대통령의 초청으로
준비된 것으로서, 양국은 '사적인' 성격을 언급하였지만 정상회담시에는 베이커 미
국무장관과 국가안보회의 의장인 SCOWCROFT 양인이 배석하였다함. 콜 수상의 방미가
이루어진 것은 부쉬 대통령으로서는 UR 의 농산물 협상타결이 금년 대통령선거에
영향을 미칠 것이라는 고려와, 콜 수상은 UR 협상이 실패할 경우 독일의 수출이

구주국	장관	차관	미주국	구주국	통상국	외정실	분석관	청와대
안기부								

타격을 받을것을 우려하여 이루어진 것임. 미국은 UR 협상의 실패를 막기 위해 독일의
중재를 요청하였다 함

6. 콜 수상이 3.23. 귀국후 기자회견에서 발표한 방미 결과를 별첨 FAX 송부함. 끝
(대사-국장)
별첨:GEW(F)-052

—7—

주 독 일 대 사 관

GEW(F) - 052

수 신 : 장 관 (구헌, 통구헌, 미헌, 통기)

발 신 : 주 독 대 사

제 목 : 　　　　별첨물

　　　　(표지 포함 총 7 매)

0055

I.

Ich bin heute morgen von einer zweitägigen Begegnung mit Präsident Bush in Camp David zurückgekehrt, wo wir in einer sehr freundschaftlichen Atmosphäre außerordentlich intensive Gespräche geführt haben.

Vorab möchte ich festhalten:

Erstens: Wir stimmen in der Einschätzung der weltpolitischen Entwicklung in hohem Maß überein.

Zweitens: Wir wollen die enge Abstimmung vor allem im Hinblick auf wichtige internationale Entscheidungen in den kommenden Monaten verstärkt fortsetzen.

1. GATT
Ein zentrales Thema unserer Gespräche war der Stand der Uruguay-Runde im GATT.

Ich möchte auch hier klarstellen, daß ich in den USA keine Verhandlungen geführt habe. Dies ist für die Europäische Gemeinschaft Sache der EG-Kommission

Präsident Bush will – ebenso wie Präsident Mitterrand und ich wie auch die anderen Partner in der EG – daß die GATT-Runde Ende April erfolgreich abgeschlossen wird.

Er teilt meine Auffassung, daß ein Erfolg der GATT-Runde von außerordentlicher Bedeutung für die weitere Entwicklung der Weltwirtschaft ist und daß wir einen Rückfall in Protektionismus unter allen Umständen verhindern müssen.

Dabei sind wir uns einig, daß eine erfolgreiche Uruguay-Runde nicht nur für Europa und die USA, sondern vor allem auch für die Entwicklungsländer entscheidend ist.

Über diesen Teil meiner Gespräche werde ich jetzt unsere europäischen Partner sowie die Brüsseler Kommission unterrichten.

2. UNCED-Konferenz in Rio
Ein weiteres wichtiges Thema war die bevorstehende UNCED-Konferenz in Rio. Präsident Bush und ich stimmen darin überein, daß diese Konferenz ein bedeutsamer Schritt auf dem Weg zu einer weltweiten Umweltpartnerschaft werden muß. 0056

Dabei geht es insbesondere darum,
- eine Klima-Rahmen-Konvention
- eine Konvention über die biologische Vielfalt sowie
- Grundsätze für die Erhaltung der Wälder
zu verabschieden.

3. Wirtschaftsgipfel München
Wir haben ferner eingehend über den diesjährigen Wirtschaftsgipfel in München gesprochen.

Präsident Bush unterstützt meine Überlegungen, in München mehr Zeit für informelle Gespräche zu haben. Wir wollen uns auf die wirklich globalen Themen konzentrieren.

Diese sind:
- Die weltwirtschaftliche Entwicklung;
- Die Lage in der GUS und in den Staaten Mittel- und Südosteuropas.
- Die Probleme der Dritten Welt.

4. GUS und MOE
Die Lage in der GUS sowie in den Staaten Mittel- und Südosteuropas war ein weiteres zentrales Thema.

Wir waren uns einig, daß die jetzt zum zweiten Mal angelaufene Nothilfe für Rußland und andere Republiken kein Dauerzustand werden kann.

Wir müssen vielmehr das Potential vor Ort stärken, vor allem in der Landwirtschaft. Zugleich müssen die Infrastruktur und nicht zuletzt die Sicherheit der Kernkraftwerke verbessert werden.

Wir brauchen ein Gesamtkonzept "Hilfe zur Selbsthilfe".

Präsident Bush und ich haben ausdrücklich die Bedeutung unterstrichen, die dem von unseren beiden Regierungen und Rußland initiierten Internationalen Wissenschafts- und Technologiezentrum zukommt.

0057

5. Rüstungskontrolle

In diesem Zusammenhang haben wir auch die Probleme der Kontrolle, der Zerstörung und der Nicht-Verbreitung von nuklearen und chemischen Waffen der früheren Sowjetunion erörtert.

Wir sind uns einig, daß hier vor allem verantwortliches Handeln seitens der Republiken gefordert ist, auf deren Territorien diese Waffensysteme noch lagern.

Ich habe dies auch in einem Telefongespräch mit Präsident Jelzin heute morgen noch einmal deutlich gemacht.

6. Bilaterale/Transatlantische Beziehungen

Ich habe gegenüber Präsident Bush, aber auch in der Öffentlichkeit noch einmal unterstrichen, daß Freundschaft und Partnerschaft mit den USA für Deutschland von existentieller Bedeutung bleiben und daß auch in Zukunft Freiheit und Sicherheit Europas nur durch den Transatlantischen Verbund garantiert sind.

Ich habe dabei nachdrücklich unseren Wunsch bekräftigt, eine starke und sichtbare Präsenz amerikanischer Truppen in Europa zu erhalten.

Gleichzeitig wollen wir unsere Partnerschaft durch einen verstärkten Austausch in Kultur, Wissenschaft, Forschung und Technologie vertiefen.

Präsident Bush und ich sind daher übereingekommen, eine deutsch-amerikanische Akademie der Wissenschaften zu gründen

Eine breit angelegte Zusammenarbeit zwischen den USA und Europa liegt nicht nur in beiderseitigem Interesse, sondern ist ein entscheidender Beitrag zu Stabilität und Sicherheit in einer sich rasch wandelnden Welt.

II.

In Camp David haben wir zugleich über die wirtschaftliche Entwicklung in unseren beiden Ländern gesprochen.
Lassen Sie mich deshalb auch hier einige Bemerkungen zur wirtschaftlichen Situation in Deutschland machen:

0058

Erstens: Die Wirtschaft in den alten Bundesländern befindet sich in einer Konsolidierungsphase.

Nach einer starken Expansion in den vorangegangenen Jahren hat sich das Wirtschaftswachstum verlangsamt.

Insgesamt rechnet die Bundesregierung 1992 für ganz Deutschland mit einem Wachstum von rund 2 % (bei rund 1 1/2 % in den alten Bundesländern).

Gleichzeitig wollen wir die Inflationsrate in den alten Bundesländern wieder deutlich unter 4 % drücken. Die Bundesbank, mit der ich in der vergangenen Woche hierüber gesprochen habe, sieht hierfür gute Chancen.

Angesichts eines weniger günstigen wirtschaftlichen Umfeldes sind auch die Verteilungsspielräume enger geworden.

Ich erinnere an meine Aussage hier in der Bundespressekonferenz am 10. Januar 1992:
"Dieses Jahr 1992 ist kein Jahr für Verteilungskämpfe und Anspruchsdenken, sondern ein Jahr der Vorsorge für Wachstum, für Arbeitsplätze und für Stabilität."

In dieser Situation sind die Tarifpartner besonders gefordert.
Wie Sie wissen trägt die Bundesregierung im Rahmen des öffentlichen Dienstes als Arbeitgeber jetzt selbst unmittelbar Verantwortung.
Deswegen wiederhole ich: "In dieser besonderen Situation haben für mich Stabilität und Sicherheit der Arbeitsplätze und die Schaffung neuer Arbeitsplätze eindeutig Vorrang vor allem anderen."

Zweitens: In den neuen Bundesländern verzeichnen wir eine positive Entwicklung bei Dienstleistungen, Bauwirtschaft und Handwerk.
Nachdem Industrieproduktion und Industrieaufträge im letzten Jahr den Tiefpunkt erreicht haben, geht es hier langsam aufwärts.

Für 1992 wird für die neuen Bundesländer ein Wachstum von rund + 10 % erwartet.

Nach wie vor schwierig ist die Lage auf dem Arbeitsmarkt. Es sind zuletzt 1,3 Mio Arbeitslose und 0,5 Mio Kurzarbeiter registriert worden.

0059

Unser wichtigstes Ziel bleibt deshalb, mehr neue Arbeitsplätze zu schaffen, als alte wegfallen.

Nach Einschätzung des Wirtschafts Sachverständigenrates und anderer Experten kann das noch in diesem Jahr erreicht werden, wenn alle Beteiligten diesem Ziel Vorrang einräumen.

Wie notwendig dieser Vorrang ist, verdeutlichen drei zentrale Kennziffern. Das Statistische Bundesamt hat jüngst für 1991 festgestellt,

- daß die Produktivität Ost 29 % des Westniveaus entspricht,
- daß Löhne und Gehälter je Beschäftigten 44 % des Westniveaus ausmachen und
- daß damit die Lohnstückkosten in Ostdeutschland 55 % höher als in Westdeutschland liegen.

Dies bedeutet: Die Wettbewerbsposition der Unternehmen in Ostdeutschland ist stark belastet.

Um so mehr bleibt es gerade in dieser schwierigen Situation Aufgabe der Tarifpartner, Produktivität und Lohnhöhe stärker als bisher in Übereinstimmung zu bringen.

Drittens: Selbstverständlich müssen in den neuen Bundesländern zugleich enorme Investitionsanstrengungen unternommen werden.

1992 planen westdeutsche Unternehmer Investitionen in Höhe von 44 Mrd. DM. Das sind zwei Drittel mehr als im Vorjahr.

Bis 1995 wollen westdeutsche Unternehmen neuesten Umfragen zufolge 113 Mrd. DM investieren (Institut der Deutschen Wirtschaft).

Viertens: Mit einem staatlichen Nettotransfer von weit über 100 Mrd. DM pro Jahr dokumentieren wir unsere Entschlossenheit, den Aufbau Ostdeutschland voranzubringen.

Damit haben wir aber zugleich die Grenze unserer finanziellen Leistungsfähigkeit erreicht.

Die neuesten Bundesbankzahlen machen ebenso unmißverständlich klar, daß der Bund mit Abstand die größte Belastung bei der Finanzierung des Nettotransfers von West nach Ost trägt - nämlich 74 von insgesamt 180 Mrd. DM in 1992. Dagegen ist der Beitrag der westdeutschen Länder und Gemeinden mit 12 Mrd. DM vergleichsweise bescheiden.

0060

...

Vor diesem Hintergrund muß darauf geachtet werden, daß künftige Belastungen
zwischen allen Beteiligten - Bund, westliche Länder und Gemeinden, östliche
Länder und Gemeinden - fair aufgeteilt werden.
Das Steuerpaket 1992 war ein erster Schritt in diese Richtung.

Für mich ist selbstverständlich: Bei den künftigen Belastungen muß alles berück-
sichtigt werden: Die direkten Leistungen aus den Haushalten des Bundes, der
westlichen Länder und Gemeinden - aber eben auch Kreditabwicklungsfonds, Fonds
Deutsche Einheit und Treuhandanstalt.

Dabei muß jeder sehen: Der notwendige finanzpolitische Spielraum ist nur durch
Sparsamkeit auf der Ausgabenseite herzustellen.
Der Bund hat deshalb bis 1995 sehr niedrige Zuwachsraten vorgesehen, durch-
schnittlich 2 1/2 % pro Jahr.
Eine ähnliche Ausgabenzurückhaltung müssen ebenso die westlichen Länder und
Gemeinden üben.

Ich fasse zusammen:
Wenn alle Beteiligten jetzt ihrer Verantwortung gerecht werden, haben wir alle
Chancen, in den neuen Ländern einen entscheidenden Schritt weiter voranzukom-
men.
Für diese Bundesregierung bleibt im übrigen die Solidität der Staatsfinanzen
zentrales Leitmotiv!
Daran müssen sich alle finanziellen Leistungen orientieren - sowohl in den
alten wie auch in den neuen Bundesländern.

외 무 부

종 별 :

번 호 : ECW-0405   일 시 : 92 0323 1900

수 신 : 장 관 (봉기,경기원,농수산부,상공부)

발 신 : 주 EC 대사 사본: 주미, 제네바대사(중계요망)-중계필

제 목 : BUSH-KOHL 회담

    KOHL 독일수상이 연호 BUSH 대통령과 미국에서 가진 회담을 마치고 귀국하여 가진기자회견 내용을 아래 보고함

    1. 미.EC 는 교착상태에 빠진 UR 협상을 4월말까지 마감한다는데 원칙적인 의견의 일치를 보았으나 주요 핵심문제에 대한 타협에는 상당한 견해차이가 상존함

    2. 미국이 요구하고 있는 농산물 보조금 감축, 특히 물량기준 감축과 관련 가장큰 저항을 보이고 있는 불란서로 하여금 양보하도록 압력을 가하는 문제와 관련,이는 불란서 정치의 속성상 아주 위험한 일임

    3. 금번 회담에서 아래 3가지 분야에서 진전을 보임

    가. EC 측의 소맥수출 감축

    나. EC 에로의 저가의 대체곡물 수입제한

    다. EC 의 농가소득 보조계획 보장

    4. 현싯점에서 양측간에 UR 협상의 성공을 위하여 가장 필요한 것은 타협 (COMPROMISE) 이며 타협이란 양측 모두의 양보 (CONCESSION) 를 의미하는바, 문제는 어느측도 양보없이 타협만을 모색하고 있는 것임. 현재로서 협상의 성공을 보장할수없으며 아직도 협상은 진행중이므로 비관론에 빠질 필요는 없음

    5. 자신이 의장을 맡게될 7월 뮌헨 정상회담전까지 UR 협상이 타결되지 않을 경우, 동 정상회담에서 타결을 기대하는 것은 현실적으로 불가능 할 것인바 그 이전에협상타결을 위하여 미.EC 양측의 정치적 의지를 가지고 최선을 다해야 할것임. 금주중 주요 회원국 정상및 DELORS 집행위원장과 미국방문 결과및 향후대책을 협의할 것임. 끝

    (대사 권동만-국장)

롱상국   경기원   농수부   상공부   고재선   장관

PAGE 1   92.03.24   05:09 DS

                                        외신 1과 롱제관

                                        0062

| 관리번호 | RL-240 |

외 무 부

종 별 :

번 호 : USW-1473   일 시 : 92 0323 2034

수 신 : 장관(통기,통이,경기원,농수산부,상공부,),사본:주제네바,

발 신 : 주미대사   EC대사(중계필)

제 목 : UR 협상 동향

대 WUS-1286

1. 당관 장기호참사관은 3.23 USTR 의 SUSAN EARLY 대표보를 면담, 3.21-22 간의 미.독 정상회담 결과등 최근 UR 협상동향에 대해 문의한바 결과 하기 보고함(김중근 서기관 배석)

1. BUSH-KOHL 회담결과와 관련, 동대표보는 본인으로서는 언로에 보도된 내용 이외에는 아는바가 없다고 언급하면서 양국정상이 기자회견에서 4 월중순까지 UR 타결전망을 낙관 한다고 발표한것은 정상회담을 장식하는 수사학적인 의미 정도일 것이라는 반응을 보였음.

2. 콜수상이 금번 회담에서 '미국이 대 EC 대체곡물 (CEREAL SUBSTITUTE) 수출을 동결한다는 조건으로 EC 측이 수출물량 감축을 받아들이겠다'는 제안을 하였는가 하는 장참사관의 질문에 대해 동대표보는 콜수상이 이를 제안 하였는지의 여부는 알수없으니 이러한 제안은 REBALANCING 과 동일한 효과를 가져오므로미국으로서는 결코 받아들일수 없는 제안이라고 일축하였음.

3. 국내보조문제와 관련동인은 미측이 기간 및 감축폭에 조건을 붙여 보조금 지급을 허용하는 SAFE BOX(BLUE BOX)를 제시한데 대해, EC 측이 아직도 구체적대안을 제시하지 않고 있는등 미.EC 간 교섭에서 '볼'은 EC 측에 넘어가 있다고 강조하였음.

4. 향후 UR 타결전망에 관한 동대표보의 개인적 의견을 문의한데대해 동인은 최근 EC 와의 협상에 진전이 없어 비관적인 의견이 대두될수도 있겠으나 미.EC 고위층에서 아직도 UR 의 성공적인 타결을 기대하고있으므로 자신으로서는 아직 희망을 버리지 않고있다 하였음.

또한 UR 협상이 타결될 경우에도 의회 동의를 위해서는 최소한 11 개월이 소요되므로 EAST TRACK 만료일의 93.6.30 인점을 감안할때 4 월말까지 협상이

통상국 안기부	장관 경기원	차관 농수부	1차보 상공부	2차보 중계	경제국	통상국	분석관	청와대

PAGE 1   93.6.11 이년기   92.03.24   13:15

외신 2과 통제관 BZ

0063

타결되어야만 의회동의가 가능하리라 보여진다고 전망하였음. (의회의 심의에는 행정부와 의회의 비공식 협의기간 90 일 (CALENDAR DAYS)과 UR 협정과 관련 법안에 대한 심의기간 60JAULUKUV(LEGISLATIVE DAYS)이 소요되는 바 금년의경우 선거준비를 위한 조기 회기종료 (10.2. 예정)및 하계휴회를 감안하면 60 일 회기일은 실제로 약 8 개월에 해당될 것이라함).

5. 또한 동대표보는 농산물 협상과 관련 일본을 포함 현재 28 개국이 COUNTRY PLAN 을 제출하였다고 설명하고 한국도 조속히 COUNTRY PLAN 을 제시하여 줄것을 요청하였음.

이에 대해 장참사관은 한국의 농업여건을 감안할때 아직 미.EC 간에 기본적인 문제도 타결되지 않은 시점에서 한국이 협상을 주도해 나갈 입장이 되지 않으며 미.EC 협상의 진전을 보아 대응해 나갈것이라고 하고 UR 협상의 성공적인 타결을 기대한다고 언급하였음. 끝

(대사 현홍주-국장)

예고:92.12.31 까지

검 토 필 (199. 6. 30.) 홍

PAGE 2

0064

외 무 부

종   별 :

번   호 : FRW-0616   일   시 : 92 0325 1000

수   신 : 장 관 (통기)

발   신 : 주 불 대사

제   목 : UR 협상 동향

연:FRW-0505

1. KOHL 독일 총리는 3.23 연호 BUSH 대통령과의 정상회담을 통해 UR 협상 타결을 위한 어느정도의 진전은 있었으나 타결에 이를 수준은 아니었다고 말하고, 앞으로도EC의 이익을 보전토록 노력할 것이나 UR 타결을 위해 불란서의 양보를 강요할 의향은 없다고 밝힘.

2. 또한 총리는 7월이전에 UR 이 타결되지 않을 경우 7.6-7, 뮌헨 개최 G-7 정상회담에서 동건이 해결될수는 없을것임을 지적함으로써 G-7정상회담이 UR 문제로 영향을 받아서는 안된다는 입장을 강력히 표명함.

3. 상기와 같이 미.독간 UR 타결을 위한 막후협상이 전개되고 있는 가운데 당지유력 경제일간지 'LA TRIBUNE D'EXPANSION'은 불란서가 EC 공동농업정책(CAP)에 있어 독일로부터 보상을 받는 댓가로 UR 타결 필요성을 강조하는 아래 내용의 논평기사를 3.23 게재함.

가. UR 농산물 분야 협상이 시작될때부터 그기능이 문제시 될것으로 예상된 CAP가 30년간 회원국에 대한 기여후 재검토되는 것은 당연함.

나. 그간 EC 는 CAP 개혁의 자체적 당위성에도 불구하고 회원국 특히 불란서의반대로 집행위가 준비한 최소한의 이니시어티브 조차 수용치 못한 결과,EC 는 농산물 문제에 있어 거부할줄만 알지 제안할줄은 모른다는 국제적비난에 봉착하였음.

다. 이러한 가운데 EC 자체간 분열이 노정되어 독일은 최소한 2회에 걸쳐 불란서와 합의한'농산물 협약'을 위반하였으며, 미국은 독일(농산물의 자급자족 목표)과 불란서(농산물 수출 추진)간 상이한 이해관계를 이용하여 독일을 회유하고 있는바,불란서는 점차 EC 내외에서 고립되고 있음.

라. 4월중 타결코자 하는 농산물 협상결과는 EC와 불란서 입장에서 보면

통상국   2차보

PAGE 1   92.03.25   20:01 DS

외신 1과 통제관

0065

불만족스런 내용이 될것이며,CAP 는 미국으로로부터 상응할만한 진정한 보상없이 그 중요한 부분을 상실하게 될것임.

　　마.　　한편,불란서의　경우　자국의　반대로　농산물협상이　타결되지　않을 경우,곡류.설탕등 주요농산물 교역의 새로운 전쟁에 있어 최대의 피해자가 될 가능성이 큼.

　　바.　불란서로서는 UR 이 타결되든 안되든 농산물분야의 손익계산서는 적자가 분명한바,현재로서 유일한 대안은 불란서를 이탈한 독일로 하여금 CAP 개혁에 있어 값비싼 댓가를 치루도록 하는 방법뿐 임.끝.

　　(대사 노영찬-국장)

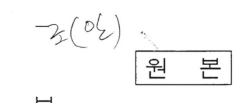

관리번호	92-24P

외 무 부

종 별 :

번 호 : ECW-0426　　　　　　　　　일 시 : 92 0326 1730

수 신 : 장관 (봉기,정보,경기원,재무부,농림수산부,상공부)

발 신 : 주 EC 대사　사본: 주 미,제네바대사(중계필)

제 목 : 갓트/UR 협상

연: ECW-0405, 0388

3.25 당관 이관용농무관은 EC 대외총국의 GUTH 농산물담당 과장을 면담하고, 표제협상 관련 협의한바, 동인의 발언요지 아래 보고함

1. BUSH-KOHL 회담등 미.EC 양자협상

가. KOHL 수상의 타협안 즉, EC 의 보조 수출물량 감축을 수락하는 대신에 미측의 CEREALS 대체품의 대 EC 수출을 동결하는 방안은 불란서정부와도 협의된바 있으나, 미측은 이를 REBALANCING 과 같은 내용이라는 점을 들어 거부함

나. BUSH-KOHL 회담결과 표제협상 전망은 불투명해지고 있으나 EC 는 협상의 돌파구마련을 위한 노력을 계속할 것이며, 협상타결의 관건은 미측에 달려있다고 볼수 있음

다. 미.EC 간 고위협상은 계속될 것이며 (차기회담 일정은 미정), 3.26-27 간 PARIS 에서 개최되는 OECD 회의시 MACSHARRY 위원과 MADIGAN 미농무장관의 접촉뿐 아니라 BUSH 대통령과 DELORS 집행위원장간의 전화협의등을 통해 미.EC 간의 정치적타협을 위한 노력은 계속될 것임

2. UR 협상전망

가. BUSH-KOHL 회담에서 4 월말까지 협상종결에 노력한다는 방침에 불구하고 DUNKEL 총장의 시한이 지켜질 것인가에 대하여는 대다수가 회의적임

나. 4 월말 시한후의 추진일정은 갓트/TNC 회의를 개최하여 결정할 문제이며 DUNKEL 과 미.EC 간의 접촉이 있을것으로 전망됨

3. CAP 개혁문제

가. 이론상으로는 UR 협상과 관계없이 CAP 개혁이 추진될수 있고, DELORS II PACKAGE, 과잉농산물문제등 내부적으로도 동 개혁문제가 금년내에 확정될 필요는 있음

통상국	차관	2차보	외정실	분석관	경기원	재무부	농수부	상공부
중계								

PAGE 1　　　　　　　　　　　　　　　　　　92.03.27　04:02

나. 그러나 현실적으로 UR 협상이 불부명한 상태에서 CAP 개혁의 진전은 어려우며, 동 문제에 대하여는 EC 정상들간의 정치적인 결정이 필요할 것임

4. 바나나문제등 기타

가. 바나나문제는 EC 단일시장 발족시기가 93.1.1. 로 박두하고 있어 일부 회원국들의 ACP 국가및 해외영토로 부터의 바나나의 순조로운 수입을 염두에 둔 내부정치적인 사안이나 UR 협상과 관련된 감축이행 계획서 제출시기와 중복되었기 때문에 더욱 복잡한 문제로 제기된 것이며, TARIFF 쿼타도입등 방안이 마련될것으로 전망됨. 한편, 3.25 EC 집행위에서 바나나의 수입제도 개편문제가 토의결정될 예정이었으나 뒤로 미루어졌음   oilseed?

나. 최근의 제 2 차 갓트/ 대수 패널 결과는 CAP 개혁방향및 미.EC 간의 농업교역상 큰 영향을 미칠것이며, 특히 패널결과에서 제시된 이해당사국에게 보복권한 부여는 EC 관계자들을 당황하게 만들고 있음. 끝

(대사 권동만-국장)

예고: 92.6.30 까지

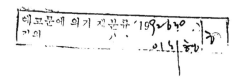

외　무　부

원　본

암호수신

종　별 :

번　호 : ECW-0444　　　　　　　　　　일　시 : 92 0330 1700

수　신 : 장관 (통기, 경기원, 농수산부, 상공부) 사본: 주미, 제네바대사(중계필)

발　신 : 주 EC 대사

제　목 : UR 협상동향

　　1. 3.27.FRAIRA DE OLIVERA 폴투갈 통상장관 (EC 의장국) 과 ANDRIESSEN 집행위 부위원장은 표제관련 회담후 양인 공동명의 발표문을 통하여, 현재 교착상태에 빠진 UR 협상에 대하여 심각한 우려를 표명하고 4 월말까지 협상종결을 위하여 미국의 태도변화를 촉구함. 동성명은 또한 미국이 지금까지 협상타결을위한 정치적 의지를 말로서만 반복하고 실제 행동이 없었음을 지적하고 최근 미국이 서비스협상에서 은행, 해운등을 제외할것을 주장하여 동협상의 주요 실질분야를 제외시키자고 함으로서 UR 협상 전체를 위기상황에 처하게하고 있다고 비난하면서 EC 가 전세계에서 가장 개방된 시장이며 4 월말까지 협상타결을 위하여 모든 가능한 노력을 기우릴 것이라고 강조함

　　2. 상기와관련 EC 집행위 관계관은 최근 미국및 EC 가 최고위층에서 협상타결을 위한 정치적 의지를 보이며 고위실무급에서의 협상이 진전을 보이고 있는 시점에서 써비스협상에서의 주요 실질분야 제외를 주장하고 나온데 대하여 이해할수 없다고 전제하고 이는 미국이 UR 협상의 결렬을 원하고 있다는 증거가 아니냐고 반문하면서 자신의 생각으로는 양측이 협상타결 실패의 책임을 서로 전가하려는 전조로 해석되므로 향후 협상타결 전망이 아주 어렵게 되었다고 언급함. 끝

　　(대사 권동만-국장)

통상국 상공부	장관 중계	차관	2차보	구주국	분석관	안기부	경기원	농수부

PAGE 1　　　　　　　　　　　　　　　　　　　　92.03.31　　04:24

외신 2과　통제관 FM

0069

URUGUAY ROUND NON-PAPER

o   THE UNITED STATES HAS SUPPORTED DIRECTOR GENERAL DUNKEL'S
    EFFORTS TO BRING THE ROUND TO A SUCCESSFUL CONCLUSION BY
    MID-APRIL.

    -- PROGRESS HAS BEEN ACHIEVED IN THE NEGOTIATIONS AS A
    RESULT OF THIS DEADLINE.

o   CONTINUING DIFFERENCES IN AGRICULTURE CONTINUE TO AFFECT
    OUR ABILITY TO COMPLETE THE ROUND BY MID-APRIL.
    AGRICULTURE IS NOT THE ONLY AREA WHERE FURTHER WORK IS
    REQUIRED, HOWEVER.

o   U.S. NEGOTIATORS ARE PREPARED TO TAKE THE TIME NECESSARY
    TO SUCCESSFULLY CONCLUDE THE NEGOTIATIONS. WHILE THE
    DELAY IN THE NEGOTIATIONS IS DISAPPOINTING, WE CONTINUE
    TO BELIEVE THAT THERE IS MUCH TO BE GAINED THROUGH
    SUCCESSFUL CONCLUSION TO THE ROUND.

    -- WE ARE ENCOURAGED BY RECENT EFFORTS OF SOME COUNTRIES
    TO IMPROVE THEIR OFFERS IN MARKET ACCESS IN GOODS AND
    SERVICES AND BELIEVE THAT THE REMAINING TIME IN THE
    NEGOTIATIONS AUGURS WELL FOR FURTHER IMPROVEMENTS.

o   WE VERY MUCH APPRECIATE KOREA'S ACTIVE PARTICIPATION IN
    THE SERVICES NEGOTIATIONS AND THE IMPROVEMENTS KOREA HAS
    MADE TO ITS SERVICES OFFER.

    -- WE ENCOURAGE KOREA TO CONTINUE TO MAKE PROGRESS IN THE
    REMAINING AREAS OF CONCERN TO THE UNITED STATES.

    --IMPROVEMENT IN FINANCIAL SERVICES ARE ESSENTIAL TO THE
    OVERALL ACCEPTABILITY OF KOREA'S OFFER.

    --THE UNITED STATES ALSO HOPES TO MAKE FURTHER PROGRESS
    IN BASIC TELECOMMUNICATIONS, DISTRIBUTION AND SOME
    PROFESSIONAL SERVICES.

o   WE URGE KOREA TO PROVIDE NECESSARY DATA SCHEDULES AND
    IMPROVED OFFERS UNDER TRACKS 1 AND 2, AND COOPERATION IN
    TRACK 3.

3/31/92

0070

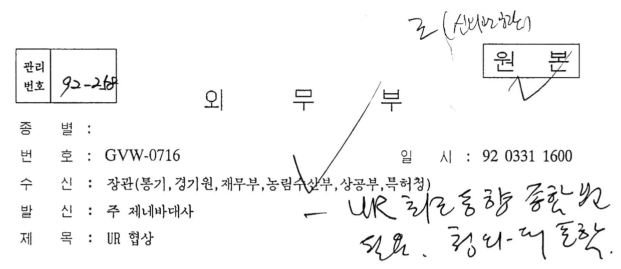

외 무 부

종 별 :

번 호 : GVW-0716   일 시 : 92 0331 1600

수 신 : 장관(통기,경기원,재무부,농림수산부,상공부,특허청)

발 신 : 주 제네바대사

제 목 : UR 협상

1. UR 협상이 별다른 진전을 보이지 않고 있는 가운데 당지 CAIRNS GROUP 대사들은 3.30 오후 DUNKEL 총장을 공동으면 면담, 협상 정돈상태에 대한 동 GROUP 의 우려를 표명한바, 당관이 파악한 동면담 요지 아래 보고함.

가. CAIRNS GROUP 대사들이 T1 및 T2 진전상황에 대한 실망 및 UR 협상 전반의 현상황에 대한 강한 우려를 표명한데 대해, DUNKEL 의장은 T1, T2 의 중요성을 강조(T4 에는 관심이 없다고 언급) 하면서 미, EC 간 타협노력이 계속되고 있으므로 인내심을 갖고 T1, T2 협상을 계속할것을 종용했다함.

나. 이에대해 JARAMILLO 서비스협상그룹 의장 및 기타국가 대사 모두가 미.EC 간 협상의 진전없이는 T1, T2 협상 진행에 한계가 있음을 지적하고 미.EC 간4 월말까지는 협상계획이 없는 것으로 알고 있다고 언급하자, DUNKEL 총장은 금명간 DENIS 의장 및 JARAMILLO 의장의 보고를 받고 INFORMAL MEETING OF HEADSOF DELEGATION(GREEN ROOM) 을 소집, 상황(STATE OF PLAY)을 1 차 점검해 보고난후 추후조치를 취할것을 검토중이라고 언급하면서, 자신으로서는 어쩔수 없는 상황인 만큼 당사국들이 적극적으로 교섭에 임해야 할것임을 재차 강조했다함.

(한편 개도국 대사들도 명 4.1.DUNKEL 총장을 면담 예정임)

2. 한편 개도국 구룹도 아국을 포함한 간부국대표들이 빈번히 회동, UR 정돈 사태 타개를 위한 대책을 숙의중인바, 현상태에 직접적인 책임을 질 나라는 미국과 EC 이므로 조만간 개도국 명의로 양자협상의 다원화(MULTILATERALIZATIONAND TRANSPARENCY) 필요성과 무역대국의 협상타결을 위한 정치적 의지를 강조하는 성명을 발표할 것을 협의중에 있음.

3. 본직은 4.3.DE LA PAIX GROUP LUNCHEN 을 주최하는 기회를 이용, SWEDEN대표등과 사전협의, DE LA PAXI GROUP 도 현싯점에서 DUNKEL 총장을 면담,

---

통상국   장관   차관   1차보   2차보   외정실   분석관   경기원   재무부
농수부   상공부   특허청

협상의 현상황에 대하여 심각한 우려를 표명하고 DUNKEL 총장이 적극적인 LEADRSHIP
을 취하도록 하는 방안등을 협의 예정임.끝
　　　(대사 박수길-국장)
　　　예고:92.6.30 까지

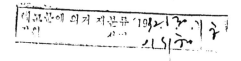

외 무 부

증   별 :

번   호 : ECW-0458   일   시 : 92 0401 1730

수   신 : 장 관 (통삼,통기,경기원,농림수산부) 사본:주제네바대사-직송필

발   신 : 주 EC 대사

제   목 : EC/농업이사회 결과

. 3.30-31 개최된 표제이사회 결과를 아래 보고함

1. CAP 개혁

가. 동 이사회는 CAP 개혁촉진 필요성에 대해 논의한바, 대부분의 회원국들은 <u>6.1.</u> <u>까지 동 개혁문제를 마무리</u> 한다는데에 의견을 같이 함.다만 벨지움, 덴마크, 화란은 마무리 시한을 설정하는 것에 반대함

나. MACSHARRY 집행위원은 동 이사회 결과에 대해 CAP 개혁추진의 전환점이 되었다고 평가함. 그러나 GUMMER 영국 농무장관은 대농에 대해 차별적인 조치를 포함하는 개혁안은 수락할수 없다는 입장을 재차 천명하였으며,벨지움은 지지가격 인하와 소득 보조제 도입이라는 개혁 기본방향에 대해 불만을 표시하였음

다. CUNHA 이사회의장은 차 기이사회 (4.28-29) 에 CAP 개혁문제에 대한 제 4차타협안을 제출하겠다고 밝힘

2. 92/93 농산물 가격안

가. 91/92 가격수준과 현행 협정등을 유지한다는 집행위의 제안설명을 청취하였으며, CAP개혁 추진상황과 연계하여 재검토키로 함

나. 동건에 대한 최종 결정은 5-6월 이사회에서 이루어 질것임

3. OILSEEDS/갓트 패널결과

0 동 이사회는 만장일치로 상기 패널결과는 수락할수 없다는 입장을 결정함. 끝

(대사 권동만-국장)

통상국   통상국   경기원   농수부   그검.ㅇ

PAGE 1   92.04.02   05:26 DS
                                            외신 1과 통제관

외　무　부

종　별 :

번　호 : POW-0170　　　　　　　　　　일　시 : 92 0401 1900

수　신 : 장관(봉기,구이)

발　신 : 주 폴투갈 대사

제　목 : 우루과이 라운드

　　본직은 금 4.1 당지 호주대사주최 아시아지역대사 초청 오찬에 참석하였는바, 동 오찬에 초청된 주재국 상무성의 FERNANDES DE SOUSA 차관(5 월초 방한예정)은 아시아 지역 대사들의 질문에대하여 다음과 같이 답하였음을 보고함

　　1. 주재국의 CAVACO 수상이 EC 의장 자격으로 DELOSS EC 집행위원장과 같이오는 4.22-23 간 미국을 방문 부쉬대통령과 우루과이 라운드를 포함한 EC. 미국간 제반 주요문제에 대하여 협의를 가질예정임

　　2.EC 각국(영, 이태리, 독)가 곧 총선을 앞두고 있고 미국역시 년말에 대통령 선거가 있으므로 이번회담에서 우루과이 라운드에서 문제되고 있는 농산물등에 대한 EC. 미국간의 이견이 정치적 타결을 볼 가능성은 희박한것으로 예상됨. 끝

　　(대사조광제-국장)

룡상국　　장관　　차관　　1차보　　2차보　　구주국　　분석관　　청와대　　안기부

PAGE 1　　　　　　　　　　　　　　　　　　92.04.02　　06:58
　　　　　　　　　　　　　　　　　　　　　외신 2과　룡제관 BX
　　　　　　　　　　　　　　　　　　　　　　　　　　0074

외 무 부

종 별 :

번 호 : GVW-0723   일 시 : 92 0401 1530

수 신 : 장관(봉기,경기원,재무부,농수산부,상공부,특허청)

발 신 : 주 제네바 대사   (사본:주 EC, 주미 대사(본부중계필))

제 목 : UR 협상 동향

　　　연: GVW-0716

　　1. 개도국 그룹간부국 비공식 회의(아국, 홍콩, 파키스탄, 브라질, 칠레, 멕시코, 콜롬비아, 우루과이, 탄자니아, 이집트 참석)가 작 3.31(화) 지난 3.24., 3.27 에 이어 재차 소집되어 연호 케언즈 그룹 대사의 DUNKEL 총장 면담 및 3.31 중남미 및 카리브 그룹 대사의 DUNKEL 총장 면담 결과 및 UR 협상 정돈 상태에 대한 개도국 차원의 대책을 협의한바 요지 아래 보고함.

　　가. 상기 양 그룹 대사의 DUNKEL 총장 면담에 모두 참석한 LACARTE 우루과이 대사는 DUNKEL 총장은 앞으로의 협상 운영 방향과 관련 T1, T2, T3 의장으로 부터 진행 현황에 관한 보고서를 받은후 내주중 GREEN ROOM 회의를 통해 상황 점검 및 의견 교환을 거쳐 4 월중 TNC 회의 소집을 고려하고 있다 하면서 아래 사항을 특히 강조했다.

　　1) T4 가동은 회피할 것(AVOID REOPENING T4)이며, 경우에 따라서는 가동을 안하겠음.

　　2) 신뢰도(CREDIBILITY) 문제가 제기될 것이므로 더이상 협상 시한의 연장문제는 거론않을 예정임.

　　3) TNC 회의는 특정국을 비난하는 SCANDALOUS 한 TNC 가 되지 않도록 하겠음.(ORDERLY FASHION 의 TNC 희망)

　　4) 자기로서는 현재 특별히 취할 INITIATIVE 가 없으며, 오히려 협상 타결을 위해서는 관계국들의 정치적 결단이 중요함.

　　나. 그밖에 DUNKEL 총장은 지난주 자신의 워싱턴 방문 결과 미국측으로 부터는 반드시 부정적인 태도가 아니라는 인상을 받았다고 언급했다 하며, EC 의 태도에 대한 일부 참석 대사의 질문에 대해서는 답변을 기피했다함.

| 통상국 | 장관 | 차관 | 1차보 | 2차보 | 외정실 | 분석관 | 청와대 | 안기부 |
| 경기원 | 재무부 | 농수부 | 상공부 | 특허정 | 중계 | | | |

PAGE 1

다. 간부 개도국 회의 참석 대사 대부분이 협상정돈상태에 심각한 우려를 표명하고, 개도국 공동의 성명을 발표하는 문제를 협의한바, 본직은 성명 발표 및 T4 가동문제에 대해 아래 요지의 논평을 함.

1) 3.27 부시 대통령의 성명도 있었고, 4 월중 부시, DELORS 위원장 회담 가능성도 거론되고 있는 만큼 현시점에서 지나치게 실망할 필요는 없음.

2) 3 개 협상 그룹 의장의 보고를 받아보고 그 내용을 평가한 결과, UR 협상 진행 전망이 확실히 비관적이라고 판단될 경우 개도국 차원에서 NON-CONFRONTATIONAL 한 방향으로 협상의 명료성 유지와 다자화 필요성 및 주요국의 정치적 의지 발휘를 촉구하는 내용의 성명을 TNC 회의에 맞추어 발표함이 바람직함.

3) T4 가동문제에 관해서는 농산물 수입국이라는 점에서 대부분의 개도국과는 상이한 입장에 처해 있는 한국으로서는 T4 활용이 긴요하므로 동 가동에 상당한 기대를 걸어 왔는바, 따라서 DUNKEL 의장의 언급에 실망을 표시하고, T4 가 미.EC 간의 독점물이 되어서는 안된다는 입장을 재차 강조함.

2. 현재 당지의 지배적 분위기는 미.EC 간 돌파구가 4 월중에 마련될 경우에는 6-7 월 타결이 아직은 가능할 수 있으나 그렇지 못할 경우에는 협상이 불가피하게 내년으로 미루어질 것이라는 쪽으로 기울어가고 있음. 일각에서는 벌써 부터 협상을 SUSPEND 하자는 의견마져 대두되고 있으나, 보다 구체적인 전망은 금주중 제출될 3 개 협상 그룹의장의 보고, 내주중 (4.6) 개최 예정인 전체 개도국 비공식 회의에서의 DUNKEL 총장의 연설 및 조만간에 있을 것으로 전망되는 GREEN ROOM 협의 과정에서 보다 뚜렷하게 나타날 것으로 예견됨.

3. 한편 미.EC 간에는 현재 농산물 뿐만 아니라 써비스 등 여타 분야에 대해서도 실무급 비공식 협상이 간헐적으로 진행되고 있으나 아직 뚜렷한 성과는 없는 것으로 파악됨. 끝

(대사 박수길-국장)

예고 92.6.30 까지

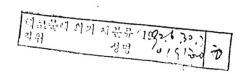

외 무 부

종 별 :

번 호 : GVW-0739   일 시 : 92 0402 1900

수 신 : 장관(통기, 경기원, 재무부, 농림수산부, 상공부, 특허청) 사본: 주미,

발 신 : 주 제네바 대사   주 EC 대사-중계필

제 목 : UR 협상 관련 언론보도

1. 금 4.2(목) INTERNATIONAL HERALD TRIBUNE 지는 별첨 기사를 통하여 미.EC 간 입장접근으로 UR 협상의 4 월말 이전 타결 가능성이 있으며, 그근거로 작4.1 미-EC 간 민간 항공기 생산에 대한 보조금 분쟁이 타결되었으며, HILLS 대표와 ANDRIESSEN 집행위 부위원장이 각각 별도로 가진 기자회견에서 처음으로 UR협상의 4 월말 이전 타결에 낙관적인 견해를 표명한 사실을 들고 있으며, 4.22 개최 예정인 BUSH 미 대통령과 DELORS 집행 위원장간의 회담이 결정적인 계기가 될것이라고 보도하였음.

2. 한편 금일판 FINANCIAL TIMES 는,

가) 4 월말 개최 예정인 BUSH 대통령과 DELORS 위원장간의 회담이 UR 협상의 교착상태를 타개할 수 있는 마지막 정치적 기회가 되어야 할것이라는 이씨 PAEMAN 부총국장의 발언을 인용 보도하면서, 그러나 아직까지는 미국이 보조금에 관한 EC 의 입장을 수용할 아무런 징후가 없다는 기사와, 나) 미-EC 간 타협을 위한 정치적 의지가 줄어들고 있기 때문에 UR협상이 마비상태에 빠졌다는 갓트 직원의 발언과 교착상태 타개를 위해서는 조그만한 기적(A MINOR MIRACLE) 이 필요하다는 당지주재 미관리들의 발언을 인용 보도함.

3. 당관이 당지 미국대표부 STOLER 공사 및 EC 대표부 JOHN BECK 부대표와 접촉, 특히 H.T. 지의 보도와 관련 의견을 문의한바

가) 금일자 H.T. 지 보도와 F.T. 지 보도가 서로 다른 방향으로 있으며

나) 미-EC 간에 협상 타결을 위해 현재 계속 노력하고 있는 것은 사실이며 빠른 시일내에 교착상태인 협상이 타결된다면 이는 환영하지 않을수 없을 것이나 현 시점에서 뚜렷한 결정적 합의가 있는 것은 아니며

다) 4.22. 미-EC 간 회담(워싱톤)은 오래전 부터 있어온 연 2 회 개최되는 정례적 회담이고

통상국 농수부	장관 상공부	차관 특허청	2차보 중계	분석관	청와대	안기부	경기원	재무부

PAGE 1   일반문서로 재분류 (1992. 12. 71.)   92.04.03   07:57
                                                        외신 2과 통제관 BZ

0077

라) 특히 새로운 협상타결 시한을 설정(4.30 로 협상 타결 시한을 설정하고있는점에 대하여) 하고 있는데 대해서는 현재 새로운 시한을 설정할 상황이 아니라는 점을 지적하는등

H.T 지의 보도가 지나치게 앞서가고 있는 것으로 본다는 견해를 직.간접적으로 밝히면서 조만간 협상 타결 가능성에 대한 회의적 반응이 있었음을 보고함. 끝

첨부: 1. H.T. 지 보도기사 1 건

2. F.T. 지 보도기사 2 건

(GVW(F)-0241). 끝

(대사 박수길-국장)

예고:92.12.31. 까지

검 토 필 (19%.6 3°.)

주 제 네 바 대 표 부

번 호 : GVF(F) - 0241   년월일 : 0402   시간 : 1800

수 신 : 장   관 (통기, 경기원, 재무부, 농립수산부, 상공부, 특허청)

발 신 : 주 제네바대사

제 목 : UR 협상

총 **5** 매 (표지포합)

배부처	장관실	차관실	이차관보	의정실	분석관	아주국	미주국	구주국	중아국	국기국	회계	통상국	문협국	외연원	청와대	안기부	공보처	경기원	상공부	재무부	농수부	동자부	외자	기획	다자협
				1	1	1					0						1	1	1				1	

Officials Say a GATT Accord Is Near

By Roger Cohen
New York Times Service

BRUSSELS — After several years of tortuous negotiations, the top European Community and U.S. trade officials believe that their positions in global trade talks are now sufficiently close for an accord to be within reach before the end of April.

The negotiations, held under the aegis of the General Agreement on Tariffs and Trade, have assumed central political importance in recent months as a barometer of relations between Europe and the United States now that the strategic threat that was long the cement to the transatlantic alliance has been withdrawn.

In separate interviews, Frans Andriessen, the European Community's chief trade negotiator, and Carla A. Hills, the U.S. trade representative, said for the first time that they were optimistic about concluding the talks successfully before the end of April. They also warned of the potentially devastating political and economic consequences of failure.

A deadline of April 15 in the Uruguay Round of talks, which have dragged on for five-and-a-half years and affect the world's $4.5 trillion in annual trade, has been set by Arthur Dunkel, the director general of GATT.

This target now seems unreachable. But the officials suggested a scheduled April 22 meeting between President George Bush and the EC Commission president, Jacques Delors, who recently exchanged letters on the trade talks, could be decisive.

Optimism was fueled by the announcement Wednesday of an outline agreement settling a bitter five-year dispute on subsidies to the commercial-aircraft industry.

"We know we have to find an answer in the GATT negotiations and the Americans agree," Mr. Andriessen, the EC Commissioner for External Relations, said. "The talks are moving and I now think we can find a way by the end of April. It will be a catastrophe if we fail."

A scheduled April 22 meeting between George Bush and Jacques Delors could be decisive.

Mrs. Hills, speaking by telephone from Washington, said, "We must find a way to bring this round to a successful conclusion and, yes, I am hopeful it can be done by the end of April."

She added that beyond its damaging effect on U.S.-European relations, a failure would seriously affect the prospects of the emergent market economies of the former Soviet bloc, which would lose both markets and the overall benefits of a more buoyant world economy.

"Trade," she said, "is more effective than aid, and an accord would add $5 trillion to world output over the next decade."

A senior U.S. official based in Western Europe, who refused to be named, added: "The consolidation of reform in Eastern Europe is our top security political objective. It will not be made easier if the EC and U.S. are bickering and in recession. The consequences of GATT for our top security objective are obvious."

The negotiations have been blocked essentially by differences over agriculture. The United States is seeking sharp cuts in the subsidies and tariff protection enjoyed by the Community's farmers. Spending on farmers — which has led to enormous stockpiles of beef, cereals and dairy produce that tend to get dumped on world markets — accounts for about 54 percent of the Community's $85 billion annual budget.

Mr. Dunkel has suggested cuts of between 20 and 36 percent in domestic subsidies to farmers and tariff protection, as well as in the volume of subsidized exports they are allowed. Washington, having initially pressed for cuts as high as 75 percent, has accepted this position. But the Community, led by France, has balked.

The impasse still exists, but the differences appear to be slowly narrowing.

Officials disclosed that in his letter last month to Mr. Delors, Mr. Bush had proposed a compromise under which the Community

See GATT, Page 13

GATT: Officials Say Pact Is Near

(Continued from first finance page)

would temporarily be able to preserve more of its subsidies.

Mr. Dunkel had already suggested what he called a "Green Box" — a category exempted from his proposed cuts — for some farm subsidies that do not affect production.

In essence, the Community is striving to move from a system that encourages unlimited production by offering guaranteed prices for all products to one in which there is no premium on output. To do so, it wants to be able to make so-called "direct payments" to farmers.

These payments would depend on the size of the farm, rather than its production, and would tend to increase for farmers agreeing to take land out of production or cut their livestock. "We still want to encourage people to stay on the land, but we want to move away from a production-based system," said a British official.

Mr. Bush, according to the officials, said the proposed "direct payments" aimed at agricultural reform could be exempt from the Dunkel cuts.

Mr. Andriessen said that in his reply to Mr. Bush, Mr. Delors had described the proposal as "very helpful." The EC Commissioner added, "I think we are now rather close to resolving the subsidy dispute, although we still have problems on the export side."

France has led objections to the proposed 24 percent cut in the volume of subsidized exports. It wants a smaller reduction, but the United States is apparently unprepared to budge on this issue. Germany is trying to mediate.

One possible area for a trade-off appears to lie in services. Europe objects to a U.S. demand that the American market in telecommunications and financial services be selectively exempt from the 108-nation GATT principle of equal access for any member country to another member's markets. The United States says it cannot open up these markets indiscriminately while U.S. companies in these fields have limited or no access to many foreign countries.

Hinting at a trade-off, Mr. Andriessen said, "How can I sell concessions in agriculture if the services question is not dealt with?" Mrs. Hills said, "If we can resolve the agricultural impasse, then other areas could move rather quickly."

Both officials said negotiations in Washington, Brussels and Geneva were currently intense.

0080

Delors may intervene over trade talks

By David Gardner in Brussels

Mr Jacques Delors, president of the European Commission, is expected to try to break the impasse in the Uruguay Round trade liberalisation negotiations in talks with President George Bush later this month.

This emerged as a senior EC negotiator, Mr Hugo Paemen, called for "last, ultimate efforts" to get a political breakthrough in the Round before the Easter deadline set by Mr Arthur Dunkel, director general of the General Agreement on Tariffs and Trade (Gatt).

Mr Paemen said a political agreement would have to resolve the main differences over agriculture, services and market access, and that detailed "implementing work" could be done in the following two months.

Commission officials said Mr Delors was likely to try to get a mandate on the Uruguay Round from EC heads of government, before meeting Mr Bush on April 22, along with Mr Anibal Cavaco Silva, prime minister of Portugal, which currently holds the EC's rotating presidency.

This meeting is one of the twice-yearly EC-US summits, but is now set to be the last chance for a Gatt break-

through if none occurs by the April 19 deadline.

It also emerged yesterday that EC-US negotiators may be making some headway on the farm subsidy row, which, along with US reluctance to open up parts of its service industries, is the main obstacle to a deal. In particular, there are signs of movement on the so-called "green box" issue – whether Washington will consent to allowing payments Brussels wants to make to farmers, in compensation for big price cuts, to be considered as non-trade distorting.

The US is understood to be considering a "blue box,"

whereby these payments would be unchallenged for six years, provided they then became degressive and the EC provided a framework ensuring they constrained rather than promoted production.

There is so far no sign the US is prepared to meet EC objections to Gatt's formula to cut the volume of subsidised exports, in addition to the subsidies. The chances of the EC accepting some volume constraint depend, some officials now believe, on the US agreeing to a partial freeze on its cheap grain substitutes coming into the Community.

See feature: miracle wanted

2 41 - 5 - 3

0081

0082

Trade talks fall on deaf ears

The Uruguay Round is deadlocked, but is too important to fail, writes David Dodwell

Negotiators in Geneva are likely to miss their Easter deadline as they struggle to break the 15-month deadlock in the Uruguay Round of talks on world trade liberalisation.

Officials at the General Agreement on Tariffs and Trade (Gatt) talk of paralysis, as the political will to make compromises among central players such as the US and the European Community appears to ebb away.

Fear that the talks face imminent collapse prompted US President George Bush last week to call for "a political push from whatever source" to rescue them. He declined, however, to offer further US concessions. American officials in Geneva say "a minor miracle" is needed to achieve a breakthrough.

At the same time, farm ministers from the 24-nation Organisation for Economic Co-operation and Development (OECD) meeting in Paris on Friday called for a swift and successful end to the negotiations. They warned of "significant downside risks for the world trading system, and costs for the world economy." If the talks fall. They too offered nothing.

The risks of failure are already apparent, as recession in 1991 led to a third successive year of faltering world trade growth: the value of trade rose by a meagre 1.5 per cent to $3,500bn — the smallest gain since 1985, according to the Gatt.

Without the boost to trade that a successful conclusion to the round should bring, recovery is likely to be retarded.

The collapse of the round — launched in 1986 to break down barriers in trade in services, agriculture and textiles, to boost international respect for patents and copyright, and to improve mechanisms for settling trade disputes — has been looming for a long time. A summit held in Brussels in December 1990 broke up in acrimony; after the EC and US failed to agree on farm trade reform. A compromise farm reform package, known as the "Final Act", was drawn up by Mr Arthur Dunkel, director-general of Gatt. It was tabled late in December 1991 and was intended to break the deadlock. All of the 108 countries that

reduced barriers to their exports — which depend on the completion of the Uruguay Round — have been an important incentive.

Although deadlines in Gatt negotiations have often been missed, the current stalemate is creating a growing sense of urgency. Beyond April, there are not enough days in the US congressional calendar to get an agreement ratified ahead of the US presidential elections in November. Officials in Geneva, including those from the US, are already talking of what might be done to minimise "backsliding" from compromises already made in the areas of services, patents and copyright, and tariff cuts if negotiations have to be postponed until January 1993

In spite of a consensus that further delay is inevitable, no one is willing to contemplate outright failure. As Ambassador Bal Krishan Zutshi, India's long-standing Gatt representative, commented: "No one can afford to abandon what has been achieved out of the round so far. Negotiators will come back sooner or later and settle it."

Even delay carries with it grave dangers:

● Protectionist lobbies in the US in particular have been held at bay largely because of the promise that trade grievances would be dealt with more speedily in the Gatt by new trade dispute procedures. If the round is put on hold, it will be hard for President Bush's administration to resist demands for unilateral action against "unfair trade".

● June 1 is a critical date, on which a two-year US Farm Bill expires. With it, commitments not to match EC farm export subsidies on a tit-for-tat basis also expire. In fact, both US administration will face a formal commitment to relaunch a subsidy war with the EC on exports of farm products. Such action would almost certainly trigger retaliation.

● The multi-fibre arrangement which controls world trade in textiles and garments expires in December. With no Uruguay Round in place, awkward renegotiation of rules for trade in textiles and garments would be needed.

● Long-sought improvements in Gatt's rules for settling trade disputes would be held up. Countries frustrated with how Gatt currently

for storage of excess production, and subsidising the price of farm

progress on the farm subsidy issue would only yield US concessions.

Many observers of the tortuous manoeuvrings within the Gatt find in addition, respect for patents

apparent, as recession in 1991 led to a third successive year of faltering world trade growth: the value of trade rose by a meagre 1.5 per cent to $3,500bn — the smallest gain since 1985, according to the Gatt. Without the boost to trade that a successful conclusion to the round should bring, recovery is likely to be retarded.

The collapse of the round — launched in 1986 to break down barriers to trade in services, agriculture and textiles, to boost international respect for patents and copyright, and to improve mechanisms for settling trade disputes — has been looming for a long time. A summit held in Brussels in December 1990 broke up in acrimony after the EC and US failed to agree on farm trade reform. A compromise reform package, known as the Final Act, was drawn up by Mr Arthur Dunkel, director-general of Gatt. It was tabled late in December 1991 and was intended to break the deadlock. All of the 103 countries that have signed up to the Gatt expressed reservation with elements of the package but, with the exception of the EC, have agreed that it is too important to be be rejected.

The issue which continues to jeopardise any agreement is farm trade, in particular the EC's Common Agriculture Policy (CAP). Reform of farm trade is essential to the successful completion of the round because many participants in the developed and developing world are seeking an end to protective farm subsidies in the EC and the US, in exchange for freeing their domestic markets to outsiders.

Mr Dunkel proposed cutting agricultural subsidies by 20 per cent by 1999, converting farm quotas and other protective devices into tariffs and then cutting them by 36 per cent by the same date. He also sought reductions in subsidised farm exports.

The EC rejected the plans in January. Mr Dunkel has refused to reopen the Final Act for fresh negotiation. He has instructed the EC to settle differences over farm trade with other negotiators — principally the US — and bring back a compromise acceptable to all.

Such a compromise would seem to be in the interests of the EC and the US. They spend billions of dollars a year supporting the prices farmers get for their crops, paying

for storage of excess production, and subsidising the price of farm products being dumped on the world market. Such policies place a heavy burden on taxpayers and consumers in the west, and damage agriculture in the Third World by depressing world prices for meat and cereals in particular.

Although the EC has made some concessions over the past few months, two contentious issues remain:

● EC demands to "rebalance" its protective regime by raising protection against the import of cereal substitutes in exchange for lower-ing protection for other farm products.

● EC demands that compensation payments to farmers (seen as the centre-piece of plans to reform the CAP)

regarded by the Gatt as a distortion of trade.

Today, compromise on both these issues appears possible, with the EC suggesting it could drop demands for "rebalancing" in exchange for compensation payments to farmers which do not distort trade. One EC spokesman in Geneva said that the remaining difference between the EC and the US are "more a matter of presentation than substance".

Many observers of the tortuous manoeuvrings within the Gatt find it hard to understand why the entire accord is being put at risk over the issue of CAP reform when the potential gains from an agreement are immense.

For the first time, trade in commercial services — worth $650bn in 1989, the latest year for which the Gatt has figures, accounting for about 19 per cent of world trade — would fall under the Gatt umbrella. A timetable would be set for the

progress on the farm subsidy issue would yield US concessions.

In addition, respect for patents and copyright — vulnerable to piracy in many developing countries — would also be built into an agreement on intellectual property rights. Trade in textiles and garments would be brought into Gatt, after having defied liberalisation for 40 years. Over 10 years the labyrinth of bilaterally negotiated quotas that determine textile trade would be dismantled, and replaced by tariffs.

Value of world merchandise trade 1991

	Exports		Imports	
	Value ($bn)	Annual change per cent	Value ($bn)	Annual change per cent
World	3,530	1½	3,660	1½
North America	555	5½	625	-2½
EC	1,565	-1	1,450	1½
Asia	885	11½	825	8½
China	70	16	65	19½

Source: Gatt

Moreover, reinforced Gatt dispute settlement rules would be expected to check the destructive proliferation of reprisals over goods that are allegedly subsidised, or "dumped" in export markets. They would tackle

cal or industrial standards, which are frequently used as a block to imports.

Perhaps most important of all, a successful conclusion to the Uruguay Round would secure the participation of much of the developing world in multilateral trade agreements. Since 1986, more than 60 countries from the developing world and former communist bloc have adopted policies of reductions in tariffs and quotas. The prospect of

largely because of the promise that trade grievances would be dealt with more speedily in the Gatt by new trade dispute procedures. If the round is put on hold, it will be hard for President Bush's administration to resist demands for unilateral action against "unfair trade".

● June 1 is a critical date, on which a two-year US Farm Bill expires. With it, commitments not to match EC farm export subsidies on a tit-for-tat basis also expire. In fact, the US administration will face a formal commitment to relaunch a subsidy war with the EC on exports of farm products. Such action would almost certainly trigger retaliation.

● The multi-fibre arrangement which controls world trade in textiles and garments expires in December. With no Uruguay Round in place, awkward renegotiation of rules for trade in textiles and garments would be needed.

● Long-sought improvements in Gatt's rules for settling trade disputes would be held up. Countries frustrated with how Gatt currently deals with trade disputes — the US foremost among them — may resort to bilateral sanctions, which again could trigger retaliation.

Delay would also hamper attempts to address new problems — such as reconciling free-trade principles with environmental concerns, and bringing competition policy under the rubrick of the Gatt.

There is a growing feeling among critics that it is time for the world's leading industrial powers to set an example to newly liberalising countries in the Third World. They should set aside narrow domestic political considerations in favour of improving the world trading system.

An old joke about Moses might prove instructive. He was sent by the Israelites to the top of Mount Sinai to negotiate with God over the commandments. He came down exhausted after 40 days with a list of 310 commandments. The Israelites angrily sent him back to negotiate a better deal. Three more days passed before a gaunt Moses reappeared: "I have good news, and bad news," he said. "The good news is I've got the list down to 10. The bad news is that adultery is still in."

For negotiators in Geneva struggling with ennui and exhaustion after six years of non-stop haggling, such a spirit of compromise could be timely.

우루과이라운드 협상 동향

1992. 4. 3.

外務部

우루과이라운드 協商은 最近 協商 參加國間 市場開放 協商의 不振으로 인해 協商 時限 延期가 불가피해지고 있는바, 關聯 動向을 아래 報告 드립니다.

---

1. 最近 動向

   ○ 4月中旬까지 終結을 目標로 推進해온 協商이 農産物 分野의 補助金 減縮을 둘러싼 美國-EC間 異見 對立으로 交錯狀態에 突入

   - 3.21-22 美國-獨逸 頂上會談, 3.19-20 美國-EC間 次官級 協商에서도 兩側間 異見 解消에 失敗

   ○ 서비스 分野에서도 主要國間 異見 擴散

   - 美國이 最近 서비스 産業의 대부분인 金融, 海運, 航空, 通信 分野에서 廣範圍한 條件附 開放 意思를 밝힘으로써 (는 상대국 시장개방수준에 따라 조건부로 개방하겠다는 입장을) 協商 妥結의 새로운 障碍要素로 登場

   ○ 開途國等 餘他 協商 參加國은 協商 不振 現象에 憂慮를 表示하고, 美國 및 EC를 非難

   ○ 조만간 協商 不振을 打開하기 위한 會議等 開催가 豫想되나 協商의 突破口는 마련하기 어려울 것으로 觀測

0084

2. 評 價

　○ 美國은 協商 時限의 遵守보다 美國의 實益 確保를 重視하고
　　있는 것으로 評價

　○ 4月中旬까지 協商 妥結은 어려우며, 美國-EC間 農産物 分野의
　　幕後 折衷이 進行되는 가운데 2-3個月間 더 協商을 繼續할
　　것으로 豫想

　　- 夏季 休暇 以前 協商 終結이 어려울 境遇 11月 美國 大統領
　　　選擧 以後까지 協商이 延期될 것으로 展望

3. 對 策

　○ 協商의 早期 妥結이 어려워지고 있으나, 協商 妥結을 위한
　　우리의 努力은 對外的으로 繼續 표명하는 것이 바람직.

　　- 우리나라는 92. 2. 17. 서비스 分野, 3. 5. 工産品 分野에
　　　대한 讓許 計劃 草案을 提出

　　- 國內的으로 敏感한 農産物 分野 讓許 計劃은 아직 未提出
　　　狀態인바, UR 協商에 대한 寄與 次元에서 빠른 時日內에
　　　提出 豫定.　　　　　　　　　끝.

- 2 -

0085

우루과이라운드 협상 동향

1992. 4. 3.

外 務 部

> 우루과이라운드 協商은 最近 協商 參加國間 市場開放 協商의 不振으로 인해 協商 時限 延期가 불가피해지고 있는바, 關聯 動向을 아래 報告 드립니다.

1. 最近 動向

   ○ 4月中旬까지 終結을 目標로 推進해온 協商이 農産物 分野의 補助金 減縮을 둘러싼 美國-EC間 異見 對立으로 交錯狀態에 突入

      - 3.21-22 美國-獨逸 頂上會談, 3.19-20 美國-EC間 次官級 協商에서도 兩側間 異見 解消에 失敗

   ○ 서비스 分野에서도 主要國間 異見 擴散

      - 美國이 最近 金融, 海運, 航空, 通信 分野는 相對國 市場 開放 水準에 따라 條件附로 開放 하겠다는 立場을 밝힘으로써 協商 妥結의 새로운 障碍要素로 登場

   ○ 開途國等 餘他 協商 參加國은 協商 不振 現象에 憂慮를 表示하고, 美國 및 EC를 非難

   ○ 조만간 協商 不振을 打開하기 위한 會議 開催가 豫想되나 協商의 突破口는 마련하기 어려울 것으로 觀測

- 1 -

0086

2. 評　價

　　o 美國은 協商 時限의 遵守보다 美國의 實益 確保를 重視하고
　　　 있는 것으로 評價

　　o 4月中旬까지 協商 妥結은 어려우며, 美國-EC間 農産物 分野의
　　　 幕後 折衝이 進行되는 가운데 2-3個月間 더 協商을 繼續할
　　　 것으로 豫想

　　　 - 夏季 休暇 以前 協商 終結이 어려울 境遇 11月 美國 大統領
　　　　 選擧 以後까지 協商이 延期될 것으로 展望

3. 對　策

　　o 協商의 早期 妥結이 어려워지고 있으나, 協商 妥結을 위한
　　　 우리의 努力은 對外的으로 繼續 표명하는 것이 바람직.

　　　 - 우리나라는 92. 2. 17. 서비스 分野, 3. 5. 工産品 分野에
　　　　 대한 讓許 計劃 草案을 提出

　　　 - 國內的으로 敏感한 農産物 分野 讓許 計劃은 아직 未提出
　　　　 狀態인바, UR 協商에 대한 寄與 次元에서 빠른 時日內에
　　　　 提出 豫定.　　　　　　　　　　　　끝.

- 2 -

0087

외 무 부

종 별 :

번 호 : GVW-0752　　　　　　　　　일 시 : 92 0403 2020

수 신 : 장관(통기,경기원,재무부,농수산부,상공부,특허청)

발 신 : 주 제네바대사

제 목 : 평화그룹회의(UR 타개책 논의)

연: GVW-0716

본직은 금 4.3(금) 평화그룹대사들은 오찬에 초치 최근 UR 협상정돈 상태 및 동 타개를 위해 평화그룹차원에서 기여가능 방안등에 관해 의견교환을 한바 , 결과 아래 보고함.

1. 우선 JARAMILLO 콜롬비아대사(T3 의장)가 금일 오전있었던 DUNKEL 총장과 3 개 협상그룹의장 회의결과를 아래와 같이 소개함.

1) DUNKEL 총장은 각그룹의장에게 분명하고 전문적인(CLEAR AND PROFESSIONAL) 협상 현황 보고서를 제출토록 요구함(동 보고서는 DUNKEL 총장의 참고용이며 GREEN ROOM 에 배포되는 것은 아님)

2) GREEN ROOM 협의는 4.8(수) 로 결정되었으며, 동 회의에서 DUNKEL 총장은 자신의 계획을 제시하기 보다 참가국들로 부터 협상현황평가, 타개책, TNC 개최시기, 진행방법등에 관한 의견을 청취할 의도임.

3) TNC 를 부활절 시한 이전 또는 이후 개최할런지의 여부에 대해 DUNKEL 총장의 특별한 복안은 없었으나, 4.22.BUSH-DELORS 회담이후 가능성이 높다고 봄.

2. 현상황의 정확한 파악에 입각한 타개책 모색을 위해 보고서의 배포가 유익할 것이라는 본직, 우루과이, 형가리등의 의견에 대해 스위스 및 JARAMILLO 대사는 공식 TNC 에는 필요할지 모르나 GREEN ROOM 에는 배포치 않겠다는 것이 DUNKEL 총장의 의도로 보인다고 함.

3. TNC 개최시기에 관해서는 던켈의 CREDIBILITY 문제도 고려, 부활절시한 이전 개최가 바람직하다는 의견(호주, 아국, 홍콩, 싱가폴)과 내실있는 TNC 를 위해서는 부활절이후 특히 부시, DELORS 회담(4.22) 이후에 개최함이 좋겠다는 의견(카나다)이 엇갈림.

롱상국	장관	차관	1차보	2차보	외정실	분석관	청와대	안기부
경기원	재무부	농수부	상공부	특허청				

PAGE 1　　　　　　　　　　　　　　　　　　92.04.04　05:42

외신 2과 통제관 FM

0088

4. 평화그룹 차원에서 공동 DEMARCHE 를 취할 필요성 여부에 관해서는 동그룹의
설립연원, 구성국가의 다양성등에 비추어 동 그룹이 어떤 형태로든 DEMARCHE 를 취할
경우 특정이해관계로 조직된 여타그룹보다 동개관성 및 비중이 높을 것이므로 ACTION
이 유익할 것이며, 현상황이야말로 평화그룹이 나서기에 가장 적절한 상황이라는 점에
대해서는 대체적인 의견의 일치를 보였으나, 구체적방식(DUNKEL 방식, STATEMENT
배포), 내용(단순한 실망표시, 절차적인 기여, 실질문제에 대한 기여등), 시기등에
관해서는 의견이 엇갈림으로써, 4.6(월) 오후 GATT에서 본직 주재로 재차회합, 토의를
계속키로 하였음. 끝
    (대사 박수길-국장)
    예고:92.12.31. 까지

검 토 필 (1992.6.30.) 기

외 무 부

종 별 :

번 호 : FRW-0714   일 시 : 92 0406 1630

수 신 : 장 관(통기)

발 신 : 주 불 대사

제 목 : UR 협상 동향

연:FRW-0271

1. 당지 4.6자 언론보도에 의하면,지난 4.3 당지개최 국제상공회의소 회의에 참석한 J.MOLLEMANN 독일 경제장관은 4.21-23간 워싱턴 개최예정인 미-EC 간 정상회담에서 UR 협상의 교착상태가 타개될수도 있을 것으로 전망하나,만약 동 회담도 별다른성과가 없을시,연호 동장관이 92.1. 주장한 G-7 특별정상회담의 개최를 통한 UR 협상 타결 필요성을 재강조 하였다 함.

2. MOLLEMANN 독일 경제장관은 P.BEREGOVOY 불신임수상의 임명이 유럽-미국간 농업보조금 분쟁해결에 도움이 되기를 희망하면서,미 BUSH대통령은 농업문제에 관해 타협할 준비가 되어있으며 일본의 쌀시장 개방 거부는 협상의 단순한 전술에 불과하기때문에 불란서가 양보할 경우 UR 협상 타결의 다른 장애요소는 없다고 강조하였음.

3. MOLLEMANN 독 경제장관의 특히 독일측으로서는 불란서를 제외한채 미측과 농업 분야 협상을 추진할수 없는
관계로 불란서측의 자발적 양보를 완곡히 촉구한 것으로보임.끝.

   (대사 노영찬-국장)

롱상국   2차보   구주국   외정실   분석관

PAGE 1   92.04.07   00:54 FN

원 본

외 무 부

종 별 :

번 호 : GVW-0759

일 시 : 92 0407 1200

수 신 : 장관(통기, 경기원, 재무부, 농림수산부, 상공부, 특허청)

발 신 : 주 제네바 대사

제 목 : 평화그룹회의(UR 타개책 논의)

연: GVW-0752

1. 연호 보고대로 UR 협상정돈현상 타개에 대한 평화그룹의 기여방안 논의를 위한 평화그룹대사간 비공식 협의가 4.6(월) 오후 개도국 비공식 회의에 이어본직 주재로 GATT 에서 개최된바 동 결과 아래 보고함.

가. 본직이 우선 4.3(금) 본직관저 오찬 협의시 평화그룹이 UR 관련 INITIATIVE 를 취할 필요성에는 전체적인 의견 일치가 있었고, 이에 입각 관련 협의시도출된 3 가지 방안(성명 발표, DUNKEL 면담, WASHINGTON 및 BRUSSELS 에 대한 직접적인 DEMARCHE) 에 관해 의견을 개진해 주도록 요청

나. DUNKEL 면담과 관련 평화그룹의 INITIATIVE 의 목적은 DUNKEL 총장을 도와주는 방향이 되어야 할것이라는 SHANNON 대사의 지적 및 그렇게 하려면 DUNKEL 총장의 전략을 잘 파악해야 된다는 ROSSIER 스위스대사 HAWES 호주대사등의 의견을 반영, 가급적 조속한 시일내에 본직 및 일부대사가 동총장을 면담, 이에관한 동총장의 의견을 들어 보기로 합의함.

다. 한편 성명발표 문제에 관해서는 ROSSIER 스위스대사가 다소 소극적 입장을 표시한 반면 여타 대사는 대체적으로 호의적인 반응을 보이며 아래 의견을 개진한바, HAWES 호주대사의 제의로 동문제는 GREEN ROOM 회의개최 결과를 본후 재론하기로 하였음.

 - 뉴질랜드: 평화그룹성격상 특정문제 취급은 곤란하며, 계속 비공식 협의를 해나가면서 TNC 개최 시점등에 맞춰 발표하는 방안 검토

 - 싱가폴, 호주, 헝가리 : 성명발표지지

 - 우루과이 : 평화그룹의 성격이 오히려 강점이 되므로 성명발표에 적극적

 - 홍콩: 좌절감 표시 및 정치적 공약 재천명에 불과한 성명은 곤란하며, 그룹

통상국	장관	차관	1차보	2차보	외정실	분석관	청와대	안기부
경기원	재무부	농수부	상공부	특허청				

PAGE 1

92.04.08   04:39

외신 2과 통제관 FM

0091

성격에 따른 제약을 고려할때 자극적이 아닌 어조로 다자협상 복귀를 촉구하는것과 늦어도 4 월말 이전 TNC 개최를 촉구하는 내용의 포함시 가능시

라. 한편 SHANNON 카나다 대사는 오찬협의에 이어 상기 협의시에도 워싱톤 및 브랏셀에 대한 각국정부의 공동 DEMARCHE 필요성을 강조하였고, TNC 개최시기에 관한 대체적인 의견은 부시.DELORS 회담이후 개최하는 것이 바람직하다는 쪽으로 기울었음.

2. 상기 1 항 "나"의 합의에 따라 본직, 스위스, 홍콩 및 뉴질랜드 대사가 4.7 오후 DUNKEL 총장 면담을 추진중임.끝

(대사 박수길-국장)

예고:92.12.31. 까지

검 토 필 (199×6 .3°.) 홍

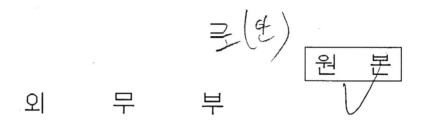

외 무 부

종   별 :

번   호 : ECW-0476   일   시 : 92 0407 1600

수   신 : 장 관 (통기, 경기원, 농수산부, 상공부)

발   신 : 주 EC 대사 사본: 주미, 제네바대사-중계요망:중계필

제   목 : UR 협상

1. EC 일반이사회는 4.6. 룩셈부르그에서 표제관련 회의를 가진후 발표한 성명에서 UR협상에서 미국과의 균형된 타협을 마련하기위한 집행위의 새로운 노력을 촉구함

2. ANDRIESSEN 대외담당 부위원장은 UR협상은 돌이킬수 없는 단계로 접어들었다(THE POINT OF NO RETURN HAS BEEN CROSSED) 라고 현시점의 협상의 현황을 설명하면서UR 협상타결을 위한 결정적인 돌파구를 마련하기 위하여 4.22. 워싱톤에서 BUSH 미국 대통령, DELORS EC 집행위원장 및 CAVACO SILVA 폴투갈 수상(EC 의장국) 간 3자 회담이 개최될 예정이며, 동 회담준비를 위한 실무협상이 내주중에 개최될 것이라고 언급함

3. 동 회의에서 EC 각료들은 UR 협상이 교착상태에 빠져있는 상황에서 미국이 해운및 금융등 써비스 협상의 주요분야에 대한 제외를 주장하고 나온데 대하여 깊은 우려를 표명함

4. 한편 동 회의에 참석한 GUIGOU 불란서 EC담당장관은 UR 협상에서 보다 신축적인 자세를 보이고 있는 BEREGOVOY 신임수상의 취임에도 불구하고 농산물관련 불란서의 입장이 변화된 것은 없으나, 지난주에 미.EC 간 항공기 보조금 문제가 해결되므로서 양측간의 분쟁이 원만하게 타결되는 좋은 선례를 남기게되어 UR 협상에서도 희망을 포기해서는 안될 것이라고 말함

5. CAVACO SILVA EC 이사회 의장은 상기 4.22.워싱톤 3자 회담에 앞서 회원국간이견조정을 위해 EC 통상장관 회의를 소집할 것이라고 말함. 끝

    (대사 권동만-국장)

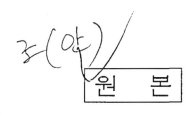

외 무 부

종 별 :

번 호 : GVW-0760 　　　　　　　　　　　일 시 : 92 0407 1200

수 신 : 장 관(통기,경기원,재무부,농림수산부,상공부,특허청)

발 신 : 주 제네바 대사

제 목 : UR/개도국 비공식 그룹회의

　　1. 표제회의가 4.6(월) 15:30- 17:30간 BENHIMA 의장주재로 개최되어, 던켈 TNC의장으로 부터 UR 협상현황을 청취하고 이에대해 개도국들이 견해를 제시하였는바,주요협의 내용은 아래와 같음.(본직, 김봉주서기관 참석)

　　가. 던켈 의장 설명 내용

　　0 현재 협상의 현황에 대하여 경고(ALARM)가 주어지고 있으나 실망할 필요가 없으며, 중요한것은 4월중순등 협상시한이 아니라 언제부터 UR협상결과가 시행될 것인지가 중요함

　　0 UR 협상결과 시행일자와 관련,섬유분야에서 MFA 의 갓트 복귀시한을 93.1.1.로잡고 있음에 비추어 아직도 93.1.1.UR 협상결과 시행이라는 목표에 도달하는데 늦지 않음.

　　0 T1 이 과거 동경라운드 보다도 훨씬 복잡한 협상이며, T2 는 서비스를 처음 SCHEDULING 하는 협상인 점을 감안할때 지난 1월 이래 매우 커다란 진전을 이루었으며,결코 협상이 교착상태에 빠졌다(ROUND IS BLOCKED)고 말할수 없음.

　　0 조만간 정치적 타결이 있지 않을 경우, T1-3작업은 어려움에 봉착하게 될것이며, T1-2 를 봉하여 정치적 타결의 대상이 무엇인지 분명하게 제시된 것이 큰 성과중의 하나임. 즉 T1을 봉하여 누가 농산물 분야의 관세화 계획을 제출하였는지를 분명히알수 있게 되었음.

　　0 현시점에서 T4를 가동할 필요가 없으며,T1-3의 모든 문제들이 극복될때 T4작업에 착수 할것임.

　　0 개도국들을 비롯한 다수국가들이 SILENT MAJORITY로서 UR 협상의 조기타결을 지원하고 있는데 감사함.

　　나. 개도국 언급내용

통상국　　2차보　　경기원　　재무부　　농수부　　상공부　　특허청

0 우루과이, 인도등은 T1-3 에 진전이 있는듯이 보이나 실질적으로는 아무런 진전이 없다고 지적하고 선진국들의 자유화 조치가 없을 경우 개도국들의 자유화 정책을후퇴시키는 결과를 가져올 것이라고 언급

0 인도, 콜롬비아등은 정치적 해결이 없는 상황은 매우 위험하며, 현재 양자협상에 대한 명료성이 결여되어 있고 갓트 밖에서 진행되고 있기때문에 2 협상자들로 인하여 98 의 협상자들이 마비 상태에 빠져있음에 우려를 표명하고 조속히 협상을 다자화 할것을 촉구

0 모로코, 탄자니아등은 T1-2 의 시한이 종료되었으며 이미 협상이 위기상황에도달하였음에 비추어 TNC 회의를 소집하여 모든 TRACK 의 협상현황을 점검할 것을 요구

다. (본직 언급내용)

0 아국은 UR 협상의 성공적 조기 타결을 바라고 있는 협상 참가국중의 하나임을전제하고 T4는 가동되어야 할것임을 촉구

0 양자협상 주도국의 양자 협상결과만을 반영,이를 기정사실화(FAIT ACCOMPLI)하여 그결과를 다른 협상참가국들에 강요함으로써 여타 참가국들이 자신의 이익을 반영할 기회를 박탈해서는 안될것임을 지적

0 또한 T1-3 은 계속되어야 하는 만큼, 협상 SCHEDU재 재작성을 위해서도 TNC 회의가 소집되어야 할것이라고 언급

2. 던켈 총장은 개도국들의 언급 사항에 대하여 아래 요지로 답함.

0 협상현황은 매우 실망스러운 상황(A SITUATIONOF GREAT FRUSTRATION) 이며 협상명료성의 결여에 대하여도 자신도 같은 입장임.

0 T4 를 가동할 경우, T1-3 협상은 진행되지 않을 것이며, 지금까지의 협상결과를 UNRAVEL할 위험성이 큼. 이와관련, 아직도 TARIFFICATION에 반대하는 국가가 있음을 우려함.

0 협상주도국들의 양자협상결과를 그대로 기정사실화 하지는 않을 것이며, 각 참가국들이 결정할 시간을 줄것임.

0 TNC 회의개최 문제는 자신의 일정을 점검해보겠음.끝

(대사 박수길-국장)

외 무 부

원 본

종 별 :

번 호 : GVW-0768

일 시 : 92 0408 1000

수 신 : 장 관(통기, 경기원, 재무부, 농림수산부, 상공부)

발 신 : 주 제네바 대사　　　　사본:주미,주이씨대사-중계필

제 목 : 평화 그룹 대사의 DUNKEL 총장 면담

연: GVW-0759

1. 본직은 연호 보고와 같이 홍콩 및 뉴질랜드 대사와 함께 금 4.7(화) 오전 DUNKEL 총장을 면담한바 동 결과를 아래 보고함.(HUSSEIN 차장보, 이성주 참사관 배석)

가. 본직이 먼저 최근 평화그룹 대사간 비공식 협의 결과 및 방문 목적을 설명하고, UR 협상 정돈상태 타개를 위한 평화그룹의 기여 방안에 관한 동 총장의 의견을 문의함.

나. 이에 대해 DUNKEL 총장은 평화그룹의 이러한 노력에 사의를 표한후 아래와 같이 자신의 견해를 밝힘.

1) 모든 협상 참가국에 대해 냉소주의(모든 국가가 UR 성공을 강조하고 있지만 협상 테이블에서의 각국 입장은 전혀 움직이지 않고 있는 상황) 및 위선(모든 국가가 UR 타결을 위해 자신이 할수 있는 일이 무엇인지 알면서도 말로만 기여하고 있는 상황)에서 벗어나라고 호소하고 싶은 심경이며, 이러한 상황하에서는 UR 타결에 대한 원론적 강조는 별효과가 없음.

2) 실제로 필요한 사항은 지금이라도 각국이 그러한 자세에서 벗어나, 특히 평화그룹의 경우에는 차기 TNC 에 자신의 양보안(BOTTOM LINE)을 밝혀 NON-MAJORS 로서 협상 진전에 실제로 기여할 용의가 있음을 행동으로 보여줌으로써 미.EC 가 이에 합류하도록 하는 SHOCK 요법이라고 봄.

3) 이는 몇몇 국가에게는 극히 어려운 주문이될 수도 있으나, 최종 순간에 강요당하는 것 보다 미리 어려운 정치적 결단을 내리는 것(유럽, 아시아, 카나다의 농업을 예로 듦)이 현명하며, UR 실패시 전면적 무역 전쟁(현 GATT 체제의 고수도 불가)이 불가피하다는 점등을 고려, 평화그룹 회원국 각자가 N/S 및 MFN 일탈등에서

통상국	장관	차관	1차보	2차보	외정실	분석관	청와대	안기부
경기원	재무부	농수부	상공부	중계				

무엇을 해야 할지 신중히 판단, 행동해주기 바람.

다. 상기에 대해 본직은 평화그룹 내에서 STATEMENT 작성에 관한 합의도 용이치 않은점을 예로 들어 현실정치(REAL POLITIK) 세계에 살고 있음을 상기시키고 그럼에도 불구 상황의 심각성에 비추어 기여 방안을 모색코자 하는 것이라고 설명하면서 BOTTOM LINE 제시시 추가적 양보를 강요당할 우려가 없지 않음을 지적함.

라. DUNKEL 총장은 상기 우려를 인정하면서도, UR 협상의 구제(SALVAGE)를 바란다면 차기 TNC 까지 아래 내용의 공약을 담은 STATEMENT 를 평화 그룹이 시행할수 있으면 유익할 것이라 함.

1) UR 협상을 종결할 시점에 와 있다는 점

(TIME TO CONCLUDE THE ROUND)

2) UR 성공을 위해 어려운 결단(입장의 변경)을 내릴 준비가 되어 있다는 점 (PREPARED TO SHIFT THE POSITION) (단, 일부분야에 있어서는 미.EC 의 상응한 조치를 전제로 한다는 단서 부기는 무방)

사. 상기에 대해 WONG 홍콩대사가 구체적으로 현 FA 의 수락용의 및 내실있는 N/S 의 제출을 의미하느냐고 질문한데 대해 DUNKEL 총장은 FA TEXT 에서의 DEROGATION 을 최소화하는 범위내에서 각국 입장의 근접화(CONVERGENCE)에 도움이되는 조치를 의미한다고 답변하면서, 협상 미결쟁점을 아래와 같이 정리함으로써 NON-MAJORS 로 부터는 TARIFFICATION 에 대한 양보가 중요함을 간접적으로 시사함.

1) TARIFFICATION: 반대하는 5 개국(일본, 한국, 카나다, 스위스, 오지리)이 양보하면 컨센서도 가능

2) 국내보조: 거의 합의에 도달한 상태

3) 수출 보조: 기본적으로 미.EC 간 잇슈로서 극복 불가능한 사항으로 보지않음.

4) 써비스: 미국의 의도는 FREE-RIDER 의 방지에 있는바, 개도국의 능력을 감안할때 선진국 시장진출 능력을 보유한 일부 국가만 움직이면 해결 가능

5) 기타 T3 등 RULE-MAKING : 정치적 돌파구만 마련되면, 5-6 주내 종결 가능

아. 그밖에 DUNKEL 총장은 TNC 운영등과 관련 아래 사항을 언급함.

- 냉정한 STOCK-TAKING 및 향후 대책을 논의할 PROFESSIONAL 한 TNC 를 운영 계획

- TNC 개최시기는 미리 밝힐 경우 그때까지 협상이 전혀 움직이지 않을 것이므로 밝히지 않을 예정.

- 그린룸 회의에서는 자신의 견해를 밝히기 보다 참가국의 의견을 주로 청취할

PAGE 2

0097

예정.

- 미국의 FAST TRACK 시한이 UR 협상 시한이라는 생각은 위험 (NON-MAJORS 로서는 오히려 FAIT ACCOMPLI 를 자초하는 결과) 하므로 계속 협상 MOMENTUM 유지 필요

2. DUNKEL 총장 면담 결과에 입각한 향후 행동 방안을 협의키 위해 4.9(목)오후 본직 주재로 재차 평화 그룹 대사 비공식 협의를 가질 예정임.

3. 상기 면담 결과에 대한 당관의 평가는 아래와 같음.

가. DUNKEL 총장 언급의 전반적 취지는, 이제까지 각 그룹 (케언즈, 라틴아메리카, 개도국/동구그룹도 본직 면담직전 동 총장을 면담)이 UR 협상에 대한 원칙론적 지지의사(COMMITMENT) 천명만 되풀이 함으로써 아무런 실질적 기여를 하지 못하고 있음을 감안, 구체적 양보에 주안점을 두고 특히 평화그룹에 대해서도 이점을 독려하는 내용임.

나. 동 총장은 일본, 한국등이 TARIFFICATION 문제를 언급한바, 특히 일본에 대해서는 7 월 선거등 요인으로 UR 협상에 극히 비협조적이라는 인식을 갖고 있다는 인상을 감지할수 있었음.

다. 동 총장은 또한 평화그룹이 자신을 돕기 위한 자세에는 사의를 표하지만, 사실은 자신을 돕는것 보다 (자신은 12.20 FA 제출로 최선을 다했으므, 더이상의 역할이 없다는 점 강조), 협상 참가국이 협상을 추진(PUSH) 해 나가야 함을강조함으로써 협상이 심각한 위기에 봉착해 있음을 간접 확인케 하는 계기가 되었음.

라. 또한 미국.EC 간 국내 보조문제는 거의 합의 단계에 와있고, 수출 보조문제가 주요 잇슈로 남아 있음을 확인함.

마. 각국의 여론때문에 TNC 회의는 조만간 개최될 것으로 보이지만, 동회의 자체가 UR 협상의 극적 타결의 계기가 될것으로는 기대할수 없다고 보며, 4.22 미.EC 정상회담 이전에는 확실한 타결 전명을 내리기 어려울 것으로 보임.

4. 한편 본직은 동 면담 기회에 아국도 농산물 C/S 를 금주내 제출 예정임을 통보하고, 협상 진전을 위해 최선을 다하고 있음을 강조함. 끝.

(대사 박수길-장관)

예고 92.12.31. 까지

검 토 필 (199✗.6.30.) 7

외 무 부

종 별 :

번 호 : USW-1776   일 시 : 92 0408 1841

수 신 : 장관(통이,통기,경일,정총,미중,외연원,경기,재무,상공,농수,경제수석)

발 신 : 주 미 대사

제 목 : UR 과 NAFTA 타결 전망

　1. 당관 구본영 공사는 4.8. 당지 소재 IIE (소장: FRED BERGSTEN) 의 선임연구원으로재직중인 JEFFREY SCHOTT 박사와 오찬을 같이하며 상호 관심사에 관하여 의견을 나누었는바, 주요내용을 참고로 보고함.(SCHOTT 박사는 UR 과 NAFTA 문제에 대하여 미국정부는 물론 CANADA,MEXCIO 정부 고위인사들에게 중요한 자문역할을 수행하는 인사중 하나이며 최근 NAFTA 문제에 관한 포괄적인 저서를 출간한 바 있음.- 동저서는 파편으로 기송부 -)

　- UR 및 NAFTA 타결 전망에 대하여 모두 낙관하며 의회가 관련법안을 승인하는 것은 새로운 정부가 출범하는 내년초가 될것임.

　- UR 타결에 관건이 되고 있는 농업보조금 문제는 결국 불란서 입장을 살려주기위하여 미국이 일부 다른 부문에 있어서 양보를 하되 실질적으로는 현재 미국입장을거의 관철하는 형식으로 매듭지어질 가능성이 높음.

　- 일단 농업보조금 문제가 매듭지어 지면 MOMENTUM을 타고 농산물 문제뿐만 아니라 서비스, 반덤핑문제등 다른 모든 문제들이 2-3개월내에 속속 타결될 가능성이 높음.

　- 4월말 던켈 GATT 사무총장, DELORS EC집행위원장등이 미국을 방문할 예정인바그때가 UR 타결의 또한차례 고비가 될것임.

　- NAFTA 문제는 기본적으로 관련 3국이 협정타결에 긍정적, 적극적이기 때문에 UR 보다 더욱 타결 전망이 밝으며 올해내 협정이 마련될 것임.

　- NAFTA 내용중 가장 논란이 많은 원산지규정(RULES OF ORIGIN) 에 대해서는 현행 미,카나다 자유무역 협정에서 합의한 내용(대부분 제조품의 경우 50 퍼센트) 이상으로 강화하는 것을 계속 반대하고 있음.

　- 한국은 UR 과 NAFTA 모두 늦어도 93년봄까지는 타결될 것을 가정하여 국내 정책을 수립하는 것이 적절할 것으로 생각됨.

| 통상국 | 2차보 | 미주국 | 경제국 | 통상국 | 외연원 | 외정실 | 정와대 | 경기원 |
| 재무부 | 농수부 | 상공부 | | | | | | |

PAGE 1   92.04.09   08:14 ED

외신 1과 통제관

0099

2. 구공사는 SCHOTT 박사에게 최근 한.미통상관계에 대하여도 대체적인 분위기를전달하고 특히 대일 역조개선 문제에 대한 한.미간 공동대응 문제에 대해서 관심을가져줄것을 부탁하였음.끝.

(대사 현홍주-국장)

외 무 부

종   별 :

번   호 : GVW-0790   일   시 : 92 0409 1900

수   신 : 장관(통기, 경기원, 재무부, 농수산부, 상공부, 특허청)

발   신 : 주 제네바대사   사본:주미, 주 EC 대사(중계필)

제   목 : UR/그린룸 회의

연: GVW-0752

1. 작 4.8(수) GREEN ROOM 회의가 예정대로 35 개 주요국 대사들이 참석한 가운데 개최되었는바, 모두에 DUNKEL 총장은 금일 회의의 목적을 (1) 협상 현황, (2) 협상타결에 대한 주요 장애요인, (3) 앞으로 협상 타결에 소요될 TIME FRAME 등 문제에 관해 각국의 의견을 듣고 솔직한 의견을 교환하는데 있다고 말함.

가. 놀웨이, 알젠틴, 인도등 많은 대사들은 이제는 거듭 연기된 DEADLINE 등 문제로 인하여 당지 대표부와 본국 정부간에 CRDDIBILITY 문제가 크게 부각되고 있으며, 이로 인하여 UR 에 반대하는 세력들이 보다 조직적인 반대운동을 전개하고 있다고 지적, 성공 여부에 대한 결단을 조속 내릴 필요가 있다고 강조하였고 우루과이등 일부 국가들은 UR 협상은 현재 마비 되어있으며 가장큰 장애요인은 1.13.TNC 시의 결정을 모든나라들이 이행하지 않고 있기 때문이라고 지적함.

나. 일본은 협상지연의 책임이 전적으로 다른 협상참가국들에게만 있다고 주장할 수는 없지만 미국-EC 간의 협상에 진전이 없으므로 본국 정부에서도 시장접근 및 서비스분야, 양허협상에서 참된 의미의 어려운 결정(HARD DECISION)을 못하고 있는 현실이라고 지적하면서, 현재 남아있는 시간을 역산해 보면 가까운 장래에 BREAKTHROUGH 가 없는한 93 년 협정 발효는 불가능할 것이라고 언급함.

다. 호주등 일부국가는 UR 의 현황은 정치적으로나 경제적으로 파국에 가까운 상황이라고 지적하고 설령 곧 BREAKTHROUGH 가 있다 하더라도 시장접근 및 서비스 분야 양허협상에 최소한 2-3 개월은 소요될 것이므로 협정의 내년 발효는 어려울 것이라고 주장했고, 서서 또한 4 월내의 돌파구 마련의 중요성을 강조함.

브라질은 이제 UR 협상이 중대한 난관에 봉착했음을 인식하고 하루속히 협상 결과에 대한 집단적 평가를 시행하여야 한다고 주장함.

통상국 안기부	장관 경기원	차관 재무부	1차보 농수부	2차보 상공부	경제국 특허청	외정실 중계	분석관	청와대

PAGE 1   92.04.10   07:47

외신 2과 통제관 BZ

0101

라. 미국과 EC 는 UR 의 다자적 성격을 충분히 인식하고 있고 그에 대한 책임을 회피할 생각은 없으나 현실적으로 쌍무적인 협상에 임하지 않을수 없으며, 자기들로서는 현상황에서 최선을 다하고 있고 양측의 정치지도자들도 협상 타결에 확고한 정치적 의지가 있다고 언급함. 또한 EC 는 협상 교착의 원인이 농업에국한 된것이 아니라고 주장하고 현 상황에 좌절하기 보다 인내심을 갖고 교섭해 나가야 할것이라는 점과 4.22 일 회의의 중요성을 강조하였으며 미국은 설령 4.22 일 회의에서 돌파구를 찾지 못한다 하더라도 협상을 꾸준히 계속되어야 할것이라고 주장함.

마. 한편 본직도 UR 교착의 주원인이 미-EC 간 합의에 도달치 못하는데 기인하는것은 사실이나 모든 참가국이 집단적인 책임감을 가져야 한다고 전제하고,특정 국가를 비판하기 보다는 각국이 UR 의 성공을 위하여 각기 시장접근, 써비스등 분야에서 할수 있는 최선은 다하여야 할것이라고 지적하고 아국도 구체적인 협력의 의지로서 금주중 농산물 SCHEDULE 을 제출할 계획임을 밝혔음.

사. 이상에 대하여 DUNKEL 총장은 MFA 유효기한의 금년말 완료등을 이유와 함께 금년안으로 협상이 성공하지 못할 경우 UR 의 전망은 극히 불투명하다고 말하고 양자교섭과 함께 다자협상도 병행해 가면서 최종 의정서를 중심으로 CONSENSUS 형성에 노력해야 할것이라고 강조하고, 각국은 이율배반적인 이중적 행동을자제하고 협상 성공을 위한 전문적이고 생산적인 (PROFESSIONAL AND PRODUCTIVE) 방식으로 현황을 진단해야 한다고 전제하고 아래 방침을 밝힘.

(1) 1.13 일 확대 GREEN ROOM 회의를 개최하여 3 개그룹의장이 제출한 보고서를 기초로 하여(참가국 수 증가) TRACK I, II, III 에 대한 솔직하고 직접적인비공식 평가(INFORMAL ASSESSMENT) 를 하겠음

(2) 동 ASSESSMENT 실시후 기자들과 회견, 정치적 돌파구(POLITICAL BREAKTHROUGH) 마련이 필요하다는 점등을 강조하겠음

(3) 공식 TNC 개최 문제는 사태진전에 따라 4 월 말경으로 고려하고 있음.

(4) TRACK 4 는 가장 마지막 단계에서 필요 최소한에서만 작동하겠음.

2. 작일 GREEN ROOM 회의를 기초로한 본직의 평가는 다음과 같음.

가. 미국.EC 간의 타결이 없는한 UR 교착상태의 타개가 거의 불가능한 현 상황에서 DUNKEL 총장은 3 개 그룹의장의 보고를 기초로 특정국가를 비난하지 않으면서 주요 애로점(BLOCKAGE)을 적시하는등 비공식평가와 함께 정치적 돌파구 마련을

호소함으로써(언론 및 각 참가국에게) 사태 전환의 계기마련을 기도함.

　　나.　4.22 일 BUSH-DELORE 회담에 큰 기대를 걸면서 그때까지 대결적인 TNC 회의(상호 비판, 각국의 강경한 입장의 재천명등)을 피하면서 비공식 GREEN 회의를 통하여 각참가국에게 사태의 진실을(FACT OF THE MATTER) 알림으로써 미국.EC 에 호소와 함께 간접적인 압력을 증대함.

　　다.　BUSH-DELORE 회담이 돌파구를 찾지 못할 경우에 대비한 전략은 현싯점에서 의식적으로 제기하지 않고 있으나 동회담 이후에는 조만간 공식 TNC 회의를소집, UR 전략 재검토가 불가피할 것으로 보임.

　　라.　금년 1 월 이래 실시되어온 불만족스러운 양자 및 다자간 시장접근 및 써비스 협상결과에 비추어 볼때 4 월안에 돌파구 마련이 되지 않을 경우 금년내 타결이 난망시 된다는점에 대해서는 많은 대표간에 이견이 없는듯함. 끝

　　(대사 박수길-국장)

　　예고:92.12.31. 까지

검 토 필 (1992. 6. 30.) 홍

외 무 부

종 별 :

번 호 : GVW-0804   일 시 : 92 0410 1800

수 신 : 장 관(봉기, 경기원, 재무부, 농림수산부, 상공부, 특허청)

발 신 : 주 제네바 대사

제 목 : UR 평화 그룹회의

　　　연: GVW-0768(1), GVW-0790(2)

　　1. 본직은 4.9(목) 오후 평화그룹회의를 재차 소집연호(1) 본직등 3개국 대사의 4.7 DUNKEL 총장면담결과를 설명하고 아래 이유를 들어 현단계에서 평화그룹 공동 STATEMENT 를 발표하는 것 보다, 일단 4.22. BUSH-DELORS 회담결과를 본후 재론하는 것이 좋겠다는 의견을 제시한바, 우루과이 대사를 제외한 대부분의 대사가 이에 동의함으로써, 4.24.우루과이 대사 주최 오찬시 재협의 하는 것으로 합의됨.

　　가. DUNKEL 총장이 GENERAL STATEMENT 의 효과에 대해서는 회의적 반응을 보이면서 구체 행동을 수반한 실질적 기여를 희망하고 있으나, 현상황에서는 일부회원국으로서는 동 희망을 충족시킬수 없다는 현실적 문제점

　　나. 4.8 그린룸협의 결과 4.13(월) 예정인 확대 그린룸협의도 역시 가급적 각국의 발언을 최소한으로 억제하고 3개협상 그룹의장 보고서에 대한 전문적 평가중심으로조용히 진행하고자 하는것이 동총장의 의도인 것으로 파악됨.

　　2. 본직은 DUNKEL 총장이 요구하는 기여방안이 농산물에 관한 아국입장의 변화 가능성을 시사할 위험성이 있다는 점 및 평화그룹을 대표해서 본직등이 DUNKEL 총장을면담 동그룹의 우려 및 협조 용의를 전달한 것만으로 상당한 성과를 거두었다는 판단에따라 상기와같은 결론을 유도한 것임.끝

　　(대사 박수길-국장)

통상국	2차보	경기원	재무부	농수부	상공부	특허청

92.04.11   04:02 FN

외신 1과 통제관

0104

발 신 전 보

	분류번호	보존기간

번   호 : WGV-0566   920411 1434 FO   종별 :

수   신 : 주   제네바   대사. 총영사///

발   신 : 장   관   (통 기)

제   목 : UR/평화그룹 회의

                    대 : GVW-0804

                                                    o

1. 대호 ~~가마치 수도로~~ statement 발표등 평화그룹의 UR 협상 관련 공동 demarche를 일단 보류키로 한것은 적절한 판단~~인 것~~으로 평가됨.

2. 본부로서도 평화그룹의 UR 협상에 대한 기여 의사는 그간의 귀직을 중심으로한 Dunkel 총장 면담등을 통해 충분히 표명 되었다고 보며, 평화그룹이 공동 statement를 통해 실질적인 기여 의사 표시등 지나치게 적극적인 태도를 보일 경우, 협상 상대국으로 하여금 아국등에 대해 필요 이상의 기대를 갖게 할 ~~수도~~

~~있다고~~ 우려~~되는~~ 점도 있다고 봄.   끝.   (제 2 차 라 과 보)
                                                (통상국장 김 용 규)

                                                (~~차관   노 창 희~~)

앙고재	92년 4월 11일	통상길과	기안자성명	과 장 신의관	국 장	차 관	장 관		외신과통제

0105

관리번호 *p2-* *281*

외 무 부

종 별 :

번 호 : ITW-0432　　　　　　　　　　　　　일 시 : 92 0411 1135

수 신 : 장관(통기,구일,상공부,농수부)

발 신 : 주 이태리 대사

제 목 : UR 관련 이태리입장및 협상 전망(자응 92-24)

일반문서로 재분류 *92.12.31*

　　1. 당관 김경석서기관은 4.9(목) 주재국 외무성 경제 5 국 BENEDICTIS 서기관을 면담, 우루과이라운드 협상관련 이태리의 입장및 동협상 전망에 관해 의견을 청취하였는 바, 동요지 다음 보고함.

　　가. UR 협상에 대한 이태리의 입장

　　O UR 협상에서 이태리의 이해와 직결되는 사항은 무엇보다 농산물분야와 섬유분야임. 농산물분야에서 GREENBOX 의 점진적 개혁과 국내보조 감축문제는 이태리가 농업국가 (전체 고용인구의 10 프로 정도 차지)임으로 매우 민감한 분야이며 특히 올리브유와 관련된 국내 보조금문제는 주요관심사항임. 그이외의 수출보조금 삭감문제는 이태리와 크게 관련되지 않기 때문에 EC 차원에서 공동보조를 취하고 있음.

　　O 한편 섬유분야는 이태리 기간산업으로 정치적인 측면에서 중요성이 크기 때문에, MFA 가 철폐되는 대신 미국, 신흥공업국, 섬유수출국등의 관세인하와 시장개방을 보장할 수 있는 효과적인 새로운 규범체계(앤티덤핑, 상계관세등) 도입을 주장하고 있음.

　　나. UR 타결 전망

　　O 던켈 GATT 사무총장이 UR 협상타결시기를 부활절로 제시한 것은 지켜지기어려울 것으로 보며, 기대할 수 있다면 4.22. 워싱톤개최 예정인 DELORS EC 집행위원장과 부쉬 미대통령간의 회담에서 어느정도 해결의 실마리가 있을 수 있다고 봄.

　　물론 양측 입장에 양보여지가 크지는 않았으므로 낙관하긴 어려우나 그동안양측이 타협점을 찾기위해 협상을 계속했기 때문에 어느정도 돌파구를 기대할 수 있다는 관측도 있음.

　　O 한편 상기 회담결과가 부정적일시 동 UR 문제는 92.7 월 뮌헨 G-7 정상회담에서

통상국 안기부	차관 농수부	1차보 상공부	2차보	구주국	경제국	외정실	분석관	청와대

PAGE 1　　　　　　　　　　　　　　　　　　　　　　　92.04.11　20:02

외신 2과 통제관 BZ

0106

토의될 예정이나 어느정도 깊이있게 다뤄질지는 의문시되며 특히 미국 선거운동이 본격화되는 시점이기 때문에 합의점 달성은 어려우며 동 협상은 결국 미국선거 이후로 연기될 가능성이 높을 것으로 봄.끝

　　(대사 이기주-국장)

　　예고:92.12.31. 까지

검 토 필 (1992. 6. 30.) 초

외 무 부

원 본

종 별 :

번 호 : GVW-0825   일 시 : 92 0413 2210

수 신 : 장관(봉기,경기원,재무부,농림수산부,상공부,특허청) 사본:주미, 주 EC

발 신 : 주 제네바 대사 주 EC대사-중계필

제 목 : UR 협상 비공식 TNC 회의(확대 그린룸회의)

연: GVW-0790

일반문서로 재분류 ('92 12 31)

1. 표제회의가 금 4.13(월) 예정대로 개최되어, 협상현황 및 향후 추진방향에 관한 DUNKEL 총장의 연설에 이어 일부국가들의 발언이 있었는바, 동 결과 아래 보고함.(동 회의에는 3 개 협상그룹의장의 보고서가 배포되었음)

가. DUNKEL 총장의 연설요지

0 던켈총장은 서두에 (1) 협상의 TRANSPARENCY 확보필요 (2) T1-3 의 MOMENTUM 이 상실되고 있다는 인식의 확산 (3) 협상표류방지 및 협상진전에 장애가 되는 문제의 해결등의 필요 때문에 금일회의를 개최, 협상현황을 평가하게(STOCK-TAKING)되었다고 함.

0 T1-2 협상의 2 가지 난점으로 첫째 FA 상의 기본적인 개념과 실제 시장접근협상에서의 상이점을 들고 포괄적 관세화를 할수 없는 참가국들은 FA 규정에맞추어 OFFER 를 수정하거나 아니면 교역상대국들과 합의하여 FA 관계규정을 수정하는 두가지 방안중에서 택일하여야 할 것임을 지적, TARIFFICATION 의 중요성을 재강조하고, 둘째, T1-2 협상과정에 내재한(IN-BUILT)한 어려움으로서는 미국, EC 등 주요 참가국들간에 진정한(GENUINE)협상지 지연되고 있는점이 시장접근 협상의 MOMENTUM 상실의 원인이 되고 있으며, T2 에서는 일부국가가 MFN 일탈을 협상의 TRADE-OFF 의 수단으로 활용하고자 하는데서 연유한 어려움, 특히 미국의 MFN 이탈의 범위와 성격이 주된 장애가 되고있음을 지적함.

0 T4 가동과 관련, T1-3 의 협상현황에 비추어 T4 작업은 무의미하여, 가동시에는 협상을 12 월 이전상태로 후퇴시킬 위험이 있기 때문에 현재 진행중인 방식에 따라 협상을 계속해 나갈 예정이라고 하면서 아직은 T4 가동의사가 없음을 재확인함.

0 향후 협상 추진 복안에 관해서는 부활절 이후 금일 제출된 각의장 보고서에

통상국	차관	1차보	2차보	외정실	분석관	청와대	안기부	경기원
재무부	농수부	상공부	특허청	중계				

PAGE 1   92.04.14 06:48

외신 2과 롱제관 BX

0108

근거한 양자, 복수, 다자간 협의(TNC 개최 가능성 포함)를 추진할 예정임을 밝히고 각참가국들은 동보고서를 충분히 검토하여 CONSENSUS 가 도출될수 잇도록각국의 입장변경을 신중히 검토할 것을 촉구함.

　나. 참가국 발언

　O 한편 금일 회의에는 주로 중남미국가만이 발언한바, LACARTE 우루과이 대사가 중남미 및 카리브국가를 대표하여 (1) 협상정돈상태에 대한 좌절감 표명, (2) 미.EC 의 주요책임 (3) UR 협상의 조속한 다자화 환원촉구를 내용으로 하는 발언을하고, 이에 이어 니카라과, 코스타리카, 알젠틴, 브라질등 9 개 중남미 제국대표가 동조 발언을 함.

　O 발언에 나선 대부분의 중남미 국가는 지난주말에 있었던 EC 집행위 차원의 수입 바나나 쿼나 설정 및 관세화 예외결정에 관하여 발언한바, 동문제에 관해서는 니카라과, 콜롬비아, 혼두라스, 과테말라등 DOLLAR BANANA 수출국(EC 의 결정은 DUNKEL TEXT 위반)과 JAMAICA, IVORY COAST 등 CAP 국가가 각각 상반된 입장을 표명하였음.

　O TRAN EC 대는 상기 바나나 문제에 관해 각국의 주장을 유의(TAKE NOTE)하겠으나, 금일회의가 동문제 논의를 위한 적절한 FORUM 이 아니며, 아직은 EC 집행위 차원의 결정(이사회 미상정)에 불과한 사항에 대해 지나치게 감정적 반응을보이는것 보다 냉정히 해결책을 모색하는 자세가 중요하다고 답변하고, 동기회에 UR 협상과 관련해서는 (1) EC 로서는 농산물이 가장 큰 문제라는 점을 재차 언급하고 (2) 미.EC 간 양자 협상에 대한 다수국의 우려는 이해되나 현실적으로 불가피한 과정이므로 지나친 압력은 바람직하지 못하다는 입장을 개진함.

　2. 한편 DUNKEL 총장은 곧이어 있는 기자회견에서도 상기 비공식 TNC 회의에서의 발언요지를 기자들에게 브리핑한후, 기자질문에 대한 답변 형식으로

　(1) DEADLINE 문제는 다시 거론않겠으나 92 년말까지 협상이 타결되어야 한다는 믿음에는 변함이 없다는 점, (2) 그간의 양자협상 결과 지난 1 월에 비하면상당한 진전이 이루어졌다느 점, (3) 예외없는 관세화에 어긋나는 OFFER 를 제출한 국가의 문제도 조만간 다루어져야할 이유로서, 이들국가의 협상입장 변경(POSITION SHIFTING)이 중요하다는 점등을 재차 강조함.

　3. 상기회의 DUNKEL 총장 발언 및 동회의에 배포된 3 개 협상그룹의장 보고서를 별첨 FAX 송부하니, 부활절 이후 DUNKEL 총장이 예정하고 있는 양자 복수 및 다자간

PAGE 2

0109

협의 및 TNC 에 대비 동 보고서에 대한 본부의 분석, 평가내용 및 아국 대처입장을 회시바람.

　4. 한편 아국의 농산물 C/S 는 예정대로 4.10 GATT 사무국에 제출함.

첨부: 1. DUNKEL 총장연설문

2. 3 개 협상그룹 의장 보고서(GVW(F)-0259). 끝

(대사 박수길-장관대리)

예고:92.12.31. 까지

검 토 필 (1992. 6. 30.)

준(검토요)

주 제 네 바 대 표 부

번 호 : GVW(F) - 0259   년월일 : 20413   시간 : 2310
수 신 : 장   관 (롱기), 경기원, 재무부, 농림수산부, 상공부, 특허청)
            사본: 주미, 주EC대사
발 신 : 주제네바대사
제 목 : 첨부

총 15 매(표지포함)

보 안	
통 제	

외신과	
봉 제	

요검토 Comment 요비

251-15-1   0111

680

13.4.1992

INFORMAL TRADE NEGOTIATIONS COMMITTEE

Heads of Delegation
Monday 13 April 1992 - 15.30 - Room D

I have convened this meeting to give an opportunity to
the chief Geneva negotiators to collectively take stock of the
situation in the Uruguay Round negotiations.

The need for such a stock-taking has arisen because of
the convergence of three factors:

(i)   our collective commitment to ensure transparency in
      the negotiating process;

(ii) the widespread perception that work under tracks
      one, two and three is losing momentum after a
      promising start; and

(iii) the general desire to stop the drift and to tackle
      the problems confronting a successful and speedy
      conclusion of this Round.

To deal with the first two factors - transparency and an
assessment of where we are in tracks one, two and three -
Mr. Germain Denis, Ambassador Felipe Jaramillo and
Mr. M.G. Mathur have each established, on my request,

0112

2TP-15-2

- 2 -

evaluations of the stage reached in their respective Groups.
They have also, as far as possible, tried to identify the main
obstacles to an early conclusion of work in their respective
areas. These reports are informal and prepared on their own
responsibility. They are available in the room in the three
working languages.

I suggest that you and your authorities examine these
reports very carefully. I intend to have bilateral,
plurilateral and multilateral consultations with you soon
after the Easter recess on the basis of these reports. My aim
will be to set the scene for what I hope will be the last leg
of our negotiating process.

To achieve this aim, your governments will have to use
these reports to clearly identify the steps they must take in
order to bridge the gap between their general policy
statements calling for the successful conclusion of the
negotiations and their national positions on specific points
which continue to defeat this objective.

Since we are in an informal meeting, let me try to make
my own contribution to the process I have just described.

The Draft Final Act has been rightly considered an
essential but not the only element on which governments can
determine their acceptance of the overall package of the
results of the Round. In other words, success in the
negotiations under tracks one and two are as important for a
successful conclusion as the Draft Final Act itself. The fact

0113

2-5f-15-3

- 3 -

that governments have entered into substantive negotiations
under these two tracks pending a final reading of the Draft
Final Act document is specially relevant. It is an indication
that what we need is an acceptable balance among and between
all elements of this Round - rule-making, market opening and
the institutional aspects.

As far as I can assess, negotiations under tracks one and
two face two kinds of difficulties. The first kind is related
to linkages between the access negotiations and certain
fundamental concepts contained in the Draft Final Act
document. The second kind are in-built difficulties within
the negotiating process under these two tracks.

One example of the first kind of difficulty, as it
emerges from the Chairman's informal report on track one, is
the way some participants have found it difficult to provide
agricultural offers based on tariffication across the board.
For these participants, it means that they will either have to
modify their offers to bring them into conformity with the
approach contained in the Draft Final Act or to convince their
trading partners to revisit the relevant concepts in the Draft
Final Act itself. I leave you with this thought.

But let me add that the very useful work done since
January this year under tracks one and two has brought out a
number of points on which choices of the same nature will have
to be considered in order to conclude the Round.

0114

- 4 -

An example of the second type of difficulty, the in-built one, is the failure of participants who appear to be principal suppliers in each other's markets to concretize their bilateral market access negotiations. The consequent delay in the start of genuine negotiations between these key countries and their other trading partners, given the rule of the m.f.n. application of results amongst all participants, is a major factor behind the loss of momentum of the market access negotiations in general.

Another example in this category - this time in track two - is the major hurdle resulting from what appears to be the trade-off being sought between m.f.n. exemptions - in particular the scope and nature of one major participant's intended exemptions - and initial commitment offers being made.

A brief word about track three would be appropriate. A great deal of technical work has been carried out. Discussions have had to take into account the view that the Draft Final Act itself recognizes a need for further work and elaboration of existing texts in certain areas. This is true, for example, in the case of the MTO Agreement and issues like non-violation.

But I shall go no further in detail. The three reports bear the stamp of professionalism and objective analysis by the respective Chairmen.

0115

2 ff-15-5

- 5 -

I have always suggested that our stock-taking be as
objective, professional and constructive as possible. I
should, therefore, point out that there is no report on track
four; and this for the simple reason that, given the
situation in tracks one, two and three, I see no evidence to
suggest that work under track four would be meaningful in
terms of carrying the work under tracks one, two and three to
fruition. To the contrary, opening track four would bring us
back to where we were before December. I do not therefore see
any reason to change the global approach we have followed so
far.

A final point - and one that does not appear specifically
in any of the papers before us - is the question of those
contracting parties and potential signatories of the Uruguay
Round agreements who, while members of the GATT community,
have not, for very understandable reasons, ever been in a
position to present schedules. I would like to take up this
question with you in the not too distant future.

This concludes my remarks. The floor is, of course, open
for those of you who might wish to take it. I do, however,
feel that a meaningful and constructive discussion would be
better engaged after you have all had time to examine the
reports, make your own assessment of the situation and to
prepare yourselves to make shifts in positions which are
indispensable for consensus. I would like, once again, to
remind you that the Trade Negotiations Committee remains on
call. I shall, of course, have no hesitation in convening it
at short notice when there is need to do so.

0116

661

13 April 1992

INFORMAL REPORTS BY THE CHAIRMEN OF THE NEGOTIATING GROUP ON
MARKET ACCESS, THE GROUP OF NEGOTIATIONS ON SERVICES,
AND THE LEGAL DRAFTING GROUP

The following three informal reports have been submitted by the
respective Chairmen of the Negotiating Group on Market Access, the Group of
Negotiations on Services and the Legal Drafting Group on their own
responsibility.

0117

- 2 -

REPORT BY CHAIRMAN OF THE NEGOTIATIONG GROUP ON MARKET ACCESS

1.   Since the TNC meeting on 13 January 1992, the Negotiating Group has
sought to complete the negotiations on all aspects of market access on
goods, including the commitments on domestic support and export competition
in the area of agriculture. Its activities have been conducted within the
framework of the draft Final Act (DFA) and the process set out in my report
of 20 December 1991 (MTN.TNC/W/93).

2.   The negotiating process envisaged that each participant would submit,
by 1 March 1992, complete line-by-line draft Schedules of concessions and
commitments for all products in HS chapters 1 to 97, together with
supporting data required by the DFA in respect of agriculture. These draft
Schedules would constitute the basis for the final balancing of concessions
in the overall market access area. Unfortunately, despite continuous
bilateral and plurilateral negotiations supplemented by regular
multilateral stocktaking sessions during the January-March period, the task
of completing the submission of draft Schedules has been slower than
expected.

Status of submission of draft schedules

3.   As of 9 April 1992, the Secretariat has received 37 submissions; some
are incomplete in terms of the substantive content concerning agricultural
or non-agricultural products as well as the precision of information
provided. Some 14 other participants have indicated intentions to table
submissions shortly.

-   Agricultural products

4.   With regard to agricultural products, 23 participants have tabled
their draft Schedules reflecting the various elements of the DFA, i.e.,
those relating to market access, domestic support and export competition,
and the provisions for special and differential treatment for developing
countries. There have been a number of deviations from the DFA on certain
specific issues, but also some departures of a more fundamental nature.

5.   Some participants have submitted base data in the areas of market
access, on domestic support and export competition without applying any
rate of reduction. A few participants have applied lower rates of
reduction than those specified in the DFA, and in one case a longer
implementation period has been proposed. Some participants have used base
periods which differ from those specified in the DFA.

6.   Most participants have converted into customs duties all existing
non-tariff measures. In a few instances, participants have indicated that
the calculation of tariff equivalents is still pending, but they have
generally indicated the products to which tariffication would apply. While
applying tariffication to a range of products, one participant has proposed
to tariffy without any exception by the end of the implementation period
only; this would involve greater minimum access opportunities than those

0118

- 3 -

indicated in the DFA for the products for which tariffication would not take place until the end of the implementation period. Some other participants have excluded a number of products from tariffication because of their perception of the relationship to GATT rights and obligations.

7. Several participants have not always followed the modalities for calculating tariff equivalents, resulting for the products in question in tariff equivalents that are higher than would otherwise have been the case. Most participants have claimed the application of the special safeguard provisions in connection with tariffied products, but some have interpreted this provision also to be applicable to some products currently subject to ordinary customs duties only.

8. The current and minimum access elements set out in the DFA have generally been provided although in some cases without all required details. In several cases the amount of current access to be consolidated does not equate to current access used to establish new minimum access. The interpretation of what would constitute low or minimal in-quota tariff rates differs among participants. One participant has not provided any quantitative commitment on the maintenance of current access opportunities nor the basis on which minimum access opportunities should be undertaken.

9. Concerning the binding of agricultural tariffs, almost all participants have followed the approach set out in the DFA. One participant has made the implementation of this element of its draft Schedule, especially in relation to tariffs at less than 5 per cent, subject to reciprocal efforts. Another participant has indicated that only products subject to tariff reductions should be bound. One participant maintains that some adjustments to bound customs duties on products not subject to tariffication are necessary to balance the level of protection across certain agricultural product sectors.

10. A number of developing countries have offered ceiling bindings on agricultural products subject only to unbound ordinary customs duties, in accordance with a flexibility envisaged in the DFA. In addition, several developing country draft Schedules contain ceiling bindings over the whole tariff Schedule (both agricultural and non-agricultural products).

11. The basic elements of the DFA related to domestic support commitments have generally been provided. The policy coverage of domestic support for which exemption from the reduction commitments is claimed in the submissions (the "green box") differs in some respects among participants. Some participants put in the green box also policies they believe appropriate rather than only those fulfilling the criteria set out in the DFA. With respect to domestic support subject to reduction commitments, some participants have made claims for credit for actions taken since 1986. A few participants have claimed credit for supply control measures. In some cases, equivalent commitments are offered while the use of an AMS may have been practicable. Most developing countries have resorted to the provisions for special and differential treatment in the DFA to claim exemptions from reduction commitments for a range of domestic support measures.

0119

- 4 -

12. With regard to export competition, the information provided covers data on both budgetary outlays and quantities of subsidized exports. In two cases, the flexibility for implementing the reduction commitment has been applied in a manner not envisaged in the DFA. Participants which do not maintain measures relevant to these commitments have generally stated so. In terms of additional commitments in this area, some participants explicitly offered not to introduce export subsidies on new products. One participant was not prepared to subscribe to such an undertaking.

- ### Non-agricultural products

13. While 37 participants made submissions covering resource-based and other industrial products, not all provided revised line-by-line draft Schedules. Some major participants have provided only qualitative assessments on the grounds that their bilateral and plurilateral negotiations have not yet reached the stage where progress could usefully be reflected in their Schedules; they also wish to have further improvements in the quality of other participants' offers before providing their own revised offers. Some other participants did not consider that it would be equitable to provide their own draft Schedules until major participants had done likewise.

14. Unfortunately, this situation has resulted in continuing gaps in the offers covering certain product areas and uncertainties on specific tariff reductions and has delayed bilateral negotiations. It also means that there is not yet an adequate basis for undertaking a comparative evaluation of the various offers.

15. Nevertheless, on the basis of the draft Schedules and of the qualitative assessments available, there remain good prospects for a substantial and broad-based package of trade liberalization results. For example:

- Many participants have confirmed their expectation of being able to meet, and in some instances to significantly exceed, an overall one-third reduction of tariffs. They have also confirmed their readiness to make substantial reductions of high tariffs, tariff peaks and tariff escalation.

- For a number of major product areas, including some resource-based sectors, the bargaining continues to be focused on meeting each others conditions so as to achieve tariff reductions going beyond one-third. This includes tariff elimination or harmonization at low rates.

- Many developing countries are negotiating important liberalization commitments, including tariff bindings at meaningful rates and the reduction and elimination of non-tariff measures. Also a number of developing countries have offered to bind their whole tariff across the board at ceiling rates, with a few exceptions.

- The elimination of product-specific non-tariff measures continues to be an important part of the bargaining process, as it has been in the autonomous liberalization undertaken by many participants. Some participants have offered to bind the elimination of non-tariff measures under Part III of the Protocol in the DFA.

0120

- 5 -

- The submissions by developed countries have also confirmed the importance attached to maximising market access in tropical products. Nevertheless, some gaps in the draft Schedules are causing serious concerns to a number of developing countries.

Concluding remarks

16. As will be apparent, a number of developments will need to take place soon if we are to be able to establish the necessary conditions and momentum to bring about the many hard decisions still required for a successful market access conclusion. Such developments include:

- a political breakthrough in the major bilateral market access negotiations in both agricultural and non-agricultural products, such as to allow commensurate multilateral progress;

- in the light of this, improving and completing the coverage and content of existing draft agricultural Schedules of concessions and commitments, and the submission of Schedules by those who have not already done so;

- completing the submission of revised line-by-line draft Schedules of concessions on non-agricultural products by those participants who have not already done so, particularly by all major participants;

- further improving a number of individual tariff and non-tariff measures offers in the light of the common trade liberalization objectives of the Round.

17. The question of the earliest implementation of concessions or, where necessary, minimum staging in relation to products of export interest to developing countries, has to be examined.

18. In addition, as soon as an adequate basis exists, the Secretariat will need to carry out the evaluation of the emerging market access package.

19. In view of the importance of obtaining, as soon as possible, a good trade liberalization package as a basis for participants to judge the acceptability of the overall draft Final Act, I intend to continue an active and flexible process of bilateral, plurilateral and multilateral negotiation and monitoring. This will need to be focused increasingly on specific obstacles standing in the way of a successful overall market access outcome.

0121

- 6 -

REPORT BY THE CHAIRMAN OF THE GROUP OF NEGOTIATIONS ON SERVICES

1.   In the meeting of the TNC held on 13 January 1992, "intensive non-stop negotiations" on initial commitments were envisaged. Accordingly, a GNS work programme of 30 January 1992 provided for the three rounds of bilateral negotiations, as well as dates and procedures to deal with draft lists of intentions with respect to m.f.n. exemptions. Dates were also established for the presentation of revised offers and draft schedules to be submitted to the secretariat for verification (10 February and 16 March respectively). The final content of the schedules and the lists of m.f.n. exemptions were to be agreed among participants and submitted to the secretariat by 31 March.

2.   Offers on initial commitments have now been tabled by 47 participants. In 24 cases participants have revised offers, 20 such revisions having been made since the last TNC. In addition, 32 draft lists of intentions with respect to m.f.n. exemptions have been presented to, and distributed by, the secretariat.

3.   While there was considerable progress in the first two rounds and a positive momentum was clearly evident by the end of February, this was not carried over into the negotiations which took place in March. No submissions indicating the final content of schedules and the lists of m.f.n. exemptions have been received by the secretariat. The impetus has been lost and at best the negotiations can be characterized as having reached a standstill.

4.   It is apparent that there is a clear link between m.f.n. exemptions and initial commitments. In the stocktaking carried out last month while many participants considered that the level of commitment contained in the offers had improved considerably, they also indicated that the scope and nature of the intended m.f.n. exemptions proposed by one major participant called into question the structure of the GATS and risked undermining the overall level of commitments. In this respect, that participant made clear that to reduce the m.f.n. exemptions would require others to improve their offers - particularly in those sectors where exemptions were sought. Other participants considered that a scaling down of their own offers was appropriate given the commercial significance of the sectors concerned.

5.   It is clear that this situation has contributed to the lack of impetus and the standstill currently experienced. This is true both with respect to the initial commitment negotiations and m.f.n. exemption lists, as well as other work of a technical nature. It is also clear that the lack of progress elsewhere in the Uruguay Round had also affected the environment in the services negotiations.

6.   The annotations to MTN.TNC/W/FA identified further technical work to be undertaken in respect of the Agreement on Trade in Services. Accordingly, work has proceeded with respect to Article XXI (Modification of Schedules) and Article XXXIV (Definitions). Technical work has also proceeded with respect to the Annex on Air Transport Services and consultations have taken place on the Telecommunications Annex. With

0122

- 7 -

respect to these two sectoral issues, decisions will be required in order
to finalize the work, In addition, the secretariat is undertaking
consultations with delegations in order to bring additional precision to
the explanatory note on scheduling of commitments.

REPORT BY THE CHAIRMAN OF THE LEGAL DRAFTING GROUP

At its meeting on 13 January, the TNC established the Legal Drafting
Group to carry forward what has been described as "Track Three" of work in
the Uruguay Round. The Group was required to review the texts in the draft
Final Act (MTN.TNC/W/FA) in order to ensure their legal conformity and
internal consistency, it being understood that its work should not lead to
changes in the balance of rights and obligations established in the
agreements. The Group has met very intensively since its establishment.
It has held five formal meetings as well as numerous informal meetings open
to all delegations.

The work programme before the Group has five principal elements.

(i) _Review of the Agreement establishing the Multilateral Trade
Organization and of the relationship between it and other agreed
texts_

Since the MTO will provide the institutional framework for the
implementation of the Uruguay Round results and the future operation of the
multilateral trading system, a priority task for the Group has been the
review of the MTO Agreement. A footnote to the Draft Final Act recognises
the MTO texts as requiring further elaboration to ensure a proper relation
to the other results of the Round. Progress has been made in the Group in
clarifying a number of provisions of the MTO text; notably those relating
to the basic purposes to be served by the MTO and to its administrative and
institutional structure. However it has not yet been possible to reach
full agreement on the formulation of a number of important provisions
relating to requirements for accession, procedures for amendments, grant of
waivers, non-application of obligations under the GATT as it will emerge
from the Uruguay Round, and the GATS and the Agreement on TRIPS, and on
such matters as the treatment of pre-existing mandatory legislation.

An important part of this work is the clarification of relationships
between the MTO Agreement and the other agreements or legal instruments in
the Draft Final Act which will now form part of the MTO framework. The
Group's discussions have served to elucidate the treatment to be given to
these agreements or instruments as annexes to the MTO text or as Decisions
to be adopted by Ministers when the Final Act is opened for acceptance.
The Group has also made progress in defining what the integration of the
texts of the individual agreements with the MTO text will mean in terms of
adjustments in terminology in these agreements and of the deletion or
adjustment of provisions on such matters as accession, entry into force,
amendments or withdrawals - the so-called "Final Provisions". On the other
hand, a few questions relating to the relationship between the provisions

0123

- 8 -

in the MTO text and those in covered agreements - notably, for example,
whether there is need to provide for any situations of conflict between the
two sets of provisions - still remain.

(ii) Integration of the Dispute Settlement Texts

Three separate texts in dispute settlement were included in the Draft
Final Act: the Understanding on Rules and Procedures Governing the
Settlement of Disputes under GATT Articles XXII and XXIII, drawn up over
the whole period since the launching of the Uruguay Round, and two texts -
one on Elements of an Integrated Dispute Settlement System and another on
the suspension of concessions - which were formulated in the final weeks of
1991. The Group is working on the establishment of a single integrated
text. The Group has made substantial progress but will need to define more
precisely the application of the integrated Understanding to the covered
agreements so that where dispute settlement will take place is in
accordance with the provisions of the Understanding and where the special
procedures or provisions relating to dispute settlement in these agreements
will continue to apply is entirely clear. Some other issues also remain,
such as for example, provisions on non-violation complaints or for action
by a panel where it is found that a fundamental conflict exists between the
substantive provisions of two or more agreements.

(iii) Review of individual agreements

Although work on the MTO text and on the Dispute Settlement
understanding has not yet been completed, it has been carried far enough to
permit the Group to start reviewing and rectifying the individual (or
covered) agreements in the Draft Final Act. This has meant attention to
such matters as use of terminology, adjustment or deletion of clauses
relating to final provisions, dispute settlement etc. as may be called for
or found necessary. A number of texts have already been reviewed and a
timetable has been established for completing review of the remainder by
the end of the month. The results of this exercise shall also facilitate
the finalization of the Dispute Settlement Understanding, notably by
clarifying how it will relate to the individual agreements.

(iv) Cross-cutting issues

The Group's review of the individual texts should benefit from an
earlier examination carried out in it of cross-cutting issues. Similar
issues or terms sometimes appear in more than one text but are treated or
defined differently. The Group has agreed, as a general guideline that
each text should be interpreted individually and in its own specific
context, and differences in such matters as the way in which certain
concepts are defined therefore need not necessarily be a matter of concern.
However, problems may arise if different texts impose conflicting
obligations with respect to the same measures, leading to uncertainties or
difficulties in the implementation of commitments. Until now, very few
such inconsistencies have been identified by the Group but a full picture
should be available once the review of the individual texts has been
completed.

0124

- 9 -

(v)   Trade Policy Review Mechanism

In the context of the footnote at page 100 of the Draft Final Act, the Group has agreed to work on the establishment of the MTO Annex describing the Trade Policy Review Mechanism so that it takes into account the extension of the coverage of reviews to all subjects covered in the Annexes to the MTO Agreement.

Concluding remarks

It will be seen that the Legal Drafting Group has carried out a great deal of detailed technical work in pursuance of its terms of reference. The discussions in the Group and the nature of the issues brought up for clarification have however had to take into account views of delegations that the Draft Final Act recognises the need for further work and elaboration of existing texts in certain areas such as the Dispute Settlement System and the MTO Agreement. Also in the view of delegations, the Agreement establishing the MTO and the decision to establish an Integrated Dispute Settlement System involve a review and adjustment of a number of provisions in the texts of the original agreements. The Group continues to make progress and there is more detailed work of a technical character that needs to be done. The completion of the Group's task will depend on a readiness to take decisions on outstanding issues and on the existence of a clear timeframe for concluding its efforts.

0125

외 무 부

종 별 :

번 호 : ECW-0517   일 시 : 92 0415 1700

수 신 : 장 관(통기,경기원,재무부,농림수산부,상공부)

발 신 : 주 EC 대사   사본: 주미,제네바,폴투갈대사(중계필)

제 목 : 갓트/UR 협상

표제협상과 관련한 최근 당지의 동향을 아래보고함

1. DUNKEL 총장 구주의회 방문

가. 4.14. 동 총장이 구주의회를 방문,대외경제 위원회에서 연설한바 요지 아래와 같음

0 표제협상중 농업보조금 감축문제는 매우 어려운 사안이나 이 문제의 해결 없이는 전체협상의 성공은 불가능하며 농업보조금 문제의 해결은 다른 분야협상의 촉매제가 될것임.농업보조금과 관련하여 미.EC 간에 합의되지 못한 사항은 2-3개로 알고 있으며, 조만간에 해결되길 희망함

0 표제협상 종결시한을 재설정하는 것은 불필요함

0 EC/바나나 문제는 선개도국간에 새로운 갈등요인이 되고 있으며 동 문제가 협상장애요인이 되지 않길 희망함

나. 동 총장은 4.16. 폴투갈을 방문하여 SILVA수상및 OLIVEIRA 무역장관과 표제관련회담을 가질 예정임

2. 미.EC 양자협상

가. 4.14. 미국과 EC 는 런던에서 고위급협상(미측: KATZ 및 CROWDER 차관, EC: LEGRAS총국장및 PAEMEN 부총국장) 을 가짐. 동협상결과에 대해 양측은 밝히기를 꺼려하고있어 그 내용을 파악하기 어려우나 당지의 언론은 4.22. 미.EC 정상회담의 사전준비를 위한 모임일 것으로 관측하고 있음

나. 4.15. EC 집행위 대변인은 최근 언론이 DELORS-BUSH 회담을 표제협상 타결을위한 마지막 기회라고 보도하고 있는데 대해 현재로서는 미.EC 간에 농업문제에 대해 합의를 이룰만한 조짐이 없으며, 성급한 기대를 갖는것은 곤란하다고 말함. 동인은또한 런던에서 개최된 미.EC 고위급 협상에서도 BUSH-DELORS 회담시 도출할

통상국   2차보   경기원   재무부   농수부   상공부

결과를찾지 못한 것으로 알고 있다고 언급함. 끝
(대사 권동만-국장)

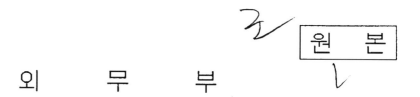

외 무 부

종 별 :

번 호 : ECW-0532   일 시 : 92 0417 1220

수 신 : 장관(통기, 경기원, 농수산부, 상공부)

발 신 : 주 EC 대사 사본: 주미, 일, 제네바대사(중계 필?)

제 목 : UR 관련 동향

1. EC 집행위는 4.16. 성명을 통하여 일본 WATANABE 외상이 ANDRIESSEN 부위원장에게 발송한 서한을 통하여 현 UR 교착상태에 대한 책임이 EC 에게 있다는 비난에대하여 강한 반발을 보이고, 오히려 현 UR 협상을 성공적으로 타결하기 위하여는시장접근 분야에서의 일본의 추가적인 양보가 더 긴요하다고 강조함

2. 일본 WATANABE 외상은 ANDRIESSEN EC 부위원장및 CARLA HILLS USTR 대표에게각각 보낸 서한을통하여 EC 측에는 관세인하 조치와 관련, 구체적인 제안이 없고서비스 분야 (특히 해상운송분야)에서 예외를 설정하였으며 농산물분야에서 미국과이견을 조정하지 못하고 있는데 대하여 비난하였으며 미국측에는 INDUSTRIAL SECTOR에서의 OFFER 제출서한을 이행치 못하였고 서비스분야에서의 OFFER가 적절치 못하여농산물등 몇가지 분야에서 EC 와 이견을 조정치 못함으로서 UR 이 교착상태에 빠졌다고 비난하였다 함.

3. 한편 EC 집행위 관계관에 의하면 UR 의 교착상태 타개를위한 EC, 미국, 일본및 카나다 4국 통상장관 회의가 4.22. 워싱턴 미국. EC 회의등에 이어 4.26. 동경에서개최될 예정이라 하며 동관계관은 동 회의에서 극적인 타협이 이루어질 것으로는생각지 않는다고 언급함. 끝

    (대사 권동만-국장)

통상국   2차보   경기원   농수부   상공부

PAGE 1   92.04.17   22:57 DW

                                                  외신 1과 통제관

                                                  0128

외 무 부

종 별 :

번 호 : POW-0204   일 시 : 92 0420 1900

수 신 : 장 관(통기,통삼,구이)

발 신 : 주 폴루갈 대사

제 목 : DUNKEL 가트사무총장 폴루갈 방문

　　1.DUNKEL 총장은 4.2 워싱턴에서 있을 UR관련 미-EC간 정상회담의 최종점검을 위해 4.15-17간 EC의장국인 주재국을방문, CAVACO수상 및 OLIVEIRA 상무장관과 회담을가졌기에 보고함

　　2.동 총장은 회담직후 가진 기자회견에서 양측간의 회담에서는 농업보조금,서비스자유화,시장접근 문제등이 주로 다루어졌으나,특별한 합의사항이 도출된것은 없다고 말하고,그러나 양측은 내주에 있을 워싱턴 정상회담이 UR협상타결의 마지막기회이며, 반드시 정치적인 결단이 이루어져야 한다는데에는 전적인 의견의 일치를 보았다고 밝힘. 한편 원래 CAVACO GEH상의 미국방문을 수행예정이었던 OLIVEIRA 상무장관은당초계획 을 변경 수행한기로 했다는바, 이는 UR타결이 각국의 정치적인 결단만을 남겨놓고 있다는 사실을 반증하는것으로 보임.

　　3.이와관련, 금 4.20자 주재국 최대일간지 D/N는 UR의 교훈 제하의 사설을 통해 UR은 6년간의 긴협상을 거쳐, 완성단계에 와 있으며 이제는 각국의 서로의 입장을 이해하고 양보하여야 할때라고 주장하면서 각국의 양보에 입각한 정치적인 결단을 촉구함.끝

　　（대사조광제-국장）

통상국　　　2차보　　　구주국　　　통상국

PAGE 1   92.04.21　　04:08 FN

外신 1과 통제관

0129

최근 UR 협상 동향

1992. 4.22.
통상기구과

1. 제네바 협상 동향

   o 미.EC간 농산물 협상 타협 실패로 인해 금년 1월이후의 시장접근 및 서비스
     분야 양허협상도 부진

   o 4.13 비공식 TNC 회의가 개최되어 협상 현황 검토
     - 협상 참가국들은 협상의 정돈상태에 좌절감과 미국.EC의 책임을 거론
     - 던켈 사무총장은 부활절 휴가이후 협상을 재개 하겠다 하고 각국이
       기존 입장을 재검토 할 것을 촉구

2. 주요국간 협상 동향

   o 4.14 런던에서 미.EC 정상회담 준비 성격의 고위 실무회담(차관급)이 개최
     되었으나, 양측간 이견을 좁히지 못함.

   o 4.16 던켈 사무총장이 포루갈 방문, Silva 수상 및 Oliveira 무역장관과
     회담 EC측의 협조 요청

   o 최근 와타나배 일본 수상은 미국(Hills 통상대표) 및 EC(Andriessen 집행위
     부위원장)애 서한 발송, 미국의 서비스 분야 MFN 일탈(금융, 통신, 해운,
     항공) 및 공산물 양허계획 미제출, EC의 해운 서비스 분야 예외 설정 및
     미흡한 관세인하 계획등애 대해 불만을 표시하고, 미.EC간의 농산물 분야
     이견이 UR을 교착상태에 빠트렸다고 비난
     - 이에대해 EC 집행위는 4.16 성명을 통해 UR 협상 성공을 위해 일본의
       추가적인 양보가 필요하다고 반발
     - 미국은 내주중 Hills 대표의 서한 전달 예정

0130

o 4.22 미.EC 정례 정상회담(Bush 대통령 - Delors 집행위원장, Silva 폴루갈
  수상)에서 농산물 협상 관련 쟁점에 대해 타협 모색 예정

  - 수출보조 감축 문제 (미국이 농산물 수출 물량 감축을 개별 품목이 아닌
    품목군 기준으로 할 수 있도록 허용할 경우, EC는 수출물량 15% 감축
    용의 시사)

  - 국내보조 감축 문제(EC의 생산과 관련된 직접소득 보조를 허용보조(green
    box)로 분류할지 여부인바, 미국은 제한적인 허용보조(safety box)로
    할 것을 제안)

  - 평화조항 문제 (농산물 감축 계획 이행기간 동안에는 갓트제소, 301조
    발동등 법적인 대응조치 억제)

  - rebalancing 문제 (EC는 미국이 사료곡물의 대EC 수출을 동결할 것을 요구)

3. 전 망

o 4.22 미.EC 정상회담에서 획기적인 타협이 도출되기 보다는 UR의 조속한
  타결이 필요하다는 선에서 합의가 이루어지고 7월경까지 협상을 계속하게 될
  가능성이 크다는 것이 일반적 관측.   끝.

외 무 부

종 별 :

번 호 : ECW-0537　　　　　　　　일 시 : 92 0422 1530

수 신 : 장관(통기, 경기원, 농수산부, 상공부)

발 신 : 주 EC 대사 사본: 주미, 일, 제네바대사(중계필)

제 목 : UR 관련동향

1. EC.미국 및 일본의 업계를 대표한 기관들이 4.21. 당지에서 UR 협상의 성공적인타결을 지지하는 별첨 공동성명을 발표함

2. 동 성명은 EC 회원국 업계를 대표한 UNICE와 일본의 KEIDANREN, 미국의 NATIONAL ASSOCIATION OF MANUFACTURES, U.S. COUNCIL FOR INTL BUSINESS, U.S. CHAMBEROF COMMERCE 등 공동명의로 되어 있으며, 현 UR 협상이 주요 협상국가의 국내정치와관련된 원인으로 표류되고 있다고 지적하고 UR 협상의 성공이야 말로 세계경제의성장과 번영에 필수적이며 DUNKEL 타협안이 여러가지 문제점을 내포하고 있으나 협상타결의 기초로서 올바른 방향제시를 하고 있다고 강조함

3. 당지언론에 의하면 동 성명은 금 4.22. 워싱턴에서 개최되는 미.EC 정상회담에서 양측 정상들이 UR 협상타결을 위한 정치적 의지를 촉구하기 위한 것이라 함

(대사 권동만-국장)

첨부: 동 성명

POLITICAL LEADERS AROUND THE WORLD HAVE GIVEN THE HIGHEST PRIORITY TO AN EARLY AGREEMENT ON A SUBSTANTIAL AND COMPREHENSIVE OUTCOME OF THE URUGUAY ROUND MULTILATERAL TRADE TALKS. YET, THE NEGOTIATIONS ARE STALLED BECOME OF DOMESTIC POLITICS. IF THIS PERSISTS, IT WILL THREATEN THE VERY EXISTENCE OF THE CONTRACTUAL GATT MULTILATERAL TRADING SYSTEM. FOR BUSINESS, THE GATT SYSTEM IS THE BESTDEFENCE AGAINST THE TIDE OF GROWING PROTECTIONISM WORLDWIDE, WITH ITS INHERENTDANGERS FOR WORLD TRADE AND COOPERATION. SUCCESSFUL COMPLETION OF THE URUGUAY ROUND IS A PREREQUISITE FOR WORLD ECONOMIC GROWTH AND PROSPERITY AND THEREFORE, FOR JOBS. IT WOULD:

통상국　2차보　경기원　농수부　상공부

PAGE 1　　　　　　　　　　　　　92.04.23　07:50 DW

외신 1과 통제관

0132

- RESTORE BUSINESS CONFIDENCE BY REDUCING UNCERTAINTIES AND THE RISK OF TRADE CONFLICTS ARISING FROM DISCRIMINATORY ARRANGEMENTS:

- SUPPORT THE DEVELOPING COUNTRIES AND THE FORMER COMMUNIST STATES, WHICH ARE LIBERALISING THEIR ECONOMIES AND TRYING TO OVERCOME THEIR HUGE ECONOMIC PROBLEMS:

- ENCOURAGE ECONOMIC COOPERATION BETWEEN NATIONS IN TACKLING NEW TRADE RELATED CHALLENGES.

THE DRAFT FINAL ACT, DESPITE ITS IMPERFECTIONS, IS A MAJOR STEP IN THE RIGHT DIRECTION. IT STILL NEEDS TO BE COMPLETED BY OBTAINING FURTHER RESULTS IN A NUMBER OF NEGOTIATING AREAS. AMERICAN, EUROPEAN, AND JAPANESE BUSINESS ORGANISATIONS JOIN TOGETHER, AS DID CHIEF EXECUTIVE OFFICERS AND THE INTL CHAMBER OFCOMMERCE IN THEIR APRIL 14 APPEAL TO GOVERNMENTS, TO URGE THE LEADERS OF THE CONTRACTING PARTIES TO DEMONSTRATE THE POLITICAL WILL TO BRING THESE NEGOTIATIONS TO A SATISFACTORY CONCLUSIONS AS SOON AS POSSIBLE HEADS OF GOVERNMENT CANMAKE HISTORY BY SIGNING THE MOST AMBITIOUS AND MOST COMPREHENSIVE TRADE AGREEMENT EVER KNOWN.끝

외 무 부

종 별 :

번   호 : USW-2060
　　　　　　　　　　　　　　　　　　일   시 : 92 0422 2112

수   신 : 장 관(봉이,봉기,봉삼,경일,동구이,미일,정총,경기원,상공부,농수부,
　　　　　　　　　　　　　　　　　외교안보,경제수석)

발   신 : 주 미 대사

제   목 : 미. EC정상회담

　　금일(4.22) 개최된 부시 대통령과 DELORS EC집행위원장 및 CAVACO SILVA 포르투칼 수상(현EC 의장)간의 정상회담 관련, THOMAS NILES 국무부 유럽.카나다 담당 차관보가행한 대언론 브리핑 내용 요지 및 당관 평가를 하기 보고함.(동브리핑 전문은 별첨 FAX 송부)

　　1. 언론 브리핑

　　가. UR 문제

　　- 금번 회담에서는 UR 타결을 위해 농산물문제에 국한해서 협의를 진행했으나 협상 타결돌파구는 마련되지 않았음.

　　- 다만 양측이 몇가지 새로운 유익한 안(IDEA)을 제의했으며, 이를 토대로 협상의 조기 타결을 위해 계속 협의해 나가기로 합의함(NILES대사는 기자들의 새로운 IDEA 의 구체 질문내용에 대해 언급을 회피함)

　　- UR 타결 관련 미측이 생각하는 시한(DEADLINE)은 없으며 미 국내정치 일정이 UR협상 타결에 장애요인이 되지 않을 것임.(NILES 대사는 협상타결이 지연되는 경우 금년 7월 뮌헨에서 개최 예정인 G7정상회담에서도 논의될 가능성이 있다고 시사)

　　- 협상 타결에 필요한 타협은 어느 일방의 양보가 아닌 균형있는 타협(BALANCEDDEAL) 이 되어야 하며, 미. EC 뿐만 아니라 모든 참가국에 수락 가능한 타협이 되어야함.

　　- 비록 금번회담에서는 구체적인 돌파구가마련되지 않았지만, 양측이 협상의 타결 싯점이 도래했다는 공통된 인식하에, 협상타결을 위한 상대방의 성의있는 노력(GOOD FAITHEFFORT)을 인정하고 보다 유연한 입장을 취할 필요성에 공감함.

　　나. 기타 정치문제

　　- UR 외에 금번 정상회담에서는 유고사태, 대 CIS 관계, 중동문제, 앙골라 사태에

통상국 정와대	미주국 안기부	구주국 경기원	경제국 농수부	통상국 상공부	통상국	외연원	외정실	분석관

관한 논의가 있었음.

- 유고사태 관련 구체 제재조치에 대한 논의는 없었으나, 미. EC 양측은 보스니아 내전과 관련 현 세르비아(유고)정부의 대응태도에 우려를 표명하고 이같은 사태가개선되지 않는 경우 4.29.개최 예정인 구주안보협력회의(CSCE) 시세르비아의 참가박탈문제를 EC 의 지지하에 미측이 제기할지 모른다고 시사함.

- 아울러 EC 는 미국의 중동 평화노력에 적극적인 지지를 표명함.

2. UR 관련 당관 평가

- 동 언론 브리핑에서 미국은 UR 타결전망에 대한 언론의 부정적 시각을 인식, 금번회담의 긍정적 측면(현상태를 '교착상태'로 보기보다는 점진적인 진전으로 평가하거나 또는 양측의 성의있는 노력을 인식했다는 발언등)을 부각시키는데 주력했으나구체적인 협상타결 돌파구가 마련되지 않았다는 점에서 일단 소기의 목적 달성에 실패했다는 평가를 면키 어려울것임.

- 특히 협상타결 전망 관련 NILES 차관보는 양측의 조기 협상타결 희망에도 불구하고, 금년 7월 뮌헨에서 개최 예정인 G7 정상회담시 UR 논의 가능성을 배제하지 않으므로써 협상기장기 지연 가능성을 시사함.

- 한편, 미측은 구체내용은 밝히지는 않았으나 상호 흥미있는 새로운 제안이 있었으며 이를 토대로 협상타결이 가능하다는 여운을 남기므로써, 표면적인 협상타결 돌파구 마련 실패에도 불구하고 향후 미. EC 간 막후 교섭에 의한 타결 가능성을 시사하고 있음에 주목해야 할 것임.

3. 금번 정상회담 관련, 미. EC 간에 논의된 내용 및 미측 평가에 대해서는 명일(4.23) USTR등 미정부 관계관과 접촉후 추보 위계임.

첨부: USW(F)-2522(10 매).끝.

(대사 현홍주-국장)

주 미 대 사 관

USW(F) : 2522   년월일 :   동조이   시간 :

수 신 : 장   관(통이. 통기. 통상, 경밀. 미일. 정종)
        사본: 상성부, 기기원, 한수연,
            대한건 1공계3과

발 신 : 주 미 대 사

제 목 : 4620 - 2060 리취록 (예)

| 보 안 | |
| 통 제 | |

(출처 :   )

(2522 - 10-1)

| 외신 1과 | : |
| 통 제 | |

0136

WHITE HOUSE READOUT ⫤THE VISIT OF PRIME MINISTᴸᴸ ANIBAL CAVACO SILVA,
PRESIDENT OF THE EUROPEAN COUNCIL, AND EC PRESIDENT JACQUES DELORS
BRIEFER: THOMAS NILES, ASST SECY OF STATE FOR EUROPEAN AND CANADIAN
AFFAIRS   THE WHITE HOUSE   WEDNESDAY, APRIL 22, 1992
WR-3-1 page# 1
    dest=swh,mwh,dos,eurcom,fns11182,fns00725,portu,angol,mideast,ussr,yugo
    dest+=fortr,gatt,usag,forag,commtrade
    data

        MR. NILES: The discussion today between the President and the
European leaders, President Delors of the Commission and Prime
Minister Cavaco Silva, was divided into -- there were two major
sections: One, the **Uruguay Round**; and the other, the variety of
other political issues where the United States and the **Community** are
working together: principally Yugoslavia, the relations with the
republics of the former **Soviet Union**, the **Middle East**. And there
was a brief discussion of developments in **Angola**, given the
important **Portuguese** interest in developments in that country.

        On the Uruguay Round, some new ideas were advanced by both
sides. Both sides agreed on the need to pursue an agreement as
rapidly as possible. The President made clear that he saw no reason
why in an election year the United States could not move ahead
quickly to conclude an agreement. The European leaders welcomed
that assurance and, on their side, said that they were certainly
prepared to work with us and the other contracting parties in the
GATT to reach an agreement.

        On Yugoslavia, there was agreement that we needed to press
ahead in efforts to maintain the deployment of the UN force that's
going into Croatia, and at the same time to support efforts to reach
a cease-fire in Bosnia-Hercegovina. Prime Minister Cavaco Silva
advised that the Foreign Minister of Portugal, Foreign Minister
Deus Pinheiro; Lord Carrington, who is running the constitutional
conference on Yugoslavia for the European Community; and the Special
Negotiator for Portugal, or for the European Community, Portuguese
Ambassador (Putillero ?) will be visiting Bosnia, Sarajevo, Zagreb
and Belgrade beginning tomorrow. We will be in touch with the three
officials and with the Community to see if there are ways in which
we can support this effort.

        The European leaders told the President, as they have before,
that the Community strongly supports the United States effort to
bring peace to the Middle East, an effort in which the Community is
participating.

        Questions?

        Q   What are the new ideas?

        MR. NILES: I'm not in a position to get into the details of
that, as you might imagine.

        Q   I'm not surprised --

        MR. NILES: You're not surprised to hear that. Well, I didn't
want to surprise you with anything. But the discussions will go on,
okay?

2522-10-2

0137

WHITE HOUSE READOUT O THE VISIT OF PRIME MINISTER ANIBAL CAVACO SILVA,
PRESIDENT OF THE EUROPEAN COUNCIL, AND EC PRESIDENT JACQUES DELORS
BRIEFER: THOMAS NILES, ASST SECY OF STATE FOR EUROPEAN AND CANADIAN
AFFAIRS   THE WHITE HOUSE   WEDNESDAY, APRIL 22, 1992
WR-3-1 page# 2

      Q   (Inaudible) -- to a category, like on agriculture --

    MR. NILES: No, that's what we're talking about. The --
surprise, yeah. The area of discussion today was -- or the
discussion on the GATT today was exclusively on **agriculture**. I
think there's a general recognition on both sides that if we are
able, the United States and the Community, to reach an agreement on
agriculture, that the other outstanding issues on the Uruguay Round
negotiations -- whether you're talking about market access for goods
or market access in the area of services -- would very likely fall
into place fairly quickly. So the concentration was on
agriculture.

    Yeah?

    Q   Were you able to accept any of the proposals that they
brought? Do you embrace any of these?

    MR. NILES: No. Neither did they embrace any of our ideas.
But I think there was agreement at the table that some interesting
ideas had been put forward that deserved further consideration.
And that will be given in the period immediately ahead. There was
an agreement that we should continue the negotiating process as
quickly as possible.

    Q   So is this -- can we characterize this as a stalemate?

    MR. NILES: No, not at all. I think it's --

    Q   Why?

    MR. NILES: Why? Well, I think we made clear -- the briefing
prior to the meeting, which I guess was yesterday, we made clear
that we were not expecting a breakthrough at this session, and nor
was one achieved. But as we have seen, I think fairly steadily
since the President and the European leaders met in The Hague last
November 8, we've had steady progress and we believe we can continue
to make progress. The differences are there. There's no reason to
minimize them. But we believe we made some more headway and we're
going to continue to work on it.

    Yeah?

               CONTINUED

2522- 10-3

WHITE HOUSE READOUT⌐ THE VISIT OF PRIME MINI☰ R ANIBAL CAVACO SILVA,
PRESIDENT OF THE EUROPEAN COUNCIL, AND EC PRESIDENT JACQUES DELORS
BRIEFER: THOMAS NILES, ASST SECY OF STATE FOR EUROPEAN AND CANADIAN
AFFAIRS   THE WHITE HOUSE   WEDNESDAY, APRIL 22, 1992
UR-3-2   page# 1
    dest=swh,mwh,dos,eurcom,fns11182,fns00725,portu,fortr,gatt,usag,forag
    dest+=ustroff,easteur,latamer,commtrade,mexico,envrmt
... data   , .*

        Q   Carla Hills gave the impression yesterday that at least
in the minds of the press the problem is the failure of the European
Community to reach a consensus on the agriculture issue, and yet the
President today had to reassure them that the American election
wouldn't cause a problem. So where is the problem? Is it really
their failure of a consensus or is it our failure to compromise?

        MR. NILES: The Community as an institution has had difficulty
coming forward with a position, but there's a related problem, and
that is the fact that while the Community is negotiating in the
Uruguay Round, it's also attempting to reform the common
agricultural policy in a major way. And one of the problems that
President Delors and Prime Minister Cavaco Silva made clear that
exists on the Community side is this relationship between the
international negotiations and the internal reforms.

        The President noted at the table that the Europeans and other
GATT contracting parties need not fear that the United States lacks
the commitment to the conclusion of the round. But that's not I
don't think the problem that we face.

        There are differences in our approach and theirs on the
question of how the agricultural system should be reformed, but
we're in the process of trying to overcome those.

        Yeah?

        Q   With those new ideas, how early are you expecting --

        MR. NILES: I'm sorry, I didn't understand.

        Q   With those new ideas -- new ideas on the table --

        MR. NILES: Yeah, yeah.

        Q   -- how early do you expect an agreement now? Before the
G-7 meeting?

        MR. NILES: We're ready for an agreement as soon as we can
reach one. And if we can reach one next week, we'd be delighted.
Next month there will be, as you suggest, an important meeting of
the G-7 in Munich from the sixth through the eighth of July. And if
that -- an agreement is not reached prior to the Munich meeting,
obviously the Uruguay Round would be a subject on the agenda. But --

        Q   (Off mike.)

        MR. NILES: I beg your pardon?

        Q   Is it a possibility that --

                2522- 10-4

                                                        0139

WHITE HOUSE READOUT UW THE VISIT OF PRIME MINISTER ANIBAL CAVACO SILVA,
PRESIDENT OF THE EUROPEAN COUNCIL, AND EC PRESIDENT JACQUES DELORS
BRIEFER: THOMAS NILES, ASST SECY OF STATE FOR EUROPEAN AND CANADIAN
AFFAIRS   THE WHITE HOUSE   WEDNESDAY, APRIL 22, 1992
WR-3-2 page# 2

MR. NILES: Well, if you don't reach an agreement between now
and Munich, obviously you can't say we're not going to discuss the
Uruguay Round in Munich. That will be a subject on the agenda, as
has the Uruguay Round at every G-7 summit since 1986.

Q   Are you saying now that for sure that will be a subject?

MR. NILES: No, I'm not saying that, because I would hope that
maybe before the sixth through the eighth of July we would be able
to reach an agreement so that we wouldn't have to have a long
discussion of agriculture at the Munich summit.

Yes, ma'am?

Q   The President repeatedly said an early agreement, an
early agreement. It suggested that he had some timeframe or some
deadline in mind. Can't you help us with that a little bit more?

MR. NILES: Well, there is no deadline. There is a desire on
the part of all of the contracting parties, not just the United
States and the European Community, to wrap up these negotiations as
quickly as possible. Negotiations began, after all, in 1986. So
we've been at this for a while. And I think there's a feeling --
Director General Dunkel has certainly expressed it in recent days
that the time has come to conclude the negotiations with the success
and with an agreement. The President shares that view, but
obviously there are some important points that need to be resolved
before we get there.

Yes, ma'am?

Q   These new ideas, the President said in a speech yesterday
that he would compromise to some extent, but not carry the whole
burden of compromise. Are these compromised ideas, and did the
other side bring the same, and was there -- in general from Europe
or was in from France or one particular country?

MR. NILES: I think the Prime Minister and the President of the
Commission spoke for the Community as a whole, not for one country.
So this was a European proposal or some European ideas that were put
forward to deal with those remaining areas of difference on the
agricultural negotiations.

As far as who carries the major weight of the compromises, I
think there's a recognition that both sides have to be prepared to
be flexible.

Q   Well, would these ideas actually bring it to a
conclusion?

MR. NILES: I think there's a possiblity that we can -- I have
always felt, and I think that's the view of the President and the
other senior officials who participated in this process for several

2522 - 16 -5

0140

WHITE HOUSE READOU━━N THE VISIT OF PRIME MINIU┃┃R ANIBAL CAVACO SILVA,
PRESIDENT OF THE EUROPEAN COUNCIL, AND EC PRESIDENT JACQUES DELORS
BRIEFER: THOMAS NILES, ASST SECY OF STATE FOR EUROPEAN AND CANADIAN
AFFAIRS   THE WHITE HOUSE   WEDNESDAY, APRIL 22, 1992
WR-3-2 page# 3

years now, that there is a basis there to reach an agreement. That
is one of the reasons why the President has spent so much time
personally in this effort. The meeting at The Hague last November,
the meeting here today, I think demonstrate his personal commitment
to success here. So we think there is a basis for success.

We also think, and this was something where we found full
agreement on the European side, that the world economy needs a
success in the Uruguay Round. Prime Minister Cavaco Silva talked
about the implications of a Uruguay Round success with the economies
of Eastern Europe and Latin America, and that's a view we share,
that the United States and the European Community would not,
certainly, be the only beneficiaries of a success in the GATT. The
world economy as a whole would benefit.

Yeah.

Q   Since you haven't given us the parameters of these new
proposals, can you at least tell us whether they are convergent in
any way? Are they in the same areas of disagreement or are they
very separate matters?

MR. NILES: (Laughs.) Same areas of disagreement?

Q   Well, that is to say, are they on the same --

MR. NILES: We're dealing with the same -- yeah, well, of
course. Of course. They -- we have certain areas where we and the
Community disagree on the nature of what the agricultural agreement
should look like. Your community has put forward some ideas in that
area, we put forward some ideas. Now, we're going to be talking,
following up on the discussions today, to see whether there's a way
in which we can bridge the gaps. And there are still some gaps
between us. And there's --

Q   Sometimes -- sometimes ideas can be divergent.

MR. NILES: No. Well, let me -- I can -- I think I can answer
the question that we did not end up further apart at the end of the
day than we were when we went in. There was a feeling at the end
that a goof faith effort had been made by both sides to bridge the
gap and that the ideas put forward were sufficiently promising to
justify further discussion, which is what's going to take place now.

Q -- When the President talked about compromises, already
agricultural groups are saying, oh, well sure, he's going to open up
our markets and not get us anything. Do you --

MR. NILES: Well obviously, it has to be a balanced deal. I
mean, balanced for us and acceptable to them. And not just
acceptable to the United States and the Community, but to another
100 participating countries -- or 96 participating countries.

Yeah.

2522 - 10-b

0141

WHITE HOUSE READOUT ||| THE VISIT OF PRIME MINISTER ANIBAL CAVACO SILVA,
PRESIDENT OF THE EUROPEAN COUNCIL, AND EC PRESIDENT JACQUES DELORS
BRIEFER: THOMAS NILES, ASST SECY OF STATE FOR EUROPEAN AND CANADIAN
AFFAIRS   THE WHITE HOUSE   WEDNESDAY, APRIL 22, 1992
WR-3-2   page# 4

Q   If -- if you ever get this agreement, you're still going
to have to work with the Congress. Apropos with that, I'd like to
ask you to respond to a full page ad that was in the Washington Post
this morning placed there by a collection of consumer and
environmental groups criticizing the entire Uruguay Round and
charging that in essence it's going to force the weakening or
dismantling of a number of US environmental laws, bringing higher US
standards down to lower standards outside the country. They cite
the Marine Mammal Protecton Act and Mexico's activities there, they
cite things involved with -- also the -- regarding pesticides on
imported food. What sort of reassureance are you going to be able
to offer on that support?

MR. NILES: Well, I think I could point to the fact that, for
instance with our principal partner, the European Community today,
their regulations in these areas are in most cases at least as
stringent as ours. I mean, it's not a question when we negotiate
with the European or discuss with the Community GATT issues, we're
not talking about weakening standards of consumer protection or
environmental protection. Their regulations, I can tell you from
experience over there, are at least as stringent in most cases of
which I'm aware, as ours are. So we and the Community go into these
negotiations with a common pont of view.

Now, it's true that the -- it's true that the community
disagreed with the secondary boycott aspects of the Marine Mammal
Protection Act -- the dolphin, a problem with the yellowfin tuna --
but that was not because the Community disagreed with what we're
trying to do. They share our objective of protecting Marine
mammals. They disagree with the element in the Marine Mammal
Protection Act which imposed a secondary boycott on countries which
import yellowfin tuna from countries that don't comply with our act
and wish to export yellowfin tuna to the United States.

The administraton opposed that particular provision of the
Marine Mammal Act, as well. We went to court, and for a while we
had an injunction against it and then we lost finally on appeal. So
we and the Community have a very, I think, common, consistent view
on the need to ensure that trade liberalization does not conflict
with environmental interests or consumer protection.

CONTINUED

2522 - 10-7

0142

WHITE HOUSE READOUT C■THE VISIT OF PRIME MINIST■ ANIBAL CAVACO SILVA,
PRESIDENT OF THE EUROPEAN COUNCIL, AND EC PRESIDENT JACQUES DELORS
BRIEFER: THOMAS NILES, ASST SECY OF STATE FOR EUROPEAN AND CANADIAN
AFFAIRS   THE WHITE HOUSE   WEDNESDAY, APRIL 22, 1992
WR-3-3-E page# 1
    dest=swh,mwh,dos,eurcom,fns11182,fns00725,portu,fortr,gatt,usag,forag
    dest+=ustroff,easteur,latamer,commtrade,mexico,envrmt,yugo
... data   , :

    Q   I understand that, but the point of the GATT here is that
laws passed by the United States Congress are likely to be
overturned by a bunch of (people ?) who didn't vote for the
Congressmen or anybody else.

    MR. NILES: Well, you really can't -- I mean, you have to be
able to demonstrate how that would happen, and I haven't seen it
happen in previous rounds, GATT rounds. I don't see it happening,
frankly, in the current GATT round. In fact, I think in a way you
could argue that a strong multilateral trading system where we have
agreement on the rules can be used to support unified standards,
worldwide standards, not just United States standards for
environmental protection, consumer protection, whatever it is, bring
the developing countries into a system of rules and regulations.
And so I think we would probably have fewer problems in the outyears
as a result of a GATT agremeent, and particularly as regards
consumer protection and environment, than we have today.

    Yeah?

    Q   On Yugoslavia, we were told yesterday that you were going
to coordinate a position for Serbia. Was there any discussion and
agreement on the steps that could be taken as to pressure on Serbia
to stop this support of aggression? For instance, beyond the CSCE,
measures that could be taken, what about diplomatic relations and --

    MR. NILES: No, there was no -- there was no discussion of
specific steps. There was a commitment to work together. There was
a -- I think a generally shared view that the behavior of the
government of Serbia, as relates to the situation in
Bosnia-Herzegovina was unacceptable, inconsistent with Serbia's
obligations under the CSCE and under international law, and a
commitment on the part of the United States and the Community to
stay in very close touch.

    Now, we've just had a senior US official visiting the area,
Ralph Johnson, he'll be coming back today. The European Community
officials, as I said, will be in Yugoslavia tomorrow. We're going
to keep in close touch with the Europeans.

    You mention the CSCE. The Helsinki meeting reconvenes on the
29th of April, and at that time there will be a proposal on the
table, which was put forward by the United States, with the support
of the European Community, to examine Serbia's participation or
Yugoslavia, Serbia's participation, in light of the way in which
Serbia is carrying out its or not carrying out, not fulfilling its
CSCE obligations in the case of Bosnia.

    So I think although there will be quite a bit of discussion,
perhaps some actions between now and then, I can't say for sure the

2522 - 10-8

0143

WHITE HOUSE READOUT   THE VISIT OF PRIME MINIST― ANIBAL CAVACO SILVA,
PRESIDENT OF THE EUROPEAN COUNCIL, AND EC PRESIDENT JACQUES DELORS
BRIEFER: THOMAS NILES, ASST SECY OF STATE FOR EUROPEAN AND CANADIAN
AFFAIRS   THE WHITE HOUSE   .WEDNESDAY, APRIL 22, 1992
WR-3-3-E page# 2

    next, perhaps important point in this process would be on the 29th
of April, when CSCE reconvenes in Helsinki.

        Yeah?

    Q   The administration put money in the budget this year for
extra export credits to compete with the Europeans if there's not a
deal in the GATT by the end June. Is the administration going to
spend that money?

    MR. NILES: Well, we have to see what happens at the end of
June. You're talking about enhanced -- Exports Enhancement Program
sales? I think we'll have to evaluate where we are at the end of
June to see what the situation is in the negotiations, and also what
the market situation is, to what extent US markets are being
undercut by subsidized exports by the European Community. It's hard
to predict right now what grain markets are going to look like on
the first of July.

    Q   Mr. Secretary? A couple of questions on the new ideas.
You said they didn't leave you further apart. Did they bring you
closer together? Have they reduced the gap?

    MR. NILES: I think they provided a basis for further
discussion. And as you can imagine, at the table today with the
ideas first put forward, it was not possible to determine whether
any or all of the ideas that were advanced will be helpful in
bringing us together or not, and that's the purpose of the follow-on
discussions, which we will conduct with the Community. So it's
very hard to say. But the spirit, I think there was a feeling on
both sides that these ideas or these suggestions were advanced in a
good spirit, and that there is a desire, a mutual desire to get on
with this and to resolve all the remaining issues as soon as
possible.

    Q   Without going into the specific details of.the new ideas,
we've been told already by the administration that what you're
suggesting and what you have been suggesting to the EC is basically
to decouple subsidies of commodities and have them subsidize the
farmer without interfering with --

    MR. NILES: Decoupled payments.

    Q   -- decoupled payments.

    MR. NILES: Right. Break the link between subsidy and
production.

    Q   Okay. Are these new ideas from the United States under that
general rubric?

    MR. NILES: I think that one of the things that has happened
during the Uruguay Round negotiations and as a consequence of CAP
reform in -- CAP reform discussions in Europe is that our original

2522 -10 -9

0144

WHITE HOUSE READOUT ON — VISIT OF PRIME MINISTER BAL CAVACO SILVA,
PRESIDENT OF THE EUROPEAN COUNCIL, AND EC PRESIDENT JACQUES DELORS
BRIEFER: THOMAS NILES, ASST SECY OF STATE FOR EUROPEAN AND CANADIAN
AFFAIRS   THE WHITE HOUSE   WEDNESDAY, APRIL 22, 1992
WR-3-3-E page# 3

objective -- one of our original objectives, not the only one by
any means -- but one of our original objectives, which was to
convince our European friends of the need to break the link between
subsidy and production, has been achieved, not necessarily in full
but that that concept is very much in the proposals that are being
discussed now in Europe for the reform of the Common Agricultural
Program. And the decoupled payments which Commissioner MacSharry
has suggested are part of that process. Now, of course, it also
involves setasides and other devices to reduce the enormous
subsidies in Europe which -- grain subsidies and other subsidies
that are posing such a burden on Europe and a burden on the
international agricultural market.

So we see, if you will, philosophically, some breakthroughs in
terms of the way the Europeans look at agriculture and the way they
look at the role of agriculture in international trade. Now, the
details, that's where we are now, trying to work them out.

STAFF: Last question, please.

Q   -- follow on the Yugoslav question. Is the US prepared
to deny the Belgrade government, either Serbia or Yugoslavia, a seat
in CSCE?

MR. NILES: This is an issue that will be discussed on the 29th
of April. We've raised the possibility. Ambassador Kornblum at the
last meeting before the Easter break in Helsinki pointed to the fact
that its behavior in Bosnia-Hercegovina put Serbia at variance with
its CSCE obligations, and there was a general agreement among the
now 51 countries participating in the CSCE that this was a serious
problem that would be taken up at the time the meeting reconvenes on
the 29th of April.

Now, obviously what we hope is that between now and then the
government of Serbia will change its policy, will cease and desist
from the activities it's undertaking in Bosnia, seeking to
destabilize the situation there. If that doesn't happen, obviously
we'll be prepared to draw the consequences when the CSCE resumes; we
advance the proposal.

Q   And the consequences are to deny them a seat?

MR. NILES: It would be our proposal. But obviously we would
hope that between now and then there would be sufficient changes in
the way in which the government of Serbia is behaving so that would
not be necessary. We're not seeking to exclude Serbia from
anything.

Thank you very much.

                    END

25LL - 10 - 10

長官報告事項

報告畢

1992. 4. 23.
通 商 局
通商機構課(27)

題 目 : 美.EC 頂上會談 結果 (UR 協商)

4.22(수) 워싱톤에서 개최된 미.EC 정상회담에서 UR 협상 타결을 위한
돌파구 마련에 실패한 것으로 보도 되었는바, 동 내용을 아래 보고합니다.

---

1. 회의 결과

   O UR 농산물 분야에서의 새로운 타결안이 제시 되었으나 타협에는 실패

   - 논의된 타결안 내용은 밝혀지지 않았으나 상금 입장 차이가 큰 것으로 보도

   O 상호 조속한 협상 타결 의지를 공동 확인하고, 이를 위해 계속 협의키로 합의

   - 미측은 오는 11월 미 대통령 선거 때문에 UR 협상 타결을 위한 노력이
     저해되지 않을 것임을 강조

   - 그러나 협상 시한은 설정치 않음.

2. 평가 및 전망

   O 금번 정상회담에서 돌파구 마련에 실패 함으로써 협상의 조기 타결 가능성은
     희박해졌으나, 4극 통상장관 회담 (4.24-26, 동경), 미.EC간 양자협의,
     서방 7개국 정상회담(7.6-8, 뮌헨)에서 연내 협상 종결을 위한 정치적 절충을
     계속할 것으로 전망

3. 조치사항 및 언론대책 : 해당사항 없음.   끝.

공람	92 통 상 기 구 과	담 당	과 장	심의관	국 장	차관보	차 관	장 관
	조현							

0146

GLGL
o0581 ASI/AFP-AI12-----
u i U.S.-GATT-EC 2ndlead■ 04-22 0303
  Bush and European leaders discuss new ideas but fail to achieve
breakthrough on GATT
  by PASCAL TAILLANDIER

  WASHINGTON, April 22 (AFP) - President George Bush and European Community
leaders discussed "new ideas" on the stalled GATT talks here Wednesday but
failed to achieve a "breakthrough" on agricultural subsidies.
  "We agreed to continue this process" of negotiation," Bush said after a
two-hour session at the White House with Portuguese Prime Minister Anibal
Cavaco Silva, the current EC president, and Jacques Delors, president of the
European Commission.
  One result of the bi-annual meeting was that the two parties will stay in
close contact on the problem in former Yugoslavia, where Serbian-led
aggression against Bosnia-Herzegovina was called "unacceptable" by a
high-ranking U.S. official.
  The focus of the meeting, however, was the reduction of agricultural
subsidies, which have been holding up the latest round of the General
Agreement on Tariffs and Trade, which began in Uruguay in 1986.
  "We are convinced ... that the EC leaders are committed to an early
agreement and I hope they know that I am committed to such an early
conclusion," Bush said, his sentiments being echoed by Cavaco Silva.
  Bush added that "new ideas" for reaching a compromise had been put forward
by both sides and Delors later confirmed this without providing any details on
what was discussed.
  While Bush and the EC leaders attempted to sound positive, one
high-ranking U.S. official warned that the two sides were still far from
reaching an agreement on farm subsidies.
  "We made it clear that we were not expecting a breakthrough at this
session, nor was one achieved," said Thomas Niles, assistant secretary of
state for European affairs. "Differences are there."
  more

AFP 222252 GMT APR 92

GLGL
o0582 ASI/AFP-AI13-----
u i U.S.-GATT-EC 2ndlead-2-last 04-22 0209
  (WASHINGTON)

  Niles added, however: "There was a feeling at the end that a good faith
effort had been made by both sides to bridge the gap and that the ideas put
forward were sufficiently promising to justify further discussion."
  While both sides would like to have an agreement as soon as possible,
Niles emphasized that, "there is no deadline," but that by resolving the
agricultural problem, the remaining issues could quickly be ironed out.
  The United States is asking for a 24 percent cut in the volume of
subsidized European agricultural exports, which the EC opposes.
  Washington asserts that the EC has not succeeded in adopting a common
position on the matter, while the Europeans insist that their proposals have
been rejected by the United States and stress that Bush has little room for
maneuver in an election year.
  Bush reassured his European colleagues that U.S. policy would not be held
hostage by the November balloting, Niles said.
  Earlier, Delors expressed little optimism about the talks, saying that his
chances of persuading Bush to soften his position were no greater than were
German Chancellor Helmut Kohl's when he met with the U.S. president March 21
at Camp David.
  pt/lb/g
AFP 222253 GMT APR 92

0147

외 무 부

종 별 :

번 호 : FRW-0865   일 시 : 92 0423 1720

수 신 : 장 관 (봉기)사본:주제네바대사-직송필

발 신 : 주 불 대사

제 목 : 미.EC 정상회담(UR 협상)

연:FRW-0831

1. DELOR EC 위원장은 4.22 표제회담에서 UR협상에 POLITICAL IMPULSE 를 주기위해 미측에대해 '적절한 제안'을 하였으며,BUSH 대통령도 양측은 새로운 아이디어를교환하였으며 협상은 이를 기초로 계속될 것이라고 언급하였으나 협의내용에 대한 구체적 설명은 없었음.

2. 회담과정에서 DELOR 위원장은 EC 가 독자적으로 추진하고 있는 공동농업정책(CAP)개혁 전망에 대한 정당한 평가와 EC 의 새로운 제안에 대한 미측에 상응양보를 요구하는 한편,EC 가 협상타결을 위해 모든 의무를 부담할수 없으며,특히 불란서의 경우 충분한 농민층의 유지는 필수 불가결한 사항으로 희생대상이 될수 없음을 분명히하였다 함.

3. 금번 회담에서는 예상했던대로 UR 교착을 타개할만한 중요한 진전은 보지 못하였으나 양측이 협상의 조기타결 필요성에 재공감하는 가운데,DELOR 위원장은 6월말까지 협상이 타결될 가능성을 전망함으로써 새로운 협상시한을 설정하였으며 7월초 G-7 정상회담에서 UR 재협의에는 부정적 입장을 표명함.

4. 한편 당관이 4.23 접촉한 불 외무성 UR담당관은 미.EC 협의내용이 상금 상세파악되지 않은 상태에서 협상결과를 평가하기는 이르나,1주전 미.EC 실무대표간 런던회담에서 별다른 성과가 없었으며, 금번 회담후 농산물 문제에 관한 명확한 언급이 없음에 비추어 성공적인 협상으로 보기는 어렵다는 의견을 피력함.

5. 또한 동 관계관은 미측이 7월 G-7정상회담시 UR 문제 재협의 가능성을 배제하지 않고 있음에 비추어 DELOR 위원장이 언급한 6월말 타결 가능성 시사는 다소 낙관적인 견해로 본다고 하며,불란서로서는 협상이 7월이후로 연기된다 하여도 문제될것이 없다는 입장이라 함.

통상국   2차보   외정실   분석관

PAGE 1   92.04.24   06:20 DQ
                                         외신 1과 통제관
                                              0148

6. 당지 언론은 금번 회담에 대해, 미.EC 양측이 UR 협상의 종료를 선언할수 없는 입장에서 미대봉령선거와 CAP 개혁 실현까지 협상의 교착을 방관할수도 없는 실정이므로 일단 상호부분적인 제안을 봉해 UR 협상에 대한 구제조치를 외견상 취한것으로평가함.

7. 또한 향후 전망과 관련, EC 집행위의 윤곽이 확정되지 않은 상태에서 보조금 제도에 관한 내부 논란 및 12개국을 대표한 협상 MANDATE 등 대내외적으로 어려움에처하게 될것이며, BUSH 대봉령 역시 선거를 앞두고 대 EC 양보 인상을 줄수는 없는형편이므로 금번 상호 제안에도 불구하고 UR 의 조기타결이 쉽지는 않을 것으로 분석함.

8. 관련사항 파악되는 대로 추보함.끝.

(대사 노영찬-국장)

외 무 부

종 별 :

번 호 : USW-2064   일 시 : 92 0423 1038

수 신 : 장관(통기, 통이, 경기원, 농수산부, 상공부, 재무부)

발 신 : 주미대사   사본:주제네바, EC 대사(WOI 요QSP)-중계필

제 목 : UR/농산물협상 동향(미-EC 정상회담)

당관 이영래농무관은 4.23 미농무부 GRUEFF 자자협력과장을 접촉, 표제관련미-EC 정상회담 결과를 타진한바, 동결과 및 당지 언로 보도등을 종합한 요지 하기 보고함.

1. 미-EC 정상회담결과

0 4.22 개최된 BUSH 미대통령과 DELORS EC 집행위원장 및 SILVA 폴투갈 수상간의 회담은 당초 예상했던대로 교착상태에 빠진 UR 농산물협상 관련 문제들을 타결하는데 실패하였음.

0 BUSH 대통령은 정상회담후 가진 기자회견에서 새로운 제안들(SOME NEW IDEAS) 이교환되었다고 항면서도 구체적으로 이야기하지 않았으며 앞으로도 회담을 계속해 나가기로 합의하였다고 말하였으나 DELORS EC 집행위원장은 나중에 양측의 제안들이 'MODEST' 하다고 표현함으로서 그동안 실무선에서 오고간 제안들을 종합해서 REVIEW 하였음을 암시하였음.

0 DELORS 위원장은 새로운 계기를 마련하기 위하여 6 월말까지 협상시한을 정하여 UR 협상을 계속하고 7.6 독일 문헨에서 개최되는 G-7 경제정상회담에서 주의제로 다룰것을 제의했으나 미측은 계속 협상을 하되 시한설정은 동의하지 않았다고 함.

2. UR 협상 전망

0 GRUEFF 과장은 UR 농산문 협상에서 EC 의 CAP REFORM 과 관련한 국내보조부분은 EC 측과 협상이 가능하나 수출보조 부문은 현재의 및그입장이 최저선으로 보고있다고 말하며 EC 측에서 새로운 대안이 제시되어야협상이 진척될수있다고함.

0 또한 금번 미-EC 정상회담 결과 합의에 도달하지 못함이 따라 오는 11 월의 미국대통령선거까지는 UR 협상이 합의되기가 어려울 것으로 보고있음.

0 아울러 동과장은 새로운 협상시한은 자연적으로 FAST-TRACK AUTHORITY 가 끝나는 93.6 이될것으로 보고 이에 맞추어 고위 실무협상이 앞으로도 계속 있을

통상국 정와대	장관 안기부	차관 경기원	1차보 재무부	2차보 농수부	미주국 상공부	통상국 중계	외정실	분석관

PAGE 1   92.04.24   06:09

것으로 전망하고있음. 끝
(대사 현홍주-국장)
예고문 92.12.31 까지

0151

외 무 부

종 별 :

번 호 : USW-2083

일 시 : 92 0423 1938

수 신 : 장 관 (통기,통이,미일,경기원,농수산부,상공부)

발 신 : 주 미 대사

제 목 : UR/미.EC 정상회담

1. 당관 장기호 참사관은 4.23. USTR 의 D. DWOSKIN MTN 협상담당 부대표보를 면담, 작일의 미.EC 정상회담의 UR 관련 협의 내용을 타진한바, 동일 발언 요지 하기 보고함.(김중근 서기관 동석)

가. (금번 정상회담 결과에 대한 평가를 문의한데 대해)

- 금번 회담의 주요 목적은 UR 협상의 최대의 난관인 농산물 문제에 대한 돌파구를 마련하는데 있었으나 뚜렷한 성과는 없었고, 양측이 협상을 계속해 나간다는 원칙에 인식을 같이 한 것이 뜻이 있다고 봄.

나. (일부 언론에서 협상시한을 6 월말로 합의하였다고 보도한데 대해)

- 미측이 7 월 G-7 정상회담 이전까지 미.EC 간에 합의도출이 이루어지지 않으면, 미.EC 에 대한 CREDIBILITY 문제가 제기될 수도 있으므로 EC 내 (불란서, 독일등) 일부국가들간에 이견이 있다 하더라도 이제는 EC 가 정치적인 타결을 모색할 단계에 와 있다고 강조한데 대해, EC DELORS 위원장도 협상이 상당기간교착상태에 있음을 인정하면서 협상의 MOMENTUM 을 주기 위해서는 시한설정 (6월말까지)이 필요하다고 언급한데에서 비롯된 것이며, 양측이 협상타결 시한에대해 합의한 것이 아니라고 언급함.

다. (연호 "새로운 제안"에 대해 문의한데 대해)

- W.P 지 보도에서 HILLS 대표가 절충 가능성을 기대하지는 않지만 여러가지 의견 교환이 있었다고 언급한데에서 나온 애기일 것이라고 하고, 어떤 방안이협의되었는지에 대해서는 언급을 회피함.

라. (향후 UR 협상 전망 문의에 대해)

- 부쉬 대통령은 작년 FAST TRACK 연장이후, EC 정상들과 수시로 접촉하는등 UR 협상 타결을 위해 최대의 노력을 기울이고 있으며, 비단 국내적으로 선거를 앞두고

통상국	장관	차관	1차보	2차보	미주국	통상국	외정실	분석관
청와대	안기부	경기원	농수부	상공부				

92.04.24 09:52

외신 2과 통제관 BZ

0152

있지만 UR 협상은 어떠한 정치적 게임과도 연결되어서는 안된다는 의지를 분명히 하고 있기 때문에, 현재로서는 EC 등과 이견 조정에 어려움이 있다하더라도 결과에 대해서는 낙관적인 생각을 갖고 있다고 강조함.

마. 동 부대표보는 먼저 일본에 대해 언급하면서 와다나베 일본 수상이 2 주전 미국및 EC 에 서한을 보내 농업분야 이외에 기타 상품및 서비스 협상을 조속히 추진하라고 촉구하였다고 하며, EC 와 마찬가지로 미 행정부내에서도 일본이 농업분야 협상에서 방관자적인 자세를 취하면서 미국과 EC 에 이러한 서한을 보낸데 대해 분노하기도 하고 일면 이를 냉소적으로 받아들이고 있다고 일본을 비난함.

바. 장참사관은 한국이 3 주전 농업분야 SCHEDULE 을 GATT 에 제출하였음을 상기 시키면서, 한국이 경제적으로 발전되었다고는 하지만 한국 농업 현실의 낙후성을 들어 농업분야에서는 여타 선진국과 다른 예외(개도국 대우)가 인정되어야 할 것이라고 언급한바, 동인은 한국측의 계획은 전보다는 다소 완화된 느낌을 주고 있으나 (LESS LIMITED) 기본적으로 CONCEPT 는 종전과 동일하며 미국내에서는 한국의 경제성장에 대한 인식이 팽배해 있어, 비록 농업분야라 할지라도 한국을 개도국 수준으로 인정하자는 분위기는 결코 기대할수 없는 것이라고 강조함. 또한 UR 협상 과정에서 한국측이 보다 적극적인 자세에서 CONSENSUS 형성에 참여하길 바란다고 부언함.

2. 언론 반응및 평가

- 작일 정상회담에 대하여 일부 언론(F.T)은 미.EC 양측이 6 월말까지 농업분야에서의 이견을 해소하기로 하였다고 보도함으로써 동 회담에서 진전을 이룬 것으로 평가하기도 하였으나, 대부분 언론의 공통된 반응은 금번 정상회담이 협상의 돌파구 마련에 실패한 것으로 평가하고 있음.

- 양측 관계자들은 새로운 제안의 내용에 대해 언급을 회피하고 있으나, NYT 지는 미측 관리의 말을 인용, EC 가 농산물 수출물량 감축을 종래의 15 % 에서 18 % 로 상향조정 제의한 것으로 보도하고 있음.(DUNKEL 안은 24 % 감축으로 제안)

그러나, 미측 관계자들은 EC 측의 제안은 미 의회및 업계가 결코 받아들일수 없는 지나치게 MODEST 한 것으로 평가하고 있어 향후 협상타결이 용이치 않을것으로 관측됨.

- 종래 USTR 측은 미.EC 농업협상에 있어 BALL 은 EC 측에 가있다고 주장하여 왔으나, 상기 DWOSKIN 부대표보는 앞으로 미.EC 가 상호 FLEXIBLE 한 입장을 취한다면 절충의 여지가 있다고 언급하였던바, 이는 작일의 정상회담시 논의되었다는 여러가지

PAGE 2

0153

절충안을 염두에 둔 반응으로 관측됨

- 또한, USTR 측은 금번 정상회담에서 진전이 없었음을 인정하면서도 UR 타결에 대한 부시 대통령의 강한 의지를 강조함으로써 UR 협상의 전망이 결코 비관적이 아니라고 언급하고는 있지만, 미측으로서도 UR 협상의 전망에 대한 뚜렷한 평가를 내리지 못하고 있는 것으로 관측됨.

3. 언론관계 기사는 USW(F)-2537 참조바람. 끝.

(대사 현홍주-국장)

예고: 92.12.31. 까지

검 토 필(1992.6.30.)

외 무 부

종   별 :

번   호 : POW-0215   일   시 : 92 0423 1900

수   신 : 장 관(통기,통이,통삼,구이,구일,북미일,사본-EC 대사:직송필)

발   신 : 주 폴투갈 대사

제   목 : 미 - EC 정상회담 개최

    1. 주재국 CAVACO 수상은 현 EC이사회 의장자격으로 DELORS EC 집행위원장과 같이 4.22 워싱턴에서 부쉬 대통령과 정상회담을 갖고 UR문제등 미-EC간 현안에 관하여중점논의 하였는바 양측은 UR 문제타결을 위한 합의점을 찾지는 못하였으나 새로운세계무역질서를 확립하기위해 미국과 EC가 협력하여야 한다는데 인식을 같이하고,UR 협상시한을 6월말로 연기하여 상호 이견에 대해 계속 협상해 나가기로함.

    2. CAVACO 수상과 DELORS 위원장은 회담후 가진 기자회견에서 EC측이 농산물 생산제한,수입증가 및 수출자재등 미국의 요구를 인정 하였으므로, 이제는 EC가 인내를가지고 미국의 회답을 기라려야 한다고 언급하고 회담시의 우호적인 분위기로 미루어 6월말 협상타결을 낙관한다는 견해를 피력함. 부쉬 대통령도 UR 협상타결로 미국내 취업기회 증가가 예상되며, 미-EC간 동반자 관계가 미래의 신세계 질서에 결정적으로 중요하다고 언급하는등 미국의 정치적 협상 가능성을 시사함.끝

    (대사조광제-국장)

통상국	2차보	미주국	구주국	구주국	통상국	통상국	외정실	분석관

PAGE 1   92.04.24   21:16 FN
                                                          외신 1과 통제관 ✓
                                                                      0155

해(02)

외 무 부

종 별 :

번 호 : JAW-2443

일 시 : 92 0424 2129

수 신 : 장관(통기)

발 신 : 주 일 대사(일경)

제 목 : UR 협상 동향

대 : WJA-1796

대호, 표제관련 당관 김현명 1 등서기관이 4.24(금) 외무성 경제국 국제기관 1 과 이시카와 수석사무관을 면담확인한바, 대호 신문기사는 근거 없는 관측기사로서 농업보호율 삭감 및 예외없는 관세화 수정문제를 TRACK 1 협상을 통해 교섭한다는 방안은 전혀 검토되고 있지 않다고 한바 참고 바람. 끝

(대사 오재희-국장)

통상국 아주국

PAGE 1

92.04.25 05:44

외신 2과 통제관 FK

0156

외 무 부

관리 P2-
번호 309

종 별 :

번 호 : GVW-0879

일 시 : 92 0424 1930

수 신 : 장관(통기,경기원,재무부,상공부,특허청),사본:주미,EC 대사(중계필)

발 신 : 주 제네바 대사

제 목 : 평화그룹 월레오찬

연: GVW-0878

본직은 금 4.24. LACARTE 우루과이 대사 주최, 평화그룹 월레 오찬에 참석한바, 동 오찬에서 있었던 미.EC 정상회담 결과에 대한 평가 및 향후 UR 협상 전개방향에 대한 협의결과를 아래 보고함.

1. 미.EC 정상회담 결과와 관련(1) 연호 DUNKEL 총장의 긍정평가에 대한 당지 언론 보도에도 불구하고, 대부분의 참석대사는 강한 실망과 좌절감을 표시하였으며, (2) DELORS EC 집행위원장이 제시한 6 월말 시한 이전 협상의 본격화 가능성에 대해서도 회의적 의견이 지배적이었고, (3) 미국 선거 이후 협상이 본격화하더라도 미.EC 간 쟁점이 쉽게 타결될수 있을지의 여부에 관한 전망도 불부명하다는 것이 다수 의견이었음.

2. 상기 1 항과 같은 평가를 기초로 향후 UR 협상 추진방향 및 협상정돈상태 타개를 위한 평화그룹의 기여가능 방안 모색문제가 지난달 본직 주도로 논의가 진행된데 이어 아래와 같이 다시 제기된바, 참석대사의 의견이 엇갈려 합의점을 찾지 못함.

가. 현싯점에서 당분간 협상중단(SUSPENSION) 문제

- 협상 정돈상황해 대한 충격(SHOCK)을 주고, 이를 통해 미.EC 에 압력을 가한다는 취지에서 약 3-4 개월 협상을 일시 중단해야 한다는 의견이 우루과이, 스웨덴 대사등으로 부터 제기됨.

- 이에 대해 본직 및 파키스탄 대사등은 협상의 중단은 본의 아니게 정치적으로 과도한 부정적 충격을 미칠 위험성이 있으며, 고위실무 협상을 계속한다는 것이 미.EC 양측의 방침이고, 기타 4.24. QUAD 통상장관 회담등 타결노력이 계속되고 있는 상황이므로 앞으로 전망이 보다 가시 될때까지 기다련 보면서 신중히 대처할 문제라는

통상국	장관	차관	2차보	~~중계~~	외정실	분석관	청와대	안기부
경기원	재무부	상공부	특허청	중계				

PAGE 1

92.04.25   07:53

외신 2과 통제관 CE

0157

입장을 피력함.

　나. TNC 조기 개최 필요성

　- 상당수 대사가 조기개최 필요성을 지지하였으나

　- 본직은 대안없는 TNC 개최는 상호 비난등 협상 분위기를 저해할 가능성만높일뿐 실익이 없으므로 바람직하지 못하므로, 인내심을 가지고 조금더 두고 보는 것이 좋겠다는 의견 개진

　다. 평화그룹 차원의 성명서 발표문제

　- 미, EC 양측이 또다시 여타 협상참가국의 기대에 부응치 못한 만큼 성명서 발표가 필요하다는 의견이 다수 대사로 부터 강하게 제시되었으나

　- 본직은 미.EC 간 정치적 돌파구 마련이 중요한 것은 사실이나 모든 책임을 미.EC 에게만 전가하고 협상의 의미있는 진전을 위한 건설적 제안이나 기여가없는 선언적 내용의 반박성명(HOLLOW STATEMENT)은 무의미하다는 의견을 피력. 끝

　(대사 박수길-장관)

　예고:92.6.30 까지

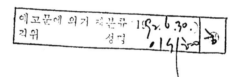

외 무 부

번 호 : GVW-0878
일 시 : 92 0424 1920

수 신 : 장관(통기,경기원,재무부,농림수산부,상공부,특허청),사본:주미,주이씨

발 신 : 주 제네바 대사대사-중계필

제 목 : 미.EC 정상회담에 관한 당지 반응

　　　1. DUN[200X 1. DUNKEL 총장은 표제 정상회담 결과에 관하여 미.EC 간 "새로운

IDEAS"가제시되고 협상을 계속해 나가기로 한점 및 자신은 더이상 시한을 거론 않겠다고 공언했지만 6 월말 시한이 제시된 점등을 긍정적 신호로 본다는 반응을 보인 것으로 언론에 보도되었으나 당지의 일반적 평가와 분위기는 DUNKEL 총장의 위치에서는 위와같이 평가할수 밖에 없지 않느냐는 의견이 지배적임

　　　2. 4.23. 본직 주최 JARQAMILLO 서비스협상 그룹(T2) 의장 본국귀임 환송오찬, 이스라엘 대사 주최만찬(4.23) 및 금 4.24. 평화그룹 대사 월례오찬등을 통하여 본직이 파악한 바에 의하면 대부분의 대사들은 동 정상회담의 결과에 대하여 강한 실망과 좌절감을 공유하고 있었으며, DELORS EC 집행위원장이 6 월말 시한을 제시했지만 사실상 미국 선거가 끝나기 이전까지의 협상 타결은 기대하기 어려우며, 미국선거 이후 협상이 본격화 된다 하더라도 현싯점에서 볼때 미.EC 간 주요쟁점이 쉽게 해결될 수 있을 것인지의 여부가 불부명하다는 것이 당지에서의 일반적인 분위기임.끝

　　　(대사 박수길-장관)

　　　예고:92.6.30 까지

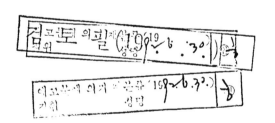

통상국	장관	차관	2차보	외정실	분석관	청와대	안기부	경기원
재무부	농수부	상공부	특허청	중계				

92.04.25　07:49

외신 2과　통제관 CE
0159

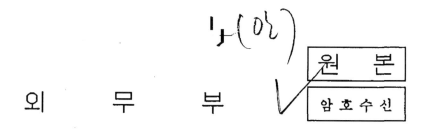

외 무 부

종 별 :

번 호 : JAW-2467   일 시 : 92 0427 1723

수 신 : 장 관(통기,통일,경일,상공부)

발 신 : 주 일 대사(일경,상무관)

제 목 : 4극 통상회의

　　　미.일, EC, 카나다간 상공장관의 4 극 통상회의가 4.24(금)-26(일)간 당지 후꾸시마현 소재 기타시오바라 호텔에서 개최되었던 바, 동 회의결과를 언론보도를 중심으로 아래 보고함.(동 회의의 공동발표문은 없으며, 일 통상장관이 회의내용을 기자들에게 발표하였음)

　　　1. 회의 참석자: 일본의 와타나베 통산장관, 미국의 힐스 USTR 대표, EC 의 안드리센 부위원장, 카나다의 월슨 국제무역장관

　　　2. 회의 주요결과

　　　（가） UR 교섭 타결문제

　　　- 일본은 금년 여름까지는 UR 교섭을 타결시키자는 목표기한 설정을 요청하였으나, 미.EC 가 기한설정에 반대하여, 다만 UR 교섭의 조기타결을 목표로 노력한다는데에 그침

　　　- 일본은 미, EC, 카나다가 현재 제출하지 않고 있는 공업제품의 시장개방 계획(국별표)을 조기에 제출토록 요청한바, 동 국별표의 조기제출이 바람직하다는데 의견일치

　　　- 일본은, 농업문제 때문에 교섭이 중단되고 있는 시장접근, 써비스등 분야의 교섭재개를 요청한바, 써비스분야등에서 가능한 조속히(6 월중이라도) 제네바에서 고위실무 교섭을 개최하기로 함

　　　- 일측은 미.EC 정상회담 (4.22)에서 상호간 제시한것으로 알려진 농업교섭의 신제안에 대해 그내용을 밝혀주도록 요청하였으나, 미.EC 측은 상세한 설명을피하고, 다만 '쌍방의 제안이 실망스러운 것이라기 보다는 교섭타결을 위해 고무적인 내용이었다'고만 언급

　　　（나） 무역과 환경문제

통상국 상공부	장관	차관	2차보	경제국	통상국	분석관	청와대	안기부

PAGE 1

- 와타나베 통산장관은 환경보호를 목적으로 무역제한 조치를 취할 경우에는1) 각국에서 동일한 환경보호 조치가 있어야 하며, 2) 무역제한 효과를 최소한으로 억제하고, 3) 규제조치의 내용을 다국간에 합의하자는 3 가지 원칙을 준수할것을 제안한 바, 각국은 이를 검토키로 함

다.) 무역과 경쟁정책

- 미국의 독점금지법 국외적용 방침에 대해 일, EC, 카나다는 강한 우려를 표명하고, 통상문제 해결을 위해서는 독금법의 역외적용이 아니라 다국간 무역교섭에 의해야 한다고 요청

- 동 문제는 금년 가을 카나다개최 4 극 통상장관 회의에서 계속 토의키로 함

라. 기타

- 일본이 러시아의 GATT 가맹을 4 국이 지원하자고 제안한데 대해 각국은 동의하였으며, 중국및 대만의 GATT 가맹에도 4 극이 지원하도록 협력하자는 일본의 제안에 대해서 각국은 이해를 표명함

3. 회의 평가

가. 금번회의가 UR 교섭에 큰 영향을 줄 정도의 회의는 아니었지만, 금번 회의에서는 대부분 UR 교섭 타개문제에 대해 논의하였는바, 일측(통산성)은 일본이 UR 교섭에 적극적이라는 것은 보여주고자 하여, 금년 여름까지 UR 교섭을 타결하자는 목표를 제안하였으나, 미.EC 의 반대로 UR 교섭 타결의 기한설정은 되지 않았음

나. 금번회의에 대해 4.27.(월) 외무성 국제기관 1 과에 확인한 바, 금번 회의에서 농업문제 때문에 교섭이 중단되고 있는 써비스등 분야에서 우선 가능한조속히 교섭을 재개하자는 의견이 모아지기는 하였으나, UR 교섭 타결목표의 시한이 설정되지 않았고, 미.EC 간 농업문제가 해결되지 않는한 UR 교섭 전체가 진전되지 않는 구조는 불변으로 금번 회의로 UR 교섭 타개전망이 변화한것은 거의 없다고 하였음. 끝

(대사 오재희-국장)

발 신 전 보

WGV-0658   920428 1722 FO

번   호 : _____   종별 : _____

수   신 : 주   제네바   대사. 총영사

발   신 : 장 관 (통 기)

제   목 : UR 협상 대책 (3개 협상그룹 보고서 평가)

일반문서로 재분류(1992 . 12. 31)

대 : GVW-0825

1. 대호, 3개그룹 보고서들은 각 분야별 협상 현황을 사실적으로 기술하고 분석한
    것으로서, 이에대한 평가에는 일응 모든 참가국의 양허 계획 조기 제출 필요성,
    기제출된 양허 계획의 내용 및 질에 대한 논평과 함께 금후 협상 타결의 돌파구
    마련을 위한 제안으로서 시장접근 및 서비스 분야에서의 각국 양허의 개선 노력등을
    언급하는 방안을 고려할수 있을것으로 생각됨.

2. 이와관련 현재 미.EC간 농산물 협상 관련 의견 대립외에 협상 부진의 주요 원인으로
    거론될 수 있는 사항은 미국.EC의 시장접근 분야 구체 양허 계획 미제시, 미국의
    서비스 분야 MFN 일탈 용인된바, 시장접근 분야에서의 아국의 양허 내용과 당분간
    동 양허내용을 개선하기 어렵다는 점을 감안할때, 앞으로의 협의 과정에서 협상
    부진에 대한 제3국의 책임을 강조하는 것보다는, 협상 부진 현상을 일반적 논조로
    지적하고 Track 4 협상의 중요성을 강조하는등 지금까지 아국이 대응해온 기본
    방향대로 대처하는 것이 좋을 것으로 사료됨.   끝.

(통상국장   김 용 규)

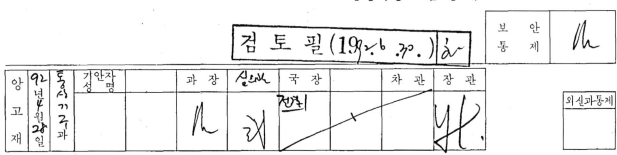

검 토 필 (1992. 6. 30.)

보 안 통 제	

앙고재	92년4월28일	통상기구과	기안자성명		과장		국장		차관	장관		외신과통제

0162

관리
번호 92-341

외 무 부

종 별 :

번 호 : GVW-0987   일 시 : 92 0513 1900

수 신 : 장관(통기,경기원,재무부,상공부,특허청)사본:주미,주이씨대사(중계필)

발 신 : 주 제네바 대사

제 목 : UR 협상

일반문서로 재분류 (1992 . 12 . 31)

　　농산물에 관한 미.EC 간 막후 절충 작업의 부진으로 협상의 정돈상태가 풀리지 않고, 부활절 협상 시한, 미.EC 정상회담이 지나고도 상당기간이 경과한 현재까지 구체적 움직임이 없어, 앞으로의 전망이 불부명한 가운데, 당지 협상 대표들간에 일반적으로 언급되는 평가 및 관측 내용을 아래 보고함.

　　1. 협상 본격화의 관건은 미.EC 간 농산물에 관한 정치적 돌파구, 마련에 있으나, 아직까지 아무런 움직임이 없음.

　　2. 5.6 및 5.7 개도국 회의시 DUNKEL 총장 및 TRAN EC 대사가 언급한바와 같이, 미.EC 양측의 정치적 결단이 요구되는 상황이나 특히 대통령 선거를 앞둔 미국의 경우 쉽게 결단을 내릴수 있을 것으로 기대하기 어려움.

　　3. 미.EC 양측은 자신들에게 책임이 집중되는 것을 의식, T1, T2 협상의 계속을 바라고 있고, DUNKEL 총장도 협상 MOMENTUM 유지를 위해 여타 참가국의 협상 계속을 종용하고는 있으나 여타국은 미.EC 절충 결과가 불부명한 상태에서 구체적 양허 협상을 추진하는 것은 무의미하다는 입장임.

　　4. 따라서 DUNKEL 총장이 4.14 TNC 회의에서 언급한 양자간, 다수국간 및 다자간 협상이 시작될 움직임이 전혀 보이지 않고 있으며, DUNKEL 총장은 TNC 개최 자체에 대해서도 소극적 반응을 보이고 있음. (다수국이 희망하고 있으므로 TNC 회의는 조만간 개최될 가능성이 없지는 않으나, 특별한 의미를 부여하기 어렵다고 봄)

　　5. EC 의 TRAN 대사 언급대로 미.EC 간 기술적 작업은 거의 끝난 단계이고 수백만톤의 곡물과 관련된 정치적 결단만이 남아 있다면, 7 월초 문헌 G7 정상회담에 대한 기대에도 한계가 있음(KOHL 수상은 UR 협상 때문에 G7 회담 분위기가까지는 것은 원치 않는다는 점을 밝힌바 있고, 최근 국내적 입지 약화에 따라 동수상의 역할에도 한계가 있음)

통상국	장관	차관	1차보	2차보	분석관	청와대	종리실	안기부
경기원	재무부	상공부	특허청	중계				

PAGE 1   92.05.14   09:53

6. 따라서 정치적 돌파구 마련은 미국의 대통령 선거가 끝나는 시점이 될 가능성이 있고, 이경우 T1, T2 작업이 약 3 개월 정도 소요된다고 보아 내년 2 월을 예상 가능한 협상 타결 목표 시점으로 잡아, 금년 하반기부터 협상이 본격화 되지 않을까 하는 것이 일반적 관측임.

7. 한편 5.18 부터 개시될 OECD 각료회의에서도 UR 협상 문제가 부분적으로거론될 것으로 예상되고, 6 월초 미.EC 각료회의가 예정되어 있는등 미.EC 간 양자적 노력도 계속될 예정이며, 6 월 중순경 약 15 개국간 서비스 양허 협상(T2) 개최 문제도 검토되고 있는 점등에 비추어 상기 미.EC 각료회의에 이어 6 월중에 T1, T2 협상이 재개될 가능성이 없는 것은 아님.

8. 미.EC 합의가 이루어질 경우 이에 따른 전체 UR 협상 타결 형태에 관해서는, 12.20 DUNKEL TEXT 의 해체(UNRAVELLING)은 곤란하다는 다수국의 공감대 및 DUNKEL 총장 자신의 확고한 입장과 EC 역시 농산물 TEXT 를 제외하고는 불만이 없지는 않으나 대체로 수락 가능하다는 입장을 보이고 있음에 비추어 농산물 TEXT 수정에만 국한될 것이라는 예상과 미국이 EC 에 대해 농산물 분야에서 양보하는 대가로 보조금, 반덤핑, 지적소유권등 일부 분야에서의 보상을 원하게 될것이라는 2 가지 가능성이 상정 가능하다고 보나, 후자의 경우 여타국의 연대적 요구에 따른 협상 붕괴를 초래할 위험성이 있음.

9. 결국 미.EC 간 정치적 돌파구가 마련되어 FAST TRACK AUTHORITY 시한내에 UR 협상이 타결될 것인지의 여부는 금년말 또는 늦어도 내년초까지는 그 전마이 분명해 질것이나, 최소한 현단계에서의 일반적 평가는 현재 미.EC 간 OILSEED문제, MSA 협상 실패 및 이에 따른 미업체의 EC 산 철강 수입에 대한 반덤핑 제소, 조선협상 실패등 굵직한 봉상현안으로 인해 양자적 봉상 마찰이 고조되고 있어 만약 UR 협상이 실패할 경우 미.EC 의정치적 관계에까지 큰 영향이 있을 것이라는 사실을 잘 알고 있는 미.EC 양측으로서는 동 협상을 타결해야 한다는 확고한 정치적 의지를 갖고 있는 만큼 결국 FAST TRACK AUTHORITY 만료전까지는 타결이 가능할 것이라고 보는 것이 당지에서의 다수 의견임. (다만, 동 시한까지 타결이 안될경우 미국이 새로운 입법조치등을 통해 FAST TRACK AUTHORITY 의 연장 조치를 취하게 될 것인지의 여부는 현단계에서 예단할수도 없고, 거론할 계제도 아니라는 분위기임.) 끝

(대사 박수길-국장)

예고 :92.12.31. 까지

김 토 필 (1992. 6. 30.)

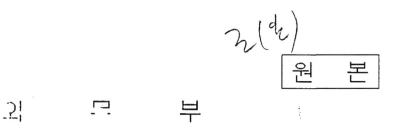

긴 급 부

종   별 :

번   호 : ECW-0619   일   시 : 92 0513 1700

수   신 : 장관(봉기,경기원,재무부,농림수산부,상공부,기정동문)사본:주미,제네바

발   신 : 주 EC 대사

제   목 : 갓트/UR 협상 표제 협상

갓트/UR 협상표제협상과 관련한 최근 당지의 동향을 아래보고함

1. EC 의 동향

가. 5.12. MAC SHARRY 농업담당 집행위원은 협상상대국들이 좀더 유연한 입장을취한다면 표제협상은 쉽게 타결될수 있으며 협상타결의관건이 되고있는 농산물 수출물량 24프로감축을 수락하는 방안을 모색할수 있다고언급함. 그 방법으로서 동인은품목별로 24프로 수출감축이행 방법이외에 품목군별, 즉 CEREALS또는 낙농제품 등으로 대별하여 감축하는 방법을 제시함

나. 동인은 CAP 개혁에따른 직접소득보조에대하여는 감축대상보조에서 제외되어야 한다는점과 PEACE CLAUSE 가 합의결과에 포함되어야함을 강조함

다. 한편, OLIVEIRA 폴투갈(EC 의장국)무역장관은 7.6-8 개최되는 뮨헨 G-7정상회담은 표제협상의 정치적인 타결계기가 될수 없으며, 각국이 처한 입장으로 볼때 비록 정상모임이라 해도 유연한 입자을 제시할수는없을 것이라고 말함. 동인은 6월말까지 미.EC양자협상에서 어떤 결론이 도출되지 않을 경우 표제협상은 93년까지 이월될수밖에 없을것이라고 말하고, 그러나 현실적으로 폴투갈이 EC의장국을 맡고 있는 기간중(6월말까지)협상이 타결되기는 어려울 것이라고 전망함

2. 미.EC 양자협상 동향

가. OLIVEIRA 폴투갈 무역장관의 대변인은 2주이내에 농업보조금관련 미.EC 간 협상을재개하며, 표제협상의 정치적 타협점을 모색하기위해 5월말경에 HILLS 미무역대표부 대표가폴투갈을 방문한다고 발표함

나. 한편, EC 집행위 대변인은 5.18. 주간에 ANDRIESSEN 부위원장이 워싱턴을 방문하여 OILSEEDS 에 관한 미.EC 간 분쟁및 갓트/UR협상 문제를 협의할 예정이라고 발표함

통상국   2차보   안기부   경기원   재무부   농수부   상공부   중계(김)

PAGE 1   92.05.14   07:41 EG

외신 1과 통제관 ✓

0165

3. 불란서동향

가. 5.12. BEREGOVOY 불란서수상은 LACOMBE 불란서농민연맹회장을 만난 자리에서불란서는 UR협상에서 계속 강경한 입장을 취할 것이며, 불란서의 세계곡물시장 점유율을 보호할 것을약속함

나. 그러나 동인은 현재 불란서로서는 농업문제뿐아니라 전체 경제문제도 중요하다고 강조하고 미대통령 선거등을 감안할때 UR 협상이조만간 종결되기는 어려울 것이라고 전망함. 끝

(대사 권동만-국장)

면 담 요 록

1. 면담일시 및 장소 : 1992. 5.19(화) 11:00-12:00, 통상기구과

2. 면 담 자

   ㅇ Ulf Sormark 주한 스웨덴 대사관 경제참사관

   ㅇ 홍종기 통상기구과장 (기록 : 신부남 통상기구과 사무관)

3. 면담내용 :

《아국의 반덤핑 제도》

Sormark 참사관

ㅇ 한국의 반덤핑 제도에 관한 법령 및 반덤핑 관세의 적용기간(sunset clause)
   문의

과   장

ㅇ 반덤핑 제도에 관한 법령으로는 88.12 개정된 바 있는 관세법 시행령
   (대통령령)이 있으며 반덤핑 관세의 적용기간은 별도로 정한 경우 또는 3년임.

Sormark 참사관

ㅇ 스웨덴 철강제품에 대해 미국이 반덤핑 관세를 부과한 바 있는바, 한국의
   경우는 ?

과   장

ㅇ 현재 철강제품 관련 미국의 반덤핑 제소를 당한 경우는 없으나, 미국 철강
   업계에서 한국산 철강제품에 대한 반덤핑 제소를 준비하고 있다는 소식에
   우리 정부는 우려를 갖고 있음. 또한 미국은 이를 상대국과의 철강 자율
   규제 협정 종료(92.3) 이후의 국내산업 보호 수단으로 삼으려는 것으로
   알고 있음.

1

0167

《UR 협상에 대한 평가》

Sormark 참사관

o UR 협상 관련 91.12 협상안에 대한 평가 문의

과   장

o UR 협상과 관련 스웨덴과 유사한 평가를 하고 있는바, 기본적으로는
  다자무역을 통해 경제를 성장시켜온 한국으로서는 UR 협상의 성공적 타결을
  중요하게 생각하고 있으며 UR 협상 실패시 국제무역환경의 악화가 예상되므로
  아국으로서는 UR 협상의 타결을 위해 최대한 기여해 오고 있음.

o 91.12 최종 협정안은 추가 협상의 기초로서 수용 가능하다는 입장임.
  즉 규범제정, TRIPs, 서비스 분야 등에서 문제점이 있지만 제일 큰 문제점은
  농산물 분야이며 특히 시장접근에서의 '예외없는 관세화' 원칙임. 쌀의 경우
  국민 감정상 개방에서 예외가 되어야 한다는 것임. 따라서 농산물 분야는
  추후 협상에서 다시 다루어져야 할 과제로 보고 있음.

Sormark 참사관

o 농산물의 관세화 예외 대상 품목 축소 여부 문의

과   장

o 현재 15개 품목으로 91.1 우리는 추후 협상 진전에 따라 15개 품목의 개방
  문제에 대해 협상할 수 있다고 언급한 바 있으며, 92.4.10 농산물에 대한
  국별 계획서 제출시에 상기 15개 품목을 관세화 대상의 예외로 하고
  cover note에 관세화 대상 예외품목의 축소에 대해서는 협상할 용의가
  있음을 언급하였음.

Sormark 참사관

o UR 협상 타결 전망 문의

2

<u>과   장</u>

o 농업보조금 문제 관련 미국과 EC간에 7월까지 타협이 이루어지면 UR 협상은
   금년말까지 타결될 수 있을 것으로 보임. 제네바 협상 전문가 및 우리 정부내
   다수 관계자들도 비공식적으로 실제 UR 협상 기한이 미국의 Fast Track이
   종료되는 내년 5월로 보고 있음. 미국과 EC는 그 전에도 예를들면 금년
   7월에 개최되는 G-7 정상회의에서 타협할 가능성도 있으나 아무도 확실한
   예측은 할 수 없는 상태임.
   (차주 Andriessen EC 집행위원과 Baker 국무장관과 회담 예정 언급)

<u>Sormark 참사관</u>

o UR 협상 각 분야에 대한 평가 문의

<u>과   장</u>

o 시장접근 분야에서 농산물등 특정품목의 관세화 대상 제외 필요. 한국의 경우
   농업인구는 8백만명으로 전체 인구의 19%임. 미국이 주도하는 무세화 협상에
   참가하고 있으나 전부 수용하기에는 개도국으로서의 어려움이 있음.

o 규범제정 분야의 경우 수용 가능하며 문제점으로는 보조금.상계관세 분야에서의
   구조 조정 보조금이 허용보조금에 포함되지 않았으며, Safeguard 분야에서의
   quota modulation은 사실상 선별 적용이므로 수용할 수 없음.

o TRIPs의 경우 우리로서는 큰 문제점이 있으나 경과기간과 관련 미국의 반대가
   큰 것으로 알고 있음.

o MTO 설립 문제는 현 갓트가 서비스, TRIPs등 신분야를 다룰 수 없으므로 MTO의
   설립이 필요하며, MTO 협약은 UR 협상 결과를 Single Undertaking 전제하에
   전부 수용하도록 규정되어 있음.

<u>Sormark 참사관</u>

o 대외무역에 의존이 큰 한국과 스웨덴은 UR 협상에 대해 유사한 입장인
   것으로 알고 있음.

o 무역과 환경에 대한 입장과 무역자유화에 대한 입장 문의

3

0169

과   장

o 무역과 환경 관련 현재 갓트에서 논의 시작 단계인 바 기본입장은 환경
  조치가 무역을 제한하는 것으로 사용되어서는 안된다는 것임.

o 최근 증가되고 있는 지역협정은 갓트를 기반으로한 다자무역체제를 대체할
  수 없으며 다자무역체제의 강화를 위해 적극 노력할 것임.

o 무역자유화 추진과 관련 어려움도 많으나 정부의 기본 입장은 무역자유화
  일정이 중단없이 계속되어야 한다는 것임.

Sormark 참사관

o 스웨덴도 지역협정이 다자무역체제를 대체할 수 없다는 것에 동조함.   끝.

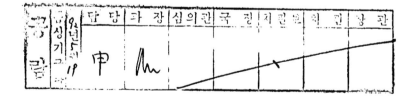

4

UR 농산물 협상 관련 (카나다) 입장

가. 기본입장 (92.3. 농산물 이행계획서)

1) 시장개방

- 11조 2C(i)의 조항은 푼타델에스테선언, 중간평가 합의의 취지에 따라 명료성을 부여하여 그 기능이 강화되고 운영면에서 효율성을 제고시켜 계속 활용 필요
- MMA, CMA는 생산조절을 하는 모든 품목을 포함해 적용
- 11 2C의 적용은 Tariff-line별이 아닌 제품별로 운용해야 함.
- T.E.의 부과는 종가세, 종량세 또는 양자를 혼용해 사용가능
- 양허대상이 되는 모든 품목에 대해 특별 긴급피해 구제제도 적용 권한을 유보
- 구체적인 T.E.는 주요협상 대상국의 수준으로 조정할 수 있는 권한을 유보하며 쇠고기에 대해서는 미국의 T.E. 수준으로 할 권한을 유보
- 특정 몇몇 품목에 대해서 적절한 수준으로 T.E.를 조정하기 위한 협상을 할 수 있는 권한을 유보
- 관세율할당, 수입량협상을 포함한 관세제도는 계절별, 시기별로 융통성 있게 운용할 수 있는 권한을 유보

2) 국내보조

- 다른 협상국들이 감축약속에 따라 감축대상 및 폭의 조정권한 유보
- 고정된 외부참조가격에 대해 적용방법, 계산등에 융통성부여 가능
- 허용대상 보조와 관련 다른 협상국들의 동등 Program에 대한 정책분류 결과를 고려해 국내보조정책의 분류기준을 재검토할 수 있는 권리를 유보

0171

나. 부문별 캐나다 이행계획 수립내용

(1) 시장접근분야

구 분	이 행 계 획 내 용
가) T.E. 및 관세감축계획	① 감축기준년도 : '86 ~ '88 ② 감축폭 : 단순평균 36 %, 최저감축 15 % ③ 이행기간 : 1993 ~ 1998 ④ 양허수준 : 전품목양허 ㅡ 단 11조2C의 비관세 조치의 관세화는 거부
나) 관세화	① 포괄적 관세화 수용여부 ㅇ 11조2C 대상품목을 제외한 모든 비관세 조치품목에 대해 T.E 산출 ㅡ 총협상대상품목(HS 8 단위) : 1154 개 ㅡ 비관세조치품목(〃) : 111 개 ㅡ T.E. 산출품목(〃) : 59 개 ㅡ 11조2C의 수입제한 조치품목(HS 8 단위) : 52 개 ㅇ 비관세조치의 유형 : 육류수입법에 의한 수입허가 ② 관세화 대상품목의 T.E. 산출 i) 국내외 가격차로 산출 ㅡ 사용된 국내가격 : 지배적 시장가격 ㅡ 사용된 국제가격 : 〃 〃 ii) 가공제품의 경우 원료T.E와 구성비를 곱하여 산출 ③ T.E.산출품목분류 : HS 8 단위의 세분류사용 ④ 감축기준, 양허세율 : 종량세, 종가세 혼용 ⑤ T.E 조정 : 가공품 T.E. 계산시 현행 세율을 추가 산업보호로 가 산 조정
다) 현행시장접근	① 대상품목 : 실품목기준 11 개(HS 4 단위기준) 품목 ② 적용관세율 : 기본관세(종가 또는 종량세) ③ 증량계획 : 없음

0172

구　　　　　분	이　행　계　획　내　용
라) 최소시장접근	① 대상품목 : 실품목기준 13 개 품목 (HS 8 단위　38 개) 　― 품목별로 관련세번을 명시 ② 초기연도　MMA 와　증량계획 　― 초기 MMA : 국내소비량의　3 % 　―. 증량계획 :　　//　　　5 % ③ MMA 적용　관세율 : 종량세 　― 최저세율 적용에 대한 명기 없음
마) 긴급피해구제제도	○ T.E. 대상품목과 일부 관세인하 품목에 적용 　― 총 적용품목 : 205 개

0173

(2) 국내보조 분야

구 분	이 행 계 획 내 용
가) 국내보조 감축계획	① 감축기준년도 : '86 ~ '88 ② 감축폭 : 20 % ③ 이행기간 : '93 ~ '98
나) 품목특정적 감축약속 (Product-Specific AMS)	① 감축약속 대상품목 : 밀(듀럼종), 보리, 옥수수, 귀리, 유채, 대두, 기타 곡물 및 유지종자와 사료, 사탕무우, 사과, 감자, 꿀, 담배, 건조채두류, 기타 농작물, 쇠고기, 돼지고기, 양고기, 기타 가축 ② AMS산출 ㅇ 시장가격지지 : (관리가격－국제가격)×지지물량 ㅇ 감축대상 직접지불 : 가격차방식, 재정지출액으로 산출 ㅇ 기타 감축대상보조 ③ 기타 : 감축대상중 감자, 담배, 쇠고기, 기타작물, 기타가축은 De- minimis에 해당
다) 동등약속(Equivalent Commitment)	① 감축약속 대상품목 : 액상우유, 가공용우유, 닭고기, 칠면조, 계란 5개 품목 ② 지원형태 : 지방정부보조 ③ 지원액 산출방법 : 감축대상 재정지출 (시장가격 지지계산은 공급량 관리품목에 대한 지지를 과다 계 산하게 되므로 제외) ④ 기타 : 액상우유, 닭고기, 칠면조고기, 계란은 De-minimis에 해당 (실제 감축은 가공용 우유에만 적용됨)
라) 품목불특정보조(Non- Product Specific AMS)	① 지원형태 : 보험, 운송, 신용공여, 지방정부 보조 ② 지원액산출 : 재정지출액

0174

구　　　　분	이　행　계　획　내　용
마) 허용대상보조 (부속서 4)	① 정부　일반서비스
	－　연구개발, 훈련, 기술자문서비스
	－　병해충방제, 검사서비스
	－　하부구조개선
	－　유통 및　판매촉진
	② 생산자에　대한　직접지불 (Decoupled Income Support)
	③ 자연재해　구호지원
	④ 탈농지원　계획하의　구조조정지원
	⑤ 휴경보상을　통한　구조조정지원
	⑥ 기타

(3) 수출보조

구 분	이 행 계 획 내 용
가) 수출보조 감축약속	① 기준년도 : 1986 ~ 1990 ② 감축기준 : 협상기초 자료로 재정지출과 보조수출 물량을 제시 ③ 감축폭 : 물량기준 24 %, 재정액기준 36 % ④ 이행기간 : '93 ~ '98

나) 감축대상 수출보조	① 대상품목 : 34 개
	
	  ㅇ 곡물 및 곡물제품 (밀, 보리, 맥아, 귀리, 호밀, 옥수수, 대두, 완두, 편두, 밀가루, 겨, 카나리씨, 메밀, 기장씨, 곡물가공품등)
	
	  ㅇ 유지류 (카놀라, 카놀라오일, 카놀라 깻묵, 가루, 아마씨, 아마씨유 아마씨깻묵가루, 해바라기씨, 해바라기유, 해바라기 깻묵가루, 겨자씨
	
	  ㅇ 사료류 (알팔파, 사료, Screening), 곡물용종자, 조식용 곡물가공품
	
	  ㅇ 유제품 (밀크파우더 농축액, 버터류, 치즈, 유제품)
	
	② 수출보조유형 : 운송보조, 생산자조달보조

다) 수출보조 제한약속	언급없음

통기

외 무 부

110-760 서울 종로구 세종로 77번지   / (02)720-2330   / (02)720-2686

문서번호 경일 20610-548

시행일자 1992. 6. 5. (금)

수신   수신처 참조

참조

선결			지시	84당대학 홍대교 ✓	
접수	일자시간		결재		
	번호		공람		
처리과					
담당자	이시경				

제목   뮌헨 G-7서미트에 대한 아측입장   일반문서로 재분류 (1992.12.31)

　　　제18차 G-7 정상회담이 오는 7.6-8간 독일 뮌헨에서 개최될 예정인 바,
귀국 소관사항중 동 회담에서 협의되거나, 발표문에 반영 시키고자 하는 아국
입장이 있으면   당국으로 지급 회보하여 주시기 바랍니다.

　　첨 부 : 최근 3년간 G-7 정상회담시 아국 관련사항.   끝.

　　수신처 : 외교정책기획실장, 아주국장, 미주국장, 구주국장, 중동아프리카국장,
　　　　　　　조약국장, 통상국장

　　예 고 : 92.12.31. 일반

국 제 경 제 국 장

전교문의A
검토필 92.6.30
홍

0177

제15차 파리서미트 (1989)

(경제선언)

The emergence of the newly industrializing economies and the
initiation of a dialogue with them are welcome. We call on those
with substantial surpluses to contribute to the adjustment of
external imbalances and the open trade and payments system. To
that end, they should permit exchange rates to reflect their
competitive position, implement GATT commitments and reduce
trade barriers.

제16차 휴스턴서미트 (1990.7)

(의장성명)

The Korean Peninsula remains an area of sharp concern, especially
because of the North has yet to sign and implement a nuclear safeguard
agreement. We welcome the recent talks between North and South Korea
and hope they mark a turning point in inter-Korean relations.

제17차 런던서미트 (1991.7)

(의장성명)

7. We look forward to North and South Korea's admission to the
United Nations and to the resumption shortly of high-level dialogue
between the two countries. North Korea's continuing failure to
sign and implement a nuclear safeguards agreement remains an issue
of major concern.

0178

외 무 부

110-760 서울 종로구 세종로 77번지 / (02)720-2188 / (02)725-1737 (FAX)

문서번호 통기 20644-194

시행일자 1992. 6. 10.(수)

취급		통 상 국 장
보존		
국 장	전 결	
심의관		
과 장		
기 안	이 시 형	협조

수신   국제경제국장

참조

제목   뮌헨 G-7 서미트에 대한 아측입장

표제건 검토결과, 당국 소관업무중 해당사항 없음을 통보합니다. 끝.

통   상   국   장

0179

외 무 부

종 별 :

번 호 : FRW-1196

일 시 : 92 0610 1800

수 신 : 장 관 (통기,구일)

발 신 : 주 불 대사

제 목 : ur 협상 동향

1. 당지 6.10자 'LE FIGARO'지는 최근 UR협상 동향과 관련, 미국과 EC 간 농업분쟁이가까운 시일내 종결되고 UR 협상타결 전망이 가시화되고 있으며, 양측간 타협이 G-7뮌헨 정상회담(7,6-7) 전에 이루어질 가능성이 있다고 보도함.

2. 동 전망의 근거로서 지난 5.27 와싱턴 미.EC 회의에서 J.BAKER 미 국무장관이F.ANDRIESSENEC 집행위 부위원장에게 EC 농산물 수출한도를 DUNKEL 안의 02:OBVA로제의하였으며, 이에 대해 EC 측은 대응입장을 준비중에 있다 함.

3. 상기 전망이 실현되기 위해서는 우선 EC내부의 의견일치를 위한 회원국간 입장조정이 이루어져야 할것이며 특히 보조금 삭감에는 동의하나 수출물량 한도 설정에는강력 반대해온 불란서의 태도변화가 관건인 바, 이를 위해 EC집행위는 회원국들로 하여금 불란서에 대해 공동압력을 가하도록 요청할 것으로 보임.

4. 미국과 EC 는 농산물 갈등이 해결방안 모색에 있어 국내정치에 미칠 영향을 우려하고 있는 바, EC 측은 유럽 농민의 희생에도 불구하고 미측 압력에 굴복한 것으로비판받아왔던 92.5. CAP 개혁에 이어 또다시 농민들의 감정을 자극하지 않도록 신중을 기할것으로 보이며, 미측도 EC 와의 타협이 부시대통령의 선거운동에 미칠 부정적영향에 대한 우려를 불식하지 못하고 있음.

5. 동지는 UR 협상 일정과 관련, 92.11.월중 미대선 직후에 타결안이 최종 확정,서명되고 93년 봄 미의회에서 비준될 것으로 전망하면서, 미 대선 결과 및 불란서의93.3 총선으로 인해 동 일정이 다소간 영향을 받을수도 있으나, 지난 6년간의 UR협상이 이룩한 성과는 이제 포기될수 없다는 국제사회의 인식이 UR 협상의 최종타결을반드시 성사시킬 것으로 봄.끝.

(대사 노영찬-국장)

통상국 　 구주국

92.06.11 　 02:48 DW

외신 1과 통제관 ✓

0180

외 무 부

종   별 :

번   호 : ECW-0789   일   시 : 92 0612 1730

수   신 : 장관(봉기, 경기원, 재무부, 농림수산부, 상공부)

발   신 : 주 EC 대사 사본: 주 미, 제네바대사-중계필

제   목 : 갓트/UR 협상 추진동향

　　　최근 당관 이관용농무관이 당지에 주재하고 있는 각국의 주 EC 대표부 농무관
모임에 참석한 결과및 언론보도등을 종합한 표제 협상동향을 아래 보고함

　　　1. 7 월초 뮨헨에서 개최되는 G-7 정상회담에서 표제협상의 농산물분야에 대한
정치적 합의여부가 동 협상의 연내 종결여부와 직결되리라는 예상이 높아가고 있음.
한편 당지의 일부 전문가들은 OILSEEDS 분야에대한 미.EC 간의 분쟁, EC 의
바나나제도개편 문제가 표제협상 타결에 미칠 부정적인 영향을 우려하고 있음

　　　2. 최근 합의한 EC 의 CAP 개혁내용이 미측을 충분히 만족시키지도 못하였고 또한
동 개혁시행시 CEREALS 수출물량을 어느정도 감축할수 있는지에 대한 분석
(가격인하의 생산감축 효과및 15% SET ASIDE 의 확고한 이행여부 불부명) 도 어려우나
미대봉령선거, KOHL 수상의 정치적 입지및 EC 의 결속강화 필요성등 정치적인 측면을
고려할때 뮨헨 G-7 정상회담이전 즉 6 월중에 미.EC 간 농산물분야에 대한 정치적
합의를 이룰수 있다는 전망이 지배적임 (미, 카나다, 호주, 이스라엘 농무관은
공정적, 스위스, 오지리 농무관은 부정적의견)

　　　3. 미.EC 간의 농산물관련한 미해결분야는 수출보조금, CAP 개혁에따른 소득보조의
GREEN BOX 및 PEACE CLAUSE 문제이나 수출보조금 감축량 문제가 관건이며 미국은 24%
감축량을 고수하는 대신에 감축기간을 연장하자는 입장이고 EC 는 소맥수출물량
감축폭을 약간 줄이는 대신에 보리등 곡물의 감축물량을 늘리자는 입장이나 양측의
입장을 조화한 방안을 강구하는 것은 어려운 과제는 아니라고 분석하고 있음 (다음주
BAKER 장관의 브랏셀방문시 동문제가 심도있게 협의될것으로 봄)

　　　4. OILSEEDS 와 관련한 미국의 발표는 정도가 지나치다는데 의견을 같이하고 동
발표는 미대봉령 선거에서 BUSH 대봉령의 열세등 내부 정치적 전략이며 동OILSEEDS
문제와 UR 협상은 별개 사안이므로 UR 협상에 큰 영향을 미치지는 않을 것이라는

통상국	장관	차관	2차보	구주국	분석관	정와대	안기부	경기원
재무부	농수부	상공부						

PAGE 1   92.06.13   05:41

분석이 지배적이었음. 한편 OILSEEDS 문제는 미.EC 양자협상을 통해 해결될 것으로 전망하고 있음

　5. EC 의 바나나 시장제도 개편과 GATT/UR 협상

　가. EC 의 바나나문제는 수입제도와 단일시장 발족에따른 바나나시장 통합이라는 두가지 문제가 있는바 시장통합 측면에서 독일및 베네룩스 국들이 바나나의 소비자 가격상승을 강하게 반대하고 있으며 수입제도 개편문제를 갓트규범과 UR 협상에 조화시키는 방안도 쉬운 과제가 아님

　나. 지난번 워싱턴 회담시 BAKER 장관은 달라바나나 생산국입장을 대변하여ANDRIESSEN 위원에게 EC 의 바나나 시장개방을 강력히 요구한바 있으며 그이유는 달라바나나 생산국들중 3 개국가가 갓트 회원국이 아니기 때문에 동 국가들이 공동으로 갓트 체제내에서 해결방안을 강구하기 어렵기 때문임

　다. 바나나수입제도 개편과 관련하여 EC 는 WAIVER 획득, TARIFFICATION 적용예외및 TARIFF 쿼타적용 방안등을 검토하고 있으나 TARIFF 쿼타를 활용하는 방안이 채택될 것으로 전망됨 (7 월중 결정예정) 한편 EC 는 UR 협상에서 계속 예외없는 TARIFFICATION 을 공약한바 있고 미국과의 관계때문에 갓트 11 조 2 항 개정제안국에 합류할 가능성은 없으며 바나난 TARIFFICATION 을 적용하되 TE 를 200% 이상으로 갓트에 제출한후 DUNKEL 타협안에 따라 TE 를 감축하는 한편, ACP 국가및 EC 해외영토의 바나나 생산및 유통구조 개선을 위한 보조금을 지급하는 방안이 채택될 가능성이 높다고 분석함 (카나다, 이스라엘, 노르웨이, 일본농무관). 끝

　(대사 권동만-국장)

이미(외)

관리 번호	92-421

외 무 부

종 별 :

번 호 : GVW-1207 일 시 : 92 0617 1700

수 신 : 장관(통기,경기원,재무부,농림수산부,상공부,특허청)

발 신 : 주 제네바 대사

제 목 : UR 협상 일정

1. 최근 UR 협상과 관련 이미 확정되었거나 당관이 파악하고 있는 당지 주요일정은 아래와 같음.

- 6.17(수) DUNKEL TNC 의장 주최 주요국 만찬

- 6.10(수) 이후 써비스 분야 다자간 및 양자간 협의 진행중

- 6.17(수) 시장접근 분야 CS 제출국 비공식 협의(6.16 사전 지역별 비공식협의개최)

- 6.18(목) 미(WARREN LAWOREL 대사), EC(PAEMAN 총국장), 일(ENDO 대사), 카나다(DENIS 의장)간 QUAD 고위 실무급 회의

- 6.28(일) CAIRNS GROUP 각료회의

- 6.25(목) 경부터 법제화 그룹 협의 재개 검토중

2. 한동안 정체 상태에 있던 UR 협상이 6.17 DENKEL 만찬을 중심으로 분야별로 재개되고 있는 것은 아래 2 가지 사항이 복합적으로 고려된것으로 당지에서는 일반적으로 관측하고 있으나, 앞으로의 협상 추진 방향 및 이에 따른 전망등은 동 사항이 논의될 것으로 보여지는 DUNKEL 만찬이후 종합 보고 예정임.

- CAP 개혁합의, BAKER-AUDRIESSEN 회담이후 7 월초 문헨 정상회담을 앞두고 미.EC 간 합의가 이루어질수도 있다는 다소의 가능성에 대비, 제네바에서도 가능한 노력을 전개 및 대미.EC 압력수단

- GATT 의 하계 휴가기간등과 연계되어 UR 협상이 장기 정체 상태에 빠짐으로써 협상의 전기(MOMENTUM) 가 상실되는 위험을 사전 예방. 끝

(대사 박수길-국장)

예고 92.12.31. 까지

일반문서로 재분류 (1992. 12. 4)

검 토 필 (199 . . .)

통상국 재무부	장관 농수부	차관 상공부	1차보 특허청	외정실	분석관	정와대	안기부	경기원

PAGE 1

92.06.18 05:42

외신 2과 통제관 FK

0183

외 무 부

종 별 :

번 호 : GVW-1240   일 시 : 92 0619 1930

수 신 : 장관(통기,경기원,재무부,농림수산부,상공부,특허청,청와대 외교안보,

발 신 : 주 제네바 대사   경제수석,사본:주미,주이씨대사(중계필)

제 목 : UR 의 현황 및 전망 협의(DUNKEL 총장과의 만찬)

1. DUNKEL 총장은 6.17(수) 아국 , 미국, 일본등 20 여개국 대사를 만찬에 초대, UR 현황 및 전망을 평가하고, 향후 대처 방안에 대하여 협의한바, 던켈총장은 각국대사의 의견을 청취한 후 하기와 같은 평가를 내림

가) 현재 UR 협상은 완전 정돈 상태에 빠졌다는 의견에 대체적으로 동의함.

나) 7 월 G-7 정상회의 이전에 미국, EC 간에 농산물에 관한 합의가 이루어지고, 또 동 합의내용이 최종 의정서(DFA)와 큰 거리가 없을때에는 UR 타결의 전망은 극히 밝아짐.

다) 7 월전에 미국, EC 합의가 없을 경우에는 TRACK 1,2,3 등을 실질적으로가동시킬수 없으며 UR 전망은 극히 비관적일 수 밖에 없음

라) 7 월 이전 타결이 없고 협상이 11,12 월로 연장될 경우에는 미국 FAST TRACK AUTHROITH 시한에 비추어 실기가 되어 최악의 사태가 발생할 것임.

마) UR 의 교착의 책임을 정치인에게 돌리는데는 동의할 수 없으며 사태 해결의 관건은 당지 제네바 대사급 협상자에게 전적으로 달려있다고 봄.

사) 협상이 7 월 이전까지 타결되지 않을 경우에는 7 월중 TNC 회의를 소집하여 모든 대처방안을 토의해 보겠음.

2. DUNKEL 총장은 위의 결론을 내린후 현재 TRACK 1,2 협상에서 전혀 진척이 없는 이유중의 하나는 자기의 전술적 실책에도 기인한다고 전제하고, 1.13.TNC 회의에서 네개의 TRACK 을 설정한 이유는 규범적인 기초(RULE-MAKING BASIS)에서 결론을 내리기 보다는 시장개방, 써비스에서 상화 균형된 이익을 교환케 함으로써 DFA 의 수락을 촉진시킬려는 의도였으나 차라리 네개의 TRACK 을 설정하기 보다는 DFA 에 대한 각국정부의 "TAKE IT OR LEAVE IT"의 입장을 요청하는 것이 옳았다는 사후 평가를 함

3. 한편 각국대사의 평가는 대체로 아래와 같았음 일반문서로 재분류 (19__.12. 31

통상국 농수부	장관 상공부	차보 특허청	분석관 중계	청와대	청와대	안기부	경기원	재무부

O 호주: TRACK 1,2 를 아무리 가동해 봐야 미국, EC 간에 합의가 없는한 협상에 진척이 있을수 없으며, 현재 협상은 완전히 정치적 차원에서 BLOCK 되어있음. 이런 현실을 가장없이 솔직하게 각국 정부에 알려서 대책을 강구해야 할것이며, 진척이 없는 것을 무엇인가 움직이고 있다는 인위적인 인상을 만들 필요가 없으며, 사태 타개책이 조속 발견되지 않으면 UR 은 중대한 위기에 처한다는 분명한 MESSAGE 를 각국 수도에 보내야 함.

O 인도: TRACK 1,2,3 중에서 TRACK 3 만 가동하고 있을뿐이며, 1,2 는 완전히 공전하고 있음. 아울러 신문에서 UR 협상이 재개된 것 처럼 가장을 하더라도 농업문제와의 연결로 인하여 진척임 불가하며, 농업문제가 여타문제의 해결을 촉발해야 함.(TRIGGER). 인도로서도 TEXTILE 등 많은 분야에서 문제점을 갖고 있는데 농업등 시장접근 분야에서 감지할 수있는 이익을 확보하지 않고는 무엇을 양보할 수 없음. TRACK 1,2 의 역할이 중요함에도 불구하고 이분야에서 진전이 없는 것이 타결을 더욱 어렵게하고 있으며, UR 은 현재 완전마비상태임.

O 미국: 작년 12 월, 금년 1 월에 비해 협상은 크게 후퇴하여 당시만 하더라도 UR 타결의 전망은 아주 밝은 것으로 보였으나, 그후의 사태추이와 각국의 정치적 상황(POLITICAL BACKDROP)은 불행스러울정도로 UR 타결에 도움을 주지 못하고 있음. 어느나라도 현 DRAFT 를 본격적으로 수정할려고 기도한다면 그것은 UR 의 UNRAVELLING 를 뜻하는 것임. EC-미국 교섭의 지지부진한 현황으로 보아 일단 교섭을 재내바로 갖고와서 다시 다원화 할 필요가 있을 지도 모르겠음.

EC-미국 협상의 전망은 현재로서 밝지 못하다고 보아야함.

O 우루과이: 신문에 UR 이 진척이 있는것 처럼 보도토록 하는 것은 일종의 사기임. 자신은 금일 MA, 써비스 회의가 개최되었으나 진척이 있을수 없다는 것을 알고 있기때문에 아예 참석도 하지 않았음.

차라리 UR 교섭을 6 개월 이라도 연장하여 새로운 MOMENTUM 을 찾도록 하는것이 좋을것임. 그리고 현교착의 책임 소재를 분명히 밝혀서 정직하게 사태를 정면으로 직시하고 대책을 강구해야 할것임. 7 월 G-7 정상회담 이전에 타결책이발견되지 않으면 UR 은 실패할것임.

O 일본: 지금은 UR 을 개시한 이래 가장 어려운 시기이며, UR 은 완전교착 상태라는 견해에 전적으로 동감함. 우리는 사태를 직시하고 현황을 정직하게 진단해야 함. 예외없는 관세화만 하더라도 일본은 DELIEVER 할수 없다는 사실을 인식해야 함.

0185

농산물 분야 BREAKTHROUGH 없이 씨비스 분야 진척이 있을수 없으며, MA 등에 어떤 진전도 기대할수 없음.

매일매일 아무런 성과없이 시한만을 잃어가고 있는바 UR 타결은 더욱 멀어져가고 있음.

0 항가리: 오늘의 사태는 특정국가만의 책임이 아니고 모든 참가국의 집단적 책임으로 봐야 함. 모든국가가 함께 노력하여 양자간에 BREAKTHROUGH 가 있도록 해야 함. 호주대사의 진단은 전적으로 옳은바, 현상을 그대로 본국에 보고하여 결단을 촉구하는 것이 좋을것임.

0 홍콩, 알젠틴: 우선 OFFER 제출국 수를 봐도 홍콩등 23 개국에 지나지 않으며, 이것이 현실임. 이젠 DEADLINE 은 하도 많이 연기해서 우리가 본국정부에 대해서 모든 CREDIBILITY 를 잃어버렸음. 정직하게 본국정부에 현황을 보고하고 TNC 도 빨리 개최하여 대책을 강구해야 할것임.

0 뉴질랜드 : 미국, EC 합의없이 TRACK 3 를 개최하거나, 교섭을 GENEVA 로갖고 온다고 하여 문제가 해결되는 것은 아님. 양자간의 조속한 정치적 타결을촉구함.

0 멕시코: TRACK 1,2 의 진전은 농업문제에 대한 명백한 타결없이는 불가능하다는 의견에 전적으로 동감임. TRACK 3 은 향후 동향에 대비, 계속 가동하여 결실을 쌓아가야 할것이며, MOMENTUM 을 계속 유지한다는 면에서도 중요한 역할을 하고 있음.

(GVKW-1241 로 계속됨)

외 무 부

종 별 :

번 호 : GVW-1241   일 시 : 92 0619 1930

수 신 : 장관(통기, 경기원, 재무부, 농림수산부, 상공부, 특허청, 청와대 외교안보,

발 신 : 주 제네바 대사   경제수석, 사본:주미, 주이씨대사(중계필)

제 목 : GVW-1240 호의 계속

태국: 협상때마다 본부에서 많은 대표를 파견토록 건의하였으나 그동안 실적이 없어 본국정부에 대해 CREDIBILITY 를 모두 잃었음. 조속 대책 강구 필요함.

0 EC: 미-EC 간에 진척이 상당히 있으며, 가까운 장래에 타결 가능성이 없다고 할수 없는바 각국은 EC 의 입장을 도와주어야 할 것임. 농업 분야는 말할 필요도 없고, MA, 써비스등 분야에서 EC 의 어려운 입장을 이해하고, 타결을 도와야 할 것임. EC 에 관한한 사안의 GLOBALITY 가 극히 중요한바, 미국도 이점을분명히 이해해야 할것임.

0 파키스탄: 정돈 사태 타개를 위해서는 UR 을 정적으로 당분간 연기하든지또는 DEADLINE 를 다시 설정, 새로운 노력을 경주해야 하며, 전체 교섭을 GENEVA 로 갖고 와야 할 것임.

0 한국: 정돈 상태 진단에 원칙적으로 동감이나 현 싯점에서 지나친 좌절은금물이며, 정돈 상태의 주된 책임은 EC, 미국에 있으나, 여타 참여국도 각자의몫을 다하고 있는지를 성찰해보아야 할 것임. 아직도 C/S 를 제출치 않은 국가가 있을 뿐만 아니라, 제출하였더라도 내실이 없는 경우가 많음 아국의 예외없는관세화에 대한 반대는 확고하며, 아국에서는 작년 40 일 동안에 1300 만명이 쌀시장 개방에 반대 서명 하였는바, "기네스북"에 수록될 정도로 반대의 강도가 강했다는 점을 지적함.. 전 참여국이 예외없는 관세화에 동의함으로서 아국이 유일한 반대자로 남는 경우를 상정할 수 있으나 그러한 경우에 취할 입장은 현싯점에서 밝힐수 없음(DUNKEL 및 미국대사의 질문에 대한 답변)

4. 관찰 및 평가

0 동 모임에서 DUNKEL 총장의 평가는 언제나 여운을 남기면서 다소 희망적인 평가를 하던 지금까지의 태도와 대조를 이루었는바, 그것은 EC, 미국간의 7 월전 타결

통상국 장관 2차보 분석관 청와대 청와대 안기부 경기원 재무부
농수부 상공부 특허청 중계

전망이 현재로서는 극히 불투명하고, 또 이런 상황에서 TNC 를 개최한다 하더라도 별다른 묘책을 찾을수 없다는 현실적인 평가 때문일 것으로 관찰되었음.

O 모든 참여자가 UR 이 현재 BLOCK 되어 있다는데 의견의 일치를 보이고 대치 방법에 대해서는 EC-미국간의 조속 합의를 촉구하는 이외에 뚜렷한 방안 제시치 못하였으며, EC 는 다소 낙관적이었으나, 미국은 협상의 GENEVA 복귀등 사실상 EC, 미국 타결 가능성에 상당히 비관적 견해를 전제로 사태를 분석함.

O 7 월 G-7 정상회담시까지 미-EC 농산물 분야의 이견이 타결되지 않을 경우, 협상의 금년내 타결이 불가능할 것이라는 것이 참석대사들의 대체적 평가임에 비추어 당분간 G-7 정상회담때까지 협상은 현 상태로 계속 될 것이며, G-7 정상회담 결과를 보아 7 월중 TNC 개최등 대책을 마련할 것으로 보임.

5. 참고로 동회의 참가국은 미국, 카나다, 일본, 멕시코, 알젠틴, 홍콩, 태국, 모로코, 인도, 스위스, 한국, 파키스탄, 호주, EC 등 20 여개국임. 끝

(대사 박수길-장관)

예고 92.12.31. 까지

검 토 필 (1992.6.??.)

상 공 부

503-9457

427-760 경기 과천시 중앙동 1번지 / 전화(02)500 - 2423 / 전송(02)504 - 6280

문서번호 산정 28010 - 283

시행일자 1992. 6. 20.(   )

(경 유)

수신 외무부 통상국장

참조

선결			지시	인그리	
접	일자시간	92.6.22	결재·공람		
수	번호	22603			
	처리과				
	담당자	신복남.			

제목 UR 최종협정문안중 의문사항 확인

'91.12.20 TNC에 제출된 UR 협상 최종협정문안중 section I. Subsidies and Countervailing Duties 내용의 해석과 관련하여 다음과 같은 의문이 제기되고 있는 바, 귀부에서 제네바 현지대표부를 통하여 그 정확한 의미를 파악하여 우리부에 알려주시기 바랍니다.

* 다   음 *

해 당 부 분	해 석 필 요 사 항
Article 8.2(a)중 "the assistance covers not more than"	"assistance"의 의미가 총지원금액인지 순지원금액(실질적 수혜금액)인지 여부
Article 28(ii)	협정문 Part III의 Actionable Subsidies에 대해서도 협정발효후 3년간 상계조치대상에서 제외되는지 여부
Article 2.1	Specific industry의 기준이 SITC 2단위인지 4단위인지 여부
Article 3.1(b)	중간소재.부품산업에 대한 지원도 금지보조금에 해당되는 여부

끝.

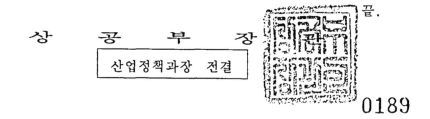

상 공 부 장

산업정책과장 전결

0189

관리
번호 92-440

외 무 부

종 별 :

번 호 : USW-3180   일 시 : 92 0623 1856

수 신 : 장관(봉기),봉이,봉일,경기원,농림수산부,상공부,경제수석)

발 신 : 주 미 대사

제 목 : MOSCOW USTR 부대표 접촉 결과 보고

1. 당관 구본영 공사는 6.23. USTR 의 MICHAEL MOSCOW 부대표와 오찬을 같이하며 상호 관심사에 대하여 의견을 교환하였는바, 그 주요내용을 보고함.(BOB CASSIDY 대표보 동석)

- 동 부대표는 UR 전망에 대해서 '이제 공은 EC 쪽에 있다', '결렬되기 보다는 시간이 다소 지연되더라도 언젠가는 끝나지 않겠느냐' 하며 비교적 담담한 반응을 보였음.

- 7 월초 뮌헨 G-7 정상회담이 하나의 계기가 될 것이라고 지적하기는 하였으나 큰 희망을 거는 표정은 아니었음.

- 구공사가 회담을 결렬시키는 것보다 조금 더 양보해서 타결짓는 것이 낫지 않겠느냐고 반응을 타진한데 대해 미국내의 반발, 타농산물 수출개도국들의 반발로 더 이상의 양보가 불가능하며, 농산물 협상이 성공적으로 이루어지지 않을 경우 UR 의 성공은 있을수 없다고 단언

- 한국이 제출한 농산물 OFFER LIST 는 너무도 기대에 못미치는 수준이라고 실망을 표시하며 한국측도 미.EC 협상결과만을 기다리지 말고 보다 적극적으로 기여해 줄 것을 촉구(구공사는 이에대해 모든 나라가 미.EC 농산물 협상결과를 기다리는 상황에서 한국측에 적극적 기여를 요청하는 것은 현실적인 기대가 아니라고 지적)

- NAFTA 가 곧 타결될 것이라는 전망이 자주 보도되는데 대해서 의견을 문의한바, 동 부대표보는 '그렇게 희망하고 있기는 하나 아직도 어려움이 많이 남아 있다' 하고 이 역시 최근 언론보도 보다는 다소 조심스러운 반응을 보임.

- 동 부대표보는 쌍무관계에 대해서는 PEI 진전상황에 대하여 만족을 표시하며 쇠고기 협상 전망과 관련, 97 년 한국측의 국내적으로 전면개방 준비를 하고 있는지 문의

일반문서로 재분류 (1992 12. .31)

통상국	장관	차관	2차보	통상국	통상국	분석관	청와대	안기부
경기원	농수부	상공부						

PAGE 1

92.06.24   10:17
외신 2과 통제관 BX
0190

- 구공사는 이에대해 올해 협상에서는 SBS 제도 개선과 '쿼타' 증량제도를 기대할수 있을 것이며, 5 년후의 일인 97 년의 쇠고기 시장 전면 개방문제에 대해서는 합의를 기대하는 것이 비현실적이라고 답변

- 한편 동석한 CASSIDY 대표보는 한국측이 지적재산권 문제에 대해 보다 적극적으로 대처하여야 할 것이라고 강조하며 최근 대만의 지적재산권 보호 강화 노력을 크게 평가

2. 한편, MOSCOW 부대표와 구공사는 일본문제에 대해서도 상호 의견을 교환하였는바, 동 부대표는 한국정부의 일본과의 접촉 내용에 대해서 큰 관심을 표명하며 앞으로 일본과의 통상협상 관련 상호 정보를 교환하기를 희망하였음. (이와관련 6 월말로 예정되어 있는 것으로 알려진 한. 일 산업기술협력 강화 방안이 마련되는 대로 당관에도 통보바람). 끝.

(대사 현홍주-국장)

예고: 92.12.31. 까지

검 토 필 (19~1.30.)

외 무 부

종 별 :

번 호 : JAW-3659   일 시 : 92 0624 1903

수 신 : 장관(경일,봉기,미이,정특,동구일)

발 신 : 주 일 대사(일경)

제 목 : 뮌헨 G-7 서미트

대 : 1) WJA - 2773, 2) WJA - 2767

연 : JAW - 3421

대호, 당관 정성배 참사관이 6.23(화) 표제관련, 주재국 외무성 경제국 미네 총무참사관(뮌헨서미트 일본 SHERPA 보좌)을 접촉한 바, 동 접촉결과를 아래 보고함

1. 뮌헨서미트 관련 아측입장 전달

가. 아측의 한반도 평화정착 및 북핵문제에 대하여, 지난 6.11. 허승차관보가 마쓰우라 외무심의관 면담시 아측 기본입장을 기 전달한 사실을 우선 상기 시키고, 대호 1) 문안(영문)을 수교하면서 아측 입장이 필히 정치선언 또는 의장 SUMMARY 에 포함되도록 요청하였음.

나. 이에 대하여 동인은, 아. 태지역 문제에 대하여는 서미트에서 주로 일본이 관례적으로 제기하여 왔다고 하면서, 금차 회의에서도 한반도 및 캄문제 등이 제기될 것이며, 한반도 문제 특히 북한 핵문제에 관하여는 일본의 입장도 확고한 만큼, 금번 회의결과에 아측 입장이 표명되도록 검토, 조치 하겠다 함.

2. 뮌헨서미트 의제별 논의동향

가. 세계경제 거시정책 조정

1) 금번 뮌헨서미트 의제중 러시아지원 문제와 공히 가장 주요한 이슈로서, 작년에 마이너스 성장을 보인 세계경제가 금년들어 다소 호전의 기미는 있으나 상금 불안정 상태인 바, 세계경제의 지속적 성장을 유도하기 위하여는 G-7 의 개별적인 일시적 재정적자 증액을 통한 성장 추진보다는, G-7 내의 전체적인 경제정책 조정이 매우 긴요하므로, 이에대한 집중 토의가 예상된다 함.

2) 현재 G-7 각국이 처한 경제 현안은, 미국의 금년말 선거대비 실업해소 문제, 일본의 내수확대 및 무역흑자 축소, 독일의 인프레억제, 재정적자 축소, 프랑스의

경제국	장관	차관	1차보	미주국	구주국	룡상국	외정실	분석관
정와대	안기부							

PAGE 1   92.06.24   22:35

외신 2과 룡제관 FM

0192

금리인하와 주로 EC 각국의 금리인하를 통한 성장률 제고 및 실업 감축방안문제등인 바, 특히 동구 및 NIS(구쏘련내 NEWLY INDEPENDENT ST.) 지원으로 경제적 곤란을 겪고있는 독일의 금융정책 문제가 금번 서미트에서 중점 협의될 것이라 함.

나. NIS 지원

1) 원전 안전성 제고문제

현재 동구 및 구쏘련내 소재 원전 25 기(체르노빌형 15 기, 경수로형 10 기)가 응급수리를 요하며, 동 발전소 관리 요원에 대한 훈련소 설치 연수를 통하여 원전의 안전성 확보가 시급한 바, 이러한 사업에 필요한 약 7 억불의 자금과 관련, 동 자금의 조달방법, 운영방안(EBRD 협력 또는 양자간 협력 등)에 대한 협의가 있을 것임.

2) 핵물질 유출방지

특히, 러시아가 많이 보유하고 있는 핵무기 및 핵물질의 관리태세 정비로, 방사능의 여타국에로의 유출 방지를 위한 방안이 협의될 것임.

3) 과학자지원 문제

현재 러시아내 핵관련 과학자 지원을 위한 센터가 미.일.러간 합의에 의하여 설치되었는 바, 핵이외 분야의 과학자에 대한 지원확대(프랑스의 제안) 여부 문제가 협의될 것임.

4) 대러시아 지원

(1) 금번 회의시 IMF 를 통한 대러시아 금융지원(240 억불)이 합의되어, 발표될 것임.

(2) 대러시아 지원과 관련하여는, 현재 원조국 협의체 구성을 위한 원칙합의 단계에 와 있는 바, 원조공여 방식에서 EC 주도 방식과 미국주도 방식 등 각국의 입장이 다소 상이하므로, 금번 회의시 협의될 것임. 일본은 금년 가을 동경개최 예정 제 3 차 CIS 지원 회의, 일.러간 관계 정상화 등 현안문제 등이 있어 양국간 지원 방식을 희망한다 함.

다. UR

현재 미국과 EC 간 농업문제로 교착 상태에 있는 UR 은, G-7 수뇌가 모인만큼 협상촉진 의지 표명선에서 의제에 포함, 토의될 것이나, 금번 회의시 구체적 타결안이나, 타결 기한 설정 등은 어려울 것으로 관측된다 함.(이는 주최국 독일이 금번 회의의 많은 시간을 NIS 지원 문제에 할당하려는 의도를 보이고 있기 때문이라고 언급)

PAGE 2

라. 지역분쟁 및 유엔기능 강화

유고 및 캄보디아 사태등 지역분쟁 해결을 위한 유엔의 역할강화 방안이 협의될 것임.

마. 인권, 지구환경

금차 회의시에는 인권관련 문제는 크게 제기되지 않을 것으로 본다하며, 환경문제는 최근 리우서미트가 끝난만큼 이를 환영하는 정도에서 언급될 것이며, G-7 에 의한 특별한 추가적 조치는 기대되지 않는다 함.

바. 아. 태지역 문제

일본의 관심 사항으로서, 동서 화해가 진행되어 가고 있는데도 아. 태지역의 정치적 경제적 질서가 아직 확립되지 않은 현실을 감안하고, 특히 러시아의 향후 대아. 태정책과 관련하여, 아. 태지역의 국제정치 질서확립, 개발문제 등을 거론, 협의코저 한다함. 끝.

(대사 오재희 - 국장)

예고: 92. 12. 31. 일반

검 토 필 (1992. 6. 30.)

이시(안)

원 본

외 무 부

종 별 :

번 호 : USW-3327

일 시 : 92 0630 1917

수 신 : 장관(봉기 봉이, 경기원, 농수산부) 사본: 주제네바, EC대사-중계필

발 신 : 주 미 대사

제 목 : UR 동향

당관 이영래 농무관과 김중근 서기관은 6.30. 농무부 해외농업처 RICHARD SCHROETER 처장보를 면담, G-7 정상회담에 즈음한 UR 관련 동향을 협의하였는바, 요지하기 보고함.

1. 최근의 UR 협상 진전사항 문의에 대해, 동 처장보는 J. OMERA 미 UR 농산물협상 실무대표가 지난주 제네바에 출장, EC 측등과 비공식 협의를 가졌으나 아무런 진전이 없었다고 하고, G-7 정상회담까지는 앞으로 일주일 밖에 남지 않았는데 향후 1 주일간 미-EC 간 UR 관련 협의가 예정되어 있지 않아, 현재로서는 G-7 정상회담에서 UR 협상과 관련한 극적인 타결을 기대하기는 거의 불가능할 것이라 전망함.

2. 또한 동인은 작년 7 월 런던 G-7 정상회담에서 각국 정상들은 UR 의 중요성을 재차 강조하고 이에대한 개인적 관심을 표명하는 내용의 GENERAL STATEMENT 를 발표하였음을 상기시키면서, 현재까지의 협상 진전상황에 비추어 각국 정상들이 개별 현안에 대해 구체적인 협의를 갖는 어렵고, 작년과 유사한 내용의 GENERAL STATEMENT 를 발표하는 수준에 그치게 될 것이라고 전망함.

3. 향후 UR 타결 전망 문의에 대해, 동 처장보는 현재의 상황으로 보아 금년 여름에 협상의 돌파구가 마련되기는 사실상 기대하기 어려우며, 9 월의 MAASTRICHT 조약 준비를 위한 프랑스 국민투표 및 11 월 미대통령 선거 일정등을 감안할때, 금년 11 월 까지는 진전이 없을 것으로 전망함.

4. 동 처장보는 개인적으로는 결국 UR 이 타결될 것으로 본다고 언급하며, 그 이유로는 CAP 개혁과 UR 협상에 적극성을 띠고 있는 영국이 금년 하반기에 EC의장을 맡게 되고, 주요 협상국들은 UR 실패시 예견되는 GATT 의 기능 축소, 보호무역주의 강화, 지역주의의 대두를 결코 방관치 않을 것이므로, 내년초 (2 월말 이전)까지는 어떠한 형태로든 정치적 타결이 이루어질 것으로 전망한다고 언급함.

통상국 농수부	장관 중계	차관	2차보	통상국	분석관	청와대	안기부	경기원

PAGE 1

92.07.01 09:28

외신 2과 통제관 BX

0195

5. FAST TRACK AUTHORITY 와 관련한 협상일정 문의에 대해, 동 처장보는 FAST TRACK 이 93.6.1. 종료되므로 FAST TRACK 발동 요건인 '의회의 행정부및 업계와의 90 일간(CALENDAR DAYS) 협의' 기간을 감안하여 역산할때

. 늦어도 2 월말까지는 UR 협정안에 가서명하고, 대통령이 협정체결 의사를 의회에 통보하여야 하며

. 상기 90 일간의 협의기간 이후에 관련 국내법이 준비되는 대로 FAST TRACK 에 의한 '90 회기일 (SESSION DAYS) 동안의 의회심의 및 무수정 표결'이 있게된다함. 끝.

(대사 현홍주-국장)

예고: 92.12.31. 까지

60.

PAGE 2

정 리 보 존 문 서 목 록

기록물종류	일반공문서철	등록번호	2020030179	등록일자	2020-03-16
분류번호	764.51	국가코드		보존기간	영구
명 칭	UR(우루과이라운드) 협상 동향 및 TNC(무역협상위원회) 회의, 1992. 전5권				
생 산 과	통상기구과	생산년도	1992~1992	담당그룹	
권 차 명	V.3 7-10월				
내용목차	* 1.13. TNC 회의 　　- 수석대표: 조일호 농림수산부 농업협력통상관 　　- Dunkel 협정문 초안(91.12.20.)을 기초로 협상(양자.다자) 추진 결정 　　- 4 track(상품 양허, 서비스 양허, 협정조문 법적 정비, 협정초안 수정 작업) 협상 전략 제시 　11.10. TNC 회의 　　- 미국.EC 간 양자협상 타결 촉구 　11.20. 미국.EC 농산물 협상 타결 　　- 공산품, 서비스 등 여타 분야 협상 결렬 　11.26. TNC 회의 　　- 협정문안 연내 확정 일정 승인 　12.18. TNC 회의 　　- 1992년 초 협상재개 결정				

0001

관리 번호	P2-416

외 무 부

종 별 :

번 호 : ECW-0902   일 시 : 92 0703 1700

수 신 : 장관 (봉기, 경기원, 재무부, 농림수산부, 상공부)

발 신 : 주 EC 대사   사본: 주 미, 제네바대사-중계필

제 목 : 갓트/UR 협상동향과 전망

    7.6-8 뮨헨 G-7 정상회담을 앞두고 표제협상과 관련, 최근 당지의 동향을
아래보고함

    1. 7.3 영국(EC 의장국) 정부 관계관에 의하면 MAJOR 수상은 KOHL 수상과
협조하여 G-7 정상회담 이전(주말)에 표제협상 타결방안을 모색하기 위한 미.EC간
양자협상 개최를 주선코자 노력하고 있으나 현재로서는 성사될 가능성이 희박한
것으로 알려짐. 한편 HURD 영국외상은 의회에서의 보고를통해 표제협상 타결을위해
최선을 다하고 있으며 CAP 개혁으로 말미암아 미.EC 간의 농산물분야에 대한 이견도
상당히 접근되어 있는 상태이므로 협상타결 가능성이 있다고 평가하고 뮨헨 G-7
정상회담에서도 논의될 것으로 본다고 말함

    2. 또한 7.3 EC 집행위 대변인은 DELORS 위원장은 7.7 G-7 정상회담과는 별도로
BUSH 대통령과 회담을 가질 것이라고 말하고 ANDRIESSEN EC 집행위 부위원장도 BAKER
미국무장관과 별도회담을 가질것임을 시사함. 동 대변인은 미.EC 간 정상회담의
의제에대해 밝히기를 거부하였으나 당지 관계관들은 표제협상 문제도 거론될 것으로
전망은 하나, 실질적인 성과는 기대하기 어려운 것으로 보고 있음

    3. 7.2 BUSH 대통령은 G-7 정상회담시 표제협상의 중요성에 비추어 논의될것으로
보나 주의제로 다루어지지는 않을것이며 금명간 타결방안이 도출되지 않을 경우,
단순히 협상을 지속할 것이라고 언급한 점등을 감안할때 미국은 표제협상의 추진에
소극적인 자세를 견지하고 있는 것으로 평가되며, 한편 불란서는 MAASTRICHT
조약비준을 위한 국민투표및 CAP 개혁에 반대하는 농민들의 움직임등국내
정치적문제로 인하여 표제협상과 관련한 현재의 입장변경에 난색을 표명하고 있어 EC
의 경우도 비록 영국, 독일등 다수 회원국들의 적극적인 움직임에도불구하고
표제협상의 조기타결 전망은 불투명한 것으로 보임

통상국 재무부	장관 농수부	차관 상공부	2차보 중계	구주국	분석관	정와대	안기부	경기원

PAGE 1   92.07.04   04:16

외신 2과 통제관 FM

0002

4. 뮨헨 G-7 정상회담에서 표제협상과 관련한 당지동향은 추보하겠음. 끝

(대사 권동만-국장)

예고: 92.12.31. 까지

외 무 부

종 별 :

번 호 : ITW-0880

일 시 : 92 0703 1910

수 신 : 장관(경일,통기,미이,정특,기정)

발 신 : 주 이태리 대사

제 목 : 뮌헨 G-7 서미트

1. 표제회의 관련 본직은 7.3.(금) 이태리측 차석 SHERPA 인 ALOISI 대사와 (외무성 경제부총국장) 면담하였는 바, 요지 다음 보고함.

2. 동대사는 금번 G-7 회의에서의 취급될 중요한 문제는 구소련지원, 세계경제활성화, UR 교섭, 환경문제등인 바, 이태리측이 특히 중점을 두는 측면은 구소련 지원문제라고 말하였음.

    가. 구소련 지원

    O 선진 7 개국 정상과 엘친대통령간 회담직후 대러시아 IMF 10 억불 지원이 발표될 예정인 바, 이는 엘친정부의 안정도를 높이는데 도움이 되는 한편, 대외적으로는 러시아의 지불능력을 제고, 그동안 러시아에 원조를 약속한 선진국들의 대 러서아원조를 계속토록 하는데도 기여할 것임.

    O CIS 지원조정회의는 올 가을 동경회의를 마지막으로 해체되고, 그대신 IMF, WORLD BANK 가 주관하는 자문그룹(CONSULTATIVE GROUP OF DONORS CHAIRED BY IMF-WORLD BANK)이 설치되어 운영될것임.

    나. 세계경제 활성화

    O 이자율 문제를 둘러싸고 미국, 독일간 현격한 입장의 차이가 있으며 이를 해소하기가 당면 불가능하기때문에, 금번 정상회담의 공동성명에서는 일반적인 표현을 사용하며 대외적으로 G-7 내부에 의견이 대립되어 있다는 인상을 피하는 문안, 즉 "세계경제를 활성화하는데 적극 노력키로 하며, 각국은 각자의 사정을 고려, 적절한 활성화 조치를 취해 나가기로 한다"는 내용이 될 것임.

    다. 우루과이 라운드

    O 최근 미국측이 EC 에 대하여도 일방적인 규제조치를 강화하고 있어 미.EC 간 UR 문제에 합의할 분위기가 조성되어 있지 못하며, 따라서 어떠한 실질적인 성과도

경제국   장관   차관   2차보   미주국   통상국   외정실   분석관   정와대
안기부

PAGE 1

92.07.04   04:34

외신 2과 통제관 FM

0004

기대되지 못하고 있음.

3. 대호 지시에 따라, 본직은 북한 핵문제가 정치선언에 포함되도록 적극 협조해 줄 것을 요청하였음. 끝

(대사 이기주-국장)

예고:92.12.31. 일반

이시 (の)

외 무 부

종 별 :

번 호 : GVW-1322   일 시 : 92 0702 1900

수 신 : 장관(통기) 사본:주미,주EC대사(중계필)

발 신 : 주 제네바 대사

제 목 : G-7 정상회담과 UR 협상 전망

　　　오는 7.6-8 간 개최 예정인 뮌헨 정상회담을 앞둔 현싯점에서 UR 협상의 전망에 대해 주요국 대사들의 한결같은 평가는 G-7 정상회담에서도 돌파구를 마련할수 없을 것이며 결국 오는 11 월 미국 대통령 선거시까지는 별다른 진전이 없을 것으로 보고 있는바, 요지 아래 보고함.

　　　1. 지난 5 월말 베이커-안드리이센 워싱턴 회담이후 미국의 LAVORELL 대사와 EC 의 PAEMAN 대외담당 부총국장간에 당지에서 일차 고위 실무접촉이 있었으나 아무런 진전을 보지 못하였으며, 현재로서는 G-7 정상회담을 전후해서 미.EC 간 접촉 계획도 없는 것으로 파악되고 있음.

　　　2. 리스본 EC 정상회담시 미테랑 불 대통령은 코 독일 수상과 가진 조찬회등에서 불란서로서는 오는 9 월 개최될 마스트리트 TREATY 에 대한 국민 투표 가격 통과에 최우선 순위를 두어야 한다는 입장 설명에 대해 콜수상도 이해를 표시한것으로 알려졌으며, 따라서 UR 협상과 관련한 입장 변경이나 진전은 기대할수 없는 상황인바, 현재로서는 UR 문제가 G-7 정상회담에서 정식 의제로 포함될 가능성도 거의 없으며, 불가피하게 논의된다 하더라도 작년 7 월 정상회담 수준에 준할 것이라는 의견임.

　　　3. 따라서, 지금부터 오는 11 월 미국 대통령 선거가 끝나는 싯점까지는 사실상 UR 에 관한 의미있는 협상의 진전은 어려울 수 밖에 없으며, 다만 9 월 이후 협상의 재개설이 DUNKEL 총장 중심으로 조심스럽게 거론되고 있으나, 미국 EC간의 합의없이는 실질적 협상이 불가능하다는 것이 당지의 지배적인 의견임.

　　　4. YERXA 미국 USTR 당지 대사 및 EC TRAN 대사는 오는 12 월 부터 내년 2 월 사이에 협상의 타결 가능성을 언급하고 있으나 인도, 북구, 아세안등 여타국 대사들은 시장접근협상의 현황에 비추어 부정적인 견해를 보이고 있으며, 특히 개도국 대사들은 12 월 이후 짧은 시간내에 본격적인 협상을 거치지 않고 미.EC 간에 합의된 결과를

통상국	장관	차관	1차보	구주국	분석관	청와대	안기부	중계

92.07.03   02:52
외신 2과 통제관 FK

0006

여타국에 강요하는 사태가 발생하지 않을까하는 우려를 가지고 있음.

5. 11 월 미 대통령 선거결과 부쉬 대통령이 재선에 실패하거나 대통령 선출이 의회의 손으로 넘어가게 되는 사태가 발생하는 경우에는 지금까지 이루어 놓은 UR 협상 결과는 거의 의미를 상실하며, 전혀 새로운 상황이 전개될수도 있을 것이라는 견해를 보이고 있음.

6. USTR 의 YERXA 대사는 6.24 당지 AMERICAN INT'L CLUB 에서 실업인들을 상대로한 연설에서 최근 EC 의 CAP 개혁안은 불충분하며, EC 가 새로운 제안을 제시해야 한다고 주장하였으며, 한편 6.27 자 ECONOMIST 는 UR 협상의 교창에 대해 미국의 책임을 부각시키고 있는등 미.EC 간에 교착 책임에 대해 홍보전이 강화되고 있는듯한 인상임. 끝

(대사 박수길-국장)

예고 92.12.31. 까지

PAGE 2

0007

외 무 부

종 별 :

번 호 : FRW-1431   일 시 : 92 0708 1720

수 신 : 장 관 (경일,구일,통기,동구일)

발 신 : 주 불 대사

제 목 : 뮌헨 G-7 정상회담

연:FRW-1390,1421

대:WFR-1270

표제회담 주요 의제의 7.7 논의결과 아래 보고함.

1. UR 협상

0 G-7 은 7.7 영국 MAJOR 수상의 중재안을 놓고 미국-EC, 영-불등 양자간 차원에서 UR협상의 교착타개를 시도하였으나 우선 EC 공동 농업정책에 대한 미측의 긍정적평가를 요구하는 불란서의 입장이 완강함에 따라 타협에 이르지 못함.

0 영국측의 제안은 농업보조금 감축기간을 6년이상으로 하고 수출물량 감축도 다소 완화(6년간 20프로,8년간 24프로) 하는것으로 골자로 하고있는바, 이에대해 미국은 긍정적 반응을 보인 반면 불란서는 9.20 'HAASTRICHT 조약' 비준을 위한 국민투표이후에야 본격적 협상이 가능한 국내 정치사정에 비추어 금번 회담에서 UR 의 타결을 원하지 않는다는 입장을 분명히 표시함.

0 G-7 은 이에 따라 UR 의 연내타결 노력을 최종 선언문에서 재천명할 것으로 보이나, 금번회담 과정에서 농산물 협상 주요 이견분야에서 상당한 진전을 보임에 따라 9.20 불란서의 국민투표 이후 본격적인 재협상을 통해 UR 의 년내타결 가능성이 커짐.

2. 대러시아 원조

0 엘친 대통령은 금일 G-7 정상에 대해 7.5 IMF 와 타결된 경제개혁 합의 내용을 직접 설명할 것인바 재정적자 감축(현재 GDP 의 17프로), 인플레 억제(현재 월평균15-20프로), 에너지 가격의 점진적 자유화 및 민영화 추진계획등 분야별로 구체적 내용이 될것임.

0 이에 대해 G-7 은 러시아의 자조노력을 돕기위한 구체적 지원방안을 표명할

경제국   2차보   구주국   구주국   통상국

92.07.09   07:30 DQ

외신 1과 통제관 √

0008

겄인바,애너지 분야 기술원조와 함께 단계별 신규차관 제공,91년이전 도입 외채에
대한 ' 관대한' 수준의 상환 재조정등이 포함될 것으로 예상됨.

　　3. 대개도국 원조

　　0 불란서가 가장 적극적으로 주창한 결과,중소득개도국에 대해서는 케이스별로
외채 감면조치를 계속 취해나가는 한편(이미 코트디브와르,카메룬,콩고에 대해
긍정적결정),최후진국(특히 사하라 이남 국가)에 대한 IMF '구조조정 강화 기금'을
1년 연장키로 합의함.

　　0 한편 일본은 향후 3년간 7억불 규모 아프리카 무상원조 계획을 발표함.

　　4. 동구 핵발전소 안전성 제고

　　0 7억불 기금설치 계획과 관련,연호 미국과 일본의 부정적 입장에 대해 불란서와
독일은 이는 새로운 기구창설이 아니며 현재 EC 가 여사한 원조를 이미 시행중에
있음을 지적코(91/92년 2.7억불 제공 약속,93년 1.3억불 예정),사안의 심각성에
비추어미,일의 양보를 촉구함.

　　0 이에 따라 G-7 은 각국 및 여타 기설립 국제기금으로 부터의 지원금으로 충당될
여사한 목적의 다자기금은 설치하되(금액 미정) 이를 G-24(대동구
원조조정기구)와EBRD 가 공동 관리토록 타협함.끝.

　　(대사 노영찬-국장)

관리
번호 92-114

외 무 부

종 별 :

번 호 : ITW-0905   일   시 : 92 0708 1820

수 신 : 장관(경일,봉기,미이,정특,기정)

발 신 : 주 이태리 대사

제 목 : 뮌헨 G-7서미트(자음 92-60)

연:ITW-0880

일반문서로 재분류 (1992. 12.31)

1. 연호 뮌헨 정상회담 관련 당지 언론평가내용을 다음 요약 보고함.

가. 세계경제 활성화방안(특히 이자율, 환율면)에 대해 정책 합의점을 찾지못하고 UR 문제도 타결하지 못한것과 관련 전반적으로 동성과를 부정적으로 평가하는 분위기임. 또한 구유고연방문제 해결에 있어서도 유럽국가와 미국간 이견이 대립, 헬싱키 CSCE 정상회의, 평화회의등 여타 국제회의로 미루어졌음에 대해유감을 표시하고 있음.

나. 그러나 다만, 세계경제문제에서 G-7 국가모두가 경기회복 노력필요성에인식을 함께하고, 실업해소등을 위해 적극 노력키로 한점, UR 문제 연내타결 목표설정, 소련원조 문제및 구유고 연방문제에 대해 일부 진전을 이룩한점을 부분적인 성과로 평할수 있을것임.

2. 상기 정상회담에 대한 주재국 정부의 평가는, 동회담에 참석한 대표단이7.9(목) 귀임하는대로 접촉, 추보하겠음. 끝

(대사 이기주-국장)

예고:92.12.31. 일반

경제국 안기부	장관	차관	2차보	미주국	롱상국	외정실	분석관	정와대

PAGE 1   92.07.09   02:06

외신 2과 롱제관 BZ

0010

외 무 부

종 별 :

번 호 : FRW-1441   일 시 : 92 0709 1700

수 신 : 장관(경일,구일,봉기)

발 신 : 주 불 대사

제 목 : 뮌헨 G-7 정상회담

대:WFR-1270

연:FRW-1390,1421,1431

표제회담 경제분야 결과에 대한 당지 평가 주요내용 아래 보고함.

1. G-7 은 각국의 상이한 정치, 경제적 이해관계에 비추어 조정된 입장을 통한 국제상황 대처에 있어 점차 무기력성을 나타내고 있음. 금번 회담에서도 세계경기 진작을 위한 총론적 당위성에는 공감하였으나 금리인하, 재정적자 감축, UR 협상등 세부 협조사항에 있어서는 어느하나도 구체적 합의에 이르지 못함.

2. 특히, 미국은 금번 회의직전 자국의 경기회복을 위해 금리인하 조치를 단행하였는 바, 이는 G-7 간 금리정책 합의 전망이 희박함에 따라 독자적으로 취한 조치로서 G-7 의 세계 경제문제 조정역할에 대한 미측의 불신을 반영한 것으로 보임.

3. 다자협의의 유용성에 대한 의문이 제기되는 가운데, 향후 G-7 간 협의는괄목할만한 합의도출 보다는 금번 동구 핵발전소 안전기금 창설과 같이 크게 부각되지는 않으나 효과적인 국제협력 사안과 함께 과거의 전통적 거시경제 정책조정보다는 미시경제 분야의 협력방안 모색등으로 점차 협의의 촛점이 옮겨갈 것으로 보임.

4. UR 협상은 금번 회담에서 정상간 특별한 타개노력이 없을 것이라는 일반적 예측과는 달리 회의시작 이전부터 불,미 정상회담을 비롯, 미.독, 영, 불, 미.EC 등 양자 차원에서 활발한 협상이 전개됨. 동 협상과정에서 미국은 자국 경기부양책의 일환으로 UR 타결 필요성에 대한 새로운 인식을 갖고 예상보다 적극적으로 협상에 임한 반면, 불란서는 92.9. 국민투표등 급박한 국내정치 일정상 소극적 자세를 견지할수 밖에 없었으며, G-7 내 불란서의 입장이 점차 고립되고 있는 것으로 보임.

5. UR 이 현단계에서 타결되기 위하여는 기술적인 협상보다는 미국과 EC (특히

경제국	장관	차관	2차보	구주국	통상국	분석관	청와대	안기부

92.07.10   02:08

외신 2과 통제관 BX

0011

불란서) 정상의 정치적 결단이 요구되는 바, 동 시기는 9.20 불란서 국민투표이후로 부터 미 대통령 선거 이전까지, 또는 미 대통령선거 직후로 예상되는 가운데 UR 의 년내 타결전망이 커짐.

6. 91 년 런던 회담시 고르바쵸프가 사실상 아무런 원조를 득하지 못한데 비해 금번 회담에서 옐친 대통령은 러시아 경제개혁에 대한 G-7 의 이해를 재고시키는 한편 신규차관, 외채상환 재조정 허용등 소기의 성과를 득하였는 바, 이는 러시아와 신뢰할수 있는 파트너 관계를 구축코자 하는 G-7 의 협력의지를 나타낸 것으로 보임.

7. 특히 금번 회담에서는 러시아를 G-7 에 포함시키는 문제에 관한 합의는 없었으나, 러시아의 국제 정치 경제적 위상에 비추어 향후 G-7 과 러시아간 공식,비공식 협의 관계가 더욱 강화될 것으로 예상됨.

8. 불란서는 금번 회담직전인 6.28 미테랑 대통령이 사라예보를 전격 방문한 외교적 이니시어티브와 여타 G-7 국가에 비해 상대적으로 건전한 경제상태를 배경으로 비교적 여유있게 금번 회담에 임함. 불란서는 비록 UR 협상에서는 수세입장에 있었으나 동구 핵발전소 안전성 제고, 대개도국 경제지원등에서 자국의입장을 강력히 피력하여 상당부분 반영될 것으로 평가하고 있으며 금번 회의 결과에 만족을 표함. 끝.

(대사 노영찬-국장)
예고:92.12.31. 까지

관리
번호 92-461

외 무 부

종   별 :

번   호 : ECW-0927   일   시 : 92 0709 1800

수   신 : 장관(봉기,경기원,재무부,농림수산부,상공부)사본:주미-중개필

발   신 : 주 EC 대사   주제네바대사(직송필)

제   목 : 뮨헨 G-7 회담결과(갓트/UR 협상)에대한 EC 의 반응과 협상전망

　　표제관련 당지언론및 당관의 관찰을 종합한 EC 측의 반응과 UR 협상 전망을아래
보고함

　　1. 일반적인 평가

　　가. G-7 회담개최 이전부터 BUSH 미대통령과 MITTERAND 불란서 대통령은 금번
회담에서 갓트/UR 협상의 구체적인 내용이 거론되는 것은 적절치 못하다는 의견을
제시한바 있고, 9.20 불란서의 국민투표, 11 월 미대통령 선거이전에 동 협상타결의
계기가 마련되기는 어렵다는 것이 일반적인 관측이었음

　　나. 그러나 금번 회담초부터 MAJOR 영수상, DELORS 위원장이 적극적인 입장을 취한
반면 BUSH 대통령과 미테랑 대통령이 소극적인 자세를 견지하였음에도 불구하고
협상의 새로운 DEADLINE 제시, 구체적인 미해결분야의 명시및 EC 의 CAP 개혁에 대한
긍정적인 평가등 종전의 G-7 회담에 비해 구체적이고 전진적인 내용이 회담결과에
언급되어 있는점을 긍정적으로 평가하고 있음

　　2. EC 의 반응

　　가. EC 집행위의 DELORS 위원장과 ANDRIESSEN 부위원장은 UR 협상의 조속한타결이
개도국및 구공산권 국가들을 포함한 세계경제 활성화에 기여할수 있으나 당분간 동
협상추진이 어려워졌음 (ANDRIESSEN 부위원장은 당분간 미.EC 의 구체적인 양자협상
계획은 없다고 밝힘) 에 유감을 표시하면서 EC/CAP 개혁이 동협상추진에 긍정적으로
기여한다는 점이 언급된 것을 높이 평가하고 미국및 불란서의 국내정치 일정으로
미루어 92.10 월경 부터는 협상이 본격적으로 이루어질 것으로 전망함. 한편 DUGIMONT
집행위 대외총국의 UR 협상담당 수석심의관도 주요 협상국들의 입장을 고려할때
최선의 결과가 아니겠느냐는 반응을 보임

　　나. MAJOR 영국수상은 UR 협상에서 각국간의 이견은 30 분 이내에 타결될수있을

| 통상국 | 장관 | 차관 | 2차보 | 분석관 | 청와대 | 안기부 | 경기원 | 재무부 |
| 농수부 | 상공부 | 증계 | | | | | | |

PAGE 1   92.07.10   03:07

정도로 근소하므로 EC 의장국으로서 자신은 앞으로도 동 협상의 조기타결을위해 세계정상들을 계속 접촉하고, 고무하여 협상을 촉진해 나갈것이라고 언급함

다. 한편, MITTERAND 불란서 대통령은 금번 정상회담에서 UR 협상타결에 재동역활을 했다는 여론을 부정하면서 9.20. 국민투표와 동 협상과는 무관함을 주장하고, 협상시한을 재설정한데 대해 환영을 표시하였으며, 협상타결을 낙관적으로 본다고 말함. 그러나 동 대통령은 EC/CAP 개혁에 상응하는 미측의 양보를 계속 요구하면서 연말까지 타결되지 않을 경우 내년까지도 동협상은 지속되어야 할것이라고 말함

라. KOHL 독일수상은 금년말까지 동 협상이 타결될것을 낙관한다고 말함

3. 향후 UR 협상전망

가. 금번 G-7 회담결과 MAJOR 및 KOHL 수상등의 활동이 적극성을 띨 것으로예상되나 UR 협상은 당분간 활성화되기는 어려울 것으로 보이며, 9.20 불란서 국민투표가 실시되고 미대통령 선거 막바지단계인 10 월경에나 미.EC 간의 양자협상이 재개될 것으로 예상됨. 그러나 이경우에도 미대통령 선거실시 이전에 실질적인 협상 또는 합의가 도출되기는 어려울 것으로 보이며 실질적인 협상은 11-12 월중 이루어질 것으로 전망됨

나. 그러나 금년말경의 협상의 미대통령 선거결과, 즉 BUSH 대통령의 재선여부에 따라 양상이 달라질 가능성도 있음. 끝

(대사 권동만-국장)

예고: 92.12.31. 까지

외 무 부

원 본

(안)

종 별 :

번 호 : GVW-1372   일 시 : 92 0710 2000

수 신 : 장관(통기, 경기원, 재무부, 농수부, 상공, 특허청)

발 신 : 주 제네바 대사

제 목 : G-7 정상회담관련

<del>일반문서로 재분류 (19</del>

1. 7.8 던켈 갓트 사무총장은 G-7 정상회담과관련하여,' G-7 정상들이

세계경제의 장래와 다수국들의 경제 개혁을지원하기 위하여 UR 성공의
중요성을강조한것을 환영하며, 동회담 COMMUNIQUE 에 제시된협상부진에 대한 유감과
균형된(BALANCED)합의가 진정 도출 가능하다(INDEED WITHINREACH)는 의견에 동감을
표하나,금번 회담에서보다 구체적인 진전이 없었음에

실망을 표시한다' 는 내용의 별첨 성명을발표하였음.

2. G-7 정상회담에 대하여 당초 부터도 커다란기대를 걸지는 않았으나, 협상
타결의 하나의중요한 계기로 일말의 기대를타결의 하나의중요한 계기로 일말의 기대를
걸고 있던 당지협상가들은 G-7 결과,

구체적진전이 없음에 상당히 실망하는 분위기이며

7.20(월) - 22(수) 사이에 농산물 주요국(8개국)회의 및 그린룸 회의 (개최 일자
미정)를 개최 향후 대책을 협의할 예정임. 끝.

(대사 박수길 - 국장)

첨부: 상기 성명 1부(GVW(F)-0428)

통상국   경기원   재무부   농수부   상공부   특허청

PAGE 1   92.07.11   08:14 BD

외신 1과 통제관

0015

주 제 네 바 대 표 부

번 호 : GVW(F) - 0428   년월일 : 20710   시간 : 2000

수 신 : 장   관 (통기, 경기원, 재무부, 농림수산부, 상공부, 특허청)

밤 신 : 주 제네바대사

제 목 : GVW-1372 첨부

총 2 매(표지포함)

브 안	
통 제	

외신과	
통 제	

428 - 2 - 1

Arthur Dunkel - Director-General of GATT

"I welcome the way in which the Heads of State and Government have stressed the significance of a success in the Uruguay Round for the future of the world economy and as a means of supporting the many governments undertaking economic reforms. This can only plead in favour of urgency.

Naturally all the participants in the Round share the regrets expressed in the Communiqué of the slow pace of negotiations and each one of them agrees that a balanced agreement is indeed within reach. Therefore, there will certainly be disappointment that this recognition has not led to a more substantial step forward in Munich. All participants must be committed to turning the expectation of agreement into reality."

Geneva, 8 July 1992, 13.40

0017

외 무 부

관리
번호 92-473

원 본

종 별 :

번 호 : USW-3524

일 시 : 92 0713 1926

수 신 : 장관(봉기, 경일, 경기원, 상공부, 농림수산부, 경제수석)

발 신 : 주 미 대사

제 목 : UR 동향

인반문서로 재분류 (1992. 12. 31)

1. 7.13. 당관 구본영 공사는 부쉬 대통령을 수행 뮌헨 G-7 정상회담 참석후 귀국한 ERIC MELBY NSC 국제경제담당 선임보좌관을 면담, UR 관련 동향을 청취하였던바, 동인 발언 내용중 언론에 기보도된 내용 이외의 참고사항을 보고함.

- 현재 언론에서는 UR 전망에 대하여 회의론이 지배적이나 G-7 정상회담에서 UR 문제가 수차례 걸쳐 논의되고 조기 타결의 필요성에 대해서 CONSENSUS 가 이루어진 것은 과거 정상회담에 비해서 큰 진전임.

- 특히 G-7 공동성명 내용에 '수출 보조금 물량과 관련한 문제에 진전이 있었다'는 표현이 구체적으로 삽입된 것은 중요한 발전으로서 미테랑 대통령은 그간 수출보조금 문제와 관련한 어떠한 문귀에도 합의한 적이 없었음.(미측은 처음에는 'REDUCING THE VOLUME OF SUBSIDIZED EXPORTS'라는 문귀를 주장하였으나 불란서의 반대로 'DEALING WITH...'로 바꿔었음)

- 현재 미.EC 간 수출보조금 문제를 둘러싼 입장의 차이는 매우 미미한 정도로 좁혀졌기 때문에 머지 않은 장래에 타결이 가능할 것으로 보임. 다만 현재로서는 EC 가 일체 입장을 변경하려고 하지 않고 있기 때문에 타결이 지연되고 있음.(5 월 BAKER-ANDERIESSON 회담시 미측 제안에 대해 아측 EC 측 반응 없음)

- 앞으로 6 개월만 영국 MAJOR 수상이 EC 의장 역할을 수행하면서 EC 내부적으로 합의도출을 위해 노력 예정이므로 EC 입장 변화를 통한 타결 기대(미국은지난 5 년간 계속 양보만 하여 왔으므로 미측의 양보를 촉구한 6.27. ECONOMIST 지 주장에 동의할수 없음)

- 9 월 불란서 국민투표는 UR 에 대한 것이 아니고 EC 통합에 대한 것이기 때문에 동 행와 관련없이 앞으로도 계속 미.EC 간에 협상이 계속될 것임.(미.EC 간 고위접촉 필요성에 대해서 미측은 G-7 공동선언에 구체적으로 포함하기를 원하였으나 EC 측

통상국 장관 차관 2차보 미주국 경제국 분석관 청와대 안기부
경기원 농수부 상공부

PAGE 1

92.07.15 00:04

외신 2과 통제관 EC

0018

434 우루과이라운드 협상 동향 및 무역협상위원회 회의 3

반대로 무산)

2. 동인은 현재 정상들의 UR 타결 의지가 그 어느때보다 강하기 때문에 년내 정치적 타결, 93.1-2 월중 타부문 포함 최종 UR 협상안 합의, 그리고 3.1. 미의회제출이라는 SCHEDULE 이 가능할 것으로 생각한다고 하였으나 EC COMMISSION 이 현재 역내 국가들을 효과적으로 대변할수 없는대 대해 우려를 표시하는등 낙관적인 입장만은 아니었음.

3. 동 보좌관은 또한 구공사와 면담시 CARLA HILLS 미 USTR 대표가 이번 정상회담에서 UR 관련 아무런 진전이 없다고 발언, 국무성과 의견이 다른 것으로 7.12. NYT 에 인용 보도 (USW(F)-4617)된 사실에 대하여 불만을 표시하며, 미 행정부내 부처간 시각차이도 UR 협상의 효과적 수행에 또하나의 문제점이라고 지적하였음. 끝.

(대사 현홍주-국장)

예고: 92.12.31. 까지

이시(여)

외 무 부

종 별 :

번 호 : USW-3527   일 시 : 92 0713 2021

수 신 : 장 관 (봉기, 봉이, 봉삼, 경일)

발 신 : 주 미 대사

제 목 : UR 동향

연 : USW-3524

1. 금일 (7.13) 당관 장기호 참사관은 USTR 의 DOROTHY DWOSKIN UR 담당 부대표보를 면담, 최근 G7 정상회담시 UR 관련 논의사항및 이에 대한 미측 평가를 문의하였는 바, 동인의 발언요지 하기 보고함.

- UR 에 한정시켜 볼때 금번 정상회담은 각국 정상들이 세계경제의 성장문제에 관심을 표시하여 간접적으로 UR 타결을 위한 분위기를 조성했다는 점에서는 긍정적으로 평가할 수 있으나, 구체적인 UR 타결 복안을 제시하지 못했다는 점에서는 실패 (BAD NEWS)로 평가할 수 있음.

- 메이저 영국 수상은 정상회담에서 UR 타결을 위해 새로운 제안을 하려고 하였으나 마스트리히트 조약 비준과 관련 9.20. 국민투표를 앞둔 미테랑 프랑스 대통령의 요청에 따라 이를 자제하였음.

- UR 농산물 분야의 핵심문제는 EC 측이 CAP 개혁안 (특히 국내보조금 삭감)을 던켈안에 어떻게 수용시키는가 하는 것이나 언론은 마치 EC 는 CAP 개혁으로 주어진 소임을 다했으며 이제는 미측이 움직여야 할 차례로 보도하고 있는데 이는 적절치 않음.

- 현재 미국조야에는 년내 UR 이 타결되지 않으면 영원히 안된다는 분위기가 싹트고 있으나 선거해에 미정부는 미국내 반응을 의식, 고정된 협상시한에 맞추지 보다는 좋은 협정을 얻는데 주안점을 두고 있음.

- 실무자의 입장에서는 설사 9.20. 프랑스의 국민투표 이후 UR 협상에 돌파구가 마련되더라도 농산물 분야는 물론, 아직도 미결문제가 많이 남아 있는 서비스와 시장접근 분야의 마무리 작업과 던켈안의 수정작업에 많은 시간이 소요되는 만큼, 년내 타결을 위해서는 많은 노력이 경주되어야 할 것임. (특히 동인은 서비스 분야의

통상국	2차보	미주국	경제국	통상국	통상국	분석관	청와대	안기부

PAGE 1

성과는 오히려 후퇴하는 인상을 주고 있다고 첨언)

 - 현재 9.20. 이후의 회의개최등 구체 협상일정이 잡혀 있지는 않으나 미측은 영국측이 계속해서 독일과 프랑스에 압력을 가할 것으로 봄. (동인은 EC 가 UR 타결을 위한 작업을 조용히 추진하고 있는 것으로 생각한다며, 미국도 UR 타결을 위해 EC 와의 이견해소에 계속 노력해 갈 것이라고 언급)

 2. 동인의 발언은 실무선에서의 의견을 피력한 것으로 UR 타결 전망에 대해종전의 낙관적이던 입장에서 다소 후퇴한 매우 신중한 반응을 보인 것으로 감촉되었음. 끝.

 (대사 현홍주-국장)

 예고 : 92.12.31. 까지

PAGE 2

이시

駐 日 大 使 舘

(Page / ―

JAW(F):　　2514　　日 時；

受　信：長　官（동기, 동인, 경인 ）

発　信：駐日大使（　　일정,　（일경） ）

題　目　UR 관련

'92 7-15 -9 00

7.15 ㊊ 夕

17日に大使級会合

新ラウンド

【ジュネーブ14日＝吉田記者】多角的貿易交渉（ガット・ウルグアイ・ラウンド）は十七日に主要国の大使級会合（通称グリーン・ルーム）を開く。先進七カ国首脳会議（ミュンヘン・サミット）が交渉の年内合意を確認したのを受け、交渉の過の方法について詰める。七月中の閣僚級会合では事前に根を詰め、グリーン・ルームでは「FTS前後での交渉の区切りが「交渉進む」とみなされかが会合が大きい。

ドンケル事務局長の任期延長を正式決定

ガット理事会

【ジュネーブ14日＝吉田記者】ガットは十四日の理事会で、年末に切れるドンケル事務局長の任期を来年六月末まで半年間延長することを正式に決めた。多角的貿易交渉（ウルグアイ・ラウンド）の合意のメドがつかないため、現在を求めない公算して、各国が事務局長続投を受け入れた。

정한 서메트의 연대 합의 목표설정에 따라
가상방향 노의. 여름축가 개최까지의
가상 방안 노의 제소여

日本経済新聞 ┌面

0022

외 무 부

종 별 :

번 호 : GVW-1401   일 시 : 91 0715 1800

수 신 : 장관(봉기, 경기원, 재무부, 농수부, 상공부, 특허청)

발 신 : 주 제네바 대사

제 목 : UR/그린룸 회의 개최

　　　연 : GVW-1372

　　　던켈 사무총장은 92. 7. 17(금) 11:00 그린룸회의를 개최

　　　UR 협상 현황을 STOCK-TAKING 할 것임을 통보하여 왔는바, 동 회의 결과

　　　보고하겠음. 끝.

　　　(대사 박수길 - 국장)

통상국　　경기원　　재무부　　농수부　　상공부　　특허청

PAGE 1

92.07.16　　04:53 FE

외신 1과 통제관

0023

이서(인)

외 무 부

종 별 :

번 호 : GVW-1421   일 시 : 92 0718 1300

수 신 : 장관(봉기,경기원,재무부,농림수산부,상공부)

발 신 : 주 제네바 대사   사본:주 EC 대사,주미대사-중계필

제 목 : UR 협상 그린룸 회의

일반문서로 재분류(1992. 12. 31)

연: GVW-1401

연호 GREEN ROOM 회의가 금 7.17(금) DUNKEL 총장 주재로 30 여개국 대사 참석리에 개최되나, 동 결과 및 당관 분석 평가를 아래 보고함.

1. 회의결과

가. DUNKEL 총장은 TRANSPARENCY 유지 목적으로 금일 회의를 소집했다고 전제한후, 그동안 미.EC 간 양자 협상 및 G-7 정상회의등 주요 정치 일정과 연결되어 UR 협상이 거의 정돈상태에 있었던 것이 사실이나, (1) 불란서 국민투표, 미대통령 선거 등 일부 정치일정이 남아 있긴 하나 더이상 주요 핑게거리(PRETEXTS)도 없고, (2) 남아있는 시간적 제약(미국의 신속 승인 절차를 의미) 및 미.EC 간 농산물 분야 타협만 이루어지면 기타 잇슈는 자동적으로 해결된다는 믿음 아래 동 타협만 기다려온 이제까지의 협상 전략이 아무런 성과도 없었던점을 고려할때, 더이상 좌시하고 있을 수만은 없다고 하면서, 9 월 이후의 협상추진과 관련 아래와 같이 자신의 의견을 제시하고 이에 대한 참석대사의 의견 개진을 요청함.

1) UR 협상을 다시 다자화하여 9 월부터 제네바에서 협상을 재개함.(MULTILATERALIZATION)

2) 농산물, 시장접근, 써비스, 섬유 포함 전분야에 걸쳐 협상을 진행하며, 이를 통해 핵심문제점(HARD CORE DIFFICULTIES)를 찾아내고 양자적, 다자적 협상등 가용한 수단을 동원, 이에 대한 해결책을 모색하되 T4 는 최후의 순간에만 가동함 (GLOBALIZATION)

3) 상기 제네바 협상에는 각국의 정치 지도자가 아니라 전권을 가진 수석대표가 책임지고 협상하며, 동 결과를 각국의 최고 정책 결정자에게 수락토록하는 BOTTOMS-UP 전략을 취함.

통상국	차관	2차보	분석관	경기원	재무부	농수부	상공부	중계

PAGE 1   92.07.19   01:00

외신 2과 통제관 BS
0024

나. DUNKEL 총장은 또한 절차적 문제와 관련, 현 시점에서는 TNC 개최가 의미가 없다는 다수국 의견에 따라 TNC 를 개최치 않기로 하였으며, 9 월에 가서도일단 9.14 시작주간 이후 절절한 시점에 GREEN ROOM 회의를 소집하여, TNC 개최 문제를 포함한 협상추진 일정, 절차등을 결정할 예정이라하고, 자신은 각국의 입장을 잘 파악하고 있고 의문점이 있으면 개별접촉을 통해 추가로 확인하겠지만 각국도 입장 변경이 있으면 수시 알려 줄것을 당부 한후, 9 월 이후의 협상에 대비하여 각국이 자국입장 정리등 사전에 철저한 준비를 미리 마쳐줄것을 특히강조함.

다. 이에 대해 대부분의 참석대사는 특별한 대안이 없는 상황에서 DUNKEL 총장의 상기 제안이 유일한 길임을 인정하면서도 아래와 같은 의견을 피력하.

1) 스위스, 말레이지아, 인도, 호주등은 DUNKEL 총장의 의도가 사실상 1.13TNC 이후의 협상 방식으로의 복귀를 의미하는 것으로 이해되나, 당시의 T1, T2 협상이 미.EC 의 협상결과와 직접 연계되어 아무런 성과를 거두지 못했던 경험에 비추어 의문을 표시함.

2) 홍콩, 칠레는 TNC 개최에 많은 관심을 피력한바, 특히 칠레는 자유무역을 지지하는 다수 협상 참가국의 입장 표명 기회 제공 및 협상의 다자화를 위한 공식적인 FORUM 마련 필요성에 비추어 9 월 이후 TNC 개최가 필요하다는 의견을 개진함.

3) 브라질은 GLOBALITY 주장과 T4 가동을 억제하려는 의도가 상호 모순된다고 하면서, T4 포함 모든 문제의 동시 협상이 공정(FAIR) 하지 않겠느냐는 의견을 피력함.

4) 뉴질랜드는 협상 정돈의 원인이 각국의 현격한 입장 차이보다는 주로 정치적 이유에 있으므로 9 월 이후의 협상과정에서 DRAFT FINAL ACT 의 INTEGRITY 를 파괴하는 일이 없어야 할 것임을 언급함.

5) 상당수 국가가 T1, T2 협상에 대해서는 이미 충분한 준비와 용의가 되었던 점을 상기 시켰으며, 특히 알젠틴은 사전 준비는 오히려 협상 주역국(미.EC 등을 지칭)에 촉구해야 할 사항이라는 의견을 표명함.

6) 미국은 현재의 상황이 어려운 상황(HELPLESS)임을 인정하고 DUNKEL 총장의 계획에 최대한 협조할 용의가 있다는 점을 언급함.

라. 본직은 아국은 시장접근, 써비스 양허협상에서 이미 충실한 내용의 양허 LIST 도 제출했을 뿐만 아니라 신축성있는 자세로 동 협상에 임할 자세가 되어 있음을 상기시킨후, 협상 타결을 위한 DUNKEL 총장의 고육책을 이해 못하는 바는 아니나, 동

PAGE 2

총장의 T4 전략에 관해서는 강한 불만을 갖지 않을수 없다고 언급함. (일본대사는 DUNKEL 총장의 계획이 현재로서는 유일한 대안으로 보인다고만 언급하고, 일본의 어려운 입장에 관해서는 잘 알려져 있으므로 되풀이 않겠다고 발언)

2. 분석 및 평가

가. 9월 이후 협상 추진방향 관련 1.13 TNC 이후의 실패 경험에도 불구 DUNKEL 총장이 상기 BOTTOMS-UP 전략을 제시한 것은 G-7 정상회의가 아무런 성과 없이 폐회되고 불란서 국민투표, 미국의 대통령 선거등 UR 협상의 진전을 막는 장애 요소가 가로놓여 있는 상황에서 더이상의 협상 CREDIBILITY 상실을 억제하기 위한 마지막 대안으로 제시된 것으로 보임.

나. 미.EC 양자 협상 및 DRAFT FINAL ACT 내용과 T1, T2 협상간의 연계를 의도적으로 과소 평가하고 있는 점등에 대해 회의론도 대두대고 있으나, 별다른 대안이 없는 상황에서 유일한 가용 수단으로 대부분의 참석국이 강한 이의를 제기치 못함.

다. 또한 DUNKEL 총장 계획의 근저에는 9.20 불란서 국민투표 이후 불란서 및 EC 의 입장이 다소 유연해 질 가능성에 대한 강한 기대감 및 동 부표이후 미대통령 선거까지의 기간을 최대한 활용하려는 의도도 깔려 있는 것으로 평가됨.

라. 현재로서는 9월 이후의 협상 형태에 관한 확실한 전망을 내리기는 어려우나 DUNKEL 총장이 수석대표의 역할을 수차 강조한 점에 비추어, T1, T2 협상과 함께 수시로 GREEN ROOM 회의를 통한 핵심문제점 파악 및 이에 대한 분야간 TRADE-OFF 를 시도하는 형태(브랏셀 각료회의 개최직전 절차)를 동 총장이 의도하고 있는 것으로 감지됨.

마. DUNKEL 총장 T4 는 마지막 단계에가서 제한적으로 가동한다는 입장에 변함이 없다고 한것은 협상의 다자화에도 불구하고 협상 성공의 관건은 역시 미.EC 간 농산물 분야 타협 성패 여부에 달려 있다는 인식 및 동 타협 도출시 이를 모든 협상 참가국에 강요하려는 의도가 아직도 강한 것으로 평가됨.

라. 따라서 아국도 9월 이후 재개될 협상과정에서 아국의 최대관심 사항인 농산물 분야 관세화 예외 반영문제가 T4 가동 이전에 어떠한 형태로든 논의될수 있도록 하는 협상 전략 강구를 포함한 철저한 사전 대비책 강구가 필수적이며, 기타 분야에 대해서도 핵심적 이해 사항에 대한 내부적 우선 순위 설정등 종합적 입장 정립작업도 사전에 완료해 두어야 할것임. 끝.

PAGE 3

(대사 박수길-장관)

예고 92.12.31.까지

외 무 부

종 별 :

번 호 : USW-3640   일 시 : 92 0721 1914

수 신 : 장관 (통이, 통기, 통삼, 미중, 정총, 외연원, 경기원, 상공부)

발 신 : 주 미 대사

제 목 : USTR 수석보좌관 면담

1. 당관 구본영 공사는 7.21. USTR 수석보좌관 (CHIEF OF STAFF)인 STEPHEN FARRAR (전 백악관 국내정책 담당 보좌관)과 오찬 면담을 가졌는 바, 동 오찬시 동인의 발언 내용중 참고 사항을 아래 보고함. (동 보좌관은 HILLS 대표에게 주요 현안에 대해 자문하고 백악관과의 관계를 조정하는 중요한 위치에 있음)

- NAFTA 관련 금주말 3 국 통상장관 회담이 '멕시코시티'에서 개최 예정이나 이번 고위급 협상이 최종 협상이 될 가능성은 매우 적은 것으로 생각함.

- 수주내 NAFTA 협상이 마무리 되더라도 양국 정상이 가서명한 협정을 금번의회 회기내 (9-10 월) 제출할지 혹은 선거후 내년 차기의회에 제출할지는 아직 결정되지 않았음 (동 협정 의회 제출시 '부시' 대통령 입장에서는 동 협정을 국제경제분야의 주요 성과의 하나로 거론할 수도 있을 것이나 동 협정 내용이 민주당 의원들 혹은 기타 이익단체들에 의해 선거 '잇슈'로 악용될 가능성에 대한 우려도 상존함)

- UR 과 관련하여서는 9 월부터 다자간, 양자간 (미.EC 간) 협상을 병행, 재개할 것이나 FAST-TRACK 기한내 협상이 마무리 될수 있을지는 현단계에서 매우 불투명함.

- 특히 EC 가 회원국들간의 의견조정에 어려움을 겪고 있어 9 월 불란서 국민투표이후에도 농산물 분야에 새로운 제의가 나올수 있을지 개인적으로는 회의적임.

2. 동 보좌관은 HILLS 대표가 9 월 '방축' APEC 각료회의에는 참석하지 못할 것이나 년내 아시아를 방문할 가능성은 있다고 언급함. 끝.

(대사 현홍주-국장)

예고 : 92.12.31. 까지

통상국 정와대	차관 안기부	2차보 경기원	미주국 상공부	통상국	통상국	외연원	외정실	분석관

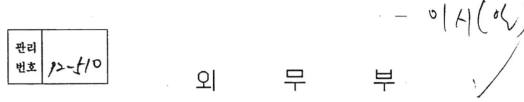

외 무 부

종 별 :

번 호 : ECW-0995   일 시 : 92 0729 1830

수 신 : 장관(통기,통삼) 사본:주제네바-직송필

발 신 : 주 EC 대사

제 목 : UR 협상동정

연: ECW-0987,0994

연호 7.29 본직의 EC PAEMEN 다자관계 부총국장 면담시 UR 협상전망에 관하여도 의견을 교환한바, 동인의 견해를 하기 보고함

1. DUNKEL GATT 사무총장이 최근 일본경제지와의 회견에서 9.20 프랑스 국민투표후 UR 협상의 진전이 잘 이루어져 93.2 월 까지는 UR 협상이 완료되기를 바란다고 천명한 것과 관련, PAEMEN 부총국장은 자신이 작 7.28. DUNKEL 사무총장과 전화접촉을 가졌다하며, DUNKEL 사무총장은 그간 미국과 EC 앞으로 넘겨졌던 협상의 중심을 제네바로 다시금 끌어들이고자 시도하고 있으며, 이의 일환으로 곧 중남미제국및 일본등을 순방, 여건 조성작업을 갖는등 9 월중 다자협상 재개를위해 준비하고 있는바 EC 로서도 동 사무총장의 노력을 지지하고 있다함

2. 농업문제가 UR 협상전반의 핵심문제로 남아있으나 그간 미-EC 간의 쟁점축소를 위한 노력결과, 실질문제에 대한 의견접근이 상당히 이루어진 것으로 평가하고 있다하면서 EC 는 앞으로의 추가협상을 통해 상호간 타협점이 모색되기를바라고 있다함. 동인은 미국의 태도도 최근에와서 더 PRAGMATIC 한 방향으로 접근하고 있으므로 EC 는 앞으로 미국의 중요한 조치(IMPORTANT STEP) 가 있기를기다리고 있다함

3. 다만 미국의 민주당 CLINTON 후보가 92.9 월말경 여론조사에서도 현재와같이 BUSH 대통령대비 높은 지지율을 받게될 경우는 UR 협상에 대해서도 CLINTON후보의 발언권이 높아질 것으로 생각된다함. 즉 CLINTON 후보는 원내다수를 점하고 있는 민주당의 우위를 바탕으로 FAST-TRACK 연장조치를 취하면서 UR 문제는자신이 직접 해결하겠다고 주장할수도 있을것이며, 그 경우는 UR 추진이 지연될 가능성도 배제할수 없을 것이라 함. 끝

통상국	장관	차관	2차보	통상국	분석관	정와대	안기부

PAGE 1   92.07.30   06:56

                                                    외신 2과 통제관 BZ
                                                    0029

(대사 권동만-국장)
예고: 92.12.31. 까지

0030

외 무 부

관리
번호 92-182

종 별 :

번 호 : CPW-3665   일 시 : 92 0814 1355

수 신 : 장관(통상국장, 아주국장)사본:주 홍콩총영사-본부중계필

발 신 : 주 북경대표 경유(박수길)

제 목 : 홍콩 정부초청 HK방문 평가

    본직내외는 1992. 8.5 - 11 까지 홍콩정부 (DONALD TSCHANG 무역청장) 초청으로
홍콩을 방문하여, TSCHANG 청장 및 CHAU 무역공업 장관등과 회동하는 등 일정을
가졌는바 특이내용 다음 보고함.1. 홍콩 / 중국관계 및 홍콩 / 한국관계 (홍콩측
언급요지)

    가. 홍콩 / 중국관계

일반문서로 재분류 (1982. 12. 31

    (1) HK 경제는 공전의 도약기를 맞고 있는바, 그 주된 이유는 중국의 경제 개혁
정책 및 중국경제의 급속한 발전 (90 년 평균 성장율 9-12 퍼센트, 광동지역 18
퍼센트 - 20 퍼센트)의 영향과 중국.홍콩간 상호 부자를 통한 견인차역할 때문임.

    (2) HK 의 대중국 부자 금액의 정확한 수자는 알수 없으나 대체로 과거 수년간 200
여억 미불에 달하고 있으며 (공장수는 약 2 만 7,000 여개, 중국인 고용인원 약 300
만명), 현재 에는 부자 지역이 상해등으로 북상하고 있고 또 내용에 있어서도
제조분야에서 써비스 분야로 이행하고 있음.

    (3) 중국의 급속한 경제 성장은 또한 그들의 대 HK 부자도 증가시키고 있는바,
현재까지 중국의 대 HK 부자 총액은 약 100 억불에 달하고 있는 것으로 알려져 있으며
(부자 주체는 주로 중앙 정부 관계 부서, 광동성 등), 특이사항 은 동부자에 현 중국
지도층 (등소평, 진운등)의 제 2 세 들이 적극 개입되고 있다는 사실임.

    (4) 이러한 중국경제의 성장세에 힘입어 HK 경제는 앞으로 4 퍼센트
까지의성장세를 보이는 호경기 (BULLISH ECONOMY) 를 보일 것이며, 이러한 경향은
중국의 개혁정책이 전국적 으로 확산 되어감에 따라 더욱 촉진 될것임.

    (제 14 차 전인대에서 헌법에 시장경제요소 도입을 본격화 할것이라는 예상도
있음.)

    (5) 중국의 개혁 정책에 대하여서는 외부 세계에서 현 지도 층의 사후에 변화가

───
통상국   장관   차관   2차보   아주국   분석관   정와대   안기부   중계

PAGE 1   92.08.15   13:14

                                             외신 2과   통제관 FR
                                                        0031

있을수 있다는 견해도 있으나, 개혁 정책이 갖고온 엄청난 성과를 부정하는정책 반전은 있을수 없고, 또 현재 차세대 지도층의 개혁 정책 추진 의도는 확고 부동하므로 중공경제와 HK 경제의 전망은 극히 좋다고 보아야 할것임.

(6) 이러한 경제 전망은 89 년 천안문 사태이후에 잠시 있었던 HK 의 BRAINDRAIN 및 외국에로의 자본도피 경향을 완전히 반전시켜 현재에는 오히려 역유입 현상이 증가하고 있으며, 1997 년 HK 의 중국반환에도 불구하고 HK 사람들은 아무런 불안감을 갖고 있지 않으면서 97 년 이후의 원만한 HK-중국 관계의 발전에 큰 희망을 갖고 있음.

(7) 광동성등 중국 남부지역의 경제는 이미 HK 경제와 신속한 INTEGRATE 의과정을 밟고 있는바, 이러한 통합과정의 촉진은 중장기적인 관점에서 정치개혁에도 영향을 주지 않을수 없을것이므로 중국의 정치적 민주화도 필연적 이라고 보아야 할것임. 따라서 HK 으로서는 1997 년 이후의 HK 의 특수지위가 중국적으로는 중국의 민주화와 함께 평준화 될것으로 믿고 있음.

(8) 홍콩이 대중국 경제 발전 특히 제조업, 써비스업 등 투자 면에서 일본,미국을 압도하고 있는 이유는 역시 지리적 근접성, 문화, 관습, 언어, 성격등의 동질성에 기인한 바가큰바 그것은 오랜 세월 계속된 이념적인 대립에도 불구하고 중국민족으로서의 공통성에 기인한다 하겠음.

나. HK - 한국관계

(1) HK 과 한국은 그들의 경제적 특징을 백분 활용하여 JOINT VENTURE 등 형식으로 중국에 진출하는 방향도 업계에서 검토, 실천 되어야 할것인바, 이러한면에서 한국의 "진도"와 HK COUNTERPART 가 심천 지구에서 JOINT 로 하고 있는CONTAINER 제조업은 좋은 본보기가 되고 있음.

(2) HK / 한국간의 무역고가 작년 50 억 미불을 초과하고 있는바 한국의 독자적인 대중국 경제관계 증진에도 불구하고 대 HK 관계도 경제구조의 상호 보완성으로 인하여 계속 발전해 나갈것이 확실함.

다. APEC 에서의 상호 협력과 사무국 유치 문제

(1) 작년 한국의 노력으로 중국, TAIPEI 등과 함께 HK 도 APEC 회원국이 되었는바, 앞으로 APEC 내에서도 HK - 한국협력 관계가 크게 증대될 것으로 봄.

(2) 지금 APEC 의 사무국유치와 관련 한국을 비롯 5 여개국이 경쟁하고 있는바, HK 으로서는 이 문제에 대하여 9 월 방콕 회의까지는 CONSENSUS 가 나올 것으로 전망하고

PAGE 2

0032

있으며 한국의 협력 요청에 대해서는 "CAREFUL AND SYMPATHETICCONSIDERATION" (CHAN 장관 언급)을 하고자함.

라. GATT 에서의 HK - 한국협력 문제

(1) 한국은 GATT 에서 규범제정, 써비스, 섬유등 많은 분야에서 공통적인 이해 관계를 갖고 있어 저간 양자간에 긴밀한 협력 관계가 이룩되고 있는 것을 크게 평가함. 특히 EC 가 거론하고 있는 한국, 홍콩, 싱가폴 3 개국에게 개도국 지위 불부여 문제에 대해서는 앞으로 공통 전략을 수립 실천 함으로써 EC 의 기도를 좌절시켜야 할것임.

(2) MFA 연장 문제에 대해서도 HK, 한국은 공통적인 이해관계를 갖고 대처 하고 있는바, 양측은 함께 MFA 의 불연장기도에 단연히 반대하고 1 년 - 2 년 연장안에 합의 하도록 9 월에 있을 제네바에서의 ITCB 에서 힘을 합쳐 노력하여야 할것임.

(3) UR 의 성공이 HK, 한국의 이익에 부합하기 때문에 이 방향 에서 공통노력을 할것이고, UR 협상 특히 TRACK I -II 협상은 불란서에서의 9 월 20 일 국민투표 이후 특히 11 월 대통령 선거 이후라야 본격화 될것으로 예상됨.

(4) 홍콩으로서는 UR 농산물 분야 TEXT 이외 여하한 개정 기도 에도 강력히반대 할것이며 이 분야에서도 한국측과의 협력을 기대함.

2. 본직의 홍콩 공식 방문은 주로 GENEVA 에서의 양 공관 간의 협조 관계 강화를 목적으로 DONALD TSCHANG 무역 청장의 INITIATIVE 에 의해 이루어진바, 홍콩 정청 측은 본직으로 하여금 장관급 인사, 상공회의소, 홍콩 무역 개발협회,산업계 등 주요 인사와의 면담 및 오.만찬 등을 주선하고 또 SHATIN 지구등 신개발 지역 사찰과 광동지역의 HELICOPTER TOUR 등을 주선 함으로써 최선의 대우를 해주었음을 감지할수 있었음.

3. 또한 본직은 홍콩정청의 주선으로 주홍콩 한인 상공회의소 주최 오찬 에서 "한국과 UR"에 관하여 연설하고 교포 상공인들의 질의에 응답 하였음.

4. 홍콩정청이 본직을 위하여 마련한 주요 일정은 다음과 같았음.

가. 면담 인사

EDUARD LEE - GOVERNMENT ECONOMIST

JOSEPH YAN - ACTING SECRETARY FOR

MONETARY AFFAIRS

DONALD TSANG DIRECTOR GENERAL OF TRADE

DAVID BROWING DISTRICT OFFICER, DEVELOPMENT

PAGE 3

OF SHATIN

PETER LAI ACTING SECRETARY FOR CONSTITUTIONAL AFFAIRS

T.H.CHAN SECRETARY FOR TRADE AND INDUSTRY

WK CHAN SECRETAY, HK CHAMBER OF COMMERCE DENNIS YAU, DEPUTY DIRECTOR, HK
TRADE DEVELOPMENT COUNCIL

나. 주요일정

DONALD TSCHANG 무역청장 (부부) 주최 HK 실업인과의 만찬

DENNIS YAU IC LAU (ASSISTANT DIRECTOR GENERAL OF TRADE) / 헬기 시찰

한인 상공회의주최 오찬 연설등 끝.

예고 : 92. 12. 31 일반,

PAGE 4

0034

British Embassy
Seoul

Mr Ho Seung
Assistant Minister for
 Economic Affairs
Ministry of Foreign Affairs
Seoul

17 September 1992

My dear Assistant Minister,

    I enclose with this letter a copy of a letter from the
Chancellor of the Exchequer in London, Mr Norman Lamont to the
Minister of Finance. I have sent on to Mr Rhee the original of the
letter. But since its contents concern the trade in financial
services and activities at the next round of Uruguay Round talks in
Geneva, I thought that the Ministry of Foreign Affairs ought to be
aware of the contents of the letter.

Yours sincerely,

David Wright

D J Wright
HM Ambassador

0035

chex.kf/jh1/11=

Treasury Chambers, Parliament Street, London, SW1P 3AG
071-270 3000

8 September 1992

Mr Rhee Yong Man
Ministry of Finance
171 760 Chungang Dong
Kwachon
Kyonggi'do
Republic of Korea

Dear Rhee

A number of recent international meetings, including the
G7 Summit, the ASEAN Ministerial conference, and the meeting of
Cairns Group ministers, have reaffirmed the importance of
achieving an early successful conclusion to the Uruguay Round.
Although in most cases, as in the UK, it is trade ministries who
are in the lead, Finance Ministers also have a particular interest
in the negotiations, because of the contribution a successful
Round will make to the revival of the world economy and of our own
national economies. In addition, in many cases, Finance
Ministries are responsible for the regimes governing financial
services, and so take a close interest in this particular aspect
of the General Agreement on Trade in Services being negotiated as
part of the Round. It is with financial services in mind that I
am writing to you, as a fellow Finance Minister.

I am firmly convinced that with increasing integration of the
global economy, significant benefits will accrue to all countries
if financial services are made subject to GATT disciplines.
However, for this to happen, a clear commitment by all parties to
the goal of liberalisation is essential. Without this commitment,
there is a risk that some countries will question the value of
including the sector in the agreement, and resort to
discriminatory arrangements in which market access opportunities
are traded on a bilateral and reciprocal basis. I believe that
exclusion of the sector in this way would have serious
consequences not only for the development of international trade
in financial services, but also for the Round as a whole.

0036

Clearly, financial services is not the only, or even the main, obstacle to agreement in the Round. A settlement of the outstanding issues in agriculture remains essential, and the UK, as a member of the European Community, is playing its part in helping to resolve these. But the main lines of the final agreement are, in my view, sufficiently clear to enable progress to be made in other areas, notably services. Indeed, such progress is vital, given the shortage of time and the substantial amount of work still remaining to be done in the bilateral negotiations on initial commitments. This is on the basis that parties are not committed to anything until agreement has been reached in <u>all</u> areas.

I hope therefore that when negotiations on initial commitments resume in Geneva at the beginning of October, you will come ready to indicate where there may be scope for improving your existing offer. It is a matter of concern, for example, that many offers still do not cover all sectors, or do not offer a standstill of the existing regime.

Accordingly I would ask you carefully to review your own offer on financial services. Even if only small changes are possible in particular cases, these could together add up to a substantial improvement in the benefits to be gained from including this sector in the agreement. In turn, that will contribute to the gains from the Round as a whole which, from the wider perspective, we as Finance Ministers wish to see.

NORMAN LAMONT

8

0037

외 무 부

종 별 :

번 호 : ECW-1063   일 시 : 92 0901 1630

수 신 : 장관 (봉기, 경기원, 재무부, 농림수산부, 상공부)

발 신 : 주 EC 대사   사본: 주제네바-직필

제 목 : 갓트/UR 협상

9.1. EC 집행위 대변인은 HILLS 미무역 대표부 대표가 당지를 방문중이며, 8.31.MAC SHARRY 집행위원과 회담을 가진데 이어 금일ANDRIESSEN 부위원장과 만나, 표제협상 추진방안에 대해 협의 하였다고 말함. 동인은 금번 회담에서 양측은 UR 협상은 금년말까지 완전히 종결하고, 미.EC 간의 현안인 OILSEEDS문제는 9월말까지 해결한다는데 입장을 같이하였다고 말함. 끝

(대사 권동만-국장)

롱상국   경기원   재무부   농수부   상공부

PAGE 1

이서(EC)

외 무 부

종 별 :

번 호 : USW-4455   일 시 : 92 0910 1920

수 신 : 장관(통기,통이,미일) 사본:경기원,농수산부,주제네바,EC 대사

발 신 : 주 미 대사   -중계필

제 목 : UR 동향

일반문서로 재분류 (1992.12.31)

1. 당관 장기호 참사관은 9.10 USTR DOROTHY DWOSKIN 부대표보를 면담, 최근 CARLA HILLS 미 USTR 대표의 EC 방문 관련 특히 UR 협상에 대해 어떤 논의가 있었는지에 대해 문의한바, 동 부대표보는 상세 언급은 피하고 요지 아래와 같이 언급하였음.

가. HILLS 대표는 EC 방문시 영국의 MAJOR 수상, ANDRIESSEN EC 부위원장 MACSHERRY 위원등을 접촉한바 UR 협상과 관변하여서는 현재 어디에 문제가 있고 앞으로 어떤 방향으로 협상을 진전시켜야할것인지를 알기위해 주로 FACT FINDING 에 목적을둔 것이었으며, EC 의장국인 여국의 MAJOR 수상에게는 UR 타결을 위한 영국의 역할이 중요하므로 영국의 보다 적극적인 역할을 당부하였다함.

나. HILLS 대표는 EC 국가들이 최근 NAFTA 문제에 대해 많은 우려를 표명하고 있기 때문에 NAFTA 내용에 대한 설명과 아울러 이것이 UR 타결의 방해가 될 수 없음을 강조하고 특히 미국으로서는 행정부의 신속협상권 시한이 얼마 남지 않았기 때문에 금년말까지는 UR 협상을 마무리 짓는다는 일정을 잡고 있으므로 관계국들이 가급적 빨리 제네바에서 분야별 양자협상등을 추진, UR 협상을 재개하도록 노력해야 한다는 MESSAGE 를 EC 에 전달한데 뜻이 있다고 하였음.

다. 영국의 MAJOR 수상도 MAASTRICHT 조약에 대한 불란서 국민부표의 향방에 대해 우려를 표명하고 결과가 좋지 않으면, UR 협상에도 영향을 미칠 것으로 우려가 된다고 하였지만 미국과 영국은 이것이 UR 협상의 커다란 장애가 될수 없으며, 불란서도 현재로서는 국내정치적으로 어려움이 있지만 기본적으로는 UR 협상타결을 BLOCK 하는 역할은 하지 않을 것이라는데 인식을 같이 하였다고 하였음.

라. DEWOSKIN 부대표보는 HILLS 대표가 NAFTA 타결을 BUSH 대통령에 보고 했을 때 BUSH 대통령은 UR 협상은 언제 타결할 것인지에 대해 강한 관심을 표시했음을

통상국 중계	장관	차관	2차보	미주국	통상국	분석관	청와대	안기부

PAGE 1   92.09.11   21:40

상기시키면서 불란서가 국민투표가 끝나면 재차 UR 협상타결을 위하 노력을 기울려야할 것이라고 하였음.

2. 장기호 참사관이 최근 BUSH 대통령의 소맥 수출 보조금 지급 발표에 대한 EC 등 주요국으로 부터의 반응을 언급하고 이에 대한 미측의 입장을 문의한데대해 동 부대표보는 이러한 지원계획은 새로운 것이 아니고 전에부터 내려온 EEP(EXPORT ENHANCEMENT PROGRAM) 계획의 일환으로서 금번의 EEP 발표는 사전에 그 내용에 대한 상세한 설명이 없어 미국이 지원보조금을 상당히 증액한 것으로 오해를 받게된 것이라고 하였음. 동인은 또한 금번의 발표금액(10 억불 상당)은 여러개의 관련 보조금을 묶어서 내놓은 것이므로 전체 액수를 증액시킨 것이 아니라고 설명하면서 이것이 UR 협상에 결림돌이 될수 없을 것이라는 의견을 피력하였음.

(대사 현홍주-국장)

예고:92.12.31 까지

PAGE 2

0040

456　우루과이라운드 협상 동향 및 무역협상위원회 회의 3

이시(안) ✓

외 무 부

종 별 :

번 호 : FRW-1836   일 시 : 92 0915 1830

수 신 : 장관(봉기), 사본:주제네바, EC(직송필), 주미대사(본부중계필)

발 신 : 주 불 대사

제 목 : UR 협상

일반문서로 재분류(19**92**. **12**. **31**.)

연:FRW-1868

(연호) 미국의 농산물 수출보조금 지급 결정 관련, 주재국 정부의 반응 및 UR전망 아래 보고함. (9.15 조참사관, 외무성 DENIS SIMONNEAU 경제국 UR 담당관 접촉)

1. 미테랑 대통령은 연호 부시 대통령앞 서한에서 금번 미정부의 농산물 수출보조금 지급 결정은 매우 실망스러운 조치로서 종자유 분쟁외에 미.EC 간 새로운 무역 분규를 야기시킴으로써 UR 타결을 더욱 어렵게 만들고 있음을 지적하고, UR 타결을 위해서는 미국의 양보가 필수적인 만큼 미측의 새로운 협상자세를 촉구하였음.

2. 동 서한은 미테랑 대통령의 직접 지시에 의해 외무성 실무진이 초안을 작성하였으나, 대통령이 일독후 불측의 불만을 보다 강하게 표현하라는 지시에 따라 재작성하여 9.10 미측에 발송하였음.

3. 미국이 UR 협상의 타결을 원한다면 9.20 불란서의 마스트리트 조약 국민투표 이후 11 월 미 선거전 사이에 실질적인 제안을 하여야 할것이나, UR 이 미 선거전에서 양후보 모두의 관심 대상이 아닌 현 상황에 비추어 11 월 이전에 협상타결을 위한 주요한 전기가 만들어지리라고 보기 어려움.

4. 이와같이 11 월 이전 미정부의 태도 변경이 없다면 금년 하반기로 예정된(일자 미정이나 년말개최 가능성) 미.EC 의장국(영국)간 년례 정상회담이 사실상 UR 타개의 마지막 기회라고 볼수 있으나 불 정부내 실무진에서는 점차 비관적인 전망이 우세해 지고있는 실정임.

5. 한편, 미국의 농산물 수출보조금 지급 결정후 불란서는 자국 수출시장의잠식을 우려하여 강경한 입장을 취하고 있으나 EC 내에서 그간 고립되었던 자국의 입지가 오히려 강화되는 반사적 이익을 받았다고도 볼수 있음.

6. 이와관련, 91.12 월 DUNKEL 보고서 발간 이후, 미국은 보조금 지급 결정등 점차

통상국	장관	차관	1차보	2차보	외정실	분석관	청와대	안기부
중계	농수산부.	상공부						

PAGE 1

92.09.16   08:39

외신 2과 통제관 BX

0041

UR(우루과이라운드) 협상 동향 및 TNC(무역협상위원회) 회의, 1992. 전5권(V.3 7-10월) 457

동 보고서 내용으로 부터 이탈되는 경향을 보이는 반면 EC 는 공동 농업정책 개혁등을 통해 오히려 이에 접근하려는 노력을 보이고 있는바, EC 가 보호무역적 이라는 일방적인 비난은 수용키 어려움.

7. 불란서는 9.20 국민투표가 성공적으로 치뤄진다면 EC 내 UR 협상의 조기타결을 희망하는 독일등의 입장을 고려하여, EC 내의 UR 협의에 있어 다소 유연한 입장을 취할수 있는 정치적 여유를 갖을수 있을것임.

8. 다만, 미국이 현재와 같은 고압적인 협상자세를 유지하는 한, 불 농민에대한 추가 양보 설득은 전혀 가능성이 없으므로(미테랑 대통령은 9.10 입원전 불 농민단체 대표를 접견코 추가양보 불가 및 대미 강경자세 유지 입장을 밝혔다함), 본격적인 협상 재개를 위해서는 여하한 경우에도 미측의 사전 양보가 필수적이라는 기존입장을 유지할 것임. 끝.

(대사 노영찬-국장)

예고:92.12.31. 까지

이시 (안)

외 무 부

종   별 :

번   호 : USW-4688　　　　　　　　　　　일   시 : 92 0921 1728

수   신 : 장 관 (통기,통이,경기원,농림수산부) 사본: 주제네바, EC 대사(중계필)

발   신 : 주 미 대사

제   목 : UR/농산물 협상 동향과 전망

　　　당관 이영래 농무관은 9.21. 미 농무부 해외농업처 RICHARD B. SCHROETER 처장보를 면담, 표제관련 동향과 MASSATRICHT TREATY 에 대한 불란서 국민투표 후의 협상 전망등을 문의한바, 요지 하기 보고함.

　　　1. 그간 협상 동향

　　- SCHROETER 처장보는 그동안 미국과 EC 간에 계속 UR 협상을 추진한 결과 동산물 수출보조 부문에서 물량기준 24% 감축은 기히 합의하였으나 EC 측이 요구하는 품목군별 감축(예: CEREAL, DAIRY 등)은 미국과 CAIRNS GROUP 에서 도저히 받아들일수 없고 종전의 개별품목(WHEAT, BARLEY 등) 감축을 계속 주장하여 현재 상호간에 이견이 많이 근접된 상태이며 감축시기는 6 년 또는 7 년을 협의하고 있다고 함.

　　- 그리고 국내보조금 감축의 경우 미측은 종전과 같이 탄력적으로 대응하고 있으나 CAP REFORM 과 관련하여 EC 측이 주장하는 GREEN BOX 인정은 실제로 받아들이기 어렵고 미측은 BLUE BOX 인정을 계속 주장하여 의견이 맞서고 있다고함.

　　　2. 국민투표후의 협상전망

　　- SCHROETER 처장보는 금번 불란서 국민투표 결과에 따라 MAJOR 영국수상이 10 월초에 EC 특별 정상회담을 개최한다고 하므로 이에 맞추어 UR 협상도 진척될 것으로 전망하면서 현재 EC 의장국인 영국의 역할을 기대하고 있다고 말함.

　　- 아울러 MADIGAN 미 농무장관과 CARLA HILLS USTR 대표도 현재는 구체적인 협상계획이 수립되어 있지 않으나 10 월에는 UR 협상타결을 위하여 EC 집행부와 협의하기를 희망하고 있다고 함.

　　- 또한 동인은 미국 대통령 선거 일정에 구애됨이 없이 UR 협상이 진행될 것이라고 하면서 UR/ 농산물 협상은 금년내에 마무리 할수 있을 것이라고 낙관적(OPTIMISTIC)인

통상국	장관	차관	2차보	통상국	분석관	정와대	안기부	경기원
농수부	중계							

* 원본수령부서 승인없이 복사 금지　　　　　　　　　　외신 2과　통제관 FS

0043

견해를 보임.

  3. OILSEED 분쟁과 관련하여 미국과 EC(미국의 JOE O'MARA SPECIAL NEGOTIATOR 와
EC 의 GUY LEGYAS 농업총국장)간에 브뤼셀에서 계속 협상을 하고 있다 하니 참고바람.
끝.

  (대사 현홍주-국장)

  예고 : 92.12.31. 까지

관리
번호 92-633

외 무 부

종 별 :

번 호 : GVW-1753   일 시 : 92 0921 1800

수 신 : 장관(봉기, 경기원, 재무부, 농림수산부, 상공부) 사본:주EC대사,

발 신 : 주 제네바 대사   주미대사-중계필

제 목 : 불란서 국민투표 결과와 UR 협상 전망   일반문서로 재분류(1992·12·31)

　　구주통합 조약안에 대한 9.20 불란서 국민투표 결과가 나온것과 관련 앞으로의 UR
전망에 관한 당지의 일차적 반응등을 아래 보고함.

　　1. 동 국민투표가 상당히 근소한 표차로 가결되고, 동 투표 과정에서 통화문제, EC
집행위의 독주문제등 다수의 문제가 노정되었으며, 반대표의 상당부분이 불란서
농촌지역에서 나온것으로 나타남에 따라, 앞으로 UR 협상에서의 EC 의태도와
관련해서는 (1) 근소한 표차이긴 하나 일단 가결된 만큼 EC 로서는 전보다는 적극적인
자세로 대미 협상에 임할 수 있게 될 것이라는 분석과 (2) 93.3. 국회의원 선거를
앞두고 있는 불란서 및 투표과정에서 독주론과 관련 상당한 비판의 표적이 되었던 EC
집행위로서는 당초 기대했던 만큼 협상의 신축성을 갖기가 어렵게 되었기 때문에 UR
협상의 조기 타결을 낙관할수 없다는 엇갈린 반응이 나타나고 있으나, 일단 EC 로서는
협상에 임할 수 있는 내부 사정이 상당히 호전되었다고 볼 수 있음.

　　2. 반면 미국의 경우에는 표면적으로는 11 월 대선과는 무관하게 대 EC 협상의
준비가 되어있다고 공언하고 있기는 하나, 미.EC 간 협상 돌파구 합의는 결국 쌍방
모두의 양보를 전제하지 않을수 없기 때문에 미국이 어렵게 전개되고 있는 대통령
선거를 앞두고 대 EC 양보로 받아들여 질수 있는 결단을 내릴수 있겠느냐의 여부가
의문시되고 있으며, 이와관련 EC 를 포함한 주요 UR 협상 참가국으로서도 불투명한
미국 선거 결과를 앞두고 진지한 노력을 기울일 수 있겠는가 하는 의문도 제기되고
있음.(반대로 미.EC 간에는 농산물 보조금 관련 대체적인 합의를 마친 상태이며
발표하는 시점의 선정만 남았다는 관측도 일부에서 제기되고 있다함)

　　3. 한편 앞으로의 당지에서의 협상 일정과 관련해서는 7.17 그린룸 회의석상에서의
DUNKEL 총장의 공언뿐만 아니라 남아있는 협상 가용 기간을 고려할때 어떠한
형태로서는 농산물 분야 G8 실무자 회의 (9.21-23) 및 일부국가간 양자협의 그리고

| 통상국 | 장관 | 차관 | 2차보 | 분석관 | 청와대 | 총리실 | 안기부 | 경기원 |
| 재무부 | 농수부 | 상공부 | 중계 | | | | | |

PAGE 1   92.09.22   21:13

* 원본수령부서 승인없이 복사 금지   외신 2과 몽제관 EC

0045

10.5 재개 예정인 서비스 분야 양자협상 일정이외에는 구체적 움직임이 가시화되고 있지 않음), 10 월중 재개된다 하더라도 미.EC 간 타결시점 또는 미대선 결과가 나올때까지는 의미있는 협상이 어려울 것으로 보임.끝

(대사 박수길-국장)

예고: 92.12.31. 까지

이시

관리
번호 92-638

외 무 부

종 별 : 긴 급

번 호 : GVWBQ-209

일 시 : 92 0923 0930

수 신 : 본부

발 신 : GV 담당

제 목 : 연: GVW-1753

연호건 3 항 아래 재타전함.

3. 한편 앞으로의 당지에서의 협상 일정과 관련해서는 7.17 그린룸 회의석상에서의 DUNKEL 총장의 공언뿐만 아니라 남아있는 협상 가용 기간을 고려할때 어떠한 형태로든 당지 협상이 조만간 재개될 것으로 일반적으로 관측되고는 있으나(현재로서는 농산물 분야 G8 실무자 회의(9.21-23) 및 일부 국가간 양자협의 그리고 10.5 재개 예정인 서비스분야 양자협상 일정 이외에는 구체적 움직임이 가시화 되고 있지 않음), 10월중 재개된다하더라도 미.EC 간 타결시점 또는 미대선 결과가 나올때까지는 의미있는 협상이 어려울 것으로 보임.끝.

(대사 박수길-국장)

일반문서로 재분류 (1992. 12. 31.)

통상국	장관	차관	2차보	외연원	분석관	청와대	총리실	안기부
경기원	재무부	농수부	상공부	중계				

PAGE 1

92.09.23 17:00

외신 2과 통제관 EC

0047

외 무 부

종   별 :

번   호 : ECW-1154   일   시 : 92 0923 1800

수   신 : 장 관(통기, 경기원, 재무부, 농수부, 상공부, 기정동문)

발   신 : 주 EC 대사 사본: 주미-중계필, 주제네바-중계필

제   목 : EC/농업이사회 개최결과

9.21-22 개최된 표제이사회 결과를 아래 보고함.

1. 갓트/UR 및 OILSEEDS 분쟁

가. MAC SHARRY 위원은 동건 관련한 7월이후 진전상황을 보고함. 동인은 미정부의 소맥수출 보조금 증액결정에 대하여 유감을 표명하고, OILSEEDS 패널 결과에 따른 EC의 입장은 동품목에 대한 EC의 보조체계를 변경 하는 것이 아니며, 지난 8월에 갓트에 제시한 보상방안을 추진하는 것임을 재천명함. 다만, 동인은 미국이 OILSEEDS분쟁과 관련하여 발표한 보복 LIST를 이행할 것으로는 보지 않는다고 말하고, 따라서 불란서가 주장하고 있는 EC의 보복조치에 대하여는 반대 입장임을 밝힘.

나. 상기 MAC SHARRY 위원의 보고에 대해 동 이사회는 집행위 의견을 지지함을 표시하고, UR협상 및 OILSEEDS 문제에 대해 이해 관계국들이 수락할 수 있는 적절한 해결 방안을 모색하고 이해 관계국들과 협상을 추진할 것을 요구함. 또한, 동 이사회는 MAC SHARRY 위원에게 미국이 대통령 선거 이전에 진실로 UR협상을 타결하려는 의지를 갖고 있는지를 재확인 보고해 줄 것을 요청함.

2. 단일시장 관련 사안

0 금번 이사회 에서는 신생 가축의 등록 규정안, 농업보조금의 종합관리를 위한 보조대상 작물의 파종면적 보고에 관한 규정안 및 AGRI-MONETARY 관리체계 개정안을 상정하여 토의한 바, 각 회원국의 의견이 다기하여 COREPER 및 관계특별위원회에서 재 검토키로 함.

3. CAP 개혁관련 사안

가. 이태리의 우유생산 쿼타 증량문제와 관련하여 이태리는 95년까지 자국의 현행 우유생산량 11.5백만톤을 9.9백만으로 감축키로 결정한 내용을 보고함. 이태리의 우유생산 쿼타 증량 문제는 차기 이사회(10.26-27)에서 재검토 키로함.

통상국   안기부   경기원   재무부   농수부   상공부

PAGE 1   92.09.24   03:25 FN

외신 1과 통제관

0048

나. 불란서가 요청한 바 있는 CEREAL과 OILSEED의 소득손실 보상방법 차등화 및젖소 PREMIUM 지급방법 변경 문제에 대하여 집행위는 젖소 PREMIUM 지급방법 변경에관한 제안을 신규로 제출하였는 바, 동 제안 및 기타 불란서 요청사항은 관계 전문가로 구성된 특별위원회의 검토를 가진 후, 차기 이사회에 재상정키로 함. 끝.

　　(대사 권동만 - 국장)

PAGE 2

외 무 부

종 별 :

번 호 : ECW-1153   일 시 : 92 0923 1800

수 신 : 장 관 (통기,경기원,재무부,농림수산부,상공부)

발 신 : 주 EC 대사 사본: 주미-중계필, 주제네바대사-필

제 목 : 갓트/UR 협상동향

9.20 불란서 국민투표 실시이후 표제관련한 당지의동향을 아래 보고함

1. 최근 미국이 UR협상의 재개촉구 및 미대통령 선거 실시 이전에 동 협상의 타결을 희망 (9.22 뉴욕 에서의 DUMAS 불란서 외무장관 회담후 EAGLEBURGER 미 국무장관서리의 발언등)한다는 의사표시를 하고 있음에도 불구하고 당지 전문가들의 견해는아래와같이 양분되어 있음.

가. 긍정적 으로 보는 측에서는 불란서 국민 투표결과 상당수의 농민들의 반대투표는 있었으나,국민투표 의 통과라는 긍정적인 결과가 도출 되었으므로 미대통령 선거 이전에도 표제협상의 타결 계기가 마련될 수 있다는 의견을 표시하고 있음

나. 다른 한편 에서는 미국이 대통령 선거 이전에는 실질적이고 적극적으로 협상에 참여할 수 없고 또한 EC 로서도 불란서 국민투표의 찬성율 이 근소한 차이에 불과했을 뿐 아니라, 상당수의 농민들이 반대 하였기 때문에 불란서 정부가 앞으로의 국내적 어려운 입장에 비추어 UR협상에서 어떤 양보를 하기는 어려우며, 계속 강경한입장을 고수할 수 밖에 없을 것으로 전망 되므로 동 협상의 타결 계기가 조기에 마련되기는 어려울 것으로 보고 있음.

2. 한편, 9.22. 개최된 농업 이사회에서 회원국의 농무장관들은 MAC SHARRY 위원에게 미국이 대통령 선거 이전에 UR 협상을 타결 하려는 의지를 갖고 있는지 여부를 확인, 보고할 것을 요구 하는등 UR 협상 관련된 당지의 움직임은 다소간 활발해지고 있는 바 주요 동향은 아래와같음.

가. GUMMER 영국 농무장관(이사회의장)은 EC가 UR 협상 MANDATE를 변경하는 것은 어려우나, 미측이 협력 하는 경우 10월말까지 동협상은 타결될 수도 있으며, EC는이를 위해 노력할 것이라고 말함.

통상국   경기원   재무부   농수부   상공부

PAGE 1   92.09.24   03:20 FN

나. MERMAZ 불란서 농무장관은 미국의 소맥 보조금 증액결정이 UR 협상 타결을 더욱 복잡하게 만들고 있다고 비난하면서 미국이 동협상에 대한 입장을 변경 해야 한다고 강조하고, 그러나 대통령 선거운동 기간중 미국의 입장을 바꾸는 것은 어려울 것이라고 전망함.

다. BURKMAN 화란 농무장관은 불란서 국민투표 결과로 인해 EC의 UR 협상 입장을 변경 하는 것은 어렵게 되었다고 평가하고, 동협상이 정체될 수 밖에 없는 요인은 미 대통령 선거와 NAFTA 협정에 있다고 말함.

라. MAC SHARRY 집행위원은 UR 협상의 적극적인 추진 방안을 모색하되, 여하한 희생을 무릅쓰고까지 타결을 추진하지는 않을 것이라고 말함.

3. 동건관련, EC 집행위 관계관들을 접촉, 결과 추보 하겠음. 끝.

(대사 권동만 - 국장)

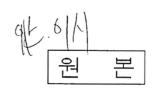

외 무 부

종 별 :

번 호 : USW-4778   일   시 : 92 0925 1955

수 신 : 장 관(봉기,봉이,미일,경기원,농림수산부,상공부)

발 신 : 주 미 대사 사본: 주제네바, EC 대사(중계망)

제 목 : UR 동향

1. 9.25. 당지 언론은 HILLS USTR 대표가 UR 농산물 협상의 타결 시한을 <u>10월말로</u> 설정 ,적극적으로 EC측과 접촉하고 있다고 보도하여 주목을 끌고 있음. (종래 HILLS 대표는 UR 타결 시한 설정을 자제하여 왔음)

2. HILLS 대표가 10월말로 농산물 협상 타결 시점을 잡은 것은 미국은 FAST TRACK 만료일 (93.6.1) 90일 이전 (3.1)에 의회에 협상안을 제출하여야 하는 바, 농산물협상 타결후 서비스 및 시장접근 분야의 협상에도 수개월이 소요될 것임을 감안한 것임.

3. 미 행정부의 10월말 시한 설정은 FAST TRACK 재연장이 사실상 어렵다는 전망하에 (FAST TRACK 권한 부여시 의회가 각 이익집단의 다양한 이해를 조정, 수용하기가 어려우며 레이건 행정부가 의회로 부터 UR 협상을 위한 FAST TRACK 권한을 획득하는 데에 2년이 소요된 점등 감안), UR 타결을 위한 마지막 시도라는 점과, 미대통령선거 직전에 협상 타결의 돌파구를 마련하여, 부시대통령 의 재선을 돕는다는 정치적 고려를 감안할때, 종래 수차례 반복되어 왔던 타결 시한 설정보다는 의미가 있는것으로 보여짐.

4. 이와관련 HILLS 대표는 9.23. EC ANDRIESSEN 대외 총국장에게 전화, 협상 타결이 가능한 대안(FORMAL, UNIFIED POSITION ON AGRICULTURE) 을 10월중 제시하라고요청 하였으며, ANDRIESSEN 총국장도 이를 긍정적으로 받아들이고 이번 기회가 협상성공을 위한 마지막 기회가 될 것이라고 하였다 함.

5. 한편, 지난주 미. EC 간에는 농무부 SPECIALNEGOTIATOR 인 OMARA 와 EC 의 LEGRAS 농업국장간에 국내 보조 감축문제, OILSEED 문제를 주 의제로 브랏셀에서 비밀협상을 가졌으나, 뚜렷한 성과가 없었다 하며, 9.29. 제네바에서 미. EC 간 재 협상이있을 예정임.

6. 관련 언론기사 별첨 송부함.끝.

통상국   2차보   미주국   통상국   경기원   농수부   상공부

PAGE 1   92.09.26   11:10 WH

첨부 : USW(F)-6143
(대사 현홍주 - 국장)

USW(F) : 6143   년월일 :   시간 :

수 신 : 장 관 (통기, 통이, 1리안, 1통기원,   보 안
                                            용 제

발 신 : 주 미 대사 농림수산부 · 상공부) 국제경제국, 주미대사

제 목 : USW-4778, 첨부   (출처 : CSM, 9/25/92)

US Prods Europeans To Wrap Up GATT During October

American and French elections could hamper bid to complete Uruguay Round

By Ron Scherer

Staff writer of The Christian Science Monitor

NEW YORK

BOTH European and United States trade negotiators are hoping the French "oui" vote on European unity will clear the way for a push next month on stalled world trade talks.

If the talks, which are to be convened in Geneva, are not successful, negotiators believe the entire Uruguay Round of the General Agreement on Tariffs and Trade (GATT) may fall. The negotiations began six years ago in Punta del Este, Uruguay.

In order to succeed, the negotiations will have to overcome some sizable hurdles. After six years, both sides are still deeply split over the issues of agricultural subsidies. The issues involved in the split are complicated by politics: the US election this fall and a spring election in France. Because of the potential political difficulties, US Trade Representative Carla Hills is encouraging the Europeans to develop a strategy to complete the round. On Sept. 23, Ambassador Hills phoned Frans Andriessen, commissioner for external affairs of the European Community (EC), suggesting that the Europeans develop a strategy aimed at reaching a deal next month.

"I suggested to him that there was a window of opportunity in the month of October and assured him that our elections were no impediment to moving forward. I had heard that some people in Europe were saying it was an impediment," Hills said in an interview. After the phone call with Hills, Mr. Andriessen met with reporters and stated that the French vote "may have a positive impact," since it removes a major uncertainty. Echoing Hills, Andriessen said October may be the last chance "to strike a political deal."

After October, negotiations would be hampered by the US election and its aftermath. For example, if Arkansas Gov. Bill Clinton were elected, he would not be sworn in until Jan. 20. "Promoting GATT is an important priority for Bill Clinton," says Paula Stern, a Clinton international economics and trade adviser.

Negotiations will effectively be halted until the new president can get Congress to approve a new US trade representative. The

See GATT page 4

new trade representative will face a tight deadline, since "fast track" approval, under which Congress essentially must vote yes or no on the new treaty, expires May 31. Since it will take at least 90 days to get treaty details to Congress, this means the final negotiations deadline is March 1.

Once the fast-track approval deadline expires, Congress can make changes to the treaty - potentially delaying its final approval for years. For this reason, Hills says, "October is really crucial."

IT is considered unlikely that Congress would vote for fast-track approval again, since fast-track approval limits Congress's ability to respond to interest groups. "Congress is essentially fed up with fast track," says Michael Aho, a trade specialist at the Council on Foreign Relations in New York. It took two years for the Reagan administration to convince Congress to give it fast-track authority for the GATT round.

Some analysts believe reaching an agreement will be very difficult, since France has elections in the spring. "With the Socialists way behind in the polls, they may reason: Why alienate another farmer or two by going very far in agriculture?," Mr. Aho says.

외신 1과
동   제

6143-11-1

However, Hills says her message to the French is: "I would do everything I could to strengthen the French economy, and the best thing you can do to that is a successful conclusion to the Round, since trade is the best motor."

Agricultural subsidies remain the balkiest item to negotiate. The US and free traders such as Australia want to move toward elimination of all subsidies. However, the US provides at least $25 billion in subsidies to its farmers. On Sept. 2, President Bush said he would spend an extra $1 billion in new export subsidies for farmers. Initially, the EC, which heavily subsidizes its farmers, objected. But, on Wednesday, Andriessen said, "The $1 billion is less disquieting than at first glance." Without agreement on agriculture, there has been slow progress in other areas such as services and intellectual properties. "No one is showing their bottom line until agriculture breaks," explains Aho.

The EC, as part of its negotiating strategy, maintains that a total package must be negotiated. Andriessen calls it "indispensable" to reach agreement on market access and services. Hills says the US also wants a total package. But, without agreement on agriculture, she says, "there are at least 50 nations who will not allow access to service providers, construction companies, bankers, or lawyers." She notes that France is the second-largest provider of services in the world. "If I were [French President] Mitterrand, I would do everything possible to ensure a successful outcome to the Round," she adds.

The next major round of talks will begin Sept. 29. At the moment there are no ministerial talks scheduled. Hills says: "At the high level is not where we make all the progress." However, if the negotiations get into high gear, Hills and possibly President Bush will have to become involved, since they will have to make political decisions.

0055

USW(F) :

년월일 :   시간 :

수 신 : 장 관
발 신 : 주 미 대 사
제 목 :

보 통 안 제 ㄴㅅ

(출처 : WSJ, 9/29/92

Hills Warns Of a Deadline For Trade Talks

By BOB DAVIS
Staff Reporter of THE WALL STREET JOURNAL.

WASHINGTON—U.S. Trade Representative Carla Hills said world trade talks would fail unless the U.S. and European Community reach a breakthrough on agricultural issues by the end of October.

"We must strike a deal in October," she said, or the U.S. won't have enough time left under negotiating authority granted by Congress to finish an agreement under the General Agreement on Tariffs and Trade.

Mrs. Hills's statements were clearly meant to increase pressure on the Europeans—particularly the French—to make further concessions in agriculture. At the same time, however, other U.S. officials dangled the possibility that the U.S. might be willing to make some concessions in a separate dispute over the EC's subsidy of soybeans as part of a broad agreement on agriculture. "They are separate issues, but they could be done politically as part of a package." said a senior trade official.

Pessimism is nothing new in the GATT talks, which have seen one deadline after another pass without a resolution. But it's unusual for Mrs. Hills, who has managed to stay upbeat in the face of repeated setbacks, to set one. "The wheels are spinning in the administration to produce an October surprise" in the GATT talks, said C. Fred Bergsten, director of the Institute for International Economics, a free-trade think tank here. However, he said that the political disarray in Western Europe made it highly unlikely the Bush administration could pull it off.

U.S. negotiators had held off pressuring the Europeans over GATT until the vote in France Sunday on the Maastricht treaty on European unity. After the vote, U.S. officials hoped, France would be more willing to make concessions — and Germany would be more willing to pressure the French to do so. But the slim margin of victory in France, and the continuing turmoil in currency markets throughout Europe, dashed those hopes.

Moreover, said Mr. Bergsten, the French have started to use the prospect of a Clinton victory in the U.S. presidential election as a reason to avoid making concessions in GATT. "They say, 'Clinton is going to win; how can we sign a deal with Bush?'" said Mr. Bergsten.

Nevertheless, the U.S. has begun efforts to get the EC to move. Mrs. Hills said she spoke with Frans Andriessen, the EC's trade chief, Wednesday, urging the EC to adopt a formal, unified position on agriculture. "I could put together a deal in two hours if someone wanted to negotiate a deal." she said. "I can't develop a position for other parties."

At the same time that the U.S. is pressing Europe on trade talks, it is pressuring the Europeans over soybeans and other oilseeds. This spring the U.S. said it would impose prohibitively high tariffs on $1 billion of farm goods and other EC products as compensation for EC soybean subsidies, which a GATT resolution panel has twice found improper. The U.S. was expected to levy the sanctions in August, but put off action until after the Maastricht vote in France. The EC pegs the value of the damages caused by its soybean subsidies at $400 million.

On Wednesday, U.S. officials said, the U.S. offered to put the damage question to binding arbitration. Next Tuesday, at a meeting at the GATT in Geneva, the EC is expected to respond to the U.S. offer.

Under the plan, the arbitration panel would have 30 days to issue a ruling — giving the two sides another month to negotiate their dispute before the panel decision. Under some scenarios suggested by U.S. trade officials, the U.S. would be willing to accept a lesser settlement on oilseeds, if the Europeans would make concessions on export subsidies and other disputes at the heart of the trade talks.

But it isn't at all clear that the Europeans would look favorably on such a package. U.S. officials say they expect the EC to ask for another mediation panel on Sept. 29, which wouldn't have power to issue binding rulings. In that case, says one official, "We've just about come to the end of the road; I don't see anything left" but retaliation over oilseeds. That would clearly set back, and possibly kill, negotiations over GATT's agricultural provisions.

The U.S. has very little room to negotiate over soybeans because of domestic pressure from farm-state lawmakers to get the EC to remove its soybean subsidies. Last week, 60 senators, including Republican Leader Robert Dole of Kansas; Finance Committee Chairman Lloyd Bentsen, (D, Texas); and Republican John Danforth of Missouri wrote Mrs. Hills asking that she impose sanctions Sept. 29—unless the subsidies are removed.

Agriculture has become the heart of world trade talks. The U.S. and other industrialized countries think they must open their agricultural markets to get

6143-11-3

less-developed countries to welcome Western banks, insurance companies and other service businesses. But the U.S. and the EC have been at loggerheads over just how much change is necessary, with the U.S. pushing for more than the EC says it can swallow politically.

Mrs. Hills says that agriculture must be resolved by October because the U.S. and other nations must still face tough negotiations over services and tariffs, which could take several months. Moreover, she estimated it would take three or four months simply to translate a general agreement into the precise legal language required in trade accords. Under the bargaining authority granted by Congress, known as fast-track, all of that must be concluded by March 1 so the administration can formally notify Congress it intends to sign a GATT treaty. Under fast-track — which is considered crucial to winning approval of trade accords — lawmakers can vote yes or no on a pact, but can't amend it.

6143 — 11-4

ADMINISTRATION MAKES ALL-OUT EFFORT TO STRIKE GATT DEAL BEFORE ELECTION

High-level Administration efforts to break a deadlock in the Uruguay Round increased this week as at least two cabinet officials pressed their European Community counterparts to strike a political deal before the U.S. presidential election, according to informed sources. President Bush may also launch a personal initiative to reach a deal by the middle of October, which he could then hail as a strategic breakthrough for halting 40 years of growing EC agricultural subsidies, sources said.

Agriculture Secretary Ed Madigan telephoned EC Agriculture Commissioner Ray MacSharry on Sept. 21 after secret negotiations for an agriculture compromise broke down last week despite a new U.S. proposal aimed at making internal support cuts easier for the EC, sources said. These secret negotiations also focused on finding a solution to the U.S.-EC dispute over oilseeds subsidies, where officials discussed target figures for cutting EC production between 8, 9 and 9.5 million tons, sources said.

After the Madigan-MacSharry phone call, senior U.S. and EC agriculture negotiators resumed their meetings in Europe with the aim of developing a list of "talking points" that Madigan and MacSharry will try to settle at a future meeting, according to a Madigan spokesman. The effort would cover a number of disputes between the two sides, he said. Major trade disputes outstanding between the U.S. and the EC at this time involve the renewal of a deal on U.S. feed grain sales to Spain negotiated as compensation for trade lost when that country entered the EC, and a dispute over the access of U.S. corn gluten feed into the EC. At press time, there were reports that the MacSharry and Madigan meeting could be taking place as early as the weekend.

In addition, U.S. Trade Representative Carla Hills telephoned EC Commissioner Frans Andriessen on Sept. 23 to emphasize the U.S. willingness to make a deal. Andriessen in turn made a commitment to take stock of efforts so far and assess whether a deal can be struck in the next five to six weeks (see related story). President Bush said that a conclusion of the Uruguay Round is one of the central priorities of his "strategic trade policy" in a policy statement released on Sept. 10 (*Inside U.S. Trade*, Sept. 18, p 11).

The new U.S. proposal on internal supports, discussed in secret meetings last week between U.S. Department of Agriculture negotiator Joe O'Mara and EC Agriculture Director-General Guy Legras, sets out commitments that would be easier for the EC to meet than the commitments proposed by a draft agriculture text developed by the top official of the General Agreement on Tariffs & Trade last year. Instead of insisting that internal support cuts be applied to individual commodities, such as wheat or dairy, the new U.S. proposal would create an aggregate category of commodities to which the internal support

cuts would be applied. This would give the EC the flexibility to meet the new commitments with cuts in cereal or oilseeds supports, which it approved in the reform of the Common Agricultural Policy, while avoiding further cuts on supports for beef or dairy, where the CAP reform cuts were smaller. The U.S. proposal appears to be based on the recognition that the EC will not agree to cuts in addition to those taken in the CAP reform.

But the U.S. proposal is likely to raise a host of issues for Australia and other agricultural producers, who export commodities such as dairy and sugar, informed sources said. These countries want assurances that some of the internal support cuts are made in these areas, and they are likely to seek additional concessions in the area of tariffication and minimum market access to offset the reduced concessions the EC is likely to make in internal support cuts for these products.

The meeting of senior U.S. and EC agriculture negotiators last week at which the new U.S. proposal was discussed, however, failed to resolve the issue of whether the compensation payments made to farmers to offset their income lost from price cuts would be reduced after six years or permanently exempted. The U.S. has signaled it would be willing to fix the required internal support cuts at a level, possibly at 16 to 18 percent, which would make it easy for the EC to meet the target without touching the compensation payments. The Dunkel draft calls for internal support cuts of 20 percent. But the U.S. is offering to leave the option open, with the implicit understanding that the compensation payments would be on the table if a farm reform agreement were renegotiated. This ambiguity would allow the U.S. and EC to sidestep the one issue that has blocked the negotiations since earlier this year.

The EC apparently has refused to agree that the payments could be subject to cuts after six years, sources said. Instead, the EC seems to be pressing for wording that would leave it free to claim that the compensation payments would not be subject to cuts in the next farm reform negotiations, but would leave the U.S. free to claim the opposite. EC officials have insisted they cannot be seen agreeing to cutting the compensation payments, which were necessary to have EC member states agree to any cuts in internal supports made in the CAP reform package. The EC had promised that the payments would be secure, and to revoke this promise would undermine the credibility of the CAP reform.

U.S. sources said MacSharry's insistence on having the compensation payments permanently protected was the reason that last week's agriculture negotiations between the U.S. and EC broke down. In contrast, EC officials indicated that the deal broke down over the solution to the oilseeds dispute, where negotiators had not agreed on a target figure, but discussed a possible EC cut in oilseeds production to 9.5 million tons from 13 million tons in 1991. In addition, the deal is said to have included additional access for U.S. corn sales to Portugal, as well as additional access to the EC market for products such as vegetable oil and pork, sources said (see related story).

In a related development, all but two agriculture ministers of EC member states insisted in an Agriculture Council meeting held on Sept. 21 & 22 that the compensation payments had to be secure and could not be reduced over time. According to one source, only Britain and France failed to support that demand. At the same time, the French agriculture minister insisted that he could only agree to an Uruguay Round compromise if it did include a commitment to cut the volume of subsidized exports. Member states also expressed some doubts that the Bush Administration will be able to make the concessions they consider necessary to strike a deal acceptable to them.

The U.S. this month has also informally floated the idea of no longer requiring internal support cut commitments in an Uruguay Round agriculture deal, although that possibility had already been raised in U.S.-EC talks in May, informed sources said. It is unlikely that the EC would consider such an option, because it considers it a concession to the U.S. that would help the Administration solidify farm support behind a farm deal that would then only cover market access and export subsidy cuts, they pointed out.

High-level U.S. and EC officials this week acknowledged the confidential efforts to strike an Uruguay Round deal in a number of public comments. MacSharry told the Agriculture Council this week he hoped to have a package deal with an Uruguay Round compromise and an oilseeds deal in the near future. EC Commissioner Frans Andriessen told *Inside U.S. Trade* in a Sept. 23 interview that MacSharry was deeply involved in exploring the agricultural issue. EC Commission vice president for economic and financial affairs Henning Christophersen told a Washington, DC audience on Sept. 21 that the latest talks on the Uruguay Round took place the preceding week and Hills alluded to the talks in a Sept. 21 speech to the Institute of International Economics. Commenting on efforts to move the Uruguay Round forward, she said that it is important for the U.S. and EC to resolve their differences, and "in fact that is happening." She also highlighted the importance of the Uruguay Round and said it is "possible and politically feasible" to strike a deal before the elections, and to conclude the negotiations before the end of the year.

Australian trade minister John Kerin told reporters on Sept. 21 that he had spoken to Hills and

'S ∩ ʞOꓤᗺW∃   : 0Ⱶ:6Ɩ : ϛᘔ-6 -ᘔ6

0059

Madigan about U.S.-EC efforts in agriculture. He said the U.S. has been "literally exploring every element of the Dunkel text" with the EC. But despite the efforts, Kerin said it is apparent there is no "breakthrough."

In addition, chief negotiators for the U.S., EC, Japan and Canada met in Geneva on Sept. 23. And the ministers for the four countries are expected to meet in the middle of October, which the Administration hopes will be an opportunity to pull Japan and Canada into the political deal the U.S. hopes to strike with the EC.

The extent of the U.S. willingness to accommodate the EC was also revealed in a draft communique on the Uruguay Round the U.S. proposed for a ministerial meeting of the Asia Pacific Economic Cooperation initiative held earlier this month, according to informed sources. The U.S. sought wording on the Uruguay Round that would have downplayed the status of the draft Dunkel text by making reference to the Uruguay Round agreement that was emerging, they said. However, that effort was not successful because the final APEC communique on the Uruguay Round does not contain that language and calls the Dunkel text a "key document" for a final agreement. That appears a weaker formulation than calling it the "basis" for an agreement. *By Jutta Hennig*

주 미 대 사 관

USR(F) :　　　　　년월일 :　　　　　시간 :

수　신 : 장　관

발　신 : 주 미 대 사

제　목 :

보안	안제	
동		

（출처 :　　　　　　）

GERMAN AGRICULTURE MINISTER SPELLS OUT CONDITIONS FOR URUGUAY ROUND DEAL

German Agriculture Minister Ignaz Kiechle late last week drew a hard line on one of the major stumbling blocks between the U.S. and the European Community to an Uruguay Round agriculture deal by insisting that compensation payments to be made to European farmers as part of the Common Agricultural Policy reform must be permanently preserved. The direct income payments must be "secured in the framework" of the General Agreement on Tariffs & Trade to ensure that they are not cut, Kiechle told reporters on Sept. 18.

He said that protecting the compensation payments is one of three "essential" conditions Germany must see in an Uruguay Round deal. He also cited the need to curb the imports of feed grains into the EC at current levels, and argued that export subsidy cuts must be applied to product groups, not to individual products. The EC is not able to absorb further imports of foreign feed grain substitutes into its markets, because these additional imports would undermine the program of cutting production through set-asides, he said. Kiechle spoke to reporters after meeting with U.S. Trade Representative Carla Hills and Agriculture Secretary Ed Madigan.

The minister said he doubted that a solution to the U.S.-EC dispute over oilseeds could be achieved this month, and said that Hills told him that without a solution on the oilseeds issue, the U.S. could not make any new proposals to move along the Uruguay Round. He said, however, that Hills told him the two issues are not directly linked, and Hills also told reporters Sept. 18 that the two issue are not linked. Nonetheless, U.S. and EC negotiators this week continued their efforts to strike a deal on both the Uruguay Round and the oilseeds dispute, exploring a reported target figure of cutting EC oilseed production to about eight or nine million tons (see related story).

Kiechle said neither Madigan nor Hills raised the issue of U.S. retaliation over the oilseeds dispute and he did not ask him about it. He hinted that the EC could further tighten set-aside requirements for oilseeds to bring about a deal, but ruled out any drastic production cut. He said that France, Spain and Italy would never agree to a U.S. demand that oilseed production be cut by 50 percent, and that a cut of this magnitude would be hard for Germany to accept. The 50 percent cut is a U.S. demand provided the entire compensation for damage done by EC oilseeds subsidies would be offered in the oilseeds sector, which the U.S. has not proposed. Kiechle also rejected the notion of a third GATT panel to determine the level of compensation, saying he was "sick and tired" of panel reports. The EC this week rejected U.S. requests to a binding arbitration panel (see related story).

6143-11-8

Kiechle implied that the extent of the CAP reform essentially met the U.S. demands for cuts in EC production and insisted that European farmers could not be asked to make more sacrifices. He pointed out that CAP reform would cut production of cereals by 20 million tons and would take an addition 10 million tons off the market by having it used as feed in the EC.

He emphasized that Germany is one of the EC members that wants a quick resolution of the Uruguay Round on the basis of a balanced package, but said other members have a different attitude. And he implied that the efforts to strike the Uruguay Round deal were set back by the U.S. announcement of increased agricultural export subsidies made by President Bush earlier this month. Kiechle said that Hills and Madigan emphasized to him that the deal did not provide additional money, but came out of a previously earmarked fund for export subsidies that would have otherwise been announced later. The subsidies also came under attack from French finance minister Michel Sapin, who told reporters Sept. 21 that the subsidies were a step backwards.

Separately, EC Commissioner Frans Andriessen said the export subsidy announcement did not have a decisive impact on the Uruguay Round. Speaking to reporters in a September 23 press conference, he said the announcement was not helpful because it came at a time when the U.S. is pressing the EC to reduce the volume of the subsidized exports. But Andriessen said that an analysis of the $1 billion export subsidy package shows that it is less "disquieting" than it appears at first glance.

USR(F) :　　　　　년월일 :　　　　시간 :

수　신 : 장　관

발　신 : 주 미 대 사

제　목 :　　　　　　　　　　　　　　　〈출처 :　　　　）

보안	
통제	

SENIOR EC OFFICIAL TO ASSESS CHANCES OF REACHING GATT DEAL BEFORE U.S. ELECTION

European Community Commissioner Frans Andriessen this week told U.S. Trade Representative Carla Hills that he will assess the status of high-level U.S.-EC efforts to break a deadlock in international agriculture negotiations, as well as talks on market access, to see if a political deal on the Uruguay Round can be struck before the U.S. presidential elections. Andriessen said he was planning to meet with Agriculture Commissioner Ray MacSharry, who is "very deeply" involved in exploring a possible U.S.-EC compromise on agriculture, late this week.

Andriessen said he would be able to tell by this weekend whether there is a "window of opportunity" for a political deal in the next five to six weeks.

He told *Inside U.S. Trade* in a Sept. 23 interview that if he concludes that the U.S. and EC could "work cooperatively in some manner," the Commission would have to decide internally how to proceed.

6143 — 11 - 10

외신 1과	
등제	

92- 9-25 ; 19:13

EMBROK U. S. ;#39

0063

Andriessen said he laid out his plans to Hills in a Sept. 23 phone call, which she had initiated to discuss the Uruguay Round. He spoke to Hills during a stay in New York, where he was ending the United Nations general assembly meeting. Andriessen emphasized that the phone conversation did not cover substantive positions on the negotiations, and that he did not discuss the Uruguay Round issue with Acting Secretary of State Lawrence Eagleburger when the two met in New York this week.

Andriessen publicly discussed his efforts on the Uruguay Round in a Sept. 23 press conference, where he said he intended to "launch a new initiative" to move the negotiations ahead. He did not spell out the specifics of his efforts, but emphasized the need to bring the negotiations to a successful conclusion soon. He also conceded that the Uruguay Round negotiations had been stalled by the French referendum on the Maastricht Treaty, which was narrowly approved by French voters Sept. 20.

In the interview, Andriessen said his effort to work on moving the negotiations forward was based on a "very strong commitment" by the White House to strike a deal, which he said is shared by the EC. In addition, he said that negotiators recognize that time is running out for the Uruguay Round, particularly in light of the U.S. political calendar. Separately, Hills told an Institute for International Economics audience on Sept. 21 that the negotiations had to move forward now to conclude the negotiations by the end of the year. In two months, reaching that goal will not be possible, regardless of the election outcome, Hills warned.

Andriessen warned that U.S. retaliation on oilseeds could ruin the possibility of striking a GATT deal in the next five to six weeks. He indicated it would be difficult to convince his "European constituency" that the EC should strike a deal that will be seen as a major concession in agriculture if the EC faced retaliation at the same time. He did not directly link the resolution of the oilseeds dispute to the Uruguay Round. But he emphasized repeatedly that if the U.S. and the EC came to an agreement in the Uruguay Round, it would be a "major step" toward a solution of the oilseeds dispute because an international farm deal would set the level of internal supports for EC farm production in the future.

Andriessen hinted that the EC would seek few changes in a draft Uruguay Round agreement beyond the area of agriculture by saying the EC would not be "too difficult" with that text. He said that the EC had "deep concerns" in the draft agreement on subsidies, but he did not think he would be able to change that text. He did concede that issues needed to be resolved in regard to the Multilateral Trade Organization and to dispute settlement, where he said there needed to be "some more precision" to ensure that unilateral measures would not be used in disputes that should be settled in the GATT. Andriessen refused to specify EC demands, but said he wanted to prevent unilateral action in all areas where it went against the rules and the spirit of the GATT.

The potential political deal that could be struck in the next five to six weeks would be broader than agriculture, and would include the areas of market access and services, Andriessen said. He pointed out that once agriculture is resolved, the other issues may fall into place, despite some difficulties. He also said the deal should include parties other than the EC and U.S., pointing out that in agriculture, the Cairns group of agricultural producers had to be involved. On market access, the U.S. and the EC still have to resolve the issue of tariff peaks, and the zero for zero initiative, where some of the demands by the U.S. for tariff-free trade are "extremely difficult" for the EC, said Andriessen. He said the EC was "very unsatisfied" with the Japanese position on market access. In a related development, informed sources said the U.S. hopes to bring Japan and Canada into the Uruguay Round deal at a mid-October meeting of trade ministers of the so-called quad--the U.S., EC, Japan and Canada.

And he said the Uruguay Round process should return to Geneva for multilateral negotiations "the sooner the better," a sentiment echoed by Hills in her Sept. 21 IIE speech.

Andriessen emphasized that a GATT agriculture deal cannot undermine the credibility of the Common Agricultural Policy by making subject to cuts the compensation payments farmers would receive to offset income lost from price cuts. The U.S. and EC negotiations have stumbled for months over how to treat the compensation payments, which the U.S. wants to subject to disciplines and the EC wants sheltered from cuts permanently.

He also identified two potential problem areas the EC could have with the North American Free Trade Agreement, emphasizing that the rules of origin could prevent imports of "spare parts" from the EC to Mexico. The EC will examine the provisions of the rules of origin "very carefully," he said. In addition, the EC is concerned over the financial services rules that demand foreign firms must be "fully established" in another NAFTA country to have access to Canada's financial markets. Andriessen also said that the EC would raise in the GATT the NAFTA's restrictions on access for third country sugar producers in the Mexican market, which begin in the seventh year after the agreement. In the NAFTA, Mexico is committed after year six to establishing import restrictions for sugar equivalent to those in the U.S., which offers minimal access for foreign sugar. *By Jutta Hennig*

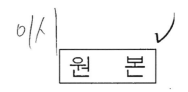
외 무 부

종 별 :

번 호 : USW-4721 　　　　　　　　　일 시 : 92 0922 1855

수 신 : 장관(통기,통이,통삼,경일,경기원,상공부) 사본:주 EC, 저네바대사-필

발 신 : 주미대사

제 목 : UR 관련 주재국 언론 보도

　　마스트리히트조약이 UR 협상에 미치는 영향과 관련, 금일 (9.22)자 주재국 언론의보도 내용 요지를 하기 보고함. (관련기사는 USW(F) - 6049 참조) 배포필

　　1. W.P. 지

　　. 동지는 HILLS USTR 대표의 말을 인용, 그간 프랑스 정부가 마스트리히트 조약비준에 관한 국민투표를 이유로 UR 협상에 적극적이지 못했으나 선거가 끝난 이상 년내 UR 타결가능성이 높아 졌다고 보도함.

　　. 한편 동지는 UR 과 프랑스 국민 투표와는 아무런 관련이 없으며 오히려 미국의 선거가 UR타결에 실제적인 장애가 되고 있다는 프랑스 SAPIN 재무상의 말을 인용 보도함.

　　2. JOC 지

　　. 동지는 프랑스 국민의 마스트리히트 조약 비준 찬성에도 불구, 아주 근소한 차이의 국민투표 결과로 인해 EC 가 자신있게 UR 협상에 임할수 없으며, 특히 부시 대통령의 9월초 소맥 보조금 증액 발표와 국민투표와 UR 과의 연계를 부인하는 프랑스정부의 태도에 비추어 협상 진전이 의문시 된다는 취지로 보도함.

　　. 또한 동지는 미국 관리의 말을 인용 미국은 EC 가 93.1월 새로이 구성되는 집행위가 자리잡을 때까지 UR 협상을 지연시킬 것으로믿고 있다고 보도함.

　　3. F.T. 지

　　. 동지는 UR 협상 참가자들과 브뤼셀에서 회합중인 EC 농업상들의 반응을 인용하면서 금번 프랑스의 국민투표가 UR 협상 진전에 긍정적인 영향을 미치지 못할 것으로 보도함.

　　. 동지는 미국의 FAST TRACK 절차에 따라 93.3.1.까지 UR 협상을 완료해야 함에도 불구하고 유럽내의 마스트리히트 조약 반대 움직임, 최근의 통화 위기와 독일,

---

통상국　　차관　　　　　　2차보　　경제국　　통상국　　통상국　　경기원　　상공부

PAGE 1　　　　　　　　　　　　　　　　　　92.09.23　　08:35 CR

　　　　　　　　　　　　　　　　　　　　　외신 1과 통제관

0065

프랑스, 영국과 이태리의 복잡한 국내적 어려움으로 인해 EC 가 UR타결 관련 단안을 당분간 내리기 <u>어려울것</u> 이라고 협상 관계자의 말을 인용 보도함.

    (대사현홍주 - 국 장)

외 무 부

종 별 :

번 호 : GVW-1759

일 시 : 92 0922 1000

수 신 : 장 관(통기, 경기원, 재무부, 농림수산부, 상공부)

발 신 : 주 제네바대사

제 목 : UR/농산물 협상(최근동향)

9.21. 당관 최농무관은 당지 불란서 대표부의 HENRY 농무관과 접촉, 최근의 표제 협상 동향 및 미-EC 간 유지작물 분쟁경과등에 대하여 의견 교환 하였는바 동인 언급 요지 하기 보고함.

1. 불란서 국민투표이후 UR 협상 전망

- 국민투표결과 매우 근소한 차이로 통과되었기 때문에 불란서 입장에서는 협상에 융통성을 보여주기가 매우 어려운 상황임.

O 또한 미국 대통령 선거 이전에는 미국측이 융통성을 보이지 않을 것으로 예상되기 때문에 11 월 이전까지 실질적인 진전을 기대하기는 어려움.

- 미-EC 간 가장 큰 쟁점은 수출보조 물량 감축문제임.

(BLUE BOX 는 비교적 쉽게 타협점을 찾을 것이고, REBALANCING 문제는 수출 보조 협상과 연계된 일종의 LEVERAGE 성격의 강함)

O 품목군내 융통성 부여는 미국측이 거절한바 있음.

O 8 년간 24 퍼센트 또는 6 년간 18 퍼센트 감축안은 지난번 G7 정상회담시 독일 농무장관이 제시한 것임.

- 금일부터 당지에서 개최되는 G-8 회의는 WOLTER 농업국장이 주재하며, 별다른 진전이 없을 것으로 예상됨.

O DENIS 의장은 9.21. 주말경 당지에 와서 9.28 주간중 시장접근그룹(MA) 회의를 개최할 것으로 예상됨.

2. OILSEED 분쟁

- OILSEED 문제는 CAP 본질과 직결되므로 EC 의 CAP 개혁안을 재조정 하지 않은 범위내에서 타결되기를 바람.

- 9.16(수) 당지에서 개최되었던 미-EC 간 협의는 별다른 결론없이 짧게 마쳤는바,

통상국	장관	차관	2차보	외정실	분석관	정와대	안기부	경기원
재무부	농수부	상공부						

PAGE 1

92.09.22 19:18

* 원본수령부서 승인없이 복사 금지

외신 2과 통제관 BS

0067

금일부터 개최되는 EC 농업이사회에 해결방안을 기대한 것으로 보임

- OILSEED 생산 감축은 여타곡물 생산과 연계되기 때문에 약속을 이행하기 어려운점이 있음. 현재까지 타결 방안을 찾지 못했다고 해서 미국의 HIT LIST 를곧 발표하지는 않을 것으로 봄. 계속해서 28 조에 의한 해결방안을 모색할것임.

3. BANANA 문제

- EC 의 200 만톤 QUOTA 제안을 중남미 국가들이 거부하고 있으나, 갓트 22 조에 의한 협의는 계속해 나갈것임. (아직 확정된 내용이 아니므로 23 조 대상은 아님)

0 금년말까지는 어떤 형태로든 결론을 내야 할 문제임.

(UR 과 관련해서는 명시적인 관세화의 예외 규정방법보다는 해당국가와 별도의 AGREEMENT 형식으로 해결지을 가능성이 있음)

4. 미국 소맥수출 보조금

- EC 에 별다른 타격이 없음.

0 일부 중동국가, 아프리카국가에 대하여 EC 와 경합이 있지만, 호주, 알젠틴등이 더 큰 타격을 받을 것으로 예상됨.

- 그러나 UR 정신 및 중간 평가 합의사항(STANDSTILL) 에 위배되므로 금번 9.29 이사회때 강력하게 항의할 것임.끝.

(대사 박수길-국장)

예고:92.12.31. 까지

외 무 부

종 별 :

번 호 : USW-4709   일 시 : 92 0922 1538

수 신 : 장관(봉기,봉이,경기원,농수산부)

발 신 : 주 미 대사

제 목 : 농협중앙회 방미 결과 보고

　　　IMF 연차총회 참석차 당지를 방문한 한호선 농협중앙회장은 9.22 USTR 의 CARLA HILLS 대표와 MACHAEL MOSKOW 부대표를 면다, UR/ 농산물협상과 관련하여 한국농촌 실정등을 설명한바 요지 하기보고함.

　　1. 농협 한호선회장의 한국 농촌실정 설명

　　0 한국은 미국 제 5 위의 농산물 수입국이며 남북한이 대치된 상태에서 6 백만 한국농민들은 식량안보를 항상 의식하면서 농업분야에 생계를 유지하고있음.

　　0 지난 9.3 서울을 방문한 DUNKEL GATT 사무총장을 만났을때도 강조한 배와같이 각국의 농업은 각자 그특성이 있으며 한국이 강조하는 쌀농사의 경우에도 몬순기후로서 농민들의 70 프로가 쌀농사에 종사 (이중 85 프로는 소규모 농가)하고 쌀이 농업소득중 50 프로이상의 비중을 차지하고있는 점을 감안해야하며 지난번 BUSH 미대통령의 방한에 즈음하여 40 일의 짧은 기간동안 쌀수입개방 반대 서명운동을 전개하여 1300 만명의 호응을 받았던 바와같이 쌀은 우리국민들에게는 아주 민감한 품목이며 최근 BUSH 대통령의 10 억불 소맥보조금 지급 확대도 이러한 맥락에서 이해하고자함.

　　0 지난번 DUNKEL TEXT 에서 제시된 예외없는 관세화와 최소시장접근등에대하여 한국으 이를 시장개방으로 생각하고있는바 한국은 UR 협상을 기본적으로 반대하는것이아니고 각국 농업의 특성과 입장이 충분히 반영되기를 희망함.

　　0 따라서 한국이 금년부터 10 개년 계획으로 농업구조조정 사업에 착수한 점을 감안하여 충분한 유예기간의 확보가 필요함을 강조하였음.

　　2. USTR CARLA HILLS 대표 및 MOSKOW 부대표 반응

　　0 UR 협상은 미국이 무엮분야 협상에서 제일 우선순위로 추진하고있으며 세계 100 여개 국가가 동협상이 성공되기를 바라고있음로 한국도 UR 협상에 적극 참여하기를

통상국 　　장관　　　차관　　　2차보　　　통상국　　　분석관　　　청와대　　　안기부　　　경기원
농수부

PAGE 1   92.09.23　07:44

외신 2과　롱제관 BX

0069

희망함.

0 한국의 쌀이 일본과같이 아주 민감한 품목임을 인정않나 모든 국가가 예외를 인정할경우 UR 협상은 성공할수없으며 관세화는 UR 협상에서 가장 중요한 항목임.

0 따라서 미국은 관세화의예외를 인정할수없으며 한국은 가장 빨리 발전한 성공적인 국가로서 개도국 조항을 적용할수도없다고봄.

0 따라 한국이 쌀의 경우 어렵더라도 서서히 수입을 시작하므로서 현재의 국제 쌀 가격의 5-6 배나되는 국내 쌀 가격을 적절히 조정할 필요가 있다고 보며석고기도 1997 년에는 수입자유화를 하여야할것이며 이렇게 하므로서 한국은 장기적으로는 이익을 볼수있을것임.

3. 미측의 상기 반응에 대하여 한호선 회장은 MOSKOW 대사가 한국농업을 잘알고있어서 다행스럽게 생각하며 한국노업이 일본과 다를뿐아니라 DUNEKL TEXT 에서 금유, 유통등 SERVICE 분야에서는 예외가 있는데 가장 예외를 인정받아야할농업분야에서 예외없는 관세화를 주장하는데 대해서 우리농민들은 이해할수없음을 강조하면서 UR 협상은 성공되어야하며 그과정에서 다소의 예외가 인정되는 가운데 타결될것으로 희망한다고 하였음.

4. 한호서 회장은 IMF 정기총참석 및 NATIONAL COUNCIL OF FARMER COOPERATIVE 의 WAYNE BOUTWELL 회장은 면담하고 오는 9.24 귀국예정임.끝

(대사 현홍주-국장)

예고: 92.12.31 까지

외 무 부

종 별 :

번 호 : ECW-1171   일 시 : 92 0925 1730

수 신 : 장 관(통기, 경기원, 재무부, 농림수산부, 상공부, 기정동문)사본;주제네바 대사

발 신 : 주 EC 대사

제 목 : 갓트/UR 협상

1. 9.24-25 당지 및 영국을 방문(당지 방문직전에 워싱턴도 방문)한 KEPIN 호주무역장관은 CAIRNS 그룹대표로서 MAC SHARRY 집행위원등과 회담을 가진후, 기자들과가진 간담회에서, 세계 지도자들의 UR 협상문제에 대한 관심이 고조되고 있어 조만간UR 협상이 타결될 가능성이 높아지고 있다고 말함. 동인은 금번 순회 일정을 갖기이전에 생각했던 것보다 미국.EC 방문후 동 협상의 타결 가능성에 대해 보다 확신을 갖게 되었다고 말하고, 미국의 대통령후보 두사람 모두가 협상의 중요성을 이해하고 있어, 미대통령 선거가 동협상 타결의 장애 요소는 아니라고 말함. 그러나, 동인은 UR이 타결되려면, 미.EC간에 어려운 협상이 남아 있는 것은 사실이라고 말하고 양측의정치적인 결단과 농업 문제뿐 아니라 <u>서비스 분야</u>에서도 공히 탄력적인 입장을 보여주어야 할것이라고 말함.

2. 한편, MAC SHARRY 위원은 동회담에서 협상의 조기타결 가능성에 대해 회의적인 입장을 표명하고 EC도 연내에 타결되기를 희망하나 여하한 희생을 감수하면서 까지 협상의 타결을 추진하지는 않을 것임을 다시 밝히고, 미측이 새로운 탄력적인 입장을 제시하기 전까지는 동협상에 커다란 변화를 기대하기는 어려울 것이라는 입장을 강조한 것으로 알려짐. 끝.

(대사 권동만 - 국장)

통상국   2차보   외정실   안기부   경기원   재무부   농수부   상공부

외 무 부

종 별 :

번 호 : ECW-1174　　　　　　　　　　　일 시 : 92 0925 1730

수 신 : 장관 (봉기, 경기원, 재무부, 농림수산부, 상공부, 기정동문)

발 신 : 주 EC 대사　　　　사본: 주 미-중계필, 주제네바-직송필

제 목 : 갓트/UR 협상

연: ECW-1153

일반문서로 재분류 (192. 12. 31)

9.25. 당관 이관용농무관은 EC 집행위 대외총국의 GUTH 농산물 담당과장을 방문, 표제관련 협의한바 동인의 주요 발언요지 하기 보고함

1. 미.EC 양자협상

가. 9 월초 HILLS 대표가 브랏셀을 방문한 이후, 미.EC 는 보안통제하에 총국장수준 (EC 는 LE GRAS 농업총국장 참석) 의 양자협상을 하고 있음. 동 협상에서는 OILSEEDS 문제를 포함한 UR 협상과 관련된 전반적인 문제가 검토되고 있으나 진전이 없는 것으로 알고 있으며, 7 월초 뮨헨 G-7 정상회담이전의 상황과 다른것이 없음

나. 미.EC 간의 농업분야에 있어서의 쟁점은 수출보조금 감축방법과 CAP 개혁에따른 소득보조금의 GREEN BOX 적용문제이며, PEACE CLAUSE 문제에 대하여는 어느정도 의견접근이 이루어졌음. 상기 현안쟁점 중에서도 소득보조의 감축보조 제외여부 (즉, 미국은 BLUE 또는 YELLOW BOX 적용을 주장한 반면, EC 는 GREEN BOX 적용을 주장) 가 가장 중요한 문제이며, EC 가 BLUE 또는 YELLOW 적용을 받아드린다는 것은 가격보조 인하로 인한 소득손실 보상을 한시적으로 지급한다는 의미이므로 불란서나 독일의 경우 이를 정치적으로 수용하기 어려울 것임. 한편 수출보조감축문제에 있어서 EC 의 입장은 품목군별 감축과 장기유예기간 부여나 동건에 대해서도 의견접근이 이루어지지 않고 있음

2. 협상전망

가. UR 협상이 정치적인 결단과 밀접한 관련이 있다는 것을 부정하기는 어려우나, 93.3 월 프랑스 총선거등 EC 회원국들의 국내정치 일정이 계속되므로 어느 특정국가의 정치적 일정과 UR 협상을 계속 연계시킨다면 동 협상의 타결은 어려워질 것임. 동

통상국 재무부	장관 농수부	차관 상공부	2차보 중계	구주국	분석관	청와대	안기부	경기원
								✓

PAGE 1

* 원본수령부서 승인없이 복사 금지

92.09.26　05:37

외신 2과 통제관 FM

0072

협상타결의 관건은 EC 의 소득보조 감축문제에 대한 미국 또는 EC 의 정치적 결단여하에 달려있음

나. 9 월초 HILLS 대표가 브랏셀을 방문한 목적은 UR 협상이 미대통령 선거이전에 타결되면 BUSH 대통령의 지지도확대에 도움이 될 것이라는 미측의 입장을 전달하기 위한 것으로 알고 있음. 따라서 미국으로서는 대통령선거 이전에 동 협상이 타결되기를 희망하고 있는 것으로 알고 있으나 다만 동 협상이 타결되려면 미국이 기존입장을 어는정도 양보하여야 하나 그 결정이 용이하지는 않을것임

다. 상기와같은 미국과 EC 의 미묘한 입장을 고려할때, 미대통령 선거이전 또는 연내에 동 협상타결 여부를 예측하는 것은 매우 어려우나 개인적인 판단으로는 회의적으로 봄. 끝

(대사 권동만-국장)

예고: 92.12.31. 까지

이서(년)

외 무 부

종   별 :

번   호 : GEW-1818

일   시 : 92 0929 1200

수   신 : 장관(봉기) 사본:주제네바대사(직필)

발   신 : 주 독 대사

제   목 : UR 협상 동향

대:WGE-1274

연:GEW-2185(91.10.24)

일반문서로 재분류(1992 . 12.31)

1. 대호관련 당관 정문수 참사관은 9.28. 연방경제부 GATT(농산물담당) KIESOW 부과장과 면담한바, 아래 보고함

가. UR 협상 전망

지난 7 월초 뮌헨 개최 G-7 정상회담시, 금년말까지 UR 협상타결 목표 실정에 의견일치를 보았으나, 특히 농산물협상과 관련, 불란서측은 9.20. 마스트리히트 조약 비준에 관한 국민투표에 미칠 영향을 고려 동 국민투표 이전까지는 기존입장 변경에 난색을 보인것으로 알려짐.

그러나 불 국민투표의 긍정적 결과에도 불구, UR 협상의 연내타결 가능성은 희박한 것으로 보이는바, 협상일정상 연내타결이 이루어지기위해서는 늦어도 10월 중순까지는 주요쟁점에 관한 정치적 절충이 이루어저야 할것이나, 미대통령선거 실시일인 11.3. 까지 불란서측 및 현 미 행정부의 주요한 입장변화를 기대하기 어려운 상황임에 비추어 결국 빨라야 내년 2 월 이후에나 협상진전 전망이 가능할 것으로 봄

나. 미.EC 간 OIL SEEDS 보조금 관련 분쟁 확대

연호 보고 미국및 EC 간 현안인 OIL SEEDS 보조금 관련, 최근 미국을 위시한 카나다, 브라질, 알젠틴 등 국가들이 EC 국가들에 대해 전면적인 시정조치 또는 피해보상을 요구하고 있어, UR 협상과는 별개 사안이긴 하나, UR 협상 분위기에 크게 부정적 영향을 주고 있음.

지난 89 년 미국등의 GATT 제소로 발단이된 동건은 GATT 의 EC 관계규정 개정요구(89.12.14. 자 GATT PANEL 판정, 90.1.25. 자 GATT 이사회 결정)에 부응, 지난 91.10. EC 측이 CAP 개혁차원에서 종래 가공업자에 대한 가격

통상국   장관   차관   2차보   구주국   분석관   정와대   종리실   안기부

0074

보조방식에서경지면적을 기준으로한 생산자 보조방식으로 전환하는데 합의한바(813)있음.

그러나 미국등은 상기 EC 측 조치를 받아들이지 않고 GATT 에 제 2 차로 제소, 92.3.16. 자로 GATT PANEL 에서는 미국등의 피해를 인정 EC 측의 동 보조금 제도 개선또는 배상을 권고하는 결정을 함으로서 동문제는 금 9.29. 제네바 개최GATT 이사회에 회부되어 주요 논쟁사로 부각될 것이 예상됨.

GATT PANEL 판정관련, 미국측은 EC 측의 OIL SEEDS 보조로 인한 피해액을 약 10 억 20 억불로 추정하고 향후 1 개월내로 정확한 피해액 산정을 요구하는 한편, EC 생산 여타 농산물에 대한 보복관세 LIST 를 준비한 것으로 알려지고 있고, EC 측은 특별대책위를 구성, 대응책 강구에 부심하고 있어 향후 UR 협상 진전을 더욱 어렵게 한들고 있음.

다. UR 농산물 협상의 미해결 쟁점사항

현재의 UR 농산물 협상에서의 미국측및 EC 간의 주요이견은, 미국등 케언즈그룹의 정부보조 농산물 수출 24 프로 감축 요구및 국내보조에 있어서 GREEN BOX 인정범위에 관한 이견등이며, 기타 바나나 수출보조 문제및 PEACE CLAUSE 문제가 주요쟁점사항으로 남아 있음

2. 표제관련, 특이 진전사항은 수시 보고코저 함. 끝

(대사-국장)

예고: 92.12.31 까지

0075

외 무 부

110-760 서울 종로구 세종로 77번지 / (02)720-2188 / (02)720-2686 (FAX)

문서번호 통기 20644-*339*

시행일자 1992. 9.30.(   )

취급		장 관	
보존		澲	/
국 장	전 결		
심의관	(서명)		
과 장	(서명)		
기안	이 시 형		협조

수신 수신처 참조

참조

제목 UR 협상에 대한 미국입장

1. 주한 미국대사관 Morford 참사관은 9.30(금) 우리부 통상국장을 방문, UR 협상에 대한 미국입장을 아래 요지로 설명하였습니다.

    가. UR 협상을 연내 타결 하는것이 미국의 입장임.

    나. 미.EC간 농산물 협상에서도 균형있는 타협안이 도출 될 것임.

    다. 미국 대통령 선거에서 누가 승리하더라도 UR 협상은 연말 까지는 타결될 것이므로 모든 협상 참가국들은 관망적 태도를 버리고 조속히 마지막 협상에 임해야 함.

2. 상기 미국입장을 담은 Talking Points를 별첨 송부하오니 참고 바랍니다.

첨 부 : 미국입장 설명서 1부. 끝.

(검열 스탬프: 1992. 10. 02 등기관)

외 무 부 장 관

수신처 : 경제기획원장관, 재무부장관, 농림수산부장관, 상공부장관, 특허청장.

0076

발 신 전 보

번 호 : WGV-1454   921001 1523 WG   종별 :

WUS -4496

수 신 : 주   제네바, 미 대사. 총영사

발 신 : 장 관 (통 기)

제 목 : UR 협상에 대한 미국입장

1. 주한 미국대사관 Morford 참사관은 9.30(금) 통상국장을 방문, UR 협상에 대한
   입장을 아래 요지 설명하였음.

   가. UR 협상을 연내 타결 하는것이 미국의 입장임.

   나. 미.EC간 농산물 협상에서도 균형있는 타협안이 도출 될 것임.

   다. 미국 대통령 선거에서 누가 승리하더라도 UR 협상은 연말 까지는 타결될
       것이므로, 모든 협상 참가국들은 관망적 태도를 버리고 조속히 마지막 협상에
       임해야 함.

2. 상기 Morford 참사관의 Talking Points를 별첨(FAX) 송부함.

첨 부 : Talking Points 1부. 끝.

(통상국장 홍 정 표)

0077

長官報告事項

報告畢

1992. 10. 2.
通 商 局
通商機構課(55)

題 目 : UR 協商關聯 美國 立場

주한 미국대사관 Morford 참사관은 9.30(수) 통상국장을 방문, UR 협상에 임하는 미국의 입장을 아래 요지로 설명(non-paper 전달)하였음을 보고 드립니다.

---

1. Non-Paper 요지

   ㅇ UR 협상을 年內에 妥結하겠다는 미국 입장은 여전히 確固함.

      - 7월의 뮌헨 G-7 정상회담시 EC측의 희망에 따라 그동안 협상을 촉진하지 않았으나, 불란서 국민투표가 종결되었으므로 조속한 협상재개 필요

   ㅇ 그간의 미.EC간 협의결과, 농산물 문제에 대한 균형된 타협안 도출이 가능하다고 보며, 농산물을 포함한 UR 협상의 모든 분야에서 진전을 기대함.

   ㅇ Fast Track 협상 권한의 시한 및 협상의 복잡성을 고려할때 실질협상을 11월 중순까지 미룰 수 없음.

   ㅇ 미국은 대통령 선거에 관계없이 년내에 협상을 종결하기 위해 노력할 것임.

      - 행정부, 의회, 업계 모두가 "좋은 UR 협상결과 (GOOD Uruguay Round Agreement)"가 국익에 도움이 된다는데 공감.

   ㅇ EC를 비롯한 여타 참여국도 연내 협상 종결을 위해 적극 노력해야 할 것임.

2. 언론대책 : 해당없음.

3. 조치내용 : 상기 미측 입장을 관계부처 및 공관에 통보.

첩부 : non-paper 사본 1부. 끝.

0078

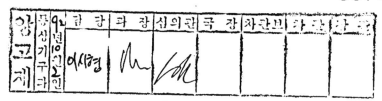

-- THE UNITED STATES REMAINS COMMITTED TO CONCLUDING THE
URUGUAY ROUND BEFORE THE END OF THE YEAR. TO ACHIEVE THE
COMPREHENSIVE AGREEMENT THAT WE ALL NEED, WE CANNOT DELAY
NEGOTIATIONS ANY FURTHER.

-- THE U.S. DID NOT PRESS THE NEGOTIATIONS OVER THE PAST THREE
MONTHS BECAUSE OF THE EC'S DESIRE TO AWAIT THE OUTCOME OF THE
FRENCH REFERENDUM ON MAASTRICHT. NOW THAT THE FRENCH VOTE IS
OVER, WE FULLY EXPECT EUROPEAN GOVERNMENTS WILL REENGAGE AND
MAKE GOOD ON THE COMMITMENT OF LEADERS AT THE G-7 SUMMIT TO
CONCLUDE THE ROUND BY THE END OF THE YEAR.

-- FAILURE TO TAKE ADVANTAGE OF THE TIME REMAINING PUTS THE
NEGOTIATIONS AT RISK. MOVEMENT NOW WOULD SIGNAL RENEWED
COMMITMENT TO GROWTH-ORIENTED POLICIES AND INTERNATIONAL
COOPERATION.

-- AT THE MUNICH ECONOMIC SUMMIT, EUROPEAN LEADERS MADE CLEAR
THAT NEGOTIATIONS WOULD HAVE TO BE DELAYED UNTIL THE FRENCH
REFERENDUM ON MAASTRICHT, BUT NEVERTHELESS AGREED TO CONCLUDE
NEGOTIATIONS BY YEAR END.

--· THERE SHOULD BE NO FURTHER DELAYS - EUROPE, AND THE WORLD,
MUST FINALIZE THESE NEGOTIATIONS.

-- THE UNITED STATES IS RETURNING TO THE NEGOTIATING TABLE IN
GENEVA AND REMAINS READY TO WORK BILATERALLY AND MULTILATERALLY
TO ACHIEVE AGREEMENTS IN ALL AREAS OF THE ROUND.

-- AGRICULTURE HAS BEEN THE CHIEF OBSTACLE TO PROGRESS SINCE
THE TABLING OF THE DRAFT FINAL ACT. U.S. DISCUSSIONS WITH THE
EC LEAD US TO BELIEVE THAT IT SHOULD BE POSSIBLE TO ACHIEVE A
BALANCED COMPROMISE ON AGRICULTURE, THAT WILL THEN ENABLE
NEGOTIATIONS IN THIS AREA TO PROCEED. INDEED, WE SEEK PROGRESS
IN ALL AREAS OF THE NEGOTIATIONS.

-- THE POSSIBILITY TO CONSIDER THE URUGUAY ROUND UNDER FAST
TRACK PROCEDURES, WHICH WERE ALREADY EXTENDED ONCE FOR THE
URUGUAY ROUND, WILL EXPIRE EARLY NEXT YEAR, AT THE BEGINNING OF
A NEW CONGRESS AND ADMINISTRATION.

-- SOME OF OUR TRADING PARTNERS MAY WANT TO USE OUR ELECTIONS
AS ANOTHER REASON TO DELAY THE ROUND. TOO MANY DETAILS AND
SUBSTANTIAL NEGOTIATIONS REMAIN ONCE A POLITICAL BREAKTHROUGH
IS MADE. WE CANNOT WAIT UNTIL MID-NOVEMBER TO MOVE AHEAD IN
COMPLETING A COMPREHENSIVE PACKAGE ENCOMPASSING ALL AREAS OF
THE ROUND WITH 108 PARTICIPANTS AND FINISH BY YEAR-END.

0079

-- THE PRESIDENT HAS REPEATEDLY SAID THAT THE ELECTION IS NOT A FACTOR IN OUR WILLINGNESS TO NEGOTIATE A CONCLUSION TO THE ROUND. THE ROUND HAS NOT/NOT BEEN AN ISSUE IN THE PRESIDENTIAL CAMPAIGN, JUST AS IT WAS NOT AN ISSUE IN THE 1988 CAMPAIGN. THE FACT IS, THE PRESIDENT AND THE ADMINISTRATION HAVE WORKED CLOSELY WITH THE CONGRESS AND THE PRIVATE SECTOR AT EVERY STEP OF THESE SIX-YEAR NEGOTIATIONS' INCLUDING OUR SUCCESSFUL EFFORT TO SECURE AN EXTENSION OF FAST TRACK PROCEDURES. A GOOD URUGUAY ROUND AGREEMENT IS IN OUR NATIONS' INTEREST, AND ALL RECOGNIZE THAT FACT.

-- IT IS EVIDENT THAT THERE IS AN URGENT NEED FOR POLITICAL DECISIONS TO BREAK THE IMPASSE IN THE ROUND IF WE ARE TO ACHIEVE A COMPREHENSIVE URUGUAY ROUND AGREEMENT IN ALL AREAS THIS YEAR.

-- WE INTEND TO PURSUE AGREEMENT BY RETURNING NEGOTIATIONS TO GENEVA AS QUICKLY AS POSSIBLE, TAKING FULL ADVANTAGE OF THE NEGOTIATING SESSIONS CONVENED BY GATT DIRECTOR GENERAL DUNKEL, OCTOBER 5-16 ON MARKET ACCESS FOR GOODS AND SERVICES, AND OTHER CONSULTATIONS TO BE SCHEDULED ON AGRICULTURE AND OTHER ISSUES, EITHER BILATERALLY OR UNDER THE DIRECTOR GENERAL'S AUSPICES.

-- IT IS OUR EXPECTATION THAT THE EC, WITH THE LEADERSHIP OF THE UK PRESIDENCY, WILL NOW BE READY TO NEGOTIATE IN EARNEST WITH A VIEW TO CONCLUDING THE URUGUAY ROUND BY YEAR END. FOR THIS REASON, NO PARTICIPANT IN THE NEGOTIATIONS CAN AFFORD TO DELAY PROGRESS ON OUTSTANDING ISSUES. ALL COUNTRIES NEED TO RETURN TO GENEVA READY FOR THE FINAL PUSH TO CONCLUDE THESE IMPORTANT NEGOTIATIONS.

0080

長 官 報 告 事 項

題 目 : UR 協商關聯 美國 立場

주한 미국대사관 Morford 참사관은 9.30(수) 통상국장을 방문, UR 협상에 임하는 미국의 입장을 아래 요지로 설명(non-paper 전달)하였음을 보고 드립니다.

---

1. Non-Paper 요지

   ○ UR 협상을 연내에 타결하겠다는 미국 입장은 여전히 확고함.

      - 7월의 뮌헨 G-7 정상회담시 EC측의 희망에 따라 그동안 협상을 촉진하지 않았으나, 불란서 국민투표가 종결되었으므로 조속한 협상재개 필요

   ○ 그간의 미.EC간 협의결과, 농산물 문제에 대한 균형된 타협안 도출이 가능하다고 보며, 농산물을 포함한 UR 협상의 모든 분야에서 진전을 기대함.

   ○ Fast Track 협상 권한의 시한 및 협상의 복잡성을 고려할때 실질협상을 11월 중순까지 미룰 수 없음.

   ○ 미국은 대통령 선거에 관계없이 년내에 협상을 종결하기 위해 노력할 것임.

      - 행정부, 의회, 업계 모두가 "좋은 UR 협상결과 (Good Uruguay Round Agreement)"가 국익에 도움이 된다는데 공감.

   ○ EC를 비롯한 여타 참여국도 연내 협상 종결을 위해 적극 노력해야 할 것임.

2. 언론대책 : 해당없음.

3. 조치내용 : 상기 미측 입장을 관계부처 및 공관에 통보.

첨부 : non-paper 사본 1부. 끝.

0081

외   무   부

종   별 :

번   호 : USW-4864   일   시 : 92 1001 1844

수   신 : 장관(통기),통이,통삼,경일,경기원,농수산부,상공부)

발   신 : 주 미대사

제   목 : UR 동향

　　1. 10.1자 FINANCIAL TIME 지는 미국과 EC 가 10.16.EC 정상회담을 앞두고 UR 타결 돌파구 마련을위해 마지막 노력을 기울이고 있는바, 10.10(잠정)브랏셀에서 ANDRIESSEN EC 대외총국장, HILLSUSTR 대표, MACSHARRY EC 농업집행위원,MADIGAN 농무장관간에 미. EC 각료회담을개최 예정이라고 보도함.

　　2. 또한, 동지는 미국과 EC 가 UR 타결의정치적 의지를 보이고 있는 것은 UR 타결을통해 부쉬 대통령은 재선에 도움을 얻고자 하며,미테랑 대통령은 농민 이외의 여타 분야 종사자의지지확보를 목표로 하고 있으며, EC 전체로서는회원국의 경제회복과 MAASTRICHT 조약 비준을둘러싼 최근의 EC 내부의 위기를 해소하려는의도라고 평가함.끝.

　　첨부: USW(F)-6273(2 매)

　　(대사 현홍주-국장)

통상국   경제국   통상국   통상국   경기원   농수부   상공부

외신 1과 통제관 ✓
0082

주 미 대 사 관

USW(F) : 6273　　 년월일 :　　　　 시간 :

수　신 : 장　관 (통기. 통~1. 특보, 경아)

발　신 : 주 미 대 사　　 사본: 경기원, 농림수산부

제　목 : 청부 (USW - 48641)

　　　　　　 (2매)

보안통제

(출처 :　　　　)

(6273　 - 2 - 1)

외신 1과 통제

주 미 대 사 관

USW(F) :   년월일 :   시간 :

수 신 : 장 관 (통기, 통1, 통상, 경2)   보 안 통 제

발 신 : 주 미 대 사   경기다, 상공부

제 목 : UR추진동향 (10개).   (출처 : FT ¹⁰/1/92)

EC, US push for Gatt deal by mid-month

By David Gardner in Brussels

THE EC and the US intend to try for a breakthrough on the Uruguay Round world trade talks early this month, in time for endorsement by European Community heads of government at the Birmingham summit on October 16, should the talks prove successful.

European Commission officials in Brussels are approaching the meeting with the caution born of a series of previously-billed breakthroughs which turned into impasses, but with genuine belief that a deal could now be done.

"The political will is now there" to get through the farm subsidies maze which has held up the Round, since the Brussels summit collapsed in December 1990, a European Community negotiator said last month.

In Washington, Mr Julius Katz, deputy US trade representative, said the United States was "neither optimistic nor pessimistic" about the possibility of a compromise over agriculture to move the Round ahead.

No meetings were scheduled, although "conversations" were continuing, he added. EC officials disclosed the bilateral talks are provisionally scheduled for October 10 in Brussels. So far, they say, these would involve Mr Frans Andriessen, EC external affairs commissioner, Mrs Carla Hills, US special trade representative, Mr Ray MacSharry, EC agriculture commissioner and Mr Ed Madigan, US agriculture secretary.

The talks are intended to exploit the so-called "window of opportunity" for settling the Round, between the French referendum on Maastricht on September 20 last, and the US elections on November 3.

In spite of EC-US brinkmanship in their worsening oilseed subsidies row, and a last-fomenting dispute over steel subsidies which the Commission discussed yesterday, the main players on the Community side still believe a deal is possible.

On the row over oilseed subsidies, which a Gatt panel has twice condemned as against Gatt rules, the US has given the EC until noon today to agree to binding arbitration.

There are said to be several reasons for renewed political impetus towards a Uruguay round settlement:

● President Bush's wish to improve his fading chances of re-election through what could be presented as an economic success for the US, which might allow him to present his opponent, Governor Bill Clinton, as a protectionist.

● The fact that the French referendum on Maastricht revealed France's farmers to be so alienated from EC farm policy that there is almost nothing President Francois Mitterrand can recover from this constituency.

● The EC's need for a success which could help it get member states' economies moving again and shift attention from the crisis over the Maastricht Treaty.

(6273 - 2 - 2)

외신 1과 통 제

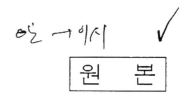

외 무 부

종 별 :

번 호 : GVW-1833   일   시 : 92 1002 1130

수 신 : 장 관(봉기, 경기원, 재무부, 농림수산부, 상공부, 특허청)

발 신 : 주 제네바 대사

제 목 : UR/개도국 비공식 그룹회의

1. 표제회의가 10.1(목) 10:00-12:30간 BENHIMA 의장주재로 개최되어, UR 협상현황을 점검하고 향후 대책을 협의하였는바, 주요 요지는 아래와 같음.

(본직 및 김봉주서기관 참석)

0 우루과이, 탄자니아등은 년내 UR 협의가 종결되지 않을경우 시간적으로 미행정부는 새로운 FAST TRACK 절차를 필요로 하게되며, 새로운 FAST TRACK 하에서는 새로운 TEXT 도출이 필요하게 되는등 매우 복잡한 상황에 빠지게 될것임을 지적하고, 협상의 년내 종결의 중요성을 재삼 강조함.

0 싱가폴, 모로코등은 년내 협의 종결을 위해서는 10.5 이후 협상이 중요하기는하나 미.EC간 농산물분야에서의 합의가 없는한 10.5 이후의 협상에서도 진전을 기대할수 없음을 지적하고, 이런관점에서 10.16 버밍험 EC 정상회담 결과가 UR 협상에 중요한 영향을 미칠 것이라는 의견을 개진함.

0 특히 싱가폴은 최근 미국으로 부터 10.5 이후 협상이 중요한 만큼 적극참여할것을 권유 받았다고 밝히고 UR협상의 성공을 위하여 개도국들의 적극적 참여를 촉구함.

0 모로코, 홍콩은 10.9 그린룸 회의 이후 협상 현황평가를 위한 개도국 비공식그룹 회의를 다시 개최하여 UR 협상 성공에 대한 개도국들의 강한 의지를 담은 메시지를 발표할 것을 주장함.

0 아국은 협상의 년내 종결의 중요성에 공감을 표시하고 이를 위해서는 (I) 미국, EC 양당사국특히 10.16 일로 예정된 특별 EC 정상회담이 UR에 어느정도의 비중을두고 있는지 파악하는것이 중요하며 (II) 시장접근 분야에서 아국등다수 개도국들이 LINE-BY-LINE C/S 를 제출하였음에도 불구하고 일부 선진국들은 이에 상응하는 기여를 하지못하고 있으며 (III) 일부개도국들이 T4의 가동에

통상국   2차보   구주국   경기원   재무부   농수부   상공부   특허청   외정실

반대하고있으나 아국은농산물 협상의 예외없는 관세화와 관련, T4 개방이 매우 중요함을 강조함.

0 싱가폴은 푼타델 에스터 선언상 UR 협상을 통하여 서비스 분야의 점진적 자유화를 지향하고 있음을 상기시키고 선진국들이 개도국들에게 너무 지나친 양보를 요구할경우, 협상은 어렵게 될것이라고 지적함.

0 탄자니아는 UR 협상결과에 대한 SINGLE UNDERTAKING과 관련, 푼타델 에스터선언상 서비스등 신분야는 상품 분야와는 별도 TRACK임을 규정하고 있음을 언급하고LLDC 는 모든 협상결과에 참여할 능력이 없음을 언급함.

2. 의장은 금일 회의결과에 따라, 10.9 그린룸회의이후 개도국 비공식 회의를개최하여 협상진전 현황을 평가하고 개도국들의 분명하고도(CLEAR-CUT) 강한 의지를담은 메시지를 발표하는 문제를 협의키로 함.끝

(대사 박수길-국장)

외 무 부

관리
번호 92-661

종 별 :

번 호 : GVW-1847   일 시 : 92 1003 1200

수 신 : 장관(통기,경기원,재무부,농수산부,상공부,특허청) 사본:주미,주이씨

발 신 : 주 제네바 대사   -중계필

제 목 : UR협상 동향 및 전망

대: WGV-1454

연: GVW-1833

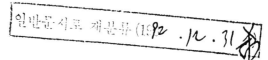

1. 내주부터 당지에서 MA, 서비스 분야 비공식 협의가 개시되는 것과 동시에 미.EC 간 막후 접촉 움직임도 활발해지는 기미를 보임으로써, MAASTRICHT 선거직후 UR 전망을 크게 불투명하게 했던 분위기가 연내타결 가능성을 조심스럽게거론하는 분위기로 전환하고 있음.

2. 연내 타결 가능성을 관측하는 근거로서는 아래와 같은 요소들이 언급되고 있음.

- 미국의 선거전 양상에 비추어 BUSH 행정부로서는 선거전에 유권자의 환심을 살수있는 경제안건을 제시해야 할 절박한 사정에 있음.(미국의 주요 협상국에대한 대호 DEMARCHE 도 이러한 맥락에서 해석)

- 상기 미국의 다급한 사정은 EC 에게는 BEST DEAL 을 얻어낼 호기로 작용할수 있으며, UR 협상의 돌파구 마련은 분열된 EC 내부의 관심을 전환시킬수 있는 소재로도 활용 가능함. 아울러 농민들로부터 이반당한 미테랑 대통령 입장에서도 더이상 잃을 것이 없다는 해석도 가능함.

- OILSEEDS 분쟁에 있어서 미국이 보복조치를 강행하지 못하는 것도 UR 협상을 타결하려는 미국의 의지가 있음을 보여주고 있음.

3. 이와 관련 당지 유력대사들(호주, 뉴질랜드등)은 10.10-11 브랏셀 개최 예정인 MCSHARRY, ANDRIESSEN, MADIGAN, HILLS 4 자 회담은 UR 협상의 년내 종결여부를 가름할 결정적 계기가 될것이며, 동 회담에서 돌파구가 마련될 경우 이는 버밍햄 EC 긴급 정상회담에서 추인 받아 년내 타결의 방향으로 나가게될 것이고, 동 4 자 회담에서합의에 이르지 못하면 UR 협상은 불가피하게 연장될수 밖에없다는 의견을 피력함. 다만 인도의 ZUTSHI 이사회 의장등 일부 대사들은 아직도 동 회담에 대하여

통상국	차관	2차보	경기원	재무부	농수부	상공부	특허청	중계

낙관론을 피하고 있음.

4. 당지의 호주, 뉴질랜드 협상 대표도 최근 KERIN 장관(호주) BOURIN 뉴질랜드 통상 장관의 브랏셀에서의 MCSHARRY 집행위원과 회담을 통해 EC 도 정치적 타결 용의를 가지고 있다는 인상을 받았으며, 미대통령 선거 이전인 10 월 중순경에 돌파구 마련 가능성이 높아지고 있으며, 10 월을 넘길 경우 선거이후의 사정 때문에 특정 후보 당선 여부에 관계없이 합의를 보기 어려울 것이라고 전망함.

5. 이에 따라 개도국들도 10.1 연호 비공식 회의에 이어 10.8 다시 회의를 소집하는등 미국, EC 의 타결 가능성에 대비한 제반조치 강구 필요성을 강조하고있음.

6. 반면 상기 움직임에도 불구하고 년내 타결을 비관적으로 보는측은 아래 사실을 지적하고 있음.

- 불란서의 국내적 어려움은 변함 없으며, 최근 영, 독간 마찰은 EC 내 불란서 입지를 더욱 강화해 주고 있음.

- 미국이 선거를 앞두고, 의미있는 양보를 할수 있을지 여부가 회의적이며,미국의 선거전 양상이 UR 에서의 돌파구 마련으로 반전 가능한 것이라고 보기 어려움.

- EC 가 미국 선거결과가 불투명한 상황아래 결과여하에 따라 번복될 가능성도 없지 않은 진지한 DEAL 을 하려고 하겠다는가 하는 의문

7. 이상과 같은 상황에서 UR 협상 전망은 아직도 확실히 단정짓기 어려우나, 10.10-11 의 브랏셀 각료회담과 버밍햄 회담을 계기로 급진전 될 가능성도 상당히 많다는 관측이 강하게 대두되고 있으므로 이에 적의 대비함이 좋을 것으로 사료됨.

8. 한편 현재 UR 협상과 관련 예정된 주요 일정은 아래와 같음.

- 10.5, 10.12 주간 시장접근 및 써비스 분야 비공식 협의
- 10.8 법제화 분야 협사일정 논의를 위한 소규모 협의(MATHUR 의장 주재)
- 10.8 개도국 비공식 그룹 회의
- 10.9 GREEN ROOM 협의
- 10.10-11 미.EC 간 각료급 회담(브랏셀)
- 10.17-18 QUAD 각료급 회담(토론토)
- 기타 CAIRNS GROUP 도 내주경 PARIS 및 당지에서 별도 회의 예정

(대사 박수길-국장)

예고:92.12.31. 까지

PAGE 2

0088

आ→이시 (기획원,농수산부)

```
관리
번호  32-669
```

외 무 부

종   별 :

번   호 : FRW-2001   일   시 : 92 1005 1830

수   신 : 장관(봉기) 사본:주EC, 제네바대사-직송필

발   신 : 주 불 대사

제   목 : UR 협상 동향

일반문서로 재분류(1992. 12. 31.)

연: FRW-1836

1. 연호 미테랑 대통령의 부시 대통령 앞 친서전달 이후, 최근 UR 협상 관련 동향 아래 보고함.(10.2. 조참사관, DENIS SIMONNEAU 외무성 경제국 UR 담당관 접촉)

가. UR 의 년내 타개 가능성이 여전히 극히 불투명한 가운데 최근 미국 및 불란서의 입장변화가 시사되는 동향이 있어 주목됨.

나. 미국이 최근 개최된 갓트 이사회 이후 대 EC 농산물 분규 있어 다소 유화적 자세를 보인 가운데 HILLS 봉상대표부 및 MADIGAN 농무장관이 10.10-11 간 브랏셀을 방문 각료급 협상을 갖을 계획인 바, EC 측으로서는 10.16. 런던 EC 특별 정상회담을 앞두고 미국의 입장변화 여부를 타진할수 있다는 점에서 기대를 갖고 있음.

다. 미테랑 대통령은 마스트리트 조약에 대한 불 국민투표 통과 과정에서 독일 KOHL 총리 및 영국 MAJOR 총리로 부터 직.간접적 지원을 받은 바 있어 이에대해 적절한 정치적 보답의 부담을 안고 있는 한편 일단 국민투표 통과로 다소간 정치적 여유를 갖을수 있게 되었음.

라. 이와관련, 약 1 주일전 미테랑 대통령은 DUMAS 외무장관등 관계 각료들에게 미국이 양보한다는 전제하에서 불란서가 양보할수 있는 분야를 검토해 보라는 지시를 하였으며, 불 외무성 실무진은 농산물 수출 물량의 감축 (예 : 24 % 에서 20 % 로 조정 수락) 방안을 작성 DUMAS 장관에게 보고한 바 있음.

마. 상기 불측 양보안은 내부 실무검토 시안에 지나지 않으나, 미국이 양보할 경우 (불측이 보기에는 GREENBOX LIST 확대 및 PEACE CLAUSE 수용 형태로 나타날 가능성이 큼) 불측도 협상의 타개를 위해 구체적으로 움직일 용의가 있다는점을 불 대통령 자신이 시사하였다는 점에서 주목된다고 봄.

2. 불측이 상기와 같이 내부적으로 양보안을 검토하는 것은 최근 소맥수출

통상국	장관	차관	2차보	외정실	분석관	청와대	안기부

보조결정등 미국의 고압적인 무역조치에도 불구하고 EC 내 독일 및 영국등으로 부터 년내 협상타결 압력이 제고되고 있어 EC 특별 정상회담을 앞두고 이에 사전대비하기 위한 것으로 보임.

이에따라, 미[84f이에따라, 미국이 여하한 형태로든 기존입장에 가시적 변화를 보일경우 불란서는
EC 가 새로운 양보입장을 수립하는데 있어 종전에 비해 보다 유연한 입장을 취할수 있는 가능성을 시사함. 끝

(대사 노영찬-국장)

예고:92.12.31 까지

관리 번호 92-665

외 무 부

증 별 :

번 호 : USW-4915   일 시 : 92 1005 1916

수 신 : 장 관(통기,통이,미일,경기원,농수산부,상공부,경제수석)

발 신 : 주 미 대 사   사본: 주 제네바, EC 대사(중계망)

제 목 : UR 동향 전망

일반문서로 재분류 (1992 · 12 · 31)

1. 최근의 UR 교섭동향과 관련 당관 장기호 참사관은 이영래 농무관과 함께 10.5 DOROTHY DWOSKIN USTR 부대표보 및 MARY RICKMAN 담당과장을 접촉, 미측 동향을 파악한 바, 요지 아래 보고함.

가. (신문에 보도된 10.10. 미.EC 각료회담 전망에 관해)

O FAST TRACK AUTHORITY 에 따라 앞으로 UR 협상을 위해 남은 시간이 매우 제약되어 있으며, 10.16. 버밍햄 EC 긴급 정상회담 이전에 미.EC 간 고위수준에서의 토의가 필요하다는 판단하에 동 각료회담이 개최될 것으로 보나 CARLA HILLS 대표가 이에 참가할 수 있는지는 아직 미지수임.

나. (앞으로 미.EC 각료회담, EC 정상회담등이 예정되어 있고 마스트리히브조약에 대한 불란서의 국민투표 결과 등으로 보아 UR 타결이 가능하다는 일부 견해에 대해)

O 지난 G7 정상회담에서 UR 의 성공적 타결을 위해 주요국들이 정치적 결단이 필요하다는 인식을 같이 한 바 있으므로, EC 국가들은 금번 EC 긴급정상회담에서 지엽적인 문제에 집착하기보다는 보다 더 큰 정치적 지도력을 발휘하여야 할 것임.

앞으로 불란서의 향배가 중요한 변수로 작용할 수 있겠으나, 영국이 EC 의장국으로서 적극적인 역할을 하고 있으며, 독일로부터도 어떤 역할을 기대하고 있으므로 EC 정상회담에서 전기가 마련될수 있기를 기대한다고 언급하고, UR 타결 전망을 조심스럽게 긍정적으로 ("CAUTIOUS OPTIMISM") 평가하였음.

O 자신으로서는 금번 EC 정상회담이 앞으로 UR 협상의 전망과 향후의 계획에 중요한 영향을 미칠 것으로 생각함.

다. (최근 미.EC 간의 농산물 협상의 진전사항에 대해)

O 최근 미.EC 간 실무선에서는 OIL SEEDS 문제를 포함 UR 협상과 관련 기술적인 협의가 진행되고 있지만 미.EC 간의 기존입장에 변화를 줄 만큼 양측 의견이 접근이

통상국	장관	차관	2차보	미주국	통상국	분석관	정와대	총리실
안기부	경기원	농수부	상공부	중계				

되어 있다고는 볼 수 없음.

　　그러나 앞으로의 상기 각료급회담, EC 정상회담에서 양측간의 주요 쟁점에 대한 문제를 어떻게 풀어가느냐에 달려 있으며, UR 협상이 농산물 분야타결에만 국한된 것이 아니고 서비스, 금융, ANTI-DUMPING 등 여러가지 분야를 포함한 하나의 PACKAGE 가 되어야 하므로 전체의 균형이라는 측면에서 보아야 할 것이라고하였음. 그러나 농산물의 타결이 없이는 UR 의 성공적 협상은 어려울 것이라는기존입장을 되풀이 하였음.

　　라. (OIL SEEDS 문제와 관련 대 EC 보복 조치가능성등 미측의 입장)

　　0 보복 조치여부에 대한 상반된 견해가 미행정부내에 있는 바, 보복 조치시에는 UR 협상진전에 부정적인 영향을 줄 우려가 있으므로 신중한 검토가 필요하다는 입장이 있는 반면, 아무런 조치도 취하지 않음으로서 UR 에 대한 진전은 물론 오히려 문제의 해결을 어렵게 하는 결과만 가져오므로 공세적인 조치가 미측에 도움이 될 것이라는 견해도 있음. 따라서 보복 조치여부는 선거를 앞두고 있는 BUSH 대통령이 어떤 카드를 구사할 것인지에 달려 있다고 봄.

　　2. 상기 면담시 미측은 EC 정상회담에서의 정치적 결단을 강조하고 있으며 UR 협상의 시한이 매우 제한되어 있다는 점에서 앞으로의 전망에 대해 매우 조심스런 표현 ("CAUTIOUS OPTIMISM")을 하고 있는등 UR 에 대한 확실한 전망을 하지 못하고 있는 것으로 보임.끝.

　　(대사 현홍주 - 국장)

　　예고: 92.12.31.까지

PAGE 2

0092

외 무 부

종 별 :

번 호 : ECW-1213   일   시 : 92 1007 1600

수 신 : 장관(통기, 정보, 경기원, 재무부, 농림수산부, 상공부, 기정동문)

발 신 : 주 EC 대사   사본: 주 미-중계망, 주제네바-필

제 목 : 갓트/UR 협상 (자료응신 92-80)

    1. 10.6. 룩셈부르그에서 개최된 EC 일반이사회는 폐회후 발표한 성명서에서 UR 협상은 양자및 다자간 접촉을통해 합의에 접근하고 있다고 평가하고 연말까지 동협상을 종결시킨다는 목표를 달성하기 위해서 최종적인 노력이 필요한 시점이며 이러한 점에서 금주말 당지에서 개최되는 미.EC 고위회담을 환영한다고 밝힘. 동 성명은 또한 EC 이사회는 모든 협상분야를 포괄하여 <u>균형된 결과가</u> 도출되도록 UR 협상이 추진되기를 바란다고 하면서, EC 각료들은 집행위에 대해 분명한 협상방향 지침을 주었다고 하고 금번 미.EC 고위회담 결과를 10.16 의 EC 긴급 정상회담에 보고토록 집행위에 대해 요청함

    2. 상기 이사회에서는 UR 협상의 조속한 타결을 강력히 희망하는 독일(MOELLEMANN 경제상) 과 동 협상의 종결은 바라나 EC 의 입장은 더이상 양보될수 없다는 프랑스(STRAUSS-KAHN 무역상) 간의 심각한 의견대립이 있었으며, 프랑스의 완강한 입장때문에 UR 협상 진전의 장애를 제거할수 있는 새로운 제안은 나오지 못한 것으로 알려짐

    3. 이사회 종료후 EC 각국이 밝힌 주요입장은 아래와같음

    가. MOELLEMANN 독일경제상은 KOHL 수상이 각회원국 정상들에게 UR 협상타결의 중요성을 강조한 서한을 발송한바 있다고 밝히면서 세계경제가 불황국면에 접어드는등 UR 의 실패시는 위기국면의 위험이 있으므로 동 협상을 더이상 지연시킬수 없으며 협상타결로 세계경제를 성장추세로 전환 시키기 위한 계기를 마련하는 것이 시급하다고 말함. 동인은 BUSH 미대통령도 동 협상을 연내에 타결한다는 분명한 의지를갖고 있으므로 현재 상황은 협상을 촉진할수 있는 좋은 기회라고 분석하면서 동 이사회는 ANDRIESSEN 대외관계 위원에게 대미협상을 추진함에 있어 보다 폭넓은 협상권을 부여했다고 말함

통상국	장관	차관	2차보	외정실	분석관	정와대	안기부	경기원
재무부	농수부	상공부	중계					

PAGE 1   92.10.08   04:38

나. STRAUSS-KAHN 프랑스 무역상은 자국도 UR 협상의 타결을 원하나, EC 가희생을 감수하는 협상타결은 있을수 없다고 말하고 EC 는 이미 CAP 개혁을통해 미측의 요구에 충분히 양보한바 있다고 말함

다. JONES 영국 무역상은 BUSH 대통령이 선거개최이전에 동 협상타결을 진실로 희망하고 있어 미.EC 간에 타협을 모색할수 있는 기회가 주어졌음으로 이를실기해서는 안될 것이라고 강조함

라. 화란과 룩셈부르그는 EC 내에 실업율이 증가되고 있는것이 가장 큰 문제이며 UR 협상의 타결은 이를 해결하는데 도움이 될것이라고 하고 동 협상타결을 봉쇄하는 것은 위험하다는 입장을 표명함

마. EC 집행위 ANDRIESSEN 위원은 모든 상황으로 보아 UR 협상이 조속히 타결되어야 하나 OILSEEDS 문제등 최근 미측의 조치들을 감안할때 협상분위기가 개선된 것은 아니라고 평가하고 금주말의 미.EC 양자협상은 미측이 얼마나 양보할 의사를 갖고 있는지를 평가할수 있는 좋은 기회가 될것이라고 말함

4. 상기 독일 KOHL 수상의 EC 회원국 정상앞 이니셔티브와 미 BUSH 대통령의 일본 MIYAZAWA 수상앞 친서발송등 국제적으로 미대통령 선거전 UR 협상의 막바지 타결점 모색을위한 노력이 가속화되고 있는 가운데 금주말 당지개최 미-EC 각료 4 자회담이 UR 의 조기타결 여부의 관건이 될것으로 전망되는바 이와 관련된 동정은 추보하겠음. 끝

(대사 권동만-국장)

외 무 부

종 별 :

번 호 : FRW-2025   일 시 : 92 10 07 1830

수 신 : 장관(봉기) 사본:주EC, 제네바대사-직송필

발 신 : 주 불 대사

제 목 : UR 협상 동향

연-FRW-2001

표제건 관련 당지 동향 및 전망 아래 보고함.

1. EC 외무통상장관 회담

가. 10.6. 룩셈부르크 개최 EC 외무, 통상장관 회담에서 영국과 독일은 미대통령 선거이전 UR 타개를 서두르는 미측의 분위기를 적극 활용해야 할것임을 주장한 반면, 불란서 STRAUSS-KAHN 상공장관은 ''미국이 농산물을 포함한 전분야에서 보다 유연한 자세를 보이지 않는한 협상 타결은 불가능하다''는 기존 입장을 고수함.

나. 동 회의에서는 UR 협상을 10.16. 버밍검 개최 EC 특별 정상회담의 의제에 포함시키기로 합의하였는 바, STRAUSS-KAHN 장관은 최근 미국 및 EC 여타 제국으로 부터 협상타결 압력이 고조됨에따라 자국입장이 더욱 고립되어 가고 있음을 인정코 EC 가 미국으로 부터 상응하는 양보없이 협상이 타결될 가능성에 우려를 표함.

다. 이와관련 JEAN-PIERRE SOISSON 신임 농업장관 역시 현재 불란서의 입장이 고립되어 있다고 말하고 미테랑 대통령이 KOHL 총리에 대해 미 대통령 선거이전 조기 타결을 서두르는 미측의 압력에 양보하지 말것을 직접 촉구하고 있다고 주장함.

2. 당관 전망

가. 금주말 개최되는 미.EC 통상 각료회담은 사실상 금년말 UR 타개 여부와관련 양측입장을 최종 타협할수 있는 마지막 기회로 관측됨. 특히 EC 특별정상회담을 앞두고 동 회담에서 긍정적 결과가 나오면 UR 협상이 예상보다 빠르게 단기간내 진척 될수 있을것으로 예상됨.

나. 비록 불란서는 대외적으로 기존 입장을 상금 유지하고 잉나, 최근 미국이 일반적 예상과는 달리 UR 협상 타개를 위해 EC, 일본등에 공세적 입장을 취하고 있음을 주목코 내부적으로 대책마련에 부심하고 있는 형편이며 연호 미테랑 대통령의

통상국   장관   차관   2차보   외정실   문석관   정와대   안기부

지시도 이렇한 차원에서 이루어지고 있는 것으로 보임.

다. 이와관련 불란서는 EC 내 자국의 정치 경제적 입지가 종전과 같지 않음에 따라 (특히 불란서는 최근 독일로 부터 '마스'조약 국민투표 통과. 불 프랑화가치유지를 위한 대규모 외환 시장개입등 정치경제적 지원을 받은바 있음) 금번 미.EC 회담에서 미국이 어느정도 양보 입장을 표하면 불란서도 협상타결을 위해 EC 의 추가 양보에 궁극적으로 동조할 것으로 예상됨. 끝

(대사 노영찬-국장)

예고:92.12.31 까지

외 무 부

종 별 :

번 호 : ECW-1223   일 시 : 92 1008 1830

수 신 : 장관 (통기, 통삼, 경기원, 농림수산부, 상공부, 기정동문)

발 신 : 주 EC 대사 사본: 주미-중계필, 주제네바-필

제 목 : GATT/UR 협상

당관 주철기참사관은 10.8. EC 집행위의 PASCAL GATT 담당과장과 접촉하고, 금주말 당지개최 EC-미국간 UR 협상회담 관련 동정을 탐문한바 동인 언급내용 아래 보고함

1. 금번 EC-미국간 회담의 사전준비를 위하여 USTR 의 LAVOREL 조정관 일행이 10.8. 당지에 도착, EC PAEMEN 부총국장등과 사전 준비회담을 가질 예정이며, EC 집행위 UR 관계관들은 주말 대기지시를 받고 있음

2. 금번회담의 주요 의제로서는 농산물분야, 시장접근문제, 서비스문제및 OILSEEDS 문제등이 거론될 것으로 전망함

3. EC 로서는 미국 BUSH 행정부가 금번 브랏셀회담에서 보다 진전된 타협안 (CONCESSION) 을 제시하기를 기대하고 있음. 그 경우는 EC 집행위로서도 10.6. 이사회의 MANDATE 에 따라 보다 융통성있는 협상대응이 가능할 것임

4. 프랑스는 국민투표 과정에서의 독일등의 후원과 특히 그간 프랑화 위기의 방어를 위하여서 독일측이 적극 개입, 도와준데 대한 부담감등에 비추어서도 이번 EC-미국간 협상에 어느정도 성의있는 태도를 표명하지 않을수 없다는 분석도 있으며, 10.5-6 의 EC 이사회 회의에서 프랑스가 UR 관련 이사회의 결론도출을 강하게 끝까지 반대하지 않은 것은 긍정적 측면으로 생각됨

5. 금번 회담에서는 주로 UR 농산물 문제의 타결을 모색하게 되겠으나 EC 가 중요하게 생각하는 서비스, MARKET - ACCESS 분야를 포함하여 종합적으로 균형된 타결방안이 모색되어야 할것이며, 또한 OILSEED 문제해결은 UR 협상타결과 분리될수 없는 것임으로 미-EC 포괄적 합의의 일환으로 동문제 협상이 이루어져야할것임

6. 시장접근및 관세분야관련, 미국은 산업분야중 다국적기업 소관사항은 전적인 자유화를 주장하는 반면, 국내적 보호가 필요한 전통산업 (섬유등) 은 고용보호의 측면에서 관세적 보호를 계속 주장할 것으로 전망됨

통상국	장관	차관	1차보	2차보	구주국	통상국	외정실	분석관
정와대	안기부	경기원	상공부	중계				

PAGE 1   92.10.09   18:33

외신 2과 통제관 DI
0097

7. 자신의 개인적 견해임을 전제하고 REBALANCING 문제는 향후 협상의 진전을 보아가며 여타 분야에서의 균형된 이익이 충분히 확보된다면 EC 로서도 양보할수도 있는 분야가 될수 있을 것으로 추정함

8. 집행위는 금번 EC-미국간 회담결과를 10.13(화) EC COREPER 회의에서 보고하고 이어서 10.16 버밍험 정상회의에 보고, 향후 협상추진에 대한 정상회의 차원의 지침을 받게 될것임. 끝

(대사 권동만-국장)

예고: 92.12.31. 까지

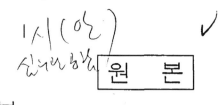

```
관리
번호  92-683
```

외 무 부

종   별 :

번   호 : GVW-1889   일   시 : 92 1008 1900

수   신 : 장관(통기, 경기원, 재무부, 농림수산부, 상공부) 사본:주미,주EC,주불,

발   신 : 주 제네바 대사   주독,주영대사-중계필

제   목 : UR 협상동향 평가

일반문서로 재분류 (1992 . 12 . 31

1. 본직이 DUNKEL 사무총장(10.8 면담) 및 CARLISLE 차장(10.6 오찬)을 접촉 DUNKEL 총장의 방한 결과 및 최근 UR 협상 동향 및 전망에 관해 협의한 결과 양인은 10.10-11 브랏셀 미.EC 각료급 회담과 관련 UR 협상의 조기 타결에 조심스런 낙관론을 개진하면서, 이에대해 아국도 신축적인 대안 마련이 필요함을 강조한바, 동 결과 아래 보고함.

　　가. DUNKEL 총장 면담

　　1) 미.EC 로 부터 구체적 신호가 있었다기 보다는 UR 협상 타결이 조만간 가능하리라는 자신의 직감에 따라 이를 한. 일 양국에 미리 알려주는 것이 공정 (FAIR) 하다는 판단하에 방문을 추진함.

　　2) 방문결과 솔직한 의견교환이 유익했다고 보며, 특히 농업구조조정 10 개년 계획에 대한 설명을 중요한 INFORMATION 으로 받아들였음.

　　3) 방한직후 미측 고위실무진으로 부터 미 대선 일정과 관계없이 협상의 재개 및 다자화를 희망하는 강한 메세지를 받아왔음. 이에대해 자신은 미.EC 양측으로부터 분명한 결의 표명이 없으면 추가로 할수 있는 일이 없다고 대응하면서 ~~특히 미국의 구체적 OFFER 제시를 할수 있는 일이 없다고 대응하면서 특히 미국의 구체적 OFFER 제시를~~ 촉구해 왔음.

　　4) 최근 미국 선거전 양상 및 OILSEEDS 분규등은 미.EC 양국으로 하여금 더이상 진지한 타결 노력을 미룰수 없는 상황을 가져왔다고 보며, BUSH 대통령의 금년내 UR 타결 결의도 이러한 맥락에서 이해함.

　　5) EC 의 경우에도 10.10-11 브라셀 각료회담을 앞두고 현재 113 위원회가 UR 문제 대책 마련에 부심하고 있으며, 10.16 EC 긴급정상회담을 대비 10.13(화) 동 위원회가 재차 소집될 예정으로 있는등 진지한 자세를 보여주고 있음.

통상국	장관	차관	2차보	분석관	청와대	안기부	경기원	재무부
농수부	상공부	중계						

PAGE 1   92.10.09   07:11

6) KOHL 수상은 UR 협상의 조기 종결의지를 굳히고 BUNDESBANK 의 "프랑"화 지지 및 앞으로도 계속 지지를 약속해 주는 댓가로 UR 에서의 불측 양보를 종용하고 있는 것을 비롯 국내경제, 통화 사정상 UR 의 타결 필요성을 절감하고 있는 MAJOR 수상을 포함 EC 전 회원국이 강력한(TREMENDOUS) 대불 압력을 가하고 있음 (최근 EC 회원국간 MFA 연장 문제 논의시 불 대표가 퇴장하는 사례가 벌어진 것은 대불압력의 강도를 보여주는 좋은 예임)

7) 이상에 비추어 자신은 UR 협상에 관해 <u>조심스런 낙관적 견해</u>를 갖고 있으며, 따라서 <u>한국도 예외없는 관세화 문제에 관한 대책 마련이 시급함.</u>

8) 예외없는 관세화는 미.EC 간 쟁점 사항이 아니며(미국은 바나나에 관한 예외를 인정할 수 없다는 점을 EC 에 불명히 전달함) 따라서 한국도 이문제에 관해 기존 입장만 반복할 것이 아니라 미.EC 간 수출보조 물량 관련 24 퍼센트- 8 년 또는 20 퍼센트 - 6 년등 기술적 대안을 협의해 나가고 있는것과 같이 신축성을 가지고 대처해 나가는 것이 현명할 것으로 봄

9) 본직은 동 총장의 신중한 낙관론과 미.EC 간 브랏셀 각료회담과 다수의 실무 접촉 및 최근 당지에서의 비공식 협의(특히 EC 가 무세화 및 관세조화 협상에 다소 성의를 보이고 있는점)등 긍정적 징후가 보이고 있는 것은 고무적 현상이라고 전제한후 아래사항을 언급함.

- 아국이 농업 구조조정 계획을 수립, 시행하고 있는 것은 사실이나, 아국의 농산물 협상 입장을 수정할수 있는 사정은 아님

- 예외없는 관세화 문제는 아국의 UR 협상 결과를 수락 또는 거부를 결정짓는 변수가 될 정도로 중차대한 문제임.

- 동문제 관련 공동이해국과 대책협의해 나가고 있지만, 미.EC 간 돌파구가마련되더라도 이를 기초로 ROLLOVER 를 시도한다면 좌시할수 없음.

- 따라서 한국으로서는 T4 에 큰 기대를 걸고 있으며 평소 사무총장이 언급하고 있는 T4 의 단기운영 가능성에 크게 우려를 가지고 있음.

10) 이에 대해 동 총장은 아래와 같이 답변함.

- 미.EC 간 돌파구가 마련되더라도 이를 여타 협상국에 강요치는 않을 것임.

- 다만, 동 결과에 대해 전회원국의 동의를 구할것인바 아무도 이에 대해 이의를 제기하지 않을 것으로 봄.

- 한국의 T4 개방에 대한 관심은 예외없는 관세화 문제 때문이겠지만, 미.EC간

PAGE 2

0100

쟁점사항 이외의 T4 개방은 반덤핑등과 관련 관심을 보이고 있는 미국을 제외하고는 어느국가도 원치 않고 있으며, 개방시 협상결과의 UNRAVELLING 을 초래할 성질이기 때문에, T4 불개방은 공정성 (FAIRNESS) 여부의 문제가 아니라 STRATEGY 의 문제임.

- 한국의 예외없는 관세화관련 진정한 어려움이 있으면 미.EC 의 경우와 같이 이해 관계국과 합의를 모색한후 가져오는 방법밖에 없음.

- 그보다는 다른방법을 통한 해결을 모색하는 것이 현명하다고 보며, 이는 한국 스스로가 모색해야 할 사항임.

나. CARLISLE 사무총장 오찬

1) 자신은 DUNKEL 총장의 방한을 아래 2 가지 이유로 반대하였고, 방한결과도 자신이 예상했던 바와 같았다고 언급함.

- 한국입장은 이미 잘알려져 있고, 방한으로 동 입장이 변경될 것으로 기대치 않았음.

- 한. 일의 강경한 입장에도 불구하고, 양국은 UR 협상의 타결은 봉쇄하지는 않을 것이라는 점에 확신을 가지고 있음.

(이에대하여 본직은 동인의 분석은 아국 사정을 지나치게 단순화한 판단이며 예외없는 관세화 문제는 UR 협상 결과에 대한 아국의 수락여부에 까지 영향을 미칠 심각한 사항이라는 점을 강조함)

2) 브랏셀 미.EC 각료회담등 최근사태 진전과 관련 협상 성공의 가능성을 반반으로 보나, 수년내 가장 높은 가능성을 보여주고 있는 것만은 사실임

3) 동 회담에서 돌파구가 마련되지 않더라도 BUSH 대통령이 재선될 경우에는 FAST TRACK 시한 및 OILSEEDS 분쟁이 보여주듯이 미국의 실질적 이해가 관련되어 있기 때문에 타결가능성이 없지 않음.

4) 다만 CLINTON 후보가 당선될 경우에는 이제까지의 협상결과를 단순 추인한다고 기대하기는 어려우며, 따라서 환경, 노동문제 포함 협상은 수년간 연장이불가피하다고 봄.

2. 한편 김대사가 접촉한 DENIS 시장접근협상그룹 의장도 아래와 같은 견해를 표명하였으며, LINDEN 고문도 타결 가능성이 상당히 높아진것만은 사실이라는 신중한 낙관론을 피력함.

가. DENIS 의장은 향후 전망을 반반정도로 평가하면서도, 미.EC 간 기술적 사항에 대한 이견은 상당히 좁혀졌다 하더라도 정치적 여건이 좋지 않다하면서 다소 비관적

견해를 갖고 있다는 인상을 풍김.

나. 미.EC 간 돌파구가 마련될 경우 대부분의 분야(반덤핑 포함 모든 규범분야, TRIPS)에서 별문제가 있으리라 보지 않음

다. 써비스협상에서도 기본 통신.해운등은 큰문제가 없을것이며, 금융(특히 BANKING) 써비스가 다소 시간을 요할것으로 봄.

라. 자신이 주도하는 무세화 관련 협의는 미.EC 에 대해 C/S 제출을 촉구하는 분위기 조성에 의미를 부여함.

마. 예외없는 관세화에 관한 카나다 정부의 입장에 변경이 없는것으로 알며 10.26 헌법개정에 관한 국민투표가 있는등 정치적 여건이 어려움 (개인적 의견임을 강조하면서), 스위스 접근 방식 (일정 유예기간후 관세화 수락방안)이 협상 가능한 대안이라고 봄.끝

(대사 박수길-장관)

예고:92.12.31. 까지

관리 번호	92-677

외 무 부

종   별 :

번   호 : USW-4965　　　　　　　　　　일　시 : 92 1007 2016

수   신 : 장 관 (통기,통이,미일) 사본: 주EC,제네바대사(본부중계필)

발   신 : 주 미 대사

제   목 : UR 동향

연: USW-4966

1. 당관 장기호 참사관은 연호 10.7. 국무부 S. KRISTOFF 부차관보와의 면담시 미행정부의 최근 대 UR 정책 진전사항을 문의한바, 동 부차관보는 HILLS 대표가 10.10. 미.EC 각료회담 참석을 위해 10.9. 브랏셀을 향발 예정이라고 확인하였음.

2. 또한, 동 부차관보는 10.17. EC 긴급정상회담을 앞둔 금번 미.EC 각료회담은 UR 타결의 돌파구를 마련하는 마지막 기회가 될 것이라고 평가하며, 최근 부쉬 대통령은 UR 타결을 촉구하는 콜수상 및 미테랑 대통령 앞 친서를 작성하였다 하고 HILLS 대표가 이를 휴대할 가능성도 있다 하였음을 참고로 보고함. 끝.

(대사 현홍주-국장)

예고: 92.12.31. 까지

일반문서로 재분류(1992.12.31.)

통상국 중계	장관	차관	2차보	미주국	통상국	분석관	정와대	안기부

PAGE 1　　　　　　　　　　　　　　　　　　92.10.08　　11:35

외신 2과 통제관 BX

0103

외 무 부

종 별 :

번 호 : GVW-1890   일 시 : 92 1009 1500

수 신 : 장 관(봉기, 경기원, 재무부, 농수부, 상공부, 특허청)

발 신 : 주 제네바 대사

제 목 : UR/ 개도국 비공식 그룹회의

　　1. 표제회의가 10.8(목) BENHIMA의장 주재로 개최되어, UR 협상 현황을 점검하고명 10.9개최 예정인 그린룸 회의대책을 협의한바, 주요 요지는 아래와 같음.

　　0 탄자니아 대표는 LLDC의 현재 경제능력에 비추어 신분야 특히 서비스, 지적소유권 분야의 협상 결과를 수용할 능력이 없음을 강조함.

　　0 우루과이, 홍콩등은 금번주말 브랏셀 개최예정인 미.EC 협상 및 10.16개최 버밍햄 EC 정상회담이 UR협상의 성공적 종결에 기여하기를 희망하면서, 미.EC양자 협상이 조속 다자화되어 UR 협상의 진전을 가속화 시킬것을 촉구함.

　　0 싱가폴은 개도국들은 년내 타결을 위한 진지한 노력에 참여할 준비가 되어있음을 명일 그린룸 회의에서 밝힐것과 현재의 낙관론이 실현 될수 있도록 모든 협상 참가국들이 노력할 것을촉구함.

　　0 아국은 시장접근 분야에서 아국등 다수 개도국들이 LINE-BY-LINE C/S를 제출하여 몬트리올 중간평가시 합의 사항인 33의 관세인하 목표에 합치 하였음에도 불구, 상응한 기여를 선진국들이 하지 못하고 있음을 지적하고, 내일 그린룸 회의에서 여사한 개도국들의 우려를 밝힐것과 금주말 미.EC 회담후 즉시 개도국 비공식 그룹회의를 개최, 동회담 결과를 평가할 것을 촉구함 (우루과이, 싱가폴도 동일의견)

　　2. 의장은 명일 그린룸 회의시 상기 개도국들의 우려를 발표하고 내주에 개도국비공식 그룹회의를 재소집하여 금주말 미.EC 협상 결과를 점검키로함.

　　(대사 박수길 - 국장)

통상국　　경기원　　재무부　　농수부　　상공부　　특허청

PAGE 1   92.10.10　　06:26 FO

외신 1과 통제관 ✓

0104

외 무 부

종 별 :

번 호 : GVW-1903 일 시 : 92 1009 2250

수 신 : 장관(봉기,경기원,재무부,농림수산부,상공부,특허청)

발 신 : 주이씨,주불,주독,주영(직송필),주미(중계필)

제 목 : 주 제네바 대사

제 목: 주제네바대사 GREEN ROOM 협의

연: GVW-1847,1889

표제회의가 금 10.9(금) DUNKEL 총장주재하에 T1,T2,T3 협상 진전상황 점검 및 향후추진방안 협의 목적으로 개최된바, 현재의상황에서 실질적 논의가 큰 의미가 없으므로 약10일후 회의를 재개하겠다는 DUNKEL 총장의제의에 따라 ~~큰 의미가 없으므로 약10일후 회의를재개하겠다는 DUNKEL 총장의 제의에 따라~~ 금주말 브랏셀 미,EC 각료회담의의미, 성격등에 관한 미,EC 의 배경 설명을청취하고 별다는 논의없이 종료된바 동 결과아래 보고함.

1. DUNKEL 총장은 최근 미,EC 를 포함 다수국이협상 타결을 위해 노력하고 있는것은 바람직한현상이나 아직까지도 아무런 성과없이 WAITING GAMES만 계속되는 상황이라고 평가하고, 아래사항을언급함.

- 아직도 93.3. 까지 WINDOW OF OPPORTUNITY 는 있으며, 동 시한내 타결이 이루어지려면 제네바에서의 다자협상은 그보다 훨씬 이전에 진행되어야 함.

- 미, EC간 돌파구 마련시 이를다자화(MULTILATERALIZATION)해야 할것인바, 다자협상 절차를 거쳐 합의요소(INGREDIENTS: T1,T2의 양허 협상을 의미)를 도출할 것임.

- 브랏셀 회담 및 EC 정상회담이 끝나는 약10일후 재차 GREEN ROOM 회의를 소집,정세평가를하되 내주부터 시장접근등 분야에서 구체적협상계획(WELL-STRUCTURED PROGRAMME OF WORK)을놓고 토의를 가질 계획임.

2. YERXA 미대사는 금주말 브랏셀 회담에관심이 집중되어있으므로 이에 대한 배경설명이필요하다고 본다 하면서 아래 사항을 언급함.

- 미,EC간 브랏셀 회담의 목적은 최종 단계다자간 협상의 재개에 필요한

통상국 경기원 재무부 농수부 상공부 특허청 요치선 장관

미,EC간입장차를 좁히는데 있으며, 이를 위해 최대노력중임.

- 양국은 모두 진지한 자세로 금번 협상에 임하고있으며, <u>진정한 양보 가능성을논의중에 있음.</u>

- 양국 모두기한내 협상 종결을 희망하며 미,EC간 이견이 극복되더라도 제네바에서의 다자간절차에 진전이 없으면 협상은 실패할 것임

- <u>브랏셀 회담에 대한 지나친 기대는 금물이며,</u>금번 회담에서 성과가 다소 미흡하더라도 이를협상의 실패로 간주해서는 안될것임.

3. TRAN EC 대사도 미국의 FAST TRACK 시한뿐아니라 불란서의 총선 일정도 있으므로 협상은반드시 조기 종결되어야 한다고 한후, 현재 협상이미묘한(DELICATE) 국면에 접어들었으므로신중한태도(DISCRETION)가 절실히 요청되는바따라서 <u>지나친 기대감및 성급한 예측을 자제해줄것을 당부함.</u> 동 대사는 기타 협상의GLOBALITY(농산물뿐만 아니라 시장접근, 써비스포함) 및 년말이전 실무작업 완료 필요성등을강조함.

4. 참석 대사중에서는 개도국 그룹의장인 모로코대사가 개도국입장을 대변 협상의 다자화 및개도국 관심사항 반영 필요성을 강조하였으며, 브라질대사는 시장접근 협상의 접근방법(무세화협상은 개도국에 원천적으로 불리) 및 T2협상을 통해, T4 의 목적을 달성하려는선진국의 태도에 불만 및 우려를 표시하였고, 알젠틴 대사도 이에 추가 하여 주요협상 참가국의 OFFER 불제시, 과도한 MFN 일탈요구등에불만을 토로함.

5. 본직은 10일후 'GREEN ROOM 재개계획을환영하며, 그때까지는 브랏셀 회담, EC정상회담등을 통해 협상의 전망이 보다밝아지기를 기대한다고 언급한후, 현재 진행되고있는 시장접근 협상 특히 분야별 무세화협상이개발수준 및 적응능력을 감안치 않고 개도국과선진국을 동일한 기준에 두고 진행되는 것은균형을 상실한 조치라는 점을언급함.끝

(대사 박수길-장관)

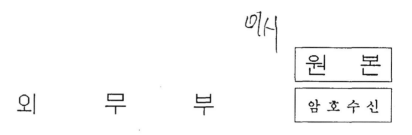

외　무　부

원　본
암호수신

종　별 :

번　호 : ECW-123**6**　　　　　　　　　일　시 : 92 1011 2230

수　신 : 장 관(통기,통삼,경기원,재무부,농림수산부,상공부)

발　신 : 주 EC 대사　　　사본: 주제네바-직송필, 주 미-중계필,

제　목 : UR 협상

연: ECW-1223

　　1. UR 협상 타결을위한 연호 미.EC 각료회담이 금 10.11(일) 당지 EC 집행위원 회의실에서 개최되었으나 금일회담에서는 별다른 합의를 보지못하고, 내일 11(월) 10:00 회담을 재개키로 함

　　2. 금일 오전 11:00 부터의 ANDRIESSEN 부위원장과 HILLS USTR 대표간의 회담을 시작으로 MACSHARRY 농업담당 집행위원및 MADIGAN 농무장관이 동석한 오찬회담과 오찬후 다시 ANDRIESSEN-HILLS, MACSHARRY-MADIGAN 간의 별도회담이 각각진행되었으나 농업장관간의 회담은 오후 5 시경 종료되었으며, ANDRIESSEN-HILLS 회담은 만찬까지로 연결된 것으로 알려짐

　　3. 18:10 분경 ANDRIESSEN 부위원장및 HILLS 대표 대변인들은 기자들에게 명 11 일 10:00 부터 회담이 재개될 것이라는 내용만 발표하고 회담의 진전여부등에 대해서는 일체 언급을 회피했음. 명일회담 동향은 추보하겠음. 끝

　　(대사 권동만-국장)

통상국	장관	차관	1차보	2차보	구주국	통상국	외정실	분석관
청와대	안기부	경기원	재무부	농수부	상공부	중계		

PAGE 1

92.10.12　17:58

외신 2과　통제관 BS

0107

UR(우루과이라운드) 협상 동향 및 TNC(무역협상위원회) 회의, 1992. 전5권(V.3 7-10월)　523

관리
번호 92-695

외 무 부

종 별 :

번 호 : FRW-2070   일 시 : 92 1012 1850

수 신 : 장관(통기),사본:주EC,제네바대사-직송필

발 신 : 주 불 대사

제 목 : UR 협상 동향

연:FRW-2001,2025

　　10.11-12 간 브랏셀 개최 미.EC 간 UR 협상 타개를 위한 각료급회담과 관련, 불 정부는 여하한 경우에도 불란서의 이익이 침해된 협상결과를 수락할수 없다는 강경입장을 천명하고 있는바 관련동향 아래 보고함.

　　1. SOISSON 신임 농업장관은 10.9 브랏셀에서 DELOR 집행위원장 및 ANDRIESSEN 부위원장을 면담코, 미국의 명확한 양보가 없는 가운데 금번 협상결과를 불란서에 강요시 미테랑 대통령은 10.16 EC 특별정상회담 참석을 보이코트 할수도 있다는 강경입장을 전달한 것으로 보도됨. 동 장관은 또한 마스트리트 조약비준을 위한 국민투표 과정에서 나타난 농민층의 절대적 불만(약 70 프로 반대)을 고려시, 도.농간 화합차원에서도 불 농민에 대한 추가양보 요구는 정치적으로 불가하다고 주장함.

　　2. DUMAS 외상은 10.11 TV 회견을 통해 아직은 협상이 타결될 시기가 아닌데다, 불란서의 중대한 이익이 무시된채 협상이 타결될수는 없으며, 미국의 압력에도 불구하고 EC 회원국간 연대감이 재차 표명될 것으로 기대한다고 언급함.

　　3. 또한 불 농민단체는 이미 CAP 개혁으로 상당한 불이익을 감수하게된 차제에 EC 집행위가 미국에 대해 추가 양보시 극한 투쟁을 통해서라도 이를 저지할 것임을 재차 강조함.

　　4. 한편, 불 정부측 관계자는 EC 정상회담에서 가중다수결에 의한 협상결과 처리 가능성과 관련, 비록 불란서가 동 회담에서 즉각적인 거부권은 행사할수 없다하여도,1966 년 룩셈브루크 합의를 원용 국가 중대이익 침해 차원에서 최소한 결정을 상당기간 연기할수는 있을 것임을 시사함.

　　5. 불란서가 상기와 같이 초강경 자세를 표명하고 있는 것은 불란서를 제외한 영국, 덴마크, 화란등 여타 EC 농산물 수출국이 EC 의 추가양보를 통해서라도

통상국　　장관　　차관　　2차보　　구주국　　외정실　　분석관　　정와대　　안기부

PAGE 1

92.10.13　　05:13

외신 2과 통제관 FM

0108

협상타결 용의를 표명하는등 불란서를 제외한 모든 회원국의 조기 협상타결 희망 분위기에 따라 EC 집행위가 미국에 대해 양보할 가능성을 사전에 적극 견제하기 위한 의도로 보임.

6. 이에대해 불란서는 현재까지 해결되고 있지 않은 유럽통화제도(EMS) 문제와 함께 UR 회담이 EC 통합의 새로운 위기를 조성할 가능성을 경고하는 한편 독일의 협조를 확보키 위해 노력하고 있는바, 이와관련 불 BEREGOVOY 총리는 금일 오후 독일을 방문 KOHL 총리를 면담 설득 계획임.

7. 표제 회담결과는, 미국측이 상당한 양보의사를 표명하였다 하나 10.12 오후 현재 주요회담 내용은 알려지고 있지 않은바, 회담 종료후 금일밤 DELOR 위원장이 주요 협상결과를 12 개 회원국 정상에 통보후 동건 논의를 위해 10.14(수) 브랏셀에서 113 조 위원회가 개최될 예정임. 또한 이와는 별도로 10.16 EC 특별 정상회담에 앞서 10.14(수) 18:00 미테랑 대통령은 DELOR 위원장을 면담 예정임. 끝.

(대사 노영찬-국장)

예고:92.12.31. 까지

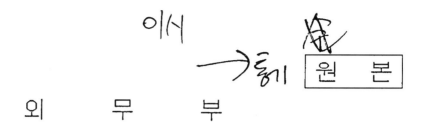

외 무 부

종 별 : 지 급

번 호 : ECW-1242   일 시 : 92 1012 2200

수 신 : 장관(통기,통삼,경기원,재무부,농림수산부,상공부)사본:GV,UK,FR,GE필

발 신 : 주 EC 대사

제 목 : UR 협상

　　1. 금 10.12(월) 오전 속개된 EC-미국 회담은 21:00 경까지 계속되었는바, 동 회담종료직후 개최된 기자회견에서 양측 대변인들은 금번회담에서 양측의 이견해소에 다소 진전(GOODPROGRESS) 이 있었다고 발표하였으나, 실무차원의 협상이 계속될 것이라고 말함으로써 최종 합의 도출에는 실패하였음을 시사함

　　2. 또한 동 대변인들은 상기 실무차원의 협상결과를 토대로 추후 양측 농업장관회담을 다시 갖기로 하였으나, 동 회담일자는 아직 결정되지 않았다 말하고, ANDRIESSEN 집행위원 및 HILLS 대표는 10.17-18 카나다 토론토에서 개최되는 미.일.카나다.EC 4개국 통상장관 회담시 재회동 할 예정이라고 밝힘

　　3. 금번 협상의 좀더 상세한 내용은 추보하겠음.끝

　　(대사 권동만-국장)

통상국	통상국		경기원	재무부	농수부	상공부

관리 번호	92-174

외 무 부

종   별 :

번   호 : USW-5079   일   시 : 92 1013 1946

수   신 : 장 관(통기,통이,미일,경기원,농수산부,상공부,경제수석,외교안보)

발   신 : 주 미 대사   사본: 주 제네바, EC 대사-본부중계필

제   목 : UR 협상

연: USW-5045

1. 당관 장기호 참사관은 금 10.13. USTR SUZANNE EARLY 농업담당 대표보를 이영래 농무관과 함께 면담, 연호 미.EC 각료회의 결과에 관해 의견 교환한 바, 동인의 반응 요지 아래 보고함.(이하 동인의 발언 요지)

    가. (브랏셀 각료회의 결과에 대한 평가 문의에 대해)

    0 아직 브랏셀로 부터 상세 결과를 보고 받지못해 아직 시기적으로 이른 감이 있지만 자신은 금번 협상에서 농산물에 대한 돌파구 (BREAKTHROUGH)가 마련되지 못하여 실망을 금치 못하며, 앞으로 UR 협상이 커다란 난관에 봉착하게 되었다고 봄.

    나. (미국이 앞으로 UR 협상과 관련 어떤 구체적인 계획을 갖고 있는지 문의에 대해)

    0 CARLA HILLS USTR 대표와 MADIGAN 농무장관이 어떤 복안을 갖고 있는지 알 수 없지만 곧 있게될 카나다에서 개최되는 4 개국 통상장관 회담과 EC 긴급정상회담에 기대를 걸어보는 수 밖에 없으며, 사견으로는 급진전이 있을 것으로 기대하지 않음.

    0 불란서가 수출보조금 문제등에 있어서 강한 입장을 견지하는 한 타결이 어렵다고 보며, 이는 내년 3 월 불란서 선거가 끝난후에 가능할 것으로 봄.

    0 EC 와의 각료회의에서는 농산물을 제외한 여타 서비스, 시장접근등에 있어서 진전이 있었다고 하지만, 농산물협상의 타결없이는 UR 의 협상이 큰 의미를가질 수 없으며, 농산물 협상의 실패가 결국 여타분야 협상의 진전에도 영향을줄 것으로 봄.

    다. (UR 협상에 대한 향후 전망과 관련 최근 비관적 의견이 크게 대두되고 있다고 지적한데 대해)

    0 현재와 같은 상태가 계속되는 한 UR 타결 전망은 PESSIMISTIC 하다고 생각되며, 앞으로는 미 대통령 선거결과를 보아야 할 것임.

통상국	장관	차관	2차보	미주국	통상국	정와대	정와대	안기부
경기원	농수부	상공부	중계					

외신 2과   통제관 FR

0111

O BUSH 대통령이 재선되면 UR 협상이 다시 활기를 찾을 것으로 보지만 10.11. 대통령 후보 TV 토론회에서 재선시 BAKER 백악관 비서실장을 경제팀의 총수로 임명할 것이라는 BUSH 대통령의 언급은 USTR 내에 대외통상교섭 LINE 에도 영향을 미칠 것이므로 신행정부 출범후 UR 협상이 다시 열기를 되찾을때까지 상당기간이 소요될 것으로 우려됨.

O CLINTON 후보의 대통령 당선시 지금까지의 UR 협상이 후퇴될 것이라는 일부의 견해도 있지만 CLINTON 후보 역시 UR 협상을 조속 종결시키는 것이 좋다는 생각을 갖고 있는 것으로 보이며, 또한 NAFTA 협정에 대해서도 조건을 담고 있지만 이를 지지하고 있는 것으로 보아 결국 BUSH 대통령이 추진해온 방향과는 크게다르지 않을 것으로 예상되나 대통령 선거 결과를 지켜보아야 좀더 확실한 전망을 가질수 있을 것임.

라. (OILSEEDS 문제 협상에 진전이 있었는지와 앞으로의 대처방향 문의에 대해)

O OILSEED 문제도 이번에 별다른 성과가 없었으며 앞으로 어떤 조치를 취할것인지 하는 문제는 CARLA HILLS 대표가 어떤 구상을 갖고 있는지에 달려있음.

2. 장참사관이 금일 오후 SANDRA KRISTOFF 국무부 부차관보 접촉 기회에 UR협상에 대한 전망을 문의한데 대해 아래 요지 반응을 보인바 참고로 보고함.

가. 직접 협상에 간여하질 않았기 때문에 조심스럽게 느껴지지만 이번 미.EC 각료회의 결과 아무런 성과가 없으므로 현재로서는 매우 비관적으로 봄.

다만 11 월 대통령선거 결과에 따른 어떤 변화가 있길 기대하며, 금년중 타결이 어려우면 94 년까지도 협상이 계속될 수 있다는 것을 상정해 볼수 있을 것임.

나. BUSH 대통령 재선시에는 분명히 미 행정부가 UR 협상을 위해 미지막 PUSH 를 가할 것이 확실하다는 전제하에, 사견으로는, 비단 CLINTON 후보가 대통령에 당선되더라도 UR 협상에 부정적인 영향을 가져올 것이라는 일부의 견해와는달리 결국 취임후 2-3 개월내에 대외정책의 PRIORITY 를 검토, UR 협상을 최우선의 대외통상 과제로 취급하지 않을 수 없을 것으로 전망되며, 이때에는 의회에FAST TRACK AUTHORITY 재연장을 신청, UR 협상을 계속해 나갈 것으로 봄.. 끝.

(대사 현홍주 - 국장)

예고: 92.12.31. 까지

PAGE 2

0112

관리
번호 92-697

외 무 부

종 별 :

번 호 : GVW-1920   일 시 : 92 1013 1920

수 신 : 장관(통기, 경기원, 재무부, 농림수산부, 상공부)

발 신 : 주 제네바 대사   사본:주미, 주EC, 영, 독, 불, 일대사-중계필

제 목 : UR 협상동향

연: GVW-1903

10.11-12 미, EC 간 브라셀각료회담이 UR 협상 돌파구 마련에 이르지 못하고 종료된데 대해 GATT 사무국, 주요국 협상대표의 반등등 당지 분위기 및 평가내용을 아래 보고함.

1. 연호 10.9 그린룸회의에서 미.EC 양측대사가 상기 브랏셀 각료회담을 협상과정상의 한 단계일뿐 이에 대해 지니찬 기대감을 자제해줄것과 동 회담이 실패하더라도 UR 협상의 붕괴를 의미하는 것으로 받아들여서는 안된다고 언급한바 있기 때문에, 당지 일반적 분위기는 예상한 결과가 나왔을 뿐이며, 따라서 성급한 결론을 내리기 보다는 앞으로의 협상방향등 추이를 당분간 더 기다려 보아야 할것이라는 분위기 임.

2. EC 대표부 관계관은 동결과가 협상의 결렬 또는 언론 보도와 같이 비관적 상황은 아니라는 반응을 보이면서, 협상의 구체적 내용은 밝힐수 없으나 시장접근 및 써비스분야에는 진전(GOOD PROGRESS)이 있었고 농산물분야에서도 시장접근 및 수출보조문제에 관해서는 기본방향(BASICS)에 관한 어느정도의 의견접근이 있었으나, OILSEEDS 문제 및 CAP 개혁에 따른 손실보상 직접보조금 처리문제가 미결로 남아 있는것으로 알고 있다고 하면서 앞으로 실무책임자급 회담을 계속해 나간후 내주 또는 그이후 양측 농무장관 회담을 개최할 것으로 보인다함.(미.EC 양대표부는 사안의 민감성에 비추어 회담내용을 밝히기를 꺼려하고 있음)

3. 호주대사는 사태진전을 비관적으로 보지 않는다 하면서 자신이 파악하고있는 바를 아래와 같이 언급함.

가. 양측입장이 점차 접근해 가고 있으며, 양측 모두 진지한 협상의지가 있음.

나. 협상은 시장접근, 써비스, 농산물 전분야를 대상으로 하고 있으며, 따라서

통상국	장관	차관	2차보	분석관	정와대	안기부	경기원	재무부
농수부	상공부	중계						

PAGE 1   92.10.14   05:13

외신 2과   룡제관 FK

0113

미.EC 합의가 나올경우 이는 UR 협상 전분야를 포괄하는 GLOBAL 한 내용이 될것임.

다. 미측이 EC 에 대해 구체적 제안을 하였고 이를 EC 가 검토중에 있다하며, OILSEEDS 문제에 관해서는 아직도 의견차가 심한것으로 알려짐.

라. 토론토 4 국 봉상장관회담 이전에라도 미.EC 농무장관회담이 또한차례 개최될 가능성도 많음

마. 버밍험 EC 긴급정상회담에서도 UR 문제가 부분적으로(AT THE MARGIN) 취급될 것으로 보임.

4. 반면, 인도대사는 미.EC 간 협상진행상황, 미국의 선거전 양상(BUSH 대통령의 재선 실패가능성) 등 제반상황에 비추어 UR 협상이 <u>2 여년간 지연될</u> 것으로 본다는 견해를 피력함.

5. 한편, 시장접근 비공식 협의는 지난주 종료되었으나 앞으로의 일정은 DENIS 의장이 DUNKEL 총장과 협의결정할 전망이고, <u>서비스협상도 금주말까지 계속되는</u> 양자협상 일정 이외의 구체계획이 없는 상태(향후 협상 일정논의를 위해 <u>10.15 GNS</u> <u>공식회의가 소집 봉보된</u> 상태이나, 금일 CARLISLE 차장에게 문의한바 자신은 현재로서는 <u>아무런 복안도 없으며</u> 다만 참가국들의 의견만을 청취할 예정이라함) 이며, 법제화 그룹 또한 10.8 소수국 비공식 협의시 조금더 사태를 관망해 본후 향후 일정을 수립키로 합의된바 있어, <u>현재로서는 앞으로의 당지 협상 일정도 불투명한</u> 상태임.

6. GATT 사무국 담당관은 사무국으로서는 미.EC 간 협상이 계속된다는데 의미를 부여하고 있다고 하면서, 지난 10.9 그린룸협의시 DUNKEL 총장이 약 10 일이후 재소집키로한 그린룸협의와 관련, 현재로서 동 개최시기를 예단키는 어려우나, 미.EC 가 협상을 계속하는 상황하에서는 협상의 다자화(MULTILATERALIZATION)가 어렵고 DUNKEL 총장이 언급한 WELL STRUCTURED PROGRAMME OF WORKS 도 나오기 힘든 것이 사실이므로, 미.EC 간 협의가 나오지 않는한 그린룸 회의는 이달말또는 미대통령 선거 이후로 미루어질 가능성도 없지 않다함. 끝

(대사 박수길-장관)

예고:92.12.31. 까지

외 무 부

관리
번호 92-698

종   별 :

번   호 : ITW-1294   일   시 : 92 1013 1735

수   신 : 장관(통기,구일,기정)

발   신 : 주 이태리 대사(사:주EC,제네바대사(송필))

제   목 : UR 협상 동향(자응 92-81)

　　10.11.-12. 브럿셀에서 개최된 미-EC UR 협상 각료회담 관련 당관 김경석서기관이
10.13. 주재국 외무성 BARUCCO 참사관과 면담하고 주재국 정부의 견해를 문의한 바,
동참사관의 발언 요지 다음 보고함.

　　1. EC 측은 금번회담에서 미국측이 미대통령 선거전 UR 타결을 목표로 어느정도의
타협안을 제시할 것으로 기대했으나, 별다른 태도 변화를 보이지 않음에 따라
협상타결의 실마리를 찾지 못함. 따라서 미국이 금번 회담을 제의한 것은, 대통령
선거를 의식, 유권자들에게 UR 타결을 위한 이니시아티브를 발휘하고 있다는 인상을
주기위한 의도인 것으로 보임.

　　2. 양측은 곧 협상을 재개키로 했으나, 그시기가 선거를 불과 며칠 앞둔시점이라는
점, 그리고 협상타결의 관건인 수출보조금 삭감문제에 가장 민감한 불란서측이
융통성을 보일 가능성이 적다는 점등에 비추어 미선거이전 또는 년말까지의 UR
협상타결은 어려울 것으로 전망됨. 끝

　　(대사 이기주-국장)

　　예고:92.12.31. 까지

인반문서로 재분류(1992 .12 .31

통상국　　차관　　1차보　　구주국　　분석관　　정와대　　안기부

92.10.14　　05:02
외신 2과 통제관 FK

0115

외 무 부

종   별 :

번   호 : ECW-1255   일   시 : 92 1014 1830

수   신 : 장관(봉기),통상,경기원,재무부,농림수산부,상공부,기정동문)

발   신 : 주 EC 대사   사본: 주 제네바,미,불,독,일본대사-중계필

제   목 : 갓트/UR 협상동향

연: ECW-1242

당관이 EC 집행위및 당지 미대표부등을 접촉하여 탐문한 10.11-12 의
미.EC양자협상 결과및 향후 전망등을 아래 보고함

    1. 양자협상 결과

    가. 동 협상에서는 미.EC 간의 최대현안이 UR/ 농산물협상 뿐 아니라, 써비스,
시장접근및 OILSEEDS 분쟁의 처리방향등이 폭넓게 취급되었는바, 12 일밤 늦게까지
양측이 매우 진지하고 끈질기게 협상타결을 모색했으나 결국 농산물문제에 대한
이견조정을 이루지 못해 합의점을 도출치 못했음

    나. 써비스, 시장접근분야 협상

    HILLS 통상대표와 ANDRIESSEN 집행위원이 주관한 동분야 협상에서는 양측간이견이
어느정도 접근되었다고 함. 분야별로 특히 금융 써비스분야에 있어서는양측의견이
일치되었다 함. 통신분야는 상호협의를 거쳐가며 입장을 추가 조정키로 했다하며,
해운분야에서는 EC 제국이 미국의 MFN 복귀를 계속 주장 했으며,기타 AUDIOVISUAL
문제와 정부조달문제에 대해서 많은 토론이 있었다 함. 시장접근 분야의 의견접근이
있었으나 농산물협상과의 PACKAGE DEAL 을 위해 결론을 보지 못했다고 함

    다. 농산물협상 분야

    0 농산물협상분야에 있어서는 미국이 EC 의 CAP 개혁에따른 소득보조를 감축대상
보조에서 제외하는 문제에대해 양해하겠다는 양보입장을 준비해 왔으나 수출보조금에
관한 이견조정 실패와 OILSEEDS 문제로 대립되었다 함

    0 소득보조: 미국은 EC 가 미국의 DEFICIENCY PAYMENT 를 인정하는 대신에 EC 의
지지가격 인하및 SET-ASIDE 시행에따른 소득보조문제에 대하여는 감축기간을 설정하지
않고 인정할수 있다는입장을 보여줌으로서 양측의 입장차이가 많이축소되었으며, 또

통상국	통상국	분석관	안기부	경기원	재무부	농수부	상공부	중계

PAGE 1

92.10.15   06:45

외신 2과 통제관 BZ

0116

EC 가 15% SET-ASIDE 계획을 시행할 경우, EC 의 CEREALS 생산량은 10% 정도 감축되는 효과가 있을 것이라는 분석결과도 제시한 것으로 알려짐

　O 수출보조: 미국은 93-99 기간중 보조수출물량 감축을 23% 수준으로 제시하는등 다소 양보한다는 입장을 보인 반면, EC 는 14% 이상은 감축할수 없다는 당초 입장을 견지함으로서 의견차이 조정에 실패하였다 함 (특히 불란서는 물량기준 감축공약은 수용할수 없다는 의견을 보이고 있음)

　O REBALANCING: EC 는 CAP 개혁의 기본원칙이 수입곡물 수요를 역내산 곡물로의 대체를 촉진한다는 데에 있음을 강조하면서, REBALANCING 의 인정 필요성을역설 하였으나, 미국은 관세인하등 새로운 무역장벽의 설정을 받을수 없다는 입장을 견지함

　O PEACE CLAUSE: 미국은 공식적 또는 다자적으로 일방적 무역보복 조치를 포기 한다는 공약에는 반대한다는 입장을 보였으나, 비공식적, 쌍무적인 측면에서는 받아드릴수 있다는 입장을 취한 것으로 알려짐

　라. 한편, OILSEEDS 문제관련, 미국은 EC 가 동 품목 생산량을 7 백만톤 수준까지 감축할수 있는 조치를 취해줄것을 요구한바 있으나, EC 는 CAP 개혁에따른 소맥 생산량의 감축과 동시에 OILSEEDS 의 생산량의 감축을 초래하는 여하한 조치도 어렵다는 입장을 보임으로서 의견조정에 실패하였으며, 수출보조금문제와더불어 미.EC 간의 핵심적 대립문제가 된 것으로 알려짐

　2. 동향및 전망

　가. 미.EC 양자협상 회담이후 HILLS 미무역대표부 대표는 10.13. 독일을 방문, MOELLEMANN 경제상과 회담을 가졌음. HILLS-MOELLEMANN 회담후 독일경제성 대변인은 회담내용을 밝히기는 거부하면서도, UR 협상을 종결시키기 위한 정치적결단을 내릴 시기임을 강조함. HILLS 대표의 프랑스 STRASS-KAHN 무역상과의 10.14. 회담 추진설도 있었으나 실현되지 않게된 것으로 탐문됨

　나. EC 집행위는 10.14(수) 113 조 위원회 회의를 개최, PAEMEN 부총국장으로 부터 대미협상 결과를 보고받고, 10.16. 정상회의앞 보고내용을 채택예정이며, ANDRIESSEN 집행위원이 정상회의에 동 보고를 할 예정임. EC 집행위는 동 보고서에서 미측의 양보내용을 중심으로 협상내용을 보고하고, 앞으로의 협상에 EC집행위가 보다 융통성있게 임할수 있도록 어느정도 재량권 부여를 요청케 될것으로 보이나, EC 정상회의의 결과는 결국 프랑스가 어느정도까지 강경한 입장을 계속 고수하느냐에 달릴 것으로 전망됨

PAGE 2

다. 현재 EC 와 미측 전문가들은 계속 협상을갖고 농업문제에 대한 실무접촉을 가지고 있으며, 그결과를 기초로 내주중 MDIGAN 미 농무장관및 MAC SHARRY 집행위원간의 농업관계 회담재개가 추진되고 있으나 그 개최여부도 버밍햄 정상회의의 결과에 따르게 될것임

라. 한편, EC 의장국인 영국은 10.16. EC 긴급정상회담에서 UR 협상 타결방안의 도출을위해 적극 노력할 것으로 예상되나, 프랑스가 미.EC 협상이 결렬된 것은 미국의 과도한 요구때문이었다고 비난하면서, EC 및 자국이익에 반하는 미국의 요구를 수용할수 없다는 강경자세를 견지하고 있으며, 또한 10.16. EC 정상회담 에서도 미국의 요구및 불균형한 결과를 거부해 줄것을 EC 집행위및 회원국들에게 강력 요청하고 있음이 주목됨

마. 이러한 상황에서 당지 전문가들은 일반적으로 EC 의 가장 큰 관심분야인 농업분야 소득보조문제에 대해서는 상당한 진전이 있었음을 평가하면서도 수출보조금등 여타문제를 포함한 미-프랑스및 프랑스-EC 회원국간의 큰 입장차이로말미암아, 미-EC 간의 타협이 미대통령 선거이전에 과연 이루어질수 있을지에 대해서 의구심을 갖고, 10.16 의 버밍햄 정상회의를 지켜보고 있음. 끝

(대사 권동만-국장)

예고: 92.12.31 까지

관리 번호	92-706

외 무 부

종 별 :

번 호 : GVW-1929 일 시 : 92 1014 1900

수 신 : 장관(통기, 경기원, 재무부, 농수산부, 특허청)

발 신 : 주 제네바 대사 사본: 주미, EC, 영, 불, 독일대사-중계필

제 목 : UR 협상동향

연: WGV-1920

1. 연호 10.11-12 미.EC 간의 브랏셀 각료회담 이후의 UR 전망에 대한 당지 USTR 대표부 및 케언즈그룹의 평가를 아래 보고함.

가. USTR 측

- STOLER 공사는 브랏셀 각료회담은 별진전이 없었으며 실무진이 협상을 계속하여 내주중에 양측 농무장관간의 회담을 갖기로 하였으나 동회담에서도 돌파구를 마련할 가능성은 불투명하며 또한 토론토 4 국회담도 UR 진전에 계기가 될것으로 보이지 않는다는 비관적인 견해를 표명함.

- CHRISTOPHER PARLIN 법률 자문관은 농산물의 브랏셀 회담의 주요 의제였으며 그중 특히 수출보조금 문제가 논의의 핵심이었으나, 합의를 보지 못하였는바, 이는 브랏셀회의전 불란서의 강경입장 표명이 EC 의 협상 신축성을 크게 제약한 결과를 가져왔고 미국 역시 일방적 양보만 할수 없었던 상황이었기 때문이라고 본다고 하면서, 미국은 계속 협상할 용의가 있으며 FAST TRACK 시한내의 UR 종결을 위해서는 금년내에 제네바에서의 실무협상이 종결되어야 한다고 보나 전망은 불투명하다고 평가함.

나. 케언즈 그룹

- 당지 뉴질랜드 및 태국 대표부측에 의하면 미국은 작 10.13(화) 개최된 케언즈 그룹 당지 협상대표들간의 회의에서 브랏셀회담 결과를 설명하면서 동 회담은 언론 보도와는 달리 상당한 진전이 있었으며, 수출보조 감축물량에 대한 숫자만 남아 있는 것으로 설명하였다 함.

- 반면 동 케언즈 그룹회의에서의 일반적인 평가는 아래와 같았다고함.

. 버밍험 EC 긴급정상회담에서 EC 정상들이 EC 위원회의 확고한 지침을 주지

통상국 농수부	장관 특허청	차관 중계	2차보	분석관	청와대	안기부	경기원	재무부

PAGE 1 92.10.15 07:33

외신 2과 롱제관 CM

0119

않는한 정상회담 자체는 UR 진전에 큰 도움이 되지는 못할 것으로 보이며, 토론토 4국 회담도 농산물 보조금 문제해결에 직접 관련이 적은 카나다, 일본이 참가한다는 점에서 볼때 UR 진전에 커다란 도움이 되지는 못할 것으로 보이기 때문에, UR 의 향후 성패는 미.EC 간에 계속될 협상의 결과에 기대를 가질수 밖에 없음.

    2. 참고로, 브랏셀 회의 결과를 보아가며 향후 법제화 그룹(T3) 일정을 논의하기위해 잠정적으로 10.16(금) 개최키로 한 소규모의 T3 비공식회의는 GREEN ROOM 회의 (개최일자 미정) 이후로 연기되었음을 금일(10.14) 갓트 사무국으로부터 통보 받았음.

    (대사 박수길-국장)

    예고:92.12.31. 까지

PAGE 2

0120

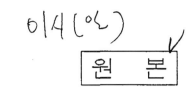

관리
번호 92-709

외 무 부

종 별 : 지 급

번 호 : FRW-2088   일 시 : 92 1014 1930

수 신 : 장관(통기) 사본:주 EC , 제네바대사-직송필

발 신 : 주 불 대사

제 목 : UR 협상 동향

대:FRW-2025, 2070

1. 미.EC 회담의 상세내용이 상금 대외적으로 알려지고 있지 않은 가운데 당지 일부 언론은 농산물분야 협상에서 양측간 상당한 진전 (GREENBOX 확대 및 EC 의 수출물량 감축분야) 이 있었던 것으로 보도하고 있음. 주재국 정부 UR 담당관은 금번 회담후 후속 협상이 계획되어 있음에 비추어 동 협상결과를 일부 언론보도와 같이 '실패' 라고 속단할수 없으며 동 회담결과에 대한 평가는 금일 브랏셀 개최 113 조 위원회에서 있을 것이라 함.

2. 금번 회담에서 EC 측의 조급한 양보 가능성을 극히 우려하였던 불정부는 회담에서 양측간 구체적 합의가 없었다는 점에서 다소 안도하고 있으나, 오히려 향후 1-2 주내 협상이 급진전될 가능성을 경계하고 있음.

3. 이와관련 DRIEUX 불 대외무역장관은 미국이 바람직한 방향으로 일부 양보하였으나 아직은 충분치 않은 상태라고 지적하였으며, SOISSON 농업장관 역시 미측은 11 월 대선이전에 UR 타결이 불가능하다는 점을 인식해야 할 것이라고 주장하는 가운데 금일 불 농민단체는 UR 협상에서 대미 양보불가 및 CAP 개혁에 따른 보완조치 촉구 목적으로 지방 곳곳에서 대규모 시위를 벌임.

4. UR 협상관련, EC 집행위로서는 10.16. EC 특별정상회담을 앞두고 불란서를 지나치게 자극하는 수준으로 협상을 타결할수가 없다는 현실적인 부담을 갖고있는 반면, 불란서 입장에서 보면 자국의 이익이 무시된 UR 협상의 진전은 협정부의 진퇴에 까지 영향을 미칠 중대사안임에 따라 (협상타결시 야당측의 즉각적인 불신임안 상정 가능성까지도 보도되고 있음) EC 집행위와 불란서 정부는 미측의 상응하는 양보폭을 놓고 한동안 대립할것으로 예상됨.

5. 한편 10.6. EC 통상장관 회담시 나타난 바와 같이 EC 내 불란서의 고립이 더욱

통상국   장관   차관   2차보   구주국   분석관   정와대   안기부

PAGE 1   92.10.16   04:57

분명해지고 있는 가운데 불란서는 독일의 협조를 크게 기대하고 있으며, 이와관련 당지 언론은 KOHL 총리가 10.12. BEREGOVOY 총리 면담시 UR 관련 불란서의 국내 정치경제적 어려움에 충분한 이해를 표한 것으로 보도함.

　　6. 10.16. EC 특별정상회담시 의장국인 영국은 UR 문제를 적극 거론할 가능성이 있으나 불측은 현안 EMS 문제외에 EC 회원국간 입장이 분열되어 있는 UR 협상문제까지 깊이 논의하는 것은 바람직하지 않다는 점을 강조하여 동건의 논의를 92.12. EC 정례 정상회담까지 연기토록 시도할 것으로 예상되며 이점에서는 독일도 어느정도 입장을 같이하고 있는 것으로 알려지고 있는 바 관련 동향 추보함. 끝

　　(대사 노영찬-국장)

　　예고:92.12.31 까지

PAGE 2

0122

외 무 부

종 별 :

번 호 : USW-5109   일 시 : 92 1014 2023

수 신 : 장 관(통기),통이,통삼,경일,경기원,상공부,농수산부)

발 신 : 주 미 대사

제 목 : UR 동향(언론보도)

연: USW-5079

1. 연호 미. EC 간 각료회의 결과와 관련 금일(10.14)자 당지 JOC 지와 F.T 지는 일반의회의적인 관측에도 불구 협상 참가자들이 협상타결 전망에 긍정적인 반응을 보이는등 금번 회의에서 미. EC 간 적지않은 진전이있은 것으로 보도하였는바, 양지의 보도내용 요지하기 보고함.

가. 써비스 분야와 일부 농산물 분야에서 의견접근

- 양지는 미국과 EC 관리의 말을 인용, 미국이 EC 의 농가소득 직접 보조를 감축 대상이 되는 국내 보조금에서 제외하는데 합의했다고 보도

- JOC 지는 EC 관리의 말을 인용, 써비스분야에서도 사실상 이견이 해소되었다고 보도 (동지는 영국 관리의 말을 인용, 써비스 분야의 경우 프랑스 정부가 프랑스 국민을 충분히 납득시킬수있을 정도로 이견이 좁혀졌다고 보도)

- 한편, F.T 지는 EC 의 보조금 지급 농산물 수출물량 감축과 관련 미. EC 양측이 융통성있는 입장을 보이고 있으며, 아래 3가지 방식이 검토되고 있다고 보도

. EC 는 6년간 각 농산물에 대해 24 퍼센트의 물량감축에 합의하되 연도별 감축량에 있어 10퍼센트 내외의 변동폭 (SWING) 허용 요구 (일부 농산물의 경우는 여타 농산물 보다 24 퍼센트 감축을 조기달성)

. 미측은 상기안에 대해 년간 변동품목을 4퍼센트내로 제안할 것을 주장

. 6년간 21퍼센트의 물량 감축을 하는 잠정협정 (이안은 합의 가능성이 거의 없다고 보도)

- 현재 미. EC 간 입장이 대립되는 분야는 EC의 종자유 생산물량 감축으로 미국은 현 13백만톤에서 7백만톤으로 생산감축을, EC는 9.5백만톤으로 생산감축을 주장하고 있다고 보도

통상국   경제국   통상국   통상국   경기원   농수부   상공부

PAGE 1   92.10.15   10:37 WG

외신 1과 통제관 ✓

0123

나. UR 타결을 위한 영국의 노력

　　- JOC 지는 익명의 소식통을 인용, MAJOR영국수상이 금번 미. EC 통상.농무장관회의의 성과를 기초로 10.16. EC 정상회담시 EC 국가, 특히 프랑스에 대하여 UR의 신속한 타결을 촉구할 것이라고 보도

　　- 동지는 부시 대통령이 침체된 재선운동에 활기를 불어 넣기 위해 11월 선거전 UR 타결에 관심을 보이고 있으며, F.T 지도 UR 이 타결되려면 11월 선거이전에 양측의 합의가 이루어져야 한다는 양측 관리의 말을 인용 보도 (F.T 지는 브뤼셀에서는 부시 대통령이 선거 일주일전에 UR 타결을 발표하길 희망하고 있는 것으로 관측하고 있다고 보도)

　　2. 관련기사는 별첨 FAX 송부하며, 미. EC 간 의견접근에 관해서는 USTR 및 관련기관과 접촉후 추보하겠음.끝.

　　첨부: USW(F)-6562 (3 매)

　　(대사 현홍주-국장)

PAGE 2

0124

주 미 대 사 관

USW(F) : *6562*　　년월일 :　　　　　시간 :

수　신 : 장　관 (통기, 통이, 통상, 경안)사본 : 경기원,
　　　　　　　　　　　　　　　　상공, 농수산부

발　신 : 주 미 대 사

제　목 : *USW - 5109* 의 첨북 (304)　　(출처 JOC 10/14/92)

보　안　　통　제

Britain to Press GATT Issue at Summit

LONDON — Britain will press its European Community partners, particularly France, to take a more flexible negotiating position in the long-stalled global trade talks, according to informed sources.

At a special EC summit Friday in Birmingham, England, British Prime Minister John Major will stress to the attending heads of state and government that the opportunity to get a deal in the Uruguay Round is fading fast and the narrow differences over farm trade must be bridged in the coming weeks.

"Never again will we be in a position where the Americans (alone can) take the required measures. We will talk of the need to get a GATT deal, and we will put some pressure on the French," said one senior British official.

The GATT, or General Agreement on Tariffs and Trade, is the 105-nation, Geneva-based body that governs most world trade in goods and under whose auspices the Uruguay Round has been conducted.

While the GATT round will not be the principal area of discussion at the summit, which will be dominated by efforts to put the program for closer EC unity back on track, Mr. Major will attempt to build on the slight progress that has emerged from talks in recent days.

The six-year round has lain dormant for nearly two years due to a U.S.-EC dispute over the size and scope of agricultural subsidies included in any deal. But President Bush is keen to cut a deal in hopes that it may provide some lift to his flagging re-election bid.

Renewed U.S. enthusiasm for a package was evident last weekend in Brussels, when senior U.S. and EC negotiators narrowed their differences on trade in services and on some agriculture issues.

One official close to the talks said both sides made compromise proposals in an effort to bridge the gap. A European official said the differences on services have been virtually eliminated.

The United States had accepted that income support payments for farmers, negotiated during the strenuous efforts to reform the EC's Common Agricultural Policy, would not be subjected to reductions, the European official said.

But two key agricultural issues remain unresolved — the question of cuts in the volume of subsidized grain that is exported, and EC insistence on raising tariffs or quotas on oilseeds to offset cuts in other farm sectors.

One U.S. official strongly stated that Washington was not prepared to allow the 12-nation community to implement an oilseeds program that hurts U.S. farmers.

Equally, French officials are adamant they cannot accept a deal that goes beyond the support cuts accepted for a reformed Common Agricultural Policy. French Trade Minister Bruno Durieux said Tuesday that while U.S. proposals made in Brussels this week were a step in the right direction, they did not go far enough.

"In order to reach this agreement, the American side must make a few more concessions. They are making proposals that are not ac-

ceptable for France and for countries belonging to the European Community," he said.

One British official said the gap between the sides had narrowed considerably on a deal that would offer potential gains for French service industries and even for the efficient French farm sector. This British official asserted that President Francois Mitterrand could easily sell the package to his countrymen.

"There is no reason why the French can't do a deal and present it as a triumph. But there is equally no suggestion that the French are in a mood to play," the official said.

France cannot technically veto the desire of other EC members for a GATT deal, but it can insist on a ratification procedure known as the Luxembourg compromise, which would greatly delay the process of approval. In any event, British officials do not see much likelihood that other EC countries will clash with France on the issue.

(*6562* - 3 - 1)

외신 1과
등　　제

주 미 대 사 관

USW(F) :　　　　　　년월일 :　　　　　　시간 :

수　신 : 장　관

발　신 : 주 미 대 사

제　목 :

보　　안
동　　제

(출처 FT 10/14/92)

EC and US closer to farm trade deal

THE European Community and the US have all but resolved two of the three remaining disputes over subsidised farm trade, according to EC officials.

Hopes are high that this could soon clear the way for agreement on the Uruguay Round world trade liberalisation talks under the General Agreement on Tariffs and Trade, despite intense lobbying by farmers on both sides.

According to senior EC officials and leaders of the US Farm Bureau, the influential US farm lobby, Washington has agreed that compensation to European farmers for big price cuts agreed in May's reform of the EC farm regime will be exempt from the Gatt requirement to reduce overall domestic subsidies by 20 per cent.

The Uruguay Round "final act" will be rewritten to reflect this breakthrough, which nevertheless must be endorsed by the other Gatt negotiating participants, which number 108 in all.

The two sides are also now examining the legal texts of three formulas for cutting subsidised exports by up to 24 per cent. According to one senior official, this is very close to being agreed.

They still differ, however, on the extent to which the EC must cut its oilseeds output, to comply with a separate Gatt ruling. The main problem here is that the US is not confident that the EC's farm reform can deliver sufficient cuts.

Talks in Brussels between the two sides' top negotiators were suspended late on Monday night after 21 hours, with both sides divulging nothing except that the gap between them had narrowed.

It is now clear that a deal could have been clinched then, but for last minute pressure from the US Farm Bureau. Mr Dean Kleckner, president of the Farm Bureau, agreed yesterday that he had been "kicking his heels" in Brussels on Monday.

Meetings are planned between Mr Frans Andriessen, EC external affairs commissioner, and Mrs Carla Hills, US special trade representative, in Ontario at the weekend, and between Mr Ray MacSharry, EC agriculture commissioner, and Mr Ed Madigan, US agriculture secretary, probably next week.

Officials from both sides say agreement has to be reached before the US presidential election in November 3 if the round is to be concluded. The betting in Brussels is that President Bush would like to announce an agreement in the week beforehand.

The EC is under strong pressure from France to concede nothing to the US which will affect its cereals exports, pressure which will be highlighted by today's "day of action" by protesting French farmers.

A senior official pointed out that even if the EC agrees to a full 24 per cent cut in subsidised cereals exports the EC will still be able to export 23.5m tonnes in six years' time, when projections based on the reform show it will need to export only 19m tonnes.

(6562 - 3 - 2)

외신 1과
제

0126

주 미 대 사 관

USW(F)　:　　　　　　　년월일 :　　　　　시간 :

수 신 : 장 관

발 신 : 주 미 대 사

제 목 :

（출처 FT 10/14/92 ）

보　안
동　제

Oilseeds still block agreement on Gatt

GATT The principal stumbling block to a settlement of the Uruguay Round of talks on world trade liberalisation is a still-yawning gap between the US and the EC on Europe's oilseed subsidy regime, according to a leading US farm lobbyist.

Mr Dean Kleckner, president of the American Farm Bureau, said, at the end of two days in Brussels lobbying US-EC trade and agriculture negotiators as they fought to settle a 20-month dispute over the EC's subsidised farm trade regime, that he was not optimistic that differences on oilseeds could be settled.

His mood yesterday contrasted with that of the negotiators, who despite the apparently inconclusive end to negotiations on Monday night, appear confident agreement can be reached.

This confidence has been underpinned by significant progress in settling two issues at times felt to be intractable: US demands that the EC cut the volume and the value of its subsidised farm exports, and EC demands that compensation payments to European farmers for price cuts under the Common Agriculture Policy reform should not be seen as subsidies, and so exempt from any agreement on subsidy cuts.

"You don't have anything until you have everything," Mr Kleckner warned, pointing to considerable differences between the US and the EC on oilseed production. US negotiators are demanding the EC cuts its output from the current 13m tonnes a year to 7m tonnes in six years.

EC negotiators are currently refusing to cut below 9.5m tonnes.

He warned that failure to reach agreement in the next 10 days would "make it a dead certainty" the US will carry out threats to impose punitive tariffs amounting to $1bn (£587m) on EC farm exports in retaliation for alleged damage done to US farmers by the EC oilseeds regime.

"There's a little more time, but we are counting in days," he said. "If we failed to reach an agreement, that would be dreadful for the Uruguay Round, and for economies throughout the world."

He insisted negotiators could be even further apart on the oilseeds dispute than the public realised, largely because the EC's target of 9.5m tonnes annual output will be based not on firm policy objectives, but on an assumption that the CAP reforms, intended to reduce the acreage sown with oilseeds, will automatically achieve the targeted reduction.

"It would create a firestorm of protest among US farmers if the administration were to settle for anything less than a cut to 7m tonnes," Mr Kleckner said. "The gap may not seem great, but we just can't believe the EC figures are accurate."

EC officials did not share Mr Kleckner's pessimism yesterday, as they weighed the significance of the breakthroughs achieved on farmer compensation and volume cuts for farm exports.

It is understood that US negotiators, in accommodating EC demands on compensation, have agreed to nothing less than a re-drafting of relevant parts of the draft Uruguay Round agreement published in late December last year.

It will allow direct payments to farmers under production-limiting criteria to be exempt from year-by-year reduction in subsidies.

In settling differences on the US demand for the EC to cut the volume of its subsidised farm exports, three formulae have apparently been tabled:

● the EC is willing to agree a 24 per cent cut in all farm products by the end of six years, provided annual progress to that eventual target allows for 10 per cent "swings", with certain products moving towards 24 per cent faster than others.

● the US accepts this proposal, but insists on the annual "swings" being limited to 4 per cent.

● a standby proposal for volume cuts to be limited to 21 per cent at the end of six years. This appears the least likely to be agreed upon.

(6562 - 3 - 3)

외신 1과
동　제

외 무 부

증   별 :

번   호 : USW-5113   일   시 : 92 1015 1533

수   신 : 장관(통기,통이,경기원,농림수산부,재무부,상공부)

발   신 : 주 미 대사   사본: 주 제네바, EC 대사(중계필)

제   목 : UR/농산물 협상 동향과 전망

1. 당관 이영래 농무관은 10.15. 미 농무부 해외농업처 RICHARD SCHROETER 처장보와 JAMES GRUEFF 다자협력 과장을 면담, 표제관련 미.EC 각료회의 결과 및전망을 문의한바, 요지 하기 보고함.

가. 미.EC 각료회의 결과

- 금번 브랏셀 회담에서 미측은 UR/ 농산물 협상과 관련하여 EC 의 CAP 개혁에 따른 손실보상 직접 보조금을 GREEN BOX 에 포함시켜 면제하도록 제의하는 대신에 수출보조금의 수량기준 24% 감축은 계속 고수코자 하였으며 OILSEED 문제는 MAGA(MAXIMUM GUARANTEE AREA) 개념을 도입, 이를 환산하여 EC 가 현재의 13 백만 M/T 생산량에서 7-8 백만 M/T 수준으로 감축시키도록 요구하였음.

- EC 측은 수출보조금의 수량기준 감축분야에서 24% 감축을 더 낮추어 주도록 요구하고 종전의 PEACE CLAUSE, REBALANCING 을 다시 주장하는 한편, 바나나의 QUOTA 허용도 요구하였으며, OILSEED 문제도 9.5-10 백만톤 수준으로 감축코자 하였음.

- 양자협상 결과 미측은 국내보조금 감축분야에서 신축적으로 대응한데 대하여 EC 측은 수출보조금 감축분야에서 DUNKEL TEXT 의 물량기준 24% 감축안에 많이 근접(22-23% 수준으로 추정)되었으나 합의에는 이르지 못했으며, PEACE CLAUSE 와 REBALANCING 은 타협이 가능한 분야로 보고 있고 바나나의 QUOTA 인정은미측에서 받아들이기 어렵다고 하였으며, UR 협상에 앞서 반드시 해결해야할 OILSEED 문제에 양측의 입장이 맞서 협상이 타결되지 못했다고함.

나. 앞으로의 계획과 전망

- 오는 10.20. 워싱톤에서 미.EC 간 농무장관 회담(MADIGAN 미 농무장관과 MACSHARRY EC 농업담당 집행위원)이 재개될 것으로 잠정적으로 예정하고 있다함.

- 10.16. 영국 버밍햄에서 개최되는 EC 정상회담과 캐나다 토론토의 QUAD 통상장관

통상국	장관	차관	2차보	통상국	분석관	정와대	총리실	안기부
경기원	재무부	농수부	상공부	중계				

회담에서의 UR 협상 진전 가능성에 대해서는 크게 기대하고 있지 않다고 말하고 다음주 초에 있을 상기 미.EC 간 농무장관 회담에서 최선을 다할 것이라고 말함.

- 미측은 대통령선거 전에는 금번의 미.EC 간 고위협상이 마지막이 될 것으로 보고 이의 타결을 위해서 현재 MADIGAN 농무장관이 미국 OILSEED 관련 생산업자들에게 CAP REFORM 의 실행측면에서 EC 가 더 이상의 감축이 어렵다는 점을 설득하고 있는 중이라고 하며 EC 측에서 PEACE CLAUSE, REBALANCING 과 바나나 문제를 양보하고 근접된 수출보조금 감축분야만 합의되면 양자간 타결 가능성이 있다고 말함.

- 만약 미국 대통령 선거전에 UR/ 농산물 협상이 타결되지 못할 경우 금년내에 UR 협상은 타결이 어려울 것으로 보고 있다고 전망하고, OILSEED 문제의 미해결시 보복 여부는 정치적인 결정이 뒤따라야 할 것이라고 말함.

2. 이 농무관은 QUAD 통상장관 회담과 관련하여 금일 주미 일본대사관의 YOKOYAMA 농무관과 오찬을 하면서 일본의 입장과 전망을 문의한바, 일본도 쌀수입개방 반대등 기본입장에 변함이 없다고 하면서 미.EC 간 타결이 되지 않은 현상황에서 QUAD 회담에 특별한 성과를 기대하기는 어렵고 10.20. 경(잠정)에 있을미.EC 농무장관 회담결과가 중요하므로 이를 예의주시하고 있다고 말하였음을 참고바람. 끝.

(대사 현홍주-국장)

예고: 92.12.31. 까지

외 무 부

관리
번호 92-712

종 별 :

번 호 : USW-5121

일 시 : 92 1015 2011

수 신 : 장 관(통기),통이,미일,경기원,상공부,농수산부)

발 신 : 주 미 대사

제 목 : UR 동향

연: USW-5109

1. 연호 관련 당관 장기호 참사관은 금 10.15. 미.EC 브랏셀 각료회의에 CARLA HILLS USTR 대표를 수행 출장한 후 작일 귀임한 DOROTHY DWOSKIN 부대표보를 접촉, UR 협상 동향에 대한 미측반응을 파악한 바, 동인의 발언 요지 아래 보고함.

가. 금번 양자협의를 계기로 협상의 돌파구를 마련하지는 못했지만 의미가 있었다고 보며 양측이 의견을 좁히는데 도움이 되었음. 농산물을 포함 서비스분야에 대한 광범한 협의가 있었는데, 농산물 이외의 분야에서는 상당한 진전이 있었으며 협상이 매우 순조롭게 진행되어 별다른 어려움을 느끼지 않았다고 봄. (PRETTY EASY, NO STUMBLING BLOCK)

0 서비스 분야중 금융분야는 미.EC 의 입장이 거의 동일했으며, MARKET ACCESS 분야는 무세화 협상을 포함하여 보다 더 포괄적인 PACKAGE 를 만든다는데 의견을 모아 앞으로 제네바에서 보다 더 구체적으로 협의를 진행시키기로 하는등진전이 있었음.

0 다만, 농산물 문제만 아직도 타결의 실마리를 찾지 못하고 있으나 금번 협의시 양측은 농산물 관련 던켈 TEXT 의 INTEGRITY 는 그대로 유지한다는데 의견을 같이하고 주요현안중 국내보조금 감축분야에

대해서는 미측이 다소 융통성 있는 자세를 보여 양측 차이점을 좁혔음. 수출보조금 감축 분야와 관련 물량기준은 던켈 TEXT 의 24% 감축안에는 근접하였지만 결국 타결을 보지 못했음. OILSEEDS 문제는 양측입장이 아직도 큰 차이를 갖고 있고 미국으로서는 이 문제를 매우 중시하고 있으므로 양측간에 해결을 보지 못하면 UR 협상에도 부정적인 영향을 줄것이 우려됨.

나. EC 국가들도 그간 농산물 문제에 대해 강한 반발을 보여온 불란서의 태도에 실증을 느끼는 (FED UP WITH FRANCE)상태인 바, 내주 수요일에 있게될 불란서 국회의

통상국   미주국   경제국   통상국   경기원   농수부   상공부   차관   장관

PAGE 1

92.10.16   10:33

외신 2과 통제관 FR

0130

현 미테랑 정부에 대한 신임투표 (CONFIDENCE VOTE)가 어떤 결과를 가져올지 주목이
됨. ㄴ 확인요.

　다. 명일(10.16) 있게 될 EC 정상회담에서는 ANDRIESSEN EC 집행위원장이 그간의
미.EC 간의 협상결과를 보고하여 EC 국가들의 반응을 타진할 것이며, 그 결과를 보아
미.EC 간 농산물 문제에 대해 한차례 더 협상을 갖는 문제를 협의중인 바, <u>미.EC 간의
농무장관 회담이 내주경 있을 것으로 봄.</u> 10.20.경

　2. 한편 DWOSKIN 부대표보는 금번 미.EC 회의시 미측은 협상타결을 위한 미측
PROPOSAL 을 EC 측에 제시하였으므로 이제 <u>공은 EC 측에 있고</u> UR 타결여부는 EC 측의
반응에 달려 있다며 현재로서는 타결 전망을 예측하기 어려운 상태라고조심스럽게
언급하였음. 끝.

　(대사 현홍주-국장)

　예고: 92.12.31. 까지

PAGE 2

0131

관리
번호 92-7ﾑ└

외 무 부

종 별 :

번 호 : GVW-1948   일 시 : 92 1016 1630

수 신 : 장관(통기,통이,통삼,경기원,재무,농수산,상공부)

발 신 : 주 제네바대사   사본:주미,EC,영,독,불,일대사(중계필)

제 목 : UR 협상 동향

1. 당관이 당지 미국 및 불란서 대표부 및 호주,태국등 CAIRNS GROUP 대표부를 통해 파악한 미.EC 간 브라셀 각료회담 결과를 아래 보고함.

가. 수출보조와 관련, 미측은 아래 2 가지 대안을 제시하고 EC 의 선택을 종용한바, 합의에 이르지는 못하였으나 입장차이를 좁히는 효과는 있었음.

- 1 안: 93-99 년간 수출물량을 24 퍼센트 감축하되, 육류, 곡물, OILSEEDS, 낙농제품의 4 개 품목군은 각 품목군내에서 품목간에 상호전용(SWING)이 가능토록 하며 동 전용폭은 1-2 차년도에는 당해년도 감축 대상폭의 10 퍼센트 한도내, 3-4 차년에는 7 퍼센트한도내, 5 차년 3 퍼센트 한도내, 6 차년 0 퍼센트 로함(단, 4 개 품목군 이외의 품목은 DFA 내용대로 감축)

- 2 안: 93-99 년간 22 퍼센트 감축하되 품목간 상호 전용 불인정

나. 국내보조 대해서는 미측이 CAP 개혁에 따른 EC 의 직접소득보조를 GREEN BOX 에 인정하는 대신 DEFICIENCY PAYMENT 의 인정을 요구하는 타협안을 제시함.

다. OILSEEDS 문제에 대해서도 미국이 EC 의 생산량을 종전 500 백만톤에서 7 백만톤으로 양보하는 신축성을 보임으로써, 다소의 진전은 있었으나 아직도 양측간 상당한 입장차이가 남아있음.

라. PEACE CLAUSE 관련, 미국이 갓트상의 모든권한을 유보한다는 입장을 표명함으로써 진전이 없었음.(불란서측 답변)

2. 불란서 대표부는 브랏셀회담 결과와 관련 수출보조를 물량으로 제한하는방식자체에 강한 불만을 갖고있으며, CAP 개혁에 따른 직접소득보조와 DEFICIENCY PAYMENT 를 연계하는 제의도 원칙적인 차원에서 수락하기 어렵다는 것이 불란서 정부의 입장이라 언급하면서, EC 집행위가 UR 타결에 적극성을 보이고있으나 불란서 뿐만 아니라 스페인, 아일랜드등 일부국가도 이를 집행위의 월권이라고

통상국   차관   2차보   통상국   통상국   분석관   청와대   안기부   경기원
재무부   농수부   상공부   중 계

PAGE 1   92.10.17   05:38

* 원본수령부서 승인없이 복사 금지   외신 2과 통제관 BZ

0132

보고있으며, 독일의 경우에도 대외적으로는 UR 타결에 열성적이라는 인상을 보이고 있으나, 불란서의 EC 내 고립을 원치않고 있기때문에 적극적으로 나설것으로 보지않는다 하였음.

3. 한편 당지 협상대표 일각에서는 미국이 그간 UR 을 선거전에 활용하련 의도에서 적극적인 입장을 취했으나, 이제는 시간도 없고 극적 타결이 이루어지더라도 BUSH 대통령측의 열세 만회에 큰 도움이 되지 않는다는 판단에서 <u>소극적인 자세로 전환할</u> 가능성도 있다고 보는 시각도 있음을 참고로 보고함. 끝

(대사 박수길-국장)

예고:92.12.31. 까지

외   무   부

종   별 :

번   호 : GVW-1949   일   시 : 92 1016 1630

수   신 : 장 관(통기, 경기원, 재무부, 농림수산부, 상공부, 특허청)

발   신 : 주 제네바 대사

제   목 : UR/개도국 비공식 그룹회의

1. 표제회의가 10.15(목) BENHIMA의장 주재로 개최되어 UR 협상 대책을 협의한바 주요 요지는 아래와 같음.

0 인도, 모로코는 UR협상 결과는 모든 협상참가국들의 이익을 균형있게 반영한것이어야 할 것임을 강조하고, 이런 관점에서 미.EC간 양자협상이 타결될 경우, 이를여타 참가국들이 다자적으로 검토할수 있는 충분한 시간이 주어져야 할 것과 미.EC양자 협상을 조속히 다자화 할 것을 촉구함.

0 싱가폴은 UR협상 관련 각종 비공식회의가 개최되어 주요사안들을 협의하고있기때문에 협상의 명료성이 저하되고 있음에 우려를 표명하고 여사한 비공시 그룹회의에서 거론되는 사항에 대한 정보공유의 필요를 강조함

2. 의장은 상기 개도국들의 우려를 사무총장에게 전달하는 한편 다음 그린룸 회의에서도 밝힐것이며, 버밍햄 EC긴급 정상회담 이후에 개도국 비공식 그룹회의를 재소집하여 동정상회담 결과를 점검키로 함.

(대사 박수길 - 국장)

통상국   경기원   재무부   농수부   상공부   특허정

PAGE 1   92.10.17   06:17 EF

외신 1과 통제관

0134

550   우루과이라운드 협상 동향 및 무역협상위원회 회의 3

외 무 부

종 별 :

번 호 : GEW-1929

일 시 : 92 1016 1800

수 신 : 장관(통기),통삼) 사본:주제네바대사-직송필

발 신 : 주 독 대사

제 목 : UR 협상동향

일반문서로 재분류(19) 92 . 12. 31

연:GEW-1818

1. 당관 정문수 참사관은 10.16. 연방경제부 GATT 농산물 담당 KIESOW 부과장과 면담, 11.11-12. 브랏셀 개최 미.EC 협상결과 관련, 탐문내용을 아래 보고함

가. 농산물 분야 협상

1)동부과장은 미.EC 협상결과에 관해 상금 공식발표된바는 없음을 전제하고동협상에서 구체합의가 이루어지지는 않았으나, 농산물 분야의 일부문제에 있어서는 상당한의견 접근이 이루어졌다함

2)미.EC 간 의견접근의 성과가 있은 사항은 EC 측이 CAP 개혁차원에서의 농산물(곡류, 우유, 우육, 양육등)에 대한 생산자 직접 소득보조로의 전환관련, 동 소득보조를 보조감축대상에서 제외하는 문제(GREEN BOX)에 미국측의 기본적인 양해를 얻은대신, EC 측은 미국측의 농산물가격 하락에 대한 DEFICIENCY PAYMENT 를 인정해 주는 선을 타협됨

3)미국측의 EC 보조 농산물의 24 프로 수출물량 감축요구문제는 불란서측이 수출물량 감축에는 무조건 반대하는 입장을 계속 고수한 관계로 전혀 진전이 이루어지지 않음. EC 국가중 불란서 이외의 아일랜드도 반대입장을 취하고 있으나, 불란서처럼 완강한 자세는 아닌것으로 봄.

4)EC 측 주장 REBALANCING 문제는 전기 1)항의 수출무량 감축문제가 타결될 경우 동시적으로 해결될 사안이며, 독일측은 동문제 관련 보다 유연한 입장 수립을 내부 검토중임.

나. 써비스, 시장접근분야

미.EC 간에 써비스 분야에는 상당한 의견접근이 이루어졌으나, 사장접근 분야는 특히 미국측이 EC 측의 섬유제품 관세인하 요구를 계속 거절하고 있어 진전을 보지

통상국 장관 차관 2차보 통상국 분석관 청와대 안기부

PAGE 1

92.10.17 05:14

외신 2과 통제관 FM

0135

못했으며, 세부사항 협의를 11.3. 미대통령 선거이후 계속하기로 함.

다. OILSEEDS 문제

UR 농산물 협상테두리 밖의 미.EC 간 주요 현안사항인 동시에 UR 협상진전과도 결부되어 있는 OILSEEDS 보조문제 관련, 미국측은 EC 의 CAP 개혁차원의 생산자 소득보조 전환방식을 원칙적으로 수용하는 입장을 보임으로서 금번 협상에서 양측간 이견해소 방안 도출에 상당한 진전이 있은 것으로 평가됨. 이와관련, 미국측이 최소한의 휴경면적율 10 프로 보장을 요구하고 있어 상호 의견접근의 성과가 있었는바, 미대통령 선거후 11 월 초경 GATT 이사회에서 다시 협의될 것으로 봄(EC 측은 CAP 개혁에 따라 연간 15 프로 휴경율을 정하고 있으나, 소규모농에 대한 예외인정등으로 실제는 10 프로 휴경율에 미치지 않고 있음)

라. UR 협상 진전전망

금 10.16. 버밍험 개최 EC 긴급 정상회의에서도 동문제가 다루어질 예정이나 불란서측의 특별한 입장변화가 없는한 동회의를 계기로 협상진전을 낙관할수 있는 근거는 희박한 것으로 봄. 금주말 토론토 개최 일.가 포함 4 자 협상에서도 MADIGAN 미 농무장관, MAC SHARRY 집행위원이 불참할 것으로 알려진 만큼 농산물 분야의 이견이 극복될수 있을 것으로 예상키 어려우므로 UR 협상의 새로운 구체진전이 있을 것으로 보기는 어려움. 현재 UR 협상타결의 관건은 미.EC 간 정치적 절충이 전제되어야 할것임에도 불구, 11.3. 미 대통령 선거 이전까지 촉박한 시일내에 협상 돌파구의 계기마련이 어려운 상황임과 또 불란서측이 농민의 반발우려와 93.3 월 대통령 선거을 의식, 종래의 완강한 입장에 변화를 보이지 않고 있음에 비추어 금년내 UR 협상 타결 전망은 어려운 것으로 본다함.

2. 한편 MOELLEMANN 경제장관은 10.13. 독일을 방문한 HILLS 미 무역대표부 대표와의 회담에서 UR 협상 조속타결 필요성을 강조하고 더이상 농산물 분야에대한 고려는 곤란하다는 입장을 개진한 것으로 보도됨.

3. 동건 관련, 수시 추보할 것임.끝

(대사-국장)

예고:92.12.31. 까지

PAGE 2

0136

외 무 부

종 별 :

번 호 : ECW-1273   일 시 : 92 1016 2315

수 신 : 장관(통기, 통삼, 경기원, 재무부, 농림수산부, 상공부)사본:주미,주제네바-필

발 신 : 주 EC 대사

제 목 : EC 긴급 정상회담(UR 협상)

10.16 영국 버밍햄에서 개최된 표제정상회담에서의 UR협상 논의동향을 아래보고함.

1. 동 정상회담후, EC 집행위 대변인은 EC정상들은 집행위가 보고한 대미협상의기본입장을 만장일치로 지지키로 결정하였다고 말하고, 불란서의 반대입장등에 대해구체적인 토의를 한 바는 없다고 말함. 한편, MAJOR영국수상은 DELORS EC 집행위원장과 가진공동기자회견에서 동 정상회담은 EC집행위에게 금년말까지 UR협상 타결을 위한 교섭 MANDATE 를 부여하였다고 밝혔으며,지난주말 개최된 미.EC 양자협상에서 농산물,서비스, 시장접근등 여러분야에서 상당한 진전이있었다고 평가하고, 동 협상이연말시한보다 조기에 타결될 가능성도 있다고 낙관적으로 전망함.

3. 한편 KOHL 독일수상도 회의종료후 낙관적인 전망을 피력했으나, 다만 프랑스 MITTERAND대통령은 동 정상회의 최종선언문 초안의 UR 관계 표현 협의시, '집행위가상기 MANDATE를 일탈해서는 안된다'는 조항을 넣을것을 주장한 것등 강경입장을 견지했음.

4. 한편, 10.15 BUSH 대통령이 EC 정상들에게 보낸 서한(양측의 협상대표들은 최대한의노력을 다했으며, EC 정상들의 정치적 결단만남았음)에 대해 동 정상회담에서 어떠한 반응이 있을 것으로 기대되었으나, 이에 대한 직접적인 논의는 없었던 것으로 보임. 한편 10.15 미국이 발표한 대두유 수출보조금 지급결정에 대해 EC 집행위대변인은 UR협상 타결에 도움이 되지 못하는 결정이라고 언급함.

5. 표제 정상회담에서의 UR협상 관련한 상세논의 동향은 관계관 접촉후 추보 하겠음. 끝.

(대사 권동만 - 국장)

통상국   통상국   경기원   재무부   농수부   상공부

PAGE 1   92.10.17   08:07 FY
                                            외신 1과 통제관 ✓

이시(외)

1

외 무 부

종 별 :

번 호 : USW-5142   일 시 : 92 1016 1916

수 신 : 장관 (봉이(봉기),미일,경기원,상공부,농수산부,경제수석,외교안보)

발 신 : 주 미 대사

제 목 : 미국의 대외 통상정책

연: USW-5109, 5121

1. 당관 장기호 참사관은 금 10.16. 국무부 경제국 JOANNA R. SHELTON 부차관보를 면담, 표제관련 협의한 미측 반응요지 아래 보고함.

가. UR 협상

- 연호 보고와 같이 미측은 서비스등 비농산물 분야에서 EC 측과 상당한 의견 접근을 보았으나 농산물은 특히 불란서의 반대로 어려운 난항을 겪고 있으며, 금일 있는 EC 정상회담에서도 불란서의 태도가 완화되지 않는 한 어떤 결과가 나올 것으로 예상되지 않는다고 하였음.

- BUSH 대통령은 선거를 의식 UR 협상의 타결을 서두르고 있으나, 금주말의 4 개국 통상장관 회담과 미.EC 간의 마지막 절충이 농산물 타결의 중요한 전기가 될 것이며 이때에 실마리를 찾지 않으면 UR 협상은 그 전망이 매우 비관적임.

나. 대외 통상정책의 방향

- 금년중 UR 타결이 실패한다면 앞으로 미국내 선거결과 누가 대통령에 당선 되느냐에 관계없이 주요한 현안(농산물등)이 양자협상의 테이블에 올려지게 될것이며 이는 오히려 일본과 한국에는 더욱 불리한 결과를 가져올 것으로 봄.

- UR 협상 실패는 결국 미의회에서 거론되어 왔던 SUPER 301 조 협상을 부활 시킬 것이며 쌀시장 개방문제와 관련 301 조 압력 수단에 의존하는 강경 통상 정책으로 발전하지 않을 수 없다고 전망함.

- BUSH 대통령이 재선되더라도 최근의 국내경제의 어려움과 국민들의 관심에 부응하기 위해서 대외통상정책은 더욱 TOUGH 해 지지 않을수 없음. 더우기 CLINTON 후보가 당선되면 FAIR TRADE 에 대한 비중을 더욱 높이게 되므로 교역장벽을 가진 국가에 대한 보복 조치등의 강경 수단을 택하지 않을 수 없을 것이며, 미국민의 경제적

통상국 경기원	장관 농수부	차관 상공부	2차보	미주국	통상국	청와대	청와대	안기부

PAGE 1   92.10.17   09:37

위기의식을 해소시키고 대외교역이 국내 고용창출에 가져오는 효과와 연결시켜 대외
봉상관계를 관리해 나갈 것으로 봄. 이러한 맥락에서 CLINTON 당선시에는 SUPER 301
조 협상과 쌀시장 개방 301 조 교섭은 당선후 2-3 개월내에 우선 순위 과제로
다루어질 가능성이 높을 것으로 봄.

다. 한. 미 관계 점검

- 금년은 한. 미간에 큰 잇슈가 없이 PEI 를 잘 타결하였으나 아직도 투자문제에
대해서는 미측의 기대 수준에 미흡하며, 특히 상무성으로 부터의 불만이 표명되고
있음.

- 또한 앞으로 있을 무역실무회담에서 IPR 문제를 잘 타결하여 93 년 SPECIAL 301
조상 한국의 지위가 다시 UPGRADE 되는 일이 없도록 관리하는 것이 중요함.

2. 당지 CONSULTING 회사인 C AND M INTERNATIONAL CO. 의 사장인 DORAL COOPER
(전 USTR 대표보)와 금일 오찬을 가진바, 동인은 UR 협상의 타결은 거의 기대하기
어려운 것으로 판단하면서, 93 년 미국의 대외봉상정책과 관련 상기 국무부의 의견과
동일한 견해를 표명하고 CLINTON 후보가 당선될 경우에 차기 미국의 신행정부는 SUPER
301 조 협상, 쌀개방 문제와 관련한 301 조 법안 봉과를 최우선의 과제로 추진할
것으로 본다고 언급하였음을 참고바람. 끝.

(대사 현홍주-국장)

예고: 92.12.31. 일반

외 무 부

종 별 :

번 호 : ECW-1273   일 시 : 92 1016 2315

수 신 : 장 관(통기,통삼,경기원,재무부,농림수산부,상공부)사본:주미,주제네바-필

발 신 : 주 EC 대사

제 목 : EC 긴급 정상회담(UR 협상)

10.16 영국 버밍햄에서 개최된 표제정상회담에서의 UR협상 논의동향을 아래보고함.

1. 동 정상회담후, EC 집행위 대변인은 EC정상들은 집행위가 보고한 대미협상의기본입장을 만장일치로 지지키로 결정하였다고 말하고, 불란서의 반대입장등에 대해구 체적인 토의를 한 바는 없다고 말함. 한편, MAJOR영국수상은 DELORS EC 집행위원장과 가진공동기자회견에서 동 정상회담은 EC집행위에게 금년말까지 UR협상 타결을위한 교섭 MANDATE를 부여하였다고 밝혔으며, 지난 주말 개최된 미.EC 양자협상에서농산 물,서비스, 시장접근등 여러분야에서 상당한 진전이있었다고 평가하고, 동 협상이연 말시한보다 조기에 타결될 가능성도 있다고 낙관적으로 전망함.

2. 한편 KOHL 독일수상도 회의종료후 낙관적인 전망을 피력했으나, 다만 프랑스 MITTERAND대통령은 동 정상회의 최종선언문 초안의 UR 관계 표현 협의시, '집행위가상기 MANDATE를 일탈해서는 안된다'는 조항을 넣을것을 주장한 것등 강경입장을 견지했음.

3. 한편, 10.15 BUSH 대통령이 EC 정상들에게 보낸 서한(양측의 협상대표들은 최대한의노력을 다했으며, EC 정상들의 정치적 결단만남았음)에 대해 동 정상회담에서

어떠한 반응이 있을 것으로 기대되었으나, 이에 대한 직접적인 논의는 없었던것으로 보임. 한편 10.15 미국이 발표한 대두유 수출보조금 지급결정에 대해 EC 집행위대변인은 UR협상 타결에 도움이 되지 못하는 결정이라고 언급함.

4. 표제 정상회담에서의 UR협상 관련한 상세논의 동향은 관계관 접촉후 추보 하겠음. 끝.

(대사 권동만 - 국장)

통상국 상공부	통상국	외정실	분석관	청와대	안기부	경기원	재무부	농수부

외 무 부

종 별 :

번 호 : USW-5152   일 시 : 92 1019 1745

수 신 : 장 관(통이,통기), 경기원, 농수산부, 상공부)

발 신 : 주 미 대사

제 목 : 우루과이라운드 (UR) 협상 동향

　　당지 주요 언론들은 10.17-18간 캐나다 온타리오에서개최된 미, EC, 카, 일 4개국
통상장관회담결과　그동안　정체되었던　UR　협상의조속한　타결과　관련　중대한
진전이있었으며,금주중 와싱톤에서 개최될 것으로 알려진 미. EC농업장관 회담에서
농업보조금　에　관한합의가　이루어질　가능성이　큰　것으로　보도하였는바,동　관련
진전사항 추보하 겠음. (관련보도 별첨)

　　첨부: USW(F)-6658. 끝.

　　(대사 현홍주-국장)

통상국　　통상국　　경기원　　농수부　　상공부

PAGE 1   92.10.20   08:05 FX
　　　　　　　　　　　　　　　　　　　　　　외신 1과 통제관 　✓

0141

주 미 대 사 관

USW(F) : 6658   년월일 : 92. 10. 19 시간 :

수 신 : 장 관 (통미, 동기, 경기원, 농수산부, 상공부)

보 안	
통 제	

발 신 : 주 미 대. 사

제 목 : USW-5152 의 첨부물 (UR 동향 3 매)(출처 :   )

(6658 - 3 - 1)

외신 1과	
통 제	

0142

Trade Talk Progress Expected

Officials Optimistic But Give No Details

By CLYDE H. FARNSWORTH

Special to The New York Times

CAMBRIDGE, Ontario, Oct. 18 — The United States trade representative, Carla A. Hills, met here today with her counterparts from the European Community, Canada and Japan, then said she expected a breakthrough in stalled world trade talks "in a matter of days."

She and the other ministers offered no specific details to back up their optimism or information on how they might overcome the firm statements by France that it would offer no further compromises to break the stalemate.

The broad talks aimed at liberalizing world trade, now in their sixth year, have been stalled by a disagreement between the United States and the European Community over farm subsidies, which Washington is trying to curtail sharply.

Political Forces

President Bush, whom opinion polls show trails in his bid for reelection, has been hoping for a global trade agreement that he could point to as evidence of how his Administration is effective overseas and stimulates economic growth.

Asked whether there had been talk of the Nov. 3 election at the meeting this weekend, Canada's Trade Minister, Michael Wilson, said with a grin: "What happens on Nov. 3?"

The strongest opposition to a deal has come from France, where farmers are a potent political force and a general election is scheduled within six months. At last week's European Community meeting in Birmingham, England, France's President, François Mitterrand, appeared unyielding in his opposition to any deal that would require further concessions to Washington.

Periodic Meetings

During the prolonged stalemate, negotiators, trade ministers and national leaders have met periodically and expressed hope or optimism that the impasse could be broken — with little evident progress.

Still, the expectation that a compromise would be reached "in a matter of days" was the most optimistic statement yet.

The officials meeting here said they expected the breakthrough would come when the United States Secretary of Agriculture, Edward Madigan, meets with Ray MacSharry, the European Community Agriculture Commissioner. They are expected to meet this week, probably in Washington.

The global negotiations involving 108 countries, known as the Uruguay Round because they began in that nation in 1986, are under the auspices of the General Agreement on Tariffs and Trade, the Geneva-based world trade organization.

It was not clear how to reconcile the apparently intractable French position with the optimism shown by the trade ministers at their weekend meeting at an Ontario country estate here called Langdon House, about a 90-minute drive west of Toronto.

Asked about the apparent conflict, Frans Andriessen, the European Community's External Relations Commissioner, referred reporters to the final communiqué from the Birmingham meeting, which "invited the commission to work within its existing mandate for an early, comprehensive and balanced GATT agreement by the end of the year."

"I think we will be in a position to make a deal within the mandate we have been given," Mr. Andriessen stressed. He noted that Mr. Mitterrand was among the signatories of the Birmingham communiqué.

'Progress Has Been Made'

Joined by ministers from the United States, Japan and Canada, he told a news conference here that the optimism was "based on the determination to bring things to a good end and secondly the fact that progress has been made in all the sectors concerned."

The community has refused so far to accept deep cuts sought by the United States in payments to growers of wheat, oil seeds, dairy products and other foods. Washington, with support from most other farm exporting nations, contends that the subsidies lead to grave distortions of world trade and impoverish treasuries of rich and poor countries alike.

Mrs. Hills, asked if the European and American farm ministers were about to meet, said Mr. Madigan and Mr. MacSharry had been "in contact," though she added that she was "aware of no meeting that has been firmly scheduled."

Seeking a Framework

The issue now, she said, was whether the major trading nations could "create a framework to agree among ourselves to go to Geneva." The formal negotiations broke off earlier this year, and a return to the multilateral bargaining table would be a sign that the parties believe a full-scale accord is close.

"We're looking for a breakthrough in those issues that have blocked progress to date in a matter of days," Mrs. Hills said, "and that would then take the negotiations to Geneva where other parties must make their contribution."

Mr. Wilson of Canada, the host at Langdon House, said the ministers discussed accelerating the negotiations.

"With the impending conclusion this year, it's important to move expeditiously," he declared. Another sign of the American optimism is a United States decision to hold back on retaliation against the European Community in a six-year old dispute over oil seeds.

The Bush Administration calculates that oil seeds subsidies paid to European farmers cost American and other exporters about $2 billion annually, and under strong Congressional pressure has threatened to retaliate against $1 billion of European exports to the United States.

But Washington has yet to push the reprisal button. "We are weighing our future steps very carefully," Mrs. Hills said. "Quite honestly, we are very much beyond time, but we're trying to look for a solution because a settlement would be in the interests of the U.S. and Europe."

92.10.18
N.Y.T.

ɛ-ɛ-8599

0144

Breakthrough Near on Reform of Global Trade

Weekend Talks in Canada Address U.S., European Deadlock Over Agriculture Subsidies

By Robert Kozak
Reuter

CAMBRIDGE, Ontario, Oct. 18—A breakthrough in stalled talks to reform global trade is possible within days, officials from major world economies said today.

"We are looking for a breakthrough in those issues that have blocked progress to date within a matter of days," U.S. Trade Representative Carla Hills said at a news conference.

Trade chiefs from the European Community, the United States, Japan and Canada said after two days of talks that a breakthrough between the United States and the EC over agricultural subsidies could come as early as this week.

The officials said the focus of the negotiations could then move back to the stalled General Agreement on Tariffs and Trade (GATT) talks in Geneva. The negotiations to reform the world trading system and boost global trade by $200 billions face a year-end deadline.

"What we have to do is to try and break the deadlock we have in agriculture in the days ahead," chief EC trade negotiator Frans Andriessen said. "We do not have much time left and then we have got to get this back to Geneva and work out the rest."

The United States and Europe have disagreed over how to cut subsidies to farmers and other issues, a dispute that has threatened to tie up any new overall deal in the Uruguay Round of the GATT.

Agriculture was the last remaining major issue holding up a resumption of talks, Hills said.

"On the non-agriculture side, on market access and services and procurement, there are no profound differences between the United States and the EC," she said.

The ministers said they wanted to move the talks away from being a squabble between the United States and Europe and back into the world forum at the GATT.

"We expect sufficient progress to be made in agriculture in the days ahead between the United States and the European Community so that at an early date the negotiations can be brought back to Geneva within the multilateral process," said Michael Wilson, Canada's minister of trade.

Agriculture ministers from the EC and the United States are expected to get back together soon, but no time has been set, the trade ministers said.

Wilson, speaking on behalf of the other trade chiefs, said they had agreed to work with negotiators to create a "globally balanced package" that could be put forward by December.

Reaching an overall accord on

GATT has been difficult as issues, particularly over how to protect farmers in various countries, has held up progress.

An accord on agriculture would be beneficial, particularly for farmers in France, where much of the protest over reforming the rules on agriculture has come from, Andriessen said.

"An agreement on agriculture in the Uruguay Round could be very advantageous" for France, he said.

The economies represented at the weekend meeting account for almost two thirds of world trade in goods and services.

Recent talks between the United

States and the EC in Brussels failed to reach an agreement, but Friday the European Community met in Britain and called for an early end to the talks. The pressure to have a deal reached on agriculture before the U.S. presidential election in November has increased, but President Bush has said Washington has conceded as much as it could.

Talks on the Uruguay Round of the GATT have dragged on for six years, with first one deadline then another falling. But with many of the world's largest economies facing slowdowns, many governments want to lower barriers and increase trade.

92.10.18.
W. P.

관리
번호 *92-229*

외 무 부

종 별 :

번 호 : GVW-1972

일 시 : 92 1020 1500

수 신 : 장관(통기, 경기원, 재무부, 농림수산부, 상공부)

발 신 : 주 제네바 대사

제 목 : UR/농산물 협상

　　10.19(월) 최농무관은 당지 불란서 대표부 HENRY 농무관을 오찬에 초대하여최근 표제 협상 동향에 대하여 의견 교환하였는바, 동인 언급 요지 하기 보고함. (김농무관보 동석)

　　1. 10.11-12 미-EC 양자 협상 내용

　　가. 국내 보조

　　- 미국은 EC 의 소득보상 직접 지불 정책, 미국의 결손 지불 정책 (DEFICIENCY PAYMENT)등 직접 지불 정책에 대하여는 AMS 삭감 약속 대상에서 제외시키도록 하는 제안을 하였음

　　0 어느국가든지 현행 보조정책을 상기 특수한 직접 지불 정책으로 수정(MODIFY)할 경우는 삭감 약속 대상에서 제외시킨다는 것임 (GREEN BOX 와는 별개의 개념)

　　- 불란서의 경우는 허용정책 (GREEN BOX)의 인정 범위에 큰 이해 관계가 없음.

　　0 불란서는 종래부터 허용정책을 확대하는데 적극적 입장이 아니었음.

　　0 CAP 개혁이 계획대로 추진된다면 소득 보상 직접 지불 정책이 허용정책으로 분류되지 않더라도 던켈 초안 삭감 목표를 충족하는데 별 문제가 없음(곡물의경우 6년간 23-28 % 삭감이 예상되며, 소득 보상 직접 지불 정책이 허용될 경우는 30-35 % 삭감이 예상됨)

　　- 미국의 결손 보전을 삭감대상에서 제외시킬 경우는 케언즈 그룹 국가등의반발이 예상됨.

　　나. 국경조치(시장접근)

　　- 동분야에 대해서는 깊은 논의가 없었음.

　　- 미국과 EC 는 TE 계산방법에 차이가 있음(EC 의 경우 국내 개입가격 더하기 10 %)

통상국 농수부	장관 상공부	차관	2차보	분석관	정와대	안기부	경기원	재무부

PAGE 1

* 원본수령부서 승인없이 복사 금지

92.10.21　03:02

외신 2과 통제관 FR

0145

O 각국의 입장 차이에 대한 추가적인 기술적 논의가 필요하다고 봄.

- EC 는 바나나를 제외하고는 동 분야에 대하여별 문제가 없음.

다. 수출 보조

- 수출보조와 관련해서는 삭감폭 문제와 REBALANCING 이 논의되었음.

- 삭감폭과 관련해서는 하기 2 가지 방안이 논의되었음.

O 관세항목(TARIFF LINE) 별로 삭감하되 24 % 삭감폭을 조정하는 방안

O 품목을 묶어서 삭감하는 방안 (AGGREGATION)과 년도별 삭감 약속을 전용 (SWING)하는 것을 인정하는 방안(미측이 다소 융통성을 보였음)

- REBALANCING 과 관련해서는 독일 농무장관이 제시한 방안(물량 기준 약속)에 대하여 미측이 다소의 융통성을 보였음.

O 곡물 대체품에 대한 수입량이 증가할 경우 수출물량을 억제하는 방향으로의견 근접 (당초 EC 안은 관세율을 재조정하는 것이었으나 현재는 물량을 통한재조정 방안 모색)

라. PEACE CLAUSE

- EC 입장에서는 매우 중요한 사항임.

- UR 협상에 의한 삭감 약속 의무와 함께 PANEL 에 의한 의무이행을 동시에부담하는 것은 부당함. 따라서 UR 이행기간중 보조수준 삭감 약속을 이행할 경우는 같은 보조문제를 이유로 PANEL 등 분쟁해결 절차에 의거 추가적인 의무를 부담하지 않아야 함.

- 금번 양자 협상과정에서 이문제에 대한 진전는 없었음.

O 미국이 다자간 약속대신 양자간 약속을 한다는 것은 과거 동경 라운드 경험에 비추어 무의미함.

O 갓트하에서 분명한 다자적 약속이 있어야 함.

마. OILSEEDS

- 미국은 종전 입장과는 달리 동문제를 UR 과 연계시켜 타결하려는 의도를 갖고 있음.

O UR 과 연계시킬 경우 여타 EC 회원국에게 UR 타결 당위성을 들어 수용 압력을 높일수 있으며, OILSEEDS 에 대한 제재 조치를 받지 않으려면 조속히 UR 이타결되야 한다는 논리를 주장

- EC 는 현 OILSEED 보조체제의 기술적 측면을 다소 수정하여 미국과 타협할

PAGE 2

0146

용의가 있으나 생산량 QUOTA 를 정하는 것은 반대입장임.

0 미국은 이와 관련 최근 EC 의 OILSEED 생산량을 현 13 백만톤에서 7 백만톤으로 줄이는 방안과 생산면적을 현 5.6 백만 HA 에서 3 백만 HA 로 줄이는 방안을 제시해 왔음.

- EC 는 기본적으로 생산량 제한 보다는 생산면적 제한을 원칙으로 하여 세부 기술적 보완을 할 의향임. (SET ASIDE 등)

0 EC 의 OILSEED 생산성 증가 가능성을 감안하면 후자가 유리

- 또한 국제 경쟁력이 가장 높은 브라질, 알젠틴등은 쇠고기, 옥수수등의 EC 시장접근 개선에 큰 관심을 보이고 있음.

2. 미, EC 농무장관 회담

- MADIGAN 미 농무장관과 MACSHARRY EC 집행위원과의 회담은 10.22(목) 개최될것으로 알려짐.

3. 바나나 문제

- 바나나는 EC 의 문제라기 보다는 ACP 국가와 중남미 국가 사이의 문제임.

(한국 및 일본의 쌀과는 상황이 다름)

- 현 상황에서는 관세화가 적절한 해결책이 되지 못함.

0 바나나를 관세화하면 미국에도 유리할 것이 별로 없음 (카리비아 국가의 경제가 악화되면 미국에 대한 밀입국 증가등의 문제가 생길수 있음.)

첨부: EC 정상회담(버밍햄) 커뮤니케 사본 1 부

(GVW(F)-625)

(대사 박수길-국장)

예고 92.12.31. 까지

이시(외)

원 본 ✓

외 무 부

종 별 :

번 호 : GVW-1979   일 시 : 92 1020 2200

수 신 : 장관(통기, 경기원, 재무, 농수산, 상공부)사본:주미,EC, 영,독,불대사-중계

발 신 : 주 제네바 대사

제 목 : UR 협상동향

인만공시로 재분류 (1992. 12. 31)

연: GVW-1948, 1929

1. 10.19-20 본직이 접촉한 카나다, 멕시코,싱가폴 대사 및 기타협상 실무차등은 10.16 EC 긴급정상 회담에서의 년내 타결의지 재확인, CARLA HILLS 및 ANDRIESSEN 양인의 협상돌파구 합의 임박 시사발언, 10.17-18 QUAD 회담결과등이 전해지고 있는 것과 관련, UR 협상의 관건인 농산물 분야에서 미.EC 양국간 돌파구 마련이 가능할 것으로 평가하면서, 미국의 FAST TRACK 시한내 UR 협상이 종결될수도 있을것이라는 조심스러운 희망적 관측을 하고 있음.

2. 이들은 아직도 OILSEEDS 생산량 및 수출보조 감축물량에 관한 양측입장에 거리가 있는것은 사실이나 , 미국의 입장에서는 선거전 열세만회라는 BUSH 대통령의 절박한 사정과 EC 측으로도 불란서의 강한 반대가 있음에도 불구하고 대통령 선거일 이전까지의 기간이 미국으로 부터 최선의 양보안을 얻어 낼수 있는 호기일수도 있다는 점에서 금주 또는 내주로 예상(금 10.20 오전 현재 날짜 미정)되고 있는 MCSHARRY, MADIGAN 회담에서 합의에 이를 가능성이 상당히 있는 것으로 내다 보고있음(EC 내에서의 불란서의 반대는 미.EC 가 합의하고 동결과를 다자차원으로 가져오게 될 경우 불란서도 이를 끝까지 저지하기는 곤란할 것으로평가)

3. 이와관련 GATT 사무국도 MCSHARRY, MADIGAN 회담결과등을 보아가면서 앞으로 약 10 일내 그린룸협의를 열어 당지에서의 다자 협상 재개와 관련한 TNC 개최문제등 구체일정을 협의할 것을 검토하고 있는 것으로 보임.(한편 MATHUR T3 의장에 의하면 DUNKEL 총장이 최근 일련의 사태진전으로 상당히 고무되어 있는 느낌이라함)

4. 반면 아직도 회의적으로 보는 입장에서는 MATHUR T3 의장, ZUTSHI 이사회 의장등의 경우 현재 MIXED SIGNAL 을 받고 있으나 농산물분야 이외에는 남아있는 과제가 많으며 낙관만 할수 없다는 신중한 의견을, YERXA 미국대사의 경우에는 연호

통상국	장관	차관	2차보	분석관	정와대	총리실	안기부	경기원
재무부	농수부	상공부	중계					

PAGE 1   92.10.21   07:43

외신 2과 통제관 BX

0148

10.13 CAINS GROUP 회의에서의 미국의 설명에 대한 문의에 대해 아직도 상당한 문제가 남아있어 전망이 불투명하다는 의견을 각각 본직에에 밝힌바 있음.

5. 한편 JEAN-MARIE METZGER 불란서 GATT 대사는 미.EC 간 이견이 상당히 좁혀진것은 사실이나 아직도 농산물 각 잇슈별로 아래와같이 여러가지 문제가 남아있어 타결이 쉽지않을 것으로 내다본다 하면서도, 버밍햄 회의에서 기존 MANDATE 를 넘어선 추가적 재량권을 집행위에 부여한 바는 없지 않다는 점을(특히 금년말 퇴임을 앞둔 MCSHARRY 의 개인적 야망) 불란서로서는 가장 우려하고 있다함.

가. OILSEED 의 경우 브랏셀회담시 EC 의 현 생산수준 13 백만톤에서 10 백만톤까지 감축(CAP 개혁에 따른 SET ASIDE 이전 수준) 하겠다는 EC 제의에 대해 미측은 검토용의를 표명하였으나, 귀국후 업계와의 협의과정에서 거부된 것으로 안다고 하면서(EC COMMISSION 으로부터의 정보가 아니라 주미 불란서대사관으로 부터의 정보라고 함) 미국과의 합의 도달의 어려움를 지적

나. CAP 개혁에 따른 직접소득 보조의 GREEN BOX 포함에 동의하는 조건으로미국이 요구한 DEFICIENCY PAYMENT 인정에 대해 EC 로서는 CAP 개혁인정 자체에 만족하는 것이며, DEFIEIENCY PAYMENT 의 GREEN BOX 포함여부는 케언즈그룹의동의 획득에 어려움이 있을 것이라는 입장 표명

다. 수출보조 문제에 대해서는 미국이 제시한 연호 대안에 대한 EC 의 선택문제가 남아있으나, 어느대안을 택하든 수량합의를 인정치 않고 있는 EC 의 협상MANDATD 에는 일응 벗어나는 것임.

6. 금 10.20 오전 CAIRNS GROUP 회의에서는 토론토 QUAD 회담 결과에 관한 카나다측의 브리핑이 있었는바, 언론보도 내용이상의 특이사항은 없었다 하며, 동 회의에 참석한 YERXA 미국대사는 브랏셀회담이상의 아무런 진전이 없었다고 언급함. 끝

(대사 박수길-국장)
예고:92.12.31.

	분류번호	보존기간

발 신 전 보

WUS-4778   921020 1822 FN

번 호 : _____   종별 : WJA -4404   WEC -0755
                                          WCN -1052

수 신 : 주   수신처참조   대사. 총영사

발 신 : 장 관 (통 기)

제 목 : UR 협상 동향

　　　　10.17-18간 개최된 4극 통상회담 결과와 근간 개최 예정으로 알려진
미.EC 농무장관 회담 등 최근의 UR 협상관련 동향에 대해 ~~각자~~ 관계관을 접촉
파악, 보고바람. 끝.

　　　　　　　　　　　　　　　　　　(통상국장   홍 정 표)

수신처 : 주 미, 일, EC, 카 대사

검 토 필 (1992. 12. 31.)

검 토 필 (1993. 6. 30.)

보 안 통 제

외신과통제

앙고재	92년 10월 20일	통상기구과	기안자 성명 이시형	과장	심의관	국장 전결	차관	장관

0150

이시(역)

외 무 부

종   별 :

번   호 : USW-5181   일   시 : 92 1020 1912

수   신 : 장 관 (통기,통이,미일,경기원,농수산부, 상공부)

발   신 : 주 미 대사 사본 : 주 제네바, EC 대사(중계필)

제   목 : UR 협상 동향

대 : WUS-4778

1. 당관 장기호 참사관은 10.20. SUZANNE EARLY USTR 농업담당 대표보를 접촉, 대호 관련 미측 반응 타진한 요지 아래 보고함.

가. 카나다 개최 4 개국 통상장관 회담에서는 UR 농산물 문제가 의제에 들어가 있지 않아 공식협의는 없었으며 다만 EC 측과의 별개의 비공식 협의를 가졌지만 별다른 진전은 없었음. EC 정상회담에서도 구체적인 협의는 없었고 UR 협상의 타결 필요성에 관한 일반적 의견교환이 있었을 뿐임.

나. 지금까지 비농업 부문에서의 진전은 있었으나 농업부문중 수출보조금 감축과 OILSEED 문제는 아직도 협의중에 있고 타결전망이 현재로서는 불확실함.

다. 금주중 MADIGAN 미 농무장관과 MACSHERRY EC 농업 위원간에 회담이 예정 되어 있으며 앞으로 협의를 계속할 예정인 바, 미 대통령 선거(11.3)전에 타결 가능성은 예측이 곤란하며 EC 측과 협의를 계속해 나갈 계획이라고 하였음.

2. 한편 이영래 농무관이 미 농무부 RICHARD SCHROETER 해외농업처 처장보를 접촉한 바 카나다 통상장관 회담에서는 상기 USTR 반응과 같이 UR/ 농산물 문제가 공식적으로 협의되지 않았으며 미.EC 간 농무장관 회담은 금주중(수요일 또는 목요일경으로 예상)에 있을 예정이고 수출보조금 감축과 OILSEED 문제를 중심으로 계속 양측 농무장관이 전화로 협의 중에 있다고 하며 SCHROETER 처장보 자신도 금일 브랏셀로 출발한다고 함.

(미측 JOE O'MARA 는 현재 브랏셀에서 EC 측과 실무선에서 계속 접촉중에 있음.)

3. 농무부측에 의하면 EXPORT SUBSIDY 문제는 감축기준을 22% 선으로 하는 방안과 24% 기준으로 하되 일정한 범위내에서 SWING 의 폭을 인정하는 방안등이 협의의 중심이 될 것이며, OILSEED 관련 미측은 종전의 입장(700-800 만본) 에서 후퇴한 900

통상국	장관	차관	2차보	미주국	통상국	분석관	정와대	안기부
경기원	농수부	상공부	중계					

92.10.21   09:13

외신 2과 통제관 FS

0151

만톤 이하 수준(EC 측은 950-1000 만톤)에서의 타결등을 검토중이라고 하였음.
농무부측 반응은 USTR 반응에 비해 협상전망에 대하여 낙관적이었음을 참고로 보고함.
끝.

    (대사 현홍주 - 국 장)

    예고 : 92.12.31. 까지

관리 번호	92-128

외 무 부

종 별 :

번 호 : JAW-5588

일 시 : 92 1020 1845

수 신 : 장관(통기,통일,통이,농수산부,사본:주제네바대사-중계필)

발 신 : 주 일대사 (일경)

제 목 : UR 협상동향 및 주재국 반응

당관 황순택 서기관은 10.20(월) 주재국 외무성 경제국 국제기관 1 과 사또과장 보좌를 접촉, 표제관련 동향 및 쌀시장 개방에 관한 일본의 입장에 대해 문의 한바, 동 결과 아래 보고함.

1. 미-EC 간 교섭결과(10.11-12, 브라셀)

농산물 교섭의 최대 현안인 5 개항목(수출보조, 국내보조, OIL SEEDS 문제, PEACE CLAUSE, REBALANCING)에 관해 주로 협의가 있었는 바, 수출보조금 및 OIL SEEDS 문제외에는 거의 합의를 본 것으로 알고 있음.

수출보조금 관련해서는 2 가지 대안 (AGGREGATION 및 SWING) 을 미측이 제시한 바 있으며, OIL SEEDS 에 대해서는 생산량 제한과 경작면적 축소 제안이 미측으로 부터 제기 되어, 이를 EC 측이 검토하고 있는 것으로 알고 있음.

수출보조금 문제와 OIL SEEDS 문제는 상호 밀접한 연관성을 갖고 있어 함께 연동 타결될 가능성이 높음.

2. EC 임시정상회의(10.16, 버밍험)

프랑스는 동 회의에서 미측 제안을 받아 들일수 없다는 반응을 보인 반면, 동 회의 공동성명에는 UR 교섭의 년내 합의를 목표로 하고 있다는 등, EC 의 명확한 입장을 파악하기 힘듬.

EC 측으로서는 금후 CAP 개혁에 의해 EC 의 농산물 생산량이 감소될 것으로 전망하고, 이는 잉여 농산물 감소로 결국 수출의 감소를 의미하는 것이므로 수출 보조금도 아울러 축소될 것이나, CAP 개혁에 의해 농산물 생산량이 어느정도 줄 것인가 하는 문제는 시행하기 전에는 확실히 알수 없는 측면이 있어, 현단계에서 미측에 수량적으로 수출보조금 감소를 약속(COMMIT)할 수없는 어려움이 있는 것으로 보인다고 함.

통상국 농수부	장관 중계	차관	2차보	통상국	통상국	분석관	청와대	안기부

PAGE 1

* 원본수령부서 승인없이 복사 금지

92.10.20   20:18

외신 2과   통제관 CM

0153

3. 4 극 봉상장관회담(10.17 - 18, 토론토)

　　미국, EC 간 교섭에 대해 비교적 긍정적인 평가가 나온 것으로 알고 있으나, 일측으로서는 이에대해 그다지 낙관적으로 보고 있지는 않고 있다고 함,

　　또한, 일봉산대신의 차관급회의 개최제의 및 쌀시장 개방에 관한 일본내 결단 필요성 언급등 관련 보도에 대해 다소 오해가 있는 것으로 생각한다고 말하고, 봉산대신은 지난 7 월 SUMMIT 의 UR 협상 년내 타결 공약의 이행을 위해서는 11 월중 차관급 다국간 협의 재개가 필요할 것으로 생각한다고 언급 한 바 있으며, 또한 기자회견시 금후 미-EC 간 교섭이 타결되고 다국간 협의가 진행된다는 전제 조건하에서는 일본도 금년 12 월중에는 쌀시장 개방에 대해서 정치적 결단을 내릴 필요가 있을 것으로 본다는 개인적 견해를 피력한 것에 불과하다고 언급함.

4. 쌀시장 개방문제

　　국제적으로 볼때 한국이외에 쌀시장 개방에 반대입장을 취해온 북구국가들이 입장 변화를 보이고 있으며, 또한 멕시코, 카나다가 NAFTA 체결로 입장약화 가능성이 많으며, 스위스의 경우 타협안(10 년이후 관세화 시행)을 제시하고 있어, 일본과 한국의 전면 개방 반대 입장이 상당히 약해지고 있음.

　　또한, 상기와 같은 상황에서 미-EC 간 협상이 타결된다고 가정한다면, 일본의 입장이 매우 곤란해질 것으로 보는 바, 그 배경으로는 현재까지 일본은 쌀시장 개방에 대해 전적으로 반대한다는 입장만으로 일관하여 왔으므로, 갑자기 정책을 전환할만한 국내적 분위기가 조성되어 있지 않으며, 또한 부분시장 개방 필요성 등을 언급한 바 있는 가네마루 전의원을 비롯 정계 실력자가 자민당내 사정 등으로 쌀시장 개방문제에 대해 결단을 내릴 입장에 있지 않는 점등을 그 이유로 설명함.

　　일측은 기본적으로 미-EC 간의 타협이 이루어 진다고 하더라도 이는 다자간에 재협의 되어야 하며, 다자간의 협의시 현재로서는 구체적 방안을 고려하고 있지는 않으나, 원칙적으로 한국등과 협력 대응해 나가고자 한다고 언급함.

- 끝 -

(대사 오재희 - 국장)

예고 : 92. 12. 31. 까지

외 무 부

종 별 :

번 호 : ECW-1296

일 시 : 92 1021 1730

수 신 : 장관(통기, 통삼, 경기원, 재무부, 농림수산부, 상공부, 기정동문)

발 신 : 주 EC 대사 사본: 주 미-중계필, 주제네바, 불대사-직송필

제 목 : 갓트/UR 협상동향

대: WEC-0755

10.21. 당관 이관용농무관은 OLSEN EC 집행위 농업총국 담당관을 접촉하고, 대후 관련 탐문한바 요지 아래보고함

1. 카나다 4개국 회담

가. 토론토 4개국 통상장관 회담에서는 미.EC 간의 양자회담 결과를 청취하였으며, 서비스, 시장접근, 공공구매, 다자무역기구(MTO) 설치, 무역과 환경의 조화문제등 UR 협상타결에 직.간접적으로 영향을 미칠 제반문제가 논의되었으나, 농산물문제는 거론되지는 않았음

나. 동 회담에서는 특히 향후 제네바에서의 UR 협상추진 일정과 농산물등 모든 협상분야를 망라한 균형된 협상 PACKAGE 내용에대해 의견을 교환한 것으로 알고 있음

2. 미.EC 양자협상

가. 미.EC 간에는 농산물분야이외 사항에 대하여는 견해차이가 크지 않으며, 농산물분야에 있어서 양측의 의견대립 사항은 EC 의 농산물 생산수준을 어느정도까지 감축하느냐의 문제임. 즉, 양측은 아직도 OILSEEDS 및 수출보조 감축문제에 있어 이견을 보이고 있는바, EC 의 OILSEEDS 생산감축폭과 CEREALS 수출물량 감축문제는 결국은 EC 의 경작지 수준 또는 생산수준을 결정하는 문제와 직결되어 있음

나. 지난주말 카나다 4개국 통상장관 회담에서 농산물문제가 제외된 것은 미.EC 간의 견해차이가 있다는 것을 의미하며, 이를 타결하기 위해 MACSHARRY 집행위원이 금주말경 (동인은 10.23. 회담이 개최될 것으로 보나, 확인할수는 없다고 언급) 워싱턴에서 MADIGAN 미농무장관과 회담을 가질 것으로 알고 있으며, 동 회담결과는 10.26-27 개최될 EC 농업이사회에 보고될 예정임

3. 협상 추진전망

통상국 경기원	장관 재무부	차관 농수부	2차보 상공부	구주국 중계	통상국	분석관	정와대	안기부

PAGE 1

92.10.22 02:26

외신 2과 롱제관 FM

0155

가. 현재 BUSH 대통령이 선거전에서 어려움을 겪고 있고, 이를 만회하는 방법의 일환으로 UR 협상의 타결을 바라고 있어 EC 로서는 동 협상에서 미국의 양보를 받아낼수 있는 좋은 기회로 보고있음

나. 미대통령선거 실시이전에 미.EC 간에 농산물문제를 포함한 UR 협상 전반에 관해 어떤 합의를 이룰 가능성은 크다(50% 이상) 고 보며, 다만 어떤 합의가 있을 경우에도 EC 집행위로서는 동 결과에대해 EC 이사회를 통해 회원국의 승인을 받아야하나, 이 경우에 불란서의 농산물분야에 대한 강경입장이 문제임

다. 불란서의 관심사항은 소맥수출과 OILSEEDS 생산을 유지하며, 포도주, 주정등의 수출을 증대하는 것인바, 만약 불란서가 소맥수출과 OILSEEDS 생산문제중 하나라도 양보하지 않을 경우, 미측의 보복으로 말미암아 포도주와 주정의 수출에 타격이 있을 것이라는 것을 불란서정부도 알고있어 지난달 불란서 국민투표이후 동 정부도 최선의 방안이 무엇인가를 검토하고 있는 것으로 알고 있음. 끝

(대사 권동만-국장)

예고: 92.12.31. 까지

PAGE 2

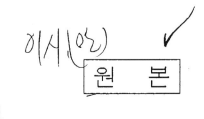

관리 번호	92-73P

외 무 부

종   별 :

번   호 : ECW-1312   일   시 : 92 1022 1800

수   신 : 장관(통기,통삼,경기원,재무부,농림수산부,상공부,기정동문)

발   신 : 주 EC 대사 사본: 주 미-중계망, 주제네바,불대사-필

제   목 : GATT/UR 협상동향

연: ECW-1311

일반문서로 재분류 (1992 . 12. 31

   연호, 미.EC 간 UR 협상 동향과 관련, 금 10.22. 당관 관계관들이 EC 집행위 관계관들을 접촉, 파악한 내용을 아래보고함

   1. 당관 주철기참사관은 EC 집행위의 DUGIMONT UR 담당 수석자문관을 면담한바, 동인의 주요 발언내용은 아래와같음

   가. 10.17-18 간 토론토에서 개최된 4 자 무역장관회의는 써비스, 시장접근분야등 일반 통상분야의 타결가능성을 포함, UR 의 연내타결에 대해 비교적 낙관적인 전망을 갖게 했던것이 사실임

   나. 10.19-21 간 당지에서 개최된 농업관계 실무회의 결과를 아직충분히 듣지 못하고 있으나 동 회의에서 별다른 진전이 없었다 하더라도 미-EC 간 협상이 완전히 결렬된 것은 아니며, 협상이 계속될여지는 남아있다고 봄

   다. 다만 10.16 버밍행 정상회담에서의 결의에따라, EC 가 미국과 정치적 타협을 아루게 된다하더라도 제네바에서의 다자협상을 즉각 재개하여 필요한 기술적 협상과 문서작업을 거쳐 이를 에딘버러 (12.16) 정상회담에 제시, 추인을 받아야 될것이나, 다자협상에 필요한 시간이 촉박한 것이 문제임 어제, 11일은?

   라. 만약 미대통령 선거일까지 협상이 타결되지 못하고 민주당이 집권하게 될경우, UR 협상과정이 지연될 것이나, 반드시 1 년이상 장기간 지연될 것으로는보지않음. 과거 동경라운드의 경우 카터 민주당 신정부와 모든분야의 협상을 기초적 단계부터 시작하여 조기 관철했던 사례가 있는바, 현재 UR 의 경우 기본적 협상은 거의 종결된 상태이므로 미국 신정부가 우선권을 부여하는데 따라서는협상이 빨리 진척될 가능성도 있음

   마. EC 의 UR 관계 실무자들은 미.EC 간 양자협상이 너무 오래 끌고 있어 제 3

통상국	장관	차관	2차보	통상국	외정실	분석관	청와대	안기부
경기원	재무부	농수부	상공부	종계				

PAGE 1   92.10.23   05:02

외신 2과 통제관 FK

0157

국들에 주는 지장등 여러요인에 비추어 가급적 다자협상으로의 조기복귀가 이루어지기를 바라고 있음

2. 한편 당관 이혜민서기관은 당지 영국대표부 UR 담당관(MADELIN 1 등서기관) 을 면담한바, 동인의 주요 발언내용은 아래와같음

가. 당지개최 농업관계 실무회의 결과 불구, MACSHARRY 와 MADIGAN 간 ~~전[84f귀. 당저 개최 농업관계 실무회의 결과 불구, MACSHARRY 와 MADIGAN 간~~ 전화협의등 미.EC 간 협의는 계속 진행될 것이며, 안드리센 집행위원은 아직도 협상전망 가능성을 낙관적으로 보고있고, 의장국인 영국도 낙관적 전망을 갖고 측면 지원하고 있음

나. EC 집행위는 금주말까지의 대미 협상결과를 10.26(월) EC 농업이사회에일단 보고할 예정임. 만약 앞으로 미-EC 간 기술적 타결이 이루어질수 있다면,그 내용이 제네바에서의 다자협상을 거쳐 PACKAGE DEAL 로 확정되어 에딘버러 정상회담에 제기될 것이므로 그 경우에는 불란서로서도 VETO 권을 행사하기 어려울 것임. 끝

(대사 권동만-국장)

예고: 92.12.31. 까지

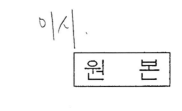

관리	
번호	92-74

외 무 부

종 별 :

번 호 : USW-5220 일 시 : 92 1022 1902

수 신 : 장 관 (통기, 통이, 경기원)

발 신 : 주 미 대사

제 목 : UR 협상 동향

1. 당관 장기호 참사관은 10.22. DEWOSKIN USTR UR 협상 담당 부대표보를 접촉, 최근 UR 협상 동향에 대해 의견교환을 가진바, 동인은 농산물 문제에서 수출보조금과 OILSEED 문제에 EC 측과 계속 이견을 보이고 있으며, 특히 OILSEED 문제에서는 EC 가 종전의 입장보다는 더 후퇴하고 있어 우려가 된다고 하였음.

2. 이어서 동 부대표보는 서비스등 비농업부문 협상과 관련 지난 카나다 개최 4개국 통상장관회담에서는 특히 한국이 금융, 시장접근, CHEMICAL HARMONIZATION 등의 분야에 좀더 진전 (IMPROVE)된 입장이 나와야 할 것이라는 의견이 있었다고 하였음.

3. 미.EC 간의 UR 협상은 농산물의 상기 2 개 분야를 제외하고는 대부분의 분야에서 매우 근접하고 있으므로 앞으로 제네바에서의 협의를 계속할 것을 미측이 제의하고 있으나, 불란서와 독일이 RELUCTANT 한 입장을 보이고 있어 전망이 불확실함.

4. 당지 10.22 자 NYT, WP, FT, JOC 등 각 신문은 UR 협상의 결렬을 보도하고 있는바, 관련기사 별첨 FAX 송부함. 끝.

첨부 : USW(F)-6757 (8 매)

(대사 현홍주 - 국장)

예고 : 92.12.31. 까지

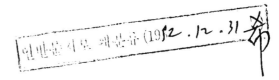

통상국	장관	차관	2차보	통상국	분석관	정와대	안기부	경기원

외　무　부

종　별 :

번　호 : USW-5246　　　　　　　　　　일　시 : 92 1023 1853

수　신 : 장 관 (봉기,봉이,봉삼,경일)

발　신 : 주 미 대사

제　목 : UR 동향

1. 당지 법률회사인 SIDLEY AND AUSTIN 사에서작성한 UR 전망에 관한 메모를 별첨 송부함.

2. 동 메모는, 미국 고위 통상관리와의 대화를기초로, 금년내 UR 타결 전망이 극히 어둡다고 보며미. EC 간 OILSEED 분쟁과 관련하여예상되는 미측의 제재와 EC 의보복조치로인해 미. EC 간 무역전쟁 가능성이 높다고예측하고 있음.끝.

첨부: USW(F)-6794(3 매)

(대사 현홍주-국장)

통상국　　경제국　　통상국　　통상국

주 미 대 사 관

USR(F) : 6794 년월일 : 시간 :

수 신 : 장 관 (통기, 통이, 통산, 경이)

발 신 : 주미대사

제 목 : 美 USTR - 526 친무(3초청)

보안통제

6794-3-1

외신1과 동제

0161

PRIVILEGED AND CONFIDENTIAL
ATTORNEY WORK PRODUCT

MEMORANDUM

FROM: Alan F. Holmer and Judith H. Bello

RE: Uruguay Round Prospects (or the Lack Thereof)

DATE: October 22, 1992

_____

SUMMARY

This memorandum reports on the status of Uruguay Round developments from Washington's perspective. The bottom line is that the gloom-and-doom reports in today's press are accurate. We see only the slimmest of prospects of a successful conclusion to the Uruguay Round this year, and are skeptical whether the momentum can be regained until well into 1993, at the earliest.

Discussion

Our report is based on conversations today with top U.S. trade officials.

They report that, in their view, progress truly had been made with the EC in Brussels ten days ago. Both top political and career officials who led discussions in Brussels are convinced that they were "quite close" to a deal. They offered a couple new proposals in Brussels, and were hopeful that they would provide a breakthrough in the stalemated agricultural negotiations.

A couple days ago, however, they learned that the EC had pulled back, as a result (they believe) of instructions from Delors. They are convinced that the French, with support from German Chancellor Kohl, have undermined the EC Commission, preventing any breakthrough in agriculture this year.

At their most optimistic, these U.S. trade officials indicate that theoretically, progress could be still made in other areas in Geneva. Hypothetically the U.S. could cease its bilateral efforts with the EC, and concentrate instead on trying to generate momentum multilaterally in Geneva. However, realistically they appreciate the enormous difficulties in doing so at a time when many who oppose the negotiations or are dragging their feet anyway are using the possibility of the election of Governor Clinton as an excuse not to negotiate meaningfully in Geneva.   67¾ — 3-2

To make prospects for success in Geneva even bleaker, the U.S. now faces the decision whether, how and when to retaliate against the EC for its failure to reform its practices or provide compensation in the Oilseeds dispute. We believe that this issue is being debated in the White House today; we further

0162

believe that USTR has strongly recommended full and prompt retaliation against the EC, even though such action is certain to provoke an equal response in kind by the EC. Regrettably, the U.S. and EC are poised on the brink of a major trade conflagration.

With President Bush continuing to trail in the polls, arguably he has relatively little to lose politically. While EC retaliation and the outbreak of a trade war could damage his credentials in foreign policy leadership, they would underscore his resolve in "standing tall" for America and American interests (which are the world's interests, too, since the recalcitrance in Brussels is preventing the conclusion of negotiations that would benefit the entire world). A trade war with the EC would not be welcome, but then it might serve as a platform for decisive and tough action by the President.

679￠— 3-3

0163

외 무 부

종   별 :

번   호 : FRW-2170   일   시 : 92 1023 1830

수   신 : 장관(통기, 경기원, 재무부, 농림수산부, 상공부) 사본:주EC, 제네바 대사-필

발   신 : 주 불 대사

제   목 : UR 협상

연 : FRW-2088

1. 최근 EC. 미국간 활발한 양자협상에도 불구하고 미 대선이전 UR 타개 전망이 더욱 불투명해져 가고 있는 가운데, UR 협상관련 당지 주요언론 보도내용 아래 보고함.

가. 지난 10 일간 일련의 EC. 미국간 UR 협상이 구체적 합의에 이르고 있지못한 가운데 미국은 본격적인 대 EC 보복조치 실행문제와 함께 무역전쟁을 상호 회피할수 있는 마지막 방안을 동시에 검토하고 있음.

나. 상금 EC 는 협상이 결렬된 것이 아니며 수일내 정치적 타결 가능성을 계속 시사하고 있으나, 불란서 DUMAS 외상은 10.23 자 당지 언론게재 대농민 앞 서한에서 본격적인 UR 협상은 (미국의 신정부가 들어선) 수개월이 지나야 가능할것임을 주장하고, SAPIN 경제재무장관 역시 UR 협상은 미대선 이후에 재개하는것이 바람직하다는 기존입장을 표명함.

다. 한편 미국은 이미 92.4 월 10 억불 상당 대 EC 보복대상 품목을 이미 준비하였는 바, 포도주, 알콜성음료, 치즈, 우유 등 불란서의 주요 수출품목이 포함됨에 따라 보복조치 실행시 불란서가 EC 국가중 최대의 피해국 (약 20 %) 이될 것으로 예상됨.

라. 한편 최근 불란서는 UR 타결을 위한 농업분야 추가양보는 커녕 기존합의된 CAP 개혁방안의 실천여부도 불투명하게 전망하는 등 농업문제에 있어 오히려 더욱 후퇴하는 듯한 인상을 주고 있음.

마. 이와관련 10.26. 개최되는 EC 농업장관 회담에서 불란서는 여타 회원국의 의구와 비난의 대상이 될 가능성이 크며, 미국의 무역보복이 시작되면 불란서에 대한 대내적 비난은 더욱 강해질 것으로 예상되는 바, 이러한 배경하에서 불란서가 소위

| 통상국 | 장관 | 차관 | 2차보 | 구주국 | 문석관 | 정와대 | 안기부 | 경기원 |
| 재무부 | 농수부 | 상공부 | | | | | | |

PAGE 1   92.10.24   05:15

외신 2과 통제관 BZ

0164

참호정책 (BUNKER POLICY) 을 계속 고수하는 것이 불 국익에 중장기적으로 유익한지 제고할 필요가 있음.

2. 한편 조참사관이 접촉한 당지 미국대사관 UR 담당관 (BRIAN BLOOD 서기관)에 의하면, 미 정부는 종자유 분쟁관련 EC 에 대해 보복조치를 취할 것이나 시기만이 문제이며, 개인적으로 보기에는 보복조치 집행전 최종 협상을 한, 두차례 시도할 가능성이 크며, 보복조치도 전면시행과 단계적 시행방안이 함께 검토되고 있다 함.

3. 또한 동 서기관에 의하면, 미 대선 이전 불란서가 기존입장을 변경할 가능성은 적으나, 향후 1 주일내 EC. 미국 간 양자협상에서 주요한 합의가 이루어지면 EC 집행위는 불란서를 우회하여 먼저 제네바에서 다자간 협의후 동 협상결과에 대해 EC 회원국의 인준을 추진할 가능성도 있다 함. 끝.

(대사 노영찬-국장)

예고:92.12.31 까지

외　무　부

종　별 :

번　호 : CNW-1158

일　시 : 92 1023 1430

수　신 : 장관 (통기, 상공부)

발　신 : 주 캐나다 대사

제　목 : UR 협상 동향

대 : WCN - 1052

연 : CNW - 1134

일반문서로 재분류 (1992 .12 .31

최근 UR 협상 동향 관련 하병근 상무관이 주재국 외무무역부 MTN BRANCHMARIO STE-MARIE 부조정관과 접촉한바 동인의 발언 요지를 아래와 같이 보고함.

1. 10. 17 - 18 간 개최된 4 국 통상장관회담 결과, UR 협상의 성공적 타결에 대한 각료들의 의지가 천명된바 있으나 교착상태에 빠진 협상에 새로운 돌파구를 마련하는 계기는 없었던 것으로 평가됨. 현재 협상 진전의 걸림돌이 되고 있는 미.EC 간 농산물 교역 현안 문제에 대한 이견해소가 급선무인데 금번 회담시 이를 깊이 있기 토의할 시간적 여유도 없었으며(금번 회담은 10.17 밤부터 10. 18 오찬까지 지속) 또한 관계국 농무장관이 불참한 상황하에서 책임있는 협의는 기대할 수 없었음.

2. 미. EC 간 유채 보조금 문제등 농산물 교역 분규에 대해 <u>10 월말경까지</u> 해결책이 모색되지 않을 경우 미국측은 10 억불에 상당하는 EC 상품(포도주, 치즈등)에 대한 보복 관세조치를 발동할 가능성이 있으며, 이경우 UR 협상의 교착상태는 상당기간 지속될 것임. 브랏셀에서 개최된 미.EC 간 실무협상이 의견조정에 실패함으로서 10. 21. 결렬 되었으며, 향후 재협상 계획이 없는 것으로 알려지고 있음. 이에 따라 근일간 개최 예정으로 알려진 양국 농무장관 회담도 성사가 될 가능성도 불투명함. 10. 22 부시 대통령은 관계각료들과 대 EC 대책을 협의한 것으로 밝혀지고 있음.

3. 미국 대통령 선거 결과 부시 대통령이 낙선하는 경우 잔임기간동안 협상추진에 적극성을 보이기 어려울 것임. 클린턴이 당선되는 경우에도 UR 협상을 추진해 나갈 것으로 보이나 FAST TRACK 이 93. 3 월 종료되기 때문에 이의 연장 승인을 의회에 요청해야 될 가능성이 있음.

통상국	장관	차관	2기보	분석관	청와대	안기부	상공부

* 원문수신부서 승인없이 복사 금지

(대사 박건우 - 작장)

예고 : 92.12.31. 까지

외 무 부

종 별 :

번 호 : ECW-1322   일 시 : 92 1023 1730

수 신 : 장관(통삼,통기,경기원,재무부,농림수산부,상공부,기정동문,사본:주미)

발 신 : 주 EC 대사   주영,불,독,제네바대사-필

제 목 : 갓트/UR 협상 동향

연: ECW-1312

표제협상과 관련한 당지의 동향을 아래보고함.

1. 미.EC 양자협상

가. O HARA 미측 실무협상 대표는 <u>10.22워싱턴으로 돌아간 것으로</u> 알려진 가운데, 10.23 EC 집행위 대변인은 수일내에 표제협상을 타결한다는 당초 목표 아래 미국과 EC는 협상을 계속하고 있다고 말하였으나, 협상 장소, 대표등 구체적인 내용을 밝히기를 거부함. 다만, 동대변인은 HAC SHARRY-MADIGAN 장관간의 전화를통한 협상가능성을 배제하지 않음.

나. 미국과 EC는 동 양자협상이 결렬된책임에 대해 상대방을 비난하고 있으나, 당지언론보도를 종합해 보면, 동 협상이 타결되지못한 이유가 EC의 OILSEEDS 감산수준, 보조수출물량감축 및 REBALANCING의 재요구 때문인것으로 알려짐.

O OILSEEDS 협상

- 미측은 EC의 동품목 생산수준을 9백만톤까지 감축할 것을 요구한 반면, EC는 CEREALS 가격인하등을 고려할 때 9.5백만톤이하로 감축은 어렵다는 입장

- EC는 SET-ASIDE 경지에 비식용 OILSEEDS생산을 허용한다는 입장 이나 미측은이에 반대

O 보조수출 물량 감축

- 미측은 품목군별로 24프로 수출물량 감축에반대하고 22프로 감축을 제의 하였으나, <u>EC는 18프로 이상 감축은 불가하다는 입장</u>

O REBALANCING

- 지난주말 각료회담시 동 문제에 대하여는 양측간 서로 양해가 된바 있었으나, EC측이 이문제를 다시 제기함으로서 동 양자협상의 결렬요인이 됨.

통상국	통상국	안기부	경기원	재무부	농수부	상공부	

92.10.24   07:33 CJ

외신 1과 통제관 ✓

0168

2. 회원국 동향

가. 금일 MAJOR 영국수상과 KOHL 독일수상은 전화회담을 가졌으며, 양인은 EC집행위가동회담을 결렬시켜서는 않되며, 미국과의회담을 계속토록 촉구하기로 합의함. 양인은 또한 미국의 보복조치는 위험스러우며 갓트협상은 성공할수 있으며, 또 성공시켜야 한다는데 의견을같이 한 것으로 알려짐. 한편, 영국정부의 관계관에 의하면 영국은 집행위에 대한 압력이외도 회원국 및 미국정부와 접촉중이며, MAJOR 수상은 UR협 상을 타결하기 위해서는 EC측이 양보하여야 할 것이라는 입장을 갖고있다고 말한 것으로 보도됨. 한편, 동국 HESELTINE 무역상은 DELORS EC 집행위원장이 친불적태도를 지양하고 UR 협상 장애요인 제거를위해 노력해줄것을 강력히 요청하였다 함.

나. 불란서정부는 입장표명을 자제하고 있는 것으로보이나, 불란서 농민 단체(CNJA)는 동 협상이 결렬된 것을 환영하고, 이는 불란서 농민들의 승리라고 표현하면서, 협상대표들은 세계농산물시장의 분배점유 및 농산물 가격인상방안에 대해 협의해야한 다고 주장함. 끝

(대사 권동만-국장)

PAGE 2

이시 (공감) ✓

원 본

외 무 부

종 별 :

번 호 : GVW-2007   일 시 : 92 1024 0840

수 신 : 장관(봉기, 경기원, 재무부, 농림수산부, 상공부, 특허청)

발 신 : 주 제네바대사   사본:주미,EC,일,영,독,불,카나다대사(중계필)

제 목 : UR 협상동향 및 전망

일반문서로 재분류 (1992 . 12 . 11)

1. UR 협상은 브랏셀 개최 미.EC 각료회담(10.10-12) 및 토론 개최 4 국 통상장관 회의(10.17-18) 이후 미대통령 선거이전 빠른시일내에 미.EC 간 농산물분야 합의에 따른 돌파구 마련으로 연내 타결 가능성이 큰것으로 기대되어 왔으나, 금주 10.19-21 간 브랏셀에서 개최된 미.EC 간 농산물 분야에 대한 고위실무대표(미국 O'MARA 및 EC LEGRAS)간의 협상이 결렬됨으로써 조기 타결 가능성이 희박해지고, 결국 미대통령 선거이후에야 향후 협상 전망이 더욱 분명해 질것으로 보이는바, 당지 협상대표들의 견해 및 당관 평가와 전망을 아래 보고함.

2. 미.EC 브랏셀 고위 실무협상 결렬 이후의 당지 전망

가. SHANNON 카나다 대사

0 토론토 4 국 통상장관 회의시 써비스, 시장접근 분야등에 대한 많은 토의가 있었으며 상당한 의견 접근이 있었음. 특히 금융써비스 분야에서 아세아, 태평양권 국가들의 양허수준을 높여야 한다는 데에 의견의 일치가 있었음.

(또한 미국 EC 양자간회담에서 농산물에 관한 의견도 상당히 접근된것이 사실임)

0 브랏셀 고위 실무협상에서 합의에 실패함으로써 UR 협상 전망이 불투명해진 것은 사실이나 미. EC 양국은 계속 접촉을 갖기로 한것으로 알며, MADIGAN MCSHARRY 전화접촉 및 회담이 예상되는등 상금 미대통령 선거이전까지 합의 도출 가능성이 없는것은 아님.

나. HAWES 호주대사

0 협상은 아직 완전 실패 한것으로 볼수없고 미대통령선거전 타결 가능성이없는것은 아님

0 작일(10.22) 미국대사의 CAIRNS GROUP BRIEFING 시에도 아직 희망을 포기하지 않고 계속 협상 하겠다는 의지를 표명했음

통상국 농수부	장관 상공부	차관 특허청	2차보 중계	분석관	청와대	안기부	경기원	재무부

PAGE 1   92.10.24   19:13

외신 2과 통제관 EC

0170

다. ZHTSHI 인도대사(GATT 이사회 의장)

0 기대를 하지 않고 있었기 때문에 놀라울 것도 없고, 실망하지도 않음.

라. ARIF-HUSSEIN GATT 사무차장보

0 미국 대통령 선거전 이후에야 상황이 더 분명해 질것이며, 결국 FAST TRACK MANDATE 를 단기간이라도 연장, 내년까지는 타결할수 있을 것으로 봄.

0 내주(10.27) 있을 GREEN ROOM 협의는 현황을 같이 논의해 보는 기회가 될것임

마. STOLER 미국대표부 공사

0 브랏셀 실무협상은 결렬되었으며, 더이상의 협상 추진 계획이 없는 것으로 알고있음. MADIGAN-MCSHARRY 회담도 개최될 가능성이 없다고 봄.

0 이로써 UR 은 사실상 끝났으며 미대통령 선거이후 시간적 여유를 갖고 새로이 시작될 수 밖에 없을 것임.

바. JOHN BECK 이씨대표부 차석대표

0 토론토 4 국통상장관 회담 직후까지의 기대는 무너졌으며, 이제 UR 의 조기타결 가능성이 거의 없어졌다고 볼수 밖에 없음.

0 미국 실무수석대표가 협상장으로 부터 WALK OUT 한것은 사실이며 현재로서는 협상 계속 계획이 없는 것으로 알지만, 이씨가 WALK-OUT 한것이 아닌 만큼 문호는 열려있음.

0 미 대통령 선거전 양상으로 보아, 10 여일 남은 현시점에서 EC 가 중대한사안을 놓고 미국과 타협할 것으로 기대할수는 없다고 보며, 미.EC 양측에서 협상 계속 가능성 내지 최종 합의 가능성을 시시하는 발언은 결국 홍보전의 의미로 볼수 밖에 없음.

사. JEAN-MARIE 불란서 GATT 대표

0 예상했던 결과이며, 미국대표가 WALK OUT 한것은 농산물 전체 PACKAGE 에대한 불만보다는 OILSEEDS 문제 때문인 것으로 알고있음.

0 미국은 OILSEEDS 문제관련 EC 와의 구두합의(CAP 개혁에 의한 SET-ASIDE 전 10 백만톤 수준)를 미 업계의 압력으로 번복하였는바, 미대통령 선거이전 BUSH 행정부와의 합의보다는 선거후 새로운 행정부와 협상 하는 것이 상호 양보에 의한 합의도달 가능성이 훨씬 크다고 봄.

아. 아. 태 10 개국 협상대표 정례협의시 표명된 일반적 견해

- 금주 브랏셀 실무 회담에서는 OILSEEDS 생산 감축문제와 함께 수출보조 물량에

PAGE 2

0171

관해 논의된바, 후자에 관해서는 18%, 21%, 23%(수치가 높아질수록 PEACE CLAUSE, SWING, 대 EC 수출무량 규제등 추가적 댓가를 미국이 부여) 방안등이 논의되었던 것으로 보임.

- 회담 결렬에 관해 미.EC 양측은 서로 상대방이 기존입장을 후퇴시켰다고 비난하고 있으나, 양측 모두에게 귀책사유가 있다고 봄.

- 미국의 경우 특히 OILSEEDS 문제와 관련, 업계의 압력에 굴복, 9 백만톤(SET ASIDE 이전 1000 만톤) 이상의 신축성을 보일수 없다는 입장을 고수한 것으로 보임

- EC 내부에서도 아래와 같은 사정이 있었던 것으로 보임

. 불란서가 강한 반발을 보이고 있는 가운데 DELORS 가 불란서 국내 정치상의 개인적 야심과 관련 소극적인 입장을 취함으로써 EC 집행위의 입지가 크게 약화됨.

. 불란서뿐만 아니라 스페인, 그리스, 이태리, 심지어 화란까지도 많은 불만을 갖고 있음.

. 독일도 MOLLENMANN 경제장관과는 달리 KOHL 수상은 다소 CONSERVATIVE 한견해를 갖고 있음.

. 버밍험 회의시 보도된 내용이상으로 깊은 토의가 있었으나, 독일의 불란서 설득노력이 양국의 이해차이로 실패함(독일은 물량규제를 받아들이는 대신 GREEN BOX 확대라는 댓가를 얻는 방향으로 불란서를 설득코자 하였으나, GREEN BOX 확대는 불란서의 이해와는 무관)

. 현재로서는 비관적으로 전망할 수 밖에 없으나 BUSH 대통령이 11.3 선거 이전에 OILSEES 에 대한 보복조치까지 강행하리라고 보기는 어렵다는 점에서 경우에 따라서는 동 결렬이 새로운 전기를 마련할 수도 없지 않다고 봄.

3. 평가 및 전망

가. 미대통령 선거전까지 미.EC 간 합의를 도출, 연내 또는 늦어도 내년 2 월말까지 협상을 마무리해 보려는 노력을 기울여 온것이 사실이나, 결국 미.EC 간 농산물 분야(OILSEEDS 및 수출보조 물량감축 문제)에 대한 이견으로 사실상 미대통령 선거이전까지 돌파구 마련 가능성은 희박함.

나. 선거이후의 경우에도 부시대통령이 재선되는 경우에는 현 FAST TRACK MANDATE 기한내에 협상이 타결될 가능성이 있다고 봄.(다만 이경우에도 내년 3 월 총선을 앞두고 있는 불란서의 정치적 입지 및 내년 1 월로 예정되어 있는 이씨 집행위원 교체등이 변수가 될것임)

0172

다. 크린톤 후보가 당선될 경우, 고위직 인사교체, 정책 우선순위 설정, FTM 연장 여부 확정등이 UR 협상의 본격화 시기 결정의 중요요소가 될 것이며 협상의 타결시기는 환경 및 노동문제등 새로운 분야의 추가 여부등 크린톤 신정부의 기본 입장의 향방에 달려 있다고 봄.

4. 홍보

당지 언론등 일각에서는 UR 의 전망이 불투명해짐에 따라 일본, 한국등 일부국가들이 UR 타결을 내심바라지 않고 있다는등 시사도 없지 않으므로 아국으로서는 특히 쌀 문제를 위요한 입장으로 인해 마치 UR 의 실패 또는 지연을 바로고있는 것처럼 대외적으로 비쳐지는 일이 없도록 정부 각 유관부서 및 해외공관에서 대 언론 관계 측면을 포함 신중히 대처해 나가는 것이 매우 긴요하다고 봄.끝

(대사 박수길-차관)

예고:92.12.31. 까지

<table>
<tr><td>관리
번호</td><td>92-753</td></tr>
</table>

외 무 부

종   별 :

번   호 : GVW-2007   일   시 : 92 1024 0840

수   신 : 장관(통기, 경기원, 재무부, 농림수산부, 상공부, 특허청)

발   신 : 주 제네바대사   사본:주미, EC, 일, 영, 독, 불, 카나다대사(중계필)

제   목 : UR 협상동향 및 전망   일반문서로 재분류 (19)92. 12 31 ㈜

    1. UR 협상은 브랏셀 개최 미.EC 각료회담(10.10-12) 및 토론 개최 4 국 통상장관 회의(10.17-18) 이후 미대통령 선거이전 빠른시일내에 미.EC 간 농산물분야 합의에 따른 돌파구 마련으로 연내 타결 가능성이 큰것으로 기대되어 왔으나, 금주 10.19-21 간 브랏셀에서 개최된 미.EC 간 농산물 분야에 대한 고위실무대표(미국 O'MARA 및 EC LEGRAS)간의 협상이 결렬됨으로써 조기 타결 가능성이 희박해지고, 결국 미대통령 선거이후에야 향후 협상 전망이 더욱 분명해 질것으로 보이는바, 당지 협상대표들의 견해 및 당관 평가와 전망을 아래 보고함.

    ② 미.EC 브랏셀 고위 실무협상 결결 이후의 당지 전망

    가. SHANNON 카나다 대사

    0 토론토 4 국 통상장관 회의시 써비스, 시장접근 분야등에 대한 많은 토의가 있었으며 상당한 의견 접근이 있었음. 특히 금융써비스 분야에서 아세아, 태평양권 국가들의 양허수준을 높여야 한다는 데에 의견의 일치가 있었음.

    (또한 미국 EC 양자간회담에서 농산물에 관한 의견도 상당히 접근된것이 사실임)

    0 브랏셀 고위 실무협상에서 합의에 실패함으로써 UR 협상 전망이 불투명해진 것은 사실이나 미. EC 양국은 계속 접촉을 갖기로 한것으로 알며, MADIGAN MCSHARRY 전화접촉 및 회담이 예상되는등 상금 미대통령 선거이전까지 합의 도출 가능성이 없는것은 아님.

    나. HAWES 호주대사

    0 협상은 아직 완전 실패 한것으로 볼수없고 미대통령선거전   타결 가능성이없는것은 아님

    0 작일(10.22) 미국대사의 CAIRNS GROUP BRIEFING 시에도 아직 희망을 포기하지 않고 계속 협상 하겠다는 의지를 표명했음

통상국	장관	차관	2차보	분석관	정와대	안기부	경기원	재무부
농수부	상공부	특허청	중계					

PAGE 1   92.10.24   19:13

                                          외신 2과 통제관 EC

0174

다. ZHTSHI 인도대사(GATT 이사회 의장)

0 기대를 하지 않고 있었기 때문에 놀라울 것도 없고, 실망하지도 않음.

라. ARIF-HUSSEIN GATT 사무차장보

0 미국 대통령 선거전 이후에야 상황이 더 분명해 질것이며, 결국 FAST TRACK MANDATE 를 단기간이라도 연장, 내년까지는 타결할수 있을 것으로 봄.

0 내주(10.27) 있을 GREEN ROOM 협의는 현황을 같이 논의해 보는 기회가 될것임

마. STOLER 미국대표부 공사

0 브랏셀 실무협상은 결렬되었으며, 더이상의 협상 추진 계획이 없는 것으로 알고있음. MADIGAN-MCSHARRY 회담도 개최될 가능성이 없다고 봄.

0 이로써 UR 은 사실상 끝났으며 미대통령 선거이후 시간적 여유를 갖고 새로이 시작될 수 밖에 없을 것임.

바. JOHN BECK 이씨대표부 차석대표

0 토론토 4 국통상장관 회담 직후까지의 기대는 무너졌으며, 이제 UR 의 조기타결 가능성이 거의 없어졌다고 볼수 밖에 없음.

0 미국 실무수석대표가 협상장으로 부터 WALK OUT 한것은 사실이며 현재로서는 협상 계속 계획이 없는 것으로 알지만, 이씨가 WALK-OUT 한것이 아닌 만큼 문호는 열려있음.

0 미 대통령 선거전 양상으로 보아, 10 여일 남은 현시점에서 EC 가 중대한사안을 놓고 미국과 타협할 것으로 기대할수는 없다고 보며, 미.EC 양측에서 협상 계속 가능성 내지 최종 합의 가능성을 시사하는 발언은 결국 홍보전의 의미로 볼수 밖에 없음.

사. JEAN-MARIE 불란서 GATT 대표

0 예상했던 결과이며, 미국대표가 WALK OUT 한것은 농산물 전체 PACKAGE 에대한 불만보다는 OILSEEDS 문제 때문인 것으로 알고있음.

0 미국은 OILSEEDS 문제관련 EC 와의 구두합의(CAP 개혁에 의한 SET-ASIDE 전 10 백만톤 수준)를 미 업계의 압력으로 번복하였는바, 미대통령 선거이전 BUSH 행정부와의 합의보다는 선거후 새로운 행정부와 협상 하는 것이 상호 양보에 의한 합의도달 가능성이 훨씬 크다고 봄.

아. 아. 태 10 개국 협상대표 정례협의시 표명된 일반적 견해

- 금주 브랏셀 실무 회담에서는 OILSEEDS 생산 감축문제와 함께 수출보조 물량에

PAGE 2

관해 논의된바, 후자에 관해서는 18%,21%,23%(수치가 높아질수록 PEACE CLAUSE, SWING, 대 EC 수출무량 규제등 추가적 댓가를 미국이 부여) 방안등이 논의되었던 것으로 보임.

- 회담 결렬에 관해 미.EC 양측은 서로 상대방이 기존입장을 후퇴시켰다고 비난하고 있으나, 양측 모두에게 귀책사유가 있다고 봄.

- 미국의 경우 특히 OILSEEDS 문제와 관련, 업계의 압력에 굴복, 9 백만톤(SET ASIDE 이전 1000 만톤) 이상의 신축성을 보일수 없다는 입장을 고수한 것으로 보임

- EC 내부에서도 아래와 같은 사정이 있었던 것으로 보임

. 불란서가 강한 반발을 보이고 있는 가운데 DELORS 가 불란서 국내 정치상의 개인적 야심과 관련 소극적인 입장을 취함으로써 EC 집행위의 입지가 크게 약화됨.

. 불란서뿐만 아니라 스페인, 그리스, 이태리, 심지어 화란까지도 많은 불만을 갖고 있음.

. 독일도 MOLLENMANN 경제장관과는 달리 KOHL 수상은 다소 CONSERVATIVE 한견해를 갖고 있음.

. 버밍험 회의시 보도된 내용이상으로 깊은 토의가 있었으나, 독일의 불란서 설득노력이 양국의 이해차이로 실패함(독일은 물량규제를 받아들이는 대신 GREEN BOX 확대라는 댓가를 얻는 방향으로 불란서를 설득코자 하였으나, GREEN BOX 확대는 불란서의 이해와는 무관)

. 현재로서는 비관적으로 전망할 수 밖에 없으나 BUSH 대통령이 11.3 선거 이전에 OILSEES 에 대한 보복조치까지 강행하리라고 보기는 어렵다는 점에서 경우에 따라서는 동 결렬이 새로운 전기를 마련할 수도 없지 않다고 봄.

3. 평가 및 전망

가. 미대통령 선거전까지 미.EC 간 합의를 도출, 연내 또는 늦어도 내년 2 월말까지 협상을 마무리해 보려는 노력을 기울여 온것이 사실이나, 결국 미.EC 간 농산물 분야(OILSEEDS 및 수출보조 물량감축 문제)에 대한 이견으로 사실상 미대통령 선거이전까지 돌파구 마련 가능성은 희박함.

나. 선거이후의 경우에도 부시대통령이 재선되는 경우에는 현 FAST TRACK MANDATE 기한내에 협상이 타결될 가능성이 있다고 봄.(다만 이경우에도 내년 3 월 총선을 앞두고 있는 불란서의 정치적 입지 및 내년 1 월로 예정되어 있는 이씨 집행위원 교체등이 변수가 될것임)

PAGE 3

0176

다. 크린톤 후보가 당선될 경우, 고위직 인사교체, 정책 우선순위 설정, FTM 연장 여부 확정등이 UR 협상의 본격화 시기 결정의 중요요소가 될 것이며 협상의 타결시기는 환경 및 노동문제등 새로운 분야의 추가 여부등 크린톤 신정부의 기본 입장의 향방에 달려 있다고 봄.

4. 홍보

당지 언론등 일각에서는 UR 의 전망이 불투명해짐에 따라 일본, 한국등 일부국가들이 UR 타결을 내심바라지 않고 있다는등 시사도 없지 않으므로 아국으로서는 특히 쌀 문제를 위요한 입장으로 인해 마치 UR 의 실패 또는 지연을 바로고있는 것처럼 대외적으로 비쳐지는 일이 없도록 정부 각 유관부서 및 해외공관에서 대 언론 관계 측면을 포함 신중히 대처해 나가는 것이 매우 긴요하다고 봄.끝

(대사 박수길-차관)

예고:92.12.31. 까지

외 무 부

종 별 :

번 호 : ECW-1324   일 시 : 92 1026 1700

수 신 : 장 관(통삼,통기,경기원,재무부,농수부,상공부,기정동문)

발 신 : 주 EC 대사   사본:주미대사(중계필),주불,제네바대사-필

제 목 : 갓트/UR 협상동향

연 : ECW-1322

표제협상과 관련한 최근의 당지동향을 아래보고함.

1. 미.EC 양자협상

가. 10.26 EC 집행위 대변인은 지난주 금요일 MAC SHARRY 집행위원과 MADIGAN미농무장관은 전화를 통하여 UR 협상과 OILSEEDS 문제를 협의하였으며, 양측이 동문제에 관해 조속한 시일내에 성공적인 결과를 달성하기 위해 계속 접촉을 희망하고있음이 명백해 졌다고 발표함. 동 대변인은또한 상기 MAC SHARRY-MADIGAN 접촉에 이어 양측의 고위실무 회담대표인 LEGRAS- O HARA도 지난주말전화 또는 FAX를 통해 접촉한바 있다고 밝힘

나. 한편, 당지 언론 및 일부전문가들은 EC농업 이사회 (10.26-27) 직후인 10.28(수)경에 양측농업 각료회담이 개최될 수 있을 것으로 예측하고있는 가운데, 10.23. ANDRIESSEN 대외담당 집행위원은 미대통령선거 개최이전에 미.EC가 농업문제에 대한 협상을 타결할 수있을 것이라고 말하였으나, DELORS 집행위원장은 조속한 시일내에동 문제에대해 합의할 수 있는 여건이 되어있지 못하다고 말한 것으로 알려짐.

2. 불란서 동향

가. 10.24 BEREGOVOY 불란서 수상은 미대통령 선거이전에 미.EC 협상이 타결될가 능성은 희박하며, 자국은 CAP 개혁내용을 초월한 어떠한 양보에도 동의 하지 않을 것이라고 말함.

나. 한편, SOISSON 불란서 농업장관은 10.25.영국, 독일, 덴마크, 스페인, 아일랜드의 농업 장관들을 각각 만나서 UR 및 OILSEEDS 관련한 불란서 입장을 설명하고,EC 의 결속을 강조한 것으로 알려짐. 동 회동후 KIECHLE 독일, TOERNAES 덴마크 및 WALSH 아일랜드 농무장관들은 EC 결속 필요성에 공감을 표명한 바 있으나,

---

통상국   통상국   ? ?   안기부   경기원   재무부   농수부   상공부

PAGE-1   92.10.27   02:54 FO

외신 1과 통제관 ✓

0178

GUNNER 영국 농무장관은 UR협상의 조속한 타결 필요성을 강조함. 특히, SOLBES 스페인
농무장관은 미대통령 선거 이전에 어떠한 합의가 이루어지기는 어려울 것이라고말함.
끝. (대사 권동만 - 국장)

외 무 부

종   별 :

번   호 : FRW-2184   일   시 : 92 1027 1840

수   신 : 장관(통기, 경일, 경기원, 재무부, 상공부, 농수산부), 사본:주EC, 제네바대사(필

발   신 : 주 불 대사

제   목 : UR 협상

연:FRW-2088, 2170

최근 UR 협상 동향 관련, DENIS SIMONNEAU 외무성 경제국 UR 담당관의 평가아래 보고함. (10.27 조참사관 접촉)

  1. 불란서 입장

  0 불란서의 입장은 일부 언론보도와 같이 농업분야에서 일체의 추가 양보를거부하며 미대선 이전 협상타결을 희망하지 않는다는 듯한 경직된 것이 아님. 불란서는 UR 타결에 의한 경제적 이득을 분명히 계산하고 있으며, 미국의 상응 양보에 따른 상호 균형된 합의 도출이 가능시 년내 타결이 최대의 목표임.

  0 10.16 EC 특별정상회담시 미테랑 대통령은 협상의 년내 타결을 목표로 미측의 REBALANCING 수락, EC 의 수출물량 조정(최대 18% 감축), CAP 개혁 내용의 GATT 내 수용 추진등 3 개 항목을 제의한바 있음.

  - 상기 제의에 대해 KOHL 총리가 종자유 분쟁과 UR 타결을 연계하는 일종의PEACE CLAUSE 를 추가로 제안했으며 이에대해 화란 총리외에는 영국을 포함한 어느 회원국 대표도 특별한 이견 제시가 없었음.

  0 UR 협상 관련, 불란서는 부처별로 입장이 다소 상이한 실정이며, 최근 불각료급 인사들의 강경일변도 발언은 부처별 이해뿐 아니라 93.3 월 총선을 앞둔 개인의 정치적 이해관계등도 반영된 것으로 해석됨.

  0 불란서의 대외정책은 미테랑 대통령 자신이 직접 결정하고 있으며, 특히 UR 의 경우 국가의 전반적 이익뿐 아니라 불란서의 외교적 입장까지도 고려하여야 하므로 오히려 대통령은 UR 협상 진전에 따라 보다 유연한 자세를 취할수도 있을 것으로 예상함.

  2. EC 집행위의 협상 MANDATE

| 통상국 | 장관 | 차관 | 2차보 | 경제국 | 분석관 | 정와대 | 안기부 | 경기원 |
| 재무부 | 농수부 | 상공부 | | | | | | |

PAGE 1   92.10.28   05:46

외신 2과   통제관 FK

0180

0 EC 회원국이 UR 협상에 있어 집행위에 부여한 MANDATE 에 명확한 한계가 없는 반면, 불란서의 입장에서 보면 EC 집행위가 기존의 MANDATE 를 초과하여 교섭하는 것을 우려하는등 상호 모순된 입장을 보이고 있음.

0 이와같이 EC 집행위의 모호한 협상 MANDATE 는 오히려 협상을[84f0 이와같이 EC 집행위의 모호한 협상 MANDATE 는 오히려 협상을 촉진시킬수있으며,
또한 추후 협상 진전에 따라 EC 회원국이나 집행위 모두가 편리한 해석을 할수 있다는 점에서 굳이 상호간에 문제점을 구체적으로 거론하고 있지 않다고 봄.

3. 미측의 농산물 협상 양보

0 EC 집행위는 최근 대미 협상에서 미측이 보여준 GREEN BOX LIST 확대 수용 의사를 상당한 양보로 평가하나, 불란서는 CAP 개혁의 분야별 주요 내용(예:국내 보조 20% 삭감)이 DUNKEL REPORT 의 기존내용에 수정없이 충분히 수용될수 있다고 판단하므로 GREEN BOX LIST 확대 필요성에 크게 공감하지 않고 있음.

0 불측은 미측이 서비스분야등에서는 일부 양보를 하였으나 농산물 분야에서는 상금 실질적으로 양보한 내용이 없다고 봄. 농산물 분야에 있어 미국의 진정한 양보는 수출물량 감축 요구의 현실화 및 REBALANCING 의 수락 형태로 나와야 한다고 생각하며, 여타 대부분의 회원국도 이에 동의하면서도 이러한 불 입장이 EC 내 점차 소수 의견화되는 경향임.

4. 향후 협상 전망

0 EC 집행위에 대한 명확한 MANDATE 부재 및 MACSHARRY 농업 담당 집행위원의 개인적인 야심등에 비추어 미대선 이전 주요 협상 OUTLINE 에 대한 합의도출 가능성을 배제할수는 없으나 여하한 경우에도 동 합의 내용을 제네바에서 다자 협의에 회부되기전에 사전 EC 회원국의 동의를 득해야 함.

0 동 협의 내용이 EC 각료회의에 회부될 경우 EC 집행위가 의장국인 영국의지원하에 가중 다수투표로 이를 인준할수도 있으나 이경우 불란서의 강력한 반발과 정치적 후유증이 예상되므로, 합의내용에 대한 결론을 유보한채 당분간 농산물이외 여타 분야 협상의 진전을 보아가며 종합적인 협상결과를 놓고 년말 EC 정상회담에서 이를 인준하는 방안도 가능할 것으로 보며 이경우 불란서가 적극적으로 반대하기는 어려울 것임.

5. 기타

0 최근 UR 협상 관련 호주내 프랑스에 대한 반감이 고조되고 있는것과 관련,GEORGES KIEJMAN 외무성 대외문제 담당장관이 11 월초 호주와 뉴질랜드를

PAGE 2

0181

방문자국 입장을 설명할 계획임.끝.

(대사 노영찬-국장)

예고:92.12.31. 까지

관리
번호 *92-756*

외 무 부

증   별 :

번   호 : GVW-2024   일   시 : 92 1027 2130

수   신 : 장 관 (통기,통이,경기원,재무부,농수산부,상공부,특허청)

발   신 : 주 제네바 대사   사본: 주 미,EC,일본,영,불,독대사(중계필)

제   목 : UR 협상/그린룸 회의   일반문서로 재분류(1992. 12. 31)

    1. UR 협상 현황점검 및 향후 추진방안 모색을 위한 그린룸 회의가 금 10.27(화) 오후 개최된바, 향후 진로와 관련 (1) TNC 개최, (2) 협상의 다자화(G8 회의)등을 활용, 농산물 분야 미.EC 간 입장차 축소노력 전개방안, (3) 그린룸회의 연속개최등의 방안이 거론되었으나, 참가국대사들의 의견이 엇갈린데다 당장 결정을 요하는 사항도 아니라는 점에서 <u>11.6 그린룸회의를 재개 계속 논의</u>키로한바, 동 토의 내용 아래 보고함.

    가. DUNKEL 총장은 10.9 그린룸회의시와 비교, 상황이 전혀 변한바가 없다하면서, 자신의 의견제시없이 참가국의 의견 개진을 요청함.

    나. 브라질(남미 수개국대표)은 EC 의 태도를 간접비난한후, 미.EC 간의 양자적 노력이 한계에 달했으므로 TRANSPARENCY 유지 및 다자화라는 차원과 미.EC 간 긴장을 해소하기 위한 목적으로 TNC 개최를 주장함.

    다. 카나다는 미국.EC 가 양자협상에서의 양국제안등 현재 안고있는 문제점을 제네바로 가져와 다자화하여 제 3 자가 동문제 해결에 기여할 수 있는 방도가 있는지의 검토를 포함한 다자차원에서 진지한 농업분야 협상 방안을 제시하면서 내주부터라도 그러한 PROCESS 를 가동시킬것을 제의함.

    라. EC 는 미.EC 양자협상이 난관에 봉착한 이유(GLOBAL DEAL 의 성격에 비추어 미국이 AD REFERENDUM 기초하에 합의한 OILSEEDS 생산 물량을 받아들일수 없다고 한데대해 EC 가 타분야 합의를 철회하는 대응조치를 취한 것은 당연한 처사임을 강조)를 간략히 설명. 브라질의 비난을 반박한후, 현단계에서 강제수단이 없는 TNC 회의의 유용성에 대해서 강한 회의를 표명. 아울러 EC 가 양자협상을 중단한바 없다는 점을 강조하면서 양자협상이 한계에 도달했다는 지적에도 반론을 제기하였으며, 미.EC 합의 가능성에 대해서는 일단 비관적이라 는 견해를 표명함.

| 통상국 | 장관 | 차관 | 2차보 | 통상국 | 분석관 | 청와대 | 안기부 | 경기원 |
| 재무부 | 농수부 | 상공부 | 특허청 | 중계 | | | | |

PAGE 1

마. 미국은 10.21 미.EC 협상결렬후 지금까지 상황이 개선된바 없으며, OILSEED 및 여타 UR 농산물 잇슈 해결 전망이 점점더 어려워 지고있다고 전제한후, TNC 회의의 유용성이 의문이 없지는 않으나 EC 의 내부적 어려움을 극복하는데 도움이 될수도 있다고 보므로 모든 나라가 원한 다면 이에 굳이 반대치 않는다는 입장을 표명함.

아울러 일부 참석대사의 미대통령 선거 언급과 관련 미국입장의 일관성(CONTINUITY) 와 UR 협상은 국내정치일정과 무관하다는 점을 언급함.

바. 기타 호주는 양국의 고위지도자가 합의에 실패한 사안을 이시점에서 다자차원에서 토의해 보더라도 큰 도움이 되지않으므로 양자간의 계속적 접촉에 좀더 기대를 걸어보는 것이 좋겠다는 의견을, 인도는 정치적 의지가 결여되어 타결을 보지 못하고 있는 현실을 직시해야한다면서 TNC 개최 및 카나다제안 모두에 대해 강한 의문을 피력하였으며, 일본은 시간부족을 우려하면서 양자간의 협의가 양자관심 사항만 토의, 기타 국가의 중대관심사항을 완전히 도외시하고 있는바, 이러한 상황에서 미.EC 간 합의가 DRAFT FINAL ACT 채택으로 이어지더라도 야당지배하의 상원등 자국 국내 정치상황에 비추어 수락될 가능성이 없다는 점을 언급함.

사. 스웨덴(북구대표)는 미.EC 양국이 합의에 이르지 못한 사실을 개탄하면서, 북구는 DRAFT FINAL ACT 에 기초한 협상용의가 있음을 표명함.

아. 본직은 TNC 개최는 유용성 측면에서 적절치 못하다고 보며, 카나다 제안을 검토해볼 필요성은 있으나 그이전이라도 미.EC 입장차를 축소하는데 DUNKEL 총장이 전체약국의 대변자 입장에서 적극적으로 개입하는 방안도 검토해 보아야 할것이라고 언급함.

자. DUNKEL 총장은 회의결과를 종합하면서 (1) TNC 개최 방안은 실효성 측면의 의문뿐 아니라 잘못 운영될 경우 PRESS GAME 화할 우려가 있으며, (2) 카나다 제안에 대해서는 이달초 DENIS 의장이 시도한 시장접근협상 재개 노력의 미진했던 성과를 상기시키면서 역시 아직 시기상조인 것으로 본다고 각각 언급하고, (3) 그밖에 그린룸 회의를 수시로 개최해 나가는 방법도 있다고 하면서, 11.6 그린룸 회의를 재소집할 계획인바, 그동안 미국 선거결과도 보아가면서 참가국이 상기 3 개 방안을 포함 향후 협상추진 방안을 광범위하게 검토해본후, 입장을밝혀줄것을 요청하는 것으로 회의를 종료함.

2. 금일 회의에서는 우선 미.EC 양국 공히 그간의 양자협상의 아무런 성과를 거둘수 없었다는 점을 토론하고 향후 협상전망도 비관적이라는 견해를 표명하였고,

특히 미국 대사는 대통령선거 결과가 미국입장에 변경을 가져올 가능성이 전혀 없다는 점을 강조하는등 앞으로의 전망을 더욱 어둡게 관망한데다가, DUNKEL 총장도 처음부터 현재의 상황에서 구체적 대안없이 TNC 회의를 개최하는것 보다는 일단 미선거이후로 미루자는 의도를 갖고 회의 도중 이를 수시로 시사함으로써, 브라질 및 카나다를 제외한 다수 참가국 대사들도 결국 좀더 사태추이를 관망하자는 동 총장의 의견을 받아들일수 밖에 없었던 분위기였던 것으로 평가됨.끝

(대사 박수길-국장)

예고 : 92.12.31. 까지

외　무　부

종　별 : 지급

번　호 : GVW-2038

일　시 : 92 1029 1900

수　신 : 장관(통기, 경기원, 재무부, 농수산부, 상공부, 특허청)

발　신 : 주 제네바 대사　　　사본:주미,EC,일,영,불,독 대사(중계필)

제　목 : UR 관련 G 7 정상에 대한 멧세지

1. 금 10.29(목) 당지 호주대표부에서 캐언즈 그룹 및 평화그룹 소속국이 모여 UR 협상의 현 난국 타개를 위해 G 7 정상들이 적극 개입해 줄것을 촉구하는멧세지를 발송하는 문제에 관한 협의가 있었는바, 본직도 일단 동 취지에 동의하여 참석함.

2. 동 협의결과 별첨 문안에 잠정적인 합의가 이루어졌는바, 당초 호주측이작성 제시한 초안에는 "AFTER 6 YEARS OF INTENSIVE NEGOTIATION, IT(DFA) REMAINS IN OUR VIEW THE ONLY VIABLE BASIS FOR CONCLUDING THE NEGOTIATIONS IN A BALANCED MANNER" 라는 문안이 별첨 별표 표시 부분에 포함되어 있었으나, 본직이 동 문안은 미, EC 중 특정 일방의 입장을 옹호하는 결과를 가져올 뿐 아니라, 아국의 경우에도 DFA 를 유일한 기초로 받아들일수 없다는 점을 언급, 삭제를 주장하고, 이에 서서, 홍콩등이 동조하여 삭제되었음.(동 문안은 최종문안은 아니나 내용상의 큰 변화는 없을 것으로 예상됨)

3. 향후 다소의 문안 수정, 멧세지의 형태, 전달 방식 결정 및 참여국 확대등을 거쳐 G 7 지도자들에게 전달하자는 것이 동 움직임의 기본 취지인바, 아국의 UR 협상 성공에 대한 확고한 의지(COMMITMENT)를 재표명하자는 의미에서도 이에 참여하는 것이좋을 것으로 사료되니 본부의견 지급 회시 바람.(명 10.30 17:00 재회동 예정임을 감안)

　　첨부: 호주 대표부 작성 G 7 에 대한 멧세지 초안. 끝

　　(GVW(F)-649)

　　(대사 박수길-국장)

　　예고 92.12.31. 까지

통상국	장관	차관	2차보	분석관	청와대	안기부	경기원	재무부
농수부	상공부	특허청	중계					

92.10.30　　09:15

외신 2과 통제관 EC

0186

주 제 네 바 대 표 부

번 호 : GVW(F) - 064P   년월일 : 21/04P   시간 : 1P○○
수 신 : 장   관 (통기, 경기원, 재무부, 농수산부, 상공부, 특허청)
발 신 : 주 제네바대사   사본 : 주미, EC, 인, 영, 불, 독 대사
제 목 : '첨부

총 2 매 (표지포함)

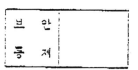

0187

6FP-2-1

DRAFT MESSAGE TO G7 LEADERS

(From the Governments of

When G7 leaders met in Munich they committed themselves to a year end
deadline to finish the Uruguay Round. Without an urgent resolution of
outstanding differences this deadline will not be met and a successful
conclusion to the entire Round will be put at risk. The Round cannot
be allowed to fail through lack of political will on the part of G7
countries.

The Uruguay Round has been stalemated since the Draft Final Act (DFA)
was tabled in December 1991. Already negotiations have dragged on for
six years - two years longer than we had all expected, denying the
world economy the boost it urgently requires.

Strenuous efforts have been made in recent months to resolve problems
which key participants have with the agriculture package in the DFA.
We understand that considerable progress has been made. The Round
has, however, encountered political difficulties which are diverting
us from the objectives to which we all committed our governments at
Punta del Este and in Montreal, and which are holding back the
necessary work required by all participants to complete the
negotiations.

The benefits of the Round will cover all sectors - agriculture, market
access, services and improved rules. All participants will gain. The
world trading system cannot risk a failure of the Uruguay Round with
all that that would entail. A successful result is needed to promote
global economic growth and to prevent a deterioration of the world
trading system. It is crucial as well to the development aspirations
of many developing countries. The remaining differences in our view
are certainly bridgeable given the necessary commitment, flexibility
and goodwill on all sides.

The economic and trade interests at stake in these negotiations are not
those of the G7 alone, but are those of the entire international
community. The world cannot afford to lose the benefits that will
flow from the Round package. Moreover the restructuring and
liberalisation underway in many parts of the world could be seriously
threatened if these processes are denied the encouragement provided by
a strengthened GATT system. Delay in concluding the negotiations is
already denying the benefits of the Round to the world economy and
damaging the credibility of the multilateral system.

We urge the leaders of the G7 countries to intervene now. Three
successive communiques have confirmed G7 commitment to the Round. It
is vital that immediate progress be made if the goal which was set at
Munich of bringing the Round to a successful conclusion by the end of
1992 is to be achieved.

648-2-2

0188

원 본

외 무 부

종 별 :

번 호 : GVW-2046   일 시 : 92 1030 2230

수 신 : 장관 (봉기, 경기원, 재무부, 농수산부, 상공부, 특허청), 사본: 주미,

발 신 : 주 제네바 대사   EC, 일, 불, 독대사(중계필)

제 목 : UR 관련 G7 정상에 대한 멧세지

연 : GVW-2038

대 : WGV-1663

일반문서로 재분류 (92 .12 .31

금 10.30(금) 표제 논의가 당지 호주대표부에서 속개되어 문안의 일부수정, 메세지의 형태, 전달방식 및 참여국 확대문제를 논의한바, 주요 결정 내용은 아래와 같음.

1. 문안 내용은 참가국들의 주요 이해가 관련되지 않는 사항(별첨 멧세지 문안의 밑줄친 부분)에 국한하여 수정함.

2. 참가국들은 아국을 비롯, 호주, 뉴질랜드, 홍콩, 북구 4 개국(놀웨이, 스웨덴, 핀랜드, 아이슬랜드) 칠레, 싱가폴, 콜롬비아, 필리핀, 체코등 13 개국이 찬성, 멕시코, 알젠틴, 태국, 인니, 볼리비아, 브라질, 페루, 베네주엘라, 말련, 항가리, 우루과이, 파키스탄등 12 개국이 본국 훈령을 기다리고 있으나 원칙적으로 찬성, 금일 불참한 나이제리아, 탄자니아, 인도, 자메이카, 이집트등 5 개국은 11.2(월) 13:00 까지 참가여부를 밝히기로 함.

3. 전달방식은 11.2(월) 13:00 까지 참가국이 확정되면, 멧세지를 완성하여 조속히 G-7 수도에 FAX 로 송부, 외교경로를 통하여 전달키로 하였으며, 원본은 추후 외교경로를 통하여 전달키로 함.

첨부 : 최종 멧세지 문안 1 부

(GVW(F)-0651). 끝

(대사 박수길-국장)

예고 : 92.12.31. 까지

통상국	장관	차관	2차보	분석관	청와대	안기부	경기원	재무부
농수부	상공부	특허청	중계					

PAGE 1

92.10.31   08:03

외신 2과 룡제관 FS

0189

주 제 네 바 대 표 부

번 호 : GVW(F) - 0651   년월일 :21.030   시간 : 2230
수 신 : 장   관 (총기, 경기원, 재무부, 농수산부, 상공부, 특허청)
발 신 : 주 제네바대사   사본: 주미, EC; 일, 영, 불, 독대사
제 목 : '첨부

총 2 매 (표지포함)

보 안 통 제	

의신국 통 제	

651 - 2 - 1   0190

URUGUAY ROUND: A MESSAGE TO THE G7

(From the Governments of   )

When G7 leaders met in Munich they committed themselves to a year end
deadline to finish the Uruguay Round. Without an urgent solution to
outstanding differences this deadline will not be met and a successful
conclusion to the entire Round will be put at risk. The Round cannot
be allowed to fail through lack of political will on the part of G7
countries.

The Uruguay Round has been stalemated since the Draft Final Act (DFA)
was tabled in December 1991. Already negotiations have dragged on for
six years - two years longer than we had all expected, denying the
world economy the boost it urgently requires.

Strenuous efforts have been made in recent months to resolve problems
which key participants have with the agriculture package in the DFA.
We understand that considerable progress has been made. The Round
has, however, encountered political difficulties among major
participants which are diverting us from the objectives to which we
all committed our governments at Punta del Este and in Montreal, and
which are holding back the work all participants must do to complete
the negotiations.

The benefits of the Round will cover all sectors - agriculture, market
access, services and improved rules. All participants will gain. The
world trading system cannot risk a failure of the Uruguay Round with
all that that would entail. A successful result is needed to promote
global economic growth and to prevent a deterioration of the world
trading system. It is crucial as well to the development aspirations
of many developing and least developed countries and economies in
transition. The remaining differences in our view are certainly
bridgeable given the necessary commitment, flexibility and goodwill on
all sides.

The economic and trade interests at stake in these negotiations are
not those of the G7 alone, but are those of the entire international
community. We all need the benefits that will flow from the Round
package. Moreover the restructuring and liberalisation underway in
many parts of the world could be seriously threatened if these
processes are denied the encouragement provided by a strengthened GATT
system. Delay in concluding the negotiations is already denying the
benefits of the Round to the world economy and damaging the
credibility of the multilateral system.

We urge the leaders of the G7 countries to intervene now. Three
successive communiques have confirmed G7 commitment to the Round. It
is vital that immediate progress be made if the goal which was set at
Munich of bringing the Round to a successful conclusion by the end of
1992 is to be achieved.

651-5-2

0191

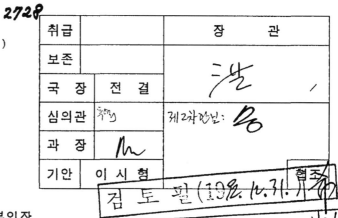

관리
번호 92-267

외 무 부

110-760 서울 종로구 세종로 77번지 / (02)720-2188 / (02)720-2686 (FAX)

문서번호 통기 20644-   2728

시행일자 1992.10.30.(   )

수신 수신처 참조

참조

취급		장 관
보존		
국 장	전 결	
심의관		제2차관보:
과 장		
기안	이시형	

검 토 필 (1992. 12. 31.)

검 토 필 (1993. 6. 30.)

제목 UR 협상 현황에 대한 정부입장

1. UR 협상의 연내타결을 위한 미.EC간의 10월 막바지 협상에도 불구하고 농산물
   분야등 주요쟁점에 대한 합의에 이르지 못하고 있으며, 미국 대통령선거를
   전후한 ~~앞으로~~ 수일간이 UR 협상 연내타결 여부의 고비가 될 것으로 전망됩니다.

2. 이와관련, 주 제네바 대사 보고에 의하면 <del>일부언론에서</del> 언론등 일각에서 최근 UR 협상의 전망이
   불투명해짐에 따라 한국이나 일본이 쌀시장 개방문제에 대한 입장 때문에
   UR 협상의 타결을 원하지 않고 있는 듯이 시사하고 있다 하는바, UR 협상의
   현황에 대한 우리정부의 평가가 대외적으로 잘못 인식되지 않도록 대언론
   관계등에 각별히 관심을 가져주시기 바랍니다. 끝

외 무 부 장 관

수신처 : 경제기획원, 재무부, 농림수산부, 상공부장관, 특허청장.

0192

발 신 전 보

WJA-4593   외 별지참조   종별: _____

번 호 : _____

수 신 : 주 수신처 참조 대사. 총영사 (사본 : 주 제네바 대사)

발 신 : 장 관 (통 기)

제 목 : UR 협상 현황에 대한 정부입장

1. UR 협상의 연내타결을 위한 미.EC간의 10월 막바지 협상에도 불구하고 농산물
   분야등 주요쟁점에 대한 합의에 이르지 못하고 있으며, 미국 대통령선거를
   전후한 ~~앞으로~~ 수일간이 UR 협상 연내타결 여부의 고비가 될 것으로 전망됨.

2. 그간 우리정부는 자유무역질서의 공고화를 위해 UR 협상이 조속히 성공적으로
   타결되어야 한다는 기본입장으로 동 협상에 임해 왔으며, 앞으로도 모든 참가국의
   이익이 균형되게 반영된 협정을 도출할 수 있도록 우리의 능력이 허락하는 범위
   내에서 적극 참여할 방침임.

3. 이와관련, ^{외국언론등 일각에서는} 최근 UR 협상의 전망이 불투명해짐에 따라 우리나라와 일본등이
   쌀시장 개방문제에 대한 입장 때문에 마치 UR 협상의 실패 또는 지연을 내심
   바라고 있음을 ^{다는 듯이} 시사하는 ^{경우가 있다고 하는바,} ~~외국 언론보도가 있었는바~~, UR 협상과 관련하여 주재국
   관계인사 또는 언론 접촉시에 우리정부의 입장이 잘못 전달되지 않도록 유의
   하기 바람. 끝.

(통상국장 홍정표)

수신처 : 주 일, 미, EC, 카나다, 영, 독, 불, 이태리, 호주, 뉴질랜드, 싱가폴,
         태국, 말레이지아, 인도네시아, 필리핀, 인도, 아르헨티나, 브라질 대사

검 토 필 (1992. 12. 31)

제2차 인보 :

보 안
통 제

앙 고 재	92 년 10 월 30 일	통상 기구 과	기안자 성명 이상조	과장	심의관 전결	국장		차관	장관

외신과통제

검 토 필 (1993. 6. 30.)

0193

0194

WJA-4593　921030 1041　WG

WUS -4890　WEC -0790　WCN -1088　WUK -1903　WGE -1519
WFR -2155　WIT -1059　WAU -0902　WNZ -0318　WSG -0695
WTH -1833　WMA -0851　WDJ -1230　WPH -1101　WND -0827
WAR -0682　WBR -0853　WGV -1659

발 신 전 보

번 · 호 : WGV-1663   921030 2004 EI 종별 긴급

수 신 : 주 제네바   재사. 총영사

발 신 : 장 관 (통 기)

제 목 : UR 관련 G-7 정상에 대한 멧세지

대 : GVW-2038

대호, 귀관 의견대로 동 멧세지 발송에 참여하기 바람.   끝.

(통상국장   홍 정 표)

	보 안 통 제	

앙고재	92년 10월 3일	통상기구과	기안자 성명		과 장	심의관	국 장	차 관	장 관	외신과통제
							전결			

0195

외 무 부

종 별 :

번 호 : ECW-1357   일 시 : 92 1030 1700

수 신 : 장관(통삼,통기)경기원,재무부,농림수산부,상공부,기정)

발 신 : 주 EC 대사

제 목 : 갓트/UR 협상동향

　　　MAC SHARRY 집행위원은 금 10.30 오후 자신이11.1(일) 시카고에서 MADIGAN 미농무장관과회담을 가질 예정이며, 동 회담에서는 UR 협상 및 OILSEEDS 문제와 관련한정치적인 타결방안을 논의 할 것이라고 말한 것으로알려진바, 구체내 용 확인되는대로 추보하겠음.끝

　　(대사 권동만-국장)

　　사본: 주 미-중계망,주제네바대사-필

통상국	통상국	안기부	경기원	재무부	농수부	상공부

외 시 ✓

외 무 부

종 별 :

번 호 : ECW-1363　　　　　　　　　　　　일 시 : 92 1030 1730

수 신 : 장관(통상,통기), 경기원, 재무부, 농림수산부, 상공부, 기정동문)

발 신 : 주 EC 대사　　(사본:주미대사-중계망,주제네바-필)

제 목 : 갓트/UR 협상동향

연: ECW-1357

1. 연호 관련, 당관 이관용 농무관은 MACSHARRY 위원실의 MINCH 보좌관을 접촉한바, 동 보좌관도 양자회담의 시카고 개최사실을 확인하면서, MAC SHARRY 위원은 MADIGAN 장관과 일요일(11.1) 만찬을 함께 하고, 공식회담은 월요일 오전중에 가질 것이라고 말함.

2. 한편, EC 집행위 관계관들은 농산물분야에 대한 미.EC 간의 견해차이는 많이좁혀졌음을 시인하면서도, 미대통령선거이전에 양측간의 정치적인 타협이 이루어질가능성은 50:50 으로 보고 있음. 끝

(대사 권동만-국장)

관리 번호	92-1의

외 무 부

종 별 :

번 호 : USW-5331   일 시 : 92 1030 1812

수 신 : 장 관 (통기,통이,미일,경일,경기원,농림수산부),

발 신 : 주 미 대사   사본: 주 제네바, EC 대사(중계필)

제 목 : UR 동향

일반문서로 재분류 (1992. 12. 31)

1. 당관 장기호 참사관은 10.29. ROBERT CASSIDY USTR 아시아 담당 대표보와 오찬을 갖고 주요 관심사항에 대해 의견교환을 가졌음.

가. 동 대표보는 UR 협상과 관련 미.EC 간에 농산물 문제에 관해 의견을 보이고 있지만 미측은 타결의 희망을 버리지 않고 있으며, 앞으로 곧 있을 미 대통령 선거 결과가 UR 협상에 어떤 영향을 줄지는 두고 보아야 하지만 USTR 은 동 선거 결과에 관계없이 UR 협상을 금년내 매듭짓는다는 방침을 견지하고 있다고 하였음.

나. 동 대표보는 만약 UR 협상이 금년말안에 타결되어 각국에 이것을 지지할지 또는 거부할지의 선택의 기회가 주어진다면 한국은 쌀등 농산물의 CLEAN TARIFFICATION 이 포함된 농산물 협상안과 금융서비스 부분의 타결안을 받아 들일수 있는지를 문의해 오면서 한국도 국내선거등의 정치일정에 영향을 받지 않겠느냐는 반응을 보였음을 참고로 보고함.

다. 상기에 대해 수일후에 있을 미대통령 선거 결과가 앞으로 UR 협상에 어떤 영향을 미칠지를 먼저 검토해 보아야 할 사안이며, 한국은 국제사회의 일원이며, 무역 자유화를 추구하는 국가라고 대응하여 두었음.

2. 당지 INSIDE US TRADE (10.30 자) 보도에 의하면 미국의 MADIGAN 농무장관과 EC MACSHARRY 농업담당 위원간에 11.1. 시카고에서 OILSEED 관련 회담을 갖기로 미측이 제의해놓고 있으며 영국 MAJOR 수상은 미.EC 간의 OILSEED 분쟁해결을 위해 미.EC 모두가 새로운 노력을 경주해야 한다고 강조하였다고 보도하였음.

(대사 현홍주 - 국 장)

예고: 92.12.31. 까지

통상국 안기부	장관 경기원	차관 농수부	2차보 중계	미주국	경제국	통상국	분석관	청와대

PAGE 1

92.10.31   09:10

외신 2과 통제관 GB

0198